IN PURSUIT OF GERMAN MEMORY

IN PURSUIT OF GERMAN MEMORY

History, Television, and Politics after Auschwitz

WULF KANSTEINER

OHIO UNIVERSITY PRESS   ATHENS

Ohio University Press, Athens, Ohio 45701
© 2006 by Ohio University Press
www.ohio.edu/oupress/

14 13 12 11 10 09 08   5 4 3 2

The cover and frontispiece illustration is a photo of wall paintings on the facade of the Thomas-Weissbecker-Haus (TWH) in Berlin Kreuzberg, which houses a number of liberal grassroots initiatives, including a center for homeless adolescents, and is one of only a few remnants of West Berlin's thriving liberal subculture of the 1970s and 1980s. Designed and realized by people living in the TWH in that era, the murals express the apocalyptic visions of the preunification, left-wing West German subculture in exemplary fashion. They depict a collective memory that combined belated antifascism and antimilitarism with a strong antinuclear bent and thus capture some of the conclusions that the Left drew from the catastrophe of World War II. It is interesting that Holocaust imagery does not figure prominently in these apocalyptic visions. Photo copyright by author.

Library of Congress Cataloging-in-Publication Data

Kansteiner, Wulf.
  In pursuit of German memory : history, television, and politics after Auschwitz / Wulf Kansteiner. — 1st ed.
    p. cm.
  Includes bibliographical references and index.
  ISBN 0-8214-1638-3 (cloth : alk. paper) — ISBN 0-8214-1639-1 (pbk.: alk. paper)
  1. Memory—Political aspects—Germany (West) 2. Memory—Social aspects—Germany (West) 3. Germany—History—1933–1945—Historiography. 4. Holocaust, Jewish (1939–1945)—Historiography. 5. National socialism—Historiography. 6. Political culture—Germany (West) 7. Mass media and history.   I. Title.
DD258.75.K36 2006
943.086.'01'9—dc22
                                                              2005024835

FÜR MEINE ELTERN

CONTENTS

ACKNOWLEDGMENTS

Parts of chapters 1 through 8 were previously published. I thank the editors and publishers of the following works for allowing me to reprint them here:

"Mandarins in the Public Sphere: *Vergangenheitsbewältigung* and the Paradigm of Social History in the Federal Republic of Germany," *German Politics and Society* 17, no. 3 (1999): 84–120.

"Finding Meaning in Memory: A Methodological Critique of Collective Memory Studies," *History and Theory* 41, no. 2 (2002): 179–97.

"The Rise and Fall of Metaphor: German Historians and the Uniqueness of the Holocaust," in Alan S. Rosenbaum, ed., *Is the Holocaust Unique? Perspectives on Comparative Genocide*, 2nd ed. (Boulder, CO: Westview Press, 2001), 221–44.

"Between Politics and Memory: The *Historikerstreit* and the West German Historical Culture of the 1980s," in Richard J. Golsan, ed., *Fascism's Return: Scandal, Revision, Ideology* (Lincoln: University of Nebraska Press, 1998), 86–129.

"Emplotment and Historicization: Recent German Histories about National Socialism and Modernity," *Storia della Storiografia* 25 (Spring 1993): 65–87.

"Entertaining Catastrophe: The Reinvention of the Holocaust in the Television of the Federal Republic of Germany, *New German Critique* 90 (Fall 2003): 135–62.

"The Radicalization of German Memory in the Age of Its Commercial Reproduction: Hitler and the Third Reich in the TV Documentaries of Guido Knopp," in *Atlantic Communications: The Media in American and German History from the Seventeenth to the Twentieth Century*, ed. Norbert Finzsch and Ursula Lehmkuhl (Oxford: Berg, 2004), 335–72.

"Nazis, Viewers, and Statistics: Television History, Television Audience Research and Collective Memory in West Germany," *Journal of Contemporary History* 39, no. 4 (2004): 575–98.

While working on this book, I received financial support from a number institutions and I am grateful for that help: the National Endowment for the

Humanities, the German Academic Exchange Service, the Holocaust Education Foundation, the Institute for Advanced Studies in the Humanities in Essen, Germany, the Mershon Center at the Ohio State University, and especially the Institute for European History in Mainz, Germany.

I also would like to thank the many colleagues who gave me opportunities to present my work and provided valuable criticism and advice: David Bathrick, Stefan Berger, David Brenner, Sande Cohen, Alon Confino, Heide Fehrenbach, Norbert Finzsch, Norbert Frei, Peter Fritzsche, Michael Geisler, Jeffrey Herf, Christhard Hoffmann, Georg Iggers, Dominick LaCapra, Judith Keilbach, Ned Lebow, Ursula Lehmkuhl, Chris Lorenz, Inge Marszolek, Vrääth Öhner, Andy Rabinbach, Steven Remy, Ann Rigney, Alan Rosenbaum, Gavriel Rosenfeld, Jörn Rüsen, Dirk Schumann, Heidemarie Uhl, Hayden White, and Richard Wolin.

It would have been impossible to do research in contemporary German media history without the help of the great staff of the historical archives at the Zweite Deutsche Fernsehen in Mainz: Holger Burghardt, Gertrud Haunz, and Hans Rink. I am also very appreciative of the generous help I have received from Ohio University Press, especially from Gillian Berchowitz and Ricky Huard.

There are many friends and family members who gave encouragement and to whom I am very grateful: Howard Brown, Nina Caputo, Scott Corley, Bonnie Effros, Mitch Hart, Friedrich Jaeger, Heiner Kansteiner, Morten Kansteiner, Kerwin Klein, Liz Lupo, Elke Michalski, Helene Mialet, Don Quataert, Jean Quataert, Harald Weilnböck, Michael Weintroub, and Oliver Withöft.

I am particularly thankful to Jennifer Cubic, who read and edited the whole manuscript, Saul Friedlander, who taught me most of what I know about research and academia, Claudio Fogu, who has been the best of friends and intellectual allies ever since I arrived in the United States, and Sonja Wolf, who teaches me about the limits of academia and the wonders of *Heimat*.

Finally, I wish to thank my parents, Heinrich and Renate Kansteiner, who provided everything from research and financial help to intellectual curiosity and emotional support.

PART ONE
GUILT AND MEMORY

THE VAGARIES OF COLLECTIVE
SYMBOLIC GUILT

Since the late 1940s, the historical culture of the Federal Republic of Germany has followed two closely intertwined but diametrically opposed trajectories. On the one hand, the political and cultural elite dealt with the Nazi past in order to leave it behind as quickly as possible. Many politicians, historians, and artists (mis)identified victims and perpetrators, settled claims for compensation, and sought explanations for the German catastrophe so that they could return to a world that no longer bore any sign of twelve years of Nazi rule. On the other hand, part of the elite did everything in its power to prevent such a return to a state of historical innocence and plastered reminders of Germany's original sin all across the media. The first mind-set invented antitotalitarianism and the economic miracle and integrated the Federal Republic into the capitalist West. This attitude was particularly pronounced among the conservative members of the war generations who had experienced the Third Reich as adults. The second mind-set reflects the historical taste of the liberal members of the postwar generations who were born during or after the war. Since the 1960s, they have continually reprocessed the Nazi past and later the Holocaust for purposes of education, remembrance, entertainment, and political gain.

The ideological and generational space between the adults of the Third Reich and postwar generations is occupied by a large number of "memory hybrids," people who have contributed to both trajectories of West German memory and who are particularly often found in the ranks of the Hitler Youth generation. Raised in the Third Reich but too young to have been perpetrators, they tend to shuttle back and forth between the desire to forget and the compulsion to remember.[1] Consider, for example, the conservative politician

Helmut Kohl, who tried to lay the Nazi past to rest by obsessively reinventing its cultural memory,[2] or liberal novelists such as Martin Walser and Günter Grass, who felt compelled to protect their "authentic" memories of German suffering from the destructive powers of commercial Holocaust memory.[3]

The first trajectory of German memory, the relentless pursuit of reconciliation and normalization, is easily understood. But the second trajectory, the sustained, collective focus on Germany's crimes, begs explanation. Why would Germans spend so much time and effort investigating, representing, and consuming stories about their past misdeeds many years before publicly apologizing for collective injustices had become an international fad? This second paradigm is a West German invention; until shortly before the collapse of the German Democratic Republic (GDR), its political elite never strayed from the path of normalization and self-exculpation. Therefore, the following study focuses on developments in the Federal Republic and touches on developments in East Germany only to the extent that they influenced the West German scene.[4]

On an abstract, metaphorical level, the German focus on memory politics can be described as the result of an unusual phenomenon—the successful sublation of large-scale personal and political guilt into collective symbolic guilt. It is neither difficult nor original to identify guilt at the center of German efforts to come to terms with the past.[5] As early as 1946, Karl Jaspers neatly categorized German guilt after Nazism into four types—criminal, political, moral, and metaphysical. After having identified the appropriate procedures and authorities for each category—ranging from the criminal courts to the victors of World War II to the individual's conscience and God— Jaspers ruled that "collective guilt of a people . . . cannot exist."[6] His honest yet defensive essay might have been an appropriate assessment of German guilt immediately after the war, but subsequent developments require a different evaluation. The Germans themselves, as well as their foreign partners, became actively involved in the construction of a new type of guilt related to the Nazi crimes—a type of guilt that was *accepted* by the West German elite and at least some segments of the population. But in contrast to past types of guilt, the new category of collective symbolic guilt was not defined in any concrete legal, political, or moral terms, and procedures of atonement and could be addressed *only* through symbolic politics and cultural memory work.[7]

The transformation of personal responsibility into transgenerational, symbolic guilt produced an exceptional historical challenge. In other cases in the first half of the twentieth century in which nations have found themselves pressured to acknowledge collective responsibility for past crimes—as happened with Japan and Turkey, for instance—the population and their representatives have largely rejected any criminal or symbolic liability.[8] In the case of World War II and the Holocaust, West German society—first through its representatives and then on a broader scale—has accepted long-term, collective moral responsibility for genocide. But for lack of precedents, the precise nature of this responsibility has remained unclear. Although standards and procedures for dealing with personal criminal guilt are well established, the process of dealing with symbolic collective guilt is uncharted territory.[9] Therefore, no one has been able to define the end point of this obligation. Many attempts to implement symbolic burials for collective symbolic guilt were based on the mistaken yet understandable assumption that symbolic guilt, like personal guilt, can be laid to rest after appropriate token punishment or atonement. This mistake informed, for instance, Helmut Kohl's and Ronald Reagan's staging of a German-U.S. reconciliation ceremony in Bitburg in 1985 that was intended to help end discussions about the Nazi past. Such attempts were motivated by the equally understandable error that unsettled symbolic charges, like unsettled criminal charges, undermine the system of (symbolic) justice and have negative effects on the integrity and self-image of the collective in question. Yet nothing could be further from the truth. The ongoing, self-reflexive debates about *Vergangenheitsbewältigung* (coming to terms with, or mastering, the past), however seemingly counterproductive, have proven to be an asset for West Germany at home as well as abroad.

The acceptance of a powerful, symbolic moral duty in combination with complete ignorance about the precise nature of this duty has caused a flurry of activity. As artists, intellectuals, and politicians have sought to identify appropriate ways of dealing with the burden of Nazism in their respective fields of expertise and institutional contexts, they have set in motion a peculiar dialectic of routine and scandal.[10] Since the 1960s, most media, professions, and institutions involved in the representation of history have developed routines for depicting Nazism—for instance, the routine of television docudramas, of historical research and writing, or of political speechwriting and political ritual. But due to the high stakes of the symbolic game, the lack of clarity, and the instrumentalization for political and aesthetic purposes, such routines are frequently punctuated by controversy when participants and commentators believe that a concrete contribution violates their understanding of Germany's historical obligation. Some of these controversies have reached national proportions and involved large segments of the West German population; the debate triggered by the miniseries *Holocaust* is one example.[11] Other scandals have concerned only the intellectual community, such as the debates about the alleged anti-Semitic inclinations of the playwright Rainer Werner Fassbinder that took place in 1976 and 1985 or the discussions about the uniqueness of the Holocaust that erupted in 1986.[12]

Describing the German obsession with mastering the past as a result of the transformation of personal guilt into collective symbolic guilt explains some of the contradictory impulses that have been expressed in Germany's historical culture. But that description hardly clarifies the historical causes of the unusual willingness to explore the nation's legacy of shame. One might be tempted to ascribe that willingness to the exceptional character of the Nazi crimes, although that explanation gives short shrift to postwar developments and hardly does justice to the highly unstable concept of the uniqueness of the Holocaust. The rise of Germany's critical historical culture since the 1960s is better understood as a truly political phenomenon—as the result of a specific constellation of ideological convictions, political generations, and strategic options. In fact, the second paradigm of German memory politics that begs explanation developed in response to the first paradigm, which became a victim of its own success. Precisely because the conservative contemporaries of the Third Reich were so successful in managing the present, that is, the challenges of economic and ideological reconstruction, they forced their critics and younger competitors to return to the sins of the past and use them as political leverage. This process started in the late 1950s, when an eclectic group of memory dissidents exposed the cracks and internal contradictions of the postwar collective memory, and gained in intensity in the late 1960s, when the activists of the student movement appeared on the scene.

Thus, the origins of West Germany's critical historical culture date back to the immediate postwar period, as a closer look at West Germany's political scene illustrates. The first West German chancellor, Konrad Adenauer, pursued politics of history that combined "extreme leniency" for the Nazi perpetrators with general "normative distancing from National Socialism."[13] For the purposes of social stability and integration with the West, he sought to settle accounts quickly with perpetrators and victims. But his pragmatic course lacked moral precision. Adenauer and the members of his administration acknowledged many victims of Nazism, including the vast majority of the German population, but recognized only a very small number of Nazi perpetrators. Therefore, their initiatives included embarrassing appeals for the release of war criminals from Allied prisons, as well as a genuine desire to make atonement and restitution to Israel.[14] This lack of moral precision is reflected in the official postwar language of memory. General and vague formulas about "unspeakable crimes" committed "in the name of the German people" and equally vague appeals to remember human suffering have informed countless official speeches directed at the citizens of the Federal Republic and foreign observers since the 1950s.[15]

The combination of communicative silence, leniency, and general acknowledgment of guilt worked wonders for the generation of Germans who lived through the Third Reich. They enjoyed social integration, stability, and renewed international recognition without taking their leaders' commitment for remembrance and atonement too seriously. In fact, most contemporaries clearly understood that the appeals constituted an end in themselves and should not be considered encouragement for additional public memory work. This moral equilibrium was only occasionally disrupted by political scandals when continuities between the Third Reich and the Federal Republic became too obtrusive to be ignored.

But the historical culture of the Adenauer era had planted a time bomb. The blatant contradiction between the repetitive, seemingly self-critical incantation about the need to remember and the general unwillingness to engage in any serious memory work offered an easy target for dissidents of the Adenauer era and for subsequent generations as they struggled to distance themselves from the disgrace of Nazism and earlier generations that had embraced it. They took the phrases about remembrance at face value and turned Vergangenheitsbewältigung into a serious historical obligation, which, because of its indeterminate nature, proved to be an excellent tool for generational, political, and intellectual strife. Some of the initial steps undertaken to advance the self-reflexive process of working through the legacy of Nazism were eminently practical. Blatant deficiencies of the postwar period were addressed through renewed attempts to bring Nazi criminals to trial,[16] to reform school education about the Third Reich,[17] and to research Nazism's historical origins.[18] These practical concerns have remained part of the process, but as subsequent generations joined the cause, more abstract questions about the appropriate representations, historical contextualizations, and political consequences of Nazism dominated the debates. From the beginning, however, these efforts were not directed at understanding and alleviating *personal* responsibility for the crimes of the Nazi period, which these generations did not share. Rather, they were intended to repair and maintain a sense of collective moral integrity for the future.

Thus, younger Germans joined Adenauer in the business of guilt management but could afford to pursue it with greater ruthlessness and rigor because the stakes and rules of the process had changed from the 1950s to the 1960s. In the postwar years, communication about the Nazi past served many purposes, including self-exculpation and political grandstanding, but the competition between different interpretations of the Nazi past was tied to a very practical benchmark, that is, the measure of economic, political, and psychological reconstruction that the respective strategies of representation helped accomplish. By the 1960s and certainly in subsequent years, that practical benchmark disappeared. Arguing about the Third Reich and the Holocaust remained a suitable venue for political and generational disagreements, but especially for the most committed memory activists, the struggle about the appropriate representation of the past became an end in itself. Given the indeterminate nature of this symbolic undertaking, this struggle was simply irresolvable and differed in that respect from the political competition of the postwar years, which had concluded with the creation of a widely shared antitotalitarian consensus.

In trying to understand the nature and shelf life of acknowledged collective symbolic guilt, many commentators have come to the conclusion that Vergangenheitsbewältigung is an ongoing, open-ended obligation. That position makes a good deal of political and didactic sense. Germans are, indeed, well advised to remember the political naïveté, lack of courage, and propensity for crime that their forebears exhibited in the Third Reich. Unfortunately, however, continued identification with the cause of Vergangenheitsbewältigung does not make a lot of emotional sense for younger Germans, who are several generations removed from the catastrophe of World War II and the Holocaust. With the exception of the relatively few individuals who find employment in Germany's institution of cultural memory, Germans born since the 1960s probably have no compelling psychological reason to engage with the legacy of the Third Reich in an intensive, sustained, and self-critical fashion.[19] For the time being, this lack of motivation is counterbalanced by the enthusiasm of professional memory activists for whom Vergangenheits-bewältigung has become a way of life and who decide how Germany's history is covered in the national media. But a closer look at Germany's political elite or Germany's media consumers illustrates that the quest for symbolic atone-ment has been transformed in the context of the second generational turnover since the war, even if the full effects of that turnover will become visible only in the media of the future.

As the intellectuals who grew up during the Third Reich conclude the most productive years of their careers, their distinct interpretations of National Socialism and the "Final Solution" are disappearing from the media that make up Germany's historical culture. The passing into history of the events of the Holocaust is not marked only by the disappearance of the voices of the sur-vivors. Equally important yet far less frequently acknowledged is the gradual disappearance of a whole generation of intellectuals who have studied events that have directly touched their lives. By exploring the Nazi period, they have tried to understand the world that shaped their childhood and adolescence years, and in the process, they have also explained that world to all of us. Their specific vision of the past transcends different national cultures and even the divide between former bystanders and perpetrators of Nazi abuses. As arbiters of the cultural memory of the Nazi era and the Holocaust, they are leaving an impressive legacy of interpretation that is remarkable for its co-herence and its emotional commitment, as well as its selective engagement with the history of the "Final Solution." This generation's pivotal role in the construction of German memories of the Nazi era is one of the conceptual foci of the present study.

The following chapters reconstruct the evolution of three key theaters of Germany's historical culture—history, television, and politics—each of which has developed very specific strategies for dealing with the challenge of collec-tive symbolic guilt. Part 2 focuses on the memory microcosm of professional historiography. After offering a diachronic survey of academic Holocaust studies in the Federal Republic, I take the Historians' Debate of 1986 and 1987 as an opportunity to provide a synchronic cut through the different layers of

West Germany's historical culture and place the professional historical discourse within its larger intellectual and social context. Chapter 5 provides a piece of intellectual archaeology by taking a close look at the texts of a new cohort of scholars who reintroduced traditional formats of narrative continuity into the field of contemporary history in the 1980s and thus advanced the historicization of the Nazi past.

Part 3 deals with the representation of Nazism and the Holocaust in the television of the Federal Republic and begins with an analysis of the most important themes, formats, and strategies of avoidance that shaped the television discourse about the "Final Solution" from the 1960s through the 1990s. This diachronic survey is then augmented by a discussion of the empirical and conceptual problems of studying television reception, which is a particularly pressing concern if one tries to integrate media history and collective memory studies. The engagement with television concludes with an in-depth look at the career and works of Germany's most successful TV historian, Guido Knopp, who, together with his production team, revolutionized the representation of Nazi history in the 1990s.

Part 4 is dedicated to the arena of national politics. On the basis of the large number of monographs that have been written about German memory politics since the mid-1990s, this part presents a comprehensive survey of the political discourse and scandals that have shaped the image of Nazism at the highest level of government. Covering the evolution of political memory in West Germany from the first postwar years to the summer of 2005, the synthesis shows how elite memories of Nazism have evolved in response to international developments, generational transformations, and shifts in political power. This chronological survey provides the foundation for the concluding chapter, which maps out the history and sociology of German memories in a systematic fashion. Together with the methodological reflections in chapter 2, the conclusion illustrates what insights the German case offers to the field of collective memory studies.

FINDING MEANING IN MEMORY

A Methodological Critique of Collective Memory Studies

Collective memory studies bring together two seemingly contradictory interests. On one side, the study of memory turns academics into concerned citizens who share the burdens of contemporary memory crises. As "memory
experts," these academics can explore the social impact of rapidly evolving
communication technologies, the uncertainties of collective belonging after
the end of the Cold War, and the challenges of coming to terms with war and
genocide.[1] On the other side, the study of memory is a bona fide intellectual
exercise that allows academics to respond to the most interesting philosophical legacies of the last century. In particular, through the concept of memory,
they can demonstrate to the few remaining postmodern critics how representations really work and how the power of representations can be explained.[2]

The rare combination of social relevance and intellectual challenge explains the popularity of the field. But though memory has obviously become
a central concept in the humanities and the social sciences, it remains unclear to what extent this convergence reflects actual common intellectual and
methodological interests.[3] This chapter lays out the state of the art in collective memory studies by analyzing the field's terminology and especially its
conceptual underpinnings. This exploration of the complex interdisciplinary
space forms the basis of three conclusions. First, collective memory studies
have not yet sufficiently conceptualized collective memories as distinct from
individual memory. As a result, the nature and dynamics of collective memories are frequently misrepresented through a facile use of psychoanalytical
and psychological methods. Second, collective memory studies need to focus
more aggressively on identifying sources and developing methods that allow
us to describe with more precision how collective memories emerge in the

process of media consumption. Since many existing works on collective memory do not pay enough attention to the problem of reception, they often cannot illuminate the sociological base of the historical representations with which they engage. And third, some of these problems can be addressed by adopting and further developing the methods of media and communication studies, especially regarding questions of reception. For this purpose, we should conceptualize collective memory as the result of the interactions among three types of historical factors: the intellectual and cultural traditions that frame all our representations of the past; the memory makers who selectively adopt and manipulate these traditions; and the memory consumers who use, ignore, or transform such artifacts according to their own interests.

Students of collective memory are, indeed, pursuing a slippery phenomenon. Collective memory is not history, though it is sometimes made from similar material. It is a collective phenomenon, but it only manifests itself in the actions and statements of individuals. It can take hold of historically and socially remote events but often privileges the interests of the contemporary. It is as much a result of conscious manipulation as unconscious absorption, and it is always mediated. It can be observed only in roundabout ways, more through its effects than its characteristics. In essence, collective memory studies represent a new approach to "that most elusive of phenomena, 'popular consciousness.'"[4]

TERMINOLOGICAL PROFUSION

Most historians who study collective memories take the work of the French sociologist Maurice Halbwachs as their primary theoretical reference point.[5] Following Halbwachs, a student of Émile Durkheim, they understand collective memories as collectively shared representations of the past. Halbwachs's emphasis on the function of everyday communication for the development of collective memories and his interest in the imagery of social discourse resonate very well with recent historiographical themes, especially regarding questions of historical representation. However, many historians are uncomfortable with Halbwachs's determined anti-individualism. They object that "Durkheimians held tenaciously that individual memory was entirely socially determined" and thus wrote the individual out of a role in the history of collective memory.[6] As a result, though Halbwachs is frequently cited, historians simultaneously seek distance from their role model in order to return to one of their favorite subjects—the objectives and actions of individuals in history.

To find alternatives to the sociologically "occupied" conception of collective memory, scholars have coined terms such as *social memory*,[7] *collective remembrance*,[8] and *popular history making*,[9] or they have altogether rejected the need for new terminology in favor of the old-fashioned concept of "myth."[10] The multitude of terms has further increased as scholars have sought to develop expressions that illuminate the social base or social function of the collective memories under consideration. Therefore, the vocabulary of memory studies includes terms such as *national memory, public memory, vernacular memory*, and *countermemory*.[11]

This terminological diversity obscures the fact that the majority of contributions to the field of memory studies continue research agendas that used to sail under separate colors. This is true of methodologically innovative work about the history of mentalities, oral history,[12] the history of everyday life and popular culture, and historical consciousness,[13] but it is particularly pronounced in areas of research that have traditionally been called cultural-intellectual history. The large-scale editorial "relabeling" explains the astonishing quantitative dimension of the memory wave and the fact that most studies on memory tend to reduce collective memory to an effect of human agency.

Many of the conceptually more interesting studies of memory gravitate toward the term *cultural memory* in order to maintain and further develop Halbwachs's emphasis on the materiality of memory.[14] In this context, Jan Assmann's juxtaposition of communicative and cultural memory is particularly useful. He designates the former as everyday communications about the meaning of the past characterized by instability, disorganization, and nonspecialization. These everyday communications have a limited temporal horizon of eighty to one hundred years; they are, by definition, strongly influenced by contemporaries of the events in question. In contrast, the cultural memory "comprises that body of reusable texts, images, and rituals specific to each society in each epoch, whose 'cultivation' serves to stabilize and convey that society's self-image."[15] Cultural memory consists of objectified culture—that is, the texts, rites, images, buildings, and monuments that are designed to recall fateful events in the history of the collective. As the officially sanctioned heritage of a society, they are intended for long-term use.

Assmann also makes an important differentiation between potential and actual cultural memories. He argues that cultural memories occur in the mode of potentiality when representations of the past are stored in archives, libraries, and museums; they occur in the mode of actuality when these representations are adopted and given new meaning in fresh social and historical contexts. These distinctions suggest that specific representations of the past might traverse the whole spectrum, from the realm of communicative memory to the realm of actual cultural memory and finally to potential cultural memory (and back). But in the process, they change their intensity, social depth, and meaning.[16] Assmann's concepts remind us that despite their power to transmit concern for historical events to future generations, collective memories have a strong bias toward the present; they dedicate disproportionate amounts of time, space, and resources to communications about events that happened within the lifetimes of its producers and consumers. Or, to use Lutz Niethammer's words, collective memories are primarily located on this side of the "floating gap" between memory and history.[17]

Pierre Nora's work in the tradition of Halbwachs lacks the conceptual precision of Assmann's contributions, but as one of the foremost practitioners in the field, Nora has advanced the most ambitious historicization of the memory phenomenon. In elegant prose, he has proposed a three-stage model that is as Eurocentric as it is simple and seemingly compelling. He divides the history of memory in three phases—a premodern, modern, and postmodern condition. Premodern times are characterized by a natural, unselfconscious relation between people and their past. Their environments of memory sustain traditions and rituals that provide a stable sense of being in time for the members of local memory communities. For Nora, the fall from memory grace occurred in the nineteenth century with the acceleration of everyday life through industrial and social modernization. As old traditions and affiliations lost their meaning, the relation between people and their past was reconstructed through first-order simulations of natural memory. Elites produced sites of memory in language, monuments, and archives that had one common referent, the nation-state, and that strove to secure the future of the nation-state through compelling inventions of its traditions. With the collapse of the ideology and reality of the nation-state in the twentieth century, these first-order simulations were replaced by second-order simulations of natural memory. The media culture of the late twentieth century spewed out identities and representations of the past that had little relation to any shared traditions, life worlds, or political institutions other than the frantic pace of media consumption itself.[18]

Attempts at historicizing memory such as Nora's indicate that our crises of memory are concomitant with crises of identity. In particular, the concern with memory in nonacademic contexts—therapeutic circles, the judicial system, post–Cold War ethnic conflicts, and so on—shows that memory is valorized where identity is problematized.[19] Despite this relatively obvious link, the connection between memory and identity has, as yet, been rarely discussed in memory studies.[20] It is not possible to fill that gap here, but it should be emphasized that rethinking memory studies from the perspective of identity construction raises two important questions. First, the focus on identity highlights the political and psychological use value of collective memories. As noted earlier, representations of the past without such use-values would more appropriately be designated as discarded traditions and/or future potential collective memories, not as collective memories per se. In addition to this crucial differentiation, the focus on identity suggests that our modern crises of memory might not be as exceptional as we tend to assume. All our efforts at historicization notwithstanding, the history of memory cannot be contained by our histories of modernity. Incidentally, this conclusion is supported by the wide range of research on collective memories in antiquity and the Middle Ages.[21]

Even historians have been forced to rethink their scholarly identity as a result of the rise of memory studies. Although most academics still maintain that "in its demand for proof, history stands in sharp opposition to memory," there are good reasons to question such a clear epistemological divide between academic and nonacademic representations of the past.[22] Perhaps history should be defined as a particular type of cultural memory because, as Peter Burke remarked in 1989, "neither memories nor histories seem objective any longer. In both cases we are learning to take account of conscious or unconscious selection, interpretation and distortion. In both cases this selection, interpretation and distortion is socially conditioned."[23] Memory's relation to history remains one of the interesting theoretical challenges in the field, a challenge we will address in the following chapters.

Another unsettled area of collective memory studies is the precise relation between the individual and the collective. At first sight, recent psychological and neurological studies give ample reason for the conflation of individual and collective memory because such research has, time and again, emphasized the social nature of individual remembering and forgetting. Even on a neurological level, our ability to store, recall, and reconfigure verbal and nonverbal experiences and information cannot be separated from patterns of perception that we have learned from our immediate and wider social environments.[24] The very language and narrative patterns that we use to express memories, even autobiographical memories, are inseparable from the social standards of plausibility and authenticity that they embody.[25] In this sense, "there is no such thing as individual memory."[26]

The impressive unanimity between psychological, sociological, historical, and artistic perspectives on human memory seems to confirm Halbwachs, who argued in 1925 that "the idea of an individual memory, absolutely separate from social memory, is an abstraction almost devoid of meaning."[27] But the fact that individual memory cannot be conceptualized and studied without recourse to its social context does not necessarily imply the reverse, that is, that collective memory can only be imagined and accessed through its manifestation in individuals. At the very least, we have to differentiate between different types of "social" memory—autobiographical memory, on the one hand, and collective memory, on the other. For lack of such differentiation, many scholars who inquire into collective memories commit a tempting yet potentially grave methodological error: they perceive and conceptualize collective memory exclusively in terms of the psychological and emotional dynamics of individual remembering.

Since the threshold between the individual and the collective is often crossed without any adjustments in method, collectives are said to remember, to forget, and to repress the past, but this is done without any awareness that such language is at best metaphorical and at worst misleading about the phenomenon under study. Historians rationalize this conflation and sidestep the theoretical and methodological challenge of thinking in terms of collectives as distinct from individuals by emphasizing the role of human agency in the construction of collective memories. They focus on acts of memorialization—for instance, in museum design—assuming the realized object and its meaning are prescribed by the maker's conscious or unconscious objectives.[28]

These category mistakes stem from a subtle but decisive confusion of the difference between "collected memory" and "collective memory."[29] A collected memory is an aggregate of individual memories that behaves and develops just like its individual composites and that can therefore be studied with the whole inventory of neurological, psychological, and psychoanalytic methods and insights concerning the memories of individuals. Unfortunately, collective memories do not behave according to such rules but have their own dynamics, for which we have to find appropriate methods of analysis.

For example, it might make sense to argue, with Sigmund Freud, that an individual's failure to work through his or her past results in unwanted symptoms of psychological distress or, put another way, that the self relies on a sense of continuity that makes it impossible to repress the past without having to pay a psychological price for this repression. But on a collective scale, especially on the scale of larger collectives, such assumptions are misleading.[30] Nations *can* repress with psychological impunity; their collective memories can be changed without a "return of the repressed." Therefore, "when speaking of social forgetting, we are best advised to keep psychological or psychoanalytical categories at bay and to focus, rather, on the social, political, and cultural factors at work."[31]

Reservations about the use of psychoanalytic methods in collective memory studies extend to the concept of trauma, which has particular relevance for our understanding of the legacy of collective catastrophes. The concepts of the unconscious and repression inappropriately individualize and psychologize collective memory processes, but the use of the concept of trauma has had an opposite yet equally misleading effect. Some recent works in trauma theory invoke the example of the Holocaust as an illustration for a more general postmodern claim about the undecidability of the nature of our historical experience and our representations of it. The very specific and unusual experiences and memory challenges of survivors—who find that their memories of the "Final Solution" form a volatile, independent realm of memory that remains painfully irreconcilable with subsequent experiences[32]—are offered as proof of the general traumatic characteristics of the postmodern condition. In this vein, Cathy Caruth has argued with regard to the Holocaust that such "a crisis of truth extends beyond the question of individual cure and asks how we in this era can have access to our own historical experience, to a history that is in its immediacy a crisis to whose truth there is no simple access."[33] Not surprisingly, such obliteration of historical specificity has met with determined criticism, even from theorists who are quite sympathetic to the use of psychoanalytic methods in memory studies. Dominick LaCapra, who has systematically and extensively worked on trauma and memory, has pointed out that "there is a great temptation to trope away from specificity and to generalize hyperbolically, for example, through an extremely abstract mode of discourse that may at times serve as a surrogate for a certain form of deconstruction, elaborate an undifferentiated notion of all history (or at least all modernity) as trauma, and overextend the concept of victim and survivor."[34]

I would go even further in my criticism and suggest that though specific visions of the past might originate in traumatic experiences, they do not retain that quality if they become successful collective memories. The concept of trauma, as well as the concept of repression, neither captures nor illuminates the forces that contribute to the making and unmaking of collective memories. Even in instances of so-called delayed collective memory (as in the case of the Holocaust or Vietnam), the delayed onset of public debates about the meaning of negative pasts has more to do with political interest and opportunities than with the persistence of trauma or with any "leakage" in the collective unconscious. Small groups whose members have directly experienced such traumatic events (veterans' or survivors' groups) only have a chance to shape the national memory if they command the means to express their visions and if their vision meets with compatible social or political objectives and inclinations among other important social groups, such as political elites or parties. Past events can only be recalled in a collective setting "if they fit within a framework of contemporary interests."[35]

Undue emphasis on the individual in psychoanalytically informed approaches to collective memory, as well as the frustration with the postmodern disregard for historical specificity, have led to attempts to rethink intentionality and agency in ways that are perhaps best described as post-postmodern methodological reflections. Nancy Wood has delineated such an approach in her account of collective memory, the unconscious, and intentionality: "While the emanation of individual memory is primarily subject to the laws of the unconscious, public memory—whatever its unconscious vicissitudes—testifies to a will or desire on the part of some social group or disposition of power to select and organize representations of the past so that these will be embraced by individuals as their own. If particular representations of the past have permeated the public domain, it is because they embody an intentionality—social, political, institutional and so on—that promotes or authorizes their entry."[36] Wood addresses a number of possible sources that "purposefully" shape public memory, ranging from social groups to institutions and dispositions of power. In this way, she has politely and diplomatically summarized the different notions of intentionality and power that have informed collective memory studies and that run the gamut from conventional historical accounts of human agency to theoretically informed inquiries into the limits of memorial culture as they are reflected in specific traditions and practices of historical representation. As Wood illustrates, the most interesting interventions in collective memory studies seek to profit from poststructural insights into cultural systems of representation but also hope to reconcile these insights with conventional methods of historical studies that emphasize agency and intentionality without returning to simplistic notions of them (including those of Freudian origins).

Still, although collective memories have no organic basis and do not exist in any literal sense and although they involve individual agency, the term *collective memory* is not simply a metaphorical expression. Collective memories originate from shared communications about the meaning of the past that are anchored in the life worlds of individuals who partake in the communal life of a social group. As such, collective memories are based in a society and its inventory of signs and symbols: "Memory seems to reside not in perceiving consciousness but *in the material*: in the practices and institutions of social or psychic life, which function within us, but, strangely, do not seem to require either our participation or our explicit allegiance."[37] Such collective memories exist on the level of families, professions, political generations, ethnic and regional groups, social classes, and nations. These examples indicate that we are always part of several mnemonic communities and that collective remembering can be explored on markedly different scales; it takes place in very private settings as well as in the public sphere. On one side of the spectrum, we might pursue collective memories of small groups, such as families whose members weave a common vision of family origin and identity.[38]

On the other side, we are beginning to consider supranational collective memories, as in the case of the (still dubious) entity known as a European collective memory.[39] On any level, however, "collective memory works by subsuming individual experiences under cultural schemes that make them comprehensible and, therefore, meaningful."[40]

Methodologically speaking, memories are at their most collective when they transcend the time and space of an event's original occurrence. As such, they take on a powerful life of their own, "unencumbered" by actual individual memory, and they become the basis of all collective remembering as disembodied, omnipresent, low-intensity memory. This point has been reached, for instance, with regard to the memory of the Holocaust in American society. As a result, millions of people share a limited range of stories and images about the Holocaust, although few of them have any personal link to the actual events. For many consumers, the stories and images do not constitute particularly intense or overpowering experiences, but they nevertheless shape the individuals' identities and worldviews.[41]

Concern with low-intensity collective memories shifts the focus from the politics of memory and its excess of scandal and intrigue to rituals and representations of the past that are produced and consumed routinely without causing much disagreement. Most groups settle temporarily on such collective memories and reproduce them for years and even decades until they are questioned and perhaps overturned, often in the wake of generational turnover. These repetitive representations form the backbone of collective memories. They are the common denominator in questions of historical taste that are disseminated widely and frequently enough to create and maintain group identities.

The study of memory routines can certainly profit from psychological models that help explain their reproduction. However, in this context, the work of Henri Bergson might prove a better point of departure than the insights of Freud, especially Bergson's concept of "habit memory"; his understanding of "the physical being as incarnation of all the possibilities of acting out the past in the present" seems to be well suited to bridge the methodological gap between individual and collective memory.[42] The concept has, among other things, significantly improved our understanding of rituals of commemoration as collective memory processes.[43]

BETWEEN INDIFFERENCE AND OBSESSION: THE MEDIA OF MEMORY

Physical and social proximity to past events and their subsequent rationaliza-tion and memorialization do not have to coincide. There is no natural, direct connection between the real and the remembered. On the one hand, collec-tive memories might exclude events that played an important role in the lives of members of the community (for instance, the memory of World War II in Japan). On the other hand, socially and geographically distant events might be adopted for identity purposes by groups that had no involvement in their unfolding (as in the case of Holocaust memory). Even if most groups do not embrace memories of events that occurred in unfamiliar or historically dis-tant cultural contexts, their memories are always mediated phenomena. All memories, even the memories of eyewitnesses, only assume collective rele-vance when they are structured, represented, and used in a social setting. As a result, the means of representation that facilitate this process provide the best information about the evolution of collective memories, especially as we try to reconstruct them after the fact.

The media of memory that help us construct and transmit our knowledge and feelings about the past rely on various combinations of discursive, visual, and spatial elements. Therefore, collective memories are multimedia collages consisting, in part, of "a mixture of pictorial images and scenes, slogans, quips, and snatches of verse, abstractions, plot types and stretches of dis-course, and even false etymologies."[44] They also include statues, memorial sites, and buildings. Since we are not able to reconstruct these fluid constel-lations in their entirety, we have to focus on one or two layers at a time. These efforts have created distinct subfields in collective memory studies. A num-ber of early theorists of collective memory, including Halbwachs, studied mnemonic landscapes and cityscapes. Their pursuits have spawned a wave of scholarly inquiry into monuments and architectural landscapes as expres-sions of cultural memory.[45]

Closely related to these concerns with spatial expressions of memory are attempts to record the images that make up our collective visions of the past. Scholars who focus on images as vehicles of memory contend that from antiquity to modern times, the media of memory have been characterized by "the primacy of the visual."[46] In their assessment, one of the reasons for the privileged status of images in memory construction derives from their exceptional ability to close and at times even obliterate the gap between firsthand experience and secondary witnessing. As Daniel Sherman put it: "Sight is the only sense powerful enough to bridge the gap between those who hold a memory rooted in bodily experience and those who, lacking such 'experience,' nonetheless seek to share the memory."[47] However, despite their evocative power, images depend on words to provide them with meaning because the relation between an image and its interpretation needs to be established. Once that connection is established and reliably reproduced, images "act as signposts, directing people who remember to preferred meaning by the fastest route."[48] Because of this close relation between images and words in the making of collective memories, such memories can also be accessed and studied through their discursive and narrative foundations. As a result, the discursive elements of collective memories are another specific focus in collective memory studies.[49]

But a reliance on the media of memory in the pursuit of past collective identities causes two problems: an unselfconscious return to the central role of human agency in history (now as the maker of representations), paired with a troubling disregard for proof (who actually shares or identifies with these representations). The formal and semantic qualities of historical representations might have little in common with the intentions of their authors, and neither the objects' characteristics nor the authors' objectives are good indicators for the ways in which users and consumers subsequently engage with these objects. In fact, it is particularly interesting to notice how often media representations are ignored or read against the grain of their intended or intrinsic messages: "Individuals are perfectly capable of ignoring even the best told stories, of injecting their own, subversive meanings into even the most rhetorically accomplished 'texts'—and of attending to only those ways of making sense of the past that fit their own."[50] Indeed, there is the distinct possibility that the monuments, books, and films whose history has been carefully reconstructed can quickly pass into oblivion without shaping the historical imagination of any individuals or social groups.[51]

The epistemological sleight of hand from representation to memory could be easily avoided, although the results of our scholarly efforts might no longer speak to memory, let alone any collective memory. It is one objective to write the intellectual history of the coming into being of a number of cultural artifacts that share certain characteristics (topic, author, place, time). It is an altogether different endeavor to tie these representations to specific social groups and their understanding of the past. The second step entails knowledge about reception processes that is beyond the conventional purview of historical know-how; it is also objectively difficult to establish.[52]

Perhaps some of the methodological problems might stand out more clearly if we briefly consider a "failed" collective memory, such as the memory of the Korean War in the United States. Unlike the collective memories of the world wars, the Holocaust, and Vietnam that have been studied extensively, stories and images of the Korean War have never filled our media and have also never been the object of particular scholarly interest.[53] The Korean War has remained a "forgotten" war, lost between the heroic fight against Hitler and the trauma of Vietnam. But the situation temporarily changed in recent years. The fiftieth anniversary of the war, the first steps toward national reconciliation in Korea, and news about war crimes committed by U.S. troops during the campaign raised interest in the history of the war, with its legacy of national division.[54] For the first time, interested parties such as U.S. veterans and their associations had an opportunity to project their own collective memory of the war into the larger public sphere and help shape a national collective memory of the Korean War in the popular annals of U.S. military interventions. However, now that the moment has passed, the memory of the Korean War will most likely again disappear, despite all these efforts to sustain it.[55]

The example illustrates two important insights about the nature of historical representations. First, most stories about the past, even those designed for fame as future collective memories, never make it beyond the group of a few initiated. In "the field of cultural negotiation through which different stories vie for a place in history," failure is the rule.[56] In addition, the example highlights one of the foundational myths of memory studies. Memory studies presuppose a rarely acknowledged but not particularly surprising desire for cultural homogeneity, consistency, and predictability. Often, we simply assume that people who have some knowledge and perhaps even a vested interest in past events such as the Korean War or the Holocaust have substantially similar perceptions of the event in question and thus form a stable interpretive community.

As one leaves behind the relatively safe epistemological ground of eyewitness memories, agency in memory politics, and concern with powerful events

such as genocide and war, collective memory begins to escape one's conceptual grasp. In fact, one faces a veritable paradox: the more "collective" the
medium (that is, the larger its potential or actual audiences), the less likely it
is that its representation will reflect the collective memory of that audience.
Frequently, the readers of a specific book or the viewers of a particular television program do not form a cohesive interpretive community because they
use the same media text for very different ends. At the same time, despite our
problems in determining the precise effect of any media event on its audience, we cannot simply exclude from memory studies the vast majority of
consumers who never take on the role of memory makers outside the confines
of their own family or profession. All these problems and challenges are best
illustrated by television, which was the most important medium of historical
reflection in the twentieth century and which, in that capacity, influenced the
historical identities of a wide range of mnemonic communities, but about
whose effects on audiences we still know surprisingly little.[57] These problems
are exacerbated by the fact that the media of representation tend to disappear
from the consciousness of the audience in the process of consumption. As a
result, consumers might subscribe wholeheartedly to certain historical interpretations, but they may not be able to identify their source even if one under-
takes the cumbersome task of asking them directly.[58]

There are some ways out of this methodological impasse. The least ambitious and most widely practiced is what Margaret Archer has called the "down-
ward conflation" of structuralism.[59] As pointed out earlier, many scholars of
collective memory conflate properties of the cultural system with sociocultural
activities. They assume that the structural characteristics of the dominant media
correlate to some extent with the perspectives of their users. This approach
acquires some validity if the representations in question are carefully contex-
tualized, that is, if it can be shown that specific representations found large
audiences and faced little competition from other media. More specifically, it
might be permissible to conclude that consistent and persistent gaps in coverage are difficult to overcome independently by the audience members and
might therefore find their way into their minds.

In addition, as a way around that problem, historians have created their
own source material. Researchers in oral history, for example, have reconstructed media biographies as a way to find out how consumers respond to
media representations and how their role as viewers interacts with other events

and activities in their lives in providing them with a historical worldview.[60] Further, historians have occasionally engaged in large-scale polling endeavors to shed light on the historical consciousness of specific collectives.[61] Short of such laborious projects, historians can, with great benefit, exploit existing data collected by commercial and academic institutions in the past.[62] One good example is the vast amount of polling and ratings data that commercial and public television systems have amassed in the last half century and that have not yet been considered as important historical sources.[63] Finally, historians of collective memory can profit from the sophisticated discussions about reception and audience behavior in media and cultural studies.[64]

Since the consumption of history becomes more and more discontinuous and fragmented in time and space, communities of memory might only rarely be constituted on the basis of shared interpretations of specific events. Increasingly, consumers are only linked through the media that they access individually and very selectively. Consequently, the media, their structure, and the rituals of consumption they underwrite might be the most important shared component of peoples' historical consciousness, although this non-confrontational, semiconscious, nonreferential, and decentralized process is extremely difficult to reconstruct after the fact.

FUTURE CHALLENGES

Scholars in memory studies must continue to design innovative ways of understanding media reception in order to study past, contemporary, and future collective memories. They have to find out what stories about the past matter to whom and how they have been distributed. In particular, historians are called on to identify new sources and put memory studies on a solid empirical basis as its practitioners leave behind the simplistic, tacit assumptions that collective memory work can be reduced to human agency or that facts of representation coincide with facts of reception. In the process, it is crucial to keep in mind that all media of memory, especially electronic media, neither simply reflect nor determine collective memory but are inextricably involved in its construction and evolution.[65]

Memory studies offer an opportunity to acknowledge that historical representations are negotiated, selective, present-oriented, and relative, while insisting that the experiences they reflect cannot be manipulated at will.[66] Put differently, the best contributions to memory studies are informed by the con-viction that "memory's imbrication with cultural narratives and unconscious processes is held in tension with an understanding of memory's relation, however complex and mediated, with history, with happenings, or even and most problematically, perhaps from a postmodern perspective, with 'events.'"[67] In this fashion, collective memory studies have evolved into an exceptionally productive meeting ground between different ways of conceptualizing society and social change. On the one hand, scholars of collective memory have suc-cessfully unraveled the semantic and narrative parameters of social remem-brance that inform and limit the historical imagination of the members of any given collective and are inscribed in the media of communication as well as our bodies and minds. These cultural formations might be variously defined as discursive formations, habitus, thought styles, archetypes, paradigms, or simply traditions. However, in one way or another, they all emphasize the im-portance of powerful impersonal factors that shape peoples' worldviews. These correlate well with constructivist and postmodern understandings of history. On the other hand, more conventional analyses of the lives and deeds of politicians, artists, and intellectuals reveal how individuals have negotiated and tested the limits of these inherited perceptions of the past. Almost by definition, these approaches pay tribute to and respect the creative energy of specific individuals. Despite their differences, the approach that focuses on cultural formations and the approach that focuses on agency are not mutu-ally exclusive in the academic subculture of memory studies.[68] In this respect, the field seems to have squared the circle. As Kerwin Klein so aptly yet per-haps too ironically remarked, collective memory studies "promises to let us have our essentialism and deconstruct it, too."[69]

Despite the need for varied methods, empirical investigations of collective memories are not *methodologically* advanced by detailed accounts about the makers of memory artifacts, although such inquiries into intellectual history are certainly important. Similarly, historical knowledge about collective memo-ries is only marginally improved by a concern with neurological insight into human memory. As impressive as such interdisciplinary efforts might be, they do not bring us closer to understanding the specific social and cultural dynamics of collective remembrance. Instead, interdisciplinary ambitions in the humanities and social sciences should be directed closer to home, toward communication and cultural studies. The study of the methods in these disciplines is more likely to yield the tools to analyze the construction of collective memories in the process of media consumption.

In the end, three important conceptual perspectives meet at the moment of reception when potential memories are turned into actual collective memories and when a selection of the large stock of standard narratives and images about the past is produced and embraced: the moment of historical consciousness. We have to further develop collective memory studies by focusing on the communications among memory makers, memory users, and the visual and discursive objects and traditions of representations. This hermeneutical triangle "implies an open dialogue between the object, the maker, and the consumer in constructing meaning."[70] All three elements should be the actors and heroes of histories of collective memory. Such an approach might also provide clear and reliable guidelines to distinguish between the vast surplus of potential collective memories and the relatively few instances of successful memory construction.

HISTORY

THE RISE AND FALL OF METAPHOR
German Historians and the Uniqueness of the Holocaust

Reviewing concentration camp research in 1998, the German sociologist Wolfgang Sofsky concluded that "historiographical academic discourse avoids irritation and destruction of historical meaning by rigidly concentrating on facts. Skeptical against large-scale interpretations it tends to focus on research of single case studies."[1] Given such proclivities in their field, historians sidestep typological and comparative research projects and are ill equipped to deal with transnational comparisons of concentration camp systems, genocides, and the other forms of modern violence that represent the most important challenge to Holocaust studies in the new century. In the case of the Holocaust, German historians have not been able to completely avoid interpretive irritation, but they have worked tirelessly to regain historiographical equilibrium and have succeeded in recent years in containing the Holocaust's disruptive potential within conventional historiographical methods and strategies of representation. The process took five decades and several generations of scholars. At the height of internal strife and methodological insecurity in the 1980s, the surprisingly speedy resolution of the crisis of interpretation must have appeared highly unlikely to all participants.

The history of Holocaust studies in Germany is divided in five relatively well-defined phases. In the initial phase, from the end of World War II until 1957, the "Final Solution" was not a central research topic for German historians. During the second phase, which lasted for a over a decade, German historiography produced an impressive record of empirical work about the Nazi genocide of European Jewry, especially its administrative implementation. In the third phase, from 1972 through 1980, the topic was again marginalized and only surfaced in a handful of publications. Then, commencing in the mid-1980s, it became the subject of heated theoretical debates and finally, in the early 1990s, the focus of the fifth and still ongoing phase of Holocaust research.[2]

The notion of the Holocaust's singularity played a crucial role in the tumultuous debates of the early 1980s. In other national settings, the overdetermined notion of the Holocaust's uniqueness has been employed to provide cohesion and purpose to a whole range of Jewish causes,[3] to help frame ambitious yet misguided research projects,[4] or to defend the discipline of Holocaust studies against nonacademic revisionists as well as academic critics.[5] None of these objectives were decisive when German historians temporarily adopted the notion of the Holocaust's uniqueness in the early 1980s, before it was effectively dismantled after the Historians' Debate that took place between 1986 and 1988. Faced with unusual and harsh methodological and political disagreements in a discipline that tended to share a common mission, German historians imported the uniqueness concept as a metaphorical crutch; it helped them define a common ground despite severe internal divisions and align themselves with interpretive tastes in other Western countries, especially Israel and the United States. At the same time, at least in Germany, the theoretical debates, including debates about the singularity of the Holocaust, "represented a sustained refusal to confront the events [of the Holocaust] directly and unprotected."[6] The generation of German historians who dominated the profession during the 1970s and 1980s and who had themselves been adolescents in the Third Reich could not bear to study the Nazi atrocities with the same detachment as their younger colleagues.

Judging from today's perspective, the history of German Holocaust studies reflects a cumbersome and protracted process of rhetorical and methodological normalization. The exceptional efforts required for this process are ingrained in the very language of German Holocaust historiography. Before German historians concluded their historiographical reconstuction process in the 1990s, they went through phases of rigid empiricism, during which they ignored doubts about the adequacy of their methods for the study of the Holocaust, as well as periods of ruthless self-criticism regarding the very foundations of their discipline. The notion of the Holocaust's uniqueness is one of the most visible signs of this identity crisis, calling into question traditional linguistic protocols for doing history and the referential illusion sustained by conventional historiographical prose.

The effect of historical verisimilitude depends on successfully merging past historical contexts with present historical writing by way of ordinary prose composition. Historical discourse is constructed on the principle that its language and topics reflect actual existential contiguities of past worlds—or at least contemporary perceptions of such contiguities. The objects, persons, actions, and themes being described, as well as the language used for the description, have to share a certain historical proximity; they have to appear to be part of the same narrative universe. Therefore, to cite one example, we do not expect to encounter anachronisms or poetic comparisons in the narrative reconstructions of past events. Roman Jacobson has used the term *metonomy* for this linguistic strategy of ordinary referential discourse, which he differentiates from the other basic linguistic construction principle of metaphor. Metaphorical texts are driven not by real or perceived contiguity but by imagined similarity; they combine and compare themes and expressions that might share certain semantic or formal characteristics but do not necessarily occur together in any given prelinguistic situation. The results are much more subjective texts that potentially defy comprehension, as in the case of modernist prose. For Jacobson, metaphor and metonomy are not mutually exclusive; they are complementary strategies that occur, to varying degrees, in any given text.[7]

German historians rarely deviated from the straight path of metonomy in the body of their texts. We find modest metaphorical ambition primarily in the margins of their writings, when they spell out the significance of their endeavors and discuss methodology and theory. In the case of the Holocaust, however, metalinguistic concerns and the search for symbols took center stage, albeit only briefly. Considered from this perspective, the prominent discussions about historical theory in the 1970s and the temporary acceptance of the negative simile—that the Holocaust is unlike any other event in history and perhaps even unrepresentable—amounted to a structural scandal. It marked the disturbing intrusion of metaphor into a decidedly metonymic discursive environment.

POSTWAR SILENCE AND THE PROTOTYPES OF HOLOCAUST STUDIES

When a new generation of university professors in unified Germany surveyed the works of their teachers and predecessors in the 1990s, they inevitably came to the conclusion, as Ulrich Herbert did in 1992, that, "taken as a whole, the West German contribution to empirical research about the persecution and destruction of European Jewry is quite small."[8] Much more work had been undertaken in Israel, Poland, and the United States. This situation has changed since the mid-1990s, primarily due to the impressive achievements of this new generation, whose members have diligently combed the archives for new insights about the origins and development of the "Final Solution." In contrast, the historians of the immediate postwar era faced a relative dearth of archival material, but in other respects as well, they were singularly ill prepared for a thorough and sustained empirical analysis of the history of the Holocaust. As we know now, many academics (including many historians) who returned to their jobs after 1945 had heavily invested in the "Nazi revolution" and were part of the functional elite who organized and implemented the military occupation, the economic exploitation, and the ethnic cleansing of occupied Europe.[9] In addition to such personal/ideological legacies, which stood in the way of historiographical inquiry into the Nazi crimes, German historians lacked the necessary methodological and philosophical prerequisites. As Martin Broszat put it, "For the language and thought style of historicism, permeated with elevated notions about History, . . . the mass executions and gas chambers represented a serious lapse in style, which one tried to leave behind as quickly as possible."[10] But even intellectuals and academics who clearly acknowledged the terrible legacy of the Nazi period felt that the best response and most urgent task was to build democratic institutions. Therefore, they refrained from further inquiry into the history of the Holocaust. As a result of all these factors, the academic publications of the postwar period present an unbalanced picture. German historians addressed the history of the "Final Solution" primarily in collections of sources and short essays.[11] At the same time, they spent considerable effort researching the history of the bourgeois resistance to Hitler in order to counter any real or alleged charges of German collective guilt.[12]

The historians' initial unwillingness to inquire about the Holocaust reflected a similar reluctance in West Germany's public sphere. Although academics limited themselves to the production of marginal texts, the wider public engaged with the Nazi crimes through two important books—*The Diary of Anne Frank* and Eugen Kogon's *Der SS-Staat*.[13] However, the former never touches on the abyss of the death camps, and the latter focuses primarily on the concentration camp universe and dedicates only a few pages to the Nazi genocide of European Jewry. This tacit agreement between academics and the educated public should not simply be construed as repression or denial; after all, the facts of the "Final Solution" had been thoroughly publicized through the media in the immediate postwar years.[14] The general avoidance of the topic in the late 1940s and early 1950s is more accurately described as a desire not to engage with the details of a shameful legacy that was quite well known in more general terms.[15] In subsequent decades, as historians probed more deeply into the history of the Nazi genocide, their work failed to reach the larger public, although academia and society seemed to follow parallel trajectories. The two most fruitful phases of Holocaust studies in Germany, in the 1960s and in the 1980s, coincided with intense public concern about the Nazi legacy in the Federal Republic.

The few scholarly texts from the postwar years that addressed the Nazi crimes attest to the profound helplessness of their authors, who tried to extract some positive meaning from the past at a time when West German society had not even found a common linguistic denominator for Nazi genocide. This quest to regain moral equilibrium certainly fit the climate of the times. The political class primarily concerned itself with the extraordinary challenge that the Nazi past represented for the recovery of Germany's moral and political standing in the world. Even the few political leaders and intellectuals who had themselves survived the camps shared this hope for national revival.[16] It is therefore not surprising that Kogon, for instance, wished that his study of the concentration camp universe might help "Germany to recognize itself: its noble as well as its horrible traits so that its contorted, disfigured face regains equilibrium."[17] In a similar vein, Alexander Mitscherlich and Fred Mielke, who edited a collection of documents about Nazi "euthanasia" and human experiments in the camps, declared that their objective was "not indictment but enlightenment, not ostracism but the blazing of a new trail—a common path into the future that may, in all our misery, at least spare us from self-abasement."[18] Such metaphorical excursions are exceptions in the scholarly, metonymic texts; they illustrate that the events under description retained a surplus of meaning that could not be expressed in conventional academic prose. The trust placed in detailed scholarly inquiry as a means of personal and national redemption coexisted in uneasy proximity with the desire to make a seemingly indifferent society understand what extraordinary events had taken place in the camps.[19] Neither survivors, who for many years were the primary researchers of the history of the camps,[20] nor academic historians, who followed in the 1960s, managed to reconcile the two different objectives and different styles of representation. The tension between metonomy and metaphor, which occasionally surfaced in the texts, was a first indirect expression of the concept of the Holocaust's uniqueness that West Germany's intellectual elite objectified and vigorously debated in the 1980s.

The texts of the postwar years anticipated future strategies for scholarly Vergangenheitsbewältigung in other respects, as well. In 1946, speaking as a sociologist, Kogon stressed that research about the camps should not deal with "parts, experiences, and this and that, but the *whole system*"—a dictum that could serve as a motto for most of the research undertaken in the 1960s.[21] Mitscherlich and Mielke, even more ahead of their times, concluded that the deeds of doctors without mercy represented "the alchemy of the modern age, the transmogrification of subject into object, of man into thing against which the destructive urge may wreak its fury without restraint."[22] This insight into the pathology of the modern era contains, in a nutshell, the critical impetus of the contemporary work of philosophers such as Theodor Adorno and Max Horkheimer, but professional historians only began to conceptualize the other side of modernity in the 1980s.[23] Incidentally, Mitscherlich and Mielke's book, initially published in 1949, was completely ignored by the German media and reached a larger audience only after it was reprinted in 1960.[24]

A closer look into the first laboratories of West German academic memory work reveals prototypes of future rationalizations and research strategies, but it also reveals a severe terminological and conceptual helplessness vis-à-vis the Nazi crimes. Completely unselfconsciously, Kogon still heralded the "extermination [*Ausmerzung*] of methodological mistakes" in his third edition, and Mitscherlich and Mielke tried to capture Auschwitz's specificity by declaring it to be "on a cosmic scale, like a shift in the climate."[25] In subsequent decades, the quest for language commensurate with the events would produce more symbolic language and occasionally involve the whole discipline, as happened during the Historians' Debate. Although German historians finally found names for the genocide of European Jewry—first "Auschwitz" and later "Holocaust"—their more ambitious attempts to agree about its historical meaning and philosophical significance proved unsuccessful. Due to its inherent structural limitations, historiography never came up with appro-

priate metaphorical language that could do justice to the feelings of the contemporaries of Nazism. Therefore, the process of historiographical normalization could only be concluded after that generation's departure from the
profession.

THE HISTORIOGRAPHY OF SOBRIETY

The silence of the postwar era ended in the late 1950s and early 1960s when
the legacy of the Nazi crimes and the question of postwar German anti-
Semitism were raised through a number of scandals and trials. A rash of
anti-Semitic graffiti between 1959 and 1960, the trial of Adolf Eichmann in
Jerusalem in 1961, and the 1964–1965 Auschwitz trial in Frankfurt, among
other incidents, indicated important transformations in West Germany's
historical culture. For the first time since the immediate postwar years, the
question of how to come to terms with Nazism topped the national political
agenda.[26] A new generation of historians, who had been young adults at the
end of the war, participated at this turning point. Several specialists in the
area of contemporary history, most of them associated with the Institut für
Zeitgeschichte in Munich, wrote expert opinions for German courts. Their
research helped settle legal disputes about compensation for the victims of
the Nazi regime and the reinstatement of former civil servants who had lost
their positions during the Allied occupation. In addition, especially in the
1960s, they supported renewed efforts to bring Nazi perpetrators to trial.[27]
Their research for the courts formed the core of the first systematic German
inquiries into the development of the "Final Solution" and the concentration
camp universe. Although many results of their work have been confirmed
and remain valid to this day, the research of the 1960s was restricted by the
needs of the courts. In their efforts to help determine matters of guilt and innocence, historians focused on administrative decision-making processes
and the role of the highest echelon of the Nazi leadership. Victims of the Holocaust never appeared on the historiographical field of inquiry, and the close
connections and interdependencies between various Nazi campaigns of ethnic cleansing, racial warfare, and mass killings eluded historical scrutiny. Nevertheless, in comparison with the previous and the following decade, the 1960s
were exceptionally productive: "Until the early 1980s very little was published
which displayed the same thoroughness and analytical sophistication."[28]

Historians who initiated research about the Holocaust in Germany in the 1960s hoped that their work would help "restore our people's moral integrity not only in the eyes of the world but also and especially in our own eyes."[29] But this interest in furthering a collective cartharsis to improve "national self-respect" was only rarely spelled out in the margins of their texts.[30] In principle, they decidedly condemned "general, moralistic and cultural critical reflections" after Auschwitz, which they identified as the deplorable, "popular style of emotional *Vergangenheitsbewältigung*."[31] Instead, they declared categorically that "for the intellectual confrontation with National Socialism and its era we in Germany require neither emotions nor moralistic revival movements but rational work based on reason and common sense," and for this purpose, they wholeheartedly embraced the "rigor of legal proceedings" because it offered the "necessary standard for rationality."[32] In their desire to understand the political and organizational preconditions for genocide and reveal the anatomy of the the the state run by the Schutzstaffel (SS) and its mechanisms of power, historians produced texts that appeared devoid of emotion but that, in terse language and in close reading of the documents, inadvertently reproduced the style of the National Socialist (NS) source material and its rationality of genocide. The modest beginnings of West German Holocaust historiography revealed more historical empathy for the mechanisms of power that facilitated genocide than for its victims. This style of engagement is illustrated by Uwe Dietrich Adam's pathbreaking study of 1972, which ends with the awkward, tautological conclusion that "the forces and tendencies which characterized Hitler's totalitarian state can only be explained—as the catastrophe of Germany and of Jewry prove—through the internal tensions and dynamics of said state."[33] Occasionally, however, the texts reveal how many questions remained unaddressed and unanswered in the rational historiography of the Nazi era. The texts inadvertently illustrate the uncomfortable proximity of genocidal rationalization and rational historiographical explanation. In his fourteen-page introduction to Rudolf Höss's memoirs, Martin Broszat helplessly and obsessively admonished Höss's propensity for "book-keeping, terse and exacting," "shocking," "apathetic," "unbearable," and "shameless rationality" (*Sachlichkeit*) without being able to counter it with anything else but terse, exacting, historical prose.[34]

Through their contributions to the court proceedings, historians helped establish Auschwitz as the first generally accepted name for the Nazi genocide.

However, committed to a "pathos of sobriety," they declined to participate in the search for suitable metaphors and philosophical concepts.[35] As a result, the scholarship of the 1960s unraveled the mechanisms of power but had nothing to say about the specificity of the Holocaust, let alone the emotional aspects of its legacy. For historians, the flight into historical objectivity might have been a natural reaction, but it increased their distance from other realms of German historical culture. In the late 1940s, Kogon could still be a scholar and a popular author in one; the scholars of the 1960s communicated largely among themselves and the courts. Yet for the contemporaries of Nazism, even those who had embraced the discourse of sobriety, an emotional surplus remained lodged within the legacy of the Holocaust; they still perceived an incommensurability between the methods of representation and the subject matter of their work. This discrepancy explains the historians' subsequent flight into metaphor, first through theoretical skirmishes and then through a temporary adoption of the negative simile of uniqueness.

FLIGHT INTO THEORY

In the wake of the student movement of the late 1960s and early 1970s, West German historiography about the Nazi past took a theoretical, nonempirical turn. The student activists pushed for a reform of those aspects of German society that had not been radically changed after 1945.[36] To this end, they emphasized and criticized the lines of continuities that linked the Third Reich and the Federal Republic. The young rebels were particularly enraged by the fact that the German elite and the capitalist order had easily survived the catastrophe they had caused. In pursuing this Marxist-inspired critique of the political status quo, the theorists of the student movement engaged in increasingly esoteric, divisive, and confusing discussions about the precise nature of the fascist phenomenon.[37]

The debates among the student activists had little direct impact on German historiography, but a number of younger professional historians who had finished their university training in the 1960s shared some of the political concerns and theoretical reference points with the student rebels. These historians were only slightly younger than the champions of historical sobriety; they belonged to the age cohorts of the Hitler Youth generation. As young academics in a rapidly expanding university system, they wanted to support social reform efforts by transforming West German academia from the inside out. In their attempts to break with the methodological and philosophical traditions of the discipline, they and their older colleagues spent considerable time discussing the merits and limitations of competing historiographical models for the study of Nazism. As a result, the historiography of the 1970s is memorable for heated debates, including ad hominem attacks, among academics who subscribed to different theoretical frameworks, methodologies, and philosophies of history.

One topic of discussion was the question of whether Nazism is best understood as a brand of fascism (and should thus be studied within the context of the history of other fascist regimes) or as a totalitarian system (and should thus be compared to the Soviet Union).[38] This question had already been discussed in other countries before it was addressed in Germany. In all these settings, the debates about fascism called into question and often even displaced the theory of totalitarianism, which had been the dominant view of twentieth-century history in the West and "the official ideology of the Federal Republic from 1955 to 1975."[39] As a result of attempts to reform their conservative discipline, German historians came to interpret the political history of Nazism and its prehistory from incompatible philosophical vantage points. The majority camp followed the conventional notion that "men make history" and therefore studied the motives, ideologies, and actions of the Nazi leadership. But a very vocal minority, mostly members of the Hitler Youth generation, developed an alternative research agenda based on an eclectic assemblage of neo-Marxist theory, sociological classics, and Anglo-American social history. The new paradigm can be somewhat simplistically summarized by the slogan "not men but structures make history." This functionalist approach, as it came to be known, proved particularly productive for the study of nineteenth-century Germany and the prehistory of the Nazi era.[40] Applied to the political history of the Third Reich, it yielded detailed studies of the power structure of the Nazi bureaucracy. Its authors emphasized, time and again, that political outcomes were primarily the result of competition and cooperation between a multitude of state and party agencies. In the eyes of the functionalists, the catastrophic policies of the Nazi government could not be satisfactorily explained through the intentions of the leaders—even if their intentions fit some of the outcomes very nicely. Rather, each statement and document had to be interpreted according to its position and "career" within the complex, polycratic governmental structures of the Third Reich.[41] The structuralist or functionalist view of history has been labeled social history by its practitioners. But the new paradigm provided few fresh insights into the social fabric of Nazi society. Instead, it offered a very productive, alternative understanding of the political history of Nazism.

FLIGHT INTO EXCEPTIONALITY

The theoretical turn in German historiography during the 1970s produced little empirical work, and at least initially, it offered no new insights into the history of the "Final Solution." German historians engaged in "wars of interpretations on an outdated, thin empirical basis."[42] Like the work of the 1960s, the abstract debates about fascism and totalitarianism and intention and structure rendered invisible the victims of the "Final Solution." In addition, unlike earlier historiographical efforts, the theoretical discussions obstructed the view of the average perpetrators of the Nazi crimes because the participants in the discussions did not focus on the concrete historical circumstances of the implementation of the "Final Solution."

In the context of the theoretical discussions of the 1970s, German historiography underwent a process of trifurcation. A steady production of monographs about the history of the "Final Solution" continued the tradition of the historiography of sobriety. As new sources became available, German historians spent less time studying the collapse of the Weimar Republic and the first years of the Nazi regime and focused instead on the period of World War II. As a result, new publications about the Einsatzgruppen (death squads), the death camps, and the war of extermination on the eastern front considerably advanced the German historiography of the Holocaust.[43] On a second historiographical scene, academic historians were challenged by the rise of the history of everyday life (*Alltagsgeschichte*). Its practitioners, located in the margins or even outside academia, rewrote the history of Nazism from the perspective of the postwar generations. In addition to these scholarly pursuits, public debates about the appropriate memory of Nazism quickly evolved into a semi-independent, third arena of historiographical practice. Especially for Germany's established academics, the participation in political and polemical exchanges became a frequent and even routine undertaking. Not surprisingly, the rise of metaphor thrived in this context. Public struggles provided the perfect outlet for representational interests that had remained unaddressed in more conventional historiographical practice.

In the early 1980s, debates still focused on the divide between functionalists and intentionalists, but now, the experts debated the origins of the "Final Solution." During the increasingly hostile exchanges of the 1970s, the opposing camps seemed to have agreed on little more than "the central role of anti-Semitism in National-Socialist ideology and politics."[44] Despite their radically different ideas about political practice and decision-making processes in the Third Reich, the centrality of anti-Semitism was generally acknowledged in monographs and handbooks. But the consensus about the importance of the "Final Solution" was merely stated in passing; with few exceptions, Nazi crimes were not the subject of original research.[45] This situation might have continued for a while if the academic experts had not been shaken up by the media event *Holocaust* in 1979. The U.S.-made miniseries depicted the everyday history of the victims and perpetrators of the "Final Solution" and raised public awareness for the Nazi genocide like no event before or since. Leading representatives of the German historical profession conceded that historians "may have paid too little attention to the problem of the 'Final Solution' and the task of distributing their insights to the wider public."[46] The surprising popular interest in Holocaust history was met with a surge of publications, but the flood of books consisted only of old classics and rapidly penned Holocaust products and thus inadvertently confirmed the need for academic self-criticism.[47] As a result of such unusual public scrutiny at home and abroad, Germany's historians went to work. But instead of hitting the archives, they did what they had done best for over a decade: they focused on one of the few original contributions to German Holocaust studies in the 1970s and began a theoretical discussion about the merits of functionalist and intentionalist interpretations of the origins of the "Final Solution."[48]

In two programmatic essays, Martin Broszat and Hans Mommsen stressed that the Holocaust was the outcome of the gradual radicalization of Nazi anti-Jewish policies in response to the failure of alternative plans for removing European Jewry.[49] They maintained that genocide resulted from a combination of general central policy decisions and local, ad hoc initiatives undertaken by competing agencies to "solve" the increasingly chaotic conditions in the ghettos and camps in occupied eastern Europe. According to their assessment, Hitler was kept informed and supported the radicalization toward mass murder—often after the fact—but he neither designed nor micromanaged the Holocaust himself, as historians had conventionally assumed. For both authors, these conclusions indicated that the political and moral responsibility for the "Final Solution" was shared by many officials, including many members of traditional elites, and could not be limited to Hitler and the top Nazi leadership. These ideas were vigorously debated and resulted in important changes in the German historiography of the "Final Solution."

When the different methodological perspectives were brought to bear on the decision-making processes of the Holocaust, it quickly became apparent that the prior formulaic consensus about "the central role of anti-Semitism in National-Socialist ideology and politics" would not survive close examination. The representatives of the opposing schools of thought could not agree on the roles played by Hitler, Nazi ideology, and the German bureaucracy in the Holocaust. In this situation of increasing division and public scrutiny, the German professoriat enlisted help from their Israeli colleagues and appropriated the idea of the Holocaust's uniqueness as a temporary and abstract, politically correct consensus. The recognition of irreconcilable differences and the adoption of a new metaphorical common ground were illustrated by an important international conference in Stuttgart in 1984. As the participants from Germany, Israel, and the United States engaged in fruitless discussions of smaller and smaller minutiae in hopeless attempts to resolve larger philosophical and methodological differences, some of the scholars from Israel became increasingly skeptical about this particular style of academic Vergangenheitsbewältigung. Saul Friedlander and Yehuda Bauer voiced uneasiness about the surreal efforts to deal with the mechanics of mass murder in a strictly academic fashion.[50] Bauer asked the assembled experts: "Don't we run away from ourselves? Don't we try, albeit of course subconsciously, to look away from the cruel reality of the most terrible mass murder in history and focus instead on easily digested, abstract conceptualizations?"[51] It is not incidental that these two scholars would provide the best, albeit very different, definitions of the Holocaust's singularity and play an important role in relating this notion to their German colleagues.

In the late 1970s and early 1980s, the Holocaust became a cornerstone of American Jewish identity and was enlisted for a whole range of Jewish and non-Jewish political objectives. The idea of the Holocaust's uniqueness was embraced by the Jewish community, and it was simultaneously employed and contested by other ethnic groups in their struggles for publicity and self-validation. Bauer "was the most prominent and outspoken proponent of uniqueness in this period,"[52] and he has forcefully stated his position ever since: "Never before in human history has a well-organized state, representing a social consensus, tried to murder, globally, every single member of an ethnic or ethno-religious group as defined by the perpetrator, for purely ideological reasons that bore not the slightest relation to reality."[53] This empirical definition must be differentiated from Friedlander's insistence on the Holocaust's incomprehensibility: "Paradoxically, the 'Final Solution,' as a result of its apparent historical exceptionality, could well be inaccessible to all attempts at a significant representation and interpretation. Thus, notwithstanding all efforts at the creation of meaning, it could remain fundamentally irrelevant for the history of humanity and the understanding of the 'human condition.'"[54] Elaborated over the years with "a peculiarly authoritative custodial voice," Friedlander's "defense of the historical and moral centrality, as well as the ultimate inexplicability, of the Holocaust" has proven particularly appealing to German historians.[55]

Since the early 1980s, the notion of the Holocaust's uniqueness has become a standard framing device in German historiography, at least for one generation of scholars. In particular, members of the Hitler Youth generation, the German contemporaries of Bauer and Friedlander, have habitually introduced their publications by acknowledging their belief in the historical singularity of the "Final Solution." The metaphor is used on both sides of the intentionalist-functionalist divide. Scholars who approach the study of the Holocaust from such different vantage points as Hans Mommsen and Eberhard Jäckel nevertheless consistently agree on its exceptional nature.[56] In addition, the status of the Holocaust as "the singular most monstrous crime in the history of human kind" is also routinely acknowledged in new surveys of the history of the "Final Solution."[57] But the agreement has never been unanimous. Andreas Hillgruber repeatedly suggested that the large number of perpetrators and more or less informed bystanders gives us reason "to think beyond the historical singularity of the events," and Martin Broszat had doubts about the usefulness of metahistorical categories stipulating the singularity of any event, including the "Final Solution."[58] Very soon after being adopted by German historians under exceptional circumstances, the notion of uniqueness was exposed as an aesthetic and political tool of limited historiographical value during the Historians' Debate, and finally, it was quite unceremoniously pushed aside by Germany's most recent crop of professional historians.

In 1986, the philosopher Jürgen Habermas delivered a frontal attack against a number of well-established conservative historians. Habermas argued that conservatives had violated the prior consensus stipulating that after Auschwitz, Germans can only selectively and self-critically appropriate elements of their national traditions.[59] He claimed that conservative historians engaged in "reviving a sense of identity naively rooted in national consciousness." For Habermas, such efforts were clearly expressed in a number of programmatic editorial essays by the historian Michael Stürmer and supported by Stürmer's colleagues Ernst Nolte and Andreas Hillgruber.[60] Nolte helped the cause by denying the historical singularity of Auschwitz, which he characterized as a reaction to and imitation of similar events in the Soviet Union and thus "a mere technical innovation."[61] Hillgruber lent support to the conservative campaign by considering the last phase of war on the eastern front exclusively from the viewpoint of the German troops, which, he argued, resisted heroically to save the German population from the Red Army's wrath. For Habermas, such histories amounted to apologetic interpretations of the Third Reich.

The details of the debate will be addressed in the next chapter. Suffice it to say at this stage that the criticized historians responded quickly and dismissed the charges lodged against them. With only a short delay, Habermas's supporters, especially prominent liberal historians, joined the battle and restated his critique. For many commentators on the Left, the scandal, as defined by Habermas, fit their favorite paranoid fantasy of a right-wing conspiracy at the center of West Germany's conservative establishment. They therefore joined the battle against the "new revisionism" without much ado. Since the conservative camp, with few exceptions, refused to continue the debate, the great majority of the articles reflected the liberal point of view.

Although the question of the Holocaust's historical singularity was not Habermas's sole or even primary focus (he spent more time and effort on the critique of conventional national forms of national identity), the uniqueness and comparability questions became the overriding concern of most commentators.[62] Very few of them were in any position to add new material to the discussion. They had neither conducted nor digested any new research about the Soviet Union or genocidal regimes other than Nazi Germany. Perhaps for that reason, the Historians' Debate soon turned into a repetitive acclamation of the historical singularity of the Holocaust.[63] The tacit agreement about the central importance of anti-Semitism had become an explicit, widely shared metaphorical dictum. Considering this development, it is not surprising that the liberal camp declared victory. Apparently, the conservative cultural trend had been resoundingly defeated. With hindsight, however, it has become obvious that the Historians' Debate did not mark any significant historiographical or political accomplishment. In the words of Norbert Frei, the debate is best understood "as the protracted political farewell—abruptly ended by German unification—of a generation of researchers and individuals who had a specific autobiographical agenda and were facing retirement at the start of the 1990s."[64]

Although liberal historians and their supporters enjoyed their success, the effort to relativize the concept of exceptionality was already well under way. A number of initiatives and research strategies called into question the simplistic notion of singularity that had triumphed during the Historians' Debate. Younger historians followed the functionalists' emphasis on the importance of modern social structures and bureaucracies and produced new research about the interdependence of Nazism and modernity and the perpetrators of the Holocaust. But the most important challenge resulted from the rise of Alltagsgeschichte. Increased interest in the history of everyday life, both within and outside academia, produced a wave of publications that provided vivid and tangible details about life in the Third Reich to generations whose members had no personal memories of the period. Designed as critical antidotes to abstract debates and lofty discussions about high politics and administrative structures, many contributions to the history of everyday life inadvertently overemphasized the seemingly normal, unproblematic daily routines of the contemporaries of Nazism.[65] At the same time, some works of Alltagsgeschichte also illustrated the pervasiveness of racism and anti-Semitism in Nazi Germany. Although West German everyday life historians did not focus on the Holocaust (at least not initially), many local and regional studies finally gave voices and faces to the victims of Nazi policies of persecution and extermination, including its Jewish victims. A fitting example is the work of

Monika Richarz, who edited autobiographical writings of German Jews about life in Nazi Germany and broke with the historiographical convention that had represented the Jews as "nameless, passive victims of an all-powerful machinery of destruction."[66]

At the end of a long phase of theoretical discussions and a short phase in which metaphor reigned, the notion of uniqueness received a last enthusiastic, over-the-top endorsement of truly epic (and epigonic) proportions: "Auschwitz is a no-man's-land of understanding, a black box of explanation, a vacuum of transhistorical significance which absorbs all historiographical attempts of interpretation. Only ex negativo, only through constant efforts to understand the futility of understanding, can we begin to grasp the break in civilization that this event represents. As a radical extreme case and absolute measure of history this event can very likely never be historicized."[67] Dan Diner's metaphorical fireworks might have been the most elegant and self-confident endorsement of the incomprehensibility claim, but it no longer rings true, precisely because it misses the element of self-doubt that had accompanied the language of some of his predecessors.

SELF-CONFIDENT EMPIRICISM

In the late 1980s and 1990s, partly in response to years of theoretical discussions, a new generation of historians returned to the study of primary historical sources, especially in the recently opened archives of Eastern Europe. Many of the younger historians had absorbed or even participated in the wave of everyday history. In addition to their interest in concrete empirical data, they resurrected the conventional historiographical research and writing strategies that had been dismissed by the first generation of social historians. Some of the best works of the 1990s provided regional studies of the origins of the "Final Solution" in occupied eastern Europe. The authors sought to understand what concrete, local factors contributed to the development of genocidal policies and how these local factors interacted with political directives from Berlin.[68] In addition to this regional emphasis, historians frequently chose conventional biographical approaches and narrative formats.

These trends and advances in Holocaust studies in Germany are exemplified by the extraacademic research pursued under the auspices of the Hamburg Institute for Social Research. Unlike their academic colleagues, its members and affiliates have kept alive the political ambitions of the student movement and the polemical tone of earlier debates. The proponents of the so-called Hamburg School set out to document the political economy at the center of the "Final Solution." They contend that an intermediate layer of academically trained professionals designed and implemented the genocidal policies of the Nazi regime in the name of modern Western science, especially economics. In their opinion, the Holocaust has to be interpreted within the overall context of state-of-the-art population policies that entailed large-scale deportations and relocations as part of wide-ranging plans to reform the political, economic, and ethnic map of eastern Europe. The attempt to realize these plans set off a chain reaction of failed social engineering that led to ethnic cleansing and genocide. Furthermore, they are convinced that the professional "ethos" and worldview of this planning intelligentsia is alive and well in Western academia, including in German historiography.[69] The work of the Hamburg School has met harsh criticism from academic historians, including generational peers, who have pointed out that material unearthed by Götz Aly and others might attest to post factum rationalizations of Nazi policy rather than actual decision-making processes.[70] Nevertheless, the work is an important part of recent research about the administrative and political personnel who realized the Holocaust. It finally addresses questions that should have been—but apparently could not have been—asked in the postwar decades.

Although clearly rooted in the tradition of Alltagsgeschichte, more recent studies about Nazi perpetrators have looked at research problems and ethical questions that were explicitly and implicitly raised in the writing of the structuralist scholars. Younger historians have zoomed in on the functional elites of the Nazi regime and researched how administrators, party officials, and academics constructed the "Final Solution." The best new works (for instance, Ulrich Herbert's 1996 study of Werner Best) combine a biographical format with a systematic exploration of the structures and worldviews that shaped the generation of young, successful Nazi functionaries.[71] Herbert's study illustrates that German historians have finally overcome the sterility of the functionalist-intentionalist debates, with their rigid, seemingly irreconcilable theoretical alternatives. Scholars such as Herbert contend that the dynamics of violence that led to the Holocaust were motivated by racial anti-Semitism *and* imperialist programs of colonization and economic modernization. The perpetrators' ideological objectives as well as their seemingly rational, utilitarian interest in social engineering—in combination with their attempts to solve pressing organizational and administrative problems caused by mass deportations—resulted in a gradual process of radicalization, a process that differed significantly in various local settings and among various groups of perpetrators.[72] Herbert has reached the alarming conclusion that acceptance of genocide did not require ideological fanaticism or mass hysteria, as alleged by Daniel Goldhagen, but that wide-scale, "escalating indifference" to the plight of minorities assured popular consent.[73]

The innovators of German Holocaust studies might differ in tone and emphasis, but they agree in their rejection of the notion that the Holocaust is an incomprehensible event. To them, such metaphorical language is useless and counterproductive. Again, Ulrich Herbert stated it well: "The study of the genocide does not just reveal information about the historically unique situation and the specific German society of the 1930s and 1940s; rather it remains a contemporary, pressing, and depressing concern, not just, but especially here in Germany. These questions will keep us busy for quite some time even beyond all short-term, topical debates and excitement. In that process the insistence on the events' incomprehensibility is as unproductive as any recourse to monocausal and seemingly radical explanations."[74] Not surprisingly, Götz Aly has been even less tempered in his criticism. He rejects the Left-liberal "feuilleton wisdom," which posits the Holocaust as inexplicable, because this approach "opens no avenues for reflection and unnecessarily restricts one's focus" in research as well as teaching.[75] Instead, he argues that the Holocaust is accessible to analysis by conventional historiographical methods partly because the conventional rules of state bureaucratic procedure applied to the "Final Solution."[76] Therefore, he concludes: "The deed and the crime is [sic] unique. However, Auschwitz is part of European as well as German history. Only when one has fully understood this context is it possible to talk meaningfully of the 'limits of understanding.' The Holocaust was not a 'reversion to barbarism,' nor a 'break with civilization,' still less an 'Asiatic deed.' But it was also far from being a 'historical black hole,' somehow beyond language, poetry and historical understanding, but rather a possibility inherent in European civilization itself."[77] As these quotes demonstrate, members of the new generation of social and everyday life historians of the Holocaust continue to invoke the metaphor of the "Final

Solution's" uniqueness. But for them, this notion of exceptionality no longer poses any extraordinary methodological or conceptual challenges. Quite the contrary, their understanding of historical uniqueness, which they routinely acknowledge in their introductions, is perfectly compatible with the traditional historicist argument that all historical events are unique phenomena whose specificity can be detected and protected by standardized historiographical methods.

In 1996, Germany's historians and many members of the educated public discussed the virtues and shortcomings of the U.S. bestseller *Willing Executioners* by Harvard political scientist Daniel Goldhagen, who presented a new interpretation of the causes of the "Final Solution." During the discussions, the country's professional historians, especially those of the older generation, appeared in a rather unflattering light, and it became quite obvious that academic experts and lay readers held very different views about the meaning of the Nazi past. The translation of Goldhagen's book remains the most successful scholarly publication about the Holocaust in Germany and the only publication of its kind that became a media event. Goldhagen very effectively communicated with his large German audiences as he explained his problematic thesis that the Holocaust was caused by a particularly vicious type of eliminationist anti-Semitism. In contrast, the doyens of the German historical profession, who took to the public stage to debunk Goldhagen's monocausal theories, appeared very awkward in front of the lay audience and the cameras and demonstrated that they had never been able to connect to the general public. Despite good intentions, not too much seemed to have changed since *Holocaust* had aired in 1979. At the same time, the debate revealed how much the ground rules within the historical profession had shifted since unification. Liberal social historians who had so vigorously propagated the uniqueness of the Holocaust had to rethink some of the basic tenets of their political and historiographical identity—for instance, regarding the role of national ideologies in postwar Germany. Now, Goldhagen's popular success further destabilized the already weakened paradigm of social history. Goldhagen's graphic prose constituted a radical metonymic and, considering the usual style of academic writing, almost pornographic performance. By explicitly rejecting sophisticated theoretical models in favor of uninhibited, extensive descriptions of the gruesome details of the Holocaust, Goldhagen mocked the cumbersome theoretical apparatus that the social historians used

to contextualize their findings. As a result, more than ever before, that apparatus appeared to be an elaborate strategy of avoidance.

The Goldhagen debate was like a prism that exposed the different generational layers of Germany's historical culture. It revealed that the intellectual
environment that had produced ambitious abstract constructs, including a
sophisticated understanding of the Holocaust's uniqueness, had inevitably
disintegrated. With renewed self-confidence about the methodological integrity
of the discipline, a new generation of German historians almost unanimously
rejected Goldhagen's thesis, but they also dismissed the metaphorical and
theoretical "frills" that their predecessors had developed in an attempt to turn
German historiography into an exceptionally self-critical and self-reflexive academic discipline.[78]

REGAINING METONYMIC EQUILIBRIUM

The rise of metaphor in German historiography that, for a short period, coexisted with conventional rhetorics of empiricism was linked to a whole range
of factors. The notion of uniqueness was adopted by a specific generation of
German historians — individuals who, unlike their predecessors and many of
their successors, either were well versed in theoretical language and applied
it in their own work or were used to debating large-scale constructs and
theoretical models with their colleagues. These theoretical inclinations were
themselves linked to the Nazi past because they reflected the ambition of a
minority among German historians who wanted to part with traditional academic practices and identities that, they argued, had been discredited during
the Third Reich. At the same time, concern with abstract historiographical
models helped them avoid direct confrontation with some of the most troubling, concrete aspects of Nazi history, including the Nazi past of some of
their teachers.[79] The peculiar mixture of selective avoidance and reformist de-
termination resulted from a specific biographical constellation. The theoretical instruments of structuralism and the concept of uniqueness were used by
historians, in Germany as well as abroad, who had themselves experienced
the Nazi era. The frustration with conventional methodology and interest in
metaphorical language reflected their desire to come to terms with exceptionally destructive events that had disrupted and devalued their own adolescence
after the fact.

The rhetoric of singularity was embraced by academics who were better informed about international professional and political developments than any previous generation of German academics—perhaps because of their innovative zeal and biographical insecurities. They were more likely to accept and identify with concepts suggested by historians from abroad. Yet the uniqueness metaphor only became popular among West Germany's historians after the historiographical crisis caused by the media event *Holocaust*. Historians recognized that they were no longer the guardians of the national historical consciousness, and they were prevented from rising to the challenge by internal division and paralysis. The concept of uniqueness and the notion of the Holocaust's inexplicability temporarily became the common denominators for a divided professoriat.

The fall of metaphor already began in the 1980s. Notions such as uniqueness and especially inexplicability are inherently unstable concepts, which became quite obvious when historians announced their belief in the Holocaust's ultimate incomprehensibility but immediately continued espousing its historical meaning in conventional historical prose.[80] In addition and more important, the language of incomprehensibility disrupts the principle of contiguity. Historians have no problem emphasizing the exceptional relevance of the case studies they have singled out for research. But this relevance is based on the belief that their results, however monographic in scope, contain insights into the larger historical context, that the historical world forms a continous whole devoid of radical qualitative shifts that require radically different methods of analysis and representation. After all, historiographical language is located at the metonymic pole of language; too much metaphor does not merely change its surface appearance and its style, it also changes the epistemological assumptions that are embedded in the very structure of historiographical discourse.

The limited value of the concept of uniqueness as a historiographical tool became obvious during the Historians' Debate when it quickly turned into a political litmus test without providing any stimulus for research. But the most important reason for the sudden demise of the idea of singularity was again generational. The second generational turnover in the discipline since the end of the war reduced the personal stakes involved in the study of the Nazi crimes and produced another generation whose members are eager to differentiate themselves from their teachers. In the process, younger historians have shed the cumbersome theoretical instruments and metaphorical language that their predecessors employed to study the "Final Solution." Recent histories of the Holocaust published in Germany illustrate this professionalization and methodological normalization in German historiography in general and Holocaust studies in particular. In the wake of everyday history and microhistory, German historians have retained their international perspective, but they have reverted to a methodological stance that preceded not just the debates of the 1970s but also the Nazi period. Fully engaged in Vergangenheitsbewältigung, they have again embraced the comforting illusion that their texts are a transparent reflection of the empirical record. With hindsight, the historiographically volatile 1970s and the subsequent short reign of metaphor appear as ripples in a sea of historiographical normality and self-confidence. The notion of the Holocaust's singularity temporarily postponed the inevitable return to business as usual and gave rise to unusually productive historiographical introspection. In this way, the short reign of metaphor attested to the extraordinary challenge that the historicization of the Holocaust posed to an academic discipline.[81]

It might take several generations of scholars (although hopefully not another event such as the Holocaust) before the unacknowledged implicit premises of the historian's craft are again tested in such a stringent fashion. In the meantime, a new consensus seems to have emerged in the discipline, a consensus that is ripe with underlying assumptions about modernity, human nature, and historical continuity and that has eliminated the historical and anthropological distance between us and the Nazi perpetrators, a distance that German historians worked so hard to maintain for over thirty years: "Perpetrator research forces one to accept the unwelcome insight that the transformation of human beings into mass murderers requires little time and will power. Neither long biographical adaptation nor time consuming indoctrination appear necessary."[82]

BETWEEN POLITICS AND MEMORY

*The Historians' Debate and West German
Historical Culture of the 1980s*

On November 10, 1988, a political scandal with unprecedented consequences erupted at the center of the West German political establishment. Literally overnight, the second-highest official of the Federal Republic, Philip Jenninger, the president of the Federal German parliament, was removed from office because the members of that body almost unanimously disapproved of the speech he delivered on the occasion of the fiftieth anniversary of the Night of the Broken Glass (Kristallnacht). The fact that a high-ranking representative of the governing conservative party was forced to resign due to "improper" remarks about National Socialism and the speed of his removal from office suggest that the speech violated some basic rules of West Germany's historical culture.[1]

Jenninger had tried to deliver a very ambitious speech, a speech that was to put him on a par with President Richard Weizsäcker, whose remarks on the fortieth anniversary of the end of World War II had brought him international acclaim.[2] Jenninger eschewed the conventional empty formulas about the need for remembrance and engaged in an exercise of self-critical memory work by focusing on Hitler's popularity with the German people. In the process, he managed to commit three major political mistakes.

In practical political terms, Jenninger's excursion into the history of everyday life during Nazism contradicted the political objectives of his own party, the Bavarian Christian Socialist Union (CSU), which was struggling to retain the loyalty of West Germany's right-wing electorate after the death of Franz-Josef Strauß, who had secured these votes for the CSU and the Christian

Democratic Union (CDU) for more than two decades. In this situation, the last thing the party needed was a self-critical analysis of Hitler's popularity.[3] In addition, the speech violated the collective identity of the German parliament. In 1988, some prominent members of parliament still belonged to the victims and opponents of Hitler's regime, and many younger members, especially on the Left, could accurately be described as ex post facto resistance fighters, that is, politicians who had spent a considerable portion of their political life fighting fascisms of all kinds to make up for the lack of resistance to Nazism in their parents' generation. Both of these groups had been very instrumental in bestowing democratic legitimacy on the West German political establishment. Naturally, both the original and the ex post facto antifascists resented Jenninger's urge to identify, albeit momentarily, with the perspective of the bystanders of the Holocaust.[4] Last and most important, Jenninger's remarks violated a tacit agreement about the nature of the Holocaust that was one of the cornerstones of West Germany's historical culture. Especially since the 1970s, the "insistence on the Holocaust's uniqueness and inexplicability [had] allowed the West Germans to see the Holocaust as something that could not be explained even in the context of the Third Reich. The Holocaust thus lost all the characteristics of a historical event and was transferred to the realm of the ahistorical that defies explanation and renders the question of responsibility obsolete."[5] Jenninger's remarks reclaimed the Holocaust as a historical and maybe even explicable event, and thus, at least implicitly, they raised the question of concrete historical responsibility.

All these "shortcomings" of the speech were exacerbated by Jenninger's poor performance. Not a gifted speaker to begin with, he lost all control over his subject matter once he noticed his colleagues' staunch opposition. In particular, he could not separate his attempt to elucidate the German population's fascination with Hitler in the 1930s and his own fascination with this topic. Past—including quotes from original documents—and present became hopelessly intermingled.[6] Thus, Jenninger not only transformed the Holocaust from an ahistorical event into a historical one; he also transformed the past into a present event and provoked an outcry among his offended colleagues, who rightly felt that his performance called into question their complacent antifascism or antitotalitarianism. Ultimately, Jenninger singlehandedly, if inadvertently, managed to undercut the elaborate defense strategies that the West German political establishment had erected in order to safeguard their democratic identity from contamination emanating from the Nazi era. This rhetorical fiasco cost him his job.

All these factors explain Jenninger's speedy removal from office, but they do not explain his ambitious objectives of describing the National Socialist anti-Semitic policies from the perspective of the bystanders and of identifying with the bystanders' passivity in the face of the persecution of Europe's Jews. I suggest that his remarks and intentions reflected the dilemma of a specific political generation—the Hitler Youth generation. This generation grew up during Nazism and was co-opted into the state youth organization, the Hitler Youth, and the majority of its members identified with the National Socialist cause during adolescence. After 1945, they faced the task of completely re-working their political and moral identity, a task they accomplished success-fully because, unlike their older compatriots, they were not held responsible for the Nazi crimes. Subsequently, the Hitler Youth generation played an im-portant part in shaping West German democracy; especially in the 1970s and 1980s, members of this generation dominated the political and professional elites of the Federal Republic.[7] In the late 1980s, however, before leaving the public arena, some of these politicians and intellectuals readdressed the issue of their double-layered identity by probing into the emotional and political proclivities of their lives during Nazism. Although these initiatives sparked an interesting research proposal, Martin Broszat's "Plea for the Historiciza-tion of National Socialism,"[8] they primarily reflected an uncritical identification with the viewpoint of the German population during Nazism. As the Jen-ninger affair and the Historians' Debate indicate, the attempts to recover and revalue memories from the Third Reich in a public setting produced a prob-lematic emotional stance that, for good reason, had been omitted from West Germany's official historical culture: they resulted in a misplaced empathy with the bystanders of the Holocaust.

THE PARAMETERS OF THE HISTORIANS' DEBATE

In November 1988, when Jenninger was forced to retire as president of the parliament, the Historians' Debate about the singularity of the Holocaust had subsided. In a nutshell, the Jenninger affair featured all the elements that had figured in the volatile discussions among German historians and the inter-ested public over the course of two years. Therefore, the following analysis and contextualization of the German Historians' Debate of 1986 through 1988 reveals a conglomeration of political, professional, and generational factors similar to that which surfaced in the Jenninger affair, albeit on a larger scale.

It is not my objective to recall and comment in detail on the arguments advanced during the Historians' Debate; such introductions and comments have been provided elsewhere.[9] Rather, I want to probe into the short- and long-term causes of the debate by offering an analysis and critique of its origins in West German party politics, by relating it to the paradigm of the history of everyday life advanced by West Germany's subculture and its mass media, by studying the political-philosophical underpinnings of the discussions, and by integrating the Historikerstreit within its wider historiographical context. Lastly, I will concentrate on the generational dynamics played out in the debate that illustrate the extent to which the issues discussed in the Historians' Debate reflected the specific experiences and attitudes of the Hitler Youth generation. The analysis of these multiple factors reveals the location of the debate within the wider context of West Germany's historical culture, that is, within the diverse representations and interpretations of the past that provided West German society with models of historical orientation and historical change in the 1980s. Understood in these terms, the concept of historical culture cuts across various institutional settings and various fields of social practice and professional expertise, including academic research and writing, the arts, the political sphere, the mass media, the educational system, and leisure activities.[10] As a public debate of exceptional proportions, the Historikerstreit affords the opportunity to study the interplay of some of these fields of historical knowledge and collective memories that hardly overlap in their day-to-day routines. Thus, the Historians' Debate gives us a chance to study historical culture "in action" and draw some conclusions on the compatibility, interdependence, and relative autonomy of different visions and concepts of the Nazi past that were in use in the Federal Republic's historical culture at the time.

Between 1986 and 1988, the Historians' Debate produced some twelve hundred texts, ranging in size from single newspaper columns to extended monographs, with as many as a hundred articles per month at one point.[11] The debate began in the feuilleton pages of the major German dailies and weeklies, especially *Die Zeit* and the *Frankfurter Allgemeine Zeitung*, and was carried over into numerous historical, political, and cultural journals before it became the focus of more than ten edited volumes and ten monographs.[12] Particularly in its early stages, the Historikerstreit continued an important cultural tradition in Germany, reflected in the close cooperation between high-brow print media and academics, especially historians. Although historians, with the exception of the philosopher-sociologist Jürgen Habermas, were the most visible and outspoken among the discussants, cultural journalists out-numbered them and played an important role in keeping the debate going.

The high profile of the Historians' Debate should not, however, deflect from the fact that at every stage, the Historikerstreit remained a strictly intel-lectual affair. The great majority of the West German population was un-aware of the course and the intellectual stakes of the debate because it "was conducted well above the heads of the wider public."[13] The local papers cov-ered the debate only very sporadically, and the electronic media paid little attention to it. With the exception of some radio debates and some TV fea-tures in the political magazines of the public German television stations, the Historians' Debate did not fill the airwaves to the same extent that it clogged the national papers and in particular their feuilleton pages. Apparently, the TV and radio journalists felt that the discussions had little entertainment value.[14] Thus, the Historians' Debate marks "one of the last triumphs of the print media" in Germany.[15]

After the fact, almost all participants agreed that the Historikerstreit had been intellectually unproductive, and in the strict sense of the term, that was certainly the case. The debate did not settle any methodological disputes nor help find new material or interpretative avenues for the study of the history of National Socialism and the "Final Solution." With the possible exception of Ernst Nolte's *Der Europäische Bürgerkrieg*, the historians and journalists never took note of the academic publications and achievements of any of the participants.[16] Instead, they focused on a few arguments and quotations from the marginal works of the historians involved, taken from textbook essays, newspaper articles, essay collections, or utterances made during the debate.[17] The impressive bibliography of the debate stands in stark contrast to the very slim textual base from which the conflict originated and from which it never departed in the course of three years. This characteristic of the dispute can also be attributed to the fact that the Historikerstreit was, after all, never much of a debate. It produced an amazing fallout but never surpassed two rounds of exchanges between the original participants. By mid-1987, both camps were repeating their initial positions and declining to engage in further discussion, especially after the liberal side, whose protagonists were more or less closely associated with the Social Democratic Party,[18] had declared victory.[19] With the distance of the years that have passed since then, it is also safe to say that the Historians' Debate has not inspired any new research. More recent research about Nazism and the "Final Solution" conducted in Germany addresses issues such as the interdependence of National Socialism and modernity and the implementation of the Holocaust in eastern Europe and thus sidesteps arguments about Nazism's singularity, which were still hotly discussed during the Historians' Debate.[20] In addition, despite the current interest in the politics of memory and commemoration, especially with regard to the Nazi past, few scholars have discussed the Historikerstreit within the context of the history of (West) German efforts to come to terms with Nazism. The few texts that have reconsidered the debate from the distance of several years were written by participants who felt that their voices were not heard in the heat of the battle.[21]

On the surface, the Historians' Debate dealt with three major issues and accusations. First, the participants discussed the concept of the singularity of the Holocaust and its comparability with other genocides, especially with the Stalinist crimes in the Soviet Union. This topic was raised in response to a number of essays by Ernst Nolte, who had argued that in implementing the "Final Solution," Hitler and the Nazi leadership acted on their fear of Bolshevik class warfare and that, above and beyond this causal connection, the extermination of the Jews represented a radicalized version of the mass exterminations in the Soviet Union. Nolte's critics, Jürgen Habermas and a number of liberal historians, denied both the causal and the phenomenological links and insisted on the Holocaust's status as an exceptional historical event.[22] Second, the discussants argued about the need for today's historians to take sides and identify with the historical actors of the Nazi period. This issue was brought about by a slim volume authored by Andreas Hillgruber, in which he suggested that German historians should identify with the perspective of the German troops on the eastern front in their defensive battle against the Red Army in 1944 and 1945. Hillgruber's critics questioned the need to identify with past actors and asserted that if they were to do so at all, historians had to empathize with victims of the regime, especially with inmates of the camps, and the many civilians and soldiers who would have survived if the eastern front had collapsed earlier.[23] Third, the critics assumed that Nolte and Hillgruber were part of an overall conservative effort to normalize the representation of the Nazi past and to remove the major conceptual and emotional obstacles to a revival of a traditional national historical identity in Germany. In their eyes, this conservative agenda had already been pursued at Bitburg in 1985, where Helmut Kohl and Ronald Reagan had staged a symbolic reconciliation between the former enemies—the United States and Germany—over the graves of German soldiers who had died in World War II, including some members of SS troops.[24] The critics thought that this agenda was clearly laid out in the recent political writings of Michael Stürmer, the historian and former adviser to Chancellor Kohl, who had argued that the Federal Republic's future depended on its citizens' identification with a national cause and a national history. Habermas and the liberal historians denied West Germany's need for conventional forms of historical identity and claimed that allegiance to the constitution, which West Germans had developed after the war, was the most appropriate type of collective identity in the present postnational environment and assured West Germany's membership in the community of Western nations.[25]

In the context of these three main concerns, the participants in the Historians' Debate raised a number of related questions. They discussed the validity of traditional geopolitical models for the interpretation of modern and contemporary German history, which had been reintroduced by the conservative historians,[26] and they questioned the allegedly defensive nature of Hitler's attack on the Soviet Union in light of Nolte's remarks.[27] And most important, the Historians' Debate overlapped with heated discussions about two national historical museum projects championed by the federal government. Shortly after having taken over the chancellorship in 1982, Helmut Kohl had announced that the new conservative government would sponsor a museum for German history, to be opened in 1987 in Berlin on the occasion of the city's 750th anniversary, and a museum in the capital of Bonn dedicated to the history of the Federal Republic. After concepts had been circulated in 1984 and 1985, both projects were challenged by liberal critics, who charged that the conservative government intended to found institutions of cultural memory that would promote the conservative national political agenda.[28]

THE POLITICAL DIMENSION OF THE HISTORIANS' DEBATE:
THE WASTEFUL DEPLOYMENT OF ACADEMIC CAPITAL

The Historikerstreit was, first and foremost, a political battle. In a country where academics in the humanities, especially in history, are often aligned with either of the established political forces—that is, the conservatives of the CDU/CSU or the Social Democrats of the SPD (Sozialdemokratische Partei Deutschlands)—it should not come as a surprise that the intellectual seasons tend to follow the political calendar.[29] Therefore, as many commentators pointed out, Habermas's initiative in July 1986 also must be interpreted within the context of the elections for the national parliament in January 1987, in which the Social Democrats hoped to regain control of the federal government (which they had lost between 1982 and 1983 under particularly humiliating circumstances).[30] However, though the timing of the debate can be understood in relation to the election, there was more at stake for the participants of the Historikerstreit than electoral results. It is important, therefore, to briefly recall West Germany's political developments since the 1960s and the impact these developments had on academic politics in order to understand the political motivations with which the historians entered into the debate.

A massive expansion of the civil service system on the state and federal levels from the mid-1960s to the mid-1970s had created a large number of well-paid jobs, especially for graduates in the humanities. These jobs were filled by members of the first postwar generation—the generation that staffed the student movement—and the majority of individuals in this generation firmly supported Willy Brandt's reform politics. As a result, the middle ranks and ultimately also large sections of the higher ranks of local, state, and federal administrations, of research institutions, of the state school system from kindergarten through secondary education, and of the media absorbed a considerable number of liberal-minded academics who would shape these institutions for several decades. Although this transformation varied widely from region to region and although it never tipped the balance in the sense that conservatives suddenly found themselves outnumbered throughout the country, it had a lasting impact on West Germany's social and political climate.[31]

Thus, the intensity and virulence of the Historians' Debate has to be partly attributed to the fact that by the mid-1980s, many conservative intellectuals

were deeply frustrated by having to deal with a well-positioned, firmly en-
trenched liberal/Social Democratic establishment in the civil service and the
media (and for conservative historians, that also included thriving new scholarly journals such as *Geschichte und Gesellschaft*);[32] this was the situation even
though the conservative parties had regained the political majority on the federal level five years earlier and had held majorities in most states throughout
the reform era. The liberal intellectuals, for their part, were highly motivated
to defend their power base in response to the conservative offensive and to
put their weight behind the Social Democratic campaign. Their strong allegiance to the liberal cause can also be attributed to the fact that almost all of
them had gained entry to the professorial elite during the expansion of the
university system in the 1960s and 1970s.[33]

These political constellations and allegiances in the Federal Republic of the
mid-1980s, in conjunction with the imminent federal elections, help explain
three political misperceptions that liberal and conservative historians held in
common. According to their habit of thinking in terms of clear-cut political
borders and close-knit political networks, both sides perceived the debate
primarily as a political campaign or even a political conspiracy, especially with
regard to their respective foes' motivation and strategy. Liberals and conservatives alike assumed that they faced deliberate campaigns designed to attain or
defend cultural/political hegemony, and thus, both failed to take note of the
more complex and more interesting aspects of the debate.[34] In addition, both
sides overestimated their influence with the electorate and their general public appeal. In fact, the intellectual skirmishes of the Historians' Debate would
have no impact at all on the outcome of the elections. Finally, conservative and
liberal intellectuals shared a political objective that negatively influenced the
course and the outcome of the Historians' Debate. The 1987 elections marked
the departure from the stable three-party system that had dominated West
German politics since the mid-1960s; with the Green Party (Die Grünen,
since 1990 Die Grünen/Bündnis 90), a political force representing the substantial but highly divided political movements located left of the Social Democrats, entering the federal arena. The defensive attitude of the political
establishment toward these movements was mirrored in the behavior of the
arguing professoriat, which, throughout the debate, ignored comments origi-
nating from the radical Left of West Germany's political spectrum.[35]

Although the Historians' Debate was strongly influenced by party politics, politicians never interfered in it. To some extent, this surprising restraint

on the part of the politicians might be attributed to their respect for the autonomy of the cultural/academic sphere; they did not feel comfortable addressing questions of historical uniqueness and comparability when even
the sociologist Habermas was chided for his alleged lack of historical expertise.[36] More probably, the politicians, unlike the historians, recognized that
there was nothing to be gained politically by entering a debate that was, for
the most part, inaccessible or uninteresting to the electorate. They engaged
in discussions about the appropriate interpretation and representation of
the Nazi past when they saw an opportunity to score politically—for instance, during the Bitburg and the Jenninger affairs immediatly prior to and
after the Historians' Debate. Finally, in distinction to other areas of West Germany's historical culture, the political establishment of the Federal Republic
was for decades closely attached to the interpretations of Nazism that had
served it very well nationally and internationally in the 1950s. Thus, especially the conservative politicians held on to the interpretive framework of
antitotalitarianism, which had eased West Germany's entry into the Western
alliance, and they declined to engage in debates that might render this useful
tool ineffective.[37]

In light of the limited political impact of the Historians' Debate, its most
tangible political effect was particularly deplorable. The Historians' Debate
marked one of the few moments in the history of the Federal Republic in
which elements of right-wing, apologetic renditions of the history of the Third
Reich found their way into the mainstream print media. Nolte's philosophical
meanderings about Hitler's right to intern the Jews and his vivid descriptions
of the Soviet threat perceived by Hitler and his followers can be distinguished
from right-wing propaganda only after close scrutiny, if at all.[38] Not surprisingly, Nolte subsequently received unsolicited but apparently not unwelcome
support from German neo-Nazis.[39] Even more important, however, Nolte's
idiosyncratic revisionism also seems to have inspired a number of younger
scholars who followed his lead.[40]

THE SUBCULTURAL AND THE POPULAR DIMENSION:
ALLTAGSGESCHICHTE AND THE MASS MEDIA

Elie Wiesel used the term *gang of four* with respect to the four conservative
historians, Klaus Hildebrand, Andreas Hillgruber, Ernst Nolte, and Michael
Stürmer, whom Habermas singled out for his attack.[41] Wiesel thus nicely

captured the conspiratorial air of Habermas's critique—but not the essence of the debate. The conservative historians' publications were never coordinated, nor did they follow the same agenda. Stürmer's contribution was the least complex, lacking any political or historiographical depth. But its one-dimensionality exposed the political/philosophical naïveté behind all the talk of national and postconventional identity during the Historikerstreit. Stürmer's call for a consistent conservative national history that would focus on the success story of the Federal Republic and provide the population with a sense of historical self was designed to render West Germans immune to right-wing ideological temptations and turn them into a reliable, predictable political entity, nationally as well as internationally.[42] As mentioned earlier, Stürmer's project can be interpreted as a historiographical extension of the government's 1985 Bitburg initiative and the two museum projects pursued by the conservative government. Stürmer's vision must have had considerable appeal, especially for politicians facing an unpredictable electorate, but it did not even come to terms with the blatant conceptual problem of Germany's division after 1945. Stürmer failed to explain how it was possible to construct a consistent national identity for West Germans and still insist on the national unity of both Germanys at the same time, a theme regularly invoked by conservative politicians in their dealings with the East German state and the East German population. Moreover, Stürmer and his colleagues in the conservative think tanks close to the government, as well as their critics on the Left, never addressed the question of how to popularize their respective designs for a West German collective identity. The conservative side apparently assumed that West Germany's political culture suffered from a debilitating identity crisis and that the existing vacuum would be filled instantaneously once the intellectuals decided to release their historical visions. The liberal side went even further by maintaining that West Germans had drawn the only appropriate conclusion from the Nazi experience by internalizing Western democratic values that superseded outdated conventional sentiments of national and historical identity. In principle, the liberals should have presumed that the population would not be tempted by the conservative campaign, although Habermas's massive intervention seems to indicate that he himself did not trust the postnational equilibrium.

There are, indeed, good reasons to believe that both sides were wrong, that at the time of the Historikerstreit, the majority of Germans did not suffer from an identity crisis nor had they given up on traditional forms of collective identity. In the late 1970s but especially the early 1980s, a large part of West Germany's historical culture underwent a massive transformation, which is only insufficiently captured by the term *Alltagsgeschichte,* or everyday history. This phenomenon was by no means limited to West Germany; in one way or another, it encompassed most of Western Europe, the United States, and Japan.[43] Alltagsgeschichte developed in West Germany in two distinct forms: as an intellectual phenomenon based in the Left subculture with few links to the academic establishment and as a popular phenomenon that encompassed all mass media, print and electronic. In either variety, Alltagsgeschichte lacked a clear conceptual focus but reflected a strong interest in relating to past events on a tangible, emotional, and subjective level and in a way that afforded the opportunity of identifying with past actors—preferably unknown or marginalized to that point—and concrete local traditions and practices. In keeping with its emotional emphasis and in distinction to more conventional ways of studying the past, Alltagsgeschichte put particular emphasis on visual records and forms of representation, such as paintings, photographs, and especially moving images. Also, for the same reasons, the producers and consumers of Alltagsgeschichte preferred conventional narrative frameworks and tried to capture past phenomena that could be considered close to home. In one way or another, often enough only in an imaginary way, Alltagsgeschichte evoked the multifaceted sounding board *Heimat;* it related to and created a sense of geographical, historical, and emotional belonging.[44] The movement dealt with diverse topics, including the early modern period and Prussian history, but in Germany, it focused primarily on the history of National Socialism.

As an intellectual movement, Alltagsgeschichte represented a critical appropriation of a number of different traditions: the neo-Marxism of the Frankfurt School, in particular Habermas's writings, and the writings of independent Marxist philosophers such as Ernst Bloch; the phenomenological and ethnological traditions of German sociology, reaching as far back as Edmund Husserl; the debates on fascism that occupied West Germany's leftist intellectuals in the 1960s; and various imports such as Anglo-American anthropology (for instance, Clifford Geertz's), Michel Foucault's theory of power, and Pierre Bourdieu's theory of practical action, as well as microhistorical and neo-Marxist role exemplars such as the works of Carlo Ginzburg, Natalie

Davis, and E. P. Thompson.[45] With few exceptions, however, the practitioners of Alltagsgeschichte took a decidedly antitheoretical stance.[46] Consequently, these traditions have often only been acknowledged in passing, and core concepts of the new movement, such as *Alltag* (everyday life) and *Erfahrung* (experience), have never been accurately defined. Institutionally, the movement had four focal points: the Max Planck Institute in Göttingen; the Open University in Hagen; the Institute for Contemporary History in Munich; and most important, a large number of local, grassroots initiatives loosely organized in an association of history workshops. Especially the latter were firmly rooted in the new social movements of the 1970s, such as the ecological, peace, and women's movements.[47] Alltagsgeschichte was launched by the first postwar generation, scholars born after 1938, many among them veterans of the student movement who—unlike their predecessors—could no longer find jobs in the shrinking university system.[48] Participation in the history workshops afforded them the opportunity to continue their involvement with leftist politics after the end of the Social Democratic/liberal reform era, to partake in a continued antifascist intellectual endeavor after theorizing about fascisms had exhausted itself and proven politically ineffectual, and to engage with history on a semiprofessional level after they had been denied access to academia proper.

As a popular phenomenon, Alltagsgeschichte went far beyond the pet projects of a group of highly motivated, unemployed, left-wing historians. It produced "a flood of literature aimed at the general audience,"[49] and it resulted in an unprecedented wave of exhibitions and new museums. Alltagsgeschichte even sparked new ways of doing history, such as the history workshops, and boosted previously marginal historical projects such as student competitions into the national limelight. Most important, however, Alltagsgeschichte changed West German television, especially its image of Nazism. German public television, which operated without any private competition until 1984, had always addressed the topic of Nazism, albeit often in a detached, "objective," and heavy-handed manner. But beginning in the late 1970s, a new generation of television producers and executives bought and produced large numbers of programs that presented the history of the Third Reich from the perspective of the average citizen. These shows were visually attractive and were cast in successful formats, such as docudramas and TV films featuring standard, popular plot types. Consequently, they were also very successful with audiences. The wave of new media images included hardly any critical probings into the population's passivity vis-à-vis the Holocaust; most of the time, they presented a vision of everyday life during Nazism devoid of many important groups of victims—Jews, Gypsies, political dissidents, and Soviet prisoners of war (POWs). By 1984, television had already achieved what historians only started to consider after the Historians' Debate: the electronic media had historicized Nazism by integrating it within the continuity of modern German history by means of pleasurable historical narratives, taking the perspective of the bystanders as the ultimate reference point without subjecting that perspective to rigorous self-critical analysis. Nevertheless, understood in these broad terms, the Alltagsgeschichte period was probably the only moment in West German history when the population as a whole and not just intellectuals or other subgroups confronted the Nazi past.[50]

Both varieties of Alltagsgeschichte developed in distinct cultural and political settings, and the popular rendition of Alltagsgeschichte lacked the clear critical, political focus of its subcultural counterpart. But both unraveled the traditional center of West Germany's historical culture by exposing the crucial blind spots of the West German historical profession, which had neither researched the intricacies of everyday life during Nazism nor been able to produce histories with popular appeal. Moreover, unlike the historical profession, the public broadcasting systems and the left-wing intellectuals were attuned to international trends, which they incorporated in their new vision of the history of the Third Reich. Not surprisingly, both varieties of everyday history received sharp criticism from professional historians.[51] Alltagsgeschichte thoroughly transformed West Germany's historical culture, but even with hindsight, it remains difficult to assess its impact; it produced self-congratulatory celebrations of local resistance groups, as well as self-critical probings into the half-forgotten histories of local concentration camps. Stated differently, it encompassed Heimat as well as Holocaust.[52]

In almost all respects, Alltagsgeschichte as a social phenomenon was the exact opposite of the writings of the participants of the Historians' Debate: it was visually instead of discursively oriented, popular instead of intellectual and academic, and concerned with subjective experience instead of objectification. Nonetheless, it is clear that the texts produced during the Historikerstreit, unlike the participants' scholarly publications, shared some of the characteristics of the genre of Alltagsgeschichte. During the Historians' Debate, the participants sought the greatest publicity they could achieve while staying within their traditional realm, the print media. Moreover, in contrast to their usual academic style of writing, their discussions featured many subjective assessments of National Socialism and were conducted on a very personal level. In this respect, the Historikerstreit was a belated reaction to the eruption of Alltagsgeschichte, which had caught the intellectuals by surprise. The conservative historians and their critics tried to reclaim lost ground and reestablish themselves in what they considered their traditional role as the primary arbiters of West Germany's historical culture. But the intellectuals of both camps misjudged the population's need for historical guidance and overestimated their own ability to provide and shape the popular historical imagination. Due to their ignorance of the historical culture in a media society, the intellectuals misconceived the process of historical identity formation in West Germany's post-Nazi society. The miscommunications and incompatibilities between the academic sector and the mass media and subcultural sectors of West Germany's historical culture will stand out more clearly if we take a closer look at the basic theoretical assumptions with which academics approached the challenge of collective identity management. Both warring factions appear to have been seriously out of touch with the actual development of collective memory and identity in West Germany.

THE POLITICAL/PHILOSOPHICAL DIMENSION:
THE MISGUIDED INTELLECTUAL QUESTS FOR WEST GERMANY'S COLLECTIVE IDENTITY

The philosophical underpinnings of the conservative agenda for the construction of a conventional national historical identity were provided by Hermann Lübbe, who was also instrumental in justifying the relative unwillingness of West German society to address the problem of the Nazi past in the 1950s. In his philosophical considerations, Lübbe strictly differentiates between historical identity and moral self-definition. According to his reasoning, the individual comes to terms with the historical forces that shape his or her life but are clearly located outside the person's own sphere of influence through the process of historical self-identification. Recognizing and adapting to these essential forces are important elements of human identity precisely because these forces define the parameters and processes the individual is exposed to without having any power to alter them. The realm of moral self-identity, by contrast, is limited to the individual's personal sphere, where his or her actions can make a decisive difference and where self-identity is indistinguishable from moral responsibility.[53] Lübbe's stance systematically unburdens the individual's historical memory vis-à-vis such a phenomenon as Nazism. Since he transposes this model onto the level of collective processes of historical and moral identity formation, he interprets the German population's postwar silence in the face of the Nazi crimes as a realistic and in this sense "responsible" tacit agreement between former victims and former perpetrators who decided to further the cause of rebuilding the shattered society and state by ignoring past struggles.[54] Lübbe's ideas are helpful in understanding the silence of the 1950s; he is its foremost apologist and—with Alexander and Margarete Mitscherlichs[55]—also its foremost theoretician. But his writings have little to say about the much more active phases of Vergangenheitsbewältigung in West Germany from the 1960s through the 1980s, which constantly interwove moral and historical issues on the personal as well as the collective levels, as the example of Alltagsgeschichte aptly illustrates. Nevertheless, Lübbe's ideas are still relevant because they render explicit the radical dissociation of moral and historical questions that informed conservative initiatives such as Stürmer's.

The leftist counterpart to Lübbe's position, developed by Jürgen Habermas, is also questionable, if for other reasons. As already mentioned, Habermas argues that the philosophical problems highlighted by Nazism call for a reflexive, postnational identity that avoids the pitfalls of traditional ideologies by generating guidelines for social action on the basis of intersubjective principles of communicative reason. For Habermas, these principles provide a healthy and necessary corrective in our dealings with the past because they put us in a position to decide which traditions we choose to continue and from which ones we choose to dissociate ourselves. More concretely, after Auschwitz, these principles help us distance ourselves and our society from the traditions that led to Auschwitz—with nationalism, racism, and authoritarianism among the most prominent. Habermas has identified two resources in contemporary German society that embody these rational principles and facilitate their future adaptation and implementation. Although Western constitutions such as the German *Grundgesetz* provide an adequate modern rendition of Enlightenment traditions, the radical democratic practice of grassroots initiatives, among them the new social movements of the 1970s, provides the necessary impetus to revise the constitutions in light of social, political, and economic change. For Habermas, the formal procedures of the rule of law and the democratic grassroots movements give us the opportunity to deal with the past in a self-critical, postnational fashion.[56] In the mid-1990s, Habermas elaborated on his earlier writings on discourse ethics in an attempt to outline a philosophy of law and ethics that would avoid the shortcomings of more traditional approaches—for instance, abstract universalist ethics and moral pragmatism. He lays the intellectual foundation for a postconventional moral consciousness rooted in rational discursive practices as well as universal procedural principles of justice that he had advocated in previous, less ambitious interventions.[57] For Habermas, in sharp distinction to Lübbe, the fact that our realm of moral responsibility extends beyond our sphere of influence represents the very essence of moral problems. In his eyes, not only the bystanders but also subsequent generations share the moral responsibility for the Holocaust.

The problem with Habermas's theoretical position on postwar West German collective identity derives from the peculiar juxtaposition of social analysis and philosophical idealization that is characteristic of most of his writings, including his texts pertaining to the issues of the Historians' Debate.[58] Habermas maintains that in addition to providing the philosophical outlines for future politics and discursive practices, his writings reflect the key aspects of postwar German history. He claims repeatedly that 1945 induced a change of mentality that led to a postnational consensus in West Germany.[59] But many elements of postwar West German history, including the events recalled earlier with regard to Alltagsgeschichte, suggest that the population never underwent a mentality change of significant proportions, let alone reached a consensus about such important matters as what lessons to draw from the Nazi period. Detlev Claussen has expressed this critique of Habermas most bluntly: "Habermas' position is weakened by the fact that he stipulates a post-1945 consensus about the National Socialist past which is completely fictitious. . . . Unfortunately, such a postwar consensus never existed."[60] In an ironic turn of events, it seems the social movements that Habermas entrusts with the development of postconventional identities and practices combine a radical democratic agenda with thoroughly conventional ways of imagining the past and passing moral judgment, as the example of Alltagsgeschichte indicates.

In sum, Lübbe and Habermas offer three choices: historical identity without ethics; moral identity without history; or formal principles of communicative action as far as possible removed from both history and ethics, at least in the traditional sense. Thus, both men systematically exclude from consideration the combination of conventional historical and moral identities that, in practice, has provided the best results in the history of Vergangenheitsbewältigung in West Germany. Whenever large numbers of West Germans have been motivated to confront the Nazi legacy, the media product that serves as a catalyst has provided them with a strong moral appeal in combination with an image of the National Socialism that they accepted, for one reason or another, as an authentic rendition of "their" history. Media events such as *The Diary of Anne Frank, Heimat, Holocaust,* and, to a lesser extent, *Schindler's List,* as well as grassroots movements such as that of the history workshops in the 1970s, offered the audience or participants a tangible sense of historical and moral identity, on the audience's or the participants' own terms. Thus, with hindsight, it has become obvious that philosophers either underestimated the population's willingness to contemplate historical responsibility with regard to actions for which it bore no responsibility (Lübbe) or overestimated the population's capacity and willingness to break radically with traditional forms of moral and historical orientation (Habermas). In either case, they underestimated the particular emotional appeal, entertainment value, didactic-philosophical pleasure, and moral historical education that perpetrators and bystanders and their descendants could derive from standardized historical narratives that interlace historical and ethical elements in very conventional ways.[61] *Holocaust,* for instance, provided moral education through the unihibited use of the genre of the soap opera for the representation of the destruction of the Jews of Europe. *Heimat,* more pleasurable than disturbing to the German audience, gave "images, history, stories, and symbolic contour to a word and concept that only exists in German."[62] Both television shows successfully appealed to the viewers' sense of justice, veracity, and historical identity.

In contradistinction to the philosophers' viewpoint, the perspective of Alltagsgeschichte as presented earlier suggests that the historical development concerning the historical identities of West Germans could be sketched as follows. The Nazi crimes, the collapse of the Third Reich, the permanent loss of formerly German territories in Eastern Europe, the division of Germany, and the Americanization of West German culture destabilized traditional forms of German national identity. But West Germans neither surrendered to a historical vacuum nor found emotional refuge in a form of constitutional patriotism. Instead, over the course of three decades, they rekindled tradition-ally stable and satisfying local and regional historical identities.[63] From this safe ground, artificially removed from the turmoil of high politics, they ad-dressed the problem of the Nazi past and constructed new, conventionally structured national identities—for instance, a fairly pervasive West German national identity. However, though the philosophers' discourse did not reflect the actual postwar development, it was a very important reference point for West German historians. In particular, the work of the social historians who joined in the critique of Nolte and others during the Historians' Debate rep-resented the historiographical equivalent to Habermas's philosophical perspec-tive on modern German history.

THE HISTORIOGRAPHICAL DIMENSION: DECONSTRUCTING THE CONCEPT OF SINGULARITY

Although the participants in the Historikerstreit were, to a large extent, politi-cally motivated, the issues under discussion reflected the themes and topics that had concerned West German historians throughout the postwar period. This applied in particular to the historiographical issues raised since the 1960s, when the methods, concepts, and interpretative frameworks for the study of Nazism multiplied. In this respect, the historians involved in the Historikerstreit focused on the historiographical past and did not aspire to shape the historiographical future. While arguing about the place of the Holocaust in German history, the participants reconsidered the theoretical, conceptual, and methodological differences that had occupied them through-out their professional careers. Since all of them were quite familiar with the applicable background, they never spelled out all the implications of their arguments. But a closer look at the historiographical context and prehistory of the Historians' Debate demonstrates in what respect the debate was the unproductive closure to a most productive phase in the history of the Ger-man historical profession.

Six historiographical issues were touched on in the Historians' Debate and concerned West German historians in the decades before the debate: the discussions about the concepts of totalitarianism versus fascism; the methodological disputes between social historians and neohistoricists and, more precisely, the clashes between intentionalists and functionalists; the debate about the notion of Germany's special path to modernity; the historiographical debates about Alltagsgeschichte; the issue of the exceptionality of the Holocaust; and the so-called Fischer Debate.[64] For the present purposes, the Fischer Debate, which occupied the West German historical establishment from 1960 through 1965, was the most important precursor to the Historians' Debate. The topic of the Fischer Debate is unrelated to the issues of the Historians' Debate, but, in both cases, the focus was on historiographical discussions that spilled over into the print media, involved the entire West German intellectual elite, and had important political ramifications. In addition, the intensity and tone of the debates, as well as the age-groups of the scholars and intellectuals involved, indicate that both debates marked a generational shift in West German historiography and intellectual life. Unlike any other historiographical disputes in the history of the Federal Republic, the Fischer Debate and the Historikerstreit destabilized a hitherto unproblematic consensus, thus opening the field to new methods and interpretative frameworks crafted according to the interests and intellectual needs of new generations of scholars.

In the early 1960s, the Hamburg historian Fritz Fischer and some of his students challenged the widely shared opinion that held all European powers equally responsible for the outbreak of World War I. Prior to Fischer's intervention, historians agreed that an exhaustive study of the archival record had proven that none of the European governments was particularly interested in starting an all-out military campaign in 1914. Only due to the specific circumstances immediately before the outbreak of the war—diplomatic mishaps, treaty obligations, the intricacies of mobilizing large modern armies, and the like—did the governments suddenly find themselves entangled in warfare almost against their will. Applying standard historiographical methods to new as well as already known archival material, Fischer revealed the particularly excessive war aims of the German government and argued that the German side was primarily responsible for the outbreak of World War I. More specifically, he exposed the parallels between the German war aims in World War I and World War II, thus proposing a continuity in German politics that was particularly disturbing to a generation of scholars who still identified with (and had grown up in) Wilhelmine Germany and who had mostly dealt with Nazism by bracketing it from its specifically German historical context.[65]

The Fischer Debate certainly changed the perception of German involvement in World War I, although Fischer could not establish a new orthodoxy as some of his students have claimed.[66] More important, however, the debate prepared the ground for the historiographical innovations of the 1960s because some of the older scholars, most notably Gerhard Ritter, undermined their credibility through their overly emotional and aggressive criticism. Also, although Fischer used conventional methods, he introduced a different, less literary, and more "objective" style of writing, which had more in common with the "scientific" style of the emerging social historians than with the style of his contemporaries and predecessors. Finally, by introducing the question of continuity within twentieth-century German history (at least up to 1945), Fischer captured the underlying motif of the younger historians, especially the social historians, who were then writing their dissertations and who were studying the nineteenth and twentieth centuries in order to understand the origins of Nazism and Germany's special path to modernity.

The comparison between the Fischer Debate and the Historians' Debate clarifies the specificity of the Historikerstreit and highlights the generational dynamics at the core of the evolution of the representation of National Socialism in West German historiography, a process that proceeded in three steps. From the immediate postwar period through the 1950s, German historians and intellectuals tended to "export" Nazism by projecting its origins onto forces and historical events external to German history, such as fate, diabolic elements, or the French Revolution.[67] Even the first systematic studies of the Nazi regime—presented by political scientists, not historians—applied a theoretical framework that linked Nazism to the contemporary Soviet system rather than the German past.[68] Thus, most of German history, with the possible exception of the last years of the Weimar Republic, was clearly separated from Nazism, remained available for positive identification and, as the Fischer Debate revealed, was also used for these purposes. This construction was destabilized by Fischer and his disciples and irreversibly overturned by the next generation of scholars, especially social historians, who constructed the prehistory of Nazism by reaching far back into the nineteenth century. Building on explanatory strategies developed during the war and in the immediate postwar period outside Germany, social historians and social scientists in the 1960s argued that the rise of Nazism was linked to a basic discrepancy between rapid technological and industrial modernization, on the one hand, and delayed social, political, and cultural modernization, on the other. Social historians considered this a detrimental combination that made Germany a special case within the context of the modernization of the Western world since the nineteenth century. In short, if the first postwar generation of German historians spent some efforts on bracketing Nazism, the next generation turned this implicit notion of exceptionality into an explicit research agenda and tried to determine the specificity of Germany's path to modernity.[69]

Unlike their predecessors, the scholars of the second generation also paid more attention to the Holocaust, although only a few made it their primary research focus. Instead, the notion of the exceptionality of the "Final Solution" became a concept that tied together West German historians of various political and methodological creeds in an increasingly diverse and competitive scholarly community. As Otto Dov Kulka put it: "One of the most remarkable developments in German historiography during the 1960s and '70s appears to have been the gradually reached, overwhelming consensus on the central role of anti-Semitism in National Socialist ideology and politics. It was identified as the only constant element and as such, a key to the understanding of the inner contradictions of the Third Reich, Hitler's unconventional war aims, and the singularity of the Holocaust."[70]

The next turning point occurred in the 1980s and took several years before reaching its conclusion in the Historians' Debate. There might have been widespread agreement among German scholars during the 1970s about the historical exceptionality of Nazism and its prehistory, especially with regard to the Holocaust, but starting in the early 1980s, the second generation of West German historians, with help from colleagues abroad, undermined, step by step, the various notions of exceptionality that had informed their work on modern German history. Thus, the Historikerstreit was just the last in a line of similar debates that relativized the interpretative framework of historical singularity. This dismantling process took place against the backdrop of the previously described historiographical and popular interest in Alltagsgeschichte, which, due to its emphasis on the "normal," everyday aspects of life during the Third Reich, provided an implicit challenge to notions of exceptionality.

One precursor to the Historians' Debate was the discussion about the aforementioned liberal master narrative of Germany's special path to modernity. The paradigm was attacked by young, Left-oriented scholars from Britain and conservative historians in West Germany, who pointed out that the theory was based on problematic assumptions about a so-called normal path to modernity that did not fit the actual development in any Western country, including Britain.[71] The second important scholarly dispute preceding the Historians' Debate focused on the structuralist interpretation of the origins of the "Final Solution," which challenged the assumption that the Nazi leaders had followed a long-term plan in their anti-Jewish policies. In their writings on the origins of the Holocaust, structural historians questioned the idea that Hitler's exceptional ideological commitments and his exceptional position within the power structure of the Third Reich were the decisive causes of the "Final Solution." Instead, they argued that many supposedly normal bureaucrats, party functionaries, and even members of the German army and the police force played a decisive role in the design and implementation of the "Final Solution."[72] Thus, at least implicitly, social historians had already challenged the limits of the concept of the Holocaust's singularity before it was contested during the Historians' Debate.[73]

Unlike prior debates in the early 1980s that addressed similar conceptual issues, the Historians' Debate, due to the relative age of the participants and audience and due to its historiographical and political context, represented a generational and intellectual divide—just as the Fischer Debate had done almost three decades earlier. In the historical profession, the Fischer Debate marked the end of the Adenauer era and the onset of the Social Democratic reform process, whereas the Historians' Debate, somewhat belatedly, attested to the end of that reform era and the onset of the neoconservative offensive in West Germany's intellectual and political life. In both cases, the younger generations were only marginally involved in the discussions. In addition, both debates paved the way to new lines of continuity in modern German history. The Fischer Debate broke the continuity barrier of "1933." After the Fischer Debate, Nazism could be conceived as a decidedly German entity, with a long prehistory in the German past. The Historikerstreit discarded the continuity barrier of "1945," which had been respected by the first *and* the second generations of West German historians who, in one way or another, believed that German history had been radically altered after the war. Since the mid-1980s, the third generation of scholars working in the Federal Republic have explored the lines of continuity that link the Kaiserreich, the Weimar Republic, the Third Reich, *and* the Federal Republic. For the first time, some scholars have pursued this question of continuity with the explicit objective of uncovering positive elements of continuity that encompassed Nazism and were worthwhile identifying with.[74]

This short survey of the debates and developments in the West German historical profession since the 1960s attests to the impressive innovative zeal and methodological diversity of the discipline. However, at the same time that the historians developed and debated the new concept of social history, West Germany's historical culture as a whole underwent massive transformations. The student movement in the mid-1960s added a critical and very distinct voice to the discussions about the meaning of the Nazi past, a voice that, by way of different metamorphoses and dead ends, gave rise to the intellectual side of Alltagsgeschichte. In addition, the mass medium of television, which only reached large audiences in the early 1960s in West Germany, added a completely new dimension to the business of representing history. As a result, the historians' contribution to West Germany's historical culture developed even more into a niche discourse addressed to an expert audience—despite the exceptional productivity of the discipline. This situation became particularly apparent during the Historians' Debate, when historians tried to reach out to a larger public but had little resonance outside academia and the highbrow national print media.

THE GENERATIONAL DIMENSION:

THE TROUBLED AND TROUBLESOME MEMORY OF THE HITLER YOUTH GENERATION

Some of the participants and commentators of the Historians' Debate pointed out that the great majority of the players in the debate belong to the age cohort born between 1920 and 1931, among them Ernst Nolte (1923), Andreas Hillgruber (1925), Joachim Fest (1926), Jürgen Habermas (1929), Eberhard Jäckel (1929), Hans and Wolfgang Mommsen (1930), Imanuel Geiss (1931), and Hans-Ulrich Wehler (1931).[75] These intellectuals are part of the Hitler Youth generation, which, in general terms, has been defined as encompassing "the age groups which were born during the Weimar Republic and raised and educated during the twelve years of the Nazi regime."[76] As mentioned earlier, members of this generation were an important segment of the West German political, economic, and cultural-intellectual elite from the late 1960s through the late 1990s. This age cohort has been repeatedly studied by West German sociologists and historians because its members have developed distinct characteristics, which had already manifested themselves in the first postwar surveys. Many factors indicate that we are dealing with a picture-perfect case study of what the sociologist Karl Mannheim, back in 1926, termed a *political generation*: an age-group whose members shared a number of formative, historical experiences in their youth that shaped their emotional and political horizon of expectation for the rest of their lives.[77] In the case at hand, these experiences included living through Nazism, World War II, and the subsequent years of deprivation—experiences shared with other age-groups—but also two experiences unique to this political generation: having grown up and been educated during National Socialism, within institutions either appropriated or founded by the Nazis, and having willingly or unwillingly served a criminal regime at a young age without, therefore, being primarily responsible for the rise of Nazism and the crimes committed under the auspices of the German state. With reference to its common educational background, this generation has been called the Hitler Youth generation. Its peculiar relationship to the complex of guilt and responsibility for the Nazi crimes, especially among its younger members, has been captured in the infamous phrase *Gnade der späten Geburt* (the mercy or privilege of late birth).[78]

The age limits set for this political generation vary from study to study, with birth dates ranging from 1918 to 1933.[79] Sociologists have pointed out that the Hitler Youth generation comprises various subgroups whose experiences differ markedly from each other; consider, for instance, the experiences of a young soldier versus a Hitler Youth member. Also and more important, the model focuses on the experiences of the male members of the generation and would have to be substantially revised in order to account for the experiences of the whole generation, male and female. Nevertheless, the model provides an excellent point of departure, especially when dealing with a still almost exclusively male profession such as the German academic elite. For the present purposes, it is not important to linger on the general characteristics ascribed to this generation, which, based on Helmut Schelsky's study of 1957, has been described as disillusioned with politics, focused on family and career, motivated by an extraordinary need for financial and emotional security, and equipped with an astute sense of realism.[80] The historians under consideration, representing only a tiny fraction of their generation and working within a small profession, do not necessarily fit this image. As a prod to further inquiry, I will focus on the peculiar situation of the historians of this generation perched uneasily, as the Historikerstreit revealed, between history and memory.

In 1926, Mannheim described in theoretical terms the case of a political generation whose "natural worldview"—acquired during youth and the yardstick against which all subsequent experiences are measured—is radically challenged by a sudden and substantial reversal of the political and social environment. He concluded that "the first impressions remain alive and predominant even if the subsequent life is spent negating and working through the 'natural worldview' acquired during youth."[81] Therefore, it is not surprising that members of the Hitler Youth generation and especially historians return to the memories of their youth and even reidentify, albeit momentarily, with the moral and political perspectives taken on during adolescence. Unlike the case of Stürmer, who was born in 1938 and does not belong to the Hitler Youth generation, Hillgruber's and Nolte's disturbing utterances in the prelude to the Historikerstreit are not so much part of a political program as they are indications of the surfacing of bits and pieces of troubled memory. After the war, most Germans came to recognize the unprecedented criminality and gigantic self-destruction they had taken part in, but from the perspective of many participants at the time, especially the committed youth, attempts to defend German territory and the German population against overwhelming odds in 1944 and 1945 amounted to the ultimate test of their patriotism, if not their commitment to the Führer. A reflection of that devotion appears in Hillgruber's need to identify with the eastern troops and in Nolte's anti-communism and anti-Semitism.

For historians of the Hitler Youth generation, the task of objectifying the Nazi past within the parameters of the discipline, on the one hand, and the interest of keeping in touch with personal memories of the period that often did not mesh with the objectified image, on the other, created a conflict that was acted out during the Historians' Debate. Thus, historians gave public testimony to their generation's troublesome position between history and memory. For the intellectuals among them, this position was exacerbated because, for professional reasons, they had spent decades producing objectifications of the past that systematically delegitimized some of their own memories. Although only a few intellectuals acted out their memories and put them into print, the harshness of the critics' response and the overall aggressive tone and ad hominem attacks launched during the Historikerstreit attested to the violence involved in a lifelong struggle with one's "natural worldview." From this perspective, in addition to the political, philosophical, and historiographical issues described earlier, the Historikerstreit also addressed the question of the legitimacy and illegitimacy of the pleasure of subjective reidentification after a total reversal of the official, collective system of values. This problem is meaningless for subsequent generations and explains why the topics of the Historikerstreit have quickly become irrelevant. The texts of the Historians' Debate became "sites of memory" only for a well-defined subgroup—the West German historians and similarly oriented intellectuals of the Hitler Youth generation.[82]

That some members of the generation felt compelled to return to their origins, even in a public setting, should not come as a surprise. However, the timing of this return is somewhat of a riddle: why did this return occur in the late 1980s? The late 1980s offered the Hitler Youth generation its last chance to influence what Jan Assmann has called the transition from communicative to cultural memory.[83] At the end of 1995, the great majority of the historians of the Hitler Youth generation were retired, thus having lost the opportunity to shape the cultural memory of Nazism ex cathedra, with the authoritative voice of the full professor and from the very particular communicative memory of their generation.

In addition, the timing of the debate, especially the late surfacing of the historians' more personal recollections, was determined by a factor that Lutz Niethammer has expressed succinctly with regard to the victims of genocidal policies but that also holds true, if in a less traumatic sense, for the members of the Hitler Youth generation. Only after West Germany's historical culture had provided an interpretative structure for the understanding of Nazism— a structure comprised primarily of mass-media representations but also historical research that provided both a protective layer between the individual and his or her troublesome memories as well as a challenge to the authenticity of these memories—did the individuals feel compelled to express their personal memories in order to amend or contradict the media images they confronted.[84] In the German case, the renewed interest in history, the wave of everyday history, the programs of West German television on the topic of Nazism, and the historians' own prior work created such a framework beginning in the late 1970s. Against this backdrop, historians of the Hitler Youth generation expressed memories they had held in check for several decades. Now, they felt challenged to tell the younger generations, who had researched everyday life in the Third Reich and who put such emphasis on the subjective angle in their pursuit of Alltagsgeschichte, what it had really felt like growing up during Nazism.

Without obliterating them, the generational factor cuts across the institutional and discursive boundaries of a given historical culture, as the parallels between the Jenninger affair and the Historians' Debate illustrate. The Hitler Youth generation as a whole, not just the historians among its members, sought explanations for the historical riddle of the rise and nature of Nazism. As a result of this concern, the generation differs markedly from the political generations preceding and following it. The generation of Germans who had been adults during the Third Reich showed little inclination after the war to come to terms with the specificity of the Nazi era. Members of the first postwar generation are primarily concerned with the question of how Nazism fits within the overall history of modern Germany and how Nazi society is related to their own social context. To this end, they pursued everyday history and investigated the ways in which Nazism represented a typically modern phenomenon. In the process of such research, the parameters the intellectuals of the Hitler Youth generation introduced for the study of Nazism were quickly displaced. Nevertheless, the Hitler Youth generation and especially its historians will most likely remain the age cohort—situated between the generation of the Nazi perpetrators and bystanders and the postwar generations—that has made the most conflicted, self-reflexive, and idiosyncratic contribution to the task of Vergangenheitsbewältigung.

HISTORIANS AND HISTORICAL CULTURE

The contribution of academics of the Hitler Youth generation to the historical culture of the Federal Republic was informed by the motive of defining a solid ground for the postwar democracy, removed as far as possible from the Nazi past. Politically, this was accomplished by excluding extremists of any kind from their own ranks and conducting their discussions within the parameters of the political mainstream; philosophically, it was done by delineating concepts of collective identity distinct from types of identity thought to be involved in the catastrophe of National Socialism; and historiographically, it was done by corroborating the decisive turning point of 1945 and by quarantining the events of the "Final Solution" through the double-edged concept of historical singularity. The consensus fell apart when some members of the profession became more actively involved in the conservative cultural offensive of the 1980s, when important developments in other sectors of the historical culture undermined key notions of this consensus, and when the historians, at the end of their careers, found themselves caught between the conflicting interests of providing objective accounts of Nazism and of relating their more personal memories of the era to the public. These factors combined brought about the Historians' Debate in 1986.

During the Historikerstreit, historians very successfully mobilized their traditional constituency, the "educated public" represented by other academics and producers and consumers of the national print media. This audience was attuned to the specificities of the historiographical perspective on Nazism and to the conflict between memories and historiography played out in the debate. But historians could not make significant inroads into other areas of West Germany's historical culture that were not compatible with the parameters of the historians' discourse, for instance, television. The abstract concepts and the elaborate historiographical models, especially those developed by social historians, are unsuitable for visual representation and could not be brought to the screen in an interesting fashion. Having spent their careers designing representations of Nazism geared toward what they perceived as the political needs of the postwar democracy, the historians of the Hitler Youth generation had been beaten to the task by a medium that barely existed at the time they received their professional training in the 1950s and early 1960s. As the earlier excursion into Alltagsgeschichte exemplifies, television and other visually based media had become the culturally and politically most relevant sectors of West Germany's historical culture by the late 1970s.[85] The hierarchical and paternalistic structure of West Germany's academic establishment, which normally works to the advantage of the professoriat, contributed to its relative isolation in this case. In the late 1980s, universities were the only significant sector of West Germany's historical culture still clearly dominated by representatives of the Hitler Youth generation. In all other sectors, with the exception of the political sphere, the image of Nazism had already been shaped by the first postwar generation. These younger intellectuals had brought Alltagsgeschichte to the screen and into the museums and had little inclination to return to the issues addressed during the Historians' Debate. The importance of the generational divide is exemplified by the fact that the younger professional historians who had initiated the study of the history of everyday life contributed very little to the Historians' Debate.[86]

After the Historikerstreit, historians had little time to contemplate the limited influence of their trade within the larger historical culture. Just like the development of the electronic media, albeit more swiftly, German unification once again radically changed the social and political context of their profession. This time, conservative historians found themselves in a better position. Once again considerably overestimating the potentials of their profession, they quickly attacked social historians for having been unable to foresee the historic events of 1989 and 1990. In response to the events and/or the critique, social historians have indeed revised their position. They have distanced themselves from the *Sonderweg* (i.e., special path to modernity) paradigm and the notion of a postnational identity and tried "to recapture nationalism for the political left."[87] Thus, some of the central ideas that were still vigorously and successfully defended during the Historians' Debate have become obsolete within the span of only a few years. The latest reshuffling of Germany's historical culture within the rediscovered parameters of national history will certainly influence future interpretations of Nazism. Perhaps the only aspects vaguely reminiscent of some of the key interpretative tools of West Germany's historiography, such as the Sonderweg theory and the exceptionality of the Holocaust, will entail an astute awareness of the specificity of Germany's postwar history between 1945 and 1989.

The different fields of knowledge and modes of representation that have been brought to bear on each other in this chapter in order to contextualize and explain the Historians' Debate have, in recent years, often been explored through the concept of memory. But as indicated in chapter 2, classical studies in the field tend to define history and memory as mutually exclusive ways of learning about and representing the past. From Friedrich Nietzsche and Maurice Halbwachs to, more recently, Pierre Nora, Yosef Yerushalmi, and Jacques LeGoff, all the classical theorists of memory have differentiated between objective, timeless, academic representations of the past and "living," collective memories sustained by social groups for purposes of historical identity formation. Even if scholars have emphasized the intertextuality between different kinds of social memory in recent years, they have rarely studied historians and their work in the same terms.[88] Thus, often inadvertently, the traditional dichotomy between history and memory has been reconfirmed. The interpretative bias inherent in the term *memory* is clearly at odds with the preceding case study on the Historians' Debate, which illustrates that the historical profession represents a very context-specific, time-bound, and socially determined approach to the study and representation of the past; in this respect, it does not radically differ from other ways of knowing the past.

RHETORICAL RECYCLING

In December 1995, Ignaz Bubis, the president of the Central Council of Jews in Germany, revealed that he himself had used large parts of Jenninger's speech on two occasions in 1989. Bubis said that after twenty years in the public arena and after having delivered numerous memorial speeches, he had been pressed for new ideas and found many of Jenninger's remarks to the point and thought-provoking.[89] This recycling of Jenninger's speech by the highest political representative of Germany's Jews was neither scandalous nor inconsistent. In 1988, many West German Jews had come out in favor of Jenninger, arguing that a German politician had finally emphasized the real problem with Nazism, that is, Hitler's popularity with the German people. In addition, as mentioned, many critics pointed out that Jenninger's failure was more a question of performance than content. Nevertheless, Bubis's revelations were remarkable for other reasons. Although his public appearances were regularly and carefully followed by journalists and politicians' aides, nobody noticed in 1989 what must have been obvious parallels between Bubis's and Jenninger's discourse. This fact completely disappeared in the context of the historic fall of the Berlin Wall. Thus, only a year after Jenninger's resignation and the end of the Historians' Debate, Bubis's—or, better, Jenninger's—speech no longer represented a noticeable transgression of the rules of West Germany's rapidly changing historical culture. It is only consistent, therefore, that six years later, in 1995, Bubis's revelations were hardly noticed by the media.

Since the late 1980s, the parameters for acceptable representations of Nazism and the "Final Solution" have changed to the point that if Jenninger's

performance were repeated today, it probably would not result in his resignation. However, after having sketched out West Germany's historical culture at
the time of the Historians' Debate, one sees more clearly how Jenninger
failed in 1988. He combined state-of-the-art conceptual models of Alltagsgeschichte with a personal interest in rectifying the negative image of the
German population's performance during Nazism. Once introduced into the
political realm of high politics, this combination formed a volatile mixture because it undermined the founding myth of the West German democracy that
had been preserved in parliament for over three decades. Inadvertently,
Jenninger had called into question the belief that the Federal Republic originated from an anti-Nazi consensus.

CHAPTER 5

NARRATIVE INVENTION AND
HISTORICIZATION

How Modern Was the Nazi Genocide?

For supporters and critics of Hayden White's work, the term *emplotment* represents the author's structural analysis of historical writing, his critique of historians' self-image, and his endorsement of epistemological relativism with regard to the writing of history. It has proven to be such a powerful, tempting, and flexible concept that it has also been used by historians who do not share White's theoretical position.[1]

Since his essay "Interpretation in History" and his book *Metahistory*, White has never systematically revised his understanding of *plot* and *emplotment*.[2] Within the formalist system proposed in *Metahistory*, "explanation by emplotment" was considered one of five levels of conceptualization in the historical work and one of three modes of explanation in the completed historical text. But in *Metahistory* itself and certainly in its reception, the tetrad of romance, tragedy, comedy, and satire, together with the corresponding tropes of metaphor, metonomy, synecdoche, and irony—became the focus of White's methodology. Critics of his tropological approach have repeatedly pointed out the limitations of his closed structuralist framework,[3] and White himself later relativized and opened it to additional plot forms and tropological structures.[4] If the tropological method he proposed in *Metahistory* seems at times too formalistic and reductive to grasp all the complexities of narrative history, it proves helpful for the analysis of narrative structures that develop in the wake of important transformations in the collective perception of the past. During such turning points—of which the historicization of National Socialism is a perfect example—historical representations display a tendency toward ideal plot types.

In 1982, White argued that different interpretations of the Holocaust, like representations of all historical events, assume the status of truthful representations of the past as a result of their compatibility with their political and social contexts. White mentioned the example of the Zionist interpretation of the Holocaust that passes as a historical truth in Israel because "of its effectiveness in justifying a whole range of current Israeli political policies."[5] At the same time, some representations of Nazism are generally considered untruthful because they cast the history of Nazism in unacceptable narrative formats, for instance, in the mode of comedy.[6] White insisted that all these restrictions solely depend on the context of the respective text. He implied that under certain circumstances, that is, a revival of Nazism, even a Nazi version of Nazism's history would be considered a truthful representation of the past.[7] His provocative assertion that the effectiveness of any given representation of Nazism determines its historical veracity has sparked heated debates among historians,[8] although few of the participants have turned to the historiography about Nazism to illustrate or refute White's arguments. The following analysis of different emplotments of the interdependence between Nazism and modernity aims at providing just such a case study. This historiographical exploration will also demonstrate that in the late 1980s, shortly after the conclusion of the Historians' Debate, younger scholars started experimenting with narrative formats that their predecessors had purposefully avoided. Not all these experiments in the margin of the discipline turned out to be successful, but together, they prepared the ground for the impressive reorientation of Holocaust historiography in Germany that was discussed in the previous chapters.

For a number of reasons, the texts and debates considered in this chapter offer strong support for White's thesis. The debate about the alleged modernity of Nazism illustrates that abstract concepts such as "the modernity of Nazism" or "the singularity of the Holocaust," as used during the Historikerstreit, cannot be proven or standardized by recourse to some commonly accepted protocol of facticity. It is impossible to determine the veracity of such abstract concepts on the grounds of the generally acknowledged facts of the NS period. In the course of their studies on Nazism and modernity, historians have delineated new fields of research and, in some cases, have produced an impressive array of new facts about the history of Nazism. Although their colleagues have acknowledged these facts, they have not accepted them as proof for the authors' specific interpretations of the interdependence between Nazism and modernity. In this case as in many others, the facticity of past events—what White called the primary referent of historical writing—and the meaningful narrative interpretation of these events—the secondary referent of historical writing—do not overlap.[9]

Rather than simply improving our knowledge, factual or otherwise, the return to theories of modernization for the understanding of Nazism represented a transformation of that knowledge according to the needs and interests of a new generation of historians.[10] The approach reflected their objective of historicizing Nazism by placing it within the continuum of modern German history. For this reason, they violated key rules that have characterized the emplotment of Nazism in most West German postwar historiography. Younger historians crossed the previously accepted plot barrier of 1945, which had assured that Nazism and the postwar period appeared to belong to two radically different, incompatible narrative universes. Returning to what White called "the Romantic apprehension of the world," younger historians used tragic and even comic plot types to integrate the histories of Nazism and the Federal Republic within a single overarching plot structure.[11] Thus, they undermined the status of Nazism as an exceptional event.

In the 1980s, three approaches advanced the historicization of National Socialism by constructing a historical continuum between the Third Reich and the Federal Republic based on the theme of modernization. In the first approach, Detlev Peukert developed his reassessment of the position of Nazism within modernity using his and others' work on the Alltagsgeschichte of the Third Reich. He interpreted National Socialism as a manifestation of the "pathologies and seismic fractures within modernity itself."[12] In the second approach, a parallel but unrelated endeavor, a number of scholars who worked together in the Hamburger Stiftung für Sozialgeschichte des 20. Jahrhunderts and the Hamburger Institut für Sozialforschung analyzed the development of modern scientific discourse in eugenics, racial hygiene, neuropsychiatry, and social and population policy before, after, and especially during Nazism. Their critique of the modern scientific paradigm was perhaps best represented in Götz Aly and Susanne Heim's concept of "the economics of the Final Solution." The third approach to the question of the interdependence of Nazism and modernity was most clearly argued in Rainer Zitelmann's work on the social and economic aspects of Hitler's worldview and their respective relevance for the social and economic policies of the Nazi regime. The analysis of the three approaches represents an intellectual archaeology of the 1980s. It emphasizes important contributions to the generational transformation of German historiography by scholars who have since departed from—or never entered—the academic scene. Detlev Peukert died suddenly at the age of forty in 1990. Rainer Zitelmenn disappeared in right-wing editorial circles, and Götz Aly continued to write influential books about the history of National Socialism as an independent author.[13]

Before presenting a detailed analysis of these three approaches, I will first take a closer look at the problems involved in the historicization of National Socialism and discuss the strategies German historians have employed since 1945 to approach the question of continuity in modern German history.

THE HISTORICIZATION OF NATIONAL SOCIALISM

The debate about the historicization of National Socialism focused on the question of how future histories of the Nazi period should be written, especially on the level of general global interpretations.[14] Martin Broszat, a member of the Hitler Youth generation, published his "Plea for the Historicization of National Socialism" before the Historians' Debate in 1985. He urged historians to contextualize Nazism within its wider historical framework and replace conventional, static, black-and-white representations of the Nazi past through more diverse approaches that better grasped the complexities of the Nazi era. In Broszat's eyes, such a reorientation would provide a more accurate picture of past reality while also being better suited for the instruction of present and future generations.

Broszat's initial proposal defined historicization in relative terms and therefore remained rather vague in some respects. Broszat suggested that future historians of National Socialism should apply *all* the methods of inquiry and representation used by historians for any other historical periods. Moreover, historians should strive for greater plasticity and flexibility in their language to convey the complexities of the Nazi past more accurately.[15] Unfortunately, during the debate that followed, the alleged shortcomings of past scholarship and thus the standards for future endeavors were never defined satisfactorily. It remained unclear whether these shortcomings manifested themselves in popular collective representations of Nazism or in historical scholarship or in both.[16] In two respects, however, the initial plea was precise enough. Future histories should inquire more closely into the lines of continuity that integrate

National Socialism into modern German history and relate these new results to the knowledge accumulated by prior research. This appeal entailed—it was argued—a shift of focus from the political-ideological record to the social history of Nazism. Broszat also suggested that the relationship between National Socialism and modernity and the theme of modernization offered a good starting point for future projects of historicization.[17]

Broszat's plea did not become an important reference point during the Historians' Debate. It was challenged by Saul Friedlander in 1987 and discussed between Broszat and Friedlander in 1988. This exchange about the historicization of National Socialism systematically addressed, for the first time, the methodological, conceptual, and ideological implications of the task of integrating the Nazi period within the history of modern Germany. In his critique of the concept of historicization, Friedlander defended the existing paradigm, with its primary focus on the political and ideological aspects of Nazism and its particular regard for the historical specificity of the Third Reich and the "Final Solution." One should not implement essential changes, Friedlander argued, until the advantages and disadvantages of the alternatives have been determined and until it can be shown that the limitations of existing scholarship are, indeed, linked to social conventions of representation and not "inherent in the phenomenon itself."[18] Broszat's intuitively convincing appeal also seemed to unduly favor the perspective of the German people in their day-to-day dealings with the regime. Thus, Broszat inadvertently valorized the problematic attitude of the bystanders of the "Final Solution."[19]

From today's perspective, it seems that both the appeal to historicize and the warning not to forsake control without prior self-reflection came too late. The next generation of German historians, part of the implied audience of the debate, had already developed a number of research projects that realized important aspects of Broszat's plea. That fact might explain the contradictory gestures in Broszat's texts—his urge for a specific kind of historicization, on the one hand, and his conviction about the inevitability of the process, on the other. The full-fledged historicizations of Nazism presented in the late 1980s and early 1990s did, indeed, justify some of the critics' concerns because they tended to relinquish complexity for coherence and consistency. At the same time, the interesting political range of the projects that will be discussed here demonstrates that the historicization of Nazism did not automatically entail a naive or apologetic emplotment of the history of the Third Reich.

WEST GERMAN HISTORIOGRAPHY AND THE CHALLENGE OF HISTORICAL CONTINUITY

With regard to the depiction of continuities in Germany's recent history, historicization defines two different but closely related projects: (1) the removal of more and more aspects of the history of modern Germany before the Third Reich from the gravitational pull of Nazism, that is, the emplotment of these aspects of the past in other contexts and plot forms than the tragic rise of National Socialism,[20] and (2) the conceptualization of historical continuities cutting across the era of Nazism and especially the symbolic border of 1945, that is, the emplotment of Nazism *and* the postwar period within one narrative universe using compatible plot types. This second aspect of historicization, which is my focus, advanced in three steps after the end of World War II.

With the restoration of the historicist tradition after the war, German historians at first refused altogether to emplot Nazism as a period within German history. Even for the more self-critical established historians, such as Friedrich Meinecke, National Socialism was a phenomenon linked to the modern European and Western tradition, not so much an aspect of the national German history.[21] But the "thesis of the radical discontinuity of German history in the twentieth century" soon gave way to a critical assessment of the prehistory of National Socialism that viewed the Third Reich as a particular German manifestation of the rise of totalitarianism.[22] Scholars such as Karl Dietrich Bracher furthered the understanding of the collapse of the Weimar Republic and the rise of National Socialism and thus had already relativized the historical border of 1933.[23] But the theory of totalitarianism offered no conceptual position from which to problematize the *Stunde Null,* that is, the notion that 1945 marked a radical new beginning in German history. As a result, even after the inauguration of study of contemporary history in West Germany, the continuities cutting across 1945 were left unexplored. Subsequently, the tragic account of the rise of Nazism was expanded to include more aspects of the German history of the nineteenth and twentieth centuries, leading to the Sonderweg theory, which, in one or another form, remained the dominant framework for most considerations of the continuities in modern German history until the 1980s. Two very popular titles of the 1950s, *Die verspätete Nation* (The Belated Nation) and *Bonn ist nicht Weimar* (Bonn Is Not Weimar), symbolized this trend and illustrate that 1945 remained an absolute limit, a barrier of emplotment that divided the tragedy ending in Nazism from the comic or even romantic return of the Federal Republic into the Western world.[24] Despite all the changes that shook up the historical discipline in Germany starting in the 1960s, the dominant emplotment of 1945 as the return to the West and the beginning of a new story line prevailed for another two decades. The structuralist social historians who presented the greatest and most successful challenge to the historiographical tradition of the immediate postwar period also developed the most elaborate version of the Sonderweg theory, tracing Nazism back to the "strange mixture of highly successful capitalist industrialization and socio-economic modernization on the one hand, and of surviving pre-industrial institutions, power relations and cultures on the other."[25]

Even in the 1960s, however, this dominant emplotment was already challenged, explicitly or implicitly, from three different vantage points. These challenges did not cause any radical change in narrative strategies of historical representation, but they do represent an important reference point for the approaches under consideration in this chapter. David Schoenbaum and Rolf Dahrendorf argued that National Socialism and its policies had an unintended modernizing effect on German society because they destroyed traditional, antiliberal loyalties and mentalities (Schoenbaum) and traditional regional, confessional, and social divisions (Dahrendorf) within the German population and thus paved the way for the postwar success of liberal democracy in West Germany.[26] Their theories caused some debate but were ultimately contained within the Sonderweg approach.[27]

The second challenge to the conventional conceptualization of the discontinuity between Nazism and West Germany was categorically rejected by most historians and remained influential only as a negative foil. The neo-Marxists of the student movement and the German New Left radicalized charges about alleged restorative tendencies in West Germany, which had already been voiced in the 1950s, and related them to similar arguments advanced in East Germany.[28] The left-wing critics violated the plot barrier 1945 with their claim that the Third Reich and the Federal Republic shared the same economic structure and the same types of political leaders. For them, the revival of fascism was an imminent danger because the two systems displayed only phenomenological, not functional, differences.[29]

The third challenge, which was only implicit initially, originated from the beginning of structural social history in Germany in the 1960s. In the long

run, the change of paradigm from traditional historiography, with its emphasis on political and diplomatic history, to the new inquiry into the underlying
social and economic structures implied a thorough investigation of the structural continuities that linked National Socialism and the Federal Republic.
This challenge, however, only materialized in the 1980s.

The turning point in the early 1980s was marked by a harsh critique of the
Sonderweg theory,[30] as well as an inquiry—parallel but independent of this
critique—into the continuities of contemporary German history from a variety
of methodological vantage points that showed little respect for the caesura of
1945. A new historical perspective developed that took the existence of historical continuities for granted and thus "move[d] across the German trauma," as
Lutz Niethammer put it.[31] All three projects that will be discussed here dared
to present a general theory about the question of the interdependence of
Nazism and modernization and its relation to postwar Germany—and this
separated them from most other contemporary historical works. Choosing previously unused plot constellations, from romance to tragedy, they also demonstrated that one of the most far-reaching implications of Broszat's plea for
the historicization of National Socialism, an increasing tropological variation
in the emplotment of Nazism, began before German unification.

EVERYDAY LIFE AND MODERN BARBARITY: DETLEV PEUKERT

Detlev Peukert followed Max Weber's definition of modernity. In his innovative work of the 1980s, he singled out four basic characteristics that have
determined the contradictory potentials of the modern era: the capitalist
economy and class structure; the rational bureaucratic state apparatus and a
high degree of social integration; scientific/technological progress and its
increasing world domination; and a rationalized and disciplined form of
everyday life.[32] On this basis, Peukert tried to sketch out the history of rationalization in Germany since the 1880s. He put particular emphasis on the
fundamental tensions between the achievements of scientific progress and
social reform and the potential for totalitarian destruction and fantasies of
scientific omnipotence.[33] In my critique, I focus on the relationship he constructed between modernity and Nazism, especially its most criminal aspects, and analyze how he dealt with the problem of continuity between the
Third Reich and the Federal Republic.

Peukert emphasized that the radicalization of the destructive potentials of modernity had been caused by special conditions in Germany: the nation's late modernization; the high degree of institutionalization and bureaucratization of the social services; and most important, the concurrence of a general European crisis of modernity with a particularly severe legitimation crisis in Germany in the late 1920s.[34] All these factors brought the National Socialists to power and were the necessary preconditions for the "Final Solution" because the policies of extermination could only have developed under the political conditions of the Nazi dictatorship and, more specifically, the conditions of Nazi warfare.[35]

Peukert singled out one causal thread—the racist dynamics in the human sciences since the turn of the twentieth century, which led to the construction of a unique and specifically modern technological apparatus for the killing of an abstractly defined category of victims.[36] His account ran as follows. Around the turn of the century, the human sciences expanded significantly due to the successes of medicine in disease control, the optimism of pedagogues and psychologists anxious to achieve similar results, the introduction of the paradigm of social hygiene, and the high degree of professionalization in the state-administered social welfare system in Germany. During the next twenty years, an integrated system of scientific thought and practice emerged that strove to solve the problems of modern society. This scientific paradigm filled the void left after the delegitimation of Christianity and became the main reference point for popular myths in secularized Germany. Thus, both science and popular culture contributed to the fantasies of scientific omnipotence and the marginalization and stigmatization of sickness, death, and old age.[37]

The scientists' optimism, however, stood in stark contrast to their frustration when confronted with the actual deaths, incurable diseases, and social deviance of their patients. This "*Praxisschock*" (reality shock), Peukert argued, led them to focus on the abstract entity of the people's "body" and its genetic "health" and to differentiate between patients worthy and unworthy of their treatment, especially in the late 1920s when research funds became scarce. As a result, the standards for categorizing and selecting patients were already clearly established before 1933.[38]

After the Nazis' rise to power, critics of this scientific paradigm were silenced, and scientists were provided with new funds and possibilities of experimenting for the construction of the master race. Soon, however, they faced the same frustrating limits they had encountered before, and they resorted again to negative selection—carried to its extreme consequence for the first time in the killing of the mentally ill after the beginning of World War II. Peukert argued that human sciences made three important contributions to the "Final Solution": the anonymous, abstract, and amoral definitions for categorizing worthy and unworthy human lives; the practice of selecting patients according to these standards; and the scientific-technological apparatus for extermination. Therefore, for Peukert, "the specific modernity of the 'Final Solution' derived from the evolution of racial-hygienic thought in the human sciences."[39]

Peukert revised and successfully integrated the different interpretive strategies that had been developed by West German intellectuals, especially on the Left, to analyze the history of National Socialism. On the basis of Max Weber's ambivalent characterization of modernity and Jürgen Habermas's differentiation between instrumental and communicative reason, he combined a revised version of the Sonderweg theory with a functionalist approach to the study of everyday life in the Third Reich, without neglecting the important integrative function of anti-Semitism and racism on all levels of Nazi society. In Peukert's narrative, the pre-Nazi and Nazi era became part of the same trajectory of the step-by-step realization and radicalization of the dark side of modernity.

Peukert mentioned two aspects of continuity that should temper any hope that 1945 marked Germany's return to a healthy, normal path of modernization—or, for that matter, the hope that such a path even exists. Although the racist utopia of a radical solution for the problems of modernity was thoroughly discredited in Germany after the war, the involvement of the human sciences in the history of racism and the National Socialist policies of extermination has never been systematically analyzed. Also, the popular myths that contributed to the lack of resistance against the policies of extermination and the marginalization of social minorities are still powerful today. The continued destructive potential of these factors, Peukert concluded in 1988, might only become apparent when we once more reach the limits of prosperity.[40]

However, Peukert never integrated the Weimar Republic, Nazism, and the postwar period within one narrative, although that option was clearly indicated and at times even demanded in his own writings. On the one hand, he identified the manifestations of the humane side of modernity in the history of the Weimar Republic and even localized aspects of communicative reason in the Nazi era, especially within the working class and youth culture. But he never linked these traditions to the reemergence of communicative reason in the culture of the Federal Republic. On the other hand, in his few remarks about the postwar period, he hinted at the troublesome continuities of aspects of instrumental reason that could be traced back to the historical constellation that caused the "Final Solution," yet he never clearly identified these traditions within the postwar context. Thus, Peukert's account falls short of a complete historicization of Nazism, although the plot form he outlined for this purpose, an oscillation between tragic and ironic emplotment, might have proven very helpful in delineating the relationship between National Socialism and the ambivalent traditions of modernity. It was Peukert's special but unfortunately unfinished achievement to have simultaneously circumvented and acknowledged the plot barrier of 1945 by projecting the historical divide of 1945 onto a dialectical narrative structure.

This undeveloped aspect of Peukert's probing into the ambiguous potentials of modern civilization might have been included in his last project, entitled "*Geschichte als historische Moralwissenschaft*" (history as a historical science of ethics), which he could not finish.[41] As a result, the first consistent historicizations of National Socialism were brought forth in the context of less subtle approaches that Peukert himself rejected for good reasons.[42]

THE ECONOMICS OF THE "FINAL SOLUTION": GÖTZ ALY AND SUSANNE HEIM

Götz Aly and Susanne Heim did not ground their study of the "Final Solution" on an explicitly developed theory of modernity.[43] They argued that the National Socialist policies of extermination had assumed a particular modern quality because they had been conceived, planned, and realized under the conceptual and practical guidance of a number of modern applied social sciences concerned with social engineering, such as economics, statistics, agrosciences, and administration. The technocrats who served the NS regime crafted scientific rationalizations and methods for the categorizing, marginalizing, expropriating, and exterminating victims, following the most advanced scientific standards.[44] In this sense, the "Final Solution" "was the specific German contribution to the development of European modernity."[45]

Aly and Heim presented their interpretation of the origins of the Holocaust in the form of the following narrative account. After the crisis between 1930 and 1932, a generation of exceptionally young social scientists entered German administration and academia; these individuals had faced a bleak professional future only a few years before. They eagerly adopted and further developed the theories for the modernization and rationalization of the European (especially eastern European) national economies and societies that had dominated the social sciences since the 1920s. Without being motivated by racism or anti-Semitism themselves, these experts, who occupied relatively inferior positions in the NS hierarchy, designed the social policies of the regime within the racist and anti-Semitic parameters set by the National Socialist leadership. For Aly and Heim, this integration of scientific reason and racist ideology determined the treatment of the Jewish population after the Nazi leaders abandoned their pogrom tactics in 1938, and they influenced the occupational policies when Germany faced the task of controlling and "restructuring" the occupied territories in the East.[46]

Heim and Aly argued that these destructive policies of modernization were first applied in Vienna, where the expropriation of Jewish businesses and the forced emigration of the Jews went hand in hand with the restructuring of the retail business.[47] The policy was radicalized in its second phase, after the occupation of Poland. Before the war, German expert opinion had diagnosed a considerable "overpopulation" in the Polish and eastern European countryside, which allegedly prevented industrialization and the accumulation of capital. Aly and Heim tried to show that the persecution and ghettoization of the Jews was intended to contribute to the reduction of the population, provide capital to turn a subsistence economy into a market economy, and increase productivity in the occupied territories.[48] The last phase—the phase of extermination—began after the attack on the Soviet Union, when the technocrats developed a plan for the systematic killing of the Jews to meet their long-term reform plans and the immediate needs of the war economy. Thus, Aly and Heim saw the "Final Solution" within the context of a number of initiatives to achieve modernization through social engineering, which also included the killing of the mentally ill, the systematic starvation of Russian POWs, and the plan to starve more than twenty million Russian civilians as a side effect of the exploitation of that country.[49]

For Aly and Heim, the Nazi dictatorship provided the technocrats with a political context in which they could realize their scientific utopias. They

conceded that the political conditions changed after the war, but in their opinion, the scientific mind-set that helped invent the Holocaust still dominated
German society: "Since 1945 the outward political conditions have changed
effectively but not irreversibly. Today, the historical constellation which facilitated genocidal policies does no longer exist in Germany. Maybe and hopefully that constellation remains unique. But the conceptual thinking that took
mass murder as a reasonable instrument of economic and political planning
and reform is still present."[50]

Aly and Heim challenged the majority opinion in the historical profession
that the "Final Solution" reflected the radical, irrational motives of the Nazi
leaders and their followers. For these two scholars, the conceptualization and
implementation of the Holocaust were developed on the basis of rational,
utilitarian, and perfectly explicable principles. And the same principles still
guided scientific practice in many academic contexts. Through this emplotment, they undermined the turning point of 1945 in the most radical way
imaginable. Not surprisingly, the authors were severely criticized for their
failure to acknowledge the structural and political differences between the
Third Reich and the Federal Republic. Their theories about the economics of
the "Final Solution" were rejected as monocausal and politically motivated.
Critics saw them as part of the intellectual tradition of the student movement
and the New Left, which focused on the interdependence between capitalism,
imperialism, and fascism and displayed the same shortcomings.[51] Aly and
Heim's texts, one critic argued, had not quite made the transition from leftist subculture to historiography.[52]

Critics also found methodological shortcomings in Aly and Heim's
work. In their mind, the two scholars failed to select a representative sample
of the lower-level Nazi administrators and therefore did not pay enough attention to the various factions that struggled for influence and political priorities. Aly and Heim received credit for having uncovered important new
sources, but the relevance of these sources for the actual decision-making
processes regarding the "Final Solution" had not been clearly established.
Due to this missing link, most scholars took the new source material to
reflect the strategies of legitimation of administrators who only adopted and
implemented decisions made at the very top of the Nazi hierarchy. Without
a clear concept of the political structure of Nazism, Aly and Heim, it was argued, took the technocrats' discourse at face value and failed to see through

the self-aggrandizement and post factum rationalizations expressed in the texts.[53]

To a certain extent, Aly and Heim contributed to the initial marginalization of their work by their overly defensive tone, their failure to integrate their work into the scholarly context, their tendency to emphasize the disturbing continuities in the careers of the involved social scientists at the expense of a closer analysis of the discursive and structural continuities, and—related to the last point—their choice to present some of their results in the form of collages rather than integrated, tight argumentation.[54] Nevertheless, like Peukert, they outlined a way of escaping the deadlock between intentionalists and functionalists that had dominated the debate about the "Final Solution" for some time. Aly and Heim kept the focus on biographical data and the motives of historical actors, and in this sense, they followed the intentionalists. In contrast to the intentionalists, however, they shifted attention from the Nazi leadership to the second- and third-level bureaucrats. Like the functionalists, Aly and Heim unraveled some of the intricacies of the National Socialist administration but parted with the characterization of Nazism as a polycratic system by presenting a homogeneous group of academics and administrators as the masterminds behind the "Final Solution."[55] Together with Peukert, they stressed that only the combination of the political system of Nazism and the rational paradigm of modern science made the "Final Solution" possible, although Aly and Heim spelled out, in greater detail, the continuing risks that modern scientific ideologies entailed. In their opinion, the particularly horrific aspect of industrial death had to be linked to the scientific tradition that was still with us and that therefore deserved close critical scrutiny.

In tropological terms, Aly and Heim's problems in being accepted by the historiographical establishment stemmed from two factors. Unlike Peukert, they completely dismissed the ironic stance toward the past that claimed the essence of Nazism could never be fully comprehended. They presented a consistent, one-dimensional tragic plot that insisted—to echo White—"on the gain in consciousness for the spectators" of the disaster of Nazism.[56] Having thus violated the conventional plot structures for the representation of Nazism, they also disagreed with their colleagues about the kind of explanation of Nazism that White identified as explanation by formal argument. Unlike intentionalists, who stressed the uniqueness of Hitler as a historical actor—a formist approach, in White's system—and unlike structuralists, who emphasized the

self-propelling tendencies toward radicalization within the NS bureaucracy—
a contextualist-organicist approach—Aly and Heim reduced the causes of the
"Final Solution" to the destructive principles intrinsic to modern science. This
argument falls within the category of mechanistic explanations of the past,
which is an unpopular mode of explanation among historians.[57] Being most
familiar and therefore more easily convinced by the formist and the contex-
tualist types of argumentation, historians clearly perceived the cognitive limits of Aly and Heim's mechanistic explanation, for instance, their failure to
conceive of any socially responsible effects of science in postwar Germany.

THE MODERN FÜHRER: RAINER ZITELMANN

Rainer Zitelmann wanted to provide a value-neutral concept of modernization that focused on the economic and social characteristics of the process,
including rationalization, industrialization, technological progress, expansion
of mass production, urbanization, increasing social mobility, and secularization. Therefore, he excluded from the definition of modernization any notion
of political progress—for instance, in terms of democratization or liberal-
parliamentary reforms. This more objective approach, he argued, opened up
the possibility to inquire into the modernizing impact of dictatorial systems
such as the Third Reich and the Soviet Union in the Stalinist era, independent of their antidemocratic record.[58] On the basis of studies about the social
and economic policies during Nazism and, in particular, his own work on
Hitler's plans for social and economic reform, Zitelmann concluded that the
National Socialist leadership had designed and launched a number of initiatives to modernize German society, some of which had been successful and
had had a lasting impact on postwar Germany.

According to Zitelmann, the mobilization and politicization of the masses
in the Third Reich was one policy initiative with long-term modernizing
effects because it helped disintegrate traditional forms of authority in German society and supported the transition of power from traditional to new
functional elites, in particular within army and state administration.[59] Zitelmann argued that the improvement of workers' social benefits and social status caused a similar homogenization and alleviated traditional forms of social
inequality, such as the difference between blue-collar and white-collar workers.[60] He also maintained that many aspects of the accelerated rationalization

of German society during Nazism had to be linked to the projects the National Socialist bureaucracy initiated to meet its responsibility for the welfare of the *Volksgemeinschaft* (national racial community). These projects reached from city development and public housing to improvements in the social welfare system and plans for its expansion after the war to new forms of organizing leisure time. But as Zitelmann pointed out, the forced sterilization program and the killing of the mentally ill sprang from the same perverted sense of responsibility. He concluded that, with the exception of those who were systematically excluded from the Volksgemeinschaft—Jews, Gypsies, homosexuals, and political opponents—the German population experienced improved social services and upward social mobility.[61] Zitelmann saw the National Socialist economic policy in the same light. In his perception, accelerated industrial and technological development and new forms of crisis management, including deficit spending to battle unemployment, made the NS era and the postwar economic miracle part of the same story of economic modernization.[62]

Zitelmann interpreted these processes of modernization in the context of the Nazi leadership's plans for political reform, especially Hitler's own plans. Through an in-depth analysis of the Führer's writings and speeches, he showed that none of the trends described previously stood in direct contradiction to the opinions about social and economic development that Hitler had voiced on different occasions. This observation applied to Hitler's intention to create a new elite on the basis of personal achievement, not social origin, and to his plans to achieve economic autarky through the conquest of "living space" in the East.[63] In Zitelmann's opinion, Hitler was primarily interested in exploiting the Soviet Union's supply of raw materials and energy sources and creating new markets for Germany's industrial products.[64] He argued forcefully that some earlier and widely held assumptions about Hitler's worldview were incorrect. Hitler had not entertained plans for the reagrarianization of Germany, as H. A. Turner argued, and his opinions about economic and social policies, organized around the theme of the social Darwinist fight for resources and survival, had been more coherent and consistent over time than previously assumed.

Although Zitelmann could show that Hitler's intentions did not contradict any processes of modernization that might have occurred, the causal relationship between the two remained unclear. As he put it himself somewhat optimistically, "The question of the extent of intended modernization during National Socialism remains to be researched more closely."[65] The direct link that Zitelmann constructed between Hitler's intentions and the actual social and economic developments was widely rejected. Even some of his intellectual collaborators, among them Michael Prinz, were not willing to follow him on that point.[66]

Zitelmann's emplotment of Nazism was the most consistent integration of the history of National Socialism and the Federal Republic under the common theme of modernization. At the same time, it was the most selective and therefore the most problematic of the three approaches analyzed in this chapter. In Zitelmann's revision of Hitler's worldview and its relation to the modernization process, the "Final Solution" disappeared from view, although it presented a crucial test case for his theories. In contrast to his predecessors who found consistency only in Hitler's anti-Semitism and his plans for the expansion in the East and consequently considered them Hitler's primary aims, Zitelmann emphasized the overall coherence and rationality of Hitler's worldview and identified the Führer's belief in social Darwinism as its underlying principle. He provided substantial proof for this interpretation with regard to Hitler's war aims but failed to illustrate how the concept and realization of the "Final Solution" could be deduced from the same rational principles. This failure is most puzzling because Zitelmann's commitment to the intentionalist paradigm left him without recourse to any alternative explanation and because the coming into existence of the "Final Solution" was an important aspect of Hitler's plans for "social reform" that Zitelmann intended to explain.[67]

The strong sense of positive continuity between the National Socialist society and the postwar society that Zitelmann's texts produced was based on his depoliticized, "objective" definition of modernity and the exclusion of the most criminal aspects of Nazism from his narrative. Zitelmann tended to argue by association. He used a number of phrases to sum up the National Socialist social and economic policies—*Chancengleichheit* (equality of opportunity), *Leistungsgesellschaft* (performance-oriented society), *keynesianische Revolution* (Keynesian revolution), and *sozialer Wohnungsbau* (public housing initiatives)—that were very familiar from postwar debates and generally viewed quite favorably. Most of the time, however, he failed to analyze the changed meaning of those phrases that had been used in both societies (such as sozialer Wohnungsbau) or to acknowledge the anachronism of the other terms when they were applied in the National Socialist context.[68] The continuity effect produced by the unreflected use of such terminology was even enhanced by the fact that Zitelmann stayed close, at times too close, to the language in his sources.

Nearly all of Zitelmann's conclusions about intended modernization during Nazism seemed untenable to his liberal colleagues. They quickly countered his emplotment of Nazism by reiterating their own ironic master narrative, which confirmed 1945 as the turning point between two incompatible narrative universes. According to the critics, Zitelmann simply reproduced the Nazis' own assessment of their contribution to the modernization of German society. Neither the living conditions of workers nor their chances for access to higher education improved during Nazism. But the possibility of perceiving social inequality and lack of upward mobility was curbed by the suppression of the labor unions and by the permanent reiteration of the alleged egalitarian spirit of the Volksgemeinschaft. The combination of these factors produced a temporarily widespread belief in the leadership's commitment to social reform and a general feeling of progress, which gave way to disillusionment during the war. None of the indicators of modernization, which could be clearly measured and for which data were available (urban growth, changes in the structure of the workforce, lasting upward mobility, expansion of the educational system), suggested any lasting change for the better. It was and is more convincing to assume that the NS period as a whole, especially its catastrophic end, left the population disturbed and disintegrated, so that there was a potential for fundamental social change once the right mixture of advice, support, and pressure was applied. Liberal critics therefore concluded that the most lasting social and economic reforms were implemented after the war.[69]

Zitelmann's tropological revolution was initially much more favorably received by conservative observers.[70] Most likely, this segment of Zitelmann's audience was won over by his attempt to be the first professional historian to replace the ironic with a thoroughly comic emplotment of the position of National Socialism within the history of modern Germany. After all, he presented an account of Nazism according to which the opposing principles, in this case, Nazism and postwar democracy, were "revealed to be, in the long run, harmonizable with one another" because they had the common goal of modernization.[71] But Zitelmann never managed to transform this partial success into an academic appointment. He embarked on a career in publishing and established himself in right-wing editorial circles.[72] In 1995, he again made headlines when he led a campaign opposing the interpretation of May 1945 as a moment of liberation. His insistence that the end of the war represented a deplorable national tragedy would have been met with considerable support from across the political spectrum just ten years earlier, but in 1995, as will be discussed in chapter 12, his position was no longer accepted within the political mainstream.

METHODOLOGICAL AND TROPOLOGICAL NORMALIZATION

The three case studies presented in this chapter demonstrate how the dominant themes and methods of the historiography of the Federal Republic were questioned and revised from the margins of the discipline at a time when members of the older generation reasserted their claim to define the parameters for the future of the German historical profession. With the exception of Götz Aly, the scholars discussed here were not key players in the impressive reorientation of German Holocaust historiography in the 1990s, but they helped set that development into motion. The historicization of Nazism that has been accomplished as the result of the generational turnover represents a conscious endeavor by younger historians to define their relation to the National Socialist past in the context of a more general social transition from the postwar period to some new era—perhaps an era of the Europeanization of collective mentalities and memories. The transition compares in importance only to the new historical perspectives and the generational change that characterized the 1960s.

Starting in the 1960s, the incorporation of new methods of historical inquiry and interpretation served a number of purposes. It helped in critically assessing and departing from the traditions of the discipline that had survived Nazism unscathed and that apparently offered no vantage point from which the immensity of the national catastrophe could be accurately measured and represented. In addition, the new methods that were "borrowed" from other disciplines served as distancing devices, allowing historians to approach the past self-critically but also from a safe psychological point of view. Due to the generational consensus to emplot Nazism in the ironic mode, the young German historians of the 1960s and 1970s could not express disagreement about the interpretation of the past by telling different types of stories. Consequently, they voiced their differences by arguing about historiographical theory. The first postwar debates about the meaning of Nazism focused on the concepts of totalitarianism and fascism and the relationship between the historicist tradition and the new social history.

The younger historians of the 1980s and 1990s again used more conventional means to express their opinions about Nazism. They returned to telling different types of stories about German history and explicitly or implicitly dismissed their predecessors' productive but cumbersome detour through difficult methodological and theoretical terrain. The transition after 1980 manifested itself as a trend toward methodological homogenization and normalization, on the one hand, and increased tropological variation, on the other. Both trends indicated a fundamental change in historical consciousness and the beginning of an efficient historicization of Nazism. All three of the approaches considered in this chapter marked a continued or renewed interest in identifying historical figures or groups of people as the decisive carriers of historical change. Along with the resubjectification of history, they displayed a particular desire to explain the past by representing its more concrete and tangible aspects. These tendencies were especially apparent in Zitelmann's and Aly and Heim's naive empiricism, and they explain the special appeal of Alltagsgeschichte. The increased tropological variation was expressed in the very disregard for the border of 1945, the careful experimentation with dialectic plot types by Peukert, and the radical comic reemplotment of Nazism by Zitelmann.[73] As a result of this methodological homogenization and narratological normalization, the analytic tools of structural history have played a less significant role in the new Holocaust historiography, whereas they continue to be featured prominently in the works of social scientists.[74]

Historians have clearly expanded the tropological space available to them in order to make the representation of Nazism fit their specific needs and interests. Nevertheless, there are still important limits to the emplotment of Nazism in scholarship today. It is not so much the comic mode—as White argued—but the romantic mode that is still excluded from the spectrum of acceptable and therefore truthful representations of the Third Reich. In scholarly contexts, Nazism has not yet been presented as "a drama of self-identification" that retroactively validates the moral perspective and political decisions of the Nazi movement.[75]

White proposed that the "Final Solution" belonged to the kind of historical and possible future events— such as "total war, nuclear contamination,
mass starvation, and ecological suicide"—that are unique to modernity and
resist conventional historiographical techniques of representation and the
categories of traditional humanism that support them.[76] To account for and
represent these types of events and the experiences related to them, White
suggested developing a new realism along the lines of the style of writing invented by literary modernism. The inadequacy of traditional historical methods vis-à-vis Nazism and the "Final Solution" was also sensed by German
historians, and it accounted for a belated but innovative crisis of representation that started in the 1960s. Apparently, however, this crisis has been settled
in more conventional terms than White expected or hoped for.

TELEVISION

CHAPTER 6

ENTERTAINING CATASTROPHE

The Reinvention of the Holocaust in the Television of the Federal Republic of Germany

HOLOKAUST

In the fall of 2000, Germany's most prominent TV historian, Guido Knopp, brought a very ambitious Holocaust documentary to prime time.[1] Knopp, born in 1948, had already had an exceptionally successful career at one of Germany's two national public television stations, the Zweite Deutsche Fernsehen (ZDF). Since the early 1990s, Knopp's name has been synonymous with expensive, high-profile documentary miniseries about World War II and the Nazi leadership. I will take a closer look at Knopp's career in chapter 8; at this point, suffice it to say that his productions were much appreciated by viewers but dreaded by historians. Knopp's staff often found spectacular new footage in the archives of the former Soviet bloc, but whenever such finds did not materialize, they staged their own visions of important events in the lives of their subjects. The resulting hybrids of fact and fiction did not reflect the current state of historical scholarship, and they depicted the German military in a relatively favorable light. Because of all these shortcomings, which weighed heavily on the minds of critical and perhaps somewhat jealous historians, Knopp was accused of producing irresponsible "Nazi kitsch."[2]

Because of this prehistory, the new Holocaust program of 2000, designed as an important highlight in Knopp's long career, was anticipated with much trepidation. Such concerns were not alleviated when the ZDF released the title of the new series. Called *Holokaust,* instead of *Holocaust,* the show's more German-sounding name was intended to signal the television producers' and their audience's acceptance of the "Final Solution" as an extremely negative yet central element of modern German history. But this play with letters was easily misunderstood as a cheap public relations gag or, worse, as an appropriation of the "Final Solution" as a German event over which German intellectuals claimed interpretive sovereignty.[3]

In the end, the actual broadcast of *Holokaust* proved anticlimactic because the series turned out to be one of the best productions about the "Final Solution" ever to be aired by German television.[4] Knopp's staff was again exceptionally successful in tracking down new footage and eyewitnesses. But, in contrast to earlier productions, the ZDF's Division for Contemporary History had enlisted the help of internationally renowned historians, had refrained from any fictitious simulations of Holocaust history, had kept the musical score within the narrow limits delineated by *Schindler's List,* and had contributed a very modest and at times even elliptical commentary. If anything, Knopp and his colleagues could be faulted for being too subdued in their interpretation of the genocide of European Jewry. They merely presented the events rather than explaining them and thus subscribed to the notion of the Holocaust's incomprehensibility as championed by some of the program's senior historical advisers.[5] The unusual restraint exhibited by the ZDF team on this occasion highlights again the exceptional status of the Holocaust in German memory. It might also explain the show's disappointing ratings. The series reached average market shares of only 8.1 percent, whereas other Knopp programs regularly had shares of over 15 percent and sometimes even up to 21 percent.[6]

The Knopp era has certainly brought some remarkable programs to the screen, comparable only to similarly accomplished British historical documentaries about Nazism.[7] But in their shortsighted debates about the documentaries, neither critics nor television producers have placed the shows within their proper historical and media contexts. During three decades of public television monopoly—the ARD (Arbeitsgemeinschaft der öffentliche-rechtlichen Rundfunkanstalten der Bundesrepublik Deutschland) went on the air in 1954, and the ZDF followed in 1963—television executives produced patriarchal television. In consultation with political elites and audiences, they designed programs that met the entertainment interests of their viewers through sports coverage, murder mysteries, and feature films. At the same time, these executives and political supervisors also defined the population's educational needs, and, among many other items, this educational agenda included the task of furthering Vergangenheitsbewältigung. Between 1963 and 1993, the

ZDF alone broadcast more than twelve hundred programs about the legacy of National Socialism and the Holocaust.[8] A number of these programs were superb, expensive, prime-time productions that attracted a remarkable number of viewers.

But the introduction of commercial television in 1984, the slow rise to prominence of the new private channels in the late 1980s, and the ensuing competition among private and public stations for funds and viewers ended the era of patriarchal television. West Germany's two public networks were forced to change their programming policies, and expensive prime-time historical coverage represented just one of the many "victims" of this commercial restructuring of the German television landscape.[9] The stations continued to produce a record number of programs about historical topics, especially documentaries about the Nazi past, but they broadcast them primarily in afternoon or late-night programming slots because prime-time hours had to be reserved for more appealing and competitive television shows. In addition, the networks no longer had the funds to produce many television plays about the history of the Third Reich because television fiction is significantly more expensive than documentary programming.

This superficial look at the development of historical coverage in the Federal Republic indicates that Knopp's greatest accomplishment consists of having skillfully carved out a prime-time niche in an increasingly competitive broadcasting environment that forced other producers of historical programming to content themselves with much smaller audiences. Against unfavorable odds, Knopp and his staff managed to survive the end of patriarchal television because of their advantageous strategic position in the ZDF and their skill in developing a new format of nonfiction television that sold very successfully in international markets. Knopp's productions have been presented to audiences around the globe, including Israel and the United States.[10] Despite all these accomplishments of the Knopp paradigm, historical self-reflection via television has clearly played a less significant role since the 1990s, after the public networks lost their captive audience and part of their funding. Therefore, it is particularly important to reconstruct the historical coverage of previous decades and to document how successfully West German television popularized the task of Vergangenheitsbewältigung and shaped the collective memory of the Holocaust. It is equally important to realize, however, that the vision of the past offered to German viewers, analyzed here on the basis of ZDF Holocaust programs aired since 1963, systematically avoided raising some of the most painful questions about German culpability and post-war responsibilities.

During the 1960s, when the Nazi past became an important topic in the political culture of the Federal Republic, the ZDF contributed to the task of Vergangenheitsbewältigung with three distinct types of programs about the "Final Solution": philo-Semitic television, imported feature films from Eastern Europe, and stories about the rescue of Jewish victims of Nazism.[11] The philo-Semitic programs, which were also produced in subsequent decades, consisted primarily of documentaries that summarized centuries of Jewish German culture and (re)introduced viewers to Jewish history and Jewish customs in order to combat postwar anti-Semitism. The programs included short references to the Holocaust for the explicit purpose of creating sympathy for Jewish culture and Israeli politics, but they did not focus on the crimes themselves. Instead, German television producers emphasized the loss Germany suffered by having murdered German and European Jewry and hoped that such modest repair efforts would improve future German-Jewish relations.[12]

Philo-Semitic and Holocaust programs were frequently scheduled in the month of March on the occasion of the annual Week of Brotherhood, which — initiated and organized by the societies for Christian-Jewish cooperation and endorsed by state and federal governments — has been a prominent part of the Federal Republic's cultural and political calendar since the 1950s.[13] Modeled after similar traditions in the United States, the societies and the Week of Brotherhood were designed to further Christian-Jewish dialogue and reconciliation. These initiatives expressed the official philo-Semitism of West Germany's political culture, and the public service stations supported them dutifully. The programs often included "pathos-laden proclamations of the exceptional importance of German Jews in the arts, literature, philosophy, medicine, journalism, etc."[14] But as with all philo-Semitic representations, the well-intended efforts could easily backfire and reinforce traditional anti-Semitic stereotypes. For instance, after having watched the 1968 ZDF feature *Die Juden von Prag* (The Jews of Prague), a reviewer came to the conclusion that "again and again one has to admire the achievements of the Jews, their intelligence, and the unwavering, tenacious consistency with which they pursue their aims."[15] In light of such highly ambivalent language in one of West Germany's leading TV guides, the value and the impact of programs designed in the spirit of reconciliation are dubious at best. In addition, the scheduling of German-Jewish reconciliation programs often revealed their status as more or less compulsory exercises in philo-Semitism: "When the Week of Brotherhood tops the calendar we encounter meaningless, unorganized interviews broadcast during the witching hour, interviews which conjure up an unimpaired and apparently unperturbed cultural consciousness and feature a great finale during which the spirit of Buber's Bible commentary floats victoriously over the mass graves."[16]

The second type of programming from the 1960s was imported movie productions from Eastern Europe. These superb, self-critical feature films told stories of failed rescue efforts and coincidental survival that addressed the traumatic legacy of the Holocaust in formerly occupied Eastern Europe. Directors such as Andrzej Wajda and Jiří Weiss explored and criticized the population's unwillingness and inability to protect their Jewish fellow citizens from Nazi persecution in expressionistic allegories of failed solidarity and ironic twists of fate under extraordinary circumstances.[17] Rather than providing accurate histories of the Nazi crimes, they explored the moral dilemmas created by the tragic events that befell the countries from abroad. In their countries of origin, these films had a strong self-critical edge, but introduced into the German context, they inadvertently supported the problematic conclusion that the German people, like their eastern counterparts, had no recourse against the Nazi policies and deserved the status of an occupied nation.

In addition to goodwill features and "displaced" allegories of persecution, the programs of the 1960s included celebrations of German rescue efforts, especially those undertaken by members of the German clergy.[18] The programs hardly reflected the complete historical record, since they omitted the churches' more impressive legacy of collaboration with the regime. Like similarly one-sided programs about the German military leadership and the conservative resistance against Hitler, the shows were designed to provide role models for the citizens of the young republic and restore hope in humanity, especially German humanity.[19]

For obvious reasons, the representation of rescue operations of Jews undertaken by Germans is a particularly thorny issue. On the one hand, television

programs highlighting the exceptional courage and integrity of Germans
who helped Jews might convincingly convey the obligations of human solidarity and resistance. Also, such programs could show, by way of concrete examples, that acting on these obligations was not as impossible as many
contemporaries of Nazism generally assumed or argued after the fact. Finally,
the programs could even help extend the deserved recognition and monetary
compensation to surviving rescuers, who were generally ignored by West Germany's historical culture—probably precisely because their very existence
called into question some fundamental defense strategies.[20] On the other hand,
any representation of this topic had to avoid the impression that the program
was providing sedatives for the German conscience.[21]

The problems with the depiction of German rescuers were aptly illustrated by the production history of the 1968 ZDF docuplay *Feldwebel Schmid*
(Sergeant Schmid). The play was based on the factual case of a German non-
commissioned officer (NCO) who provided Jews with fake identity papers in
the Vilna ghetto and was then court-martialed and executed in 1942.[22] The
ZDF editorial staff tried to avoid the impression that *Feldwebel Schmid* followed
a self-congratulatory or self-defensive agenda by diligently researching the
historical accuracy of the play and by hiring the young Israeli director Nathan
Jariv and the Jewish writer Hermann Adler, who had witnessed Schmid's actions in Vilna himself.[23] In the end, this strategy failed and caused more
problems than it solved, in part because the scriptwriter could not provide an
acceptable script.[24] Even after another writer was involved, the script was still
not satisfactory. At the same time, the production could no longer be stopped,
as the producer Hans Günter Imlau emphasized in a letter to the ZDF's director general: "The Israeli ambassador in Bonn as well as the German ambassador in Tel Aviv strongly support this ZDF project."[25]

Under these circumstances, it is not surprising that the final result was
unconvincing. The play, which was broadcast on March 22, 1968, still contained historical inaccuracies, many stereotypes, and stilted dialogue.[26] One
reviewer even came to the surprising and certainly unintended conclusion
that the play "thoroughly disproves the assumption that one could have resisted more vigorously or saved more Jews under Hitler."[27] Thus, the program illustrated what the scriptwriter Adler had expressed very succinctly
during the production process: "The contemporary Federal Republic is certainly opposed to the gassing of Jews. . . . But it also does not really know what

to do with people like Anton Schmid."[28] Faced with the moral dilemma between inappropriate self-defense and moral education and operating on politically treacherous ground between anti- and philo-Semitism, German television producers were not able to develop a compelling framework for stories about German rescuers.[29]

The extent to which the programs of the 1960s avoided any direct and self-critical engagement with the history of the "Final Solution" is remarkable. As shown in chapter 3, German historians had already begun their study of the perpetrators and the bureaucracy of genocide in the 1960s, whereas television images of the "Final Solution" were still "out of focus," providing only indirect and deflected glimpses of the Holocaust. The situation did not change significantly in the following decade. The programs of the 1970s continue to highlight fictitious and factual stories of successful rescue operations and thus focused on the most reassuring aspect of the history of the Holocaust.[30]

THE SURVIVOR PARADIGM

After 1977, German viewers encountered Jews primarily as victims or, more precisely, as survivors of the "Final Solution." This change in focus initiated a surprising expansion in the ZDF Holocaust coverage. Over the next two decades, television stories about the Nazi genocide became an ever increasing feature of German television. As a result, the survivors' perspective informed approximately 60 percent of all ZDF programs on the history of the "Final Solution" (see figure 6.1).

The first wave of survival narratives consisted of documentaries and features, which developed the dialectic of suffering and survival on the basis of individual case studies. Television producers interviewed survivors in Germany but also imported them from all over the world. Since this first wave commenced in 1978 and the programs in question had been planned and in production for at least one year, the beginning of the survival paradigm cannot be attributed to the media event *Holocaust,* which the ARD broadcast in 1979. Instead, the phenomenon resulted from a confluence of generational and political factors that produced similar paradigms of Holocaust narratives in a number of national cultures, especially Israel, the United States and, most surprisingly, West Germany.[31]

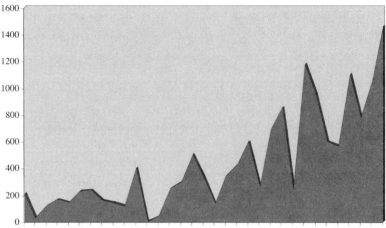

FIGURE 6.1. ZDF programs about the "Final Solution," 1963–1995 (minutes per year)

However, the second wave of survival narratives was directly linked to the success of *Holocaust* in 1979. Starting in 1983, the ZDF featured an impressive string of expensive Holocaust fiction that represented the station's political and aesthetic answer to *Holocaust*. The series of vivid, fictitious renditions of the everyday histories of Nazi anti-Semitic policies comprise some of the best visual Holocaust fiction ever produced. Beginning with the ZDF production of Lion Feuchtwanger's *Geschwister Oppermann* (The Opperman Siblings), this set of works included subsequent ZDF miniseries such as *Die Bertinis* (The Bertinis), a highlight of the station's thirty-eight-year history, and *Die Durchreise* (In Transit), a far less sophisticated but equally successful narrative of persecution and survival during Nazism. In addition, the ZDF aired and helped produce acclaimed German feature films such as *David* and *Regentropfen* (Raindrops), and it purchased some of the best-known representations of the Holocaust, among them *The Winds of War, For Those I Love, Murderers among Us, Playing for Time,* and *Sophie's Choice.*[32] This wave of Holocaust programs, which remains unsurpassed, brought entertaining, personalized fiction to the screen. The German television executives clearly followed the U.S. lead, but they also adopted the concept of Alltagsgeschichte, which had already transformed the study of contemporary history in the Federal Republic.[33]

In general, the programs on survivors, including the aforementioned highlights, conveyed the triumph of survival as much as they attested to the horror of the concentration camps. The programs focused on the exception. They
dealt with survivors, not the "average" victims who did not live to tell their
stories. Therefore, they invited identification with the exceptionally lucky, re-
sourceful, cunning, and gifted individuals who, in the fictitious world of
Holocaust films, were often also blessed with exceptional virtue.[34] In addition, many of the Holocaust stories broadcast by the ZDF, especially the
prominent prime-time shows, featured suspenseful narratives, which contained the horror by means of action-driven adventure stories. One example
of this type of coverage was the 1983 French-Canadian coproduction *For
Those I Love,* which was based on the memoirs of the survivor Martin Gray
and was aired by the ZDF in 1986. As Thomas Thieringer pointed out at the
time: "In the Warsaw ghetto, in Treblinka, during Martin's escape through
the countryside—always the same picture: individuals who are unconcerned
by the dangers which surround them and who are suddenly confronted with
difficult 'problems'—just like in any run of the mill adventure film. . . . Everything is geared towards suspense."[35]

The tendency toward glorification and suspense was particularly noticeable in U.S.-made miniseries and international coproductions. But similar
strategies of representation also informed factual programs about the "Final
Solution" in which the very presence of survivors signaled the exceptionally
positive development of their life stories—exceptionally positive, of course,
only in the context of the history of the Holocaust. The survivors' tales, fact
or fiction, formed a specific genre based on an interesting contract with the
viewer who, in watching the program, agreed to listen to accounts of extreme
brutality in combination with accounts of exceptional fortune and/or courage.
This contract integrated Holocaust stories into conventional parameters of
narrative entertainment but also provided the conventional story types with
an unusual realistic edge. Following the conventions of the genre, the visual
evidence on the screen, that is, the survivor, attested primarily to the fortuitous
part of the story, the fact of survival.[36] The personal history of Simon Wiesenthal, often represented in ZDF programs, is an apt illustration of the binary
structure of most survival stories.[37] The narrative of Wiesenthal's ordeal in
the Nazi camps was always juxtaposed to his exceptionally successful postwar
career. The viewers encountered a highly articulate, determined, intelligent

individual who fought back and almost single-handedly brought to justice hundreds of Nazi criminals. As one reviewer remarked, "For large parts of the program Wiesenthal came across as a lively conversationalist, a Viennese story teller who swiftly enumerated a number of atrocities and presented his gallery of arrested Nazi criminals."[38]

The redemptive narrative structure inherent in many survivors' stories was used not only by television journalists who approached survivors but also by survivors themselves when they took their stories to the screen. In 1975, several years before the onset of the survivor paradigm, the survivor Karel Vreba produced a documentary entitled *30 Jahre nach Auschwitz* (Thirty Years after Auschwitz) to mark the thirtieth anniversary of the liberation of the camp. The documentary exemplified the didactic problem inherent in such stories, which was succinctly expressed by Walter Jens:

> For the inmates of Auschwitz who produced the film the reminiscing documentation might indeed be a work of liberation and working through, a work which confirms their solidarity in the very process of production. But how have younger generations absorbed the film, generations for whom the "ramp of Auschwitz" is a textbook term like the "ballroom of Versailles"? For them did the horror prevail over the atmosphere of cops and robbers, of camaraderie and adventurous escape? . . . I am afraid that the decision to let the old *Auschwitzer* follow their memories was not a very good idea, at least not from a didactic point of view. The well-known story pattern—do you remember, buddy—trivialized the past for the viewer in front of the screen.[39]

"FAILED" SURVIVAL

Unlike the Holocaust coverage of earlier decades, which featured a narrow range of subject matter and genre types, the apex of Holocaust programming in the 1980s presented a wider spectrum of stories and program formats. In the course of two decades, the representation of the Holocaust on German television had become a complex, multilayered process. In addition to the dominant survivor narratives, the ZDF produced a new round of philo-Semitic goodwill programs and continued the celebration of altruistic rescuers.[40] But more important was the onset of Holocaust stories that, on a modest scale, called into question the dialectic of suffering and survival.

Starting in the late 1980s, some ZDF programs undercut the binary structure of the survival paradigm by constructing stories against the grain of the genre. These programs included documentaries that tried to reconstruct the fate of victims as a microstudy of the great crime by uncovering the hidden traces and memories of former Jewish communities.[41] The documentaries refrained from representing death in the camps and were limited to postwar interviews, postwar footage of the victims' hometowns, and a few original photos. But precisely because of their limited focus, the programs conveyed the fate of the victims much more successfully than most survivor stories had. Such self-conscious approaches to the memory of the victims from the postwar perspective formed the conceptual and chronological mirror image of the Anne Frank–type stories that chronicled the development of the Nazi anti-Jewish policies from the perspective of the victims and their failed attempts to escape deportation. Despite the differences, both types of Holocaust stories, like most programs about the topic, refrained from actually depicting deportation and death itself.[42]

A very different strategy of displacement was employed in documentaries that used survivors to elicit and capture on film powerful reflections of the pain in their faces, their gestures, and their language without offering narrative space to stories of escape and rescue. Such productions needed exceptional skill and/or a certain amount of violence—for instance, the type of violence involved in the decision to film survivors of the Holocaust who lived on as severely handicapped individuals or the type of violence involved in attempts to destroy a survivor's composure in order to bring to the surface visible reflections of abuse and guilt.[43] But for obvious reasons, few German journalists employed such interview strategies, which is one reason why the representation of survivors in the programs of the ZDF was dominated by heroic figures.

Since the German producers of TV fiction did not face similar moral limitations, the ordinariness of victimization and survival was best expressed in ZDF TV plays, in particular the 1988 production *Die Bertinis*. The author and director Egon Monk transformed Ralph Giordano's partly autobiographical novel of the same title into a didactic TV play that chronicled the history of an Italian/German/Jewish family from the late nineteenth century to the year

1945.[44] The play, like the book, focused on the family's fate during the Nazi period. As partners in a so-called interracial marriage—the mother was Jewish—the couple and their sons were safe from deportation until 1945, but they still experienced the same gradual expulsion from society that all Jewish victims of the regime did. In the end, when the mother was threatened with deportation, the family went into hiding and survived in the flooded basement of a bombed-out building until Allied troops arrived in the city. In contrast to the usual prime-time fare on the Holocaust, Monk realized a slow, obsessively precise, and detail-oriented play with heavy-handed didactics. By means of incremental repetition, Monk chronicled the increasing danger and the mounting depression as the Bertini boys were kicked out of school and the family was threatened by the Gestapo and abandoned by their friends. The distancing camera work, the slow pace, the repetitive structure, and interspersed original news clippings and photos systematically undercut easy identification and narrative suspense.[45] Not surprisingly, some critics admonished Monk's distanced style and the resulting lack of emotional involvement: "Nobody shed any tears about them [the Bertinis]. The viewers could observe their fate without any feelings as if they were stenciled figures in a picture book which precisely depicts historical reality but never grasps the emotional truth."[46] Perhaps because of the systematic distancing techniques and despite extensive advertisement,[47] the miniseries only reached a disappointing 20 percent of television households.[48] Nevertheless, Monk had developed an alternative concept to the usual prime-time representation of the Holocaust and realized his concept with rarely matched consistency.[49] He had captured the everyday life of the Nazi persecution from the victims' perspective without turning them into heroes or sublating their suffering through a suspenseful narrative.

Although Monk systematically understated the emotional impetus of the narrative, at least one potential viewer anticipated the film with considerable anxiety. Ralph Giordano excused himself from the first showing of the TV play to the press with the following remarks: "I have had a strange and unexpected experience. The anticipation of being confronted with a visualization of the family history has caused in me a deep uneasiness. . . . Over the period of 40 years I became used to the book and the process of working on it. Although that process also represented a difficult confrontation with my life story it became familiar to me as a permanent companion. Somehow the film is a very different case—I have the feeling that it will trouble me much more than the book ever did."[50]

Monk had employed the same strategies of representation when he scripted and directed the TV adaptation of Lion Feuchtwanger's 1933 novel *Die Geschwister Oppermann*.[51] Broadcast in 1983 on the fiftieth anniversary of the Nazi rise to power, the film narrated the events of 1932 and 1933 from the viewpoint of the members of an upper-class Jewish German family who lost the family furniture business in the early months of 1933 to a Nazi competitor. Some members of the family managed to escape abroad, but the company's director survived incarceration and torture only as a physically and psychologically broken man, and his son, a high school student, committed suicide rather than publicly apologize for an allegedly un-German paper he had written about German history. In his study of everyday persecution during Nazism, Monk succeeded in showing, as he suggested himself, that "the reality of the Third Reich can be adequately depicted, that the horror was and is not beyond comprehension, and that the crimes are representable because they do not exceed the scale of human behavior."[52] The question remains if Monk would have been so successful and so optimistic about our abilities to understand and represent the Nazi crimes if he had dealt with the representation of mass genocide.[53] Nevertheless, Monk's work belongs to the small group of programs that did not foreground the exceptional experiences of the survivors and that invited the viewer's identification with the fate of the many victims who did not return. These exceptions illustrate the extent to which the victims and their memory have been left underrepresented on German television. But they also demonstrate that the ZDF programs about the "Final Solution," including above exceptionally accomplished programs, have not dared to depict the core of the Holocaust. Obviously, there are good reasons for this reluctance to represent graphically the mass murder committed in the death camps. The few filmmakers who have tried to fill that gap and whose productions have reached German audiences have not found compelling strategies of representation. For instance, the Polish director Aleksander Ford chose to represent the core events of the Holocaust in his film *Märtyrer* (The Martyr), an Israeli-German coproduction that told the story of the Polish pedagogue Janusz Korczak; Korczak accompanied the children in his orphanage from the Warsaw ghetto to Treblinka, although he could have stayed behind. The overly sentimental film, broadcast by the ZDF on March 8, 1976, painted a simplistic, heroic picture of Korczak.[54]

In the end, one of the most impressive survivor stories broadcast by the ZDF predated the paradigm by several years. In the 1972 documentary *Mendel Schainfelds zweite Reise nach Deutschland* (Mendel Schainfeld's Second Voyage to Germany), the director Hans-Dieter Grabe interviewed an ordinary survivor with due restraint. Grabe followed Schainfeld as he traveled from Norway, his country of residence, to West Germany, where his ability to make a living and his entitlement to increased compensation payments would be assessed in a number of medical exams.[55] Better than any other program, the portrait captured "one's own helplessness when confronted with a survivor whose life failed through no fault of his own,"[56] a feeling that was hardly conveyed by such accomplished survivors as Simon Wiesenthal.

A GENOCIDE WITHOUT PERPETRATORS?

According to its television image in the Federal Republic, the Holocaust was a crime without perpetrators and bystanders, at least until the early 1990s. German television had made a considerable effort to give faces and voices to the survivors, but it never sought to identify the people who committed the crimes or those who watched the catastrophe unfold and remained passive. To some extent, the lack of television coverage was the outcome of obvious practical problems: very few perpetrators and bystanders would have been willing to make potentially incriminating or morally damaging statements in front of the camera. But the editorial staff never tried to counteract the lack of factual programming by producing television fictions about the motives of the perpetrators and bystanders.[57]

In the context of studies of the judicial attempts to come to terms with the past, critics often argued that the courts' failure to mete out appropriate punishment to the perpetrators of the Holocaust illustrated that postwar German society had made its peace with the Nazi murderers.[58] This critique may underestimate the modest, albeit selective, achievements of the West German judiciary and might also imply an active conspiracy when the process at hand should be more accurately described as an inability and unwillingness to face the Nazi criminals and the criminal potential of modern German society. In either case, the unwillingness to deal with perpetration and passivity is reflected in all spheres of Germany's historical culture, including television. In 1965, when the ZDF broadcast the Czech movie *Romeo, Julie, a tma* (Romeo,

Juliet, and Darkness),[59] a reviewer argued that "the effectively directed psychological study of the victims obstructs our view of the perpetrators."[60] This critique applies to three decades of ZDF programming, although it was only rarely expressed. Therefore, Barbara Sichtermann's exceptionally insightful commentary about the interdependence between the existing TV images of the victims and the lack of TV images of the perpetrators, written in the context of the 1988 broadcast of *Die Bertinis,* deserves to be quoted at length:

> The saga of the victims invites us to identify with them. It creates compassion for the innocent whose position we share with sympathy. Yet we are not entitled to this position. . . . The accomplices and opportunists also had children and worries and convictions, fears and hopes; they could also be introduced as central figures from whose perspective the audience could consider the events. But in this respect there is still a powerful taboo because these people were the majority of our people, these people were we ourselves. . . . The television play can present subjectivity, unfamiliar experiences, which touch us deeply. So far these have been the experiences of the victims whose fate only very few of us shared. If television wants to critically reflect the past, including the NS past, the perpetrators have to begin to appear on the screen, as subjects and not as caricatures.[61]

During the 1970s and 1980s, only a handful of ZDF programs, often scheduled in off-prime-time hours, probed deeper into the gray, undefined collective of perpetrators who normally appeared on the screen. Two of the productions that tried to give faces and personalities to specific Nazi criminals dealt with the case of Klaus Barbie and French attempts to come to terms with collaboration.[62] The other programs on perpetrators focused on Gustav Franz Wagner, who was the head of the Sobibor extermination camp;[63] the exciting circumstances of the Eichmann's capture;[64] and the Wannsee Conference of 1942.[65] But only one of the programs, the 1976 documentary *Dr. W.— Ein SS-Arzt in Auschwitz* (Dr. W.—An SS Doctor in Auschwitz) by the Dutch journalist Rolf Orthel, penetrated the moral enigma presented by the Nazi perpetrators and reconstructed the conflicted personality of Eduard Wirth, who volunteered for selection duty but also occasionally helped inmates and committed suicide in 1945.[66] Through interviews with the family and former acquaintances, Orthel traced the "psychological mechanisms of repression and derealization which enabled all of them to continue their normal lives after the atrocity."[67] Unlike any other program on the "Final Solution," the documentary presented the events from the perspective of the perpetrators and their social environment, made it possible to identify with their point of view, and delivered a critical yet complex understanding of the banality of evil.

In the aftermath of the Goldhagen phenomenon that focused public attention on the motives of the average Germans who had implemented the "Final Solution," German television producers finally made the perpetrators a primary focus of inquiry. ZDF series such as *Hitlers Helfer* (Hitler's Henchmen) and *Hitlers Krieger* (Hitler's Warriors) inquired into the motives of the Nazi leadership and mentioned the involvement of the German military in genocide and ethnic cleansing. However, these productions by Knopp and his staff aestheticized Nazi power and focused again on the Nazi leadership while ignoring the "average" perpetrators of the genocide.[68] In addition, the programs were produced and aired years after the introduction of commercial television, when the public networks had lost a significant share of their audience.

This silence about the perpetrators was even surpassed by the silence about the German bystanders of pogroms and deportations. The programs that dealt with bystanders of the Holocaust were primarily non-German productions that observed the persecution of the Jews through the eyes of helpless bystanders or reluctant and unsuccessful helpers in occupied countries.[69] Only one film in the sample featured an initially indifferent and later indecisive and therefore ineffective German helper, and this program became the victim of Cold War politics. Konrad Wolf's movie *Sterne* (Stars), produced in East Germany in 1959, told the story of a German NCO in Bulgaria who fell in love with a Jewish girl from Greece incarcerated in a local camp before being deported to Auschwitz. The soldier could not bring himself to cooperate with partisans who might have been able to free the girl. Only after the departure of her convoy did he finally join the resistance movement.[70] The rights to the movie were acquired by the ZDF in 1963, and the station's acquisition staff repeatedly recommended its broadcast. Nevertheless, the ZDF did not air the film until twenty years later, in 1983, because the public service stations of ARD and ZDF had agreed to boycott productions from countries that participated in the occupation of Czechoslovakia in 1968; consequently, the ZDF had returned the television rights to *Sterne* in the same year.[71] The film concluded with a politically correct East German happy ending, but it was an exceptional production in the context of Germany's historical culture. No other program in the ZDF sample specifically addressed the problem of the indifference of the German population during the systematic persecution of European Jewry.

The ZDF never confronted its viewers with their own problematic behavior during Nazism but instead invited them to identify with the victims, who, according to most stories on the screen, were preyed on by a small collective of ruthless, ideologically motivated, but otherwise strangely undefined Nazi thugs and bureaucrats. Through television, German audiences could learn about the victims' suffering and feel empathy with their fates, an empathy that had been so sadly missing during the persecution itself. However, television journalists never tried to induce the next step; they never created programs that focused on their viewers' actions (or their viewers' forefathers' actions) in light of the newly gained sympathy and respect for the survivors. Television was not the only German institution that kept its peace with the bystanders of the Holocaust, but it was certainly no coincidence that for many years, these bystanders also represented the majority of the audience.

The conscious or unconscious decision of television producers to spare the feelings of audience members and political supervisors highlights the political limits of Vergangenheitsbewältigung and raises the question of the extent to which the medium of television can function as a vehicle of social and cultural reform. In the absence of explicit, self-reflexive inquiries into the experiences, motives, and moral failures of the bystanders of the Holocaust, the memory paradigm fostered by German television created an uncanny resemblance between the passive viewers who were surprisingly willing to watch the Holocaust unfold on the screen and the actual bystanders of the Holocaust who observed pogroms and deportations with a similar stoicism. This disconcerting resemblance is clearly an effect of the technological and social characteristics of the medium of television, but it was exacerbated by the fact that ZDF television producers, despite their considerable accomplishments in educating the public about the Nazi crimes, rarely tested the limits of political taste and therefore never exhausted television's potential to support self-critical habits of historical reflection.

The last phase of Holocaust coverage thus far began in the 1990s. This phase was characterized by new subject matter—the aforementioned perpetrator coverage—and was a side effect of the overall transformation of Germany's television landscape. As commercial networks, which were first licensed in 1984, started to attract large market shares, their public service competitors rose to the challenge by banishing less popular topics and programming formats from their prime-time lineup. In the course of these transformations, historical programming in general and Holocaust subjects in particular almost completely disappeared from early evening program slots. Beginning in 1990, television histories of the "Final Solution" aired predominantly in the afternoon and late-night hours in front of small audiences. Between 1981 and 1989, the ZDF offered an average of 260 prime-time minutes of Holocaust programming per year, but in the first half of the 1990s, the prime-time figures dropped to an average of merely 50 minutes per year (see figure 6.2). That drastic reduction took place while the station's overall output of Holocaust coverage actually continued to increase, from 800 minutes of programming in 1985 to an unprecedented 1,400 minutes in 1995. Given the large number of viewers in prime time, especially in the 1980s, the ZDF thus significantly reduced its audience's exposure to Holocaust-related topics.[72] Most surprisingly, the reduction of prime-time Holocaust pro-

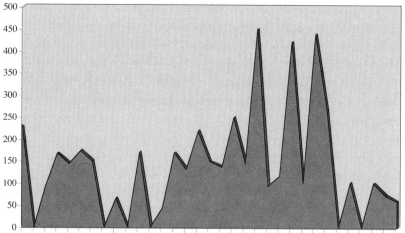

FIGURE 6.2. ZDF prime-time programs about the "Final Solution," 1963–1995 (minutes per year)

gramming, as well as prime-time historical programming in general, took place against a background of intense media coverage of Nazi history, as the elite of the Federal Republic publicly remembered the decline and ultimate demise of the Nazi regime fifty years earlier (see chapter 12).

As a result of these developments, the Nazi genocide has been reduced to a special-interest topic despite a record output of new productions on the history of the Holocaust. There have been only a very few exceptions to this trend, most notably *Holokaust* in 2000.

THE WINDOW TO THE WORLD OF PERSECUTION

The well-funded institutions of German public television informed viewers about their own society, but they also provided plenty of information about the world outside Germany. By vicariously traveling to exotic destinations or by studying the political mores of their Western allies, German audiences received an opportunity to redefine their place in the world. Occasionally, German television even provided foreign filmmakers with an opportunity to explain their culture to German audiences. Thus, British, American, and other perspectives would be introduced by German journalists looking out into the world and by foreign observers commenting and reflecting on their own culture.[73] For obvious reasons, contemporary history in general and Holocaust history in particular occupied a most peculiar place in the spectrum of alternative universes that television had to offer. All too familiar and alien at the same time, TV histories of the "Final Solution" straddled the symbolic fence between "us" and "them." German television producers handled this challenge in a particularly shrewd but also problematic way. By appropriating those aspects of the "Final Solution" that they deemed suitable for identification—for instance, the resilience of the survivors—and by leaving other, less sanguine aspects unaddressed—especially the experience of the perpetrators and bystanders—the television staff crafted a peculiarly gratifying vision of the Holocaust. This shortcoming applied in particular to the figure of the survivor, who was symbolically reclaimed for Germany but whose suffering was, at the same time, presented as part of a foreign world unfamiliar to German audiences. Neither gesture lacked moral or historical integrity in and of itself, yet the combination of the two reinforced a very selective perception of the history of the "Final Solution."

The German journalists and filmmakers who produced documentary programs about the Holocaust clearly intended to bring the survivors back home, and in this, they succeeded. The survivors often lived halfway around the globe and related episodes of their lives that most German perceived as alien to German culture. Nevertheless, the journalists' empathy for their interview partners, the moments of nostalgic remembrance on the side of the survivors, and last but not least, the cultural-linguistic familiarity between the two—all these factors turned the survivors into Germans again, in a subtle, yet powerful denial of the terrible results of twelve years of Nazi rule. For the individuals involved, mostly young German journalists and German Jews who had survived the Holocaust, the encounter might have had tremendous benefits. But for the German audiences in front of the screen, who had not engaged in such concrete and demanding memory work, the documentary programs, as well as their fictional counterparts, created the illusion that the psychological and political scars of the Holocaust could be easily removed. The programs provided German-Jewish minisymbioses, which systematically underestimated the problems inherent in postfascist German-Jewish relationships and respectfully yet efficiently used the survivors to meet the psychological needs of postwar German audiences. By selectively supplying the point of view of the survivors, German television conducted an imaginary dialogue with the victims and thus, at least on a symbolic level, circumvented the very result of the mass murder that made a real dialogue and a real reconciliation with the victims impossible.

The ZDF Holocaust programs were a vital addition to Germany's television landscape because they exposed German viewers to a historical perspective, however constructed and belated, that had been insufficiently represented in Germany's historical culture for many years. But the identification with the survivors of the Holocaust by German producers and possibly also German audiences appeared especially problematic given that the German media never sufficiently and self-critically explored the motives and experiences of the perpetrators and bystanders of the "Final Solution." While familiarizing the audience with the perspective of the survivors, the ZDF programs did not present the perspective on the crimes that was most familiar to the contemporaries of Nazism among the viewers. By means of television, Germans saw some images of persecution that they or their forebears witnessed personally—for instance, the pogroms of 1938 or the deportations of Jewish citizens. But more often, television brought eyewitness accounts and real and reenacted images of scenes that even most contemporaries had never seen with their own eyes: Jews in their embattled homes, Jews in hiding, Jews on their way to the ghettos and camps, survivors interviewed in foreign countries, and less frequently, the concentration camp universe. Television became the window to the hidden world of persecution. In comparison, some crimes that did occur close to home and right under the eyes of German citizens—so-called euthanasia, the abuse of the forced laborers and POWs, the local camps all over the country—these visually more familiar and perhaps more threatening images were not reproduced on television.[74] Most important, none of these events were ever represented from the perspective of the German population in ways that urged viewers to identify with that population's point of view. In the Nazi universe provided by the ZDF, the crimes remained distinctly foreign territory—in principle, not unlike the wonders of the New World and the tribal secrets of Africa.

After the broadcast of the unfinished movie *Die Passagierin* (The Passenger) by the Polish director Andrzej Munk, one reviewer made a peculiar comment: "Auschwitz is in Poland and the Polish directors including Munk can apparently not get over this fact."[75] The reviewer's noticeable relief over the fact that Auschwitz was, indeed, in Poland suggests that proximity between one's everyday life and the sites of the former crimes (implying, among other things, a degree of visual familiarity with realistic filmic renditions of the crimes) is potentially a very disturbing experience. In the case of Poland, the proximity is particularly troublesome, and Polish directors have clearly made a considerable effort to work through this visual familiarity. In the same vein, Ralph Giordano's reaction to the visualization of his autobiographical novel, cited earlier, suggests that familiar images are potentially more disturbing than unfamiliar ones, however gruesome they may be. This factor might explain the carefully selective vision of the Nazi crimes offered in the programs of the ZDF: crimes without perpetrators in visually unfamiliar surroundings represented from unfamiliar perspectives.

In the end, the study of television histories highlights what Vergangenheitsbewältigung is all about. Generations of German intellectuals and consumers have spent an extraordinary amount of time and effort, of elaborate avoidance and selective confrontation to advance a state of normalization and historicization. For academic historians, this normalization entails the study of the Nazi past and the Holocaust with the conventional tools of their trade, which are applied to every conceivable aspect of that past in a productive yet routine manner and which result in ambitious, complex historical narratives addressed to an international community of scholars.[76] For television producers and audiences, such normalization results in the marginalization of self-critical historical representation in off-peak hours, directed at specific, historically minded, minority audiences and ever more sensational revelations about the Führer in more commercially driven prime-time programming. Even this development, however disappointing, marks the normalization of the German media in the context of the development of international media markets.

NAZIS, VIEWERS, AND STATISTICS

*Television History, Television Audience Research,
and Collective Memory in West Germany*

Television archives represent an excellent but underused and often unattainable resource for the study of contemporary history. The media institutions that shaped everyday culture in the second half of the twentieth century control archival treasures that remain far less accessible for the researcher than rare medieval manuscripts. Especially the most important source, the visual record itself, is carefully guarded against unwanted, poor intruders who have neither the means nor the desire to purchase distribution and copyrights. Another factor hampers historical research about television as well. As salaried intellectuals, many academics still regard the plebeian pleasures of television with considerable suspicion. They might partake in these pleasures in the privacy of their homes, but they distrust the medium's political and cultural influence and consider television unworthy of their professional attention. Historians are particularly prone to such prejudice because they carry a more specific grudge. After all, television has undermined their rewarding side careers as public historians. Before the era of the tube, historians were often enlisted for the task of shaping their nations' historical consciousness. Today, this feat is accomplished in much more efficient and entertaining ways by the electronic media—a development that might well account for the remarkable consensus among historians regarding television's unsuitability for the construction of history.[1]

The critical attitude of historians explains why television in general and historical programming in particular has not received sufficient attention by specialists in contemporary history. But the many users of electronic media, whose lives and worldviews historians are trying to reconstruct, do not share this assessment. Therefore, it is high time to study the key medium of the twentieth century from a historical perspective, to tap into the underused wealth of archival data that television institutions have accumulated over the decades, and to show in detail how television has reflected and shaped historical consciousness. The present study is designed to advance this cause and engage with the difficult problem of audience reception, which is widely acknowledged in cultural studies and which has, as seen in chapter 2, recently also surfaced in research on collective memory. Increasingly, scholars have recognized that it is quite problematic to study collective memories on the basis of the representations of the past without trying to determine who has actually used and identified with such representations.

Commercial audience research institutes provide the best data about television reception, but the industry has received mixed reviews and the data have never been used for historical analysis. Many media critics and television makers insist that commercial audience measurements provide little information about the quality and success of specific shows and misrepresent audience behavior. Although this criticism is largely accurate, commercial audience research data offer great opportunities for historical research, as I will try to show in the following analysis and assessment of this new type of sources. The same data that serve dubious purposes in the power struggles of the television industry provide valuable insights into the evolution of popular tastes once they are integrated into their specific historical context.

The basis of the following inquiry is a quantitative analysis of the contents and especially the ratings of twelve hundred programs about Nazism and the Holocaust that were broadcast by the ZDF between 1963 and 1993. I will also consider the ratings of competing programs and other quantitative and qualitative audience research projects conducted inside and outside West Germany's public service stations. Together, these data provide a fascinating perspective on the development of the collective memory of the Nazi period in the Federal Republic of Germany. They indicate, for instance, that television played a crucial role in the process of coming to terms with the Nazi past because, through that medium, a larger national audience was exposed to interpretations of Nazism that were originally developed by historians, writers, and journalists in Germany and abroad. In this process, scriptwriters, directors, and TV executives served as conduits between the intellectual elite, to which they belong by training and social origin, and the mainstream national public, which they serve. They accomplished this work under close scrutiny of the political elite, whose members controlled the purse strings and top personnel decisions in the public networks.

The translation of the intellectual discourse that reached the screen in this way was heavily edited and simplified. For instance, the programs no longer bore any sign of the divisive controversies that informed many intellectual debates and instead conveyed the impression that the past had been contained within a powerful national interpretive consensus. If this message misrepresented the historical culture of the elite, which was characterized by competition and disagreement from the 1960s on, it nevertheless revealed an underlying truth. In their efforts to educate the public about its past and further their own careers, television makers proved to be excellent researchers of the largest common denominator in questions of historical taste. The journalists, administrators, and historical experts in the television stations made it their job to sift through the maze of intellectual strife and determine which strategies of representation best represented the current intellectual and political climate. More often than not, they managed to extract ideas that proved interesting and acceptable to their viewers, even as they inadvertently demonstrated that many intellectual battles, however divisive on the surface, were based on considerable agreements about the significance and meaning of the Nazi period.

As a result of their peculiar position as marginal intellectuals and respected and perhaps even envied popularizers, TV makers crafted stories about the Nazi past that demonstrated more clearly than the stories provided by any other medium how the Federal Republic had evolved from a collective of former Nazis and bystanders into a democratic society that maintained a surprisingly critical attitude toward its own past. This journey included the transformation and substitution of generations of anti-Semites by generations of Germans who felt considerable empathy for the survivors of the Holocaust and who were therefore surprisingly willing to watch and listen to stories about the Nazi past, including stories that provided accurate and detailed information about Nazi crimes.

TELEVISION CONSUMPTION IN WEST GERMANY

It took twenty years, from 1954 to 1974, before the West German television market was saturated and before television had effectively created an all-inclusive national audience. Once the threshold of one million subscribers had been crossed in 1957, the audience grew steadily by more than one million house-holds per year until the growth rate dropped rapidly in the early 1970s. At the end of the expansion process, there were over eighteen million TV sub-scribers in the Federal Republic, and only 5 percent of the population did not have access to television in their own homes. In the following decade, from the mid-1970s to the mid-1980s, the number of subscribers and viewing habits remained remarkably stable.[2]

The quantitative data on television use in West Germany correspond to a number of important qualitative changes in the consumption of television since the 1950s. During the phase of expansion, television redefined the re-lationship between the private and public spheres in West German society. In combination with other important social developments, including the mobi-lization of society through the automobile and the gradual reduction of aver-age working hours, television shaped the extended leisure time of West Germans and gave rise to new family rituals. Public television fostered cul-tural homogenization by alleviating social and regional differences, and it fa-miliarized West Germans with democratic decision-making processes.[3]

The situation changed significantly after commercial television was intro-duced in 1984. Until that point, German television had been exclusively public television. The first public network, the ARD, commenced national broad-casting in 1954; the second public station, the ZDF, went on the air in 1963. Each provided one program nationwide, so German viewers could only choose between two national channels.[4] With a delay of several years, the new com-mercial channels introduced in 1984 proved very attractive to German con-sumers. In fact, since the mid-1990s, the most successful commercial stations have frequently been market leaders in the increasingly competitive dual television landscape.[5] As a result of the multiplication of channels and the diversification of daily television routines, German television no longer creates national audiences and has lost a great deal of its integrative function for German society. This development is aptly illustrated by the fact that only 30 percent of the population watched *any* of the numerous live broadcasts of the public television stations that covered the fall of the Berlin Wall.[6] In con-trast, during the 1970s and most of the 1980s, public television still regularly united the majority of West Germans in front of the screen. Especially between the hours of 8:00 p.m. and 10:00 p.m., West Germans (and many East Germans) would not just share the experience of watching television but would also often actually watch the same programs.

In the complex constellation of economic, political, and consumer interests that have shaped West German television, policy and technological initiatives have been primarily determined by the media industries and the political elite, whereas program initiatives have remained in the hands of the stations themselves. The introduction of national television in postwar Germany in 1954, the founding of a second public station in 1963, the advent of color television in 1967, and the introduction of commercial television in 1984—all these changes resulted primarily from political and economic pressures and not from consumer lobbying. Consequently, in all cases, viewers have only gradually incorporated the new media and programs into their daily habits.

The consumers' influence on television policy and programming can be best described as veto power. The introduction of commercial television is a case in point. The collaboration between the conservative political establishment and West Germany's leading media companies was designed to undercut the political influence of public television. But the top-down reconstruction of Germany's television landscape only succeeded because commercial television did not contradict the consumers' recreational interests. Viewers welcomed the new entertainment opportunities because public television had not always offered their preferred television fare. Rather, in patriarchal fashion, public television presented programs that politicians and TV executives deemed suitable for their constituency and that viewers found acceptable given the lack of alternatives.[7]

For the majority of the viewers, this acceptable fare included historical coverage on the topic of Nazism. More than any other medium in West Germany, television forged an important and powerful connection between Vergangenheitsbewältigung and the pleasures of representation and narration. Especially in the 1980s during the last years of the public television monopoly, television was the primary vehicle for mastering the past for the German population. In these years, television provided a selective yet compelling vision of the Nazi past that proved quite appealing to German audiences.

THE ZDF PROGRAMS ON NAZISM

Between 1963 and 1993, the ZDF aired over 1,200 programs that dealt with the Nazi past and its postwar legacy, as noted earlier. The data reveal some fluctuations in output from year to year, but in general, the programs on Nazism closely followed the overall expansion of ZDF airtime. The station consistently dedicated between 1 percent and 1.5 percent of its programming to the task of educating and informing its viewers about Germany's problematic past. The programs of the ZDF on the history of the Nazi era covered a wide variety of subjects, ranging from a large contingent of almost 350 programs on the topic of World War II to a small segment of less than 30 shows on fascist movements outside Germany (see figure 7.1). Though producers and viewers were clearly interested in revisiting the military confrontation between Germany and the Allies, other key elements of the Nazi period received considerably less attention. That observation applied in particular to the history of the Nazi movement, which was not one of the foci of

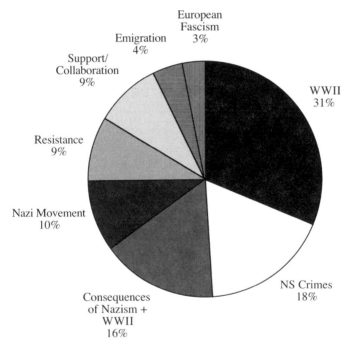

FIGURE 7.1. Topics of ZDF programs on Nazism and World War II, 1963–1993 (percentage shares based on total minutes per topic)

West German television. Thus, the core of the Nazi phenomenon was left un-derexplored, at least in the context of the ZDF program. Also, the ZDF pro-vided a strangely "balanced" rendition of the Nazi era by dedicating the same amount of airtime to programs about the Nazi movement, the popular sup-port of the regime, and the antifascist resistance. By contrast, judging by the figures, the ZDF engaged quite aggressively with Nazi crimes and the Third Reich's historical consequences.

The quantitative analysis of ZDF programming yields a number of addi-tional interesting results when one focuses on the data for prime time.[8] The hours between 7:30 p.m. and 10:30 p.m. have particular relevance for produc-ers and viewers because programs placed outside this window reach only a small fraction of television households. Since the ZDF, like its public service competitor, more than tripled its overall output and similarly expanded its editorial and production staff since 1963, the internal competition for prime-time programming slots also gradually intensified. In this increasingly com-petitive climate, the programs on Nazism did not fare badly, but they lost some ground. With increasing distance from the Nazi past, mainstream au-diences were confronted less frequently with their troublesome history, while retirees, youths, and intellectuals, who consume television off the beaten tracks of prime-time programming, had more opportunities to satisfy their historical curiosity. In short, over the decades, Nazism has become a special-interest topic.

Prime-time figures also indicate that the efforts to come to terms with the past via television evolved in four quantitatively quite distinct phases. Two pe-riods of engagement and two periods of disengagement stand out in retro-spect. During the 1960s and early 1970s, the ZDF offered an average of sixteen hundred prime-time minutes of historical programming per year. Though these figures were never reached again, the years from 1979 to 1987 represent a similarly active phase in terms of television coverage on the his-tory of the Third Reich. In contrast, during the second half of the 1970s and between 1988 and 1993, prime-time programming on the topic was markedly reduced, reaching only one thousand and six hundred minutes, respectively (see figure 7.2).

The quantity of historical programming was the outcome of many factors, including the television makers' awareness of the importance of the topic of Nazism, their attempts to respond to general societal trends, and their efforts

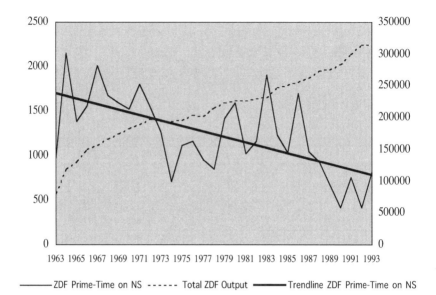

NOTE: The figure combines two different scales. The numbers on the right correspond to ZDF total output, whereas the numbers on the left correspond to ZDF prime-time programming on National Socialism.

FIGURE 7.2. Total ZDF output and ZDF prime-time programs on Nazism, 1963–1993 (minutes per year)

to repeat past successes while coordinating all programming initiatives. In addition, the periods of disengagement reflected real and perceived political and budgetary limitations. Following the saturation of the television market in the 1970s, all public service stations in West Germany experienced serious budget problems, which influenced program quality. The ZDF had to reduce the percentage of expensive, self-produced or commissioned programs, and it filled the gaps with inexpensive U.S. imports. Likewise, beginning in the late 1980s, the public stations tried to respond and preempt the rise of their commercial competition by offering more entertaining prime-time fare, which was only possible at the expense of more serious subject matter. Finally, the lull in historical coverage in the 1970s and the 1990s was also influenced by political events, especially the rise of left-wing political terrorism in the Federal Republic during the 1970s and the collapse of the Berlin Wall in 1989.

Both events caused ample discussions about their historical significance that were laced with explicit and implicit references to the Third Reich, but they also displaced in-depth historical programming that focused specifically on the history of the Nazi period. Although these economic and political events set the parameters within which the process of coming to terms with the past could unfold on the screen, the different phases outlined here also reflected substantial transformations in the content of historical coverage that were closely linked to the evolution of the Federal Republic's historical culture. Many of these changes, which will be briefly outlined in this chapter, followed generational patterns—in this case, generational transformations among television makers and television audiences.[9]

The representation of Nazism in the programs of the ZDF advanced in two steps represented by the two phases of engagement, from 1963 to 1971 and from 1978 to 1986. The first phase of engagement provided television that was made and consumed by contemporaries of Nazism. Most TV makers and viewers of those years were adults by the end of the war, and they engaged with representations of the past that helped them cope with the postwar political and moral status quo. The programs of the time reflected a decidedly anti-Nazi stance but also employed a range of strategies designed to strengthen the audience's loyalty to the new state and lift the moral burden of Nazism from its shoulders.[10] Like many contemporary interpreters of German history, ZDF experts emphasized the sacrifices endured by the German population during and after the war and searched for suitable role models in the historical record of the Third Reich.[11] The ZDF was particularly committed to the rehabilitation of the German churches, emphasizing the clerics' support for the victims of the regime while failing to point out their more extensive record of collaboration.[12] For similar purposes, the coverage transformed the conservative resisters to Hitler into democratic proto–West Germans while ignoring the Communist resistance movement.[13] Even the military was counted among these protodemocrats and celebrated for its steadfastness on the eastern front.[14] Therefore, it is not surprising that the early shows of the ZDF displayed a disturbing tendency to revisit and mourn military defeats during the war and omit the army's involvement in Nazi crimes.[15]

In their eagerness to repair the honor of the pillars of society—the churches, the military, and the conservative elite—television makers failed to engage directly with the Nazi movement and its leaders.[16] In addition, they rarely produced and scheduled more honest explorations of the positions of the former perpetrators in West German society.[17] Instead, the ZDF offered a number of shows that simply used the war as backdrop for suspenseful spy stories.[18] None of these Cold War themes originated in television—they had already dominated the West German feature films of the 1950s—but the new medium was the most powerful transmitter of the postwar historical identity.[19]

The schematic and predictable narrative universe of the 1960s programs offered audience members the opportunity to reshape their own memories or imagine their parents' experiences in terms of clearly designated types of historical actors and stereotypical situations. In more than one sense, the shows remained black-and-white illustrations of the perceived existential divisions during the Nazi period, which included the divisions on the battlefield (German versus enemy soldier, enlisted men versus officers, German versus Allied spy, and Nazi versus soldier) as well as the divisions on the home front (Nazi versus resistance fighter, Nazi versus victim). The programs always recommended to their viewers the subject position of the anti-Nazi, either as dutiful soldier, resister, or victim. In addition to "Aryan" German nationals and citizens of occupied countries, Jews were acknowledged as victims, But, as noted in the previous chapter, the Jewish victims appeared in marginal roles as objects of heroic German rescue efforts or in philo-Semitic programs that mourned the loss of Jewish culture in central Europe.[20] The Holocaust was more directly addressed in a few feature films from Eastern Europe that the ZDF aired during the 1960s. However, these excellent, self-critical films about the lack of support for the Jewish victims during the German occupation could have been easily misunderstood by their German viewers, since they seemed to indicate that resistance against the "Final Solution" had been unrealistic and futile considering that even the former enemies of the Third Reich had failed to protect "their" Jews.[21]

The 1970s marked the end of the historical coverage that had dominated the screen during the first decade of the station's existence. The ZDF had exhausted the reserves of postwar feature films and discontinued the production of docuplays, which had an important role in delivering a suspenseful and entertaining but also stereotypical vision of the past. New topics and program formats were developed, but they remained ill defined for several years. TV makers pursued other priorities, and they were not alone in their change of heart. Commenting on the scholarly production and political climate of the decade, historians have compared the 1970s to the 1950s and concluded that West German society was systematically avoiding direct confrontation with the Nazi past during both periods.[22] The disengagement of the 1970s was not as severe as the postwar communicative silence, but in the later period, the republic suffered from economic decline and terrorist assaults and faced its first severe crisis; consequently, it was focused on the present rather than the past. Clearly, the data from the television archives support this interpretation, although they also indicate that the intermittent disinterest in history represented a phase of gestation and transformation rather than deliberate silence and repression. Even during the 1970s, when historical programming played a reduced role in prime time, the ZDF's staff produced a couple of innovative, critical programs, especially on the history of the Holocaust and everyday life during Nazism, that laid the foundation for the second phase of engagement.[23] Aired in the afternoon or late at night, the shows might not have registered in the collective memory of the nation because they only reached small audiences. Nevertheless, ZDF historians deserve particular praise for these modest initiatives, since they demonstrated the station's continued commitment to the cause of Vergangenheitsbewältigung in a period when many intellectuals and journalists assumed that the time for historical reckoning had inevitably passed.

When the topic of Nazism was again more regularly addressed in prime time in 1978, many of the old themes returned, especially regarding the representation of World War II. In addition, however, a new and different vision of the past appeared on the ZDF screen, a vision that responded to the interests and the standards of historical verisimilitude of new generations of Germans. During the 1980s, for the first time in postwar history, the majority of television viewers had no personal memories of the Nazi past. This new audience was served by television makers who were either in the same position or who had experienced the Nazi period as children or adolescents.[24] Thus, in the 1980s, unlike in the 1960s, the electronic communication about Nazism was primarily conducted between Germans who were not themselves responsible for Nazism and its crimes.

Relieved of the burden of personal liability, the younger generations explored the burden of the past with less circumspection. The most important innovations of these years were prime-time fictions that vividly re-created everyday life during Nazism and a wave of programs dedicated to the suffering and endurance of Holocaust survivors. In contrast to the reflexive, schematic discourse of the 1960s, which had functioned as a rigid conceptual screen between past and present, the programs of the 1980s invited direct emotional engagement and identification. They provided surrogate memories that suggested how social life and victimization during Nazism might have felt. These historical simulations were facilitated by new television aesthetics. The second phase of engagement occurred after most viewers had purchased color television sets, and the new experience of watching in color, in conjunction with more image-driven programs, boosted the reality effect of the historical programming.

The stunning success of the miniseries *Holocaust,* which was produced in the United States by the National Broadcasting Company (NBC) and broadcast in Germany by the ARD in 1979, accelerated the rise of the survivor paradigm in West Germany's historical culture.[25] After this exceptional media event, television acknowledged the Holocaust's historical specificity and brought Jewish survivors to the screen, but the programs of the ZDF still only rarely explored the worldview of the perpetrators and the fateful decisions of the bystanders.[26] While the survivor paradigm provided strategies of representation that both acknowledged and contained the legacy of the "Final Solution," the paradigm of everyday history offered, for the first time, a conceptual strategy of collective memory that could handle the conflicted and ambivalent realities of the Nazi years.[27] In contrast to the one-dimensional programs of the 1960s, shows developed under the new approach presented explorations into the normality of life in the 1930s and 1940s as well as critical, detail-oriented analyses of resistance and conformity. The fact that television emphasized the experiences of the survivors over the motives of the perpetrators and stressed normality over conformity illustrates the limits of the new paradigms of historical reflection. The shows of the 1980s were still selective in focus and designed to stimulate consensus rather than conflict, but unlike in earlier years, the programs addressed the central issue of the Nazi past—the genocide of European Jewry.

As in the 1960s, television shared the new approaches to history with other sectors of West Germany's historical culture. The paradigm of everyday history originated in the history workshop movement of the 1970s and was adopted by a number of academic historians before it found its way to

the screen.[28] German historians were not as interested in the survivor paradigm, at least not in the specific type of narratives that had crossed the Atlantic in the wake of *Holocaust* and had become so important for German
television. But they spent a great deal of time and energy discussing the concept of the Holocaust's singularity, one of the conceptual cornerstones of the
paradigm. Many academic publications of the 1970s and 1980s acknowledged the notion of the Holocaust's singularity, and as shown in chapter 4,
the concept was vigorously discussed during the 1986–1988 Historians'
Debate.

Historical reflection via television could not have been sustained with the
same intensity for much longer, but it was suddenly undermined by the rise
of commercial television and German unification. Private stations showed
little inclination to dedicate airtime and money to historical education, and
their public competitors felt compelled to follow suit, at least in their prime-
time lineups. Thus, the end of patriarchal television also marked the end of
a particular type of historical reflection through television. The ZDF still produced a number of high-profile documentaries on the Nazi perpetrators in
the 1990s, but the remarkable success of Knopp series such as *Hitler, Hitlers
Helfer* (Hitler's Henchmen), and *Hitlers Krieger* (Hitler's Warriors) did not reverse the general displacement of self-critical historical programming into
more marginal programming slots.

TELEVISION RATINGS

Television producers and media scholars regard television ratings with great
suspicion. In Germany, the critique of television ratings has intensified in recent years, as ratings make and break careers in an increasingly competitive
television market. In particular, producers in public service networks, who
were not subjected to market pressures until the late 1980s, reject the idea
that ratings accurately reflect the quality of their work.[29] In their opinion, "the
use of ratings for the evaluation of television programs simply reflects the
laziness, the lack of imagination, and the lack of funds" among television
executives.[30]

Media scholars dismiss ratings for other reasons. They point out that ratings provide little information about actual reception processes. The simple
fact that a certain number of people share a room with a running television

set delivers no knowledge about viewing intensity or the impact of television contents and television aesthetics on the lives of consumers. Critics have therefore concluded that "there is no sophisticated public discourse that does justice to the complexity of the multiple practices and experiences that television audiencehood involves" and that audience measurements such as ratings can be more accurately described "as a central site where the television industry enacts its power to gain control over the audience."[31]

All points of criticism are well taken. At times, even advertisers and television executives, who base many decisions on ratings, concede that ratings are, indeed, a poor programming tool because external factors have a decisive impact on the measurable success of television shows.[32] Ratings are influenced by season and weather, as well as weekday and time of broadcast.[33] In addition, the specific characteristics of a given program—its contents and aesthetics— determine ratings as much as the program's context and competition.[34] However, though ratings do not fulfill the purposes they were designed to accomplish, it is wrong to deny them any interpretative value and refrain from tapping into the wealth of data that has accumulated over the years. As media scholar Elihu Katz argued in 1996: "What we know most about audience behavior is who chooses what; the problem here is that we know too much, in that the mountains of ratings have only rarely been mined for their lawfulness."[35]

In contrast to the situation in the United States, which Katz was commenting on, the mountains of German ratings are still quite modest in size, especially for the era of the public service monopoly of ARD and ZDF. Under these circumstances, the German television landscape offers a great opportunity to begin mining ratings and other audience research data as historical sources. Ironically, ratings are even more useful for historical analysis than for programming decisions because many of the external factors that undercut their value in assessing specific programs become negligible if we increase sample size and historical focus. Considered over the course of several decades and for hundreds of programs with similar content, ratings offer excellent polling data that allow us to reconstruct the tastes of German audiences.

The ARD and the ZDF initiated quantitative viewer research in 1963 by commissioning the company Infratam in Wetzlar to provide regular reports on West Germany's television viewers.[36] In a number of representative households, Infratam installed a set meter that recorded when the television was in

use and to which station it had been tuned.[37] Parallel to the quantitative research conducted by Infratam, the ARD and ZDF retained the services of
Infratest in Munich for the task of qualitative audience research, which the
company had undertaken for some stations of the ARD since the 1950s.

In the late 1960s, the work of Infratest and Infratam was severely criticized by media experts inside and outside the stations. The critics found the
qualitative research wanting because the pool of interviewees was too small
to provide any reliable information on the actual opinions of West German
viewers. In addition, the monotonous use of a small, invariable set of questions for all programs produced stereotypical, predictable results, which hardly
seem worth the financial effort of several million marks per year.[38] As a result, continuous qualitative viewer research was terminated in 1974.

The quantitative research of Infratam was not subject to similarly devastating criticism, although experts exposed a number of important limitations
of the company's work.[39] As a result, the stations commissioned a different
type of quantitative viewer research beginning in 1975. The new Teleskopie
system, run jointly by the Institut für Demoskopie in Allensbach and the
Infas-Institut in Bad Godesberg, introduced the "people-meter" to Germany.[40]
In addition to overall television consumption and station of choice, the people-
meter also recorded which members of the household convened in front of
the set at any given point in time. For the first time, the success or failure of
any program could be linked to the structure of its audience in terms of gen-
der, age-group, and educational background.[41] The latest transformation in
quantitative viewer research occurred in 1985 when ARD and ZDF retained
the services of the Nürnberg-based company GfK, which still produces the
ratings for all television channels in Germany. All commercial channels have
successively joined the new system. In principle, GfK offered the same service
as Teleskopie, albeit at a more competitive rate.[42]

When interpreting West German ratings, it is important to keep in mind
that the ZDF's efforts to match the popularity of the ARD programming were
severely handicapped for the first five years of its existence because the FM
transmitters for the distribution of the ZDF signal were still under construction. As a result, in 1963, only 43 percent of all television households could
receive the new programming. This percentage increased rapidly to 73 percent in 1965 and 95 percent in 1968.[43] Nevertheless, even years after the ZDF
reached the same potential audience as the ARD, the ratings clearly indicate

that the ZDF programming was used more selectively than that of its more established rival. At least until the early 1970s, viewers followed the habit of first tuning to an ARD program and only switching channels if they found that program unsatisfactory. Consequently, throughout the late 1960s and the early 1970s, the ZDF lagged behind the ARD; it attracted, on average, 12 percent fewer viewers than the ARD.[44] The situation changed between 1973 and 1978 when the ZDF's audience, for the first time, matched the size of the ARD's, primarily as a result of a changed prime-time lineup. Since that time, the ZDF has only trailed its competitor by an insignificant margin of 1 percent to 4 precent and occasionally even surpassed the ARD.[45] In 1988, private stations began to attract considerable audience shares, and both public networks have had to contend with much smaller audiences ever since.[46]

With this information in mind, I will compare the ratings of the ZDF's historical coverage to the ratings of the ARD shows aired at the same time. The comparison with the competition is particularly useful because the ARD very rarely scheduled similar subject matter in these programming slots. Taken together, the data should show how attractive or unattractive the topic of Nazism was for German viewers. Since many German intellectuals have been quite critical of their compatriots' willingness to confront the Nazi past, one would expect the ratings to reflect the population's distaste for the topic.[47] That hypothesis is also supported by the qualitative audience research conducted by Infratest in the 1960s and early 1970s. As mentioned, the research proved relatively worthless for the purpose of program planning, but from the present perspective, some of the findings are quite interesting. Having questioned the audience at some length, experts at Infratest concluded, for instance, that viewers rejected television fiction that destroyed the illusion of reality through abstract or satirical representations and disapproved of particularly unpleasant, negative, or violent material.[48] Thus, it is not surprising that these experts also determined the topic of Nazism was unpopular with West German audiences. The reports from the 1960s emphasized that viewers did not want to be confronted with questions of guilt, especially when programs suggested a general German responsibility for Nazi crimes and failed to make a clear distinction between Nazis and Germans. In addition, viewers complained about too much realism when Nazi atrocities were depicted in detail and objected to cold, overly didactic renditions that were difficult to identify with and offered little entertainment value.[49]

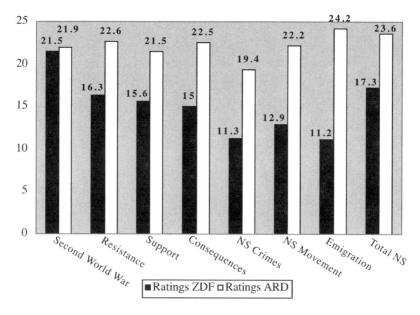

FIGURE 7.3. Average ratings of ZDF programs on Nazism by topic in comparison to ratings of ARD competition, 1963–1989 (average percentages of TV households per year)

THE RATINGS OF NS PROGRAMS

Naturally, one would expect that the ZDF sample as a whole performed significantly below its competition because the rival ARD lineup offered a much wider range of program types, including real blockbusters such as live sports coverage and game shows. Therefore, the overall discrepancy between the two stations of 6.3 percent is not particularly revealing. However, a closer look at the data indicates that German viewers indeed consumed historical programming in a selective fashion. Viewers greatly appreciated the ZDF World War II coverage, and knowing about their audience's predilections, ZDF administrators made this the most frequently addressed topic of contemporary history. In contrast, any other topic related to Nazism floundered in the ratings; the numbers are particularly interesting for the larger samples in the categories "NS Crimes" and "Consequences of Nazism" (see figure 7.3).

It is tempting to overinterpret the significance of these findings and conclude that the low ratings attest to the audience's desire to ignore the past, but that interpretation would be premature. The different subtopics were not competing on a level playing field. The programs about World War II were disproportionately made up of movies and docuplays, which were popular by definition, whereas the shows on Nazi crimes largely consisted of documentaries and TV plays, which never commanded the same audience potential. Considering this bias in the data, one can at best conclude that viewers showed a slight inclination to avoid programs that directly addressed the most sensitive issues, that is, the record of genocide and Germany's postwar responsibilities.

In contrast to the subtle gradation in ratings and appreciation that the analysis has revealed so far, a historical breakdown of the same figures returns unexpectedly stark and intriguing results. It turns out that audience resistance to historical reflection was particularly pronounced in the mid-1970s. For four years, between 1975 and 1978, viewers abandoned the historical coverage of the ZDF at a time when the station had caught up with its competitor and occasionally even surpassed the ARD in overall ratings.[50] The sudden

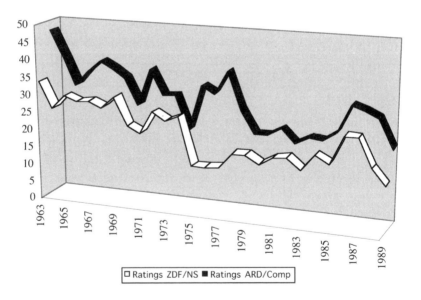

FIGURE 7.4. Historical development of ratings of ZDF prime-time programs on Nazism in comparison to ratings of ARD competition, 1963–1989 (average percentages of TV households per year)

viewer disinterest reflected changes in the ZDF program but also attested to
the general transformation of West German society and West German historical culture (see figure 7.4).

Considering the ZDF's reduced audience potential in the 1960s, it is remarkable how well the station's historical coverage performed in the ratings
during the first phase of engagement. Contrary to my expectations, viewers
did not avoid the subject of Nazism. When they temporarily abandoned the
historical coverage in the mid-1970s, they pursued other priorities for their
entertainment and displayed a general indifference or even dislike for history—a dislike that was shared by many other segments of Germany's society,
including the television makers themselves. But viewers also expressed their
dissatisfaction with the specific programs of those years. They were no longer
attracted to the old strategies of historical representation, in particular the
docuplay, and they reacted to the fact that no compelling new television format for the representation of contemporary history had been developed for
prime time. These shortcomings reflected a temporary lack of funds as well
as a temporary lack of interest and imagination on the part of the television
executives.

The situation was decisively different after the generational transformation and the general reorientation of West Germany's historical culture that
took place in the 1970s. From that point on, program makers who belonged
to the postwar generations and had replenished the budgets at their disposal
brought a new, widely appreciated vision of Nazism to the screen. As a result,
producers, programs, and audiences were back in sync during the second
phase of engagement. Therefore, with the exception of the data for the mid-
1970s, there was no indication that viewers avoided the ZDF programs on
Nazism and used their veto power to force a change in programming policy.
For most of public television's history, audiences integrated the visions of
Nazism into their television routines even when it would have been very easy
to avoid exposure with the turn of a switch.

FROM SELF-DEFENSIVE TO SELF-CRITICAL ENTERTAINMENT

The data can be interpreted in a number of ways. One option is suggested by
media experts who warn that the actual choices viewers make about their television consumption do not necessarily represent their preferences. For lack

of information or indifference, audiences might stay tuned to programs that do not reflect their tastes as they might perceive of them on other occasions—for instance, during a polling interview or in their next book purchase.[51] This interpretation is supported by the fact that postmodern audiences with multiple channel options feel easily overwhelmed by their choices and tend to use television as a stopgap medium between other, more pressing or meaningful activities.[52]

In my assessment, this interpretation does not apply to German viewers in the era of public television. The impressive variety and circulation figures of German TV guides indicate that German audiences were exceptionally well informed about their limited choices and made deliberate decisions regarding their evening entertainment.[53] In addition, the extensive correspondence and phone calls that public stations received from their viewers suggest that they were intent on having their interests heard and implemented.[54] Nevertheless, experts note that the programs of choice should not be construed as the audiences' preferred television fare. Especially considering their limited options, the programs watched by the consumers of public television would be more accurately described as the least objectionable program they could find at any given point in time.[55] Therefore, one should also not assume that the programs precisely delineate the historical pain threshold of the audience. These programs reflected the television makers' informed assessment of public opinion, but in the high-stakes game of television, TV journalists were not likely to be allowed to test the limits of historical taste, nor would they be intent on doing so. For all we know, considerable segments of the audience might have found more self-critical explorations of Nazism and the Holocaust both interesting and worth their while, especially during the 1980s.

Assuming that, at least in this specific case, ratings do reflect a link between program content and the interests of the audience, two alternative explanatory models can be considered. First, one might attribute the relative popularity of the ZDF's coverage to its many political and moral flaws. Perhaps viewers appreciated the ZDF programs precisely because they offered overly defensive and even apologetic reinventions of the history of Nazism and World War II. After all, the ZDF often provided entertaining, uncritical, and unprovocative visions of past misdeeds and present obligations that carefully avoided putting the audience on the defensive politically or morally. Very few ZDF programs aggressively questioned the interpretive status quo or emphasized the extent to which the members of the audience were responsible for the "German catastrophe" and how they had fallen short in their responsibilities toward the victims of Nazism. This interpretation would vindicate the harsh critics of West Germany's historical culture who have identified a widespread and persistent reluctance on the part of the German population to confront the Nazi past in any meaningful and honest fashion. However, the facts give ample opportunity for radically different explanations. Considering that the ZDF programs never denied Nazi crimes or German responsibility for them and occasionally even stressed the continuing obligations arising from them, it is tempting to conclude that West Germans are an exceptionally self-critical collective of former perpetrators and bystanders and that this exceptional penchant for retrospection and remorse was reflected in their willingness to watch their own crimes unfold again and again on television.

Both interpretations have their merits, but they need to be historicized and applied with more precision. Clearly, apologetic and defensive strategies of representation dominated the ZDF's coverage of the 1960s. The programs did not reflect the more honest discussions about Nazism that erupted in the public sphere at the beginning of the decade and marked the emergence of a very active phase in the Federal Republic's historical culture. These events might have been covered in the ZDF's newscasts and political magazines and prompted viewers to watch the programs discussed earlier, but the contents and aesthetics of the programs ignored the controversies among politicians and the concerned public that initiated the era of Vergangenheitsbewältigung in West Germany.[56] Programs of the 1960s had more in common with the widely shared and agreed on Cold War rhetoric, strategies of dehistoricization, and stories of German suffering that characterized the public discourse of the 1950s and that will be analyzed in chapter 9. Therefore, the indictments of West Germany's collective memory by critics such as the Mitscherlichs and Adorno who took issue with this complacent consensus of the postwar years also apply to the first decade of ZDF programming.

However, once this criticism had been taken up in some areas of West Germany's historical culture (for instance, in the history workshops of the 1970s) and finally helped transform the mainstream perception of Nazism, a different, less objectionable interpretation of the past found its way into

German living rooms. To be sure, television still avoided particularly disturbing aspects of the historical record and failed to report accurately on the many intellectual battles of the 1980s. But judging by the programs and the ratings, it is difficult to imagine that many Germans walked away from their evening entertainment without a clear grasp of the exceptionally vicious crimes committed by the German government and the Nazi Party between 1933 and 1945. In fact, it is difficult not to come to the conclusion that the German mainstream media and mainstream culture of the 1980s mark an exceptional phase in the evolution of the nation's collective memory of the Third Reich; that phase also distinguishes the German case from similar cases of modern genocide and conflicted memory. For a period of almost a decade, considerable segments of the German population were surprisingly willing to confront the national legacy of shame and acknowledge the suffering of the victims.

This self-reflection via television came too late for the generations most responsible for the crimes, but it certainly influenced the worldview of subsequent generations as they contemplated their parents' and grandparents' involvement in the history of Nazism. There are a number of reasons to assume that these topics had not played a prominent role in the informal, intergenerational transmission of family history and family lore that form the backbone of our collective memory.[57] During the 1980s, public television helped fill some of these blanks and occasionally even helped jump-start a more honest intergenerational dialogue. In this role, public television fulfilled some of the educational potential envisioned by its founders, although the founders themselves and the members of their generation were not yet ready for that dialogue about the burden of the past.

The study of the ZDF's historical coverage and its reception adds an important element to our understanding of Germany's collective memory of the Nazi period. We have conventionally assumed that minorities in the ranks of the Federal Republic's cultural and political elite advanced the self-critical confrontation with the past against the objections of more conservative colleagues and a largely resistant population. Indeed, for many artists, academics, and other intellectuals on the Left, Vergangenheitsbewältigung was becoming a way of life, initially in the 1960s and then especially in the 1980s. As will be discussed in chapter 11, in the decade before unification, these individuals eagerly criticized and debated the politics of memory pursued by the Kohl administration on the occasion of Helmut Kohl's controversial visit to Israel in 1983, the chancellor's plans for national historical museums revealed in the same year, and the public relations debacle of Bitburg in 1985. The question of how West Germany should remember the Nazi period was further pursued during the Historians' Debate between 1986 and 1988 and has concerned many intellectuals ever since.

This picture remains accurate in many ways, but the material analyzed in this chapter suggests that we might have misjudged the attitudes and interests of many Germans who did not actively participate in the intellectual debates. The image of a recalcitrant or disinterested public, an image that played such a prominent role within the intellectual discourse, might need to be amended to include a wider variety of motives and dispositions. In contrast to the assumptions of the intellectuals both on the Right and on the Left, many television viewers approached the Nazi past with considerable curiosity. Especially in the 1980s, the topic was neither a particularly pressing concern to them nor a potentially debilitating legacy of shame—but it piqued their interest. The insights they took away from their viewing experience influenced their relations to their country and their country's past precisely because the programs provided excellent entertainment about a subject that was still of some personal concern. Thus, the ZDF programs provide a window into the more sedate and consensual ways of remembering Nazism that have prevailed in the everyday lives of many Germans but have so frequently been overshadowed by the necessary and productive infighting of the professional memory seekers, who made that consensual remembering possible but often failed to see or appreciate it after the fact.

CHAPTER 8

THE RADICALIZATION OF GERMAN MEMORY
IN THE AGE OF ITS COMMERCIAL REPRODUCTION

Hitler and the Third Reich in the TV Documentaries of Guido Knopp

Since the mid-1990s, the historical documentaries of Guido Knopp have dominated the German airwaves and cable systems. No other type of historical programming, let alone any other type of historical representation, has reached as many citizens and consumers. And no other vision of history has had the same success in shaping Germany's collective memory of the Nazi era at the end of the twentieth century.[1] This outcome is the result of a complicated interaction between market forces, the evolution of modern communication technologies, and the generational dynamics of Germany's historical culture. But at the heart of the Knopp phenomenon are the radical visual aesthetics of a new type of historical documentary crafted by Knopp over the course of ten years and effectively reproduced under his supervision by a small, cohesive, and privileged group of television makers in the ZDF.[2]

The aesthetics of these programs are easily described and criticized. The numerous ZDF documentary miniseries about the Third Reich, which have been released since the early 1990s, rely on an attractive combination of fast cuts, iconic references, dialectics of color and black-and-white footage, dramatic music, an aura of authenticity, and a compelling narrative framework delivered in short, distinguished sound bites. On the visual level, the programs combine eyewitness testimony, original photos and NS footage, blurry simulations of historical events, and short clips of historical sites, often with Knopp's reassuring presence in the foreground. Constant change keeps these different elements in motion and the viewers alert. The eyewitnesses, dramatically illuminated by spotlights, are never allowed to say more than a few sentences at a time; the photos are taped so that they appear like moving images; the original footage, featuring Nazi propaganda highlights, is digitally manipulated whenever the feed is not "up to speed" or when the images are already so familiar to the audience that some alienation devices seem appropriate; the staged historical events are shot with handheld, subjective cameras that deliver unstable images with little informational value but lots of visual appeal. Each of these segments lasts less than a minute; often, a segment lasts only seconds.[3]

The ZDF staff further accentuates the dynamic visual collages through carefully calibrated sound tracks that add sound effects to silent footage, introduce dramatic scores (with a particular partiality to Richard Wagner and Klaus Doldinger), and rely on the sonorous voice of Christian Brückner (the German voice of Robert de Niro) to enact the script.[4] The voice-over as well as Knopp's remarks on the screen seem beyond reproach, since they deliver only politically correct messages. The statements eloquently express the anti-Nazi stance of their authors and impress on the audience a general pacifist worldview and the need for international reconciliation. In addition, the commentary renders explicit one of the visual and conceptual construction principles of the programs and thus ties together the potentially dispersive images. In most cases, the material unfolds along the conventional trajectory of the biography of Adolf Hitler. His actions, crimes, and neuroses—explicated in the commentary—integrate the Nazi footage, the eyewitness testimony, and the play scenes. The films feature two additional key subjects, the war and the Holocaust, but they are always visually and conceptually anchored in Hitler's objectives and obsessions. However, although the commentary links the different components of the programs and introduces one reading of the material, it never controls the semantic possibilities that Knopp's high-speed documentaries entail. In fact, as the new paradigm has taken shape, the discursive level of interpretation has become increasingly detached from the visual text. A very appealing, provocative, and transgressive vision of Nazism has emerged that belies the politically correct messages and opens venues of identification that are engaging, revisionist, and, some critics have charged, even fascist in nature.

It must be appreciated that Knopp is really the first German television maker who has focused directly and extensively on Hitler. In the past, a few important documentary films were made about the Führer, the most important being Erwin Leiser's *Mein Kampf* (My Struggle) and Joachim Fest's *Hitler: Eine Karriere* (Hitler: A Career),[5] but on television, Hitler was both omnipresent and marginal; he appeared in almost all programs about the Nazi past but was very rarely the primary subject of these shows.[6] Since the second half of the 1990s, the Knopp school has explicitly restored Hitler to his position as a central historical agent, for the benefit of generations of Germans who are quite unfamiliar with the historical record.

Even this superficial analysis illustrates that the specific achievements of the documentaries are visual in nature. The juxtaposition of familiar material with novel and surprising images—for instance, color photographs from 1938 or simulated walks through Hitler's bunker—and the acceleration of this mix to breakneck speed offer up an underappreciated feast of television editing. Unlike past productions, the films of the Knopp school are truly visual texts. Until the 1980s, German TV documentaries were primarily discursive constructs, whose producers used visual materials as illustrations or refractions of their intellectual concepts.[7] But even the best compilation, essay, or interview films produced in this tradition quickly became anachronisms with limited audience appeal as the medium evolved into a visually driven communication tool, especially in the context of the commercialization of German television after 1984. Knopp and his associates have taken the important step of bringing the genre of historical documentary up to date by relegating discourse to a secondary position, in which it assists the visual record but does not create its meaning. The resulting complex weave of visual stimuli is clearly appreciated by viewers. In fact, the films have been produced in collaboration with the audience, since Knopp has developed the new paradigm partly in response to consumer feedback.

In contrast to the general audience, many professional and academic critics of Knopp's vision of history fail to understand his innovation. Reviewers have been too critical and too forgiving simultaneously. They might appreciate the politically correct messages of the script or lash out against the intellectually insipid commentaries, but either way, they fail to understand that the script represents a marginal component in the overall design of the programs. In the same vein, critics have condemned the staged simulations of historical events and the digital manipulations of photographs and NS footage as superfluous technical frills and ridiculed Knopp's persistent search for new, unfamiliar visual material, without realizing that these elements are at the core of the new language of history. As a result, the really important questions regarding the semantics of the new visual discourse and its relationship to Nazi culture have rarely been directly addressed. How did the new discourse evolve, and how does the elaborate regimen of signs function on the primary, visual level? What interpretations of Nazism are suggested to the audience, and how do these messages differ from the messages of Nazi visual culture on which the programs rely so heavily?

THE APPRENTICESHIP OF A TELEVISION STAR

Soon after Guido Knopp started working for the ZDF in 1978, he appeared on the screen as the moderator of a TV discussion program, a role he would play frequently in the following decades.[8] In that capacity, he became involved in a high-profile project called *Narben* (Scars), whose production history illustrates the problems German television makers faced when they tried to respond to the media event *Holocaust,* which had taken everybody by surprise in January 1979.[9] Broadcast by the ARD, the ZDF's only competitor in the age of public television's monopoly, the four parts of *Holocaust* reached an average of twelve million viewers in 36 percent of West Germany's television households.[10] The audience response to the U.S. blockbuster made it painfully clear that German television had neither recognized nor satisfied a popular demand for contemporary history. Not surprisingly, the media event caused hectic activity inside the public stations, as television makers tried to get back in touch with their audience. The ZDF project *Narben,* developed in collaboration with Polish television, was one of these attempts at making amends. The docudrama focused on the tumultuous history of Danzig and Gdansk in the twentieth century and approached the topic from the perspective of two real individuals—one Polish, one German—who were born in the city before World War II.[11] Intended to advance the cause of German-Polish reconciliation and provide emotionally compelling, everyday history, the production became the subject of intense internal politics. The budget spiraled out of control, one member of the production team entered contractual agreements with the Polish partners that had not been approved by the station's administration, and the director general of the ZDF, Günter von Hase, personally requested changes in the script, a highly unusual move as he himself acknowledged.[12] In the end, the program proved to be an awkward, slow combination of documentary and docuplay, with little audience appeal. The three-part series only reached a disappointing average of 2.2 million viewers.[13] Despite these shortcomings, however, *Narben* became a modest public relations success because reviewers applauded its political objectives.[14]

Knopp was not directly involved in the design or implementation of *Narben*, but he approached his superiors with the idea of organizing a live TV discussion with prominent guests after the broadcast of the last sequel of *Narben*, for the docudrama would surely raise mixed emotions that should be addressed in an open forum.[15] Von Hase welcomed the initiative and offered some "helpful" suggestions about the composition of the group of discussants. The program was broadcast at 10:30 p.m. on May 17, 1981.[16] The discussion, like the preceding show, prompted a number of anti-Polish phone calls, but it is remarkable that none of the seventy callers personally attacked Knopp, who moderated the exchange on the screen.[17] In the following days, several reviewers acknowledged Knopp's sensitive, intelligent performance as a TV host.[18] By participating in the project, Knopp had the opportunity to pass his first test in the public arena of memory politics, and the experience gave him valuable insights into the organization of international, high-profile memory events. If subsequent developments are any indication, he made the most of that experience.

Knopp came to the ZDF at age thirty after a short career as a newspaper journalist with *Die Welt* and the *Frankfurter Allgemeine Zeitung*. By 1981, he was already the de facto leader of the small ZDF subdivision for programs on contemporary history.[19] In that capacity, he oversaw a low-profile weekly series that featured fifteen-minute interviews with German academics about all kinds of topical concerns, and he helped produce programs on subjects as diverse as the history of German liberalism and nuclear power.[20] Knopp turned to Nazi history and memory only after the broadcast of *Narben* and after a couple of years of television experience.

Throughout the 1980s, Knopp produced a string of fairly conventional documentaries that reflected his fundamental beliefs about the history of National Socialism and only occasionally foreshadowed the more radical formal innovations of the 1990s. From the very beginning, Hitler was the conceptual and visual center of these interventions. Knopp's first full-fledged TV documentaries about the lack and failure of German resistance began with spectacular coverage of the Führer.[21] Subsequent programs went to great lengths to cast the German people in the role of seduced victims of Hitler and his propaganda minister, among them the 1987 documentary about Joseph

Goebbels with the revealing title *Der Verführer* (The Seducer).[22] On that occasion, Knopp and his colleagues paraded a string of Goebbels's associates before the camera, all of whom enthusiastically attested to their former boss's exceptional intellectual powers and manipulative skills. Not surprisingly, the reviewers of the broadcast admonished Knopp for the lack of critical distance and reproached him for his refusal to explore the German people's willing participation in the dialectics of seduction.[23]

The programs of the 1980s attested to Knopp's skill in delineating interpretations of Nazism that were acceptable to large segments of German society, even if that meant projecting an anachronistic, politically correct democratic consensus into the past. For instance, when exploring Hitler's rise to power, the ZDF historians interviewed a range of contemporaries, from labor union activists and Communist Party members to industrialists and military officers, and asked them about the reasons for their failure to prevent Hitler's chancellorship.[24] That nicely balanced pool of eyewitnesses, reflecting the ZDF's permanent search for political equilibrium, gave a number of different answers to that question. The representatives of the Left openly acknowledged their political and strategic mistakes, but the more conservative interviewees seemed a little surprised by such inquiries, since they had helped Hitler gain power in the first place and had harbored no intentions of offering resistance, as least not for many years.[25] In this case, fairly conservative interpretations of Nazism resulted from a sense of fairness, the ideal of *Ausgewogenheit* (political balance) that is dear to any journalist who wants to keep his or her job in public television. On other occasions, Knopp achieved the same effect by simply championing the perspective of the average eyewitness. For this purpose, he even committed a modest infraction when he included detailed testimony about rapes perpetrated by Soviet soldiers in a program on women in postwar Germany.[26] But like other projects dedicated to the history of everyday life, the program proved severely flawed because Knopp highlighted the suffering of German civilians without providing the historical context of the German crimes in the Soviet Union. This specific pitfall of Alltagsgeschichte had already been adamantly discussed by German historians, and some reviewers rejected Knopp's highly selective representation of World War II history.[27]

By the end of the 1980s, Knopp had established himself at the ZDF as a provider of well-researched historical documentaries for late-night audiences.

With few exceptions, his programs were scheduled after 10 p.m., and in that environment, he delivered respectable but not extraordinary audience shares of between 7 percent and 17 percent of television households. The public networks were not yet facing serious commercial competition, and Knopp's ratings, which reflected audiences of between 1.5 and 5.5 million West German viewers, placed him in the mainstream of late-night nonfiction television.[28]

Among more Left-leaning television critics, Knopp had gained a reputation for his routine anniversary productions featuring apologetic interpretations of the Third Reich that demonized Hitler and exculpated his followers.[29] From their perspective, Knopp appeared as a staunch defender and popularizer of the politics of memory advanced by Chancellor Kohl, who launched an aggressive campaign of historical normalization and national revival through museums, memorials, and public rituals after he rose to power in 1982.[30] Because of these political predilections, Knopp seemed a perfect match for the ZDF, which was alleged to have particularly close relations to the new conservative government. Under the circumstances, it was not surprising that Knopp became a central figure in the media festivities during the fortieth anniversary of the Federal Republic in 1989 and the subsequent media celebrations of German unification in 1990.[31] His activism for the cause of German unity pleased his superiors and gained Knopp the Order of Merit of the Federal Republic, but the constitutional patriotism of the anniversary programs as well as the more conventional patriotism of the unification shows elicited little enthusiasm among West German viewers.[32] All programs, including Knopp's, produced mediocre ratings.[33] The lack of audience success might have encouraged Knopp to return to history and shape the popular memory of events that viewers found much more interesting than the "historic" liberation of their eastern brothers and sisters.

The large-scale visual exploration of the history of World War II, which Knopp launched in the 1990s, was planned before unification, and he had already developed ties to Soviet television to gain access to new visual sources. But the disintegration of the Soviet Union made this long-term collaboration much more attractive to the Russian partners. Over the next decade, the television historians of the ZDF pioneered the exploitation of Eastern European film archives, which proved to be gold mines for Western media corporations. Opening this vault allowed Knopp to present his viewers with a seemingly endless supply of new footage of Hitler and the Nazis, but he still faced one serious challenge. There is no indication that Knopp was particularly concerned about the critical reception of his work among intellectuals, who regularly admonished that television in general and Knopp in particular failed to provide the type of accurate, analytically ambitious historical representations they appreciated in the publications of their colleagues in academia.[34] But Knopp's public statements of the time indicate that he shared the assessments of some more supportive critics, who pointed out that German television had not found a recipe for interesting, visually and emotionally compelling historical documentaries that avoided discursive overload and had true mainstream appeal.[35] In the realm of television fiction, *Holocaust, Heimat,* and many other less famous TV plays had shown how the general audience could be integrated into the important task of collective remembrance.[36] But factual documentary television had never followed suit, and a closer look at the aesthetics of Knopp's early programs explains this shortcoming. Despite all his efforts, Knopp still produced illustrated history lectures. The voice-over commentaries—delivered in terse, fairly monotone voices—dominated the productions. The footage of historical sites and eyewitness accounts remained static. The interviewees delivered long-winded, staged testimony that occasionally exposed their shameful past conduct and dubious rationalizations for the few experts in front of the screen but had little appeal for the uninitiated.[37] When Knopp himself appeared on screen, which he did more and more frequently, he sometimes came across as an arrogant lecturer talking down to his audience or, on other occasions, like a student in an oral exam.[38] As a result, the Nazi newsreels remained the most exciting, dynamic component of the programs.

The situation began to change slowly in the late 1980s as Knopp's productions picked up speed and displayed more visual complexity. After these modest innovations, some reviewers were quick to complain about hectic story lines and visual overloads.[39] These reactions reflected the increasing impatience among intellectuals with the lack of analytical depth in Knopp's programs and were hardly representative of the opinion of the general audience. But it is quite likely that the viewers and television executives of the 1980s were also not yet ready for the radical aesthetics and reinterpretations of German history that Knopp was aiming for. Viewers' familiarity with fast-paced, commercial television and executives' fear of competition were preconditions for the development and successful reception of Knopp's later works. In 1988,

this familiarity and fear did not exist because privately owned networks, introduced in 1984, had not yet reached sizable audiences and executives in the
powerful public TV stations had not yet realized the full extent of the coming
threat. By the early 1990s, however, when Knopp achieved his aesthetic and
audience breakthrough, viewers were familiar with the pace and style of commercial television, and administrators had felt the pressure of competition.
Both groups could now appreciate Knopp's attempt to emulate and compete
with that new style of television. Consequently, only the transformation of the
West German television landscape into a dual system of commercial and
public networks created the cultural and political basis for the radicalization
of German memory after unification.[40]

Knopp's early programs featured some of the components of his later successes. In the early 1980s, Knopp added machine-gun sounds to the silent
footage of mass executions, used segments of feature films, and staged historical events (all of which the critics dutifully objected to).[41] But the programs still lacked the total-art-work-effect (*Gesamtkunstwerkeffekt*) based on
the elegant integration of image and sound and, most important, speed and
scale. For instance, Knopp had yet to realize that eyewitness testimony, which
helps to create an aura of authenticity, is best accelerated by "cutting the in-
terviewee to pieces," that is, by using only small sound bites at a time that
correspond exactly to the parallel moving images. All these innovations were
gradually introduced as Knopp focused on the dramatic subject matter of World
War II. During the 1990s, Hitler and his henchmen became the subject of a
sustained, polished, and very successful media campaign that recalibrated
many of the images produced during the original Hitler media campaign of
the 1930s and 1940s.

FINALLY WINNING THE WAR

Knopp used the many historical anniversaries of 1989 to delineate a vague
outline of his goals as a documentary filmmaker.[42] But his public commitment to suspenseful, biographically structured programs revealed very little
about his concrete media strategies and certainly did not capture the interesting aesthetic innovations that would be developed in the ZDF in the coming
years. In addition, the first sequels of Knopp's long World War II epic, *Die
Saat des Krieges* (The Seed of War), broadcast in the same year, still reflected

conventional historiographical ambition and, as a consequence, were not very compelling as visual documents.[43] The first part reconstructed in great detail the diplomatic intrigues before and during the Munich Treaty. The viewer was quickly lost in a maze of names and locations, strung together by a complicated, long-winded commentary with few visual highlights. The handful of visual gimmicks appeared completely out of place. Viewers saw blurry figures behind glass doors engaged in hectic negotiations in Czech that were conveniently summarized by the voice-over comment; a ghostlike, faceless Hitler planning military mischief; and an unintentionally comic Guido Knopp in front of the historic conference hotel pretending that Neville Chamberlain and Adolf Hitler were just behind those walls and could walk out any second. Stretching his talents as an actor, Knopp showed considerable commitment to the cause of filmmaking but little ingenuity as a filmmaker.[44]

That changed when *Der verdammte Krieg* (That Damned War) began in 1991 and the attack on the Soviet Union was jointly reenacted by the ZDF and Gosteleradio, a Russian TV station in Moscow.[45] Providing most of the funds, the German station was the dominant force of the production, and the final cut was determined in Mainz, not in Moscow.[46] Nevertheless, the public relations officers of the ZDF emphasized the themes of partnership and reconciliation and announced the project with great pathos and hyperbole. The series, they said, dealt with "the biggest battle in world history . . . which stood for many decades like an ocean of blood and tears between Russians and Germans."[47] But now, after fifty years, the pathbreaking collaboration would bring the one, indivisible truth and the message of peace and reconciliation to the viewers "between Aachen and Görlitz, between Brest and Wladiwostok."[48] The geographic ambition and pride, vaguely reminiscent of Hitler's obsession with colonial empires in the East, illustrated the uneasy combination of pacifist intentions and militaristic jargon that characterized the whole series.[49] As the language slipped from its peaceful moorings and began to celebrate the German Sixth Army (which "accomplishes its handiwork with deadly precision"), the images enacted an epic struggle that made it difficult for the German viewers not to root for "their team" as it faced extraordinary obstacles in the depth of the Russian steppe.[50]

Befitting such an exceptional competition, the coverage began with profiles of the cranky team chefs, Hitler and Stalin, and analyses of the lineup. The subsequent clash of the titans was cast in the simple, compelling, and balanced aesthetics of a sports event as German men advanced swiftly on the screen, preferably from left to right, and were met by equally determined Soviet troops, including Cossacks on horseback flying from right to left. In the "brutal, dirty war on both sides," the men served with great courage and suffered from the inhumane conditions and the destructive orders of their dictators and generals, as selected eyewitnesses confirmed repeatedly.[51] In some respects, the Germans were more brutal, but their exceptionally vicious crimes were perpetrated against bystanders of the war and therefore not of much concern for the filmmakers (or, presumably, their audience).[52] In the meantime, like cheerleaders, women were portrayed eagerly supporting the war efforts in the armament industries at home. Finally, as with all good sports events, the competition was decided by chance. An untimely uprising in Yugoslavia, the early onset of winter with all its mud and snow, betrayal by spies, and the repeated irrational decisions of the Führer sealed the fate of the German team. For the German viewers, this approach set in motion a string of attractive counterfactual questions: what if the attack had been earlier, the winter later, or the Führer brighter? These questions and their answers, clearly implied by the films, exposed the not so hidden emotional point of gravity of the whole undertaking.[53] The "we" in "we would have won" was right below the attractive visual surface and even more powerful because that affirmative pronoun in relation to World War II had no place in the official culture of the Federal Republic. Occasionally, that "we" even sneaked in through the back door, for instance, when Knopp turned to his Russian counterpart with the great line, "All the sacrifices did not count for our dictator. What about yours?"[54]

This ironic summary captures the intellectual contents of the series, but the simplistic emplotment was delivered with an exceptional wealth of finely tuned images. The subject matter and the international cooperation suggested the overall binary plot structure of the series, made possible by stunning visual material, especially from the Soviet archives. Rare color footage of the war reduced the distance between past and present and drew viewers into the events; engaging eyewitness testimony, from survivors who enjoyed returning to their sites of memory, highlighted the courage and resilience of the average soldier; dynamic black-and-white battle scenes attested to the awesome scale of the war; and the propaganda shots of the dictators reminded the viewer, like the contemporaries, just who was pulling the strings. The images

and the contrasting rhythmic editing drove the narrative, set up the epic competition, and defined the emotional stakes.

For the first time in Knopp's career as a television maker, the language of
the script, however revealing it may have been, became subservient to a very
attractive, transgressive visual text. Knopp and his associates might not have
been aware of their accomplishments—which made it easier for them to
continue to attach simple, politically correct messages to far more ambivalent, provocative productions. But when they reworked the intrinsically dramatic events of World War II with access to great material and within the
context of an international collaboration, they produced a new aesthetics for
historical documentaries. Like *Heimat* in the realm of fiction, the new paradigm was an appropriate German answer to *Holocaust* because it provided an
honest reflection of German collective memory. It was also a fitting answer
because *Der verdammte Krieg*, like *Holocaust* before, came into existence in
a commercially charged environment, which encouraged television makers
to take political risks and test the limits of historical taste. Only a few intellectual observers clearly perceived the change, and even fewer were able to
put them into words. Focusing on the explicit political and historical messages of the production, they took issue with the tiresome political correctness, the overemphasis on questions of military strategy, and the fast and
suspense-driven plot structure.[55] Occasionally, the critics went even further
and argued that *Der verdammte Krieg* simply reinforced the visual and discursive codes of Nazi propaganda, resurrected the pathos of the frontline experience, and obliterated the question of German guilt.[56] But they often
missed the real subject and achievements of the films. Knopp's documentaries had nothing to do with historical analysis, least of all historiographical
analysis, and dealt instead with honor, fate, myth, heroism, and, most important, repressed German military pride. As a sophisticated collage, *Der verdammte Krieg* did not simply mirror Nazi aesthetics and propaganda. Rather,
Knopp and his colleagues translated the topics of Nazi discourse into the visual
and political languages of the late twentieth century and presented a highly
ambivalent, suspenseful film driven by its own internal contradictions, especially between its explicit political message and its aesthetic revisionism. That
made for good entertainment for Knopp's audiences precisely because the
programs were not direct reflections of Nazism but fragmented and fractured
visions of the past that offered viewers the exceptional pleasure of remaining

within the political consensus of the German democratic mainstream while playfully exploring the perspectives of the former perpetrators in a collective setting.

The ratings of *Der verdammte Krieg* look solid but unspectacular until one takes into consideration the rapidly changing television landscape in Germany in the 1990s. The first six sequels in June 1991 reached an average of 4.2 million viewers; the second installment of five programs in January 1993, focusing on Stalingrad, was watched by 4.6 million; and the final six episodes between March and April 1995, covering the events until the end of the war, still attracted 3.8 million viewers.[57] Considering that the ZDF's overall market shares had dropped from 25.4 percent to 14.7 percent during the same period as result of commercial competition, the ratings represent an extraordinary success.[58]

The ratings indicate that many audience members considered *Der verdammte Krieg* the most interesting—or the least objectionable—program available at that point in time, but the viewers' involvement in the story on the screen could still fall anywhere within the wide spectrum between curious indifference and intense participation.[59] However, there are good reasons to assume that the latter was more likely than the former because an unusually large number of consumers of Knopp TV tended to engage in an active process of communication with the station during and after the broadcast of the shows through mail, telephone, and, more recently, E-mail. The numbers of letters and phone calls were very small relative to the total audience, and their content was hardly representative, but viewers of Knopp documentaries were more likely to contact the station than viewers of other programs on the topic of Nazism.[60]

In response to *Der verdammte Krieg*, the ZDF received a number of anti-Semitic and anti-Russian phone calls much like those that accompanied many programs on the subject matter.[61] In addition and more to the point, reactions to *Der verdammte Krieg* indicated that the audience appreciated the liberating, revisionist implications of its aesthetics and perceived (and suggested remedies for) the obvious contradiction between the visual language and the voice-over commentaries. For this purpose, many viewers picked up the phone or wrote letters recommending that Knopp look into the theory that the attack on the Soviet Union was a preventive strike. The repeated references to this standard myth of revisionist, nationalistic circles in thirty out of a total of eighty letters implies that the authors expected sympathy for these ideas among the television makers and that, in their eyes, an explicit acknowledgment of these themes would bring the commentary in line with the show's appealing aesthetics.[62] Viewers' interests and interpretations also became embarrassingly obvious during the TV discussion at the end of the series when callers were permitted to pose their questions live on the air. Instead of joining in the celebration of reconciliation, they bickered with the experts in the studio about the precise number of victims on the eastern front and insisted on the defensive nature of the campaign.[63] Knopp certainly did not create these attitudes, but, intentionally or inadvertently, he invited the post factum identification with the perspective of the German military that was reflected in these reactions from the audience.

HISTORICIZING HITLER

Taking the risk of producing expensive, high-profile, international documentary miniseries, rarely tried before, had paid off handsomely for the station and Knopp in times of tough competition with private networks. In a culture saturated with memory products in the form of memorials, museum exhibits, popular history books, newspaper coverage, and anniversary programs, Knopp made his mark at a moment when the public stations were generally losing ground because they could no longer afford the expensive investment in Vergangenheitsbewältigung that ARD and ZDF had pursued in the 1960s and especially the 1980s. Having taken the decisive step of developing real documentary television history (as opposed to what we might call distant-learning history lessons), Knopp could now use and fine-tune the recipe with other, related subjects. The first target, already the implicit center of so many earlier programs, was Hitler himself. In 1989, commenting on Hitler's hundredth birthday, Knopp had argued that the private life of the Führer was trivial and that any concentration on Hitler's personal life smacked of a personality cult. Consequently, the ZDF would not waste any airtime on the criminal.[64] Given the many ZDF documentaries that had featured Hitler, this was an astonishing statement even in 1989, but by 1995, in light of new production and commercial opportunities, Knopp had clearly reversed his opinion. His new six-part series *Hitler: Eine Bilanz* (Hitler: A Reckoning) dedicated forty-five prime-time minutes to Hitler's private life, followed by in-depth coverage of his propaganda accomplishments, his foreign and interior policies, his military leadership, and his career as a mass murderer.[65]

Knopp pursued ambitious goals with the new series. In his assessment, Germans were held hostage by their history, which handicapped them in a number of ways—by preventing them from supporting highly gifted students, discussing euthanasia in a calm fashion, and embracing gene technology without inhibitions, for example. Knopp wanted to liberate Germans from this burden by confronting Hitler's legacy directly because, in his opinion, nobody needed to be afraid of the Führer five decades after his death; as he put it, "The best weapon against Hitler-nostalgia is Hitler himself."[66] But even in the carefully edited text, which Knopp published to mark the media event *Hitler: Eine Bilanz,* the burden of the past became synonymous with nostalgia for the Führer, and fear turned into fascination. As a result, Knopp defined the purpose of his historicization campaign with peculiar ambivalence: "When we can say without inhibitions: Beethoven and Goethe were Germans, but Hitler was too—then we are on the right path."[67]

The early production *Der verdammte Krieg* was structured as an epic contest between two dictators and their countries, and that structure provided an excellent visual rhythm to the series. Agency was limited to the two leaders and the war itself, which emerged as a faceless, powerful force in its own right. For the new Hitler documentaries, Knopp and his associates invented a less obvious but similarly compelling visual structure that repeated and radicalized their interpretation of the Hitler phenomenon. The usual collage of eyewitness accounts, propaganda footage, and play scenes was divided into semantic units through Hitler close-ups and Hitler quotes, each accompanied by loud, high-pitched, monotonous sounds. Firmly established in the center of the programs, Hitler represented the only real historical agent, since all other people either deferred to his authority or responded to his challenges. Each of the six sequels of *Hitler: Eine Bilanz,* as well as many subsequent ZDF documentaries, followed the same blueprint; they presented in endless variations the one-sided, uneven relationships between Hitler and his people, Hitler and his henchmen, Hitler and his generals, and Hitler and his foreign opponents. The programs thus simply depicted what Knopp had believed all along and what he expressed very succinctly before the broadcast: "Without Hitler the Third Reich would have disappeared like a bad dream."[68]

Hitler: Eine Bilanz became a stunning ratings success. Although all but one of the six parts were aired after 10 p.m., the series still reached an average of 5 million viewers, which corresponded to 11 percent of all television households and 22 percent of all television viewers at the time of broadcast.[69] As before, the audience engaged very actively with the series. In over eight hundred phone calls, especially during the obligatory final TV discussion, the viewers expressed a wide range of complaints.[70] In addition to some anti-Semitic and anti-Turkish slurs, the audience objected to the program's anti-German tendencies, the abuse of Wagner's music, and the selection of eyewitnesses.[71] But viewers were most irate about the fact that they were unable to reach the station during the final discussion and could not intervene in the debate.[72] The ZDF had arranged for a special phone number and permitted a few lucky audience members to pose their questions live on the air, but apparently, neither the station nor the phone company was prepared for such a high volume of calls.

In contrast to the audience, the critics seemed unprepared for the media event *Hitler.* Though some reviewers magnanimously welcomed the use of cutting-edge digital technology and admitted that programs on Hitler could be entertaining, they invariably admonished the lack of historical context and explanation and dutifully, yet helplessly, pointed out that the demonization of Hitler obliterated German guilt.[73] These observations, neither new nor inaccurate, failed to grasp the specific achievement of the series. After acknowledging and even valorizing the suffering and achievements of the German military and civilians during and after the war, Knopp had finally resurrected the contemporary perception of Hitler himself and translated that image into the visual language of the late twentieth century.[74] The series captured the awe-inspiring combination of power and performance not by way of an explanation (for instance, through Weber's concept of charismatic leadership) but by way of a reinactment or a simulation: a stylized, seamless, empathetic, emotionally compelling ride without distance or irony; the flimsy safety belt of an anti-Nazi discourse only added to the thrill because it underscored the pretense that the ride was really dangerous.

THE TOTAL KNOPP

After all these successes, ZDF's executives authorized more docuseries on such diverse topics as the history of espionage, the Vatican, turning points in twentieth-century German history, and especially the Third Reich.[75] Not a year has gone by without another prominent Knopp product and another opportunity for Hitler to enthrall his people from his (nonexistent) grave. To serve that purpose more effectively, Knopp's unit for contemporary history was elevated in the ZDF administrative hierarchy, and in one of the biggest achievements, the programs from the Knopp factory were, for the first time, scheduled in prime time starting in 1997.[76] All this generosity is easily explained. Ratings and public relations interests figure prominently in the making of the Knopp phenomenon, but revenue has played the decisive role. Since ZDF Enterprises, the commercial subsidiary of the public station ZDF, has been very successful in selling the series in foreign markets (in some cases, to more than forty countries), the fairly small subdivision of contemporary history, with a full-time editorial staff of nine associates, is one of the ZDF's premier cash cows.[77] In addition, Knopp's rise to national prominence reflects the German networks' explicit strategy of creating and relying on a few television stars to define their public image and safeguard their market shares in the dual system. Since the public stations long ago lost the bidding war for German TV stars such as Thomas Gottschalk and Harald Schmidt, they have to content themselves with turning lesser stars such as Guido Knopp into brand-name products.[78] In the process, Knopp himself has become a multimedia sensation. His superiors have come to love him as much as his editors at Bertelsmann because the many books that have accompanied the many series, boosted by free advertisement on the ZDF screen, have regularly been ranked on Germany's nonfiction best-seller lists.[79] As long as these strategies work—as long as Knopp manages to sell his products all over the globe and remains an affordable and popular public television star—no German viewer will have to be without the next Knopp production.

After *Hitler: Eine Bilanz,* Knopp delivered another blockbuster with *Hitlers Helfer* (Hitler's Henchmen). The first six episodes, aired in January and February 1997, dealt with Rudolf Hess, Heinrich Himmler, Joseph Goebbels, Hermann Göring, Albert Speer, and Karl Dönitz.[80] Provided with prime-time opportunities, Knopp pulled out all the stops. *Hitlers Helfer* and the subsequent *Hitlers Krieger* (Hitler's Warriors), which presented biographies of Hitler's top generals, were exceptionally well-crafted programs.[81] The cut was even faster, the images more seductive, and the score more dramatic. As Knopp made crystal clear in an interview before the broadcast, prime time was no place to be analytical or offer background information: "We have to appeal to the audience directly and visually."[82] The first six episodes of *Hitlers Helfer* attracted almost seven million viewers every night and have remained Knopp's most successful television programs to date.[83]

The show on Erwin Rommel, the first sequel of *Hitlers Krieger*, illustrated how specific assessments and interpretations could be expressed through cutting techniques that seemed to create an innocent, pluralistic collage of diverging points of view.[84] About one-third of the way through the documentary, Rommel's military exploits in North Africa became the subject of an invented dialogue between a range of eyewitnesses who had never seen each other face to face but had been elegantly pitched against each other on the cutting tables of the ZDF. Having been informed by the voice-over that Rommel's troops took more prisoners but also sustained more casualties than any other units and that the general had therefore been criticized as an ambitious and reckless daredevil (*karrieresüchtiger Hazardeur*) by his superiors, the viewer met the first eyewitness, a German veteran, who confirmed Rommel's reckless and selfish behavior as a commander.[85] Without any further elaboration from the commentator, the next eyewitness, another German veteran of the Africa campaign, contradicted the first vehemently, maintaining that Rommel always put the well-being and safety of his troops first. At this point of impasse in the imagined dialogue, Knopp introduced testimony of superior credibility. A jovial British veteran attested that Rommel treated his own troops, as well as his opponents, with honor and integrity and that he was one hell of a general. This statement clinched the case. If even his former enemies confirmed the general's moral rectitude, the jealous superiors and disgruntled inferiors had to be mistaken or, worse, intentionally lying. The film included further snippets of critical testimony by Jewish survivors (so identified by captions) who feared for Palestine and considered all soldiers in Hitler's services criminals.[86] The viewer might have forgiven this "subjective," "special-interest" testimony in particular, since he or she learned that Rommel had shown great courage in the negotiations with his superiors and was deeply disturbed by illicit news about the "Final Solution." Sadly, a former assistant remarked, Rommel never again showed the enthusiasm and drive he had displayed in North Africa, although he tried his best when the Allies landed in Normandy. In the conclusion, the documentary staged and mourned the suicide of a German military genius in sepia colors and permitted his son, Manfred Rommel, the former mayor of Stuttgart, to ponder if he himself was a better human being than his father and if he would not have done the same.[87] An idol was reborn.

A number of reviewers perceived *Hitlers Helfer* as Knopp's answer to Daniel Goldhagen, assuming that Knopp was prompted by Goldhagen's focus on popular German anti-Semitism to retell the more conventional story about the Nazi leaders' colonial and anti-Semitic obsessions.[88] Although it is very likely that Knopp seized the opportunity and sailed on the coattails of a media event that he had helped put on stage, it is also clear that the momentum generated by the success of *Hitler: Eine Bilanz* would have brought him to Hitler's henchmen with or without Goldhagen.[89] For his stories to work, Knopp needed a clear biographical focus and a factual or imagined connection to Hitler. Therefore, his search for new subject matter made him realize that Germans other than Hitler shared responsibility for the catastrophe of Nazism. But in contrast to Goldhagen, Knopp resisted the radical move of indicting the whole German people because that interpretation went against his perception of German history, might have alienated his audience, and, most important, did not fit the conceptual and aesthetic framework that had proven so successful in his prior work. For all these reasons, the project *Hitlers Volk* (Hitler's People) that Knopp has contemplated for some years has not yet materialized.[90]

Many programs of the series *Hitlers Helfer* and *Hitlers Krieger* turned out to be the single most successful program of the evening in which they were shown in Germany, which is an exceptional accomplishment for a historical TV documentary. In an age of rapidly diversifying television offerings and fragmented audiences, Knopp's documentaries provided a common reference point for many viewers.[91] This phenomenon was part of a larger trend that Knopp might have helped create but that went far beyond the confines of the ZDF's Division of Contemporary History in Mainz. After a decade of the cheap television fiction that followed the introduction of commercial television, German viewers turned to nonfiction and especially historical nonfiction in the mid-1990s. TV executives were pleasantly surprised by this development because even a well-made documentary costs about 60 percent less than the average TV play.[92] As before, Knopp proved to be in the right place at the right time. For many years, he had developed the new type of infotainment that the ZDF could now produce very quickly to satisfy and profit from the surprising audience demand.[93] Therefore, after years in a niche market, Knopp received unprecedented airtime and broadcast opportunities in prime time.

As often happens, the historians and self-proclaimed intellectuals among the journalists came out in full force as the Knopp show had passed its peak. They only reacted after the second installment of *Hitlers Helfer* was aired in April and May 1998, perhaps because these programs featured Josef Mengele and Adolf Eichmann, and the feuilleton was not willing to have the Holocaust debased on public television. The *Süddeutsche Zeitung* in Munich objected that Knopp's programs were just too much fun to watch (too much fun-compatability, i.e., *Spasskompatibilität*), and even the *Frankfurter Allgemeine Zeitung*, certainly positively inclined toward Knopp, complained about "the enthusiasm for evil" that allegedly emanated from his work.[94] None of the critiques was particularly original, for reviewers had noted the same reservations for several years, but a media conference in Cologne in June 1998 offered a rare showdown between the historians of the ZDF and their professorial colleagues. Historian Ulrich Herbert emerged as the most outspoken critic when he claimed that the ZDF produced "Nazi kitsch" and that the adaptation of the visual language of the Third Reich had turned the ZDF from a champion of education and enlightenment into a protagonist of Nazi aesthetics.[95] Not all historians shared this point of view. Knopp and his associates found important defenders, including Simon Wiesenthal, who had been a frequently interviewed for ZDF's productions, and Eberhard Jäckel, who had offered professional advice for many of Knopp's programs.[96]

In 1998, after the broadcast of *Hitlers Krieger,* one reviewer prematurely counted his blessings when he remarked, "What good luck that Hitler was not successful with women, otherwise Knopp would present us with *Hitlers Frauen.*"[97] As it turns out, that has already happened; the ZDF aired *Hitlers Frauen* (Hitler's Women) in April and May 2001, one year after the broadcast of *Hitlers Kinder* (Hitler's Children). The former consisted of an ill-matched string of TV biographies of Eva Braun, Magda Goebbels, Winifried Wagner, Zarah Leander, and, most incongruently, Marlene Dietrich, and the latter presented another lamentation of the loss of a whole generation to Hitler's and Goebbel's seductive powers.[98] In addition, Knopp had his associates revisit World War II on a global scale in *Der Jahrhundertkrieg* (The War of the Century), produced together with the History Channel,[99] and he reached one of the implicit destinations of his whole television career when he remembered the suffering of the German refugees and expellees in *Die grosse Flucht* (The Great Escape).[100] At this stage of the evolution of German memory, such one-sided mourning about German suffering hardly raised any eyebrows. After Martin Walser's indictment of Germany's self-critical memory industry in 1998,[101] followed by Grass's recovery of his childhood trauma in *Im Krebsgang* (Crabwalk) in 2002,[102] Knopp found himself in the company of esteemed fellow travelers who are not known for their high regard for popular taste and the dictates of the marketplace. But Knopp faces another problem—he is simply running out of suitable topics and is losing his audience.[103] Throughout his career, he has experimented with subject matters other than Nazism. But his programs on the history of the Federal Republic, the power of the popes, and the biggest political scandals and espionage cases of the twentieth century have never had the same impact as those on Hitler and the Third Reich. Only Nazism has provided Knopp with an opportunity to be a taboo breaker, to present to his viewers an appealing combination of fascist and postmodern aesthetics for the alleged purpose of political education. No other topics have offered such interesting, suspenseful inconsistencies for Knopp and his audience. Knopp will likely remain the butt of many jokes about his exceptional historical staying power (*Durchhaltewillen*) and his willingness to approach the Nazi topic from any possible and impossible angle. Commentators have ironically suggested that it is just a question of time until Knopp comes forward with a production about Hitler's dogs since he has already exhausted every other possible combination, from *Hitler's Warriors* to *Hitler's Children*.[104] Even in this respect, however, Knopp has been an involuntary trendsetter. It has only been a few years since German comedians first dared to make fun of Hitler and include the Third Reich in their comedy routines.[105] At least this Hitler wave, unlike its precursor of 1977, has been entertaining and educational.[106] To a large extent, that is Guido Knopp's achievement and legacy.

The fascination with the Nazi past has continued in the new century. Many media outlets, including television, marked the sixtieth anniversary of the end of World War II with extensive historical coverage. In fact, in 2005 Hitler was more present in Germany's public sphere than ever before, and the commercialization of the Führer works.[107] There are always enough viewers for the latest Knopp documentary and enough buyers for yet another book about

Hitler's alleged homosexuality.[108] Nazi history is such a well-established genre of popular entertainment that the historical fast-food products will survive the death of the last contemporary of the Third Reich. But the authors and film producers who followed in Knopp's footsteps have to compete vigorously for market shares by promising ever-more-outlandish and sensational revelations about Hitler's life and death.[109] The mass media formats and stories about the Nazi past that were invented in the 1960s, popularized in the 1980s, and commercialized in the 1990s will have to be reinvented to attract future German consumers who will no longer know anybody who lived in the Third Reich.

HISTORICAL PORNOGRAPHY

On first sight, Knopp's vision of Nazism seems to represent a perfect illustration for Susan Sontag's 1980 critique of the culture of "fascinating fascism" and Saul Friedlander's contemporaneous concerns about the combustible mixture of kitsch and death in postwar representations of Nazism.[110] But Sontag's and Friedlander's moralistic indictments of the historical culture of the 1970s implicitly claim to have understood the social and political dynamics of Nazi culture. Their criticism is based on the conviction that the texts they analyzed—including films, photographs, and novels—duplicate Nazi culture in essential respects and therefore also duplicate the political risks inherent in Nazi culture. From my perspective, many of these concerns and the underlying political certainties and connections appear problematic. On a technical and formal level, many of the strategies of representation invented or perfected in the Third Reich have been employed by the postwar culture industry without any obvious fascist political repercussions. In addition, in their concern for elite culture, Sontag and Friedlander fail to acknowledge that many of the texts in question had limited mass appeal and therefore bore few political risks. However, even if the moral/political gesture of their interventions might be less compelling today, some of their insights help us understand the specificity of the innovation introduced by Knopp, whose own perceptions of Nazism were very likely decisively influenced by the visual culture of the 1970s and its representations of the Third Reich.

Like the texts that Sontag and Friedlander analyzed, Knopp's documentaries express a thinly veiled fascination with violence, subjugation, and death, and they lack intellectual self-reflexivity. Knopp is the antithesis of a film-maker who would invite his viewers to contemplate the specific gaps and biases in his vision of Nazism or intentionally complicate his interpretations of the past to the point of interpretive instability. In this sense, because of his subject matter and his aesthetic approach, Knopp appeals to what Sontag called the fascist desires within us and what Friedlander identified as the attractive combination of harmony and power, which characterized Nazism as well as its postwar reflections.[111] Knopp's specific, daring innovation consists of crafting documentaries for the most important medium of communication that explore the official limits of historical taste by inviting viewers' temporary identification with the Nazi perpetrators. As an ingenious mixture of historical pornography and historical education, Knopp's TV encourages viewers to join the historical actors and eyewitnesses, adore the Führer, and fight the battle on the eastern front. The visual stream—especially the simulations that have no other function—creates a slick projective surface that allows the audience to become Nazi, while that pleasure is, at the same time, rendered illegal and even more interesting through the superficial yet efficient commentary that directly contradicts the visual language. In the past, the pornographic pleasure of becoming Nazi was primarily the result of the contradiction between particular subcultural representations of Nazism and the official memory culture of the Federal Republic.[112] Now, for the first time, the contradictory messages are assembled within one seemingly endless stream of documentaries for generations of Germans who might not have internalized the representational taboos and can only experience and appreciate the pleasures of transgression if they receive the rules as well as their violations in the same media package. The illicit pleasures that Knopp's TV provides on a regular basis also explains why *Holokaust* turned out to be a critical success but an audience flop, as discussed in chapter 6. *Holokaust* only reached an average market share of 8.1 percent because even in the year 2000, a German television program on the "Final Solution" was not likely to offer the kind of transgressive pleasures that *Hitler* and *Hitlers Helfer* had presented.[113] Viewers knew that nobody, not even Guido Knopp, was likely to use the theme of the Holocaust to create an ambivalent exploration of Nazi aesthetics and Nazi power.

At this stage of the evolution of German collective memory, the seductive contradictions of Knopp's TV programs can only be produced in documentaries, not in TV fiction. It would still be impossible to have Nazis as heroes in conventional television plays, where discursive and visual levels create a harmonious narrative universe. Only the fractious, multidimensional surface of this new type of documentary, tolerated as a result of the visual illiteracy of critics and supervisors, creates the indeterminate imaginary spaces that pro-grammers call anti-Nazi education but that many consumers might use to play Nazis themselves. Also, it is easier and cheaper to attain a historical au-thenticity effect in documentaries than in fiction. Here, in a specific environ-ment, viewers produce "authentic" German memories and playfully retain the roles of perpetrators that have been so carefully edited out of all German historical culture until recently.

On one occasion, the production of a successful documentary marking the fiftieth anniversary of the 1936 Olympic Games, Knopp had reason to look closely at one of the best and most visually compelling and complex propa-ganda films ever produced—Leni Riefenstahl's *Olympia*.[114] Knopp's film, which contained extensive quotes from *Olympia*, gave no indication that he was aware of the interesting parallels between his own and Riefenstahl's efforts, but it is likely that he realized the attractive structure of the Nazi footage in his repeated search for suitable material. Like Riefenstahl, he tried to tell dramatic factual stories of competition, triumph, and defeat and exploit all the visual means at his disposal to make these stories attractive to the largest possible audience without highlighting the biases and construction principles of the stories. In addition, as in the case of Riefenstahl, Knopp's specific innovations were developed at the cutting table. Despite these paral-lels, it would be anachronistic to call Knopp a fascist, since he operates in a completely different historical context with very different political objectives in mind. But the visual language he has developed to reach his objectives has more in common with the visual language of Nazi culture than with the vi-sual structures of modern documentary classics such as Alain Resnais's *Night and Fog*, Marcel Ophüls's *The Sorrow and the Pity*, Hans-Jürgen Syberberg's *Hitler, a Film from Germany*, or Claude Lanzmann's *Shoah*.[115] Or, put differ-ently, mainstream television, as a means of communication and a political tool, has more in common with the films of Goebbels than these self-reflexive auteur documentaries, even if one of the auteurs in question (Syderberg) en-tertains reactionary, even anti-Semitic opinions.[116] That explains why so many postwar German filmmakers have tried to avoid and undercut the conventions of mainstream visual culture, especially but not only in their representations of German history.[117]

Like many media events of our time, Knopp's TV productions are the result of a careful adaptation and manipulation of the audience's taste for commercial purposes.[118] Knopp shares this pursuit of the consumer with many past and present media experts, including Goebbels.[119] Like the former propaganda minister and many postwar television makers, he mixes entertainment with the politically correct messages of the day. But unlike Goebbels, he faces a more sophisticated audience—or so we hope. Viewers might enjoy the titillating fiction of Hitler's limitless power and the tragedy of the rise and fall of his political genius in the course of their evening entertainment. However, on the morning after, their political identities and decisions are probably as dangerous or as harmless as they were before their visit to Knopp's Hitlerland.

Since the majority of Knopp viewers are over fifty years of age, it is likely that they enjoy a new perspective on a historical topic that has created lots of discussion in their lifetime and that some of them have experienced personally.[120] The programs allow them to revisit, reorganize, and reinvent their own memories, but they are not likely to change their current political identities. For this segment of the audience, the consumption of Knopp's documentaries might even have some exceptionally positive effects. As veteran consumers of the West German media, they experienced the revolution of mainstream historical representations in the 1980s, when public television brought a wide range of programs into the living rooms of Germans who thus remembered the Holocaust and might have felt sympathy for the survivors (as described in chapter 6). At that stage, despite all the efforts involving moral and cultural reparations, German mainstream culture had very little to say about the perpetrators and bystanders of the "Final Solution." It was only after Goldhagen, Knopp's television, and the Wehrmachtsexhibit, which exposed the crimes of the German military to the general public, that one could look back at a sustained interest in the perpetrators, the most challenging legacy of the Holocaust. Considering these different layers in the media consumption of older generations of West Germans, it is very possible that the audience's temporary identification with the perspective of the Nazi leaders and soldiers—in light of an earlier identification with the survivors of the Holocaust—might lead to more self-critical interpretations of

Nazism than Knopp's at times infuriatingly one-sided, apologetic representations indicate.

Ironically, however, the effects of Knopp's work might not be so productive
or harmless for the minority of youthful viewers he is particularly proud to
count among his audience, for these individuals have not experienced the
most self-critical phase of German collective memory in the 1980s.[121] Unless
they have encountered more self-reflexive approaches to the burden of the
past in their schools and families, which is unlikely at least for a substantial
part of unified Germany, they might not have at their disposal information
and interpretations that help them counterbalance Knopp's rather one-sided
celebration of Nazi power. For lack of interesting political and aesthetic alternatives, they might not return from their temporary identification with the
ordinary soldiers and the political elite of the Third Reich as easily as their
older compatriots do.

This thought experiment shows that having Knopp's TV productions without a didactic counterweight is a frightening idea and that the real challenge
for German television makers has not yet been met. It should be possible to
craft attractive mainstream representations of Nazi history that invite
identification with the perpetrators and bystanders of the "Final Solution" but
also, within the same program, offer equally attractive and suspenseful critical perspectives on their decisions and actions. These opposing perspectives
have to be developed discursively and visually (and not just discursively, as in
the case of Knopp's TV) in order to create tensions and ruptures in the
process of identification that cause at least a minimum of unease and reflection.[122] In addition—and this is the real challenge—all of this would have to
be accomplished without undermining the purpose of entertainment, which
is the primary condition for mainstream appeal. Very few popular representations of Nazi history released in the German context have ever come close
to this theoretical ideal, and one of these exceptions was *Holocaust*. After all,
Holocaust offered the families Weiss and Dorf as possible objects of projection and provided a suspenseful, entertaining, and moderately contradictory
perspective on the "Final Solution."[123]

This challenge will most likely not be tackled by Knopp, who appears to be
a fairly naive executor of a new historical paradigm of representation. He has
taken advantage of the political and aesthetic opportunities that the commercialization of German television and German unification offered to people in

his position, and very few have used those opportunities as efficiently and successfully. He established historical pornography as a new documentary genre when Germany's public television networks tried desperately to thwart competition from commercial networks, which had broken all rules of good taste since their introduction in the mid-1980s, including, among other things, through the screening of real pornography.

PART FOUR

POLITICS

HIGH POLITICS AND
COMMUNICATIVE MEMORY

Collective Guilt Management in the Adenauer Era

People with political aspirations faced an unpredictable situation in postwar Germany. They had to craft a new power structure with the help of Allied administrators, voters, colleagues, and civil servants who all pursued different interests: The Allies had understandable reservations about Germany's political elite and were themselves subject to pressure from international partners and competitors in a rapidly changing global environment. The voters had just proven their utter political unreliability—at least in the minds of most candidates for public office. The colleagues gave cause for considerable apprehension because nobody was sure how past mistakes would be assessed in the new political arena. Finally, the civil servants had dutifully and often enthusiastically served the Nazi regime, and their loyalty to the new leaders remained to be determined.[1]

These challenges were more than offset by the exceptional opportunities that the postwar conditions offered to a very specific segment of Germany's political establishment. In the West, reconstruction became the opportunity of a lifetime for the old and the second tier among the representatives of Weimar's bourgeois parties. With active Nazis and most of their outspoken critics excluded from the competition—the latter because they had been murdered or preferred to stay in exile—the development in the western zones of occupation retroactively validated the opportunism of the so-called inner emigration.[2] Notwithstanding some important exceptions, the typical officeholders in postwar West Germany had learned the business of democracy during the Weimar Republic and avoided the carnage of the front because of their relatively advanced age. In addition, they had kept a low profile during the Third Reich and displayed just the right amount of opportunism to stay alive.

For lack of alternatives, these individuals with a proven track record of political self-preservation were called on to develop a democratic system for a West German population that largely consisted of opportunists with similar skills. This rare affinity between political base and political superstructure helps explain the surprising success of the West German experiment in democracy.

The democratic politicians of Weimar had, at some point, competed against the Nazis and consequently been sidelined or had even been persecuted by them. Despite individual and collective acts of opportunism—most notably, voting for the Enabling Act in 1933—the political elite was therefore better suited for the task of moral leadership than other segments of elites, who had simply made their peace with the regime. On the basis of this relative distinction, the political opportunists of the Third Reich were now enlisted for a particularly important and tricky task: they had to design a system of guilt management acceptable to Allies and Germans alike. This task included a practical and closely related symbolic component. The new political elite needed to sort out the victims and the perpetrators of the Third Reich. In addition, they had to develop a language that conveyed these categorical decisions to the population and offered some ground rules for the construction of social relations between individuals and groups with different moral and political track records.

West German politicians became true visionaries and role models in the precarious business of guilt management because they were quite familiar with the sensibilities of the voters and because the Western Allies quickly adapted their policies to these sensibilities. In 1945, the political interests of the Western Allies and Germans differed significantly, but within a few years after the beginning of the Cold War, the political objectives and interpretations of both sides became largely compatible. With surprising speed, the German politicians, the German population, and the Western occupiers devised the compelling semantic framework of antitotalitarianism.[3] Considered from this new ideological vantage point, the conservative politicians who emerged victoriously from the postwar power struggle distinguished themselves by their relative distance to Nazism, their anti-Communist credentials, and their leadership in the process of economic recovery. These qualities gave them a slight edge over their Social Democratic competitors, who had a much stronger moral claim to leadership but had decided early on to play the role of constructive opposition.[4]

In contrast to the developments in the West, the emerging East German leaders never commanded the same political capital and further lost credibility when they failed to attain any concessions from their political overlords. Antifascism in the East never integrated popular perceptions of Nazism, leadership ambitions, and global developments as successfully as antitotalitarianism in the West.[5] Yet on both sides of the ideological divide, specific segments of the Weimar political establishment received the opportunity to develop a political system without interference from Germany's traditional elite. The situation differed from that of 1918 and 1919 in that there was no nobility or military leadership to be reckoned with, and in this very precise sense, the perception of a radical new beginning—a zero hour—made sense to the lucky few who had been handpicked by their Soviet partners or who had passed muster in the eyes of their voters and the Western Allies.[6]

The conceptual and moral framework we use today to make sense of Nazism and the "Final Solution" gives specific meaning to events that the survivors of the Third Reich—as they might have categorized themselves—saw in a very different light. The former Nazis and bystanders might have had a general understanding of the crimes of the regime, but they focused primarily on their own suffering. All victims with whom they did not identify, including the six million European Jews, disappeared behind a mountain of fallen German soldiers and civilians.[7] For these "survivors," the task of finding acceptable ways of expressing and alleviating their misery became the basis of their new identity and an excellent resource in the struggles between political systems and political parties that quickly followed the military collapse. Although the population and its new leaders therefore had no consciousness of the Nazi crimes that could compare to the popular Holocaust memory of the 1980s and 1990s, they still managed to adapt their prejudices to the radically changed political environment. That adaptation entailed, among other political U-turns, transforming one's anti-Semitic disposition into a defensive philo-Semitic habitus.[8]

Members of subsequent generations who grew up in the relative affluence of the Cold War inherited an interest in the politics of history, but they dealt with much more subtle moral and symbolic challenges, for which they invented a different set of rules and expectations. Therefore, we would expect to find two distinct paradigms of memory politics: a postwar paradigm that appealed to people who had firsthand knowledge of Nazi society and a post-1970s paradigm designed to satisfy the moral and entertainment interests of West German consumers born after the war. These two paradigms certainly existed—as shown in the past chapters—but on the level of federal politics, the situation was complicated by a number of factors.

In the Adenauer era, the political elite crafted exactly the kind of defensive and self-centered politics of history that contemporaries appreciated and that many members of subsequent generations found dishonest and distasteful. In the 1960s and 1970s, a new crop of leaders followed; for political and generational reasons, these people were stuck between memory paradigms. The Social Democratic chancellors Willy Brandt and, to a lesser extent, Helmut Schmidt reversed the foreign policy of the Federal Republic, but the reforms were undertaken from within the antitotalitarian paradigm. Occasionally, Brandt's personal political style provided glimpses into an alternative universe of self-reflexive, emotionally compelling memory politics that subsequent generations came to appreciate. But for the most part, Brandt followed the same type of pragmatic, result-oriented politics to overcome the political fallout of World War II that had already dominated the political scene during the Adenauer era. Especially during his public appearances in Germany, Brandt systematically understated the extent to which his understanding of German history informed his political agenda, and he rarely tried to cast his own vision of the past into institutions of cultural memory. All the while, other segments of West Germany's historical culture—literature, theater, and electronic media—experimented with new types of collective memory, which focused specifically on the crimes of the regime, raised the question of personal criminal and moral responsibility, and featured visually based and emotionally provocative formats of historical reflection.[9] Consequently, the task of bringing the federal government up to date with other channels of collective memory was left to the next age cohort, the Hitler Youth generation, whose most visible political representative, Helmut Kohl, assumed power in 1982.

Without wasting any time, the Kohl administration reformed the range of collective memory products that the government offered to the West German public. Starting in the 1980s, a conservative vision of German history was cast into monuments and thrust into museums to provide Germans with a stable, democratic historical consciousness. Conservative politicians had long fretted about their voters' lack of national historical identity, but among conservatives of the Hitler Youth generation, this concern assumed a particular urgency. For the adolescents of the Third Reich, who had experienced a sudden reversal of values during their formative years, the curiosity about National Socialism had a strong autobiographical component; they could not simply turn it off when it became a political liability. That explains why politicians such as Kohl doggedly pursued the historicization of the past against considerable political resistance and put so much energy into the creation of institutions of cultural memory, which we can now admire in Berlin and elsewhere. In contrast, the politicians of the first postwar generation quickly abandoned the cause of Vergangenheitsbewältigung when they reached the highest level of government in the late 1990s. For Gerhard Schröder and Joschka Fischer, who are prime examples of this generation, the Nazi past represented a political tool, not an existential challenge. Making provocative comments about previous generations and their peculiar forms of historical reflection helped them in the early stages of their political careers. But when they finally reached power in 1998, they felt no particular urge to shape the cultural memory of the past. Reinventing Nazism no longer offered any strategic advantages in the competition with political rivals who were not *personally* invested in a particular perception of the past.

As a result of these specific generational dynamics, three distinct paradigms of memory politics developed in the Federal Republic: the pragmatic and apologetic memory of the war generation; the ambivalent, objectifying, and idealistic memory of the Hitler Youth generation; and the instrumental and critical memory of the first postwar generation. The first of these paradigms was primarily developed in the context of political discourse and political ritual, whereas the last two relied heavily on visual media. Of all three, the second paradigm, the idealistic collective memory of the Hitler Youth generation, had the greatest impact on Germany's infrastructure of cultural memory.[10]

The three paradigms have not evolved in the chronological sequence one might have expected. The particular political turmoil of the late 1960s and 1970s is partly explained by the fact that the apologetic memory of the war generation clashed directly with the critical yet equally pragmatic memory of the first postwar generation. The more self-reflexive and ambivalent memory of the Hitler Youth generation had already made important inroads in academia and the legal profession, but it only became a dominant influence on the federal political scene in the early 1980s; then, it caused a decisive shift in the structure of West Germany's political culture. From that point forward, all the way through the late 1990s, the most heated political conflicts about memory were conducted between the conservative idealists of the Kohl administration and the left-wing critical activists and intellectuals who were associated with the Green Party and who carried the critical memory of the postwar generation into parliament.

Viewed from a generational perspective, the impressive German tradition of memory politics appears as a grand exercise in intergenerational miscommunication. Each paradigm reflected the political and psychological needs of the corresponding political generation, but precisely for that reason, the different collective memories did not provide a good basis for intergenerational dialogue.

BUILDING A NEW PARTY SYSTEM

The reconstruction of the political infrastructure in postwar Germany was complicated by two factors: the division into different zones of occupation, especially the division between East and West, and the fact that liberals and conservatives decided against reconstituting their old Weimar parties and instead sought to create new organizations with different profiles and voter bases. As a result, starting in the summer of 1945, a plethora of local and regional political initiatives coexisted and competed with each other.[11] The competition was often most pronounced between organizations with similar ideological orientations, especially if they happened to be on opposite sides of the quickly emerging Cold War divide. The diverging policies of the Allies also accounted for the different speeds and trajectories of the reconstruction process. In the East, the Soviet occupiers had imposed a centralized, hierarchical structure by 1947. In fact, the single most important step in this direction, the forced integration of the Kommunistische Partei Deutschlands (KPD) and the SPD, had already occurred, in the spring of 1946.[12] In contrast, U.S. administrators favored a very different, bottom-up approach, which explains why the construction of a comprehensive party system in the West was only concluded in 1950 when the Christian Democrats finally integrated all their different regional chapters.[13]

Even before they again wielded any real power, politicians were courting public attention and wooing the people through declarations and speeches in the fall of 1945 and spring of 1946. The statements focused on the present misery but also provided modest analyses of the recent past. Considering the inscrutable political constellation after 1945, it is not surprising that most political players reverted to strategies of interpretation that had informed their worldview prior to Nazism. The new leaders of the Communist and Socialist Parties felt vindicated by the outcome of the war and approached the task of reconstruction with considerable self-confidence. Emphasizing their early resistance to Hitler as well as the victims in their own ranks, they reiterated their prewar socioeconomic explanations of Nazism, which held the capitalist elite responsible for Hitler's rise to power. That approach was most pronounced in the declarations of the KPD, whose leaders recycled the old-fashioned Komintern definition of fascism as the most reactionary element of the finance capital.[14] But the SPD and the labor unions, in East and West, released compatible statements about the alleged class base of the Nazi regime. In addition, neither Communists nor Socialists saw any need to address their past political mistakes. With the exception of some vague references to possible tactical errors, the enmity between both parties never became a topic of public discussion.[15]

The reconstruction of the center of the political spectrum took more time because conservatives and liberals decided against reconstituting the denominationally defined Catholic Center Party in favor of a less narrowly conceived Christian party, which would appeal to a larger cross section of German voters. The decision attested to the tactical acumen of the politicians at the helm of the new Christian Democratic Party, but it also reflected the gist of their historical analysis. Like many church leaders, the CDU functionaries considered Nazism the consequence of the rampant materialism and secularization that had seized Germany in the nineteenth century. This explanation conveniently diluted any sense of German responsibility and contained a useful attack on the alleged materialism of the Social Democrats.[16]

Most of the new or reconstituted political parties could legitimately lay claim to some victims of the regime who had been murdered for their political convictions. In particular, the political leaders in the West projected the moral integrity of the few martyrs onto the whole population, which thus quickly metamorphosed into an innocent target of Nazi repression and Allied revenge. Consequently, without exception, the political elite in the West rejected the idea of a collective guilt of the German people, a notion that had surfaced in the foreign press during the war, was now stubbornly reiterated in the German media, and was tenaciously attacked as factually inaccurate and morally flawed.[17] For some historians, the insistence and denunciation of the charge of collective guilt reflects the common psychological denominator of a society that reacted to and on some level realized the magnitude of its political self-destruction and the enormity of the moral debts incurred in the process.[18] That hypothesis might, indeed, capture a key psychological component of postwar politics, but it does not change the fact that the suffering of the many victims who could not be easily enlisted for current political objectives was rarely publicly acknowledged. The majority of individuals with designs on public office, in the East and West, rejected the racism of the NS regime in general terms. But they either failed to mention Jewish victims at all or else included them in a generic list of war dead that emphasized the sacrifices of the German people.

The first public declaration of the KPD in the Soviet zone, for instance, referred explicitly to the many eastern European victims who died in the camps and even invoked gas vans and death ovens without acknowledging the genocide of European Jewry.[19] For KPD leaders such as Walter Ulbricht, the Nazis' ethnic-cleansing campaign against the Slavic people explained the need for extensive reparation payments to the Soviet Union and the permanent loss of the East Prussian territories. In this context, he and other party leaders were initially quite outspoken about the partial guilt of the German people, although that theme disappeared from public documents within a few months after the war.[20] In contrast to this strategically crafted KPD discourse, the East German Christian Democrats were much more honest and precise about Nazi racism. Until the political landscape was effectively streamlined by Moscow, East-CDU functionaries such as Jakob Kaiser and Andreas Hermes, who had actively resisted Hitler, acknowledged the suffering of the Jews and rejected Nazi anti-Semitism in exceptionally explicit terms.[21]

In the West, the Social Democrats were the only group that aggressively confronted the legacy of the Third Reich, including the events of the "Final Solution." The new SPD chairman, Kurt Schumacher, had spent many years in Nazi camps, which set him apart from most other postwar politicians. Occasionally, Schumacher engaged in the same tactical maneuver as his colleagues — for instance, when he released the working class from any responsibility for the Nazi crimes.[22] But more often, he used his exceptional moral clout to remind his listeners of the victims of the Nazi regime and especially the suffering of the Jewish people. Until his death in 1953, he never tired of insisting on swift punishment for the perpetrators and generous compensation for the victims.[23] In the first years after the war, the only voices comparable to Schumacher's belonged to the members of an influential circle of liberal politicians in Stuttgart. Theodor Heuss and Reinhold Maier, who were part of the group and later joined the Freie Demokratische Partei (FDP), made it very clear that Germans should not complain about their current difficulties, since they had not lifted a finger when Jews were deported.[24] Immediately after the war, Heuss, who would become the first president of the Federal Republic, anticipated his famous 1953 declaration of the collective shame of the German people when he stressed that the population's passivity during the deportations had undermined its moral and spiritual integrity.[25]

Unfortunately, Konrad Adenauer, the single most important political figure of the early Federal Republic, did not belong to this group of exceptionally self-reflexive and self-critical politicians. Adenauer differed from many of his future colleagues because he entered the political arena only after some delay. He took over the leadership of the CDU in the British zone in January 1946 and from then on pursued his career with exceptional ambition and tactical forte. Adenauer obviously understood that any explicit lobbying for Jewish causes would not improve his chances at the ballot box, although this insight did not prevent him from expressing quite critical opinions about his fellow citizens in more private settings.[26] Moreover, to his credit, Adenauer made excellent use of the political capital extended to him, enhancing his own as well as Germany's political stature and independence. He played Allied supervisors and German public opinion against each other and pushed them to the limits of their political pain threshold, but he always contained this potentially destructive strategy within a consistently pro-Western, antitotalitarian message.

DEFINING AND PUNISHING THE PERPETRATORS

The many political and administrative challenges of the postwar years can be categorized according to two general at times competing, at times complementary objectives: providing a sense of justice after the upheavals of Nazism and reconstructing German infrastructure, institutions, and identity as quickly as possible. For good reasons, the Allies initially focused on the first task at the expense of the second, but they quickly changed priorities, which brought them in line with the interest of most German people and their elected officials. The former citizens of the Third Reich expected and perhaps even appreciated that their surviving Nazi leaders faced Allied courts, although they did not seem to pay close attention or derive much satisfaction from the Nuremberg proceedings that began in 1945. According to the polls, Germans managed to hide their indifference when officially quizzed about their opinion—after all, they were well trained in public double-talk—but they could not be bothered with the details of the trials. In particular, the Nuremberg successor trials, which only ended in April 1949 when the former diplomats of the regime were sentenced, were conducted without much interest or support from the public.[27]

Although the former citizens of the Third Reich guarded their true feelings about the Nazi leadership, they openly expressed their outrage about the treatment of their military leaders who had been sentenced by Allied military courts. Once the federal government was reconstituted in the West in May 1949, politicians, church leaders, and average citizens united in an energetic and successful lobbying campaign on behalf of their generals. All were incensed that the Western Allies wooed West Germany for its military contribution to the Cold War but at the same time insisted on punishing the very people who embodied German military pride and expertise. Government and opposition politicians, Adenauer among them, helped focus and sustain the collective outrage about the judicial abuse of the "alleged war criminals." Using public opinion as well as the Allied wishes for rearmament as leverage, they succeeded in having most of the officers released by 1952 and getting the Allied military prisons closed by 1958. As a result, Hitler's military henchmen, who had planned and implemented his wars of extermination, could enjoy their pensions without any fear of further prosecution; the treaties between the Federal Republic and the Western Allies establishing West German independence specifically excluded the possibility of double jeopardy.[28]

From the start, the German population was also greatly concerned about and involved in the Allied attempts to rid German society of its average Nazis. Targeting hundreds of thousands of suspected criminals seriously disrupted the reconstruction efforts, especially in the U.S. zone, and required so many personnel that, starting in March 1946, the Germans themselves sat in judgment over their fellow citizens. The magnitude of the undertaking, the passive resistance of the population, the fateful decision to process lesser offenders before advancing to more serious cases, and, last but not least, the fact that neighbors and colleagues assessed each other's integrity—all these factors derailed the well-intended denazification plan. Regardless of their individual offenses and shortcomings, the great majority of Germans tried by the lay courts were categorized as harmless bystanders and released with a slap on the wrist. The longer the process lasted, the more difficult it became to find people willing to serve as judges. In addition, as denazification continued, more and more seriously compromised Nazis got off scot-free. In the end, almost everybody was relieved when the new federal parliament severely curbed denazification in 1950 and a few years later abandoned the process altogether.[29]

The members of parliament (MPs) showed the same generosity when they passed two amnesty laws, first regarding all crimes punishable by up to six months in prison and then, a few years later, regarding all crimes punishable by up to three years that had been committed during the last nine months of World War II. Since both laws passed with comfortable majorities, in 1949 and 1954, respectively, it is not surprising that nobody in parliament voiced any concerns when, in 1955, the statute of limitations took effect concerning all crimes punishable by up to ten years in jail, including offenses such as grievous bodily harm and unlawful imprisonment.[30] From this point forward, many crimes committed in the camps and ghettos were exempt from prosecution.

By the middle of the first postwar decade, the political elite had swiftly implemented a well-understood mandate from their voters. Considering the general suffering caused by the war and the difficulties and successes of reconstruction, the majority of the population preferred to ignore past crimes and political failures and end the process of collective (self-)incrimination as quickly as possible. As a result, however, West German society, vigorously represented by its leaders, constructed a rigid and one-dimensional image of the Third Reich that separated a few guilty leaders and henchmen from the rest of society. This collective memory contained so many holes and contradictions that it could be easily dismantled and used as political leverage by subsequent generations, if they should be so inclined.

THE VICTIMS OF NAZI PERSECUTION

The second important challenge to postwar justice, the task of making amends to the many victims of Nazism, was not abandoned as quickly as the search for the perpetrators. That difference is easily explained. Unlike the perpetrators, who were ultimately considered a German problem, the many victims of Nazism living outside Germany constituted a European or even a global problem and attracted the attention of several foreign governments. West Germany's relatively impressive track record regarding compensation for Nazi crimes emerged gradually—primarily as a result of international pressure, not as a result of German concerns about the victims' fate.

Defining and disbursing compensation payments was more complicated than punishing the perpetrators, since it involved a wide range of different claims and victims. At the end of 1945, the Allies tried to address the most pressing refugee and compensation problems by designating all gold reserves of the Third Reich for the support of displaced persons, especially Jewish survivors. But it turned out to be difficult to get to the funds, and they proved completely insufficient for the task at hand.[31] Since the Allies never agreed on another general compensation strategy, a support system for the victims developed only gradually and unevenly. In most cases, U.S. administrators took the lead and were followed, with some delay, by representatives from the other Western occupying powers. The ad hoc measures adopted in this fashion (such as preferential allocation of apartments, jobs, and food) often drew the ire of the German people who were competing for the same scarce resources.[32] It is no wonder, then, that the first ambitious compensation initiative, designed to right the wrongs committed during the so-called aryanization of Jewish businesses, met with strong resistance from German officials who categorically rejected the return of private property to its former owners. After sixteen months of fruitless negotiations, U.S. administrators finally issued a military law that took effect in November 1947 and reversed the illegal appropriation of property in Nazi Germany.[33] German business representatives and their political allies continued their resistance, especially after the founding of the republic in 1949. With an association and a journal created solely for this purpose, they lobbied for a reversal of the law, using highly inflated figures about its alleged costs to the German people. Despite these well-organized attempts, supported by influential politicians from the governing parties, the return of or compensation for aryanized properties proceeded fairly swiftly, with most cases settled by the mid-1950s.[34]

The compensation law of 1947 set an important precedent in the long history of German financial restitution efforts. The law officially addressed any loss of property suffered between 1933 and 1945 as a result of persecution on the basis of race, religion, nationality, worldview, or political opposition to Nazism.[35] The formula was more than adequate for righting the wrongs of aryanization, but the categories of race, religion, and politics proved purposefully restrictive when applied to the larger issue of individual compensation for past suffering, as the next step in the compensation process demonstrated. After long deliberations, especially by German experts, the U.S. high command accepted the first truly comprehensive compensation law in August 1949, designed to indemnify German victims of Nazi terror and their families for loss of life, health, property, and career.[36] However, by following the 1947 example and linking the rights of the victims to the categories of race, religion, and politics, the law systematically excluded many individuals with valid claims, including the victims of forced sterilization and "euthanasia," military deserters, and former camp inmates whom the Nazis had classified as "asocials" or "criminals."[37] In subsequent legislation, the formulas and their exclusions were simply repeated until, four decades later, they finally came under critical scrutiny when new political forces such as the Green Party entered the national political arena.

If the reimbursement law of 1947 set precedent in one respect, it remained exceptional in another. It is one of the few pieces of compensation legislation that was unilaterally adopted by the military government. All subsequent provisions were written and implemented by German civilian authorities and merely checked by Allied personnel. As a result, the kind of reservations that German politicians had already harbored about the antiaryanization law became an influential factor in all compensation matters. Since the population and many members of the political elite resented compensation provisions for foreigners and social minorities—often intuitively confirming the limits of the NS *Volksgemeinschaft* (NS racial community)—the postwar governments only incurred such compensation obligations when they faced overwhelming foreign pressure or believed they would gain compelling advantages through additional concessions.[38] The first Adenauer administration, for instance, took a passive, wait-and-see attitude when faced with claims for compensation by victims in what had once been Nazi-occupied Europe. Despite criticism by the SPD opposition, the government embraced a successful legalistic defense strategy, which deferred all claims by foreign nationals to an unknown point in the future, when a comprehensive peace and reparations conference would decide the fate of the divided Germany.[39] That tactic worked until the late 1950s, when all Western European countries, now social and economic partners of a prospering West Germany, insisted on an interim solution for their citizens who had suffered at the hand of the German occupying forces.[40]

Under different circumstances, however, Adenauer was quite willing to come up with unorthodox compensation solutions if the price seemed right. Thus, in 1952, against the opposition of his own finance minister and many officials involved in the negotiations, he insisted on concluding global settlements with Israel and the Jewish Claims Conference in the amount of 3.5 billion marks. The two agreements were unprecedented because one involved an association without legal standing according to the conventions of international law and the other was concluded between two states that had not existed when the crimes were committed and did not maintain diplomatic ties. Adenauer's generosity and persistence might have reflected a personal moral awakening, but his decision was certainly influenced by the fact that the Western Allies, especially the United States, had indicated that a successful settlement of Jewish claims would pave the way for Germany's reentry into the international community of nations.[41]

THE GERMAN VICTIMS OF WAR AND EXPULSION

One of the key postwar debates about social justice after Nazism is rarely addressed in the standard works on German memory politics. Scholars who have studied the history of compensation and punishment after World War II point out how much Germans perceived themselves as victims, but they often fail to explore the discussions and important legislative initiatives that addressed this question of German victimhood.[42] This omission prevents us from gaining a better understanding of the symbolic and political interaction between different compensation policies that were created side by side. The refusal to map out the politics of history in their entirety reflects an understandable distaste for the Germans-as-victims discourse, but it also represents a problematic projection of more recent collective memories into the political landscape of the early republic. None of the political actors of the time, the Allies included, felt the particular respect for the victims and survivors of the "Final Solution" that is one of the main achievements of the memory culture of the 1980s. Therefore, scholars who were socialized during and after the rise of the Holocaust paradigm need to suspend their moral judgments temporarily and view the postwar debates about victimhood from the viewpoint of the contemporaries. Obviously, it cannot be the purpose of this exercise to valorize the contemporaries' self-centered concerns after the fact, but taking their perspective seriously helps to reconstruct the complexity of the postwar environment and describe with greater precision how the history of memory has evolved since the mid-1940s.

Right after the end of the war, German financial experts began discussing solutions for the severe fiscal problems caused by the collapse of the Third Reich. While figuring out how to settle Germany's immense debts and how the surplus of worthless currency could be reduced to a sound level, they also thought about ways of evenly distributing the financial burden of the war among the population. In the end, these problems were not addressed in one general reform package because the U.S. military administration insisted on a swift currency reform to initiate the economic recovery in the West as quickly as possible.[43] But once the deutsche mark was introduced in the summer of 1948, German politicians prepared legislation to alleviate some of the economic injustices caused by the war. The initiative focused on the part of the German population that had suffered the most severe monetary losses during the war, as a result, for example, of Allied bombing or expulsion. Unlike in the case of the displaced persons and foreign victims, German politicians acted on behalf of the so-called war-damaged individuals without Allied prodding. In November 1948, the first support package for these victims passed the Frankfurter Wirtschaftsrat, the temporary parliament of the U.S. and British zones. The law was called the Burden Equalizing Law (Lastenausgleichsgesetz); it provided monthly subsidies and financial support for apartment construction, professional development, educational expenses, and the purchase of household items.[44]

In the few years since the German surrender, the composition of the war-damaged population segment had changed significantly. As a result of the expulsion of ethnic Germans from Eastern Europe, the needs of the eight to nine million refugees now exceeded the needs of the victims of warfare and

NS terror.[45] This development explains why politicians acted so swiftly. They identified with all victims of the war, but for many years, they paid particular attention to the expellees, who constituted a serious political risk. The politicians assumed correctly that, if the sizable refugee community was socially marginalized and politically radicalized, it could bring down the frail postwar democracy. This counterfactual assessment is still shared by most experts in the field; like the postwar politicians, the experts give the law credit for addressing one of the most severe challenges that the new republic faced.[46]

Whereas the first Lastenausgleich of 1948 was adopted without any lobbying by the expellee organizations, all subsequent amendments were accompanied by the powerful and at times even shrill propaganda of the refugee pressure groups. In the first years after their arrival in the West, the expellees were too fragmented and perhaps too traumatized to mount an effective political campaign. But starting in 1949, when the first national umbrella organization was founded, professional lobbyists pushed the cause of the expellees in the halls of government.[47] Initially, the relationship between the administration and the expellees was quite confrontational. Adenauer and his ministers were willing to provide assistance but not at a rate that might threaten the economic recovery process. Consequently, they favored need-based subsidies, whereas the expellee leadership demanded payments that represented at least a percentage of the expellees' actual monetary losses. To overcome the stalling tactics of the government, refugee organizations launched an ambitious public relations campaign in 1950. In addition to professing their love for their homeland and demanding the right of return, they also, somewhat contradictorily, lobbied for better compensation payments and threatened to withdraw their support for the CDU coalition government and its policy of west integration.[48] This was not an empty threat. In the summer of 1950, the expellees, together with disgruntled former Nazis, founded their own political party, the Bund der Heimatvertriebenen und Entrechteten (BHE), and won an instant election success in the state of Schleswig-Holstein, where the refugees comprised a higher percentage of the population than in any other state.[49]

The federal government reacted to this threat with a combination of material concessions and inexpensive yet fateful symbolic gestures. The more extensive second Burden Equalizing Law of 1952 provided, for the first time, a modest, regressively rated indemnification system in conjunction with other new benefits.[50] Moreover, many federal politicians who had never cared about the eastern territories, including Adenauer himself, suddenly professed their attachment to the provinces beyond Oder and Neisse and declared their commitment to the German borders of 1937.[51] Adenauer was much too pragmatic and realistic a politician to believe that the territories might be returned one day. He paid lip service to nationalistic causes to pacify the expellees and assure their support for his government and the project of west integration. The cooperation proved very advantageous for both parties. The refugee functionaries established such close ties to the minister for expellee affairs that they occasionally wrote their own amendments to the Burden Equalizing Law and had them subsequently rubber-stamped by parliament.[52] Christian Democrats and Christian Socialists, as well as the oppositional Social Democrats, helped integrate the expellees into the political mainstream and could count on them as some of their most loyal supporters for many years to come.[53] But the partnership came at a price. By embracing the refugees, the political elite fostered unrealistic expectations and, at least in theory, committed itself to a revanchist agenda. As long as the Cold War persisted, the occasional verbal radicalism proved harmless, but once the relations to Eastern Europe finally improved, the unrealistic expectations of the expellees and their officials turned out to be a serious impediment to long-overdue foreign policy reforms.

As a result of the political objectives of the new federal government and its reaction to internal and external pressures, the first federal support package for the German expellees and the first comprehensive restitution settlement for survivors of the "Final Solution" were negotiated side by side. The law to indemnify the expellees passed parliament in May 1952, and the Treaty of Luxembourg with Israel and the Jewish Claims Conference was signed in September 1952. In both cases, the measures' success depended on Adenauer's personal involvement. Starting in the spring of 1951, Adenauer held several one-to-one meetings with the leader of the expellee organization, Linus Kather, to decide on the expellee support package and lay the foundations for their future political cooperation.[54] In the spring of the following year, he prevented the failure of the negotiations with Israel and the Claims Conference by pressuring his own finance minister into accepting more generous treaty terms.[55] These developments indicate how much the chancellor democracy revolved around Adenauer, but they also show that the different groups of victims directly competed with each other for taxpayer support. Adenauer and his administration balanced obligations that they considered unavoidable in the interest of internal stability with financial responsibilities that satisfied Allied demands and could enhance West Germany's political independence. Obviously, the German political elite wanted to make progress on both fronts. However, when facing competing claims that appeared to exceed the financial resources of the Federal Republic, the conservative government decided that the investments into future West German citizens and voters took precedence over the settlements of past crimes.[56]

German politicians were less than enthusiastic about punishing Nazi perpetrators or compensating some of the victims of Nazi crimes. They assumed that they could not afford to alienate the former Nazis among their voters, and in light of the misery surrounding them, they strove to keep scarce resources in the country and focus them on the most deserving segments of the population. These priorities reflected their honest concern about the future of the second German democracy, which was launched under such adverse conditions, as well as their anxiety about their own careers. Consequently, in the deliberations about the best targets of state support, politicians showed little concern for foreigners and tended to ignore any group that lacked quantitative clout or that they preferred *not* to count among their supporters.

Left to their own devices, the new political leaders would probably have limited public support to a collective of ethnic Germans reminiscent of the Nazi Volksgemeinschaft—with the exception of the former political dissidents from their own ranks. In this sense, the political priorities of the postwar years illustrate the extent to which Nazi culture and Nazi politics had reflected and permeated German society and continued to influence the minds of the silent majority of the West German citizenry. Yet regardless of their own prejudices, the politicians of the Federal Republic simply could not ignore the millions of refugees, whereas they could have easily forgotten about the millions of victims dispersed across Europe and the world—had there not been some forceful Allied reminders about at least some of these victims.

"SAVING" THE CIVIL SERVICE

The generous application of the victim label within German society and its restrictive use for anybody outside Germany again became obvious during the reconstitution of the civil service. The Allies had pressed for a comprehensive reform of the civil service to assure its support for a democratic West Germany. But conservative politicians effectively sidestepped these demands, and even Social Democratic officials, who were, in principle, in favor of reforming the civil service, delayed action for fear that any radical reform plans might disrupt the reconstruction efforts and cost the SPD important votes.[57] With large-scale reforms postponed indefinitely, the German government still had to address the more specific question of how to treat the civil servants and public employees who had lost their jobs as a result of the war. This heterogeneous group of approximately half a million people included former professional soldiers, civil servants expelled from the East, and individuals who had been fired in the process of denazification. Even before the founding of the republic, displaced civil servants demanded their old jobs and formed pressure groups to advance that cause. Partly in reaction to this lobbying campaign, the drafters of the constitution inserted paragraph 131 into the document, which obliged the government to settle the claims of the former public employees.[58]

The first Adenauer administration discharged this obligation quickly and generously. In May 1951, long before many other compensation questions were settled, parliament passed a law that met most of the demands of the unemployed civil servants. The legislation required all state agencies to reinstate them as quickly as possible at their previous level of seniority. In addition, anybody with more than ten years of service was to receive temporary support if the reinstatement had to be postponed for organizational reasons. The law specifically excluded former members of the Waffen-SS and the Gestapo from receiving benefits, although it also offered them a convenient loophole. The civil servants in question could be rehired if they argued persuasively that they had been officially transferred to one of the blacklisted Nazi agencies and therefore had just followed orders.[59] No other group of individuals who had suffered setbacks as a result of the war managed to recoup their losses as effectively as the civil servants of the Third Reich—with one telling exception. As a fig leaf for the generous reinstitution of the civil servants, the parliament extended the same generous terms to the Jewish civil servants who had been fired by the Nazis, but the MPs conveniently excluded any individuals who had "decided" to emigrate from Germany.[60]

The swift implementation of paragraph 131 did not occur in response to popular demand. In fact, the measure was received quite critically by many citizens who faced obstacles like those confronting the displaced public employees but had nobody to bail them out.[61] By extending preferential treatment to their public servants, politicians pursued three objectives: to advance the rehabilitation of the military, to accelerate the reconstruction process, and to simply make their own jobs easier. They hoped their gift would reconcile the loyal retainers of the Nazi state with the new democratic system and provide them with the same competent staff that had already served the last administration with distinction.[62] Consequently, very few members of the political elite voiced any concerns when former Nazis, including high-ranking officials and severely compromised individuals, returned to their posts in local, regional, and federal administrations. Only in the late 1950s did the price to be paid for such generosity become apparent as Nazi perpetrators were detected in the ranks of the police and other public sector agencies. Or, more precisely, for the first time in the late 1950s, the price appeared to be too high because the media raised questions about the careers of some of the supposed victims the state had so magnanimously welcomed back into the fold.[63]

NEUTRALIZING NAZI INSURGENTS

In addition to dealing with erstwhile Nazi perpetrators, the political establishment was quickly forced to confront unreconstructed Nazis who were eager to build a political future in West Germany. Encouraged by the general climate of reconciliation and forgiveness, right-wing activists targeted voters in northern Germany, where a high concentration of refugees and above-average unemployment numbers provided a particularly fertile ground for a revival of NS ideology.[64] As a result, the democratic politicians in Bonn faced a difficult task. On the one hand, they lobbied vigorously for the release of former Nazis and military leaders who had committed crimes against humanity. On the other hand, they were expected to fight against unrepentant Nazis who might have violated laws regulating public speech but were otherwise only guilty of showing poor political judgment and producing tasteless propaganda. Such radically different standards for assessing past and present conduct could not be easily justified. The quick eradication of the Nazi resurgence, which Allied administrators and foreign observers considered a precondition for West German independence, was further complicated by the fact that the political leaders could not count on unequivocal support from the judiciary. Unlike the situation in the Third Reich, when judges had willingly accepted orders from the Nazi government, the jurists now cherished their political independence. In addition, more than a few judges identified with the neo-Nazi activists and defended their idealism for the Nazi cause.[65]

Wolfgang Hedler was the first politician who acquired national notoriety by testing the limits of political tolerance in the new republic. As a member of parliament for the Deutsche Partei, he spoke at many party rallies in the fall of 1949, calling resistance fighters traitors, rejecting any German responsibility for the war, and identifying with the aims of the Nazi anti-Jewish policies. After the national press reported on Hedler's infuriating statements, parliament quickly stripped him of his immunity and excluded him from its meetings. Hedler was charged with insulting the memory of the German resistance, threatening the public peace, and slandering colleagues, including the SPD chairman, Kurt Schumacher. Hedler's trial in January and February 1950 made national and international headlines because the list of coplaintiffs read like a who's who of the German resistance against Hitler and because the judges cleared Hedler of all charges. As a result of this setback, SPD leaders felt abandoned by the democratic state they had helped create and took matters into their own hands. When Hedler showed his face in parliament despite his suspension, a number of SPD MPs roughed him up in good Weimar tradition. In addition to these less than professional measures, the SPD introduced two laws in parliament; one was designed to nullify all NS convictions based on political and racial discrimination, and the other introduced mandatory sentences for a whole range of antidemocratic behavior, including insulting the memory of NS victims. Both projects failed on the floor because the federal government saw no need for legislative action. Perhaps as a result of the international outcry about Hedler's acquittal, the decision was reversed on appeal, and he was sentenced to nine months in jail.[66]

Adenauer appeared determined to take the same wait-and-see attitude when the second, more serious challenge appeared on the extreme right wing of the political spectrum. Founded by former midlevel officials of the Nazi Party in the fall of 1949, the Sozialistische Reichspartei (SRP) and its figurehead Ernst Remer received disturbingly high numbers in state elections in Lower Saxony and Bremen in 1951. The party's success, winning 11 percent and 8 percent of the popular vote, respectively, raised serious concerns at home and abroad, which were further exacerbated by the enthusiastic reception of

Remer's many public appearances. As a former army officer, Remer had played a key role in rounding up Hitler's opponents in the officer corps after their failed assassination attempt of July 20, 1944, and he continued to deride the resisters as traitors to the national cause. For a while, Remer was one of the best-known Germans abroad, and that fact certainly played a role in the repeated Allied demands for federal action against the SRP and its notorious leader. As a result of this pressure, the federal government finally petitioned the newly established federal constitutional court to ban the SRP as an unconstitutional political association. In truly antitotalitarian fashion, the appeal was filed together with a request for a similar injunction against the KPD. Despite tensions between the federal government and the federal court, the judges honored the requests. On orders of the court, the SRP was dissolved and its property seized in October 1952, and the KPD met the same fate in 1956. Remer and the SRP had been the most visible right-wing extremists of the postwar years because they had copied the Nazi movement in terms of style and content. As a result, they provided the political mainstream with a welcome opportunity to demonstrate its anti-Nazi disposition.[67]

Even before the constitutional court could conclude the case against the SRP, the attorney general of Braunschweig, Fritz Bauer, took the opportunity to turn a conventional criminal trial pending against Remer into a national didactic media event. With the help of many famous witnesses and distinguished experts, Bauer proved that Remer had slandered the memory of the German resistance. He used the trial of March 1952 to demonstrate to the assembled national press corps that the resisters of July 20, 1944, had made an ethically, politically, and legally exemplary decision. Thus, the trial marked an important step in the gradual transformation of the popular perception of the conspirators from traitors into political role models.[68]

The three reluctant collaborators in the battle against incorrigible Nazis— the Allies, the federal government, and the German courts—faced one more serious challenge in the early 1950s. Barred from founding a party of their own, a group of former NS officials tried to infiltrate the FDP in the state of Northrhine-Westphalia. The British, who watched these attempts closely, repeatedly urged the German government to intervene, but when their requests proved futile, they acted on their own initiative. In January 1953, British forces arrested six high-ranking former Nazis and accused them of plotting to overthrow the postwar democracy. Neither public opinion nor the political leadership

in Bonn considered the six Nazis a serious threat. Journalists and politicians
agreed that the British had overreacted and thus had de facto, if not de jure,
infringed on West Germany's emerging independence. Adenauer was specifically concerned about the possibility that the spectacular British stunt might
play into the hands of the critics of West Germany's rapid rearmament. The
negotiations about the pertinent treaties granting the Federal Republic limited sovereignty and membership in the North Atlantic Treaty Organization
(NATO) had just been concluded. Getting them ratified by a reluctant parliament was difficult enough without any high-profile Allied action that questioned West Germany's political reliability. Therefore, the chancellor went on
the offensive. In a radio broadcast on January 19, 1953, he assured his listeners about the stability of the West German democracy and predicted that
right-wing parties would be completely marginalized in the upcoming federal elections.[69]

Since the British arrests had taken place in the judicial limbo between occupational and West German law, the British high commissioner, the federal
government, and the courts spent some time figuring out who should prose-
cute the arrested Nazis. The men were finally turned over to German authorities after Adenauer personally promised a rigorous judicial investigation. As
in the past, however, the chancellor ran afoul of the federal judiciary. By July
1953, all conspirators had been released, and by December, they had been
cleared of all charges. This turn of events could have created serious problems for Adenauer if his earlier prediction had not come true. In the federal
elections of September 1953, the CDU won a resounding victory and the remaining right-wing parties were decimated. The measures taken against
Nazi insurgents, as uncoordinated and reluctantly implemented as they were,
had apparently impressed the electorate and undercut what limited appeal
the Nazi ideology still possessed.[70]

COLLECTIVE SHAME: INVENTING WEST GERMAN CULTURAL MEMORIES

While pragmatic politics of history progressed very nicely in the first years of
the Federal Republic, the new political establishment in Bonn had a tough
time coming up with rituals and symbols that expressed the mission of the
new state and the identity of its citizens in a succinct and dignified fashion.
Hoping for unification in the near future, many leaders hesitated to make

long-term decisions about the public face of the provisional West German state.[71] They were quite sure of what the Federal Republic stood against—dictatorships of all sorts—but they were uncertain what compelling positive characteristics they could bestow on the truncated, impotent federal entity they governed from a small provincial town in the Rhineland. This insecurity became obvious during the search for a new national holiday. There was general consensus that certain symbolically meaningful dates could not fulfill that purpose. May 8, for instance, marking the end of the war, was deemed a day of national ignominy, and the tenth anniversary of the collapse of the Third Reich passed without official acknowledgement.[72] As a result of such dilemmas, a national holiday and a set of West German memorial days emerged relatively slowly. In fact, the West German government only began experimenting with national rituals because it did not want to surrender the arena of symbolic memory politics to the East German Communists, who celebrated their antifascist identity with great confidence.

In August 1950, the Adenauer administration decided to organize a national memorial day on September 7 in a pitiful effort to preempt and counterbalance the Day of the Victims of Fascism that had been observed in the Soviet zone of occupation for several years and was prepared with considerable pomp and circumstance for September 10 in the GDR. The haphazardly put together West German countercelebration, marking the first anniversary of the first session of parliament, turned out to be a flop.[73] It was unceremoniously replaced in 1953 when parliament tried to solve the West German identity crisis by declaring June 17, the day of the workers' uprising in the East, the national holiday of the West. The Day of German Unity, as it was called forthwith, inadvertently acknowledged the problem involved in crafting an official West German identity because the uprising was clearly *not* a West German event. The decision to celebrate its anniversary left the core of the new identity strangely undefined. For West Germans who had experienced the division of Germany, the date inspired powerful sentiments of national belonging. Throughout the 1950s and 1960s, June 17 brought out an impressive grassroots movement, first supported by the Social Democrats and later by the Christian Democrats.[74] But subsequent generations regarded the failed rebellion of 1953, undertaken by people of questionable national affiliation, with complete indifference. As national unity appeared increasingly unrealistic and undesirable, June 17 turned into an anachronism.

As the example of the Day of German Unity illustrates, crafting the official memory of Nazism was a difficult and thankless task. Therefore, Adenauer was happy to transfer that responsibility to West Germany's president, Theodor Heuss, who wielded little real power and could focus his energies on inventing a West German identity. Heuss, another Weimar politician who had been sidelined by the Nazis, went to work with great zeal and helped design an infrastructure of cultural memory that determined the official calendar of the Federal Republic for many years to come. In a string of public speeches, he addressed three important themes: the relationship between Germans and Jews, the suffering of the German people as a result of Nazi rule, and the legacy of the conservative resistance against Hitler. With regard to all three themes, Heuss tested the limits of popular taste, although he ultimately decided—and proved particularly adept at delineating—a widely acceptable collective memory of the Third Reich.[75] Heuss's concern for consensual memory work makes him an excellent source for the study of the political culture of the 1950s, when most politicians focused on practical political challenges and left the task of formulating general historical lessons to others.

Heuss made his most important contribution to the rhetorics of memory in 1949, when he coined the phrase *collective shame*. Speaking in front of the Wiesbaden Society for Christian-Jewish Cooperation, Heuss encouraged his compatriots never to forget "the Nuremberg Laws, the Jewish star, the burning of the synagogues, and the deportation of Jewish people to foreign countries which sent them into misfortune and death."[76] His description of the crimes was relatively precise, but he never mentioned the German perpetrators. His passive constructions acknowledged the "misfortune" that had happened to Jews but failed to explain who had been responsible for their suffering. At the same time, Heuss was very precise about the misfortune and injustices that his listeners had to endure. To defend his audience against unfair accusations of collective guilt, he constructed a strange parallel between Jews and Germans. The assumption of collective guilt, he argued, represented the same type of simplification that the Nazis had used when they deemed all Jews guilty by definition. Despite this apologetic rhetoric, Heuss suggested that something like collective shame lingered in German society, and that statement prompted considerable discussion: "The worst that Hitler has done to us—and he has violated us in many ways—is that he forced us into the shameful condition of having to share the name 'German' with him and his henchmen."[77]

In the early 1950s, Heuss reiterated these themes in public speeches during memorial and dedication services and on national holidays. Trying to point his listeners in the right moral direction without alienating them, he revealed, in exemplary fashion, how carefully the conservative political leadership negotiated their voters' historical pain threshold.[78] Heuss distanced himself from the tradition of Prussian militarism but defended the honor of the German soldiers who had been sacrificed by the regime.[79] He praised the failed assassins of July 20 as role models but elevated them to such exceptional status that their actions would not reflect negatively on the passivity of the average Germans.[80] In this careful and deliberate fashion, Heuss contributed to the invention of a set of recurring national events: the week of brotherhood in the spring, the Day of German Unity in June, the anniversary of the July 20 assassination attempt against Hitler, and the National Day of Mourning in November. His successors used these dates as opportunities to reflect on the vagaries of German history in vague and abstract terms. With two exceptions, they followed Heuss's time-tested formula and spoke safely, yet unimaginatively, about "crimes committed in the name of Germany." As will be discussed, only Gustav Heinemann and Richard Weiszäcker had the courage to put their presidential authority on the line and challenge popular, apologetic perceptions of Nazism.

A SURPLUS OF VICTIMS

In the 1950s, parliament featured three major subject positions. On the extreme right of the political spectrum, expellees collaborated with former Nazis. Both groups felt that they were unfairly singled out and punished for Nazi crimes, while many Germans who had made the same contributions to the Nazi revolution were swiftly rebuilding their lives and careers. The Allies had initially prohibited the expellees and former Nazis from forming political organizations, but when the ban was lifted in 1950, these groups organized in parties such as the BHE and the Deutsche Reichspartei (DR) and crafted an aggressive, apologetic discourse of German victimhood. However, as a result of the political repression of right-wing organizations, most notably the SRP, and the social and economic integration of the "German victims" into West German society, the lamentations about past suffering became less and less

attractive to voters.[81] The victim discourse of the Right survived in the subculture of the deportee organizations and occasionally resurfaced in the
speeches of conservative backbenchers of the Christian Democrats, but it disappeared as an independent political voice in parliament.[82]

The victim discourse of the Right contradicted and competed with the
more ambivalent victim discourse on the Left, which combined elements of
victim and resistance identity and was represented in parliament by the KPD
and SPD factions. Emphasizing the sacrifices inherent in the working-class
struggle against Hitler, Communists, and Social Democrats claimed a moral
and political leadership position in the new republic and demanded extensive
economic reforms to prevent the recurrence of fascism. For this purpose,
they emphasized and reproduced the political fault lines that had divided fascists and antifascists all over Europe—with some important qualifications. In
the case of the Communists, the spirit of international, antifascist solidarity
was first extended toward the antifascist bulwark in Moscow and the victims
in Eastern Europe—many of whom were retroactively stripped of their Jewish identity—and subsequently enlarged to include the German population.[83]
In the case of the Social Democrats, the transnational component of their
working-class identity (which explains their demands for compensation for
foreign victims) was quickly overshadowed by a sustained and aggressive
campaign for German reunification and international neutrality, which the
SPD launched to challenge Adenauer's policy of west integration.[84] Unfortunately, the story of working-class resistance had limited appeal for a population that had lacked such exemplary courage. Moreover, Germans quickly
lost interest in far-flung nationalization plans, which had initially appealed to
many survivors of the Third Reich. Therefore, the political culture in West
Germany rapidly produced a memory of Nazism that was more attractive to
the majority of citizens who no longer identified with the Nazis and had
never shared the commitments of the antifascist opposition.

In the course of the Adenauer era, the victim discourses of the Left and the
Right were pushed aside by the increasingly dominant collective memory of
the bystanders of the Third Reich, who constructed an alternative myth of German victimization. True to the antitotalitarian spirit of the times, the government and its representatives in parliament argued that the Weimar Republic
and the German people had been the victims of Nazis as well as Communists.
Caught in the battle between competing radical ideologies, the bystanders
had helplessly watched the destruction of the republic and the rise and fall of

Hitler's Germany.[85] The myth had a number of very appealing implications. Although Antifascists might have suffered more than the average citizen during the Third Reich and Nazis, at least initially, might have had to bear the brunt of the Allied reform efforts, their misery appeared commensurate to the agony they had brought on Germany as a result of their irresponsible behavior. According to the logic of the myth, the innocent bystanders had earned the right to lead the postwar republic after having been pushed around by radicals for such a long time and with such terrible consequences. Only bystanders such as Adenauer could supposedly serve as honest brokers, sort out the competing claims of losers and victors, and return Germany to the nonideological mainstream.

In the political everyday life of the Federal Republic, the different concepts and ideologies of victimhood were often combined. Especially before elections, Christian Democrats as well as Social Democrats appealed to former Nazis, soldiers, and expellees by acknowledging their specific sense of victimhood.[86] This creative integration of diverging concepts of victimhood proved easier to accomplish than one might assume. Despite important ideological differences between the competing victim identities, they all appealed to past experiences of personal suffering. As long as the reasons and precise circumstances of these experiences were left unmentioned, media, politicians, and the electorate could craft the pervasive, lingering resentment about past injustices into the lowest common psychological and political denominator for the first generation of reluctant West Germans. This compromise identity turned out to be both vague and ruthlessly exclusive at the same time. Despite the occasional acknowledgment of the suffering of the Jewish "fellow citizens," the first prototype of West German national identity was implicitly directed against all groups of victims who played no significant role in the new democratic process.[87] Roma/Sinti, homosexuals, forced laborers, and other victim groups were not part of the West German social contract. In fact, it was easier for former Nazis to be accepted into this bystander/victim community than for many of Hitler's real victims.

THE END OF THE POSTWAR PERIOD?

Everything seemed to fall into place by the mid-1950s, at least from the perspective of the Adenauer administration. The comprehensive denazification plans of the Allies had been derailed, and only a handful of German leaders remained behind bars. The government had weathered the refugee crisis without any serious political or economic destabilization. The debts of the German Reich had been settled for a reasonable price, reparations were postponed into the distant future, and the few, unavoidable compensation agreements that were made improved West Germany's reputation without representing a crippling burden. The destruction of the war turned out to be less severe than it had originally appeared, and the currency reform and the influx of foreign investment jump-started the economy almost overnight, with the result that reconstruction and economic recovery progressed much more quickly than expected. In contrast to developments in the Weimar Republic, the political mainstream had successfully marginalized radical political parties and ideologies, as Adenauer's resounding election victory of 1953 demonstrated. Merely ten years after the collapse of the Third Reich, the Federal Republic had regained sovereignty and was firmly integrated into the political, military, and economic networks of the capitalist West. None of this could have been accomplished without the marvelous window of opportunity provided by the Cold War, but the federal government had certainly played its cards wisely, showing goodwill whenever necessary and using its increasing political leverage effectively, almost ruthlessly, whenever possible. Finally, all these developments made so much sense because the past, present, and future seemed to follow a simple, powerful narrative trajectory. Antitotalitarianism at home and abroad appeared to guarantee economic and political prosperity. Completely unrelated events, from the war in Korea to the workers' uprising in the GDR, made sense if viewed through this antitotalitarian lens.

Scholars of German memory often reproachfully recite the basic strategies of representation that West Germans employed in the 1950s to thwart off the guilt that they had heaped onto themselves through war and genocide. For most commentators, these defense mechanisms—for instance, the self-stylization as victims, the projection of all responsibility on Hitler and his henchmen, and the neutralization of Nazism as a natural catastrophe—were dishonest, self-serving myths that the population and its elected leaders constructed in mutually reinforcing and mutually comforting cycles of collective make-believe.[88] This dominant, liberal emplotment of the history of West German memory is occasionally amended to include an interesting psychological caveat. Some liberal critics, mostly members of the postwar generations, are willing to concede that the German people and their leaders might not have had a real choice in the matter because their own personal losses had traumatized them to such an extent that they were cut off from the historical truth of their own responsibility. Commentators who assume such collective psychological impairment rarely fail to point out that it took several genera-tions to work through the trauma and guilt.[89] In either version of this liberal master narrative, critics have conveniently cast themselves in a very privi-leged position. According to their own model of German memory and Ger-man trauma, they are the first generation that is politically and psychologically capable of fully understanding and representing the historical catastrophes of Nazism and the Holocaust—catastrophes from which their parents still had to avert their eyes in denial and disbelief. But the liberal model of Ger-man collective memory has one important shortcoming. Precisely because the model is so elegantly and compellingly constructed, it is difficult to use the historical analysis of the memory culture of the 1950s for a rigorous, self-reflexive inquiry into the limits of the Holocaust culture that came into exis-tence during the 1980s.

Obviously, there is an alternative interpretation of the politics of history of the postwar years that is psychologically less complex but similarly concerned about establishing its own moral and epistemological superiority. According to the conservative minority opinion, the new political elite, far from being psychologically or otherwise impaired, undertook the Herculean task of recon-struction with impressive zeal and success. That achievement put subse-quent generations in a position to engage in symbolic politics of memory and contemplate their own moral superiority in the comfort of their secure, middle-class existence.[90] Even if one does not want to take sides in this morally overde-termined debate, the accomplishments of the Adenauer administrations appear exceptional indeed. Rarely have politicians been so successful in deliv-ering on their promises. In his first speech in parliament, Adenauer protested against the removal of German industries by the Allies; promised support for the German war victims, expellees, and civil servants; announced a rigorous review of the military court proceedings against the German military leader-ship and the denazification process; and committed himself to a policy of aggressive economic growth to pay for the promised subsidies.[91] This prag-matic declaration of political intent was severely criticized by opposition leader Kurt Schumacher because Adenauer had only mentioned the suffering of the Jews in passing, when an acknowledgment of Jewish sacrifice and a pledge of support and compensation should have topped his agenda.[92] But after six years in power, Adenauer had realized his objectives and, along the way, even fulfilled some of the objectives of the political opposition.

In the years following the founding of the republic, the conservative politicians in power helped shape a paradigm of NS interpretation that would soon dominate the West German political scene. But despite the overwhelming success of the antitotalitarian discourse, the conservative leadership remained insecure about the popular appeal and long-term resilience of their own ideological stopgap measure. They feared that the new Cold War ideology could be easily pushed aside by interpretive paradigms that had deeper roots in German society. The two most important and obvious competitors were socialism, in its democratic Western and dictatorial Eastern varieties, and traditional nationalism. Both ideological constructs offered coherent worldviews and called into question the historical rationale of west integration. Moreover, both were pushed by the SPD, which, through the late 1950s, combined traditional Socialist demands—for instance, about the nationalization of key industries—with a strong emphasis on national unity. But the more comfortable West Germans felt in their new role as Western consumers, the more they lost interest in antifascist lore and Socialist utopias. Consequently, the SPD had to reinvent itself as a bourgeois party by dropping the rhetoric of class war and joining the pro-Western, antitotalitarian camp. Yet despite this clear ideological victory of the conservative mainstream and despite repeated CDU victories at the ballot box, conservative politicians still felt that they ideologically shortchanged their voters, who, they assumed, suffered from a debilitating identity vacuum after the collapse of the Third Reich. That ideological inferiority complex continued to haunt the conservative leadership until 1989, initially made them very nervous about East German propaganda, and prompted them to embark on numerous ill-fated attempts to construct a West German national identity for what allegedly was a politically immature population.

CHAPTER 10

THE LONG GOOD-BYE OF THE
WAR GENERATIONS AND THE SEARCH
FOR LIBERAL POLITICS OF MEMORY

From Adenauer to Schmidt

The historical culture of the 1950s presents a complex and contradictory picture. On the one hand, West German society and its elite appeared determined to remove the signs of defeat and international ostracism, and they were very successful in doing so: they cleared the rubble, integrated the refugees, won the freedom of POWs and war criminals, regained political self-determination and military power, joined the Western alliance, settled accounts with victims, and crafted ideological concepts that sustained the sudden change of fortune. On the other hand, even as the West German recovery seemed to progress most swiftly, the society shifted its trajectory, gradually but persistently. During the second half of the 1950s, the self-critical voices gained momentum and unsettled the postwar equilibrium that Adenauer and others had established with such skill. The first part of the story is easily told. It does not take much imagination to understand the motives and the exceptional drive of the "survivors" of the Third Reich in their pursuit of reconstruction, stability, and forgetfulness. But the second part of the story presents an interesting historiographical and narrative challenge. Why would West Germans question a collective memory that had served them so well?

The literature on German memory contains a wide range of explanations for the origins of West Germany's unusually self-critical historical culture. Some scholars emphasize the importance of foreign influences. They argue that in the wake of the Eichmann trial in Jerusalem in 1960–1961 and a sustained GDR propaganda campaign against former Nazis in positions of power, the West German elite was forced to revise its policy of leniency.[1] Other experts highlight the accomplishments of a small group of liberal jurists in the state administrations, who convinced regional politicians to found a central agency for the prosecution of Nazi crimes. Starting in 1958, the agency in Ludwigsburg launched the first systematic German effort to research the crimes of the regime and bring perpetrators to trial.[2] At the same time, a new democratic spirit held sway over West Germany's public sphere. Historians point to the rise of a protest movement against nuclear weapons, which brought tens of thousands of demonstrators into the streets, and a thriving intellectual scene, which produced its own critical memory events, such as the release of Günter Grass's *Tin Drum* in 1959.[3] These critical voices were amplified by the national press corps, whose members played a key role in scandalizing anti-Semitic behavior and the shortcomings of the courts in their dealings with old and new Nazis.[4]

One might add other, more speculative story lines to this historiographical mix. The success of the critical press coverage and the circulation of photos of the Nazi crimes in the popular press indicate that West German society was ready to be entertained by accounts of spectacular Nazi crimes.[5] Apparently, Nazi history became a source of popular entertainment at the same time that Germany underwent an electronic media revolution, marked by the rise of television. Finally, during the 1950s, Germans still had to deal with the many traumas of the war.[6] Perhaps the turning point at the end of the decade signaled a decisive shift in this collective mourning process. All these facets of the political and cultural history of German memory are nicely reflected in the term *Vergangenheitsbewältigung*, which was invented in the late 1950s.[7]

The turning point of the late 1950s is emphasized by scholars who have studied German memory on the basis of archival material since the 1990s. But most of them have no firsthand experience of life in postwar Germany, and therefore, it is interesting to note that their predecessors, West German intellectuals who lived through the period and studied the historical culture of the 1950s as contemporaries, have come to very different conclusions. Theodor Adorno, the Mitscherlichs, Ralph Giordano, and even Hermann Lübbe failed to notice the turning point of the late 1950s. In their opinion, West Germany continued on the road of self-serving amnesia or salutary silence far into the 1960s and 1970s.[8] This major discrepancy in interpretation might indicate that the contemporaries were blinded by their political interests and failed to notice a historical turning point for which they were prime examples. Perhaps they enjoyed casting themselves in the role of courageous critics stemming the tide of amnesia and therefore failed to notice how many fellow citizens shared their critical assessments. It is also possible, however, that today's professional memory experts exaggerate the social relevance of the stories they have uncovered in the course of their research. Appreciative of self-critical historical reflection, they seek out the lone critical voices and intellectual whistle-blowers and retroactively attribute to them political powers they might never have had in real life.

The disagreements between contemporary observers and younger scholars might also reflect their respective source base. Some of the key innovations of the late 1950s occurred, for instance, in the realm of law. A number of scandals in that period involved former Nazis who tried to use the courts to be reinstalled into their professions or who had been identified by their victims but were only reluctantly charged by competent authorities.[9] The self-righteousness of these plaintiffs and defendants outraged informed observers as much as the nonchalance of the judges. It seemed that the courts were filled with former Nazis—unfortunately, on both sides of the docket. These concerns triggered important reform efforts, including the founding of the Ludwigsburg agency and an only partially successful attempt to coax the most seriously compromised judges into early retirement.[10] Yet these developments occurred outside the purview of the general public. Many media outlets reported about the scandals, but the discussions about solutions and the halfhearted reform efforts were only covered in the sociologically circumscribed media environment of the national press.[11] The pursuit of Vergangenheitsbewältigung was initially a primarily intellectual preoccupation. Under exceptional circumstances, elite initiatives would result in national memory events, in the way that the founding of the Ludwigsburg agency led to the 1963–1965 Auschwitz trial, for example. But most of the innovations of the late 1950s were directed at relatively small audiences.

The turning point fifteen years after the war marked an increasing diversification and fragmentation of West Germany's historical culture, not a general shift in historical consciousness. From that point forward, there were at least three major and more or less independent arenas of historical reflection: the visual media of cinema and especially television, working in close cooperation with the popular illustrated press; the national political scene that was covered extensively in the national highbrow press; and a large variety of specialized yet interconnected intellectual settings, including theater, art cinema, literature, law, architecture, and academic history. For about ten years, from the late 1940s to the late 1950s, these arenas had been surprisingly compatible. But they subsequently evolved in different directions, with television and politics continuing to favor consensual, defensive formats of collective memory, whereas some of the intellectual subfields, for example, law and literature, developed more critical types of historical reflection that challenged the conservative mainstream.

One of the key issues that caused tension between different spheres of West Germany's historical culture was the question of what past behavior justified the label "Nazi." Which segments of Nazi society should have political visibility as guilty perpetrators? After 1945, politicians and other role models in the West aggressively advocated a simple, self-serving concept of Nazism that separated Hitler and his henchmen from the rest of the population. This concept initially conflicted with the interests of the Allies, who wanted to treat Germans according to their individual conduct in the Third Reich, and the interests of surviving victims of Nazi crimes, who demanded satisfaction for their suffering. The most ambitious model collapsed first; in the context of the Cold War, it proved impractical to determine the guilt of every German. The second, grassroots concept of Nazism survived longer; throughout the 1950s, the German courts dealt with perpetrators who had been recognized by their victims. But the crude dichotomy between Nazi leaders and seduced followers quickly became the dominant model and governed the actions of the West German state and judiciary. Only the most prominent Nazi leaders retained political visibility—for two simple reasons. First, their prominence had been established by the NS media and reinforced by the media event of the Nuremberg trials.[12] And second, dead or incarcerated, they no longer required judicial attention and could conveniently absorb excess guilt. The vast majority of Nazi perpetrators—unknown to the media or their victims—were systematically rendered invisible by the basic categories of historical analysis that the West German mainstream embraced. None of the soldiers, party members, and bureaucrats who had perpetrated crimes appeared on the political radar screen. In fact, even incorrigible Nazis had to go to extraordinary lengths to regain visibility as Nazis; like Remer or Werner Naumann, they had to launch raucous neo-Nazi campaigns and far-flung conspiracies to attract the attention of authorities.

But the comfortable limits of visibility that shielded all the "unknown" Nazis from detection were gradually and often inadvertently called into question by a number of different factors, such as by the critics of the dysfunctional judiciary and by an emerging popular culture that helped visualize the unknown Nazis.[13] The postwar West German cinema, which was hardly a haven of self-critical reflection, had come up with an inoffensive way of representing Nazis. The perpetrators on the big screen tended to be anonymous, ideologically driven brutes without personality or conscience.[14] This stereotype might have made it easier for the viewers to enjoy the performance, but for some observers the cinematic discourse confirmed the existence of the unknown Nazis who were also featured prominently in the judicial scandals of the times. The nameless perpetrator, hiding behind a respectable bourgeois facade, became a perceivable threat, and his existence was forcefully confirmed by GDR propaganda.

The political elite clearly faced a confluence of mutually reenforcing interpretations of the past, emanating from different spheres of West Germany's historical culture, that called into question some basic tenets of the political memory of the postwar years. As a result of these developments, politicians lost the leadership role in memory politics that they had occupied during the first ten years of the republic. But none of the changes prompted an immediate response from the federal government, despite (or because of) the fact that there were many former Nazis in the federal bureaucracy who now regained visibility because of the new public image of Nazi perpetrators.[15] Adenauer and his CDU successors either ignored or vigorously defended themselves against the charge of renazification and never deviated from the path of antitotalitarianism. Moreover, at the same time that the intellectual discourse of Vergangenheitsbewältigung took shape, the SPD embraced west integration and antitotalitarianism as West Germany's official ideologies. As a result, the party was now uneasily perched between the conservative mainstream, whose interpretation of the past the Social Democrats adopted for strategic reasons, and the intellectual critics, whose revisionism corresponded to the resistance identity that Schumacher and others had fostered in the immediate postwar years. Even during the SPD/FDP administrations after 1969, when the party collaborated closely with liberal intellectuals, antitotalitarianism remained the underlying basis of federal politics. That fact contributed to the rapid disillusionment of Brandt's intellectual supporters and explains why the intellectual critics who lived through the 1950s and 1960s did not notice a decisive shift in West Germany's historical culture. People such as the Mitscherlichs or Giordano were quite aware that, despite the best efforts of the intellectual elite, the political and the popular memory of Nazism that had been crafted in the postwar years proved surprisingly impervious to change.

There might be another reason why the changes of the late 1950s did not register too prominently in the contemporary intellectual discourse and many subsequent publications dedicated to West German efforts of mastering the past. The generational model of German collective memory, which has been used to structure the process of Vergangenheitsbewältigung from its inception and which was applied in previous chapters, helps explain the transformations from the late 1960s through the 1980s, but it fails to explain the turning point of the late 1950s—at least as elegantly as one might wish. At that point, the first postwar generation, the generation of the student movement, had not yet arrived on the political scene, and their older peers, the members of the Hitler Youth generation, were involved in the transformation but were not yet calling the shots.[16] The changes in the perception of Nazism that occur fifteen years after the war resulted from a successful collaboration among different age-groups that had experienced Nazism as adults *or* as adolescents and that now updated the antitotalitarianism consensus for a rapidly modernizing, increasingly self-confident democracy.

The recalibration of the concept "Nazi" that began in the late 1950s was just one aspect of the subtle transformation of West German collective memories that were primarily concerned with the bystanders and not the perpetrators of the Third Reich. Starting in the early 1960s, an intergenerationally produced, self-confident bystander memory arose, which would dominate the German scene for many years to come and set the agenda for the memory fights of the future. The most important political effect of the struggle about the new concept of Nazi, which now included people directly involved in the "Final Solution," incorrigible anti-Semites, and prominent politicians with NS pasts, concerned the citizens outside these targeted groups. By redrawing the border between Nazis and non-Nazis, the contemporaries of the Third Reich consolidated their identity as nonviolent, nonideological, and innocent bystanders.[17] The new line of demarcation was drawn with considerably more self-confidence than previous symbolic borders had been. By the late 1950s, the silent majority had survived Hitler *and* created the economic miracle. On the basis of those accomplishments, the intergenerational coalition aggressively protected the integrity of bystanders in many spheres of West Germany's historical culture. The well-constructed innocence of the average citizen of the Third Reich drew the ire of the postwar generation, although it was never completely dismantled. At least in the political arena, the self-confident bystander memory has remained the dominant collective memory to this date.

Considered from the bystander perspective, the tensions that developed between different arenas of collective memory in the late 1950s seem to reflect a separation of labor between different channels of communication rather than an outright competition between diametrically opposed political identities. It is true that the SPD and CDU's decision to leave the self-critical practice of Vergangenheitsbewältigung to others produced a rift in the historical culture of the Federal Republic, which still exists today. Most likely, politicians made the right choice when they kept their eyes on the voters and their distance from the intellectual skirmishes because, at least until the 1980s, an explicitly self-critical memory agenda would not have had a chance at the ballot box. At the same time, however, the decision to defend the postwar memory peace as well as the decision to challenge it were initially based on the same fundamental interest in protecting the integrity of the Nazi bystanders, who represented the majority of German voters, media consumers, and intellectuals. This subtle, pervasive, passive-aggressive bystander memory was effectively challenged by the political activists of the postwar generation who never had to face the choice between accommodation and resistance and could therefore easily imagine themselves in the role of heroic resister against Nazis, parents, and the Bonn establishment. But before that challenge could register, let alone influence the political scene, the war generations had another opportunity to strip themselves of the most overt remnants of Nazism. Judged with hindsight—and not just from the perspective of the student activists—the attempts of the late 1950s and early 1960s to combat anti-Semitism and exclude Nazis from political leadership positions were not particularly successful.

PRIVATIZING ANTI-SEMITISM

It is difficult to decide if the late 1950s were marked by a significant increase in anti-Semitic behavior or if the public perception of such behavior had changed and the media had adjusted their coverage accordingly. Most likely, both factors together explain the rise of a new type of media story highlighting the

persistence of anti-Semitic attitudes among the average citizens of the Federal Republic. After 1957, newspapers, radio, and the new medium of television reported frequently on insults that Jews and Jewish institutions suffered
courtesy of old and new Nazis. Some of the cases made national headlines
and even became the subject of parliamentary debates—for instance, the
case of a high school teacher who threatened a Jewish survivor while proudly
recalling his participation in the "Final Solution," or the activities of a Hamburg businessman who spent his profits on printing anti-Semitic pamphlets
that he distributed generously across the country, including to members of
parliament. At least as disturbing as the stupidity of the older generation
were the many acts of vandalism by youthful offenders directed against Jewish institutions, which raised the specter of a postwar generation steeped in
Nazi ideology. But all these incidents only assumed scandalous proportions
because law enforcement agencies failed to apprehend or punish the perpetrators. As in the past, the judges considered anti-Semitism a harmless pastime and, in the early days at least, released the offenders with a slap on the
wrist.[18]

The climax of the crisis occurred on Christmas Day in 1959 when two
young adults painted swastikas and anti-Semitic slogans on the walls of the
Cologne synagogue, which had just been renovated and rededicated in the
presence of the chancellor himself. The actions of the two youths were hardly
exceptional; similar offenses had been occurring all across West Germany for
several years. But the location and the timing of the crime, in addition to the
already tense atmosphere, caused an outcry in the media and a wave of copy-
cat crimes, both nationally and internationally. Critical observers in Germany
and abroad became convinced that the renazification of the Federal Republic
was well under way. In light of the international repercussions of the event,
the federal government quickly tried its hand at damage control. Adenauer
himself embarked on a whirlwind of public relations activities. In addition to
interviews with the foreign press and his first visit to the site of a former concentration camp, he gave his fellow citizens concrete didactic advice. In a
television address in January 1960, he suggested that a good thrashing would
go a long way to straightening out the hoodlums. Adenauer's message struck
a chord in his audience and elegantly transferred the problem from the political into the private realm. But his statement also reflected his honest assessment of the situation. Despite all his public assurances of swift action and

increased vigilance, he saw no need to change his pragmatic policies of national reconciliation.[19]

In response to the Christmas incident, parliament quickly adopted a new law against the incitement of racism—although not necessarily on its own volition. Other European governments had enacted similar measures to contain the wave of anti-Semitic offenses, and West Germany simply could not break rank.[20] In fact, parliament's unwillingness to change course in any more profound way became obvious in May 1960. While Eichmann was tried in Israel, the statute of limitations for all Nazi crimes of manslaughter took effect in West Germany. Parliament discussed the matter only briefly, and the government as well as a majority of the MPs saw no need for action.[21]

POLITICAL SITES OF MEMORY AND THE EAST-WEST CONFLICT: OBERLÄNDER AND GLOBKE

There have always been suspicions that the wave of anti-Semitic actions had been orchestrated by East Berlin, although no conclusive evidence has been found yet.[22] But there are no doubts about the origins of the concurrent, aggressive East German media campaign that exposed former Nazis within the West German government and accelerated the change in perception of the Nazi past in the Federal Republic. In 1959, the East German administration stepped up its propaganda efforts against the West in an effort to win back the hearts of its own population. Since the mid-1950s, an average of 250,000 East German citizens had left the country per year. Most of them were young and well educated, and they joined the economic miracle in the West and thus threatened the very existence of the GDR. The accusations hurled across the border did not solve the crisis—the construction of the Berlin Wall accomplished that in 1961—but the well-staged campaign served as an important catalyst in the development of a new type of collective memory of Nazism in the West.[23]

The poster boy for East German charges about the renazification of the Federal Republic was Adenauer's minister for expellee affairs, Theodor Oberländer. In the early 1930s, Oberländer embarked on a stellar career in political science and agroscience and joined the leadership of a number of political and scholarly associations dedicated to the study of eastern Europe and the protection of German minorities abroad. All academics working in this field wanted to strengthen the German influence in the East, and the Nazi seizure of power gave them extraordinary opportunities to participate in and profit from the construction of a neocolonial empire.[24] Oberländer became a member of the Nazi Party in May 1933, but personal and political problems with midlevel Nazi functionaries prompted him to continue his career in military counterintelligence, which needed experts to prepare for war. In this capacity, Oberländer was involved in three not particularly successful military campaigns in which he led Red Army POWs in the fight against Stalin. At the beginning of July 1941, Oberländer's unit witnessed the murder of thousands of Jews by Ukranian militia, SS, and Sicherheitsdienst (SD) in the city and vicinity of L'viv. Some members of Oberländer's battalion might have participated in the mass murder, but it has never been proven that he perpetrated atrocities or ordered others to commit them.[25]

After the war, the U.S. military secret service appreciated Oberländer's expertise in eastern European affairs, which might have helped him pass through the denazification proceedings relatively easily. Oberländer was free to pursue another extraordinary career, this time in politics. With the same ambition and adaptability that had served him well in the Third Reich, he embraced the cause of the expellees and quickly became one of the most powerful representatives of the BHE Party. In 1953, Oberländer joined Adenauer's second cabinet as secretary for expellee and refugee affairs. His appointment prompted negative press coverage in Germany and abroad and made the details of his Nazi career better known. But the criticism soon died down, despite the fact that Oberländer recruited a number of other former Nazis as senior staff members. Adenauer had been eager to get Oberländer and the BHE on board because with the BHE votes, he controlled a decisive two-thirds majority in parliament. As a matter of principal, Adenauer continued to support his minister even after the expellee special-interest party had run its course and Oberländer, ever the opportunist, had swiftly abandoned the BHE and joined the CDU.[26]

All this changed in the fall of 1959 when the Warsaw bloc unleashed a well-coordinated campaign against former Nazis in the West German government and selected Oberländer as the prime target. In several press conferences and high-profile news stories, Oberländer was accused of having tortured civilians and organized the massacre in L'viv. Although similar charges had not derailed Oberländer's career in previous years, he now faced serious criticism even from colleagues within the government and the CDU parliamentary faction. The CDU MP and editor of the weekly *Die Zeit*, Gerd Bucerius, made the most damaging public statement when he asked Oberländer to resign in order to protect the reputation of the government and the country.[27] Most West German observers, Bucerius and the SPD opposition included, did not believe that Oberländer had committed the crimes that the Eastern European press described in great detail. But people with Oberländer's record were now considered an unacceptable liability. As a onetime enthusiastic Nazi, he could no longer be accepted within a political establishment that had reinvented itself as a community of innocent bystanders. In the course of this moral makeover, the political leaders of the Federal Republic had belatedly developed a sense of collective shame, although they recast the concept of Nazi so carefully and selectively that they still only had to be embarrassed about a small minority in their own ranks. Moreover, not everybody shared the new standards of political integrity. In the end, Adenauer only accepted Oberländer's resignation in 1960 because he no longer served any important political purpose and was therefore not worth the trouble. Oberländer spent the rest of his long life fighting his accusers in court, for the most part very successfully.[28] In the 1990s, he once again became the focus of critical attention. For the historians of the Hamburg School, he exemplified the inhumane, racist disposition of twentieth-century social science. Götz Aly and Susanne Heim counted him among the academics who laid the intellectual foundation for the "Final Solution."[29]

The next target of East Berlin's campaign, Adenauer's chancellery minister Hans Globke, suffered public humiliation like Oberländer but did not have to cut short his political career. As a civil servant in the Interior Ministry of the Third Reich, Globke had coauthored a lengthy interpretation of the Nuremberg Laws, crafted legislation that added special surnames to the legal names of Jewish citizens, and participated in the negotiations with Swiss authorities about marking Jewish passports. But after the war, Globke received ringing endorsements from acclaimed conservative opponents of the Hitler regime, who praised his conspiratorial support for the assassins of the July 20, 1944, uprising.[30] Globke became the head of Adenauer's chancellery in 1949 and proved to be a loyal and irreplaceable adviser. For the opposition, he represented a prime example of the administration's failed personnel policy. Schumacher complained repeatedly that Adenauer and his ministers far too often recruited former high-ranking members of Hitler's government for senior civil service positions and thus risked West Germany's credibility as a democratic state.[31] But by the late 1950s, SPD politicians had abandoned their case against Globke and others because their criticism had not appealed to moderate voters. In democratic fashion, the bystander memory offered by the conservative mainstream had won the competition against the resistance/victim identity initially championed by Social Democrats. As a result of these developments, the final and most severe attack on Globke was carried out by East German ideologues and the West German press—each pursuing different objectives. East Berlin used the Eichmann trial in Israel to claim a direct link between Eichmann and Globke. Albrecht Norden, the Sozialistische Einheitspartei Deutschlands (SED) leader in charge of the anti-Nazi campaign, argued strenuously that Globke had written and not just commented on the Nuremberg Laws.[32] The majority of the West German press corps rejected these charges but faulted Adenauer for continuing to support Globke despite his dubious record in the Third Reich.[33] Although his case, like Oberländer's, demonstrated a shift in published opinion, Globke remained in office until his mandatory retirement in 1963, which coincided with the end of Adenauer's third and last term in office. Adenauer was determined not to hold the past mistakes of former Nazis such as Globke and Oberländer against them as long as they remained loyal *and* useful members of his administration.

In the late 1950s and early 1960s, the actions of the GDR government decisively influenced the collective memories in the West for the last time. The existence of the GDR had always played an important role in the politics of history pursued in Bonn. The physical proximity and competition with the ideological other across the border made antitotalitarianism such a successful ideology. But in 1959, East Berlin intervened in the memory politics on the other side of the border at the very moment that some of the basic categories of historical representation shifted toward a less selective and defensive understanding of the Nazi crimes. Therefore, the East German disinformation represented an important factor in the construction of a new understanding of the burden of the past. Norden continued his attacks on West German politicians, including such high-profile targets as President Heinrich Lübke and Chancellor Hans Georg Kiesinger, but none of these campaigns proved as compelling as the charges against Oberländer and Globke. Moreover, after the construction of the Berlin Wall and the self-critical turn in West Germany's memory politics, Norden's propaganda failed to make much of an impression in the West.[34] With Brandt's new foreign policy toward eastern Europe (*Ostpolitik*), East Berlin completely lost the initiative in the arena of memory politics and never regained it.

By the time his party finally forced the eighty-seven-year-old Adenauer into retirement in 1963, he had maneuvered the Federal Republic into a state of international isolation. In the first half of the 1950s, the steadfast implementation of west integration had gained him many friends and admirers, but in the second half of the decade, his government's uncompromising attitude toward Eastern Europe became a serious obstacle in an age of détente. In 1961, West Germans were as much shocked by the construction of the Berlin Wall as they were outraged by the apparent indifference of their allies in the West who passively watched the catastrophe unfold. Apparently, political leaders of the Federal Republic had to take matters into their own hands and actively pursue their interests in the East. Yet Adenauer's Christian Democratic successors, Ludwig Erhard and Hans Georg Kiesinger, hesitated to revise a foreign policy that had facilitated West Germany's unexpectedly fast recovery.

Erhard became chancellor in October 1963 and quickly fell out of favor with his coalition partners from the FDP and many leaders in his own party when he failed to find a quick remedy for the economic difficulties that the republic encountered after fifteen years of prosperity. Kiesinger subsequently took the helm of a CDU-SPD coalition in December 1966, but he and his foreign minister, Willy Brandt, failed to normalize relations with Eastern Europe against Soviet objections. The federal government signed trade agreements with a number of Eastern European countries in 1963 and established diplomatic relations with Romania in 1967, but more fundamental foreign policy reforms were left to the Social Democratic/liberal coalition that assumed power in 1969.[35]

Erhard and Kiesinger were even more reluctant to break with the politics of history of their famous predecessor. They dutifully administered the various compensation and reconciliation provisions but saw no need for new initiatives, with the exception of occasional intellectual interventions to boost the spiritual well-being of their historically challenged people. In true Adenauer fashion, Erhard immediately declared the end of the postwar era after taking office. In his mind, West Germany's material accomplishments had permanently dispelled the shadows of the past—certainly, a very suitable analysis for the designer of the economic miracle.[36] However, somewhat in contradiction to these declarations, Erhard also set out to design an appropriate postfascist German identity. Convinced that Germans had overreacted to the loss of the war and their homeland by abandoning the healthy traditions of nationalism, he now hoped to fill the gap with the idea of a "formed society." Erhard's strange mixture of liberal, technocratic, and authoritarian traditions never took off, but it illustrated how much Nazism and the war had undermined the worldview of the conservative elite.[37] Projecting their own disorientation onto the whole population, conservative politicians and academics saw the republic threatened by the destructive forces of secularism, crude materialism, and regional particularism that were no longer counterbalanced by any sense of national cohesion. It seems from today's perspective that the conservative elites could not believe how easily they had escaped from the catastrophe they had helped bring about and therefore expected the burden of the past to return with a vengeance at any moment.

On the highest level of government, the 1960s' politics of history lacked vision and ambition, but that was obviously not true for many other segments of West Germany's public sphere. Important legal and educational reforms that had been crafted on the lower levels of the Federal Republic's political infrastructure in the late 1950s were now taking full effect. In the years since 1958, the central agency for the persecution of Nazi crimes had carefully researched the historical details of the Nazi genocide. As a result, beginning in 1960, a whole string of trials involving former personnel of the extermination sites kept the "Final Solution" in the headlines for several years.[38] In addition, the release of new curricula and textbooks had at least some effect on the teaching of history in schools. It had become increasingly unlikely that German teenagers would graduate from high school without having at least a vague idea about the meaning of Auschwitz.[39] Finally, in 1963, West Germany experienced its first media event that focused specifically on the moral and political responsibility of the bystanders of the "Final Solution." Rolf Hochhuth's play *The Deputy* became a theatrical hit, and intellectuals entered into a a heated discussion of the passivity of Pope Pius during World War II and Hochhuth's interpretation of the Vatican's policies.[40] All these developments showed that the aggressive reinterpretation of Nazism by the student movement was not the only and arguably not even the most influential factor in the reorientation of West Germany's historical culture in the 1960s. However, as often happens in times of rapid intellectual transformation, the new representations of the past remained very ambivalent in their meanings and possible effects. They certainly improved the general awareness of the crimes of the regime, but they also offered effective strategies of avoidance and exculpation. The trials suggested that only a relatively few thugs were responsible for the "Final Solution"; Hochhuth highlighted the shortcomings of an influential foreigner; the new teaching guidelines contained the topic of National Socialism within a rigid antitotalitarian framework;[41] and the radical students delivered a scathing critique of the older generation but had little to say about the historical responsibilities they and their peers faced as a result of the Nazi past.

In the immediate postwar years, politicians led the German efforts to respond to the challenges left behind by Nazism. They simply had no choice in the matter. The many pressing social, organizational, and moral problems required political solutions. As these solutions took effect and many temporary measures became long-term arrangements, politicians turned their attention to the more routine, presentist concerns that were no longer directly linked to the Nazi past. At the same time, other professions and other arenas of public life became the primary sites of historical reflection and controversy. In some cases (for example, in the legal profession), the shift of momentum was at least in part the result of past political decisions. In other cases (for instance, in the literary field or the youth subculture), the new efforts of historical interpretation either evolved independently from the political realm or took shape in opposition to the dominant themes of postwar politics. As a result, in the 1960s, the political establishment assumed a more reactive and at times even defensive voice in the increasingly competitive and divisive cultural wars about the legacy of Nazism. Politics of history were no longer the politicians' primary concern or responsibility. They dealt with the past when circumstances forced them to craft new legal interpretations of the Nazi legacy or when representations of the past could be employed in reproducing or challenging existing power structures. Both factors played an important role in the 1965 parliamentary discussion about the statute of limitations for murder.

THE STATUTE OF LIMITATIONS FOR MURDER

The ground rules of West German politics, which politicians had developed in 1949, made the job relatively easy for the new parliament. By casting the Federal Republic in the role of the successor state of the Weimar Republic, members of the constitutional council had created a helpful fiction of legal continuity. Since the Nazis had never officially suspended the Weimar constitution, the founding fathers and mothers of the republic could pretend that the rule of law had survived the dictatorship unscathed.[42] This fiction had two important consequences for the prosecution of the Nazi perpetrators. The postwar political elite assumed that the Nazi crimes could be successfully prosecuted according to the laws existing at the time of the offenses — no special, retroactive laws à la Nuremberg would be required. In addition, everybody expected that the whole process would be wrapped up in a reasonable amount of time because the Weimar legal code provided clear statutes of limitations. Until 1965, parliament kept up the pretense. In the spirit of general forgiveness, one statute of limitation after another took effect with minimal discussion in parliament. In 1960, the SPD opposition suggested extending the statute of limitations for manslaughter, but the amendment was voted down by the conservative majority. At a time when the perception of the Nazi crimes had already shifted in other segments of West Germany's public sphere, most MPs still pursued aggressive politics of integration and reconciliation.[43] In contrast, by 1965, when parliament discussed the statute of limitations for murder, a new moralizing, self-reflexive discourse had found its way into the minds and hearts of a vocal minority of MPs. For the first time, even some conservative representatives challenged the legal peace of the 1950s from the perspective of a generation that had not committed any atrocities.

Although the voices in parliament now represented a wider range of opinions about the meaning of the Nazi past, the pragmatic bystander memory of the Third Reich still dominated the scene. The majority of parliamentarians maintained that changing the statute of limitations at that stage would threaten the integrity of the rule of law and undermine the credibility of the West German democracy in the eyes of its citizens. But they listened to their colleagues who passionately argued that an even more fundamental sense of justice would be violated if the democratic state did not use all legitimate resources at its disposal to punish the perpetrators of the state-sponsored genocide of

the Third Reich. The two opposing sides reflected the well-established difference between bystander and antifascist memory that had been fostered in the
ranks of the CDU and the SPD, respectively. But the critics of the status quo
also included a few young MPs, most notably Ernst Benda from the Christian Democrats, whose opposition to the existing statute of limitations tran-
scended the collective memories of the contemporaries of the Third Reich
and their focus on the sacrifices that Nazism had imposed on them.[44] For the
first time, a generation of politicians born into the Third Reich and consequently not responsible for its rise and demise considered the possibility that
some of the Nazi crimes had been exceptional events that exceeded the more
conventional terror that Hitler had waged on his own people. This new perspective on the burden of the Nazi past flourished in other social contexts, in
which members of the Hitler Youth generation became important players in
the 1970s. But in the political realm, the changing of the guard did not take
place until the 1980s.

THE TRIALS AND TRIBULATIONS OF HANS GEORG KIESINGER

The self-defensive attitude of most conservative politicians and their inability
to adapt to the changed intellectual climate in the Federal Republic played out
in exemplary fashion in the last years of the chancellorship of Hans Georg
Kiesinger. Kiesinger's career in the Third Reich as a senior bureaucrat in the
Foreign Ministry and member of the Nazi Party since 1933 made him an excellent target of memory politics. Two public events focusing on that past
stand out in hindsight because they capture the political constellation of the
late 1960s in a nutshell. In the first incident, which occurred on July 4, 1968,
Kiesinger testified as a defense witness in the trial of two former high-
ranking members of the Foreign Office who had participated in organizing
the "Final Solution" in Bulgaria. Kiesinger played the part of the defense
witness very well. Under repeated probing by the Frankfurt public prosecu-
tor, he assured the court that he had never heard about the "Final Solution"
in the ministry and that he had dismissed foreign news coverage about the
systematic murder of civilians in the East as wartime propaganda. By declaring his innocence, Kiesinger supported the defendants' assertion that
they had organized deportations without knowing the destination of the
transports.[45]

Kiesinger's appearance before the court was closely monitored by the foreign press corps and the former bureaucrats of the Third Reich. In particular, former Nazi officials under investigation by the Ludwigsburg and other prosecutorial agencies watched Kiesinger's testimony carefully because they considered themselves the victims of a judicial double standard. In their minds, the great majority of NS civil servants had been permitted to resume their careers—sometimes with exceptional success, as the case of Kiesinger demonstrated—while a handful of people had been singled out to receive punishment for the crimes of the whole nation. The accused officials failed to acknowledge that their duties had included mass murder, but they clearly had a point. The dividing line between "visible" and "invisible" Nazis was, indeed, drawn rather arbitrarily and constantly renegotiated. Moreover, these negotiations took place during a resurgence of Nazism as a political force. In 1964, a former Wehrmacht officer managed to unite a number of right-wing splinter parties under the umbrella of the Nationaldemokratische Partei Deutschlands (NPD). The party garnered up to 8 percent of the popular vote in state elections in 1966—with the result that Nazis were back in the governing business even as a few prosecutors still tried to sort out the mess they had left behind after their last stint in power.[46]

This contradictory situation was quietly resolved in favor of the civil servants. The Frankfurt trial that featured Kiesinger as the star witness ended with a guilty verdict, but the large majority of organizers of the Holocaust never had to face trial—in contrast to the lower-ranked personnel of the camps. The so-called *Schreibtischtäter* (desk perpetrators) were spared from prosecution because, as part of a routine legislative package passed by parliament in April 1968, the statute of limitations for accessory to murder charges was retroactively reduced to fifteen years, and thus, many trials against the organizers of the Holocaust had to be abandoned. It took months before the full extent of the legislative "mistake" became known, and the precise circumstances of this backdoor amnesty have never been determined. It is certainly possible, however, that bureaucrats in Bonn quickly intervened when administrators like themselves, who had devised the Holocaust from Berlin, were about to be put on trial.[47]

The second incident that highlighted Kiesinger's past and illustrated the political climate of the late 1960s in exemplary fashion lasted only seconds but garnered as much media attention as the chancellor's appearance in front

of the Frankfurt court. On November 7, 1968, the young political activist
Beate Klarsfeld, yelling "Kiesinger, Nazi," slapped Kiesinger across the face
while he addressed the CDU's party congress. The twenty-nine-year-old Klarsfeld had already pursued Kiesinger on a number of occasions, and her attack
was hardly the most memorable protest of the year. In April, Rudi Dutschke,
one of the leaders of the student movement, had been shot in Berlin by an
avid reader of the conservative tabloid *Bildzeitung,* and the radical wing of the
student movement and state authorities were well on their way to escalating
the violence against each other.[48] But Klarsfeld's action highlighted the exceptional role that references to the Nazi past played in this charged atmosphere.
For the students, analogies between past and present were a key element of
their intellectual inquiries into German history and their strategies of political provocation. In addition, both the political establishment and its critics
tried to justify their increasingly destructive and self-destructive behavior as
self-defense against the forces of totalitarianism or fascism.[49]

In attacking Kiesinger, Klarsfeld had not just singled out one of the most
successful former Nazis in the Federal Republic; she had also targeted an outspoken critic of the student movement and an aggressive advocate of the politics of national integration under the banner of antitotalitarianism. Several
times during his career as a regular MP, Kiesinger had suggested that former
Nazis and their erstwhile opponents join forces against the common enemy
in the East. In the late 1960s, he became one of the first conservative politicians to invoke the versatile paradigm of antitotalitarianism to explain and reject the political challenge of the student movement. Like many of his peers,
he believed that the Weimar Republic was destroyed as a result of a two-
pronged attack by political radicals on both sides of the political spectrum and
that a similar destructive force had reappeared in the form of the riotous students.[50] This basic narrative had two important implications. First, the political mainstream, however closely it might have collaborated with the Nazis
before and after 1933, did not bear any responsibility for Hitler's rise to power
and its long-term consequences. Second, the simple analogy between past
and present turned the students into the true heirs of National Socialism and
thus placed them beyond the pale of democracy; as enemies of the state, they
were not entitled to the privileges and protections extended to real democrats.

Kiesinger's two involuntary public performances illustrate the complex political situation of the late 1960s: A successful, conservative political estab-

THE LONG GOOD-BYE   233

lishment in the government, which had overcome the challenges of the post-war years and made peace with its involvement in the Third Reich, faced a handful of dissidents within its own ranks, a small faction of student activists, and a reconstituted Nazi movement. The situation was further complicated by the presence of foreign observers who carefully screened how the Federal Republic would master its first severe crisis and, last but not least, the Social Democratic opposition and, since 1966, coalition partner of the CDU. The SPD leadership negotiated the tricky political terrain very well by pursuing a risky and ambivalent but ultimately quite successful strategy of memory politics. On the one hand, the SPD leadership sided with the memory dissidents (and occasionally, even the student activists) and invoked the party's anti-Nazi legacy. On the other hand, the party purposefully approached the political mainstream and adopted its antitotalitarian identity. Partly as a result of this clever tactic on the part of the Social Democrats, the memory fights of the 1970s and 1980s pitched the conservative establishment against the many offshoots of the student movement and left the SPD relatively unscathed.

SOCIAL DEMOCRATIC MEMORY POLITICS

The Social Democrats were well prepared to assume power. They had dropped the class-warfare rhetoric in 1959, embraced Adenauer's west integration in 1960, and abandoned their aggressive prounification agenda after the construction of the Berlin Wall. Having also proven their ability to handle power during the CDU/SPD coalition, SPD leaders finally took over the helm in Bonn in 1969 in the midst of considerable political turmoil.[51] The crises and social changes of the 1960s and 1970s were the result of a complex generational constellation involving at least three different age-groups that used the Nazi past as their symbolic battleground. On the grassroots level of West German politics, a small group of activists, mostly members of the first post-war generation, burst onto the political scene in an unusually vigorous and creative fashion. Buoyed by their undeniable innocence of any Nazi crimes, they challenged the limits of West German society. The protests of the student movement coincided with the transfer of power from the Weimar to the war generation on the highest level of government. The first three chancellors of the Federal Republic and most of their ministers had developed their political identity before Hitler rose to power. In contrast, for Brandt and his associates, Hitler had always played a key role in their political universe; they could hardly remember a time when the Nazis or the lingering memory of the Third Reich had not dominated German politics. But people like Brandt and Egon Bahr had not just internalized the political landscape of the late Weimar Republic and the Third Reich; they had also defined their political personae in vehement opposition to the Nazis. For the first time in twenty years, representatives of the German resistance against Hitler led the federal government. This antifascist identity informed their political style and provoked their opponents. During the campaigns leading up to the 1966 and 1969 elections, the Christian Democrats viciously attacked Brandt for his decision to elude the grasp of the Nazis by escaping to Norway.[52] Brandt, for his part, never let his critics forget their past political sins. Having been elected chancellor in 1969, he declared that Hitler had now finally lost the war, implying that his predecessors in the job of chancellor had been tainted by their passive acceptance of the Nazi regime and therefore could not accomplish the necessary moral renewal of German politics.[53]

The politics of history of the Adenauer administrations and the politics of memory of the Kohl administrations have been studied in detail, but the record of the Brandt administration has never been subjected to similar scholarly scrutiny. Perhaps German academics have been reluctant to analyze the accomplishments of West Germany's only truly progressive chancellor because they considered Brandt a role model rather than a research subject. Be that as it may, a closer look at the political discourse between 1969 and 1974 reveals a contradictory picture. Despite the moralistic rhetoric about a second democratic zero hour, Brandt and his ministers tended to approach the burden of the past from a very pragmatic point of view, especially in their foreign policy. Brandt certainly intended to revolutionize the politics of history, as his personal interest in new rituals and gestures of remembrance demonstrated. But the speeches he delivered on such occasions followed fairly conventional antitotalitarian strategies of interpretation. In essence, Brandt seemed to strive for a new programmatic framework for the representation of the Nazi past, but lacking a clear alternative language of memory—or perhaps the courage to implement such a clear alternative vision—he settled for an ambivalent combination of radical new gestures of memory accompanied by traditional sound bites.

These inconclusive findings indicate that the early 1970s marked an important phase of transition in the official politics of memory of the republic—

and not just on the level of the student movement subculture. The activists on the street and their provocative reinterpretation of the past might have captured most of the limelight, but the contradictory messages of the Brandt government had similarly important long-term consequences. The Brandt administration participated simultaneously in two very different paradigms of memory politics. On the one hand, the Social Democratic evolutionaries still practiced the pragmatic, nonmoralistic politics of communicative memory that had been developed by Adenauer and that focused on the needs of the contemporaries of the Third Reich. On the other hand, people like Brandt and especially the new Social Democratic president, Gustav Heinemann, tried to shape the cultural memory of the Nazi past for the benefit of generations whose members had no personal memories of the German catastrophe. They were the first federal government officials to sponsor exhibits and museums for the teaching of contemporary German history. In this sense, Brandt and Heinemann set the precedent for the paradigm of cultural memory production that dominated the 1980s, when Helmut Kohl founded numerous government institutions with the intention of shaping the long-term popular memory of the Nazi era.[54]

STUDENT MOVEMENT AND OSTPOLITIK

During Brandt's years in office, two issues particularly enraged the political elite, and both were blown out of proportion because they turned into ill-defined proxy battles about the future of the Federal Republic and the political legacy of the Third Reich. One of these topics was the student movement and its terrorist offshoots. For CDU politicians, the crisis provided a welcome opportunity to repeat their antitotalitarian mantra that Kiesinger had already applied to the student activists. Conservative parliamentarians such as Alfred Dregger considered terrorism the result of too much liberal education, which had exposed a whole generation to the risks of spiritual homelessness. As he saw it, growing up without the benefits of a Christian value system and a positive sense of German history, some members of the postwar generation had turned into the same type of hoodlums who had brought down the Weimar Republic. Not surprisingly, the representatives of the governing coalition vehemently refused this claim. In their opinion, the misguided actions of the students were caused by the grave political mistakes of previous generations.

By attacking the republic and especially its political and economic elites, the activists overcompensated for the lack of resistance against Hitler and West Germany's refusal to acknowledge its shameful past. Consequently, liberal observers warned that an aggressive, authoritarian response by the state could cause more long-term political damage than the uprising itself.[55] But as the violence escalated, liberal politicians appeared to lose faith in their own emplotment of the crisis, and they huddled under the protective umbrella of antitotalitarianism that already sheltered their conservative colleagues. In 1972, the Brandt government adopted the infamous *Radikalenerlass* (literally, radicals' decree), which excluded members of radical left-wing groups from the ranks of the civil service.[56] In 1977, after the violent liberation of the hijacked Lufthansa plane in Mogadishu and the collective suicides of the Baader-Meinhof gang in Stammheim, even Brandt argued that the supporters of the terrorists advanced the cause of Nazism in Germany.[57] The rhetoric and enthusiasm for reform politics had fallen victim to unforeseeable political pressures. Faced with the radical antifascism of the student movement, the Social Democrats found it impossible to successfully market their own brand of moderate antifascism. Rather than extolling the virtues of the Social Democratic resistance against Hitler from the offices of the federal government, they continued the intellectual journey initiated at the Social Democratic convention in Bad Godesberg in 1959 and closed ranks with the antitotalitarian camp. As a result, the ideology of anticommunism experienced a renaissance at the precise moment that the primary target of that ideology, the East German dictatorship, appeared in a new, more favorable light.

The second bone of contention in the early 1970s was Brandt's effort to normalize relations to Eastern Europe. The negotiation and ratification of the nonaggression treaties with the Soviet Union, Poland, the GDR, and Czechoslovakia caused heated debates in parliament and in the media about the strategic objectives and political responsibilities that Brandt's bold diplomatic initiative entailed.[58] The discussions were an important turning point in West German efforts to adapt to the long-term political and moral consequences of World War II. Cold War politics had spared West Germans the painful experience of dealing directly with the resentment and the demands of the victims of Germany's war of colonial conquest and destruction in Eastern Europe. In addition, the rhetoric of anticommunism permitted West German leaders to postpone dealing honestly with the loss of German territories beyond Oder and Neisse. The belated efforts to normalize relations suddenly raised all these unaddressed questions, although none of the political players explicitly acknowledged the enormous moral stakes of the whole endeavor. Even Brandt, who was certainly inclined to mix politics and ethics, refrained from emphasizing the moral foundation and implication of his Ostpolitik, at least when addressing West German audiences. His declaration of government of October 28, 1969, announced the intended democraticization of West German society with great pathos but related the new policy of détente toward the Warsaw bloc in understated, terse language.[59] The government's struggle for sober and precise terminology continued in the following years, both at the negotiation table and in the West German media. It reflected the difficult task of crafting an understanding with the new partners in the East that would be acceptable to NATO allies and the West German population and at the same time satisfy the complicated legal restrictions that the Potsdam Accord of 1945 and the West German constitution imposed on the process.

Given the complex legal situation and the considerable resistance against the Ostpolitik among conservatives and expellees, it made perfect sense for the government to focus on legal and diplomatic technicalities in order to deflect attention from the emotional and moral stakes of the initiative. After all, Brandt pursued important objectives. The nonaggression treaties were expected to bring the Federal Republic back in line with its Western partners, enhance West Germany's foreign policy profile and diplomatic options, and, perhaps most important, reopen the lines of communications between East and West Germans in order to protect the cultural and social integrity of the German nation.[60] None of these objectives would be served by an emotional debate about German guilt. But it is interesting to note that the political opposition participated in this linguistic pact of sobriety, at least to a certain extent. CDU officials were outspoken in their resistance to Brandt's foreign policy. In their mind, the government had given legitimacy to a number of criminal regimes and shortchanged German interests by abandoning important territorial claims in exchange for tenuous returns. Occasionally, the heated debates touched on the emotional center of gravity of the issue, for instance, when critics pointed out that Hitler's crimes did not turn Soviet and East German crimes into acceptable policies or when they argued that Brandt betrayed the memory of the victims of Stalinist terror when he visited the GDR's antifascist memorial site in Buchenwald.[61] These were certainly serious charges, but all participants in the debates avoided the ultimate symbolic battleground. Neither the government nor the opposition raised the specter of the victims of war, genocide, or ethnic cleansing in any *concrete* terms. Neither side tried to bolster their case by invoking graphic visions of suffering that could provide additional moral impetus to their claims.[62] Despite some groundbreaking political innovations in the administration of guilt during Brandt's years in office, the West German political elite confirmed the linguistic protocols for the discussion of the Nazi past that had been developed in the Adenauer era for the internal West German political arena. But government officials had another, international political arena at their disposal. When addressing foreign governments and foreign media, Brandt and his officials chose to combine the circumspect, technical language of international diplomacy with much less circumspect, moralistic statements and gestures of German repentance that indirectly called into question the rhetorical status quo in Bonn.

When Brandt met Willi Stoph, a high-ranking East German politician, in Erfurt in March 1970, he emphasized the collective German responsibility for the Nazi crimes in unusually explicit terms. Brandt said that twenty-five years earlier, the world was horrified by the crimes committed in the name of Germany and that all Germans shared the liability for these events, including all who were present at the gathering in Erfurt.[63] Brandt's candid acknowledgment of German collective responsibility established a common ground for the upcoming negotiations, but it also served as a clear rejection of the East German position regarding material and symbolic reparations for Nazi crimes. Therefore, Brandt's explicit statement in Erfurt constituted a relatively aggressive political move. But in other Eastern European capitals, similar expressions of German remorse were delivered with great humility, even if such gestures did not always correspond to local protocol. When Brandt decided to kneel in front of the Warsaw Ghetto Memorial—certainly his most important and lasting contribution to the politics of memory—his hosts were disappointed that he had not shown the same reverence at the grave of the unknown soldier, a site of superior symbolic importance according to local Communist custom.[64] The response in West Germany was even more critical, albeit for other reasons. Brandt's emotional, spontaneous gesture violated the pragmatic rhetoric of sobriety that he himself had embraced in most of his statements about the burden of the Nazi past. Adopted instinctively, not by conscious design, Brandt's radical reinvention of the existing rituals of memory pointed toward the future of memory politics. In the course of the 1970s and 1980s, West Germans would come to embrace emotionally engaging, biographically concrete, and visually entertaining formats for the representation of Nazism, which explains why Brandt's visit to Warsaw or, more accurately, the footage of that visit, has retroactively assumed the status of a founding moment in the history of West Germany's celebrated, self-critical memory culture.[65]

INVENTING THE CULTURAL MEMORY OF NAZISM: THE MODEST BEGINNINGS OF A NEW PARADIGM

Most of the time, Brandt and the members of his cabinet were still occupied with the task of clearing away diplomatic rubble left behind by World War II. But on several occasions, they displayed significant concern about the future collective memory of the Nazi era. They clearly understood the important role that the interpretation of the Third Reich would play in the evolution of West German identity. In addition, they realized that the defensive mind-set and rhetoric that had helped the contemporaries of the Third Reich to deal successfully with the material, political, and emotional consequences of Nazism and World War II would not be an appropriate moral yardstick for the construction of the long-term collective memory for subsequent generations. This realization informed Brandt's spontaneous gesture in Warsaw, as well as a number of modest initiatives in the new field of cultural memory politics that were undertaken by his administration. Unfortunately but perhaps not surprisingly, the first tentative steps in the unfamiliar terrain were contradictory and proved unsuccessful.

The Brandt administration made three attempts to craft sites of memory with clearly liberal connotations. On May 8, 1970, Brandt organized an official memorial ceremony marking the twenty-fifth anniversary of the end of World War II, the first event of this kind in the history of the German parliament. The ceremony might have been intended as an opportunity to remember the end of the war as an act of liberation rather than a moment of national defeat and ignominy. Brandt certainly expressed this sentiment in other settings — for instance, after the elections of 1969.[66] But in his speech in parliament, he returned to the old, proven formulas, talking about Hitler's victims in vague, general terms and reminding the student activists to avoid the pitfalls of political radicalism.[67]

The second attempt to shape West German historical consciousness through symbolic government action turned into a complete fiasco. In 1974, the Brandt administration tried to reinvent the constitution as an emotionally charged site of memory that would foster republican values and displace more dubious nationalistic, antidemocratic traditions. But the republic's conservative political elite resented such progressive identity engineering by fiat and simply boycotted the lavish state ceremony organized on the twenty-fifth anniversary of the signing of the constitution on May 23, 1949.[68]

The third attempt, by contrast, was surprisingly successful, although it had initially been launched by Brandt's predecessor. In 1968, the cabinet of the CDU/SPD coalition had decided to commission a historical exhibit, to be displayed in the old Reichstag in Berlin, to mark the hundredth anniversary of German unification in 1971; the cabinet members also decided that the exhibit should address a few additional historical turning points of the previous hundred years, including 1918, 1933, and 1945.[69] The relatively modest project became an unprecedented audience success, profiting from a growing popular fascination with history and historical exhibits. As a result, the Brandt administration decided to transform the show into a permanent installation in the Reichstag—after adding a few self-critical remarks about German and Nazi history. All these activities expressed a serious interest on the part of the cabinet, but Brandt and his ministers only devoted limited time to the task of reinventing German history. Consequently, the field remained wide open for another federal employee with more time on his hands.

In the early 1970s, President Heinemann became the undisputed, albeit very controversial, champion of progressive memory politics, following a presidential tradition of preoccupation with history that had begun with Heuss. Heinemann was the first Social Democrat to become president of the Federal Republic. He was voted into office by one of the slimmest margins ever in March 1969, and he made no secret of the fact that he wanted to use his office for the pursuit of partisan politics.[70] Heinemann had a clear vision of German history, and unlike Brandt, he relentlessly impressed it on his many captive audiences. In Heinemann's opinion, Nazism was the result of the long-standing authoritarian and antidemocratic traditions in German history that had become particularly pronounced in the second half of the nineteenth century and caused the collapse of the Weimar Republic. He also considered the Federal Republic a real opportunity to turn this trend around and estab-

lish the first successful democracy in German history. But for this to hap-
pen, West German citizens and politicians had to stop dismissing the Bonn
republic as a stopgap measure on the way toward reunification and develop
a truly democratic, tolerant, and emancipatory civil society.[71] To contribute
to this cause, Heinemann vigorously attacked the icons of national history.
On the hundredth anniversary of German unification, he appeared on
prime-time television and argued that Otto von Bismarck and the empire he
had helped create could not serve as role models for West Germany: "One
hundred years German Empire means twice Versailles, 1871 and 1919; it also
means Auschwitz, Stalingrad, and unconditional surrender."[72] In this way,
Heinemann crafted his own succinct Sonderweg-theory of modern German
history; he created a direct link between the founding of Bismarck's empire
in Versailles in 1871 and the catastrophes of World War I (that is, Versailles
1919), the Holocaust, and World War II. On other occasions, he added that
national unity was not a value in and of itself, especially if achieved at the expense of democratic forms of government, and that the German people had
a fateful tendency to accept authority uncritically.[73] Not content with exposing
the flaws of much of recent German history, Heinemann also set out to find
positive reference points for a democratic German historical consciousness.
To that end, he sponsored a museum for the history of German emancipatory movements, which opened its doors in Rastatt in 1974 as the first federally sponsored institution of its kind.[74] Finally, Heinemann founded a student
history competition that became a raving success and has turned into an annual ritual in the schools of the Federal Republic.[75]

Heinemann's ambition as the history teacher of the nation did not sit well
with West Germany's historical establishment. Conservative in outlook, most
academic historians belittled Heinemann's naive didactic ambition and his
tendency to press the past into a ready-made ideological framework. However, a minority of younger historians, including the proponents of the future
Bielefeld School, approved of the president's vision of German history because it reflected their own opinions about the historical origins of National
Socialism. The progressive historians, as well as many other critical intellectuals, supported the search for an alternative political identity that could
compete with and ultimately replace the antitotalitarian paradigm.[76] In the
1980s, this search for a truly West German collective consciousness focused
on the idea of a constitutional patriotism, but that catchphrase had not yet

been invented in the era of Brandt and Heinemann. In addition, as became very obvious in the context of German unification in 1990, Brandt and possibly also Heinemann pursued more conventional and more realistic notions of national identity as their intellectual allies.

The honeymoon shared by the progressive political establishment and the critical intellectual elite of the Federal Republic lasted only a few years. Brandt left office in May 1974, when one of his closest advisors was exposed as a GDR spy. At that point, the ruthless attacks by his political enemies and the empty coffers of the federal government had undermined his penchant for political reform. When Helmut Schmidt subsequently took over the chancellorship, intellectuals and politicians parted ways again.[77] Schmidt belonged to a large cohort within his generation whose members were drafted into the institutions of the Third Reich and, to a certain extent, identified with their causes but became deeply suspicious of ideological commitments after the collapse of Nazism in 1945.[78] These personal inclinations, which might explain Schmidt's dislike for the moralistic political style of his predecessor, were further exacerbated by the dire political situation of the mid-1970s. Facing the twofold challenge of economic depression and political terrorism, Schmidt focused his efforts on crisis management. He had no interest in shaping the collective memory of Nazism or involving the federal government in another campaign of democratic value engineering. Consequently, his administration initially chose a minimalist approach to the politics of history more reminescent of the stance of Kiesinger and Erhard than of Schmidt's immediate predecessor, Brandt.[79]

Schmidt's reluctance made perfect sense. For first time since 1949, the government really seemed to have a choice in the matter. The ratification of the treaties with the countries of Eastern Europe had settled the most important unresolved political legacy of World War II, and the politics of history that had required so much attention in the preceeding decades could finally be brought to a close. But at the very moment that the politics of history had run their course and seemed to have settled the burden of the past on quite favorable terms, a new paradigm of political identity exposed the limits of antitotalitarianism.[80]

The most radical challenge was launched by the members of the Red Army Faction who assassinated a number of high-ranking politicians and business leaders in their failed attempts to jump-start a general uprising against West Germany's allegedly fascist ruling class. The small group of terrorists unnerved the political elite to such an extent that many of the professed democrats in Bonn lost faith in the democratic ideals they had quickly embraced in 1945.[81] But the more important challenges were waged by the activists in the new social movements, who, with the help of the media and members of the liberal political elite, invented a new communicative memory of Nazism.

The political activists who continued to explore the meaning of fascism were supported in their efforts by artists who invoked the Nazi past in provocative ways, as the first Fassbinder debate of 1975–1976 illustrated.[82] Even the mainstream media experimented with new forms of historical reflection. Some of these experiments were of a rather dubious nature, for instance, the glorifying coverage of the Nazi leadership that surfaced in the popular print media of the Federal Republic during the Hitler-wave of the mid-1970s.[83] Other innovations—the first wave of Alltagsgeschichte on German television, for example—proved much more productive.[84]

The historical culture of the 1970s reflected a new, diffuse sense of curiosity about Nazism that, among other consequences, prepared the ground for the exceptional reception of the TV series *Holocaust*. The media event itself transformed this sense of curiosity, focused it on the history and legacy of the "Final Solution," and thus helped initiate the most self-reflexive phase in the evolution of German collective memory.[85] All the uncoordinated, contradictory cultural initiatives raised questions about the Nazi past that had not been explicitly addressed in the realm of high politics.

The miscommunication between the political elite and other, more innovative segments of West Germany's historical culture stemmed from the fact that the latter were already fully involved in the politics of memory and the problem of symbolic collective guilt, whereas the former still focused primarily on conventional politics of history and only gradually adapted to the new cultural environment. In the course of the uneven and asymmetrical transition from one memory paradigm to the next, the new formats of historical inquiry developed in other sectors of West Germany's historical culture were selectively adopted in the federal political arena. That became particularly obvious during the 1978–1979 Filbinger scandal, which in the course of a few months moved from the political periphery in Baden-Württemberg and the literary sector of West German's historical culture to the hub of national politics in Bonn.

In February 1978, the weekly *Die Zeit* published excerpts from the new novel by the playwright Rolf Hochhuth, which dealt with a love affair between a German woman and a Polish forced laborer during World War II.[86] The outline of the story followed an actual case that ended with the betrayal of the lovers and the execution of the Polish man by Nazi authorities. In an aside, Hochhuth mentioned that the Nazi judges who caused this miscarriage of justice were still enjoying their pensions in the state of Baden-Württemberg. He added—and this is what caused the uproar—that the murderers had little to fear because the governor of the state, Hans Filbinger, was also one of those "terrible judges" who had upheld Nazi law.[87] Initially, Hochhuth only made references to Filbinger's record as a military judge in a British POW camp. But when Filbinger sued for libel, it quickly turned out—or perhaps it was known all along by Hochhuth—that the governor had helped sentence soldiers to death in the last months of the war. With proper symbolic guilt management, none of these facts would have ended Filbinger's career, but he committed two major public relations mistakes that made his resignation inevitable. First, Filbinger failed to reveal the full record of his service as a military jurist; the press found a total of four death sentences that listed Filbinger as an officer of the court and that he professed to have forgotten. Second, although Filbinger explained and defended his actions at length, he never apologized to his colleagues, his voters, or the relatives of the soldiers he had condemned to death.[88] He failed to realize that legal innocence no longer amounted to historical innocence. Just because he had not committed any crimes in the eyes of the law did not mean that he could survive in the court of public opinion. Because he showed no signs of remorse, Filbinger had become indistinguishable from other "hidden" Nazis who failed to make amends for their past misdeeds.

The Filbinger scandal established new rules of political conduct. As a result of subtle, yet important transformations during the Social Democratic reform era, the clear antitotalitarian differentiation between Nazis and the conservative political establishment, which had structured the political process in the postwar decades, was finally called into question. The SPD administrations never developed a compelling cultural memory of Nazism, for instance, by highlighting and objectifying the Social Democratic resistance to Hitler. Maybe that was not an attractive or important task for people who clearly remembered the war and their own defeat at the hand of the Nazis. But during the 1970s, the Social Democrats and their political allies in the media developed a new, unofficial communicative memory of the Third Reich that took its cue from the extraparliamentary political culture and revised the relationship between Nazism and the conservative mainstream. For the first time, conservatives faced a political majority that questioned their historical innocence. They were confronted with the tacit, widely shared assumption that the political tradition they represented—and perhaps even their own past behavior—contained troublesome pro-Nazi dispositions and actions. Mounting an efficient defense against this charge was difficult, because the questionable actions belonged to the ill-defined realm of symbolic guilt caused, for instance, by not displaying the appropriate shame about one's past political mistakes. That was exactly the sin that cost Hans Filbinger his job.

As a result of the political transformations of the 1970s, the pragmatist Schmidt, who had initially not shown much interest in politics of history or memory, became the first West German chancellor to visit Israel and to speak at the memorial ceremony for the victims of Kristallnacht.[89] Without showing any rhetorical ambition, Schmidt thus initiated the government's involvement in the type of Holocaust remembrance that became such an important symbolic battleground in the Kohl era. Even as these changes were taking place, however, many of the old political traditions persisted, especially in contexts in which the political elite had exclusive access to public speech.

The power of new paradigms of historical reflection, as well as the political elite's relative distance from these paradigms, became quite obvious in 1979 when the West German parliamentarians finally agreed to abolish the statute of limitations for murder in the wake of the media event *Holocaust*. By supporting an initiative they had rejected three times in the course of fourteen years, the members of parliament acknowledged a decisive change in the national and international perception of the Nazi crimes that they had not anticipated.[90] At the same time, they also used the occasion to reiterate the self-serving collective identity that parliament had crafted for itself in the course of three decades. In their speeches on the floor, parliamentarians celebrated once more their antitotalitarian worldview and congratulated themselves for having created such a successful democracy. Only one MP refused to join the party. Karl Hansen, an SPD politician closely aligned with the peace movement, argued that his colleagues' virulent anticommunism and the myth of their opposition to Nazism—all nicely wrapped up in the antito-talitarian package—had allowed them to avoid any honest, self-critical inquiry into their own involvement in the Nazi state.[91] Hansen's polemic anticipated the many entertaining performances by members of the Green Party who joined parliament for the first time in 1982. The antifascism of the new MPs, honed in the social movements of the 1970s, clashed directly with the collective identity of the West German legislature.

One could argue that the new liberal communicative memory that won the day during the Filbinger scandal reflected the historical record more accurately than previous ideological frameworks. After all, the conservative elite had indeed brought Hitler to power, the Left had mounted more meaningful resistance, and many Nazis had escaped appropriate punishment. But the liberal communicative memory represented a number of risky political choices. By precariously balancing themselves between antitotalitarianism and antifascism, between the center of power in Bonn and the center of extraparliamentary resistance in Berlin, Frankfurt, and other cities, the Social Democrats temporarily emerged as the voice of reason that could mediate between an overly defensive conservative establishment and an overly aggressive left-wing subculture. In comparison to the self-righteousness of the conservatives as well as that of their radical critics, the moderate Left finally occupied the moral high ground that it had not been able to attain after 1945. The strategy acknowledged the complexity of the new generational, political, and media context of the late 1970s, but it also raised many expectations that the Social Democrats could ultimately not fulfill. Vacillating and mediating between two antagonistic interpretations of the Nazi past offered Social Democrats tactical advantages, but it also prevented them from constructing an independent, robust liberal collective memory of the Nazi past that could have effectively replaced the antitotalitarian consensus.

Conservative politicians were obviously not happy about losing the dominant role that they had played in the historical culture of the postwar decades. They specifically resented having to defend themselves against suspicions that the paradigm of antitotalitarianism had elegantly dispelled for many years. When the federal parliament discussed Filbinger's case in June 1978, Helmut Kohl bitterly complained that Filbinger would never have become a target of inquiry if he had been a member of the SPD. He blamed Brandt for fostering dissent by "always equating conservative with reactionary and pseudo-fascistic."[92] Kohl's complaint illustrates that West Germany's political culture was split along two axes by the end of the 1970s. In addition to the more hostile relationship between Social and Christian Democrats, the West German political scene also suffered from a seemingly irreparable rift between the official establishment still dominated by members of the war generations and the diverse subcultures that had become the political home of the postwar generation. In particular the latter divide was defined in fundamental ideological terms, but after the media event *Holocaust,* all three major camps—Social Democrats, conservatives, and extraparliamentary opposition—increasingly expressed their differences in the language of collective memory.

While defending Filbinger in parliament, Kohl promised that he and his generation would stop digging up dirt about colleagues and instead build bridges across political divides. As the next chapter will show, Kohl certainly fulfilled the first part of that promise, but he failed spectacularly on the second count.

CHAPTER 11

FIGHTING ABOUT THE FUTURE OF THE PAST

The Difficult Process of Cultural Memory Production in the Kohl Era

Most scholars researching West Germany's historical culture invoke Hermann Lübbe's paradoxical dictum that the memory of the Third Reich has intensified with increasing temporal distance to the Nazi past.[1] On one level, Lübbe's assessment is self-evident. Even a superficial look at the German media landscape of the 1980s and 1990s reveals a plethora of television programs, theater productions, novels, autobiographical writings, museums, memorial sites, and anniversary speeches that focused on the Nazi past. In addition, Lübbe's remarks are irresistibly attractive for scholars who are increasingly isolated from the everyday culture surrounding them. Declaring memory politics a popular national pursuit helps them reconnect to the mainstream and bestow social relevance on their work. On another level, however, Lübbe's opaque statement is misleading. The wave of explicit and often highly visible cultural representations of Nazism constituted a cultural battleground about West German and later German identity. The struggle of interpretation between different political generations and different political factions was so intense because the opponents had set their eyes on a formidable prize—the power to shape the future of the most prosperous society that had ever existed in Germany. Most participants assumed that the transition from history to memory, from the contemporaries of Nazism to subsequent generations provided a rare opportunity for the institutionalization of cultural memories that would determine the political trajectory of the republic for many years to come. The warring factions certainly understood demographics: in the late 1970s, the contemporaries of the Third Reich represented only a minority of the West German population for the first time. But in the heat of the political battle, the memory activists overestimated their influence on the nation's historical consciousness. The great majority of cultural representations of Nazism were only appreciated by a small group of individuals. Moreover, it is difficult to determine if memory products that attracted larger audiences, such as TV programs and museum exhibits, swayed public opinion in one way or another. The mere presence of an explosive, competitive elite culture does not mean that the individual and collective memories of people who were not closely tuned into the debates changed in the way that producers, critics, and historians of historical culture have assumed.

Finally, Lübbe's statement is problematic for another, closely related reason. Since we are well advised to refrain from equating the presence of cultural production with the presence of similarly structured collective memories, we should also be very careful about conflating the absence of cultural products with the absence of memory. Although the culture of the 1950s did not produce anything comparable to the wave of representations of Nazism that hit the public sphere in the 1980s and 1990s, it is nevertheless possible and perhaps even likely that individual and collective memories in the 1950s were still greatly concerned with life and death in the Third Reich. The very surplus of memories of all sorts—sublated, imagined, reconstructed—meant that communications through memory—memories as leverage, as explanation, as excuse—did not require a process of objectification. Memory of Nazism was such a familiar and trusted currency of social exchange that it did not need to be supported by an infrastructure of standardized cultural images. Moreover, the contemporaries of Nazism had been exposed to an intense U.S. media campaign that publicized and visualized the NS crimes in the first months after the war. These images might well have served as a widely shared, ad hoc cultural memory of the past, despite the fact that the campaign was relatively short-lived and that images of Nazi crimes subsequently disappeared from Germany's public sphere for many years.[2] Considered from this perspective, the outpouring of memory products since the 1980s does not attest to the intensification of memory but "merely" its continued importance. The contemporaries of the Third Reich had voluntarily and involuntarily imparted to the next generation a sense of how much Nazism and World War II had influenced their lives. As a result, both generations now used the Third Reich as a key reference point for their discussions of the future of West German identity. In this process of intergenerational strife, they *externalized* the memory of Nazism; they created complex and contradictory, emotionally and politically overdetermined institutional memories of National Socialism.[3]

Memory transfer entails a reinvention of memory. The externalized memory of the 1980s had little in common with the internalized memories of the 1950s and 1960s. The former included, for instance, a well-developed memory of the Holocaust that had never existed in previous decades.[4] In addition, intergenerational memory transfer, especially when accomplished through a process of externalization, probably reduces the emotional investment in the memory under description and diminishes its importance in everyday life. Consider, for example, the West German political elite. It is very likely that memories of Nazism, which were rarely explicitly acknowledged, accompanied Adenauer and his associates every step of the way as they tried to negotiate a steady course within a maze of conflicting claims of victimhood. In contrast, the members of the Kohl administration, who developed a remarkable interest in shaping the cultural memory of Nazism, devoted most of their time to tasks other than the politics of memory. They probably accomplished most of their political work without thinking much about the legacy of the Third Reich.

Like many other Western countries, West Germany and later unified Germany experienced a memory revolution in the 1980s and 1990s. In museums, history workshops, anniversary ceremonies, student history competitions, and other venues, Germans retrieved and reinvented their history.[5] As a result of this sustained interest in the past, especially in the Nazi past and the Nazi crimes, a new infrastructure of institutional memory permeated Germany's public spaces.[6] In many cities and towns, local leaders erected memorials for resisters and victims of National Socialism, as was done, for example, at the sites of former concentration camps.[7] In some cases, the new infrastructure of memory complemented or superseded the first generation of memorials created at the request or insistence of survivors or Allied administrators in the immediate postwar years.[8] But many of the new objects of remembrance for the first time reminded passersby of the location of former synagogues or Nazi institutions of terror. The markers might seem unobtrusive to today's casual observer, but they only came into existence after considerable debate. In most cases, the monuments for the victims of Nazism were proposed by societies for Christian-Jewish cooperation, local grassroots initiatives associated with the new social movements, or the SPD or Green factions of local parliaments. CDU/CSU and FDP politicians almost never suggested and frequently even opposed such monuments.[9] Conservative politicians realized only belatedly that properly displayed historical guilt could be a source of cultural as well as economic capital. In the East, the development of a Western-style memorial culture, which began shortly before unification, has continued to elicit all kinds of critical reactions in an atmosphere of complex and competitive claims of victimhood.[10]

As this brief summary indicates, the federal initiatives in the realm of cultural memory production might have dwarfed all local projects, but they only represented the tip of an iceberg. The planning and construction of two national history museums, a central war memorial, and a memorial to the victims of the Holocaust took place against the background of a general resurgence of interest in history that provided both the audience and the critics for Kohl's aggressive memory agenda. The federal projects were undertaken with a great sense of urgency. Since the public finally seemed to be interested in the past, the Kohl administration could address the loss of history that had worried conservative observers since the 1950s.[11]

HELMUT KOHL AND HISTORICIZATION OF NAZISM

Like 1969, the year 1982 represents a twofold generational turning point in the development of West German politics. After the election of March 1983, representatives of the political movement and political generation that had entered the political scene in the late 1960s now brought their antifascist identity to bear on federal politics. For the first time, the Green Party was voted into parliament by the activists of the social movements and their sympathizers in the civil service who rejected the deployment of new nuclear weapons and favored more environmentally conscious policies. But the Green representatives also launched a concerted attack against the antitotalitarian identity of parliament, the first attack of this sort since 1953 when the Communists exited the federal scene.[12] The second generational turnover of the early 1980s occurred in an even more rarified political environment. In another first, the federal government was led by a politician whose relatively young age had saved him from facing the many serious moral and political challenges that the Nazi regime liberally doled out to his older compatriots. Kohl, who became chancellor in October 1982, was seventeen years younger than Brandt and twelve years younger than Schmidt. Therefore, he never had to make up his mind if and under what circumstances he would resist a Nazi government; he was never called up to defend a criminal regime and certainly never asked to commit crimes against humanity. Kohl was clearly grateful for this "blessing of late birth," as he phrased it during a visit to Israel in 1984.[13] He turned this privilege into a coherent political program, which had already taken shape before he became chancellor.

At the height of the terrorism crisis in 1977, Kohl's was one of the few voices that sought to de-dramatize the situation. He painted a much more optimistic picture than many of his colleagues, who either denounced the terrorists as Nazis or feared that a German state would once again act out against opposition from the Left and undermine its own constitutional foundation in the process. For Kohl, the terrorists did not constitute a serious challenge for the West German state. Therefore, there was nothing to be gained by comparing them to the Nazi thugs who had brought down the first German democracy. In his mind, the political reaction to terrorism was a much more fundamental problem than the terrorists themselves: West German society, including its political elite, had not yet recognized Nazism for what it manifestly was—a distant historical phenomenon that had very little bearing on the current state of affairs. Kohl advised cutting the debilitating ties between past and present by historicizing National Socialism. Once the Third Reich was acknowledged as an important but relatively short and self-contained period of German history, the German people would be free to develop a healthy, self-confident historical consciousness, which future generations deserved and which would enhance Germany's standing in the world.[14] By emphasizing the alleged historical distance between Nazism and the Federal Republic of the 1970s, Kohl helped define a new, efficient strategy of normalization intended to put West Germany on an equal footing with its Western partners. He no longer countered references to Nazi crimes by highlighting the crimes of the Soviet bloc and his own anti-Communist credentials. Unlike many of his conservative colleagues, Kohl clearly acknowledged Auschwitz—he simply rejected its continuing political relevance.[15]

Once in office, Kohl stubbornly pursued his strategy of historicization, even when facing massive resistance. Thus, even in the first years of his government, an interesting pattern emerged that contrasts with the track record of the Brandt and Schmidt administrations in the new field of symbolic memory politics. Brandt and his associates had made the first tentative contributions toward the construction of a cultural memory of National Socialism. In the context of these attempts, Brandt had shown a special gift for innovative, sparingly applied gestures of memory of great moral integrity. At the time, these gestures remained controversial, although they retroactively assumed the status of founding moments in the history of symbolic guilt management. Despite his considerable rhetorical skills, however, Brandt had not been able to follow up on the gestures with similarly compelling and innovative language and institutions of memory. In his public statements, he preferred to stay close to the well-trodden paths of antitotalitarian consensus building. In comparison, Kohl jumped into the arena of memory politics with greater enthusiasm and developed a particular zeal for the staging of emotionally pleasing gestures of memory and planning new institutions of historical education. Unfortunately, however, these gestures and plans failed in the court of public opinion (although not necessarily in the court of popular opinion). As a result of the outcry in the media, few journalists still took notice of the fact that the contents of Kohl's speeches displayed considerable moral complexity and sensitivity, even if he was not able to deliver them with appropriate rhetorical flair.

In the course of reinventing the cultural memory of the Nazi period, Kohl also drew fire for his undemocratic style of government. Unless required by law, he rarely bothered to consult parliament before making far-reaching decisions about museums, memorials, and diplomatic protocol. This autocratic approach to memory politics was not unprecedented. Neither Brandt nor Heinemann had involved parliament or the public in planning and realizing the Rastatt museum or the Berlin exhibit. But Kohl operated in a very different political context. Since the late 1970s, the West German elite had become obsessed with the Nazi past and wanted to have a say in the construction of its collective memory. Therefore, the political opposition in parliament, especially the Greens, and a considerable share of the press corps quickly interpreted Kohl's initiatives as a well-orchestrated conservative conspiracy and denounced his allegedly apologetic intentions—sometimes long before the memory object or memory ritual in question had taken shape. There is no indication, however, that the majority of the population shared this sense of betrayal. As far as can be ascertained, most citizens appreciated Kohl's political intentions as well as the institutions he helped create.

THE BITBURG DISASTER

Kohl's first major project, the reconciliation ceremony in Bitburg, established the pattern of unilateral government action, harsh criticism in the media, and tacit acceptance by the population that characterized the federal politics of memory throughout the 1980s and the first half of the 1990s.[16] Bitburg turned into a public relations debacle for the government, but it was modeled after a successful precedent. When the former Allies of World War II had convened in June 1984 to celebrate the fortieth anniversary of the Normandy invasion, they had not invited a West German representative. To make up for this slight, French president François Mitterand had organized a special French-German lovefest and photo op in Verdun in September 1984, which deeply impressed Kohl. Now, the chancellor could not wait to stage similar productions with other partners of West Germany, and President Ronald Reagan was the obvious candidate. Positively inclined toward media events in general and media events with Kohl in particular—after all, Kohl had just guided nuclear rearmament through parliament—Reagan agreed to take the fortieth anniversary of the end of World War II as an opportunity to demonstrate the depth of U.S.-German friendship.[17] Thus, the two heads of state bumbled into a political affair that seemed part classical drama and part soap opera. The production featured a diverse cast of characters: a president's wife who did not like to be confronted with the gruesome facts of Nazi repression and genocide and therefore declined an invitation to visit the former concentration camp at Dachau; the ghosts of SS soldiers that rose from their graves to haunt a historically challenged U.S. president who seemed to have no grasp of the political significance of events that happened during his lifetime; a German chancellor who stubbornly insisted on his beautiful vision of international reconciliation at the graves of the fallen soldiers; and finally, a polyphonic choir of political and intellectual critics on both sides of the Atlantic who went after their respective political leaders with a vengeance.[18]

Some lobbying groups in the United States, especially veterans' association and Jewish organizations, had already raised objections in the early planning stages of Kohl's sweeping reconciliation ceremony. But the whole affair only assumed scandalous proportions when it became public knowledge that the military cemetery at Bitburg, which had been selected for logistical reasons, contained the remains of fifty Waffen-SS soldiers among the more than two thousand German soldiers buried at the site. It is unclear when the officials learned about this potentially embarrassing fact, but in the spring of 1985, both administrations faced massive protests that were quite exceptional in the history of the politics of memory. In the United States, the government and its critics tried to sort out the tricky problem of whether the close cooperation between the government and the Jewish community in the arena of national memory politics would tie the government's hand in other affairs, such as its foreign policy toward Germany. Was it acceptable to pose as the patron saint of Holocaust memory in institutions like the future Holocaust Memorial Museum and still pursue much more pragmatic and flexible memory Realpolitik in other settings?[19] In the Federal Republic, the symbolic wars raised the important question, only addressed indirectly at this early stage, of what precise status German victims of World War II would have in the future cultural memory of Nazism. The problem of the Waffen-SS provided a particularly challenging case study for this larger memory conundrum, since the organization included in its ranks perpetrators of civilian massacres (for instance, in Oradour) but also many draftees who served as regular soldiers and might not have committed any war crimes. For Kohl's critics, especially the very vocal critics in the Green Party, the idea of honoring the German casualties of war in the context of a general ritual of mourning and reconciliation amounted to a wholesale relativizing of the Nazi crimes and offended the memory of the real victims.[20] For Kohl's supporters, canceling the Bitburg ceremony would insult the honor of the German military. From today's perspective, the notion that the Wehrmacht had any honor left that could be offended might seem like a peculiar idea, but in 1985, the myth of the Wehrmacht's innocence still dominated popular opinion.[21] At least in this respect, Kohl's insistence on the Bitburg visit made perfect sense, despite the aggressive demands at home and polite inquires from abroad that suggested a change of venue.

As a result of all these tensions and misgivings, the actual ceremony in Bitburg turned into a hurried and awkward event that featured no speeches or symbolic gestures of friendship. Even the attempt to counterbalance the ceremony in Bitburg with a considerably longer visit to Bergen-Belsen could not change the fact that the majority of the press corps, including the government's supporters, considered Bitburg an utter failure.[22] Kohl delivered a perfectly acceptable speech during Reagan's visit, in which the chancellor emphasized the German responsibility for continued remembrance of the Nazi crimes and made clear that May 8, 1945, should be considered a day of liberation for Europe and Germany.[23] In addition, an overwhelming 70 percent

of the population supported Kohl's insistence on the Bitburg visit.[24] Nevertheless, in the eyes of the media professionals and the historically interested
and literate public, Kohl had proven to be a memory klutz, and that reputation stuck with him throughout his career.[25]

BRINGING THE HOLOCAUST TO PARLIAMENT:
RICHARD VON WEIZSÄCKER'S ANNIVERSARY SPEECH

The fortieth anniversary of the end of World War II would have been remembered only for Kohl's heavy-handed and ill-fated attempt at dispensing historical closure had it not been for another weighty presidential intervention into
the federal politics of memory. The Christian Democrat Richard von Weizsäcker, the former mayor of Berlin, had been elected president in 1984 with
an impressive majority of votes from both sides of the aisle.[26] A year later, he
put that symbolic capital on the line when he delivered an exceptionally ambitious speech that has become the single most important public statement
in the history of German memory politics.[27] Weizsäcker's relatively short text
contained a number of exceptional rhetorical and political accomplishments.
He was able to acknowledge the large variety of experiences and feelings that
Germans remembered in the context of May 8, 1945, and still state unequivocally that the date represented a day of liberation. He carefully mapped out
the European and global implications of World War II but always analyzed
these developments from a specifically German perspective. He emphasized
that postwar generations shared no political responsibility for the crimes yet
expressed the continued need for self-critical remembrance in very compelling,
even appealing terms. Finally, Weizsäcker described the German suffering
before and after May 1945 with great empathy but demonstrated that, in the
German memory of Nazism, the victims of genocide took precedence over
the victims of Allied warfare and expulsion. In this way, the president established a clear hierarchy of victimhood that marked the first successful, official
endorsement and practical illustration of Holocaust memory by a high-ranking
political representative of the Federal Republic.[28]

    With hindsight, one could fault Weizsäcker for his philo-Semitic appropria-
tion of the Jewish saying that "the secret of redemption lies in remembrance,"
since the promise of redemption seemed like a problematic, premature
utopia for German society, at least in the context of the 1980s.[29] In addition,
Weizsäcker's assessment that only a few Germans participated in the imple-

mentation of the "Final Solution" has proven to be overly optimistic.[30] Yet despite or perhaps even because of these shortcomings, he crafted a carefully calibrated rhetorical monument to the exceptionality of the Holocaust that approached the "Final Solution" from a German perspective and rendered the emerging Holocaust memory palpable and acceptable to German audiences.[31] Weizsäcker's biography made him a perfect fit for this subject position of reformed bystander. As the son and the defense lawyer of a high-ranking Nazi diplomat who had been indicted at Nuremberg, Weizsäcker was clearly associated with the conservative elite that brought Hitler to power and served him so well throughout the Third Reich but largely failed to acknowledge its responsibility after the war. Consequently, when Weizsäcker delivered his speech, an heir to the old, discredited elite, a man who could also legitimately speak for West Germany's new conservative elite, finally made symbolic amends for the crimes of the regime and specifically mentioned the victims of Nazism.[32]

In the course of the next decade, Weizsäcker's sensitive remarks became the benchmark of the German official memory, although this outcome was certainly not uncontested. The long-term success of the speech reflected Weizsäcker's political and rhetorical skills and the excellent timing of his intervention. He managed to put into political speech the new assessment of the Third Reich that had emerged in academia and the liberal media as a result of generational transformations and international developments and that placed the Holocaust at the center of modern German history but had not yet been embraced by the political establishment in the Federal Republic.[33] After this accomplishment, Weizsäcker promptly received enthusiastic support from the media and his colleagues on the Left of the political spectrum, but the leaders of his own party resented the displacement of the time-tested ideology of antitotalitarianism and resisted the change of paradigm for many years.[34] In an amended format, Weizsäcker's hierarchy of victimhood was finally enshrined on a plaque at the central memorial site in Berlin in 1993 but only after the collapse of the GDR and as a result of substantial lobbying from the Jewish community.

THE MEMORY WARS AND THE ELITE CONCEPTIONS OF WEST GERMAN IDENTITY

In the six years before unification, the republic enjoyed relative political stability and economic prosperity, and the political leaders could finally address

West Germany's alleged identity gap, which had concerned them for many years. In fact, the situation seemed perfect for such an intervention. Since the late 1970s, historical exhibits, museums, and TV programs had attracted large, enthusiastic audiences. Now, the politicians hoped to be able to channel this interest in the right direction and provide future generations with a solid democratic historical consciousness. The political elite's unprecedented interest in memory—never before and never since have German politicians paid so much attention to the representation of the past—had a number of important consequences. First, the implementation of popular didactics of history required historical expertise, and the political elite turned to West Germany's professional historians for help. The ensuing, unusually close cooperation between state and academia further politicized an academic establishment that was already politically fragmented. The civil servants in government and academia agreed on the desirability and viability of some sort of historical consciousness engineering, but they certainly disagreed about its ideological orientation. At least four different and more or less incompatible blueprints for the construction of West German identity competed with each other: on the right side of the political spectrum, the old antitotalitarian ideology and the new and as yet little understood historicization model; on the left side, the new Holocaust memory and the liberal concept of constitutional patriotism.[35] With great enthusiasm for the task at hand but divided by ideological rifts and professional envy, academic historians and their political allies embarked on a prolonged intellectual war about the German collective memory of the future. In the heat of the battles, in which changing constellations of academics, politicians, and journalists recycled the same basic convictions and leveled the same charges against each other, the participants rarely noticed that the general population, for whose benefit these battles were allegedly fought, paid little attention to the intellectual fracas among the elite.

The West German memory wars of the 1980s began with the Bitburg affair, were highlighted by the Historians' Debate, and concluded with the Jenninger debacle. But the cooperation between politicians and historians in the process of cultural memory building is best illustrated by the tale of two museums, the House of History in Bonn and the German Historical Museum in Berlin. The idea of creating two museums, one focusing on the history of the Federal Republic and another on German history in general, had been brought

up repeatedly in the past and not just by conservative politicians. Many Social Democrats and liberals who held office before Kohl had made similar
suggestions, including Chancellor Schmidt, President Walter Scheel, and the
mayor of Berlin, Dietrich Stobbe, to name a few.[36] But none of these initiatives produced any concrete results until Kohl became chancellor and turned
the museums into his pet projects. Kohl explicitly mentioned the museum
plans in his first government statements and quickly acted on that prospect.[37]
He convened a committee of four historians, who developed a conceptual
blueprint for a West German history museum in Bonn and presented it to the
public in October 1983.[38] To Kohl's chagrin, things moved much slower in
Berlin. Although a local planning commission had been formed in 1982, the
project did not make any headway in the politically fragmented city government. Therefore, Kohl personally intervened in 1985, promised substantial
federal subsidies, and convinced the local CDU/FDP government to create a
new commission, which swiftly produced a first conceptual outline by April
1986.[39]

During the planning phase, the Social Democrats, the Greens, and a number of like-minded historians voiced serious reservations about Kohl's museum projects. First of all, they were dismayed by the course of action the
chancellor had chosen to implement his objective. Even before the first report
was published, several liberal historians complained about the composition
of the Bonn commission. In their mind, the four conservative members of
the panel hardly constituted a representative cross section of West Germany's
historical profession.[40] Kohl's opponents demanded that parliament play a
much more active role in the decision-making process. To some extent, the
critics' intervention was even successful. The second Berlin commission,
convened in 1985, represented a less homogeneous group of experts, although
conservative panel members were still in the majority and the whole project remained a top-down government initiative with minimal parliamentary
involvement.[41]

The concerns about process went hand in hand with serious suspicions
about the chancellor's long-term political objectives. Since the opposition had
not been invited to contribute to the conceptual deliberations, its leaders assumed that Kohl and his handpicked historical advisers planned to celebrate
the historical accomplishments of the governing political parties while giving
short shrift to the historical achievements of their competitors. Even if Kohl

were to refrain from such overt self-adulation, he certainly intended, or so the critics assumed, to cast his subjective, conservative interpretation of the past into a permanent form, thereby projecting an uplifting, nationalistic vision of German and West German history into the future. Therefore, from the beginning, the critics also presumed that Nazism and self-critical reflections about the failures of Vergangenheitsbewältigung would not occupy a prominent place in that beautiful vision.[42] As usual, the Greens were particularly outspoken in their criticism, asserting that Kohl's museum plans amounted to a wholesale whitewashing of German history.[43]

The first critics spoke up in 1983, and the debate continued intermittently until it reached its climax after the release of the Berlin commission's report in 1986. At that stage, the discussion about the museum plans overlapped with the Historians' Debate. In fact, the latter was a continuation of the former, since many of the protagonists of the Historians' Debate had already spent considerable time and energy discussing Kohl's conservative cultural revolution when Habermas detected a revisionist conspiracy at the heart of the West German historical establishment.[44] Yet despite the volatile intellectual climate of the mid-1980s, the government had no problem casting its unusual cultural initiatives into a permanent legal framework. Conservative majorities in Berlin and Bonn passed the necessary laws between spring 1987 and spring 1990, and museum construction was well under way in the West German capital. As will be discussed, the museums plans had to be amended as a result of the collapse of the Berlin Wall and German unification, without, however, changing the overall ideological mission of both institutions. When the two museums finally opened their doors to the public in 1994, their design, location, and audience differed significantly from the original plans, but the exhibits still reflected Kohl's strategy of historicization.

Up until the late 1980s, the memory battles had produced few tangible results. Even the supporters of the Bitburg ceremony had no reason to be proud of the final outcome; the museums controversy had caused a lot of political hot air but no concrete memory objects, at least not yet; and the Historians' Debate mixed simplistic political accusations with high-flying discussions about abstract concepts without stimulating historical research or the production of public history. Historians and politicians were clearly concerned about the appropriate representation of Nazism and the Holocaust, but no consensus had emerged in either field. With the exception of Weizsäcker, nobody had been able to outline compelling new strategies of representation. Younger historians just began to transform their new interest in the history of the "Final Solution" into specific research and writing strategies, but politicians were unclear how historicization would work in practice or how the successor state of the Third Reich could do justice to the new paradigm of exceptionalism. At the same time, other members of the cultural-political elite, especially in the electronic media, had risen to the challenge and found new, successful formats for representing the "Final Solution," among them the survivor narrative. Politicians were obviously lagging behind other expert communities in the race toward politically correct ways of representing and appropriating the Holocaust, which helps explain why the last political memory event of the 1980s was resolved so quickly and in such dramatic fashion.

THE JENNINGER DEBACLE

In past decades, members of the political elite had often paid their respects to the memory of the Jewish victims, especially during official visits to foreign countries or when addressing the nation in other ceremonial contexts. They had occasionally visited with Jewish congregations on the anniversary of Kristallnacht and delivered pensive, abstract speeches that reflected little conceptual or political ambition. In this fashion, the political elite had participated in the wave of commemorative events that had marked the fortieth anniversary of Kristallnacht in 1978. Ten years later, however, the event was commemorated with greater official fanfare. All political dignitaries of the republic flocked to Frankfurt to join the memorial services organized by the national Jewish organization and the Frankfurt congregation. In addition, the parliamentary leadership decided to organize a rare state ceremony in the Bundestag to mark the fiftieth anniversary of the Nazi pogrom. The highest representatives of the West German state clearly intended to take their involvement in the construction of Holocaust memory to a new level and announce the meaning of the "Final Solution" ex cathedra from the seat of the West German sovereign.[45]

Considering the exceptional circumstances, it is perhaps not surprising that the nationalization of Holocaust memory got off to a bad start. After Weizsäcker had turned down the honor—there was no chance that he could top his performance of 1985—and after some bickering about the program, Philipp Jenninger, the president of the parliament, emerged as the single speaker of the event. Jenninger could be trusted to deliver a solid philo-Semitic message. He was on very good terms with a number of Israeli politicians and the Jewish leadership in West Germany and therefore quite familiar with all the appropriate rhetorical stereotypes. Apparently, however, Jenninger's colleagues underestimated his political ambition. The president of the parliament and his speechwriters tried to move the official memory of the Holocaust a decisive step forward. Weizsäcker had self-critically reflected about the meaning of the "Final Solution" from the perspective of the former and the present political elite. Now, Jenninger wanted to take the next logical, yet radical step and explore the meaning of the Holocaust from the vantage point of the millions of bystanders who had witnessed the pogroms and deportations but never lifted a finger for the German Jews. As seen in chapter 4, Jenninger's excursion into the gloomy, ambivalent world of fascist Alltagsgeschichte failed miserably—or succeeded beyond his wildest expectations. The self-declared honorary antifascists in parliament did not want to entertain the possibility that they had been or might have been just as cowardly and opportunistic as the great majority of the citizens of the Third Reich. Rather than acknowledging the possibility that their anti-Nazi stance was a thin veneer that might easily crumble under pressure, the parliamentarians used Jenninger's lack of rhetorical finesse to turn the table on him and accuse him of anti-Semitism—much to the surprise of his many Jewish friends.[46]

The Jenninger affair illustrates that, in the 1980s, politicians in the conservative mainstream—and not just independent-minded conservatives such as Weizsäcker—for the first time sought to embrace the Holocaust as a political tool. In previous decades, only liberals had invoked the "Final Solution" to define absolute political limits and scandalize the public speech or behavior of their conservative colleagues who had allegedly violated these limits. The conservatives never responded to these accusations in kind; they leveled serious countercharges against their critics, but they almost never used references to the history of the Holocaust to defend their position or attack their opponents. The situation changed in the 1980s when public speech about the Holocaust assumed more symbolic capital than ever before. A number of conservative politicians, Kohl and Jenninger included, challenged the Holocaust monopoly of the Left and caused a turf war about the question of who could and who could not legitimately invoke the "Final Solution" to further their own political objectives. Initially, the liberal politicians and their academic allies successfully defended their territory, as the Historians' Debate and the Jenninger affair illustrate. But just a few years later, public statements about the meaning of the "Final Solution" were no longer the privilege of any specific political faction; the Holocaust had become a truly arbitrary political sign that could be attached to a wide range of political agendas.[47]

Finally, Jenninger's debacle also showed clearly that the West German politicians were not ready to contemplate the brutal facts of the Holocaust, including the abysmal failure of their own caste, without the benefit of an alleviating conceptual and rhetorical framework that would highlight residues of past moral integrity and promising venues for future political action. In the past, the paradigm of antitotalitarianism had provided just such a framework, but now, it was high time to find a new crutch, and Jenninger had certainly not been any help. It turned out, however, that the solution had been close at hand the whole time and just needed to be further developed. Since the first postwar years, West German politicians had frequently invoked the project of European integration as the perfect remedy against the political forces that had brought Hitler to power.[48] The politicians of the 1990s were even more enamored by this rhetorical strategy. Just like their predecessors who rarely failed to mention German suffering when they acknowledged Jewish victims, the political vanguard of a unified Germany reflexively confessed their love for Europe whenever they were called on to reflect about the German catastrophe. Unlike in the past, however, when West German politicians had a tough time convincing their foreign colleagues to contemplate the misery of expulsion and air warfare, the new Europeanization of the Holocaust met with enthusiastic support in all European capitals. As a result, starting in the mid-1990s, the increasing appropriation of the memory of the Holocaust for the construction of German identity went hand in hand with a projection of the historical lesson of the "Final Solution" onto the European community in which the Germans were the model students of history in a large collective of anti-Nazis. However, before Germans reached that new memory equilibrium (discussed in chapter 12), they had to come to terms with a number of political challenges—including unification, the Gulf War, and a disturbing rise in right-wing violence—that changed their perception of the Nazi past.

UNIFICATION AND MEMORY

German unification fundamentally changed the politics of memory. The West German political elites were now busy managing the political, economic, and social consequences of the sudden, unexpected implosion of the GDR. That entailed, among many other challenges, punishing GDR perpetrators of political crimes and sorting out the competing property claims that arose as a consequence of the return of East Germany into the capitalist world.[49] Thus, the politicians returned to the practical politics of history that had occupied them in the first years after World War II, although they now supervised the process of coming to terms with a past they had not experienced themselves. Unlike the situation in 1945, they could launch the operation Vergangen-heitsbewältigung-GDR from a stable home base, which enjoyed greater political independence and international recognition than ever before. One might have expected that the frequently invoked parallels between 1945 and 1989 would have improved West German sensibility in regard to the interests and insecurities of their fellow citizens in the East. After all, many members of the elite could still remember how it had felt to be welcomed back into the fold of Western democracy by sometimes helpful, sometimes vengeful, but mostly arrogant representatives of foreign occupying powers. In practice, however, the comparisons between the end of Nazism and the end of the SED regime seemed to serve very different purposes. By highlighting their undeniable success in the politics of memory, the Western champions of Ver-gangenheitsbewältigung legitimized their strategy of extending the Federal Republic eastward. References to the past helped establish a new round of hierarchical, top-down politics of history.[50]

While the West German political leaders integrated the former GDR into the West German political and economic system, they were simply too busy to pay much attention to the cultural politics of memory, which had provided such an interesting pastime during the 1980s. In addition, the rapid process of unification between November 1989 and October 1990 destabilized two of the available formats for the implementation of memory politics. On the left side of the political spectrum, many liberal intellectuals and politicians quietly abandoned the concept of constitutional patriotism.[51] Even the most enthusiastic supporters of the concept had never been able to demonstrate how it might provide an effective emotional reference point for collective identity formation. In light of the powerful resurgence of national sentiment in Germany and other parts of Europe, this shortcoming became even more apparent.

The memory activists on the other side of the political spectrum faced similar problems, although they attributed them to the overwhelming success of their own ideological model for explaining German history. The complete collapse of the Communist bloc had validated the antitotalitarian worldview of many Bonn administrations. Consequently, antitotalitarianism became the key ideological framework for the political appropriation of GDR history and the integration of East Germany's political and cultural institutions into the political infrastructure of the Federal Republic. But its very success also turned the traditional type of antitotalitarianism into an outdated, uninteresting concept for the collective memory of the future.[52] As a result, the leadership in unified Germany was left with two alternative models, which were both still in the experimental phase. If nothing else, the debates of the 1980s had clearly demonstrated that, in the political realm, the strategy of historicization and the precise meaning of the Holocaust remained illusive and highly controversial. It was not immediately obvious how either of these models could be developed into a new political consensus or how they could be deployed to bring the antitotalitarian classic up to date.

FIGHTING HITLER IN BAGHDAD: THE GULF WAR OF 1991

When Iraq invaded Kuwait in August 1990, the German government was wrapping up the complex process of unification and preparing for the first all-German elections scheduled for December. The crisis in the Persian Gulf presented an unwelcome distraction from these pressing domestic concerns. The United States quickly approached Germany with a request for troops and money for a UN-backed attack on Iraq and put the Kohl administration in a difficult position. The CDU/CSU members of the coalition government favored contributing troops, but they failed to convince their liberal coalition partners from the Free Democrats, who insisted—as all previous West German governments—that the Federal Republic's Basic Law ruled out any out-of-area deployment of German forces. Since the Social Democrats and the Greens were adamantly opposed to sending troops and changing the constitution, the government could only pledge generous economic support for the war effort. Immediately before and during the fighting, which lasted from mid-January to late February 1991, the Kohl administration increased its financial support and sent reconnaissance and defensive weapon systems to Turkey and Israel.[53]

The situation brewing in the gulf triggered a massive public debate that began in November 1990 regarding Germany's role in world affairs—a debate that would change the political memory of Nazism in significant ways. The crisis constituted the first foreign policy challenge for unified Germany and provided an excellent opportunity for staking out new claims in the unexplored political landscape of the post-Communist world. The drama of war, in contrast to the anticlimactic event of unification, offered the political players a chance to rethink priorities, reestablish relations with friends and foes, and reconnect to their political base. Very quickly, the media were filled with heated discussions about the appropriate means of resistance against dictatorial powers and about wars of aggression, a topic on which all German politicians felt very knowledgeable, even if they passionately disagreed with one another. The obvious parallels between the German past and the Iraqi present also meant that the necessary recalibration of the political system could be conveniently negotiated in the language of memory that the West German elite had developed over the preceding decade.[54]

The members and supporters of the coalition government considered the Gulf War a perfect opportunity for the Federal Republic to attain the global political stature that the country deserved on the basis of its extraordinary economic clout. In their eyes, the invasion of Kuwait was a clear-cut legal and moral case, and Germany had nothing to lose but a lot to gain from joining the war effort. Moreover, by supporting their allies, German leaders could demonstrate to the world how well they had learned the lessons of history: brutal dictators such as Hitler and Saddam Hussein had to be stopped by military force, especially if the safety of the Jewish community was at stake.[55] Some conservative politicians in the ranks of the CSU went even further and suggested that Germany become a full-scale combatant in order to achieve the measure of equality with its Western partners that West Germany had never been able to attain.[56]

The champions of normalization in the government and the media were therefore quite annoyed when the peace movement came out in full force to oppose the remilitarization of German foreign policy. A large coalition of left-wing organizations staged successful demonstrations, most notably in January 1991 when over two hundred thousand activists clogged the streets of Bonn. Like their predecessors in the 1950s and the early 1980s, who had opposed rearmament and the deployment of nuclear weapons, the peace activists insisted on a very different interpretation of German history. In their minds, Germany's wars of aggression had put an absolute limit on the use of German troops and German money for any purpose other than self-defense. By taking to the streets, they wanted to make sure that this pacifist consensus, which had informed West German politics, would remain a cornerstone of collective identity in unified Germany.[57] The peace movement might have foiled government plans for more extensive military involvement in the war—German troops were only sent to the Mediterranean—but in the end, the peace activists lost the battle about German identity because many public intellectuals and left-wing politicians who had traditionally supported the pacifist cause defected to the other side.

As a result of the Gulf War, the intellectual elites of the former West Germany faced a serious dilemma. They assumed that they could not have it both ways, that is, both uphold the long-standing antimilitaristic tradition of the Federal Republic and demand the effective protection of human rights in Kuwait and Israel. Feeling the need to choose between the two principles embodied in the slogans "Never again war" and "Never again Auschwitz," they ranked the second above the first and supported the war against Iraq.[58] This relatively sudden rearrangement of political priorities attested to the general insecurity of the Left after unification and to the new importance of Holocaust memory. Habermas and the liberal historians had spent considerable energy adapting Holocaust interpretations to the German context, and unlike other cornerstones of their identity, the commitment to the memory of the Holocaust had not been called into question by unification. Now, they acted on their philo-Semitic reflexes in the mistaken belief that supporting the war was the only way to express solidarity with Israel. In their rush to judgment, they never considered that the liberation of Kuwait and the protection of Israel might have been accomplished by means other than war. With public intellectuals such as Habermas, Enzensberger, and Biermann leading the way, the whole Left political establishment, with the exception of the pacifist wing of the Green Party, joined the coalition against Saddam Hussein. Apparently, the Left was still susceptible to fantasies of vicarious resistance; its leaders still hoped that victory in the Gulf, if sponsored by Germany, would also count as a belated, symbolic victory against Hitler.

The campaign against the Gulf War was designed to galvanize the Left and safeguard the political legacy of West Germany's social movements, including their self-critical collective memory of Nazism. But the attempt to appropriate the public sphere, which had worked so well in the past, failed decisively in the early 1990s. The reorientation toward the political center temporarily split the national liberal leadership from significant parts of its political base. It took several years before the Left again presented a united front, and by that time, a radical pacifist disposition was no longer considered an integral part of an antifascist identity, as the discussions about the deployment of German troops in the former Yugoslavia demonstrated. In the course of a few years, the Left helped dismantle interpretations of Nazism and the Holocaust that it still vigorously defended against relativization during the Historians' Debate. As a result of these and parallel efforts of the conservative political leadership, the memory of Nazism could now support a wide range of political objectives.[59]

The new semantic flexibility became obvious on a number of occasions, including during the emotional parliamentary debate about the future seat of the German government that took place in Bonn in June 1991. The representatives from the Left invoked the Nazi past in support of a wide range of positions. Like the majority of conservative MPs, Willy Brandt pleaded for the move to Berlin as a sign of national normalization, which he inappropriately compared to the return of the French government from Vichy to Paris in 1944. In contrast to Brandt's position, many younger members of the Green Party and the East German Partei des Demokratischen Sozialismus (PDS, the successor of the SED) vehemently rejected the idea that the government of the Federal Republic should return to the site of two former totalitarian regimes. They wanted to remain in the low-key environment of the Rhineland, where the first and only successful German democracy had taken root. Still others, including the former SPD chairman, Hans-Jochen Vogel, argued that the many visible reminders of German guilt made Berlin a perfect place for the kind of self-critical, self-reflexive republic that had developed in West Germany in the course of several decades and that would now have to be shared with the former citizens of East Germany.[60] The Left was clearly no longer able to unite under the banner of antifascism and force their opponents onto the defensive simply by invoking the Nazi regime.

XENOPHOBIA AND POPULAR ANTIFASCISM

Less than two years after the political turmoil caused by the Gulf War, the Federal Republic experienced another unusual display of grassroots politics. It almost seemed as if important cross sections of the population resented the fact that the political elite had implemented unification without popular consent. Now, they wanted to make sure that their own values would count in the new republic. In addition to the demonstrations against the Gulf War, the string of exceptional collective founding acts included a sharp rise in violence against foreigners and Jews and an antixenophobic counterreaction by left-wing activists and many citizens in the political mainstream. All of these actions were justified through references to the Nazi past, and all of them were at least partly directed against the political leadership in Bonn, including the leaders of the opposition.

In a rare show of German unity, radical right-wing youths in both the East and West went on the offensive in fall 1991. In the East, the violent attacks against foreigners met with open approval by many former citizens of the GDR. On several occasions, large crowds of onlookers cheered on neo-Nazi thugs as they raided dormitories and beat up political refugees and foreign workers.[61] Right-wing youths in the West could not count on similar popular support, so they tended to choose stealthier but equally deadly tactics. Official statistics for unified Germany list several thousand arson attacks in 1992 alone, which cost the lives of seventeen people.[62] The campaign of violence reflected a wide range of motives but assumed cohesion, in the eyes of the perpetrators as well as their opponents, through a simplistic ideological framework that featured a counterfactual, romantic emplotment of National Socialism among other equally unappetizing tidbits.[63] The affirmation of Nazi racism and its symbols, which had thrived in West German right-wing circles in the 1980s partly as a provocation against the increasingly successful official Holocaust paradigm, offered a ready-made ideological framework for like-minded adolescents in the East, who had had fewer opportunities to develop political organizations and a consistent neo-Nazi identity.[64]

Quite ironically, the impressive popular reaction against the racist attacks also received some of its strength from counterfactual interpretations of Nazism, albeit of a radically different kind. The pogroms and murders seemed to corroborate what the radical Left had argued all along, that is, that the Federal

Republic remained structurally compatible with its political predecessor and that fascist political practices could reemerge at any time. Given the severity of the violence, it was now relatively easy to organize a civic movement that publicly expressed its sense of outrage and historic duty. In the 1992–1993 winter, millions of citizens, representing the largest political grassroots movement in the history of the Federal Republic, participated in candlelight vigils to mourn the victims and oppose racism.[65] Through their public statements, the demonstrators also expressed their dissatisfaction with their political representatives in Bonn. In true populist fashion, the federal government had delayed action, assuming correctly that the violent campaign reflected the sentiments of important segments of the voting public. In fact, by curbing the traditionally generous political asylum laws shortly after unification, parliament had expressed its tacit approval of the concerns, if not the actions, of the neo-Nazi hoodlums.[66] As a result of these decisions, the government was now caught in the ideological cross fire between two competing subcultural interpretations of fascism that, at least for a short while, managed to displace the government's own ambitious memory agenda.

In the long run, however, there was no reason to worry, at least not about the future of Germany's cultural memory of Nazism. The popular antifascist movement quickly lost steam, and the right wing returned into its ideological ghetto. Xenophobic and anti-Semitic crimes continued at a disconcertingly high level, but they no longer caused public discussions that could derail the conservative memory agenda.[67] Moreover, the government's long-range investments in the politics of memory finally began to pay off. In the mid-1990s, Kohl could present institutions of memory that offered conservative visions of the past to large audiences and demonstrated, for the first time, how federally induced historicization would work in practice.

THE CENTRAL MEMORIAL FOR THE VICTIMS OF WAR AND TERROR

The first project to come to fruition took only ten months from start to finish—a veritable coup d'état in the cumbersome and time-consuming process of cultural memory production. In January 1993, the federal government announced its detailed plans for the creation of a "Central Memorial Site for the Victims of War and Terror," and in November of the same year, the highest dignitaries of the republic dedicated the memorial in Berlin. The building

chosen for the purpose was located at the capital's primary boulevard, Unter
den Linden. Erected after the Napoleonic Wars, it had been the official site of
mourning and hero worship for four previous German states, including the
GDR.[68] The government moved so quickly to appropriate the building for the
self-representation of the Berlin republic because many of its members, especially Kohl himself, were convinced of the need for a central memorial.
They wanted to create what the chancellor and some of his predecessors had
missed in Bonn: a dignified locale where foreign visitors could pay their respects to the victims of past wars.[69] In addition, they acted hastily and in secret because their previous attempts to realize a similar project in Bonn had
been foiled by partisan politics.

In 1982, Kohl had been approached by the conservative leadership of the
Volksbund Deutsche Kriegsgräberfürsorge, the nonprofit association tending
the graves of German soldiers at home and abroad. The association wanted
to replace the existing, makeshift, and unappealing memorial site in Bonn
with a much more impressive and expansive monument, and found a sympathetic audience in Kohl.[70] Unfortunately, all attempts to build a consensus
in parliament came to naught. In 1985, in the middle of the political wrangling about the anniversary celebrations, the representatives paid some attention to the memorial project, but they could not agree on the necessity, let
alone the design, of a new monument that would honor the victims of German crimes *and* the German victims of the war. The representatives of the
Green Party flat-out rejected the idea of a large memorial, which could be
abused for nationalistic purposes and which would inevitably and inappropriately equate victims and perpetrators.[71] In contrast, the Social Democratic
Party had come up with a particularly ingenious and, for the government,
particularly troubling proposal. Since many Social Democrats considered
Weizsäcker's 1985 speech a crowning achievement in the history of German
memory politics, they wanted the memorial to reflect the spirit of that speech
and the precise hierarchy of victimhood that Weizsäcker had developed.[72]
None of these suggestions pleased the governing liberals and Christian Democrats. They preferred a conventional war memorial featuring the traditional, vague dedication to "the victims of war and terror" that already adorned
the Bonn monument; they simply wanted to transfer this time-tested antitotalitarian message to a new, much more impressive site that would rival similar institutions in other European capitals. Considering the wide spectrum of

opinions on the matter and the divisive political climate of the 1980s, it is not surprising that no action was taken.[73]

Kohl revived the plans for a central memorial after unification and after the decision to move the government to Berlin. Now that the stately building in central Berlin offered a perfect venue, Kohl would not make the same tactical mistake again: rather than trying to square the memorial circle by bringing everybody on board, he decided to implement his own vision of German collective memory. As a result of that decision, the memorial in Berlin is probably the most accurate representation of Kohl's personal historical taste. Sooner or later, all other cultural memory projects were handed over to boards of experts who might have been handpicked by Kohl and his advisers and who might have agreed with his general political outlook but who nevertheless pursued aesthetic and professional objectives that probably did not coincide with the specific sensibilities and aims of their employer. In the case of the Central Memorial, the situation was different. Stripping the building of its socialist trappings and refitting it with more appropriate symbols did not require a complex bureaucracy. With one notable exception, nobody outside the government was involved in the decision-making process, and it is safe to assume that no important step was taken without Kohl's personal involvement.[74] However, judging by the results, one might wish that he had sought additional advice: among the institutions of cultural memory created during the Kohl era, the Central Memorial is the least compelling interpretation of the Nazi past.

When the government presented its memorial plans to the public, all details had already been settled. The interior was to be returned to its pre–World War II condition and decorated with two simple items: a plaque with the inscription "To the Victims of War and Terror" and a copy of a pietà by Käthe Kollwitz blown up to life size from its original modest height of fifty centimeters. In the weeks and months after the announcement, the political opposition largely agreed with the government plans. Some SPD representatives grumbled about the lack of parliamentary involvement and reminded their colleagues about Weizsäcker's more suitable, differentiated acknowledgment of the victims, but they raised no fundamental objections. Key players in the Green Party were even more accommodating. In a relative sudden reversal of the official party line, they applauded both the locale and the artwork selected for the future memorial.[75] This generosity reflected the general change of political tastes and priorities after unification, especially concerning themes and symbols of nationalism. But the change of mind was also a result of Kohl's strategically brilliant decision to make Kollwitz's pietà the visual centerpiece of the monument. The artist's name and works had been fixtures both in the West German peace movement and the official pacifist iconography of the East German state.[76] By appropriating her work, Kohl and his advisers appealed to the aesthetic sensibilities of their erstwhile West German opponents and signaled their appreciation of one of the more acceptable legacies of the Communist dictatorship. In one simple move, the vague memorial to the victims of war and genocide had become a celebration of reconciliation among Germans.

The political opposition thus was elegantly disarmed, and the field was wide open for the academic critics of the government's politics of memory who had lost some of their political influence in the process of unification. In addition to typical intellectual concerns—for instance, that expanding the pietà from its original size undercut its authenticity as a symbol of private mourning[77]—they argued quite compellingly that Kollwitz's statue was both historically and spiritually inappropriate for the purpose at hand. The traditional Christian icon of the mother mourning the death of her son seemed unsuitable for remembering the victims of genocide and mass death, especially the many Jewish victims.[78] The academic critics held no sway over the government, but another constituency with far more political clout had similar concerns and ultimately brought about significant changes in the design of the memorial. The Central Council of Jews in Germany, vigorously represented by its president, Ignaz Bubis, opposed the overly generous inscription that lumped together the victims of the "Final Solution" and their tormentors who had died during World War II, for instance, as a result of Allied bombing attacks.[79]

When all protests seemed futile, Bubis, himself a member of the CDU, simply threatened to boycott the opening ceremony, which almost certainly would have caused an international scandal. Faced with such an accomplished deployment of political capital, the government made two key concessions. First, Kohl promised to support the construction of an official Holocaust memorial in the capital. The idea had been debated since the late 1980s, but lack of funding and government support had thus far prevented its realization. In addition, Kohl agreed to have a second plaque installed at the entrance of the memorial that would list the groups of victims in a format similar to the famous passage in Weizsäcker's speech.[80] But the text was changed in significant ways. Rather than acknowledging the suffering of the Jews in the second sentence after the general introduction ("We mourn today the victims of war and terror. We remember especially the six million Jews"), the first five sentences of the text on the plaque focused on the suffering caused by war, mentioning specifically fallen soldiers, POWs, and expellees, before paying respect to the victims of the "Final Solution."[81] The text did not specifically highlight the sacrifices of the German people; it spoke of all the peoples who suffered in times of war. But in its current version, the inscription nevertheless subsumed the victims of genocide under the general category of war dead and thus confirmed the traditional format of national war memorials as well as the antitotalitarian consensus of West Germany's political tradition.

Scholarly opinion about the merits of the Central Memorial has not changed since the mid-1990s. Analysts who disagree with Kohl's political motives interpret the memorial as a systematic attempt to displace the self-critical West German memory of the Third Reich. In the perception of these critics, the memorial's abstract and decontextualized representation of the past renders the crimes invisible and deflects from Germany's continued moral obligations.[82] Moreover, even scholars sympathetic to the Kohl conservative politics of memory deplore the memorial's lack of democratic legitimacy and its intellectual shortcomings, including its inappropriate Christian iconography.[83] All these points of criticism are worth considering, but they do not capture the specific aesthetic and political innovations that the new institutions of cultural memory brought about in the 1990s. Most visitors might, indeed, perceive the Central Memorial as a typical war memorial, although for audiences familiar with Germany's professional memory discourse, the site presents a more interesting and more contradictory picture. As a result of political exigency and the intellectual predilections of its creators, the memorial combines the general victims discourse and antitotalitarian consensus of the 1950s with elements of left-wing pacifist memory and the Holocaust memory of the 1980s. Thus, it weaves together distinct layers of German collective memory that had originally been shaped by different political constituencies and political generations. The resulting collage might anger academic observers for its lack of consistency and political correctness, but it provides a relatively honest snapshot of the power relations in the memory politics of the 1990s, an era when a determined conservative government anticipated and alleviated the criticism of its political opposition and quickly reacted to unforeseen misgivings of the Jewish community that it simply could not afford to antagonize.

Precisely because of its intellectual shortcomings, the Central Memorial also demonstrates, in exemplary fashion, how institutions of cultural memory contribute to the historicization of the past. Since the memorial bears the obvious marks of a political compromise, it exposes current and future audiences to the competitive negotiations involved in its creation. The memorial tends to historicize specific types of collective memory by subjecting them to a process of competition, as a closer look at the memorial's most recent memory layer, the layer of Holocaust memory, illustrates. On the one hand, the memorial certainly marks the advance of Holocaust memory in the political sphere, since there had never been a federal institution of cultural memory that specifically mentioned the suffering of European Jewry. On the other hand, the memorial clearly relativizes Holocaust memory, not by denying the event or by preventing its representation but by integrating it into a plethora of memory perspectives and memory subjects that are not necessarily compatible with the memory of Holocaust as it was constructed in the 1980s. This historicization effect is especially unavoidable if the topic of the Holocaust is featured in institutions of cultural memory that cover a wide range of historical topics and perspectives. During the 1980s, the "Final Solution" had temporarily assumed the status of an absolutely exceptional event, but in the 1990s, as representations of the Holocaust multiplied, the semantics of space undercut this exceptionality. On a larger scale and therefore much more effectively than the Central Memorial, the federal historical museums in Bonn and Berlin reduced the Holocaust to one subject in a wide range of matters that clearly all deserved similar attention. The "Final Solution" was thus relativized at the precise moment when the German state for the first time paid tribute to its Jewish victims symbolically and not just financially, as it had in the past.

HISTORICIZATION, CULTURAL MEMORY, AND MUSEUM POLITICS

When the House of the History of the Federal Republic opened to the public in June 1994, the overall narrative trajectory of its permanent exhibit was more triumphant than originally intended. From its inception, the museum was designed to celebrate West German accomplishments in the aftermath of the nation's biggest catastrophe; it was always supposed to convey a Phoenix-from-the-ashes type of story to an allegedly historically insecure population. Part of this objective was accomplished by omission. As the critics had antici-pated, the exhibit systematically avoided any radically self-critical interpreta-tions of the West German democracy, especially regarding its relationship to the Nazi past. There was no mention of the severe shortcomings of the repub-lic's restitution efforts and the failure to bring many Nazi criminals to justice. The presentations glossed over the fact that the functional elites of the Third Reich had retained their leadership positions in the Federal Republic and never touched on the troublesome rise of neo-Nazi activism since the 1980s, which had become a source of great embarrassment for West Germany and unified Germany.[84]

Obviously, these flaws had nothing to do with unification. They also would have surfaced in the more narrowly conceived West German museum that the Kohl administration had originally proposed. But the collapse of the GDR made the self-congratulatory tale of West German success even more com-pelling. The events of 1989 and 1990 required the museum designers to pay more attention to the history of the GDR and gave them a chance to demon-strate West Germany's economic and political superiority in great detail.[85] Furthermore and more important, the fall of the Berlin Wall provided a fabu-lous, visually compelling conclusion to the story of West Germany's rise from the ruins of World War II.[86] In this narrative configuration, the Holocaust plays a limited, yet important role. In combination with references to other Nazi crimes, postwar expulsions, and general postwar misery, the events of the "Final Solution" demonstrate just how deep Germany had sunk and how miraculous the West German recovery had been. The crimes and the suffering are presented in a compact, iconographic format through photos, documen-tary footage, and a few objects at the very beginning of the exhibit. But the misery depicted on the ground floor of the museum is not accompanied by many comments, and as the visitors move up to the second floor, they quickly enter the glittery world of West German consumerism, which is the primary focus of the exhibit. A wealth of artifacts and electronic media displays recon-struct the life worlds of several generations of West German and East Ger-man citizens. The presentation is wonderfully engaging and entertaining, reflecting cutting-edge museum didactics and presenting just the right combination of everyday history interspersed with bite-sized snippets of political, economic, and social history.[87] But by re-creating the past with such attention to detail, the museum staff also masterfully re-created the protective layers of everyday life that the contemporaries of Nazism and their descendants had built in the postwar decades—partly in response to the disturbing legacy of Nazi history. As in the case of the Central Memorial, the permanent exhibit thus juxtaposes different layers of German memory while clearly stressing the priority of some memories at the expense of others, for instance, the priority of memories of postwar everyday life at the expense of Holocaust memory. However, unlike the Central Memorial, which lacks a compelling narrative trajectory and therefore tends to expose the cracks between incompatible types of memory, the museum teaches, in very practical terms, how to contain and historicize the memory of the Holocaust within an overall narrative of contemporary German history leading from the depths of genocide and defeat to the triumphant recovery of national unity and self-determination.

The impressive number of visitors and the positive feedback they have provided over the years show that the German public clearly appreciates the museum in Bonn.[88] It is quite possible, however, that the strategies of historicization offered in the museum are only particularly compelling for very specific generations of museum curators and visitors. For those who experienced West German everyday life, the museum systematically valorizes the political and consumer choices they made in the past. The pleasure of having your life reconfirmed at every twist and turn in the museum narrative certainly creates a lot of goodwill toward the museum's overall didactic objective, including its "advice" on how to deal with the history of the "Final Solution." But future audiences without such nostalgic attachment to the displayed life world might stumble over the marginal yet powerful depiction of the "Final Solution" at the beginning of the exhibit. They might turn the building upside down and deconstruct West German normality from the perspective of the catastrophe that preceded it or from the perspective of the East German normality that accompanied it for so many years. This thought experiment shows that strategies of historicization, which openly acknowledge the troublesome past while trying to contain it within redemptive plot types, risk losing their power of conviction when presented to audiences with little emotional attachment to the narrative contents or narrative formats chosen to accomplish the normalization.[89]

It is still too early to pass judgment on the Museum of German History in the new capital. After the decision to move the capital to Berlin, the museum could no longer be built close to the Reichstag as originally planned because the location was now reserved for government offices. Instead of moving into a shiny new building at the Spree, the staff had to make due with the historic Zeughaus, which had already housed the GDR's national museum of history but offered considerably less space than the museum plans required. As a result, construction and renovation have been under way for over a decade, and the first permanent exhibit will not be unveiled until sometime in 2006.[90] However, from 1994 to 1998, the former museum director Christoph Stölzl and his team presented a temporary exhibit that showcased some of their acquisitions. Judging by that first attempt to display the entire history of the German people, it seems unlikely that the museum will become a hotbed of nationalistic propaganda any time soon. As to be expected from a temporary installation, many of the rooms appeared somewhat haphazardly put together, but there was no indication that the museum planers intended to marginalize the history of the Third Reich. Considering the scope of the installation, the Nazi period and the Nazi crimes were presented in impressive detail. Not surprisingly, the exhibit also lacked a clear conceptual or narrative focus— with one important exception: Stölzl and his colleagues often seemed more concerned with European rather than specifically German history.[91] With that thematic emphasis, they anticipated the most important and successful historicization strategy in unified Germany. Whenever the troublesome Nazi crimes were not integrated in the success story of the Federal Republic (as, for instance, in the Bonn museum), they became part of the history of European integration. That fact was made particularly obvious in 1995 when European and world leaders shuttled from one anniversary celebration to the next, all the while congratulating themselves on their exemplary service for peace and reconciliation. In the past, German dignitaries had had to stay home alone and contemplate their historical misdeeds; now, they would be included in the festivities.

In the first half of the 1990s, the Kohl administration managed to recast the memory of Nazism by selectively integrating a wide range of historical interpretations that had a long standing in West Germany's historical culture or had recently assumed global prominence. This attractive memory package, reaching from antitotalitarianism to Holocaust memory, would never have taken shape without Kohl's personal commitment, perhaps even obsession, with the task of containing the destructive identity effects of the Nazi past. Most likely, Kohl's peculiar commitment did not correspond to some objective psychological needs of the German population. His choices tell us more about his and his advisers' craving for historical reassurance than about the intended audience of his conservative cultural revolution. Nevertheless, the institutions of cultural memory created in the Kohl era were a notable accomplishment. Politicians regained some of the initiative that they had lost in the previous decades and helped elevate the self-confident bystander memory to a new level of ideological, rhetorical, and technological sophistication. The museum discourse of the 1990s, like the television discourse since the 1980s, cast German audiences in the role of enlightened, vicarious witnesses of Nazism who—in the very act of consuming history—allegedly helped prevent its recurrence.

The externalized optimistic bystander memory of the 1980s and 1990s also represented an important step toward the nationalization of the Holocaust. For the first time, Nazi crimes provided an explicit reference point for the constitution of German identity, initially in West Germany and subsequently in unified Germany. This process of nationalization laid the foundation for the next stage in the evolution of the political memory by preparing Germany's political elite for the role of memory partner—and occasionally, even memory tutor—in unified Europe. Yet all these formidable achievements came at a hefty price. The dominant political memories of the 1990s positioned the consumers and producers of Holocaust memory in fundamental opposition to the witnesses and perpetrators of Nazi violence and thus undercut any truly self-critical reflections about the presence of the past. By identifying with the victims and survivors of the Holocaust after the fact and by embracing the romantic story of German recovery from unconditional surrender to unification, Germans developed a positive sense of collective belonging, first on a national and later perhaps also on a European scale. But this historical consciousness does not provide a good understanding of the social and psychological processes that shape(d) the perpetrators and passive bystanders of past, present, and future acts of ethnic cleansing and genocide. On the level of national politics, only the Greens—and inadvertently Philipp Jenninger, in his badly miscalibrated anniversary speech—attacked this optimistic fiction of historical discontinuity, and even their critical voices would disappear in 1995 when Europe mobilized the memory of the Holocaust to justify military intervention in Yugoslavia.

NORMALIZATION

The Europeanization of
German Political Memory since the 1990s

The important repackaging of the Nazi past that occurred in 1995 built upon time-tested strategies of memory politics. German politicians had frequently ended their relatively vague reflections about the Nazi past by publicly declaring their commitment to the process of European integration, which, they argued, would prevent the recurrence of catastrophes such as World War II.[1] But in the 1990s, these declarations were combined with detailed acknowledgments of the crimes of the Nazi regime, including the genocide of European Jewry. In addition, in the celebrations of 1995, this theme was collectively embraced by European leaders in a flurry of banquets, parades, and speeches all across the continent. For the first time, the Europeanization of the Nazi past was acted out on the level of discourse *and* ritual and by a group of leaders who proudly claimed survivor status for their countries and for Europe as a whole and now gladly bestowed the same distinction on their former opponent.

The Europeanization and internationalization of German memory that occurred in 1995 was not the result of long-term government planning. The political memory marathon began with a short parliamentary ceremony marking the fiftieth anniversary of the liberation of Auschwitz and continued with local gatherings recalling the liberation of the major concentration camps and the bombing of Dresden in February 1945.[2] Kohl and his ministers intended to mark May 8, the fiftieth anniversary of the end of World War II, with a dignified, focused ceremony in Berlin that would not involve any high-level foreign guests. Kohl himself was not even on the list of speakers, which instead comprised the Federal Republic's three presidents—the president of the republic Roman Herzog, the president of the lower house of parliament

Rita Süssmuth, and the president of the upper house of parliament Johannes Rau.[3] Such humility on the part of the German political elite can only be explained by the political "trauma" of Bitburg. Despite all the changes that had taken place since 1985—including unification, the restoration of full sovereignty, and Germany's enhanced profile in world politics—German politicians chose to revert to the subdued, understated political style that had characterized anniversary celebrations in the Federal Republic before the Kohl era. Since nobody wanted to risk repeating Kohl's mistake, a strange disconnect developed: while the German media put on an imposing and entertaining anniversary show clearly dominated by the theme of liberation, the politicians decided to stay on the sidelines and reflect on the good fortune of German liberation in the safe setting of their own simple ritual.[4] Luckily, they were rescued from their self-imposed memory cloister by friendly neighbors who intervened on their own accord and not because they had been pressured—like Reagan had been ten years earlier.

The first relief detail arrived in the person of French president François Mitterand, who, scheduled to leave office in a few months and struck with terminal cancer, invited his German colleagues to attend the Paris anniversary celebrations. As if this was not gracious enough, he also expressed his desire to participate in the festivities in Berlin and use that opportunity to deliver a parting message about the accomplishments of French-German and European reconciliation.[5] These wishes could clearly not be ignored, and diplomatic protocol required that all former occupying powers and partners in the four-plus-two negotiations would be invited as well. Thus, the celebrations took on a format that Kohl had probably not even anticipated in his wildest dreams. Suddenly, all the major international players who had supervised and intervened in German memory politics since 1945 agreed to travel to Berlin, the former and new German capital, acknowledge their erstwhile enemy as an equal, and celebrate fifty years of peace and reconciliation. This was normalization with a capital N.[6]

The second, somewhat belated relief detail arrived in the person of the Polish foreign minister Władysław Bartoszewski. But since everything had already been settled in the most advantageous terms imaginable, his suggestion that a representative from Poland should also be invited to Berlin was given short shrift by the government. The Polish and German media and the SPD opposition protested against the arrogant dismissal of Bartoszewki's initiative and prompted the chancellor to reverse his decision. In the end, an additional, second-class anniversary celebration was organized, which featured a Polish guest—who turned out to be Bartoszewski himself—and the two presidents of Germany's lower and upper houses, who had lost their spots on the original celebration ticket to the higher-caliber visitors from France, Great Britain, Russia, and the United States.[7]

A final challenge to the anniversary celebration was launched in April 1995 by an eclectic assortment of conservative and right-wing politicians and journalists who correctly assumed that their interpretation of May 8 had no place in the official memory events planned in Bonn. Brought together by the historian and journalist Rainer Zitelmann, the group represented an impressive cross section of the German Right, ranging from extreme right-wing parties with neo-Nazi inclinations, such as the Die Republikaner, to the conservative wing of the CDU/CSU. Yet the suggestions of the group were hardly radical, at least when considered in the context of fifty years of German memory politics. In an ad placed in the *Frankfurter Allgemeine Zeitung*, Zitelmann and his associates encouraged their readers to resist the dominant liberation theme and retain a more ambivalent memory of May 8, 1945, a date that, in their opinion, marked not only the end of NS terror but also the beginning of German expulsion and division.[8] Their plea certainly exaggerated the homogeneity of Germany's memory culture. As part of the extensive anniversary media coverage, the suffering of German soldiers and civilians had received a fair share of attention.[9] In essence, the group simply reminded the public of the themes and positions that had dominated the official political memory in the Federal Republic for many years but no longer corresponded to the political consensus that had gradually evolved after Weiszäcker's speech of 1985. Their modest assault on the politically correct liberation paradigm was quickly rebuffed by all relevant players, who were poised to enjoy the Europeanization of German memory without further interruptions.

The actual celebrations brought no surprises, but they impressed an unusually large audience, which watched the media coverage of the political circus as it traveled from London to Paris, Berlin, and Moscow. The German speakers all dutifully confirmed the liberation theme that had helped attract so much goodwill from the international community. One speaker after another emphasized that the regrettable suffering of the German people in the postwar years could not be separated from the grave political mistakes and exceptional crimes the government and its followers had committed before 1945. In return, the representatives of the former Allies spoke eloquently about the Federal Republic's exemplary track record and insisted that May 8, 1945, should no longer be considered the day of victory over Germany but the day of "Europe's victory over itself," as Mitterand put it.[10] The German president brought all these themes together in a speech that contained few references to the Nazi past and focused primarily on postwar developments. Herzog clearly acknowledged the German responsibility for the war and the Holocaust and emphasized that "we really do not need to discuss that question again today."[11] He obviously meant that the fact of German responsibility was recognized by everybody, including Germans, and the meaning of his statement was perfectly obvious in the specific context. Considered from a more critical angle, however, the sentence could also serve as the motto for a speech that had little to say about crimes, victims, and responsibility and talked instead about the "willing pupil" Germany that helped turn the field of rubble that was Europe into "an island of peace, freedom, and prosperity."[12]

In 1995, a memory marathon had come to an end. In the course of twelve years of fiftieth and fortieth anniversaries of Nazi history, a long struggle had been waged to develop public formats of remembrance that would satisfy three very different constituencies: the politicians themselves; their foreign colleagues, who always cast a critical eye across the border; and the German voters whose interests were no longer as easily predictable as they had been in the 1950s and 1960s. The agreement and optimism at the end of that twelve-year period demonstrated that Germany's politicians declared the struggle to be over, not necessarily because they had found the right formats—although they certainly had made some progress in that respect as well—but because they had been explicitly signaled by their foreign partners that they could now pay less attention to memory politics and focus more exclusively on the "real" political challenge of becoming a first-rate European and global power broker.

On the way toward that goal, the political elite now faced important obstacles that it had itself erected in past decades as a response to the catastrophe of Nazism. Foremost among these obstacles was the West German self-restraint in all military matters. The constitution of the Federal Republic explicitly prohibits out-of-area deployment of the armed forces, which politicians of all stripes had traditionally interpreted as an injunction against the mobilization of the Bundeswehr for any purposes other than self-defense. During the Cold

War nuclear standoff between the East and West, this policy was never seriously challenged because there was simply never any reason to send NATO troops into battle in Europe. West Germany could enjoy its pacifist, anti-Nazi identity without having to pay a serious price for that commitment. The collapse of the Soviet bloc and the war in Yugoslavia changed all that, and it is very possible that the forgiving attitude that Germany's European neighbors displayed in 1995 had a lot to do with their expectations about the Federal Republic's political and military contribution to the crisis management on the Balkan Peninsula. Be that as it may, in the second half of the 1990s, Germany's politicians slowly went down the path toward military normalization. In the process, they radically changed their interpretation of the Nazi past. If World War II had previously served as a strong reminder that Germans had better refrain from any military adventures lest they become perpetrators again, the Nazi wars were now reinterpreted as providing a strong moral obligation to help today's victims of ethnic cleansing—if necessary, even by military force.

THE BALKAN CIVIL WAR AND THE DECONSTRUCTION OF WEST GERMAN PACIFISM

Just a few weeks after the anniversary celebrations, in June 1995, the government sought permission from parliament to join the UN-authorized NATO mission in the former Yugoslavia and send medical units, transportation equipment, and administrative staff to Croatia, Bosnia and Herzegovina, and Italy. In addition, Defense Minister Volker Rühe intended to deploy fighter jets in support of NATO's rapid-response forces already in the area. This last item on the government's wish list caused heated debates in parliament, which, at least on that occasion, still followed clear party lines. For the speakers from the ranks of the CDU/CSU and FDP, unification and the restoration of full sovereignty had radically changed Germany's foreign policy options and responsibilities. They argued that the self-imposed restrictions on the use of military force had made perfect sense during the Cold War but that Germans had no longer any moral justification for refusing to return the many favors they had received over the past fifty years. Having obtained so much help in dealing with the legacy of Nazism, the Federal Republic had a moral obligation to stand shoulder to shoulder with its friends in the West and support the fight for human rights and democracy in Europe.[13]

Most representatives of the opposition were not convinced by these arguments. Speakers from the Social Democrats, the Greens, and the East German Socialists defended the political consensus that had informed West German diplomacy since the Adenauer administration. In their opinion, unification did not provide a compelling reason to abandon the lessons of the Nazi past and remilitarize German foreign policy. Since the Federal Republic could easily meet its treaty obligation without sending combat troops, the critics suspected that the conservative government was primarily motivated by political ambition and not so much by the desire to help the people of Yugoslavia.[14] Joschka Fischer, the leader of the Green faction in parliament, proved particularly apt in exposing the contradictions in the government's argumentation. He wondered why Kohl and his ministers, since they were so convinced about the need for military intervention, had not also volunteered German ground troops. Perhaps they sensed, he suggested in answering his own question, that sending German soldiers into communities that had been devastated by the Wehrmacht half a century earlier was still a bad idea.[15] In the end, the protests of the opposition had little effect on the outcome of the vote. In fact, a substantial number of SPD representatives and even a few Green Party members voted in favor of the government initiative.[16] The politics of memory that had sustained West Germany's self-reflexive and unassuming presence in world affairs no longer unified the political class in the new and enlarged Federal Republic.

On July 11, 1995, Serbian troops overran the UN safety zone of Srebrenica. Reports about the ensuing murder and expulsion of thousands of Bosnians dominated the European media for weeks. The civil war in Yugoslavia, which had raged since 1991, seemed to have assumed a new quality, and many observers demanded more decisive action on behalf of the war's victims.[17] In Germany, the events in Srebrenica caused the political opposition to abandon its pacifist principles and explore the possibility of armed intervention. One of the first prominent liberals to break rank was none other than Joschka Fischer, who explained his change of heart with a remarkable feast of memory politics. In an open letter addressed to his Green Party comrades, Fischer called the Serbian perpetrators the new fascists, who had to be met with decisive resistance if the process of European integration was to continue unabated.[18] Using all the right buzzwords, Fischer expressed his interventionist stance in the radical antifascist lingo that was attractive to Green Party members. At the same time, he signaled his colleagues in the SPD and CDU that the Green movement was joining the political mainstream and would soon be ready to assume government responsibilities.

Fischer's history lesson received praise and criticism from across the political spectrum, but in the short run, his initiative exacerbated the existing political divide in his own party. The Green moderates supported his plea, arguing that it was high time for German liberals to get their historical priorities straight. Rather than obsessing about their fathers' and grandfathers' perpetrator existence and their own fear of becoming like their predecessors, Germany's antifascists should finally pay attention to the victims of war and genocide—especially those that could still be saved.[19] In contrast, the radical wing of the party maintained, in good pacifist tradition, that the same goal could be attained much more effectively by nonmilitary measures such as embargoes.[20] In December 1995, when parliament decided about German participation in the NATO-led and UN-authorized peacekeeping force for Bosnia and Herzegovina, the Green vote split three ways: twenty-two opposed, twenty-two in favor, and five abstentions.[21] Nevertheless, it was quite obvious that Fischer had made the right strategic choice. Parliament provided an impressive mandate for military intervention, and there was no sign of significant popular opposition to that decision. A number of important liberals, including Jürgen Habermas, Günter Grass, and Ralph Giordano, had publicly expressed their support for the deployment of German troops.[22] Reading the signs of the times correctly, Fischer had helped build a political bandwagon that would deliver German troops to Kosovo, Bosnia, and Afghanistan and transport Fischer himself into the German Foreign Ministry within three years.

Ambitious liberals such as Fischer played the fascism card for the last time in 1995, but in this case, to gain access to the political mainstream and not to expose its allegedly fascist elements, as they had done in the past. At a time when everybody, including right-wing Christian Democrats, garnished their speeches with bits and pieces of Holocaust memory, posing as the only true protector of the legacy of anti-Nazism no longer offered any political advantages. Conservatives no longer felt that their actions and symbolic gestures somehow fell short of the ethical demands that foreign observers imposed on Germany but that they had often not been able to meet because of practical political concerns—for instance, concerns about the population's willingness

to engage in self-critical politics of memory. The success of Kohl's memory initiatives at home and abroad had alleviated these feelings of inadequacy, and
without them, the conservative establishment could no longer be pressured
into political concessions. The guilt factor had simply worn away. Therefore,
Fischer publicly relinquished the weapon of antifascism in exchange for political respectability, as long as it could still be used as a bargaining chip. For
politicians who had feared the weapon in the past, Fischer's gesture marked
an important turning point in the history of memory politics. West Germany's
independent Left was the third and last significant player, who had regularly
pestered the republic's conservatives about their inadequate reckoning with
the past and had finally abandoned the cause—just like the East German regime in 1989 and the former enemies and present allies in the summer of
1995.

Having found a new memory paradigm that provided political stability as
well as international recognition, German politicians managed, for the first
time, to communicate about the Nazi past across generational and political
divides. Previously, liberal representatives of the postwar generation and conservative members of the war and Hitler Youth generations had spent a lot of
time denouncing each other (for their alleged fascist inclinations, among other
things), but they had rarely listened to each other. In the context of the Europeanization of German memory and the gradual remilitarization of German
foreign policy, political actors from different age-groups and with different
worldviews displayed an unusual willingness to respect and explore each other's
point of view. That fact became quite obvious in a parliamentary debate in
March 1997 when the MPs discussed the virtues of the traveling photo exhibit, entitled "The Crimes of the Wehrmacht," that had been organized by
the Hamburg Institute for Social Research as its contribution to the super
memory year of 1995. Consisting of fourteen hundred photos and substantial commentaries, the exhibit documented the crimes against humanity that
the German army—not the SS—had committed in occupied eastern Europe.[23] The show directly attacked the popular myth of the honorable Wehrmacht that veterans, politicians, and many social institutions, including the
churches, had constructed in the postwar years and that had survived the political turmoil of the 1970s and the memory revolution of the 1980s. As with
so many other memory projects whose proponents end up preaching to the
converted, the organizers expected only a modest audience, and initially, their

expectations proved quite realistic. In Hamburg, for instance, the exhibit attracted about seven thousand visitors. That pattern repeated itself until the show reached Munich in January 1997, where the local politician Peter Gauweiler viciously attacked the organizers as unpatriotic, left-wing propagandists.[24] In three hundred thousand letters sent to Munich households, Gauweiler urged his fellow citizens to stay away from the "Crimes of the Wehrmacht," inadvertently catapulting the exhibit into the political limelight. Over ninety thousand visitors showed up in Munich, and that success recurred in many other cities. Ever since, the show has been credited with shaping a new self-critical popular memory of World War II.[25] Similar perspectives on the history of the war had informed previous scholarship and extraacademic memory work, but the myth of the Wehrmacht had never been criticized in such a compelling visual format.

Parliament discussed the "Crimes of the Wehrmacht" exhibit in March 1997 at the request of the Green Party faction, whose members were outraged by Gauweiler's attack. After the CDU conservative stalwart Alfred Dregger had lambasted the exhibit for defaming a whole generation of honorable German men as Nazi criminals, speakers from the SPD and the Green Party radically changed the tone of the debate. In very personal and emotional words, the younger MPs described the experience of growing up with parents who, in one way or another, had bought into the Nazis' national revolution and left their children with a legacy of guilt and confusion. Everybody in the house, including Dregger, was impressed by their courageous intervention; there had never been a similar moment of empathetic understanding across the generations—at least not on the topic of Nazi Germany.[26] Unfortunately, the intergenerational dialogue about World War II did not just help the war generation understand its younger critics; it also seemed to have further reduced the younger generation's skepticism about military solutions for political problems, as the subsequent discussion about the NATO intervention in Kosovo illustrated.

In the fall of 1998, parliament faced another vote on the deployment of German troops in the former Yugoslavia. The decision was complicated by two factors. In a general election, the voters had just turned the Kohl administration out of office and replaced it with an SPD/Green coalition, but the new parliament and the new government had not yet been constituted. Moreover, the anticipated NATO intervention in Kosovo lacked the support of the

UN Security Council.[27] Yet both problems were brushed aside by a grand coalition of interventionists. The old and the new governments closely cooperated in the decision-making process, and their agreement assured them of a resounding victory in parliament. In contrast to the discussion of 1995, the debate no longer included extensive, explicit references to the Nazi past. A few vague remarks about World War II supported the notion that Germany's experiences provided a compelling reason for the use of military force, but the decision was primarily justified by other arguments. One speaker after another pointed toward the broad international consensus in favor of intervention, the clear moral imperatives justifying the action, and the war's positive consequences for the process of European integration.[28] Germany's politicians felt that they could finally conduct (war) business as usual. The newest attempt at escaping the gravitational pull of Nazism again received considerable support in liberal academic circles. Intellectuals such as Habermas and Dan Diner, who had argued with the Kohl administration about West Germany's postfascist identity and the politically correct interpretation of the "Final Solution," now took the politicians' optimistic spin on the war in the former Yugoslavia to its logical conclusion. In their minds, concerted and decisive action on the Balkan Peninsula would allow Europe to leave behind the conflicting national memories of World War II and emerge as a new global player and undisputed champion of international human rights.[29]

The only political forces in Germany that resisted the war and the new historical consensus were a seriously weakened peace movement that had lost all its national leaders and the East German socialists, who made it perfectly clear that they considered the war an exclusively West German affair.[30] The NATO bombing raids and propaganda campaign against Serbia reminded PDS officials such as Gregor Gysi and Lothar Bisky of the treatment that Eastern European dissidents had received during the Cold War. Like the West German peace movement in 1991, which had projected the German suffering during World War II onto the Middle East and sympathized with the helpless inhabitants of Baghdad, the East German politicians and their voters now felt a strong kinship with the Serbs of Belgrade. Moreover, having watched a peaceful resistance movement dismantle a seemingly all-powerful regime within a few months, they put a lot of faith in nonviolent political action. In addition to all these moral and emotional concerns, the strong PDS opposition to the NATO campaign reflected important tactical objectives. By condemning the war as a breach of national and international law, Gysi and his party colleagues hoped to inherit the leaderless West German peace movement and improve their popularity among voters back home, who wanted the government to pay attention to its new citizens before it embarked on costly military adventures abroad.[31] Powerless against the grand coalition of interventionists, the PDS could not change national policy, and inadvertently, it even supported the memory politics of the new administration. By insisting on the political relevance of the GDR past and by turning that past into their historical weapon of choice, Gysi, Bisky, and their colleagues helped exclude references to National Socialism from the political battlefields of unified Germany.

Once a precedent had been established in the former Yugoslavia, German armed interventions abroad became almost routine, as the examples of Macedonia and Afghanistan illustrate. Both missions caused heated debates in Germany. In particular, the deployment of German troops in Afghanistan was resisted by a number of MPs in the ranks of the governing coalition.[32] But none of these debates have featured discussions about the legacy of Nazism. Even in matters of war and peace, the memory of World War II no longer provides useful moral and rhetorical ammunition.

The years between 1995 and 1998 marked a decisive turning point in the history of memory politics. The elusive goal of normalization had finally become a tangible reality, although "being just like anybody else" looked different from what past generations of West German politicians might have expected. In the years after the war, even the most enlightened and self-reflexive political leaders had probably resented the rigid framework of expectations within which they had to conduct their business. Every so often, they must have dreamed about an alternative political universe in which they could pursue their careers and fight for national interests without constantly having to consider the burden of the past. But now that a political life without guilt and without required public gestures of atonement seemed within reach, it turned out that silence was no longer such a desirable commodity. With the end of the Cold War, the Soviet empire could no longer lend legitimacy to Western democracies, and the West turned to its own shameful past as a source of self-validation. This process radically changed some of the rules of engagement in the international political arena. Whereas collectives and institutions had previously fought for the right to forget the unheroic aspects of their pasts, they now competed for the privilege to confess their crimes to the world. The bystanders of World War II now rigorously scrutinized their relationship to Hitler's Germany and even the pope, and the U.S. president publicly apologized for past misdeeds.[33]

The new culture of self-incrimination and humanitarian intervention was collectively affirmed during the European Holocaust conference held in Stockholm in January 2000. Twenty-two European heads of state confessed to their countries' crimes during World War II in front of an impressive international audience of journalists, academics, and a few largely ignored Holocaust survivors. All present swore allegiance to an antigenocidal pact and promptly turned their good conscience against Austria, where the xenophobic, right-wing Freiheitliche Partei Österreichs (FPÖ) had just become part of the nationally elected government. This unprecedented, illegitimate, and unsuccessful campaign shows that an indiscriminately wielded Holocaust memory can have very unfortunate and destructive political consequences.[34]

When Germany became a full member in the European anti-Holocaust club in the second half of the 1990s, German politicians, in contrast to their foreign peers, had already performed the peculiar dialectic of silence and self-accusation for a number of years. The Kohl administration, in particular, had sought to contain the power of history through ever more brazen and inclusive acts of national self-representation. Quite ironically, a conservative German government had thus inadvertently radicalized the politics of memory and become a trailblazer in the business of confessional guilt management. One might assume that German politicians would now enjoy their decisive competitive advantage and bask in the glory of their forefathers' exceptional crimes, but that never happened. The German political culture certainly produced its own share of confessional media events in the 1990s, most prominently during the Goldhagen affair when thousands of well-educated citizens almost joyfully recalled the gruesome details of the Nazi genocide.[35] In addition, some of the cultural memory initiatives of the Kohl administration (the Holocaust Memorial, for example) fit very well into the post–Cold War climate of collective self-accusation. But the German political elites had initially launched these projects in pursuit of their own narrowly conceived notion of normalization, and neither the Right nor the Left strayed far from that trajectory, even after the international context had shifted so drastically.

German conservatives and liberals followed different political programs, but they all wanted to blend into the European environment, as self-confident national leaders or postnational antifascists or, in the most recent metamorphosis, as publicly repentant *and* militarily active antifascists. The desire for international appreciation cut across all political and generational divides and explains why the coalition government of SPD and the Greens, which took power in 1998, proved particularly eager and successful in marginalizing the burden of Nazism. For the first time, members of the postwar generation wielded power in the German capital.[36] With Fischer and Gerhard Schröder, the government was led by individuals steeped in the tradition of the counterculture of the 1960s and 1970s; both had been vigorous liberal activists in their youth.[37] Yet after long careers in state parliaments and state governments, all of their antifascist enthusiasm had apparently worn off—or, more precisely, it had been funneled into antifascist military interventions abroad. In contrast to their predecessors of the Hitler Youth generation, they had no ambition to shape the cultural memory of the Nazi past and simply wrapped up the unfinished memory business of the Kohl administration as quickly as possible.

THE HOLOCAUST MEMORIAL

The Holocaust Memorial was the first piece of unfinished memory business that the liberal coalition faced. The idea of a central monument in Berlin, dedicated exclusively to the Jewish victims of National Socialism, had not been part of Kohl's memory agenda, at least not at the beginning of his tenure.[38] The memorial plans were first developed by the historian Eberhard Jäckel and the journalist Leah Rosh in the late 1980s. They managed to round up some of the usual liberal suspects in a private foundation in November 1989, just a few days before the Berlin Wall collapsed. Yet despite support from luminaries such as Günter Grass and Walter Jens, the initiative went nowhere until it was endorsed by the Central Council of Jews in Germany and the World Jewish Congress. In 1992, as a result of vigorous lobbying by the foundation and its supporters, the federal administration and the conservative state government in Berlin promised to cover half of the costs of the monument, and they donated a prime piece of real estate in the vicinity of the Brandenburg Gate. A year later, Kohl personally committed himself to the project in exchange for Bubis's attendance at the dedication ceremony for the Central Memorial for the Victims of War and Terror. Everybody assumed that a permanent marker to the uniqueness of the Holocaust would soon adorn the capital.[39]

But the first design competition, concluded in March 1995, revealed that historical uniqueness was difficult to express in concrete and steel. The jurors, handpicked by the foundation, the Kohl administration, and the Berlin senate, waded through more than five hundred entries. Somewhat overwhelmed by the task, they ultimately nominated two first prizes. The representatives of the foundation were particularly enamored of the design of a Berlin artist who suggested erecting a gigantic concrete slab and inscribing it with the names of all known Holocaust victims. Other jurors favored a slightly less ambitious, large steel construction that, given the right weather and time of day, would project the names of the former death camps onto a large public space.[40] Both designs met with massive public disapproval. Throughout the spring and summer of 1995, the intellectuals of the republic discussed and rejected the megalomaniac dimensions of the projects; many suggested that the basic parameters of the memorial should be reconsidered, including its size, location, and exclusive focus on the Jewish victims.[41] Kohl, probably influenced by Bubis, did not share these fundamental concerns, but he too had serious reservations about the outcome of the competition. He vetoed both designs and thus put the whole process on hold for many months. For once, Kohl's decision drew almost unanimous praise. In the first parliamentary debate on the project in May 1996, which only about a third of the MPs attended, speakers from all factions embraced the idea of a memorial, including its exceptional size and location, but rejected the top-seeded designs.[42]

The rare agreement across the political spectrum made it particularly obvious that there was simply no compelling architectural concept in sight. Therefore, after some deliberation and further delays, the three collaborating agencies organized a second competition. When the results came in in the fall of 1997, the critics in academia and the national press corps conceded that the new proposals were vastly superior to the previous suggestions. Nevertheless, only a few intellectuals changed their minds; most of them, including erstwhile supporters such as Günter Grass and Walter Jens, strongly advised abandoning the whole project because it would never result in a suitable site of mourning and self-reflexive memory.[43]

Unperturbed by such familiar misgivings, the chancellor and the newly constituted jury—which now included Bubis—selected a design by Peter

Eisenman and Richard Serra from an exclusive field of twenty-five invited entries. The architect and the sculptor from the United States wanted to cover the twenty thousand square meters with four thousand concrete pillars, thus erecting an abstract, oversized, symbolic Jewish cemetery in the center of Berlin.[44] But a swift implementation of their plan was now blocked by Berlin's mayor, Eberhard Diepgen, who seemed to have changed his mind about the memorial and was playing for time in anticipation of the federal elections in the fall of 1998. When Kohl was, indeed, turned out of office, the project appeared to be in jeopardy because Chancellor-Elect Gerhard Schröder had already announced he would not pursue the memorial plans any further.

But Schröder quickly changed his mind in the course of the negotiations with his coalition partners from the Green Party, which shows how relatively indifferent he felt about the whole affair. In fact, Schröder's change of heart was probably a consequence of the Walser-Bubis debate that erupted shortly after the election. Martin Walser delivered his attack against what he considered a facile and oppressive Holocaust memory in October 1998 and explicitly referred to the memorial as a prime example of the misguided memorialization of German shame. Among other consequences, Walser's intervention radicalized and polarized the debate about the memorial. The opponents now appeared to share Walser's controversial position, which was certainly an impression that the new chancellor wished to avoid. In this tricky situation, the new government made the right and opportune decision to turn the memorial question over to parliament.[45]

On June 25, 1999, the German parliament, during one of its last sessions in Bonn, ended a discussion of eleven years about the construction of a national memorial for the victims of the Holocaust. The representatives decided what juries, private sponsors, and intellectuals had not been able to settle and chose a modified version of Eisenman and Serra's 1997 design. In the years since the second competition, Serra had abandoned the project, and Eisenman had substantially revised the original plans as a result of negotiations with the foundation and the federal government. The memorial that parliament finally accepted had been reduced in size and paired with a learning center for visitors who might be unfamiliar with the history of the Holocaust. Of the four thousand pillars, only twenty-seven hundred remained, with their maximum size reduced from seven to five meters. In addition, the whole installation was lowered into the ground, which rendered it less obtrusive in the rapidly growing modernist cityscape of Berlin. The parliamentary debate itself, dominated by politicians of the postwar generations, lacked emotional highlights and illustrated that postwar Germans had dutifully absorbed the rhetoric of remembrance and the politically correct historical consciousness.[46] Deliberately seeking a path between cliché and sincerity and for the most part settling for the former, the representatives created a memorial that, as one commentator put it, "will commemorate the millions of victims but also itself" as a lasting symbol for "the best Germany that ever existed."[47] In contrast to their predecessors, the new political leaders were apparently quite confident about Germany's moral integrity and saw no need for additional memory work. Fischer did not attend the parliamentary debate, and Schröder appeared only sporadically, whereas Kohl, the former chancellor who had worried so much about his people's liberation from the burden of the past, followed the discussions with keen interest.[48]

Building the Holocaust memorial took much longer than originally planned. Most of the delays were caused by bureaucratic and technical problems that any project of this scope inevitably encounters. But occasionally, the politics of memory that had dominated the decision-making process also brought the construction work to a sudden halt. In the fall of 2003, the media reported, for instance, that the graffiti-resistant coating of the memorial pillars would be provided by the chemical conglomerate Degussa, which had supplied the SS with Zyklon B, the poisonous gas used in the concentration camps, during the war. After a short public battle that pitted different representatives of the memorial lobby against each other, Degussa lost the contract, and it took months to find a replacement.[49]

On May 10, 2005, the Holocaust Memorial was opened to the public by the president of the parliament, Wolfgang Thierse, as part of the official commemorations surrounding the sixtieth anniversary of the end of World War II.[50] In the weeks and months after the memorial opened, it quickly became apparent that the large site with its twenty-seven hundred stelae could serve many different purposes. As expected, international dignitaries flocked to the site, neo-Nazis applied distasteful graffiti, and the small exhibit on the premises attracted an impressive number of visitors.[51] But the memorial also appealed to urban dwellers with very little interest in history. To the consternation of some commentators and, presumably, to the furtive satisfaction of the memorial's two full-time guards, children and adolescents played hide-and-seek and jumped from stele to stele, while some adults appreciated the memorial as a great rendezvous and picnic site.[52] The memorial's multiple-use value illustrates how well it fits into Berlin's urban landscape. Its success might also indicate that German Holocaust memory has entered a phase of self-confident, permissive remembrance; the authorities appeared very comfortable with Peter Eisenman's open design and the ways in which it has been appropriated by Berliners and their guests. Most important, however, the reception of the memorial highlights one key ingredient of successful Vergangenheitsbewältigung that informed all venues of Germany's historical culture. Many representations of the Nazi past that became collective memories had educational and artistic merits and at least the appearance of moral integrity. But successful strategies of historical interpretation offered additional benefits, for instance, entertainment value or strategic political advantages. Vergangenheitsbewältigung was partly driven by the kind of pleasure experienced by the children who jumped across Eisenman's symbolic graveyard for the murdered Jews of Europe.

The saga of the memorial will continue for many years to come because the decision of parliament has exacerbated an unfortunate memory competition. The memorial embodies the notion of the Holocaust's uniqueness that had deeply impressed West Germany's elite in the 1980s and that established a clear conceptual barrier between the "Final Solution" and other Nazi crimes. At the same time, however, the project sets a precedent for other groups of NS victims who had not appeared on the official radar screen in the 1980s but had slowly emerged from political oblivion—often with the help of the Green Party—and now make legitimate claims about memorial representation. In response to these demands, the government quickly processed additional memorial projects without much discussion. In December 2003, parliament decided to erect a memorial for homosexuals who had been persecuted by the Nazis, and a similar project remembering Sinti and Roma victims will follow soon. The sites for the new monuments are close to the Holocaust Memorial. Once completed, the complex will highlight the folly of a memory policy that was set into motion in the 1980s but that continues to replicate the selection criteria of the Nazi state and, in a routine fashion, parcels out public recognition commensurate with the public relations prowess that the lobbying groups bring to the negotiation table.[53]

POST–COLD WAR JUSTICE AND THE FORCED LABORERS OF THE THIRD REICH

A second piece of unfinished memory business started making headlines in the fall of 1998. In a reversal of the foreign policy it had pursued for many decades, the United States exerted increasing diplomatic and legal pressure to have Germany make amends for the crimes that the Nazi government and German society had committed against millions of forced laborers in Germany and occupied Europe. In the end, these attempts succeeded, although it took three years of arduous negotiations before the victims received their first modest compensation payments—more than five decades after the defeat of the Third Reich and after most of the former forced laborers had died. Also, unlike the situation in the 1950s and 1960s when the last international compensation deals had been struck, the German business community was the primary target of the U.S. initiative, and Germany's political elite, morally fortified and politically savvy after decades of memory politics, came to the rescue of the bedraggled chief executive officers (CEOs).

The protracted negotiations about financial restitution for the surviving forced laborers were partly the result of the very success of the West German model of Vergangenheitsbewältigung. When the Western world searched for new strategies of self-legitimization after the end of the Cold War, German methods of memory management became part of a new paradigm of Western identity. After 1945, German politicians were forced to turn their country's past misdeeds into the moral basis of the postwar political status quo. Since the 1980s, foreign critics, international agencies, and internal whistle-blowers have held other countries with blemished records to similar standards and urged them to acknowledge and come to terms with their past as Nazi collaborators or their involvement in other crimes. The wave of self-reckoning encompassed all of Western Europe and intensified and expanded to Eastern Europe and other parts of the globe during the 1990s.[54] Therefore, unlike in previous decades, German sins and strategies of national reconciliation were now explored in the context of a general European, even global, process of coming to terms with the past. This process produced new standards for moral conduct and reparations,[55] and it often focused specifically on capitalist enterprises that had profited from the misery caused by Nazi Germany.[56] In addition, the collapse of the Berlin Wall had set free millions of individuals with very legitimate claims against their former German oppressors. As a result of all these developments, appropriate gestures of reconciliation and retribution were now demanded from the German business community, one of the key constituencies in Germany that had elegantly avoided taking responsibility in the past.[57] Thus, in the course of a general and final settling of accounts, the memory paradigm first developed and proudly displayed in

West Germany came back to haunt the unified republic, albeit only for a brief period.

Throughout the Cold War, West German governments repeated the same mantra when confronted with legitimate demands for compensation by foreign administrations and individuals. Any comprehensive reparations agreement, they argued, could only be negotiated as part of a final peace treaty that would solve the problem of Germany's division. This position was largely accepted in the West because none of the NATO partners wanted to see a sizable transfer of hard currency to Warsaw bloc countries.[58] The defensive maneuvering of the West German government depended on Cold War politics and U.S. approval, but it succeeded even after the collapse of communism—once small, strategic adjustments had been made. Since unification clearly solved the problem of Germany's division and since the two-plus-four accord could be construed as a comprehensive peace treaty, the Kohl administration had to come up with a different legal strategy to sidestep renewed demands for compensation.[59] Again with U.S. backing, the government now refused to pay reparations to Eastern Europe by insisting that all former Warsaw Pact partners had long ago relinquished any claims against the GDR and that unified Germany had "inherited" that waiver. At the same time, Kohl bought Eastern European acquiescence to the process of unification by funding a number of humanitarian foundations for the surviving victims of Nazi crimes in Poland, Russia, and the Ukraine, among other countries.[60]

While West German governments skillfully dodged compensation demands in the international arena, they also continued to ignore the victims of the NS regime who lived in the Federal Republic but lacked the political clout to attract national or international attention. Consequently, there were many different types of victims and hundreds of thousands of individuals in Germany and abroad who had received little or no compensation for the suffering they endured in the Third Reich. These people included Roma and Sinti, homosexuals, victims of forced sterilization and/or "euthanasia," conscientious objectors, deserters, POWs, and a large and ethnically diverse group of over a million surviving forced laborers living all over Europe as well as in Israel and the United States.[61] The latter group finally received a public apology and belated and limited financial compensation. This surprising outcome was brought about by the strange legalistic process of international memory management with which the Western world—which had developed a new relationship to historical wrongs—sought to discharge the last obligations stemming from World War II in an era of global capitalism.

Starting in 1998, U.S. trial lawyers used two legal tools against German companies that had exploited forced laborers in the Third Reich. They targeted them with class-action lawsuits of the type that had already forced the U.S. tobacco industry to its knees and had resulted in hefty settlements in the 1990s. In addition, in order to establish jurisdiction over the problem of NS forced labor in U.S. courts, the lawyers invoked the controversial Alien Tort Provision of 1789, which, in its most recent interpretation, provides U.S. courts with the ability to adjudicate human rights violations committed by non-U.S. citizens on foreign soil.[62] Since class-action suits and the Alien Tort Provision are elements of U.S. private law, they are only effective against defendants with deep pockets. Despite or, more accurately, because of this obvious shortcoming, the strategy proved quite effective against wealthy defendants outside the United States. In August 1998, pending class-actions suits convinced two major Swiss banks to pay $1.25 billion to settle allegations of having illegally profited from the Holocaust. Shortly thereafter, several European insurance companies facing similar accusations agreed to process all pending Holocaust-related claims.[63] As a result of these settlements, German companies were inundated with class-action suits, primarily regarding the use of slave labor during World War II.

Since the lawsuits interfered with diplomatic relations, Washington could have intervened on behalf of the German defendants, but that option did not appeal to the political establishment in the United States. In the 1990s, U.S. popular culture had established a close link between Holocaust memory and American exceptionalism. Through films, television programs, and federally supported institutions such as the Holocaust Memorial Museum in Washington, DC, the country had come to define itself as an anti-Holocaust nation that fought for the rights of victims of genocide.[64] Regardless of ample evidence to the contrary (for instance, during the Ruandan genocide between 1994 and 1995), this very optimistic aspect of late twentieth-century U.S. identity had become a powerful tool in the political arena. Displaying their Holocaust awareness gave officeholders an inexpensive way of appealing to voters, especially Jewish voters. Therefore, genuine concern for the lack of justice for survivors of NS crimes, the ambition to wrap up all unfinished memory business before the turn of the century, and a keen sense for potential political gain had spurred a number of Holocaust-related initiatives on the federal and the state level. A whole series of laws put pressure on European companies to reveal pertinent information and settle claims if they wanted to continue to do business in the United States.[65] But these well-advertised actions by members of the U.S. Congress and the federal government also set limits on the public conduct of U.S. politicians. Speaking out in favor of companies such as Volkswagen, Bavarian Motor Works, and Daimler-Benz, now identified as slave-labor companies during World War II, made no political sense—unless an acknowledgment of their legitimate business interests could be combined with public praise for their generosity toward their former forced laborers.

For the most part, the German business elite thought that the U.S. campaign against them had neither legal nor moral merit.[66] But the incoming SPD/Green government and a small group of CEOs did not share this defensive attitude. Gerhard Schröder was familiar with the problem of the forced laborers before he took office. In his former job as governor of Lower Saxony, he had been a member of the board of directors at Volkswagen. Consequently, he had been informed about the management's decision in the summer of 1998 to have the company's history researched by independent historians and begin the process of identifying and offering compensation to former forced laborers.[67] Unlike their colleagues in other companies and industries, the managers in Wolfsburg recognized early on that sustained media coverage about the topic could wreak havoc on the company's reputation and business dealings abroad. Like the management at Volkswagen, Schröder chose to be proactive about the whole affair. Months before the election in September, he announced plans for a compensation fund for former slave laborers, and once in power, he made the search for a political solution one of the government's priorities during his first years in office.[68]

Schröder's coalition partners had paid even more attention to the topic in past years. Consistent with their antifascist self-image, Green officials had lobbied persistently on behalf of the forgotten victims, especially in the 1980s. They had repeatedly argued that the existing compensation provisions should be extended to include the former forced laborers and even introduced legislation to that effect in parliament.[69] Yet despite parallel demands by the European Parliament, West Germany's conservative government had blocked all of these initiatives. Considering this background, the new coalition of Social

Democrats and Greens seemed ideally suited to settle the compensation question, but they would not have made much headway, especially in Germany's business community, if the United States had not exerted massive political and legal pressure.

From this very diverse set of interests and pressures, a compromise emerged in the course of three years of negotiations between the governments of Germany, Israel, the United States, and many Eastern European countries, as well as representatives of the German business community, the Jewish Claims Conference, and numerous law firms representing the interests of the victims. The contracts and treaties that were signed in July 2000 provided recognition and payments to many victims who would have otherwise never seen a dime, but it also left the German side in a very advantageous position. The German business community and the German government each paid roughly $2.5 billion into a foundation that provided the surviving forced laborers with a onetime payment of up to $7,500 per person. Since June 2001, the payments have been distributed relatively unbureaucratically to over 1.3 million victims in more than seventy countries. In addition to the payments to the survivors, the foundation earmarked about 10 percent of its resources for the settlement of remaining material claims against German companies, such as those resulting from their involvement of the so-called aryanization of Jewish businesses in the Third Reich. The remaining funds have been used for miscellaneous expenses including lawyers' fees—over $60 million in the United States alone—and to set up an additional foundation dedicated to keeping alive the memory of the victims. In return for these efforts, the German government and the German business community can expect that they will never again be forced to pay significant sums as compensation and retribution for Nazi crimes.[70]

Although attaining legal peace was the most important objective of the German negotiators, they also managed to gain a number of symbolic concessions that validated over fifty years of German compensation policy. The whole package of payments was extended as a voluntary, humanitarian gesture that the German government and German industry offered in recognition of the country's moral and historical responsibility for the Nazi past. The compensation treaties never assigned any concrete legal responsibility for the crimes and thus carefully and intentionally avoided setting legal precedent.[71] Moreover, the not-so-secret wrangling behind the scenes made it painfully

obvious that many CEOs felt uncomfortable about providing any compensation and admitting any sort of responsibility. Until some of the larger and potentially more exposed companies stepped in and made up the difference, the
voluntary contributions from the German business community fell woefully
short of the promised $2.5 billion. This foot-dragging was accompanied by all
kinds of unsavory remarks from German CEOs, who recycled well-known
strategies of German guilt evasion. There were exceptions, but the general
impression was that well-to-do businesses, which had profited handsomely
from the use of slave labor, now refused to take responsibility.[72]

In comparison to the impervious and insensitive business community,
the German politicians managing the crisis appeared levelheaded and quite
sympathetic toward the victims, and thus, they avoided any public relations
debacles. In particular, the chancellor's special envoy, Otto Lambsdorff, well
known for his conservative views and business-friendly attitude, avoided
inflammatory public statements and thus protected the government from the
type of memory scandals that the Kohl administration produced on a regular
basis. But taking note of the interesting differences between the public conduct of government politicians and their partners in the business community
should not divert attention from the important, fundamental continuities of
six decades of compensation policies. In principle, Germans with real power,
whether political or financial, only offered substantial retribution payments
either when doing so was unavoidable (for instance, as a result of U.S. pressure) or when such gestures offered tangible political advantages at home or
abroad.[73] In this international communication process, foreign governments
played the Nazi card in pursuit of all kinds of foreign and domestic policy objectives. But the German side, at least in their dealings with foreign powers
and agencies, consistently tried to improve Germany's perception abroad while
limiting the material resources—not necessarily the symbolic resources—
that had to be spent on this task. Precisely because German politicians succeeded on both accounts, they were never forced and never felt compelled on
their own volition to implement a comprehensive compensation plan that acknowledged all the victims of National Socialism. Moreover, since Germany's
elite has been so successful in advertising their country's antitotalitarian
record and democratic and humanitarian commitments, there is nobody left
who has the desire and the power to seriously challenge the results of six
decades of focused, if morally flawed political memory work.

The positive image that the government managed to project throughout the negotiations did not extend to the opposition. On July 7, 2000, the Foundation Law passed in parliament with an overwhelming majority of votes: in all, 556 MPs supported the measure, 42 opposed it, and 22 abstained. But the impressive final tally, signaling agreement across the political spectrum, tended to obscure the fact that conservative parliamentarians had harshly criticized the law during the preceding debate. They maintained, in predictable fashion, that the compensation question had to be settled once and for all and that parliament should never consider any other demands for retribution. Moreover and more surprisingly, a number of CDU/CSU speakers voiced very specific concerns. They worried about the possibility that some forced laborers, in particular Jewish survivors, might be double-dipping, that is, that they might be collecting compensation for their work as forced laborers while continuing to receive payments as Holocaust survivors and thus absorbing funds that should be directed toward other groups of victims who had never been compensated. This strange and belated concern about justice—after all, the members of parliament had long been informed about the so-called forgotten victims and apparently had not cared about them—was accompanied by another peculiar initiative. A few CDU MPs called on the government to take the final compensation agreement with the victims of Nazism as an opportunity to demand similar gestures of compensation and reconciliation from Eastern European states that had expelled their German citizens after 1945.[74]

The parliamentary debate thus illustrates the seemingly contradictory effects that the stabilization of German political memory entailed. On the one hand, the Europeanization of German memory and the success of the Holocaust human rights discourse, which had accompanied and facilitated Germany's return into positions of political and military leadership, provided the political elite with the necessary self-confidence to embrace compensation agreements like the foundation law and—as will be discussed—defend the new memory status quo against anti-Semite revisionists. On the other hand, the very stability of the new memory paradigm also gave conservative politicians the self-confidence to recycle past resentments and anti-Semitic themes they had not voiced in such explicit terms since the 1950s. Apparently, even among generations once or twice removed from the crimes of Nazism, two contradictory memory reflexes remain dialectically intertwined. Empathy for non-German victims of genocide and ethnic cleansing has been closely linked to empathy for German victims of World War II. As a result of that emotional short circuit, the two feelings of solidarity can easily and quickly switch places. That explains why a collective such as the German political elite—or the Left subculture since the 1970s—can honestly oppose and combat anti-Semitic discourse in some contexts and shortly thereafter dabble in anti-Semitism without experiencing much of a sense of contradiction.

EUROPEAN LIBERATION AND RESISTANCE:
SIXTIETH ANNIVERSARIES IN NORMANDY, BERLIN, AND WARSAW

In the summer of 2004, Gerhard Schröder and his European Union (EU) colleagues convened for another round of anniversaries and continued their attempts to streamline the continent's collective memory of its divisive past. The highlight came at the beginning of the memorial season. In June 2004, Schröder became the first German chancellor to be invited to the D day festivities in Normandy. His trip to the sixtieth-anniversary celebrations became a great success because Schröder proved to be both media savvy and memory sensitive. Before leaving for France, he had the motto of his trip broadcast by Germany's tabloid *Bild am Sonntag:* "The Allied victory," he impressed on the many readers, "was not a victory over Germany but a victory for Germany."[75] That would have been a surprising piece of news for the soldiers who had stormed the beach in 1944, but the veterans, politicians, and journalists from all over the EU (as well as Russia and the United States) who welcomed Schröder in Caen clearly appreciated his commitment to the liberation paradigm. Having loudly cited Weizsäcker, Schröder also used one of the more successful rhetorical sleights of hand that Roman Herzog had employed in 1995. He announced to the assembled dignitaries that "we in Germany know who caused the war. We know our historical responsibility and take it seriously." Without spelling out who actually was responsible and what that historical responsibility entailed—after all, we all know anyway—he quickly moved on to equate Allied and German soldiers symbolically: "German soldiers died because they were sent on a murderous campaign to repress all of Europe. But in death the soldiers from all sides have been united—united by the sorrow of their parents, wives, siblings, and friends. We bow in respect for their pain." Within a few lines of his speech, Schröder slid elegantly from "we Germans" to "we assembled here." Having thus reached his rhetorical destination, Schröder repetitively celebrated the "united and democratic Europe" that had learned its lesson and whose liberation began sixty years ago. Unlike Kohl, Schröder even managed to introduce a personal note into his speech that did not sound defensive and supported his overall message: "Nobody will ever forget the terrible history of Hitler's reign. My generation grew up in its shadow. Only four years ago my family found the grave of my father, a soldier killed in battle in Romania. I never had a chance to know my father."[76]

Schröder's appearance in Caen was well received all over Europe, but he alienated the keepers of the official memory of Germany's veterans.[77] With Bitburg in mind, Schröder had decided not to visit the large German military cemetery of La Cambe in Normandy because some of the twenty-one thousand German soldiers buried there had been members of the Waffen-SS. Instead, the chancellor traveled to a much smaller cemetery containing the remains of both German and Allied soldiers and was promptly chided as unpatriotic by some retired generals and the cemetery administration.[78]

Later in the summer of 2004, Schröder had two more high-profile opportunities to transform national into European memory, and he pursued that objective relentlessly. First, he was the keynote speaker during the anniversary commemoration on July 20 and he delivered a surprisingly precise and differentiated acknowledgment of the German resistance against Hitler. Just a few days later, on August 1, Schröder traveled to Poland to participate in the ceremonies marking the sixtieth anniversary of the Warsaw uprising. Poland had just become a member of the European Union, and Schröder was the first German politician to be invited to attend the ceremony in honor of Poland's national heroes. Quite appropriately, he used his speech in Warsaw to settle some important memory disputes that had strained the relationship between Germany and Poland.

As so often happened in the past, the memory trouble was caused in part by Germany's intellectual-literary caste. Although Europe's politicians and their speechwriters were crafting more and more harmonious and homogeneous European memories of the Nazi era, German writers and intellectuals continued revising and testing the limits of existing memory paradigms, a task they had tackled with great success since the 1960s. In the course of four decades, the process had become a comforting routine.[79] But the 1990s brought an interesting new twist to this memory routine. After unification, some of the players who had entered the scene in the 1960s now tested the limits of memory paradigms that they had themselves helped create two decades earlier. This new element of self-reflexivity informed the interventions of Günter Grass and Martin Walser, among others, who had challenged the antitotalitarian paradigm in the 1960s and now turned their critical eye on the Holocaust paradigm for which they had prepared the field. When Walser deplored "the continuous representation of our guilt in the media" and rejected "its instrumentalization for contemporary purposes"[80] and when Grass revisited the demise of the refugee ship *Gustloff* in great detail,[81] the novelists either purposefully or inadvertently called into question the predominance of Holocaust memories and directed attention toward the experiences of their own and their parents' generations, which had been temporarily relegated to a secondary position within the infrastructure of German memory.[82]

The renewed interest in the fate of the German victims of World War II and the diplomatic focus on final compensation arrangements had some interesting political side effects. Special-interest groups such as the expellee organization, which had long been considered a political anachronism, reappeared on the national scene. The expellees' renewed demands for return of property, increased financial compensation, and public acknowledgment of their suffering—for instance, in a center for expulsion history in Berlin— were covered extensively in the national press, and conservative politicians were again vying for the expellees' endorsement.[83] For obvious reasons, these developments made Germany's eastern neighbors quite nervous. Therefore, Schröder's Polish hosts must have been pleased to hear the chancellor's unusually concrete assurances: "We Germans know very well who began the war and who were its first victims. Consequently, we can not allow restitution claims from Germany which turn history upside down."[84] Schröder added that his government would gladly confirm this position in front of any court in which the expellees might try to pursue their case. Moreover, he made it perfectly clear that a center for expulsion history would never be built on his watch. The rest of his speech in Warsaw was dedicated to the theme of Europe. In a text of less than twelve hundred words, Schröder managed to mention "Europe," "free Europe," or "the European legacy" fifteen times—far more often than "Germany" or "Poland."[85] He had covered the same ground in Caen and Berlin. In fact, in his speech in Berlin on July 20, he advocated the Europeanization of the memory of World War II in a particularly compelling statement that captured the new historical consciousness in a nutshell: "Europe should understand and honor these two dates—July 20th and August 1st—as blazing signposts on the way towards a truly European ethical community. Today, 60 years later, we can and must realize the European legacy of the resistance against Hitler. The fight for freedom and the rule of law and the fight against terror and military aggression unifies all of us in Europe— now more than ever after we enlarged the European Union on May 1st."[86]

Schröder's public appearances in the summer of 2004 illustrate the fervor with which German politicians had embraced Europe as their ideological home and how elegantly they historicized and sublated the specificity of German history within the larger framework of collective European memory. Schröder reiterated the same themes in his public statement on the sixtieth anniversary of the end of World War II in May 2005.[87] With the possible exception of the 1950s, Germany's political elite had never felt as comfortable about its chosen memory of Nazism. Finally, the long memory turmoil that had begun in the 1960s and had lasted through the mid-1990s came to an end.

DEFENDING THE MEMORY PEACE AGAINST INCORRIGIBLE ANTI-SEMITES: THE HOHMANN AFFAIR

The very success of the ideological construct "Europe," with all its postnational trappings, caused misgivings among conservative, nationalistic segments of the population and triggered political initiatives designed to convert that popular resentment into electoral success. At the same time, as the new paradigm gained momentum in the years since 1995, German politicians became increasingly willing to defend it against attacks from within their own ranks. As happened so often in the past, the limits of political taste were tested and readjusted in the highly sensitive and symbolic terrain of anti- and philo-Semitism. But unlike in the past, the elite of the Berlin republic now unambiguously defined and defended these limits.

Before the federal election in the fall of 2002, the powerful deputy chairperson of the FDP, Jürgen Möllemann, reached out to right-wing voters in a carefully calibrated campaign of xenophobic and anti-Semitic innuendo. Following the examples of other European populists such as Jörg Haider and Pim Fortuyn, Möllemann tested the limits of Germany's political culture by

accusing the well-known Jewish TV talk show host Michel Friedman of foment-
ing anti-Semitism. Möllemann argued that Friedman's spiteful and intolerant
interventions on the screen caused resentment against the very constituency
that the TV host had vowed to protect in his capacity as a member of the Central Council of Jews in Germany.[88] Members of the SPD/Green coalition immediately denounced Möllemann's offensive statement, but it is even more
remarkable that the elder statesmen of the FDP gradually turned against
their controversial leader and ostracized him from the party.[89]

In the following year, Christian Democratic leaders were prompted to act
even more decisively when they had to deal with their own anti-Semitic scandal. On the national holiday of October 3, 2003, the CDU member of parliament Martin Hohmann delivered a carefully crafted speech in front of his
political constituency that was a picture-perfect example of anti-Semitic propaganda and therefore deserves to be analyzed in some detail.[90] Hohmann set
the tone of his speech, entitled "Justice for Germany," by referring to a number of seemingly egregious cases of injustice that had riled public opinion in
previous months. Among other examples, Hohmann recounted the story of
a German social welfare recipient residing in Florida and the fate of a convicted
murderer who could not be deported to his homeland, Turkey, for humanitarian reasons. For Hohmann, these cases of welfare fraud and miscarriage
of justice exemplified a general lack of community spirit in Germany that
could only be rekindled if the government would finally treat all its citizens
fairly and distribute burdens equally on all shoulders. Hohmann reported
that he had made three concrete suggestions to help the administration reach
this goal: the state should reduce its payments to the European Union, cur-
tail its support for the victims of Nazi terror in light of Germany's strained
financial resources, and demand from the international community that former German forced laborers receive the same payments as the surviving Jewish forced laborers who had just been awarded ten billion marks. Since all
three suggestions had been turned down by the governing coalition, Hohmann
concluded that the administration ranked the needs of foreigners above those
of the German population and he asserted that this strange set of priorities
was caused by a persistent misrepresentation of the German people as a collective of perpetrators.[91]

Hohmann continued by highlighting his reasonable, moderate political
disposition. He emphasized that he had no desire to whitewash or forget the

German past and professed satisfaction over the fact that neo-Nazis in Germany had never succeeded at the ballot box—unlike in other European countries. Revealing his ignorance about the evolution of collective memories across Europe and in the world beyond, he maintained that Germans were the only people who continuously focused on the dark aspects of their past and thus systematically undermined the self-confidence of future generations. For Hohmann, that was particularly unfortunate because the simplistic division of the world into German perpetrators, on the one hand, and all their victims, on the other, did not reflect historical reality. In a predictable but still stunningly brazen or stunningly ignorant excursus, Hohmann then embarked on a long reflection about the role of Jews in the history of the twentieth century that took the form of a rhetorical question and was reminiscent of the style Ernst Nolte had employed in the Historians' Debate.[92] Clearly acknowledging his source, Henry Ford's 1920 anti-Semitic pamphlet "The International Jew," Hohmann completely uncritically recalled the details of Ford's infamous attack against Jews as the instigators and primary perpetrators of the crimes of communism, especially in the Soviet Union. Even in light of all these facts about Jews, Hohmann argued, one would be mistaken to misrepresent Jews as a people of perpetrators because many Bolshevik perpetrators of Jewish background had renounced their religion. The real perpetrators of the twentieth century were neither "the Jews" nor the "the Germans" but "the godless people with their godless ideologies." This was reason enough for Hohmann to call for a return to Christianity, and in an interesting twist on the theme of Europe, he sent his listeners on their way with the slogan "With God into a good future for Europe! With God into a good future especially for our German fatherland."[93]

Hohmann delivered his speech in front of an audience of 120 listeners in his hometown of Neuhof in Hesse, part of his electoral district. His appearance was an annual local ritual; this was the thirteenth time that he had addressed his fellow citizens on Germany's national holiday. Apparently none of the listeners voiced any objections. The speech might have lingered in local memory without national repercussions had it not been for a curious coincidence. Later in the same month, a U.S. Holocaust survivor was looking for Web sites relating to a historical exhibition on the "aryanization" of Jewish property in Hesse, to which she had contributed some objects. In the course of her search, she stumbled across the text of Hohmann's speech, which the local chapter of the CDU had posted on its Web site. She promptly alerted the organizers of the exhibition, which was cosponsored by the Fritz-Bauer Institute in Frankfurt and the Hessischer Rundfunk, the regional public broadcasting service.[94] In this roundabout way, a comment about Hohmann's speech found its way into the political coverage of the national network ARD and was quickly picked up by the national press.[95] Within a month's time, Hohmann's speech became a full-blown scandal that concerned the political leaders in Berlin and Hesse for several weeks.

Representatives of the SPD and the Greens quickly called for Hohmann's resignation. Even CDU officials voiced serious concern about his continued presence in parliament.[96] But the CDU's national chairwoman, Angela Merkel, hesitated to have Hohmann expelled from the CDU parliamentary faction. In light of the considerable local and regional support for him, she was not sure if she could convince two-thirds of the CDU/CSU parliamentarians—the number required by law—to take such an unprecedented step.[97] Consequently, the national party leadership decided to issue a formal reprimand and sternly advised Hohmann to desist from making similar public statements.[98] In the meantime, Hohmann had issued an unconvincing apology ("It was and is not my intention to hurt other people's feelings")[99] and had actually reiterated his opinions in an interview with the ZDF.[100] Moreover and more important, he had provided the TV station with a copy of a letter of support he had received from an army general in charge of the Bundeswehr's rapid-response forces. Once that juicy detail became public knowledge, the SPD defense minister, Peter Struck, quickly fired the general and put the CDU leaders in a difficult position.[101] Now they had to explain to their critics— including the Central Council of Jews in Germany, the Israeli ambassador, and the head of the Protestant Church—why they still protected Hohmann even after one of his supporters had lost his job.[102] In a quick turnaround, Merkel initiated expulsion proceedings and narrowly avoided losing her own job as leader of the CDU/CSU faction in parliament when a surprisingly large number of MPs refused to back her request.[103] The motion carried with the necessary two-thirds majority, but 20 percent of the members abstained, cast invalid ballots, or voted against Merkel's proposal.[104] Hohmann became the first CDU/CSU deputy ever to be expelled from his faction, and in July 2004, he was also expelled from the party.[105]

The Hohmann affair exposed some of the layers, dynamics, and actors of German memory politics in exemplary fashion: (1) foreign observers who play an important and for the most part very productive role in German memory politics; (2) special-interest groups protecting their share of the memory business, including liberal memory activists who watch the German scene closely and are always ready to scandalize behavior such as Hohmann's; (3) the mainstream parties, including the Green Party, that use memory politics to enhance Germany's profile abroad and edge out the political competition at home; (4) the public television networks that help set the agenda in the political arena and—together with the national press—provide venues to define and resolve political scandals; and (5) the complex and variegated layer of local politics that may follow different traditions and develop different collective memories than the national political mainstream.

Since the mid-1990s, the interplay among these different entities has shaped a national political culture that has settled into a new collective memory of the Nazi past and—partly as a result of the favorable effects of that consensus—has become less tolerant of deviant memories of Nazism. In the cases of Möllemann and Hohmann, the political elite reacted relatively quickly and consistently and removed them from the close-knit network of national politics. Such consistency would have been impossible during most of the history of the Federal Republic because the success of democratic parties, especially conservative parties, depended on their ability to appeal to voters with worldviews resembling Hohmann's and integrate them into the democratic process. Sixty years after the end of the war, the CDU leaders abandoned these strategic considerations, and their assessment might be correct—for two reasons. First and most important, the key constituencies in the population that fundamentally disagree with the Europeanization of German politics and memory have opted out of the democratic political process. Neo-Nazis, skinheads, and even the extreme nationalists of the New Right are no longer interested in making the CDU their political home. Second, since the contemporaries of the Third Reich represent a rapidly decreasing percentage of the voting public, it is safe to assume that fewer voters feel very strongly about politics of memory—at least as far as they pertain to the Nazi past. They no longer expect or appreciate the contorted political discourse of previous decades, which had been designed to bridge the gap between West Germany's official historical culture and deviant memories of the past among important segments of the population.

Yet the Hohmann affair also shows that the national political leaders in Berlin, like many other members of the national elite, tend to overestimate their power to shape German collective memories. Just because the elite has settled on a new memory paradigm that fits its interests does not mean that other memory communities in the country think and feel the same way. In fact, everything about Hohmann's speech—its deliberate wording and rhetorical structure, its outrageous contents, and not least of all, the fact that it was promptly published on the Web—indicate that Hohmann addressed an audience that shared his opinion. He had probably made similar claims on previous occasions—perhaps during the other twelve speeches he delivered on October 3 in prior years. He might have actively participated, first as mayor and then as MP, in crafting a local political culture that had very different ideas about Germany's past and present than the party leadership in Wiesbaden and Berlin. Since Hohmann's infringement was only "uncovered" as result of a whole string of coincidences, it is quite likely that there are many other local communities dominated by similar views. Obviously, these communities are not exactly like Neuhof, which is part of an exceptionally conservative electoral district. Hohmann's predecessor as MP was none other than the CDU conservative heavy hitter Alfred Dregger, and Hohmann himself was already well known for his extreme views before October 2003.[106] Nevertheless, other communities in the Federal Republic might feel similarly about welfare recipients, Jews, and the so-called misrepresentation of German history, although their members are probably too knowledgeable about the limits of Germany's official historical culture to announce their beliefs in the crude fashion chosen by Hohmann and his friends.

FROM THE POLITICS OF HISTORY TO THE POLITICS OF MEMORY—AND BACK

Two different, overlapping processes shaped the political reaction to National Socialism in the Federal Republic. In the first decade after the war, German politicians had to deal with the practical problems that war, division, and occupation brought about. The perception of the problems as well as their solutions had to be negotiated with Allied supervisors and special-interest lobbyists who often disagreed about the relative importance of the challenges at hand. All these negotiations had important symbolic and ideological components and were part of the cumbersome task of constructing a postfascist (West) German identity compatible with the new form of government and geographic status quo. But like the reconstruction of the cities and the introduction of a new currency, the fundamental ideological reorientation of West German politics after 1945—from west integration to antitotalitarianism to the invention of new national symbols and a new official infrastructure of memory—served practical, utilitarian purposes. To survive in the competitive environment of the postwar years, new values and symbols had to contribute to Germany's political, economic, and psychological recovery. Strategies of representation that did not bring West Germans closer to that goal, for example, the memory of Communist resistance, were invariably relegated to the sidelines.

In essence, during the postwar years, West German politicians and their East German counterparts acted like any other elite group that had been called on to clean up the mess of a defeated regime: they tried to repair their power base and their standing in the world as quickly as possible. To assure their own and Germany's political survival, they focused on the tangible historical obstacles that the immediate postwar period offered in abundance. Therefore, the strategies of dealing with the past that dominated the political scene in the 1950s are aptly summed up as politics of history and should be distinguished from the moralistic, self-reflexive, and self-critical politics of memory that first developed in some niches of West Germany's historical culture in the 1960s and only came to dominate the political culture in the 1980s.

Even in later years, the diplomatic challenges that the Federal Republic faced offered many occasions to engage in pragmatic politics of history, as happened during the first years of Brandt's Ostpolitik or in the context of the two-plus-four negotiations. But in the course of the 1970s, West Germany's politicians adopted a new paradigm of dealing with the past, a paradigm that had slowly built up momentum over many years. It is impossible to pinpoint the precise origins of this less utilitarian, more moralistic framework of historical reflection. Was Heuss's declaration of collective shame in 1949 already part of the new framework? Or had he just miscalculated a rhetorical intervention that was designed to educate rather than provoke his audience? The majority of Heuss's speeches suggest that he preferred the role of paternalistic consensus builder to the task of dismantling West Germany's favorable image of itself. Therefore, I hesitate to count him among the trailblazers who first called into question the political status quo of the 1950s. But with Heinemann, the political scene finally featured a player who was determined to deal with the unaddressed ethical challenges of the Nazi past. The election of a Social Democratic president—in conjunction with the election of an SPD chancellor—led to the first aggressive reinterpretation of the Third Reich on the highest level of government. Heinemann and Brandt did not reverse any of the pragmatic decisions of the previous conservative administrations, and they confirmed the Federal Republic's basic political orientation. But these important continuities fade in comparison to their attempts to add ideological complexity to West Germany's political landscape, for instance, by founding the first institutions of cultural memory. Heinemann's symbolic and rhetorical interventions—and, to a lesser extent, Brandt's public appearances outside Germany—challenged the defensive, apologetic historical consciousness that West Germany's politicians had adopted in the 1950s.

By the time Heinemann became president in 1969, all pressing, practical concerns about the legacy of Nazism had been settled, and therefore, changing tack from consensus to confrontation no longer represented an existential risk. But Heinemann and those who followed in his footsteps still had a choice in the matter. They decided to take the road of more resistance in an attempt to invent a collective memory of the Nazi past that, if successful, would turn West Germany into a more democratic and more self-reflexive society. Heinemann's interventions required self-confidence, even arrogance, as well as political recklessness. In this respect, he differed from Brandt, who was not ready to take the same political risks for such a spurious goal as providing Germans with the right historical consciousness. Heinemann also differed from public intellectuals such as Grass or Hochhuth, who negotiated the burden of the past in a cultural context that was more forgiving toward political deviants. The role of West Germany's first liberal president is perhaps best compared to the whistle-blowers in the judiciary of the 1950s and the young historians and student activists of the 1960s. These individuals faced the real possibility that they would be ostracized by the political mainstream as a result of their moralistic approach to the burden of the past. Therefore, in contrast to the interpretations of Nazism that had been crafted in the 1950s, the new protest memories cannot be reduced to political or professional strategies of survival. Rather than erasing all traces of Germany's shame as quickly as possible, the memory activists raised poignant questions about the country's moral integrity and tried to find answers to the challenges of collective symbolic guilt. Their provocations marked the beginning of West Germany's second paradigm of historical reflection, which was no longer concerned with politics of history and focused instead on politics of memory.

In due time, the gesture of protest would become a finely tuned ideological weapon that efficiently served the self-interest of the Left and thus became a worthy counterpart to the antitotalitarian identity of the political mainstream. But for several decades, the politics of memory never completely lost their moralistic, antiutilitarian, and sometimes self-critical edge.[107] Quite ironically, one of the many successors of the first group of memory activists was none other than Helmut Kohl, who embarked on an ambitious attempt to reinvent the memory of Nazism and lay to rest the burden of collective symbolic guilt when it would have been much easier to avoid the contentious field of memory politics altogether. With little sensitivity and charisma but a good deal of ambition, Kohl cast West Germany's antitotalitarian consensus into a completely new infrastructure of cultural memory. His commitment to historicization and memory politics certainly did not help him stay in power (he had more efficient and illegal tools to accomplish that). Like others in the memory business, he followed deeply felt convictions about the type of historical consciousness that would best serve future generations.

In the mid-1990s, the politics of the past took another pragmatic turn, as themes of interpretation that had been developed in the previous decades were now deployed to bolster the remilitarization of Germany's and Europe's foreign policy. When the Greens joined the federal government in 1998, an echo of their original vigorous antifascism helped bring about an important reversal in the long history of reparations. For the first time, some of the forgotten victims received modest compensation payments. But neither this rare occurrence nor the overdetermined political debates during the first Gulf War and the first military intervention in Yugoslavia change the fact that self-reflexive politics of memory gradually retreated into the background. The current administration had to bring to a close memory projects launched by previous governments, but it did not start any initiatives of its own. Moreover, during the debates about Kosovo and slave-labor compensation, German politicians deployed references to the Nazi past to define German and European political self-interests and streamline the decision-making process. They no longer used the specter of Nazism as a litmus test to determine the moral integrity of their political objectives. In this important respect, today's politics of memory serve the same purpose as the politics of history in the postwar years, and the approximation of the two different paradigms of historical reflection provides an excellent measure for the normalization of the political memory of the Third Reich that has occurred since 1995.

TOWARD A SOCIAL GEOGRAPHY
OF COLLECTIVE MEMORY

Considered on the basis of cultural output—that is, on the basis of the many books, plays, speeches, exhibits, films, and TV programs that have addressed the burden of the past—German memory has evolved in five stages. With the exception of the first two years, the decade after World War II was a phase of considerable agreement about the meaning of Nazism, before a gradual reorientation of Germany's historical culture occurred in the late 1950s and 1960s in response to political as well as generational changes. In the 1970s, these reform efforts were followed by years of stagnation in key areas of cultural production, accompanied by more or less fruitful experimentation in other, more marginal environments. Partly as a result of these innovations, the 1980s marked a revolution in West Germany's memory of the Third Reich, as a wide variety of media acknowledged the history of the "Final Solution" and explored everyday life during fascism. In the subsequent phase of German memory, which is ongoing today, many collectives successfully adapted to the new paradigm, developed more or less self-reflexive routines of Holocaust remembrance, and established a new memory status quo that cut across political and generational divides. But the new memory has not remained unchallenged. It is rejected in right-wing political circles and has been dismissed as a superficial media event by some public intellectuals. Rather than undermining the new paradigm, however, such criticism has helped transform what initially was a more narrowly conceived Holocaust memory into an abstract, versatile memory of European human rights abuses. In this abstract, iconographic format, the memory of the Holocaust assisted in integrating unified Germany into the European community.

The five-stage model obscures the fact that different segments of Germany's historical culture made markedly different contributions to the task of working through collective symbolic guilt. Professional historians made the least important contributions—at least, in terms of the social relevance of their work. They first went on with business as usual, pretending that nothing extraordinary had happened in the Third Reich. When they finally began to wonder what implications the catastrophe of Nazism might have for their profession, they embarked on a prolonged theoretical tangent; only later did they write detailed studies about the implementation of the "Final Solution" which made important contributions to international scholarship but found few readers outside the narrow confines of academia. During the phase of methodological insecurity, historians also lobbied aggressively for specific cultural memories of Nazism, but they failed to take that advocacy as an opportunity to try to bridge the gap between scholarly and popular perceptions of the past.

West Germany's politicians proved particularly adept at consensus building. They excelled in that task first in the 1950s, when they helped craft the victim ideology of the former bystanders, and then in the 1990s, when they promulgated the Europeanization of German memory with very favorable consequences for their own role in European affairs. Between these two phases, however, politicians often found themselves on the defensive, especially when they championed new sites of cultural memory.

A few academics and politicians criticized the memory peace of the 1950s, but the driving force of self-critical reform has been West Germany's diverse intellectual scene, including its writers, artists, and journalists. In that group, TV makers have played an important but as yet insufficiently understood role. As a result of political pressure and self-censorship, on the one hand, and proximity to politically independent intellectual discourses, on the other, TV executives managed to square the memory circle. During the 1980s, they helped revolutionize West Germany's historical culture, but unlike similarly inclined amateur historians, left-wing political activists, museum curators, and print journalists, they carefully abided by the political limits of historical taste.

The brief survey shows that historians were most outspoken in the fourth phase and most productive in the fifth, that politicians made particularly important contributions to Germany's historical culture in the first and fifth phases, and that TV makers excelled in the fourth. One should stress, however, that all three of these relatively conservative professions would not have come as far as they did in the development of an active, more or less self-critical historical culture if they had not profited from the intellectual contributions of writers, artists, and journalists who used their relative political and institutional independence to advance much more pessimistic and demanding assessments of Germany's crimes and subsequent moral obligations (especially in the second, third, and fourth phases). Finally, it is important to differentiate the impressive range of Germany's historical culture, documented in its diverse cultural output, from the actual individual and collective memories that have developed in response to the representation of the past in print and visual media as well as in response to other, less tangible venues of historical education.

GERMAN MEMORY STUDIES

The reorientation of West Germany's historical culture in the 1980s led to an academic preoccupation with memory that started in the 1990s. In a wave of monographs, specialists of German history sliced the memory pie in almost any way imaginable. They analyzed the architectural history of former concentration camps and Nazi cityscapes, studied the evolution of official memorial days and institutions of cultural memory, and focused on the representation of Nazism in different media, including newspapers, films, and television. The study of German memory was part of the cultural turn in historical studies, but the focus on culture and memory occurred during a phase of methodological normalization. As a result, most scholars analyzing German sites of memory embraced fairly traditional notions of historical research and writing. They assumed, for example, that the history of memory represented a contiguous, consistently structured terrain without much synchronic variation. These shared methodological assumptions did not, of course, prevent substantial scholarly disagreement, especially between experts who identified with the memory politics of the 1950s and those who disdained them. But despite such differences of opinion, German historians subscribed to an aggregate vision of the history of memory. They homogenized diverse arenas of cultural production and political competition that had developed distinct visions of Nazism and had served different mnemonic communities.[1] This tendency was particularly problematic, since the field has focused primarily on elite discourses. Scholars have only recently begun to document the historical coverage in the mass media, explore the motives of journalists and editors who produced that coverage, and speculate about the possible effects of the coverage on readers and viewers.

Yet from the beginning, German memory studies has also been an interdisciplinary field. The dominant paradigm has been challenged by scholars who have called into question the tacit methodological assumptions with which historians tended to approach the history of memory. The most interesting of these challenges was provided by sociologists and political scientists who studied collective memories from the vantage point of the sociological thought of Pierre Bourdieu or German systems theory in the tradition of Niklas Luhmann.[2] In contrast to their colleagues in history, social scientists assumed that many professions and institutions involved in the interpretation of the Nazi past developed as relatively independent traditions—or systems of thought—according to their own reproductive rules. From the social science perspective, the specific contributions to Vergangenheitsbewältigung made by historians, TV makers, and politicians should be carefully analyzed within their specific, narrowly circumscribed discursive and sociological contexts before they are compared and possibly equated with other types of public memory. For outsiders, the academic world of Luhmann scholarship sometimes assumes a sectarian quality, replete with impenetrable intellectual jargon. Moreover and more important, in some applications of systems theory in German memory studies, the analyses of collective memories degenerate into a tautological celebration of the power of the system to generate meaning and defend its borders against semantic intruders.[3] Despite these occasional shortcomings, the underlying explicit assumptions that inform the social science approach to the study of memory appear more compelling than the tacit, unreflected methodological beliefs that many historians share. On conceptual as well as empirical grounds, it is prudent to assume that collective memory is, first and foremost, a "local" phenomenon. Specific interpretations of the past circulate in rather narrowly defined channels of discourse and engage quite specific audiences without, as a matter of routine, overcoming these social, technological, and ideological limitations.

THE MEMORY PYRAMID: VERTICAL COMMUNICATION BARRIERS

I imagine the social geography of German memory in the form of a pyramid with a complex interior structure. The pyramid revolves around three axes that influence all arenas of collective memory. There is the obvious divide between conservative and liberal collective memories of Nazism, which splits the pyramid into two antagonistic but dialectically related halves. In addition, all interpretations of the past have been the product of cross-generational competition and cooperation that involved at least three important age-groups — the war, Hitler Youth, and postwar generations. Finally, collective memories of the Third Reich and its crimes have been constructed in many different professional and informal social settings, which vary tremendously in size and social status and can be divided into three general, hierarchical categories. The top of the pyramid is crowded with elite discourses, such as professional historiography, that feature restrictive entrance criteria for authorized speakers. The members of such elite groups strive to reach a general public, but in practice, they either communicate among themselves — producing detailed, ambitious professional memories of Nazism — or reach an audience located in the second broad layer of the pyramid, which I would designate as the politically and culturally interested public. This interested public, representing perhaps 15 percent to 25 percent of the population, consists of the readers of the national press and the consumers of highbrow TV.[4] The people in this bracket take an active interest in the cultural products of the elite; they selectively listen to the historians, novelists, auteur filmmakers, and museum designers — often by way of the national press — who provide them with relatively complex and self-reflexive texts.[5] In the day-to-day reproduction of Germany's public sphere, this politically and culturally interested public can be relatively clearly differentiated from the majority of citizens about whom we know comparatively little. That general public includes readers of the *Bild-Zeitung* and *Hör-Zu*, viewers of Knopp's TV productions, and members of Germany's famous pub culture (*Stammtischkultur*), but actual information about the public's historical tastes is quite limited.

Whenever scholars have tried to find out how Germans who are not part of the political and cultural elites remember the Nazi past, they have come up with important and unexpected results. Popular private memories of the war and postwar years do not seem to be compatible with the externalized and objectified elite memories that have filled the public sphere of the Federal Republic for many decades. Private memories seem to differ from public memories in form and content; they appear to be based on different systems of periodization and different standards of plausibility. In the 1980s, a team of oral historians brought together by Lutz Niethammer showed that working-class memories in the Ruhr Valley did not focus on the political turning point of 1945 that has played such an important role in elite memories in the East and West. Instead, workers at the Ruhr identified the onset of aerial bombing in 1941 and the marked improvement in living conditions after 1948 as among the most important turning points in their lives.[6] More recent oral histories have had similarly intriguing results. A group of social psychologists at the Kulturwissenschaftliche Institut in Essen has demonstrated that Germans who are two generations removed from the events of the Third Reich deliberately and selectively craft images of the Nazi past based on a wide range of sources, including media coverage, formal education, and family lore. Postwar generations seem, for instance, very adept at inventing stories about the Nazi past that cast their family members in a positive light. They project their grandparents into Holocaust narratives they encounter in school or on TV, without retaining any consciousness of the fictitious nature of these family histories. It is interesting to note that these projections do not depend on an intergenerational pact of silence. They even take place in families in which members of the grandparent generation openly acknowledge their political and moral mistakes of the Nazi years.[7]

Private memories are not more self-serving than public memories. As the preceding chapters have shown, many German public memories are selective and apologetic. But the manipulation of the past seems to follow different rules on different levels of the pyramid. In contrast to objectified public memories, popular private memories appear to be particularly flexible and able to integrate diverse images and story elements irrespective of their historical accuracy. Private memories are more concerned with emotional rather than factual consistency. In this important respect, the psychological dynamics of cultural reception differ from the political and professional dynamics that govern the production of cultural products such as novels, history books, or museum exhibits. These products reflect the historical imagination of their producers and the minority of audience members who are closely attuned to the structure and rules of specialized historical discourses, but they probably do not represent the historical consciousness of the larger population. The apparent divide between private and public spheres and between elite and popular memories indicates that historical reflection in contemporary media societies takes place within different channels of communication and on the

basis of different routines of consumption, which can evolve more or less independently of each other.

Many examples in the history of German memory illustrate these communication barriers. The 1986–1988 Historians' Debate was closely followed by
all members of the elite, including those who did not actively participate in
the controversy, but the abstract debate never interested the larger public. For
intellectuals, the Historians' Debate remains an important site of memory,
but it had little impact on the popular imagination about the Third Reich.
This example illustrates that people at the base of the pyramid might be un-
aware of the divisive and emotional memory battles that take place at the top,
whereas intellectuals have difficulty imagining how few of their fellow citizens follow their discussions with keen interest. In fact, intellectuals even
tend to cherish their discursive interventions more than the institutions of
cultural memory that they are expected to create. During the years of controversy about the Holocaust Memorial in Berlin, discussants frequently suggested that their debate constituted a site of memory that was superior to the
memorial itself. But that self-centered strategy of remembrance only worked
for the debate's participants and the relatively few readers who followed the
discussion in the national press.[8] A large segment of the German public only
took notice of the memorial when clips about its construction and inauguration appeared on the evening news, and this public never paid any attention
to the discursive site of memory that the intellectuals appreciated so deeply.

HORIZONTAL COMMUNICATION BARRIERS

The professional contexts considered in the previous chapters are all part of
the top of the pyramid—at least as far as its producers are concerned. Historians, politicians, and media executives rely on exclusive networks of communication to regulate the flow of material and symbolic resources. They negotiate
their relations to the public through the national media, which provide them
with an opportunity to assess their perceptions outside their own professional domains. Even in times of increasingly fragmented audiences, the
construct of the public sphere continues to define public visibility and thus
fulfills two important functions. It influences the internal decision-making
process within different professional contexts, and it informs members of the
elite and the public about professional contexts in which they do not actively

participate. Only interpretations of the past that become part of the mainstream national media coverage have a chance to influence the evolution of historical consciousness over a wide range of professional or social settings.

But communication barriers that are particularly pronounced between collectives located on different levels of the pyramid also divide mnemonic communities of comparable status. History, politics, and television produce very different representations of the past. Historians constantly devise potential memories that are rich in detail and possess an extraordinary degree of accuracy. But since these interpretations of the past are written according to arcane and relatively inflexible rules and presented in increasingly anachronistic formats, they have only a limited influence on other social arenas of historical reflection.

In the history of the Federal Republic, there have been three phases during which historians have had the opportunity to shape the perception of the past in other professional settings. In the 1960s, they found an eager audience in the courts, which tried to understand the flow of power in the Third Reich. This collaboration triggered the first modest historiographical inquiries into the history of the "Final Solution." In the 1980s, historians working within and outside academia provided a useful research foundation for the wave of everyday history that revolutionized the representation of the Third Reich in public television. In fact, during this phase, the texts of academically trained historians and the products of journalists and TV makers reached their greatest compatibility in terms of content and form. In the 1990s, historians and media executives parted ways again, as the Knopp phenomenon aptly illustrates. But at the same time, the memory politics of the Kohl administration offered the conservative elite among Germany's professional historians a welcome opportunity to influence future cultural memories of Nazism. As members of founding committees and supervisory boards of museums and memorials, they influenced the basic intellectual strategies according to which other experts and political appointees filled the halls of museums in Bonn and Berlin and realized the Holocaust Memorial site in Berlin. All of these examples of interdisciplinary collaboration should not detract from the fact that Germany's professional historians and their colleagues abroad are the primary consumers of their research publications. With a delay of several decades, their ideas might find their way into history textbooks, and occasionally, TV makers, museum designers, novelists, and others mine historical works for material that they translate according to the aesthetic and epistemological parameters of their own ways of reinventing the past. But historians are really most useful to nonhistorians as rhetorical devices. Because of their popular image as fact fetishists, historians can be effectively deployed to enhance the reality effect of a given text—for example, when TV makers try to convince their audiences of the historical verisimilitude of their media products.[9]

Television makers, like journalists, do not enjoy the high degree of specialization that characterizes the historical profession. A few privileged TV executives, most notably Guido Knopp, deal exclusively with the representation of contemporary history and have sizable staffs at their disposal that assure them of continuous media presence. But the vast majority of scriptwriters, directors, and members of the editorial staff work on a range of political and historical topics. They focus temporarily on the memory of Nazism when important anniversaries come up or when they are involved in the production of ambitious films that take months or years of preparation. Considering this versatility, it is surprising that television executives with considerable expertise in developing cultural memories have rarely intervened in the debates about the proper ways of representing Nazism. In newscasts and political magazines, the public networks have selectively commented on the latest intellectual struggles concerning the legacy of the Third Reich. But TV makers themselves have never made their opinions known in the pages of the national press where the important discussions about museums, memorials, and anniversaries have taken place.

This reluctance is the result of a pervasive culture of political control and self-censorship within Germany's public broadcasting institutions. Politicians dominate the supervisory boards of the networks and use their power to improve their own image in the media. Although the political elite has rarely cared enough about historical programming to criticize or demand specific interpretations of the Nazi past, the climate of political supervision and intervention has caused TV executives to adopt symbolic defense strategies that influence all broadcasting decisions. When dealing with potentially controversial topics such as the legacy of Nazism, the people in front of and behind the cameras put on a carefully constructed appearance of objectivity. To protect that aura of impartiality, the written and unwritten rules of public television employment discourage lobbying efforts on behalf of specific political positions.[10] But lack of political visibility should not be misconstrued as lack of interest in intellectual debates about the legacy of Nazism. TV makers consider themselves part of the country's cultural elite, and familiarity with that elite's interests and control of an electronic medium allow them to respond to new trends much faster than historians or politicians. In practice, TV executives thus screen the diverse, confrontational intellectual field of Vergangenheitsbewältigung and rework its topics and formats into television programs that are appealing, or at least acceptable, to their political supervisors and audiences. The programs that emerge from this process are designed to cater to popular interests, but they also reflect a conservative assessment of the limits of historical and political taste. Familiarity with intellectual developments in Germany and abroad and sensitivity to political trends allowed German television executives to respond to the invention of Holocaust culture in the late 1970s and to develop a type of Holocaust memory that was acceptable to many segments of German society.

Partly in compensation for their self-imposed political silence, public television employees emphasize their power over public opinion. Ironically, this populist identity of Germany's public television executives has never triggered any real curiosity about TV viewers. People with responsibility for broadcasting decisions feel comfortable in their role as public gatekeepers, and they certainly depend on ratings as a measure of their success, but they have no strong desire to come to know their actual audiences. As a result of this indifference, we know little about the political and social effects of the educational efforts that were undertaken by public television in the 1980s and continued with reduced intensity in the 1990s. TV makers have reached large audiences with their historical programs, but they probably have not shaped their viewers' historical consciousness as much as they like to imagine.

The lack of sophisticated, qualitative audience research also makes it difficult to determine the extent to which television programming has influenced the politics of memory in other professional contexts. Until the broadcast of *Holocaust* in 1979, West Germany's historians, for example, had not paid much attention to popular perceptions of the past or considered the educational potential of television. Even after the broadcast of *Holocaust,* when some self-critical voices could be heard in the ivory tower, the institutions of higher learning only slowly shifted gears. While publishing houses encouraged the writing of Holocaust history in an attempt to respond to popular demand, the academic elite, unlike the media elite, has never fully taken advantage of these publishing opportunities.

West German politicians also had problems developing compelling forms of Holocaust memory despite the fact that, in previous decades, they had proven very adept at casting popular perceptions of the past into binding legislative frameworks. In the postwar years, a conservative majority used that power to abandon the search for perpetrators and cast the victim identity of the former bystanders into long-term legal structures. But even in the 1950s, which were characterized by considerable agreement about the interpretation of Nazism, the bystander memory had to compete with alternative concepts of victimhood. Moreover, starting in the late 1950s, the political discourse slowly diversified on some levels of government. At that stage, state administrations helped raise teaching standards and rekindled the search for Nazi criminals. Yet all efforts to build a more self-critical political culture were derailed by the political turmoil of the 1970s, which forced an initially reform-minded federal administration into a defensive position.

Given its preoccupation with crisis management, the political elite of the Federal Republic was surprised by the shift in the media discourse and public perception of Nazism in the 1980s. In an immediate, symbolic reaction to *Holocaust,* parliament abolished the statute of limitations for murder, an option politicians had rejected for several decades. During the following years, West Germany's political leaders slowly and tentatively shifted their attention toward the victims of the "Final Solution." Weizsäcker's speech of 1985 and the Central Memorial in the Neue Wache were more or less successful attempts to pay tribute to the new paradigm of Holocaust exceptionalism while retaining the focus on German victimhood that had dominated West Germany's historical culture for three decades. In addition, local governments played an important role in the reconstruction of West Germany's cultural memory of Nazism in the 1980s and 1990s. But the dictum of the Holocaust's uniqueness was only fully accepted by German politicians when it was recast as a common European legacy that no longer set Germany aside from its European partners and former victims. Since the mid-1990s, this tolerant and "democratic" Holocaust memory has helped legitimize the normalization and remilitarization of Germany's foreign policy. Under such favorable circumstances, German politicians have been very willing to praise the blessings of Holocaust memory to skeptics within their own ranks and within the business community by embracing the Holocaust Memorial and the settlement for the forced laborers of the Nazi regime. In the perception of German and European leaders, a self-critical memory of the European genocide is one of the key elements that differentiates the postimperialist countries of Europe from their U.S. ally.

A closer look at these three professional arenas of collective memory production and their interaction with each other reveals many similarities. All three professions have moved quite cautiously in questions of Vergangenheitsbewältigung, egged on by memory dissidents who urged their reluctant colleagues to pay closer attention to the legacy of the Nazi crimes. Television executives reacted first, followed by historians and then politicians. On a collective scale, however, historians, TV makers, and politicians only turned to the task of Holocaust interpretation in the 1980s, when interest in the "Final Solution" intensified nationally and internationally. Moreover, at the height of West Germany's Holocaust curiosity, the three fields provided very different types of Holocaust memory. Television makers rendered the "Final Solution" tangible, meaningful, and bearable by focusing on the figure of the survivor; historians discussed abstract questions of historical uniqueness and comparability; and politicians—the last group to react—tried to devise rituals and sites of memory, with the help of the German Jewish community, that would integrate the new demands of Holocaust remembrance with time-tested antitotalitarian commitments and notions of German victimhood. The three discourses certainly reinforced each other by emphasizing the new political relevance of the history of the "Final Solution," but they only reached a higher degree of structural compatibility when each field settled on formulas, icons, narratives, and gestures of remembrance that were reproduced in a routine fashion. Even under these circumstances, structural tensions persisted, which made mutually beneficial, intellectual exchanges between the three contexts unlikely, if not impossible.

INTERNATIONAL CULTURE—TRANSNATIONAL MEMORY?

The historical culture of the Federal Republic was shaped through international communication. West German politicians developed their first interpretations of Nazism under direct Allied supervision, and even after regaining political independence, they paid close attention to the responses that German politics of history and memory elicited abroad. That attention was directed primarily toward the West, but the political elite also listened to the government in East Berlin, with which it competed vigorously in the postwar years, and the governments in Moscow, Warsaw, and Prague, especially once relations to Eastern Europe intensified in the 1970s. The international outlook of the political elite was reflected by journalists, who themselves first depended on Allied licenses and continued to report on the perception of Germany abroad when the occupational status was rescinded. In addition, German audiences quickly became familiar with media products from the United States, Western Europe, and, to a lesser extent, Eastern Europe.

The West German media that emerged in the decades after the war were well financed and served a sizable population. As a result, West German public television networks, unlike those in smaller European countries, could afford to produce high-quality indigenous television adapted to the tastes and customs of their German audience. Despite this relative advantage, West German television, as well as the West German film business, relied heavily on imports. These imports were often "cleaned up" through dubbing and editing, but German viewers could nevertheless get a reasonably good idea of how the war, the German crimes, and Germans themselves were perceived abroad. Since the 1980s, the international exchange of media products has further intensified. Hollywood's vision of the Holocaust has traveled to Europe, and in turn, Knopp's ambivalent TV histories of Hitler's rise and demise have crossed the Atlantic and reached American audiences.

In contrast to politicians, journalists, and TV makers, West German historians acquired an international perspective with some delay. The generation of scholars who joined the profession during the 1960s, motivated by understandable feelings of ambivalence about German political and academic traditions, developed, for the first time, the necessary skills to operate successfully in an international intellectual environment. Since that turning point, German universities have reluctantly reformed a cumbersome, anachronistic teaching system that, among other disadvantages, stymied international cooperation. Nevertheless, many areas of research, especially contemporary German history and Holocaust studies, have become truly transnational pursuits based on a free exchange of scholarship. In fact, among the groups that care most about the construction of cultural memories, academics might well be the most thoroughly internationalized. Without access to national institutions of power but with plenty of contacts and travel opportunities abroad, they represent a true postnational discursive avant-garde. From that position, they can preach the benefits of a transnational ethical outlook, which, in the case of German academics, also provides a nice antidote to lingering feelings of national shame.

In light of all this international communication about German history, one might be tempted to conclude that the reproduction of collective memories and identities has been internationalized and transnationalized, especially with regard to such signature events as the Holocaust.[11] But several important aspects of the history of German memory make me wonder if that conclusion accurately reflects the dynamics of collective memory in and about Germany. Academics, for example, who feel very comfortable within the international networks of their profession and embrace the concept of transnational identity wholeheartedly, are hardly representative of the population at large or of the German elite. Many groups that do not share the academic lifestyle might prefer ideological frameworks that better reflect their own experiences and group loyalties.[12] Moreover, despite or perhaps because of an abundance of international communication, German elites have been amazingly successful in developing interpretations of the Nazi past that reflect international trends and advance national or elite interests at the same time. In the 1950s, the Adenauer administration integrated the international concept of antitotalitarianism with an aggressively nationalistic victim identity. Since the late 1990s, a liberal government, with the explicit support of its European counterparts, has enhanced Germany's influence in world and European affairs under the cover of a transnational Holocaust memory. Between those two events, the objective disagreements between German politicians and their partners abroad have, indeed, decreased, but political memories still reflect a keen sensibility for the important role that national political interests play in European affairs. When the supporters of military intervention in Yugoslavia invoked the Holocaust in the 1990s, they were concerned about an unfolding humanitarian crisis *and* saw an outstanding opportunity to project German power abroad. A similar ambivalence informed Adenauer's balancing act between international compensation, west integration, and rearmament, and there is no indication that a radical reorientation of German and European politics will occur anytime soon. Until the centers of power in Europe shift decisively from the national capitals to Brussels and Strasbourg, the manipulation of the past for elite interests will not assume an unequivocally transnational orientation, and for reasons of efficient democratic control, it is not even clear if that shift is so desirable. Precisely because West Germany developed as a country with limited sovereignty, the international orientation of its political elite has not changed much in the years since the end of World War II. In this respect, the Federal Republic differs from other European countries whose elites have more gradually adopted an international perspective in the process of European integration.

The limits of the globalization are not just apparent at the top of the pyramid; they also are obvious at its base. Consumers across Europe and the United States have often shared the same images and stories about World War II and the Holocaust. But it is far from certain that different audiences build similar identities and memories with the help of these media products. In the post–World War II environment, shared images of the Holocaust—for instance, auteur films from Poland, Czechoslovakia, and the Soviet Union—probably had quite different effects on audiences in Eastern and Western Europe. Even recent international media events such as *Holocaust, Schindler's List,* and Knopp's TV productions, which were specifically designed with global markets in mind, might not have shaped their viewers' knowledge and feelings about the past in parallel ways. Thus, for example, Knopp's visual fantasies about Nazi power clearly appeal to audiences around the globe, but the programs have the potential to provide particularly intense illicit pleasures for German viewers, for whom playful identifications with Nazism retain a taboo quality that audiences in other countries have probably never experienced in quite the same way. Knopp's TV renders the historical personal by addressing ambivalent feelings about the German past that most official venues of Germany's historical culture have carefully avoided.

As an exception to the rule, Knopp's productions highlight the structural disadvantage that media images and stories have in comparison to other more narrowly focused discourses of historical reflection. Many interpretations of Nazism circulating in German society are addressed to very specific target audiences—family members, neighbors, colleagues, high school students, political constituencies, and so on. These discursive interventions with limited visibility to outsiders carry greater potential emotional weight than anonymously distributed media products. The special quality of personal exchanges about the past explains why widely shared media products can have very different semantic effects in different reception environments and why mutually exclusive historical cultures and subcultures exist side by side. Many collectives that feel indifferent or antagonistic about Germany's official memories have successfully reproduced their own deviant memories of the Nazi past, as Germany's extended right-wing subculture illustrates. Consider, for example, the Hohmann affair discussed in the last chapter. In the communities of like-minded neighbors, voters, and backbenchers, Hohmann's anti-Semitic rant probably confirmed existing prejudices and strengthened his status within those groups. But once his speech was inserted into the national political scene, which proscribes very different, philo-Semitic attitudes about Jews, Hohmann's identity as local populist clashed with his role as national parliamentarian. Hohmann's case is unusual because he is a member of an elite, high-profile group. If they are so inclined, most Germans can embrace anti-Semitism and indulge in a sense of German victimhood with friends and family without fear of being outed in the national media.

Experts in memory studies have suggested that national memories and identities have been displaced by a dialectical, conflicted interplay between global and local memories and identities in the last decades of the twentieth century. They see this as a very positive development that has led to more self-reflexive forms of collective remembrance, especially in the realm of Holocaust memory, and has provided tangible advantages for victims of past and present human rights abuses.[13] Interventions like Hohmann's confirm one part of this equation; local memories play, indeed, an important role in the evolution of German collective memories, although that is hardly a new development. But there is no indication that transnational collective memories are similarly successful. In May and June 2005, French and Dutch voters rejected a new European constitution and the plans for political integration that their politicians had designed for them. It is reasonable to assume that many Europeans also disagree with the idea of a common European historical consciousness that political and cultural elites have championed since the mid-1990s. In Stockholm in 2000, Europe's political leaders collectively embraced the Holocaust as a key element of their collective memory. But there is no indication that their citizens have followed their lead and begun to perceive themselves as part of a Holocaust-centered European mnemonic community.

Euro-skepticism is less pronounced in Germany than in other parts of Europe because the project of European integration has helped Germans shed the negative image of the Nazi perpetrator. But even in the German context, conventional types of collective memory play a more important role in every-day life than the sense of a shared European historical trajectory—despite the fact that knowledge and feelings about the past in different parts of Europe are probably more compatible today than they were fifty years ago. To the chagrin of politicians and academics, transnational collective memories still seem to be a rare phenomenon in today's Europe.

There is no way of knowing whether the collective memories of the future will someday resemble the academic utopias of today. Considering the dizzy-ing multitude of memories and identities in divided and unified Germany, it is even difficult to determine what role national identities have played in the evolution of German collective memories since 1945. There was no single medium that united all Germans in reflection about their historical legacy. Neither television nor the official discourse emanating from Bonn or Berlin, nor, most certainly, historiography provided such a common horizon. Never-theless, there was a widely shared awareness of the Holocaust that cut across political, generational, and social divides. All postwar generations in the Fed-eral Republic have been linked by an experience that they have felt more or less intensely at different stages of their lives and that created a peculiar com-mon bond. The experience might have occurred in encounters with non-Germans while traveling abroad, it might have been the result of media consumption, or it might have been an insight gleaned from the way older Germans spoke about themselves and their country. At some point, we real-ized that others, that is, non-Germans, perceived us Germans as having a special relationship to the Nazi crimes we saw unfolding in the media with remarkable frequency. That international experience set in motion more or less productive, intense, and sophisticated reflections about questions of col-lective shame and perhaps also other, less savory and more ambivalent feel-ings about the deeds of our forebears. In this way, the Holocaust became a powerful component of the national historical consciousness of West Ger-mans in the 1980s.[14] It is difficult to study this process of identity formation objectively and determine the extent to which it reflects the experiences of former East Germans and younger generations born into the Berlin republic. But the pervasiveness of a sense of shame as a mark of national distinction highlights what is at stake, for better or for worse, in the reinvention of the Holocaust as a European human rights catastrophe. Given the opportunity, most collectives in Germany, from the politicians in Berlin to the grandchildren of the ordinary bystanders of the Third Reich, use the globalization of the German past to shield themselves from moral self-doubt. That development, though probably unavoidable, might not be in the best national interest.

NOTES

1. For a discussion of these generational ideal types, see Jörn Rüsen, *Zerbrechende Zeit: Über den Sinn der Geschichte* (Cologne, Germany: Böhlau, 2001), 291–99.

2. Rupert Seuthe, *"Geistig-moralische Wende?" Der politische Umgang mit der NS-Vergangengheit in der Ära Kohl am Beispiel von Gedenktagen, Museums- und Denkmalprojekten* (Frankfurt, Germany: Lang, 2001).

3. Günter Sauter, *Politische Entropie: Denken zwischen Mauerfall und dem 11. September 2001: Botho Strauss, Hans Magnus Enzensberger, Martin Walser, Peter Sloterdijk* (Paderborn, Germany: Mentis, 2002); Sabine Moser, *Dieses Volk unter dem es zu leiden galt: Die deutsche Frage bei Günter Grass* (Frankfurt, Germany: Lang, 2002).

4. Although the Communist leadership controlled all aspects of the GDR's historical culture, some remarkably independent voices emerged in the margins of official antifascism, especially among writers and filmmakers. These examples illustrate that state control of cultural memories of Nazism was tight but hardly total or consistent and that the evolution of East German memories deserves more attention. See Annette Leo and Peter Reif-Spirek, *Helden, Täter und Verräter: Studien zum DDR-Antifaschismus* (Berlin: Metropol, 1999); Thomas Jung, "Jenseits der Erinnerungspolitik oder Der schwierige Umgang mit dem Holocaust in der DDR," in Klaus Berghahn, Jürgen Fohrmann, and Helmut Schneider, eds., *Kulturelle Repräsentationen des Holocaust in Deutschland und den Vereinigten Staaten* (New York: Lang, 2002), 167–91; Thomas Fox, *Stated Memory: East Germany and the Holocaust* (Rochester, NY: Camden House, 1999).

5. Dan Diner, "Gedächtnis und Methode: Über den Holocaust in der Geschichtsschreibung," in Fritz-Bauer-Institut, ed., *Auschwitz: Geschichte, Rezeption und Wirkung* (Frankfurt, Germany: Campus, 1996), 11–22; see also Diner, *Beyond the Conceivable: Studies on Germany, Nazism, and the Holocaust* (Berkeley: University of California Press, 2000), 218–30, and Gesine Schwan, *Politik und Schuld: Die zerstörerische Macht des Schweigens* (Frankfurt, Germany: Fischer, 1997).

6. Karl Jaspers, *Die Schuldfrage: Von der politischen Haftung Deutschlands,* new ed. (Munich, Germany: Piper, 1987), 25.

7. The collective nature of this symbolic guilt, as defined by West Germans and foreigners, is illustrated by the constant lament of conservative West German political forces who clearly sensed that they were made part of a moral contract they did not enter into of their own free will. In this sense, their tedious complaints accurately reflect the nature of the phenomenon of collective symbolic guilt. They fail to recognize, however, that working through collective symbolic guilt has been an extremely rewarding and productive experience for the Federal Republic. See Armin Mohler, *Der Nasenring: Die Vergangenheitsbewältigung vor und nach dem Fall der Mauer* (Munich, Germany: Langen Müller, 1991), and, less shrill and less entertaining, Klaus Michael Groll, *Wie lange haften wir für Hitler: Zum Selbstverständnis der Deutschen heute* (Düsseldorf, Germany: Droste, 1990).

8. For the Japanese case, see Ian Buruma, *The Wages of Guilt: Memories of War in Germany and Japan* (New York: Farrar Straus Giroux, 1994), 293–97; for the memory of the Armenian genocide in Turkey, see Richard Hovannisian, ed., *Remembrance and Denial: The Case of the Armenian Genocide* (Detroit, MI: Wayne State University Press, 1998).

9. See Bernhard Giesen, "Das Tätertrauma der Deutschen: Eine Einleitung," in Bernhard Giesen and Christoph Schneider, eds., *Tätertrauma: Nationale Erinnerungen im öffentlichen Diskurs*

(Constance, Germany: UVK, 2004), 11–53; and Michael Kohlstruck, *Zwischen Erinnerung und Geschichte: Der Nationalsozialismus und die jungen Deutschen* (Berlin: Metropol, 1997), 31.

10. On the construction of historical debates and scandals in the media, see Werner Bergmann, *Antisemitismus in öffentlichen Konflikten: Kollektives Lernen in der politischen Kultur der Bundesrepublik 1949–1989* (Frankfurt, Germany: Campus, 1997), and Thomas Herz and Michael Schwab-Trapp, eds., *Umkämpfte Vergangenheit: Diskurse über den Nationalsozialismus seit 1945* (Opladen, Germany: Westdeutscher Verlag, 1997).

11. For the best discussion of the reception of *Holocaust* in Germany, see Yizhak Ahren et al., *Das Lehrstück "Holocaust" Wirkungen und Nachwirkungen eines Medienereignisses* (Opladen, Germany: Westdeutscher Verlag, 1982).

12. Regarding the Fassbinder controversies, see Janusz Bodek, *Die Fassbinder-Kontroversen: Entstehung und Wirkung eines literarischen Textes* (Frankfurt, Germany: Lang, 1991). The Historians' Debate is discussed in chapter 4.

13. Norbert Frei, *Vergangenheitspolitik: Die Anfänge der Bundesrepublik und die NS-Vergangenheit* (Munich, Germany: Beck, 1996), 397, 406; see also Ulrich Brochhagen, *Nach Nürnberg: Vergangenheitsbewältigung in der Ära Adenauer* (Hamburg, Germany: Junius, 1994).

14. Frei, *Vergangenheitspolitik*, 401, and Michael Wolffsohn, *Ewige Schuld: 40 Jahre deutsch-jüdisch-israelische Beziehungen* (Munich, Germany: Piper, 1991).

15. Jeffrey Herf, *Divided Memory: The Nazi Past in the Two Germanys* (Cambridge, MA: Harvard University Press, 1997), 282–83; Peter Reichel, *Politik mit der Erinnerung: Gedächnisorte im Streit um die nationalsozialistische Vergangenheit* (Munich, Germany: Hanser, 1995), 154–59 and 172–75.

16. For a description of the turning point in the criminal investigation in the late 1950s and early 1960s, see Marc von Miquel, *Ahnden oder Amnestieren? Westdeutsche Justiz und Vergangenheitspolitik in den sechziger Jahren* (Göttingen, Germany: Wallstein, 2004), and Annette Weinke, *Die Verfolgung von NS-Tätern im geteilten Deutschland: Vergangenheitsbewältigungen 1949–1969 oder Eine deustch-deutsche Beziehungsgeschichte im Kalten Krieg* (Paderborn, Germany: Schöningh, 2002).

17. Peter Dudek, *"Der Rückblick auf die Vergangenheit wird sich nicht vermeiden lassen": Zur pädagogischen Verarbeitung ds Nationalsozialismus in Deutschland (1945—1990)* (Opladen, Germany: Leske und Budrich, 1995), 260–84.

18. Ulrich Herbert, "Vernichtungspolitik: Neue Antworten und Fragen zur Geschichte des 'Holocaust,'" in Herbert, ed., *Nationalsozialistische Vernichtungspolitik, 1939–1945* (Frankfurt, Germany: Fischer, 1998), 13–14; Georg Iggers, *New Directions in European Historiography*, rev. ed. (Middletown, CT: Wesleyan University Press, 1984), 94.

19. In this context, the research of social psychologists Harald Welzer, Sabine Moller, and Karoline Tschuggnall is very insightful. They argue that the grandchildren of the Nazi generation, in the process of listening to family and media stories about the past, construct memories of the Third Reich that reflect the self-defensive strategies of interpretation that their grandparents adopted after 1945. But there is no indication that these invented memories are a psychological or political burden for the younger generation or that any media or cultural institutions will successfully challenge these collective memories; see Welzer, Moller, and Tschuggnall, *"Opa war kein Nazi": Nationalsozialismus und Holocaust im Familiengedächtnis* (Frankfurt, Germany: Fischer, 2001), 205–10; see also Kohlstruck, *Zwischen Erinnerung und Geschichte*, 281–88.

CHAPTER 2

1. These connections are emphasized in Andreas Huyssen, *Twilight Memories: Marking Time in a Culture of Amnesia* (New York: Routledge, 1995); Aleida Assmann, *Erinnerungsräume: For-*

men und Wandlungen des kulturellen Gedächtnisses (Munich, Germany: Beck, 1999); and James Young, *At Memory's Edge: After-Images of the Holocaust in Contemporary Art and Architecture* (New Haven, CT: Yale University Press, 2000).

2. See Kerwin Lee Klein, "On the Emergence of Memory in Historical Discourse," *Representations* 69 (Winter 2000): 127–50.

3. Susannah Radstone, "Working with Memory: An Introduction," in Radstone, eds., *Memory and Methodology* (Oxford: Berg, 2000), 1–22; see also Patrick Geary, "The Historical Material of Memory," in Giovanni Ciappelli and Patricia Lee Rubin, ed., *Art, Memory, and Family in Rennaissance Florence* (Cambridge: Cambridge University Press, 2000), 17–25, and compare to Assmann, *Erinnerungsräume*, 17.

4. John Dower, *Embracing Defeat: Japan in the Wake of World War II* (New York: Norton, 1999), 25.

5. Maurice Halbwachs, *Les Cadres sociaux de la mémoire* (Paris: Alcan, 1925); Halbwachs, *La Topographie légendaire des Évangiles en Terre Sainte: Étude de mémoire collective* (Paris: Presses Universitaire, 1941); Halbwachs, *La Mémoire collective*, published posthumously by Jeanne Alexandre (Paris: Presses Universitaire, 1950); see also the discussion of Halbwachs's work in Patrick Hutton, *History as an Art of Memory* (Hanover, NH: University Press of New England, 1993), 73–90, and for a general introduction and contextualization of social constructivism, see Nancy Nelson Spivey, *The Constructivist Metaphor: Reading, Writing and the Making of Meaning* (San Diego, CA: Academic Press, 1997), chapter 1, esp. 17–26.

6. Jay Winter and Emmanuel Sivan, eds., *War and Remembrance in the Twentieth Century* (Cambridge: Cambridge University Press, 1999), 23.

7. James Fentress and Chris Wickham, *Social Memory* (London: Blackwell, 1992).

8. Winter and Sivan, *War and Remembrance*.

9. Roy Rosenzweig and David Thelen, *The Presence of the Past: Popular Uses of History in American Life* (New York: Columbia University Press, 1998), 3.

10. Noa Gedi and Yigal Elam, "Collective Memory—What Is It?" *History and Memory* 8, no. 1 (1996): 30–50.

11. The term *countermemory* is derived from Foucault; see Hutton, *History as an Art of Memory*, 106–23; public memory versus vernacular memory designates officially endorsed or produced memories as distinct from grassroots memories, as in John Bodnar, *Remaking America: Public Memory, Commemoration, and Patriotism in the Twentieth Century* (Princeton, NJ: Princeton University Press, 1992); see also John Gillis, "Memory and Identity: The History of a Relationship," in Gillis, ed., *Commemorations: The Politics of National Identity* (Princeton, NJ: Princeton University Press, 1994), 3–24.

12. In the case of oral history, the connection to memory studies is aptly illustrated in Lutz Niethammer, *Lebenserfahrung und kollektives Gedächtnis: Die Praxis der "Oral History"* (Frankfurt, Germany: Syndikat Autoren und Verlagsgesellschaft, 1980).

13. For recent works on historical consciousness that are very relevant to memory studies, see Jürgen Straub, ed., *Erzählung, Identität und historisches Bewusstsein: Die psychologische Konstruktion von Zeit und Geschichte* (Frankfurt, Germany: Suhrkamp, 1996); Jörn Rüsen and Jürgen Straub, eds., *Die dunkle Spur der Vergangenheit: Psychoanalytische Zugänge zum Geschichtsbewusstsein* (Frankfurt, Germany: Suhrkamp, 1998); and Felix Philipp Lutz, *Das Geschichtsbewusstsein der Deutschen: Grundlagen der politischen Kultur in Ost und West* (Cologne, Germany: Böhlau, 2000).

14. See, for example, Mieke Bal, Jonathan Crewe, and Leo Spitzer, eds., *Acts of Memory: Cultural Recall in the Present* (Hanover, NH: University Press of New England, 1999); Dan Ben-Amos and Liliane Weissberg, eds., *Cultural Memory and the Construction of Identity* (Detroit, MI: Wayne State University Press, 1999); and especially Marita Sturken, *Tangled Memories: The Vietnam War, the AIDS Epidemic, and the Politics of Remembering* (Berkeley: University of California Press, 1997).

15. Jan Assmann, "Collective Memory and Cultural Identity," *New German Critique* 65 (Spring–Summer 1995): 125–33; see also Assmann, *Das kulturelle Gedächtnis: Schrift, Erinnerung und politische Identität in den frühen Hochkulturen* (Munich, Germany: Beck, 1992).

16. See Assmann, "Collective Memory and Cultural Identity," 130.

17. Lutz Niethammer, "Diesseits des 'Floating Gap': Das kollektive Gedächtnis und die Konstruktion von Identität im wissenschaftlichen Diskurs," in *Deutschland danach: Postfaschistische Gesellschaft und nationales Gedächtnis* (Bonn, Germany: Dietz, 1999), 565–82. Concerning the vested interest of second-generation observers, see the helpful concept of "postmemory" proposed by Marianne Hirsch, *Family Frames: Photography, Narrative, and Postmemory* (Cambridge, MA: Harvard University Press, 1997), esp. 22.

18. See Pierre Nora, ed., *Realms of Memory: Rethinking the French Past,* 3 vols. (New York: Columbia University Press, 1996–1998); for lucid discussions of Nora's project and methodology, see Nancy Wood, "Memory's Remains: Les Lieux de Mémoire," *History and Memory* 6, no. 1 (1994): 123–49, republished in Wood, *Vectors of Memory: Legacies of Trauma in Postwar Europe* (Oxford: Berg, 1999); and Peter Carrier, "Places, Politics and the Archiving of Contemporary Memory in Pierre Nora's *Les Lieux de mémoire*," in Radstone, *Memory and Methodology,* 37–57.

19. Allan Megill, "History, Memory, Identity," *History of the Human Sciences* 11, no. 3 (1998): 37–62.

20. Jeffrey Olick and Joyce Robbins, "Social Memory Studies: From 'Collective Memory' to the Historical Sociology of Mnemonic Practices," *Annual Review of Sociology* 24 (1998): 105–40, and the interesting reflections about collective identity from the perspective of international relations theory in Rodney Gruce Hall, *National Collective Identity: Social Constructs and International Systems* (New York: Columbia University Press, 1999).

21. Mary Carruthers, *The Book of Memory: A Study of Memory in Medieval Culture* (New York: Cambridge University Press, 1990); Elisabeth Valdez del Alamo and Carol Stamatis Pendergast, eds., *Memory and the Medieval Tomb* (Aldershot, UK: Ashgate, 2000); and Charles Hedrick, *History and Silence: Purge and Rehabilitation of Memory in Late Antiquity* (Austin: University of Texas Press, 2000).

22. Megill, "History, Memory, Identity," 56; see also David Lowenthal, *The Past Is a Foreign Country* (Cambridge: Cambridge University Press, 1985), 214, and the nuanced assessment of Dominick LaCapra, *History and Memory after Auschwitz* (Ithaca, NY: Cornell University Press, 1998), 19–21.

23. Peter Burke, "History as Social Memory," in Thomas Butler, ed., *History, Culture, and the Mind* (New York: Basil Blackwell, 1989), 97–113.

24. That is one of the many interesting results of neuropsychological research on memory distortion; see Daniel Schacter, ed., *The Cognitive Neuropsychology of False Memory* (Hove, UK: Psychology Press, 1999), and Schacter, *Searching for Memory: The Brain, the Mind, and the Past* (New York: Basic Books, 1996).

25. For psychological research on autobiographical memory, see David Rubin, ed., *Remembering Our Past: Studies in Autobiographical Memory* (New York: Cambridge University Press, 1996); Martin Conway, ed., *Theoretical Perspectives on Autobiographical Memory* (Dordrecht, the Netherlands: Kluwer, 1992); and Conway and Susan Gathercole, *Theories of Memory,* vol. 2 (Hove, UK: Psychology Press, 1998).

26. Michael Schudson, "Dynamics of Distortion in Collective Memory," in Daniel Schacter, ed., *Memory Distortion: How Minds, Brains, and Societies Reconstruct the Past* (Cambridge, MA: Harvard University Press, 1995), 346–64.

27. Paul Connerton, *How Societies Remember* (Cambridge: Cambridge University Press, 1989), 37; see also the discussion of neurological and psychological research for purposes of cultural history in Elisabeth Domansky and Harald Welzer, eds., *Eine offene Geschichte: Zur kommunikativen Tradierung der nationalsozialistischen Vergangenheit* (Tübingen, Germany: Edi-

tion Discord, 1999), 11–23; Winter and Sivan, *War and Remembrance in the Twentieth Century*, 10–19; and Schacter, *Memory Distortion*.

28. Susan Crane, "Writing the Individual Back into Collective Memory," *American Historical Review* 102, no. 5 (1997): 1372–85, and Winter and Sivan, *War and Remembrance*.

29. See Jeffrey Olick's excellent discussion in Olick, "Collective Memory: The Two Cultures," *Sociological Theory* 17, no. 3 (1999): 333–48.

30. This misleading assumption is nicely spelled out in Paul Edwards, *To Acknowledge a War: The Korean War in American Memory* (Westport, CT: Greenwood, 2000), 18: "When nations, like individuals, try to rewrite the past in such a way as to ignore its impact, they are likely to become sick, and their affirmations to become obsessions."

31. Irwin-Zarecka, *Frames of Remembrance*, 116. This also explains why a number of scholars have strongly objected to using methods of individual psychology and psychoanalysis for the study of collective memories, including Marc Bloch as early as 1925; see Bloch, "Mémoire collective, tradition, et coutume," *Revue de Synthèse Historique* 40 (1925): 73–83, cited in Burke, "History as Social Memory"; it also explains why some classics of Vergangenheitsbewältigung literature in Germany are methodologically (but not morally) problematic; see Margaret Mitscherlich and Alexander Mitscherlich, *The Inability to Mourn* (New York: Grove, 1975).

32. See, for example, Gillian Banner, *Holocaust Literature: Schulz, Levi, Spiegelman and the Memory of the Offense* (London: Vallentine Mitchell, 2000), and especially Lawrence Langer, *Holocaust Testimonies: The Ruins of Memory* (New Haven, CT: Yale University Press, 1991).

33. See Cathy Caruth, *Unclaimed Experience: Trauma, Narrative, and History* (Baltimore: Johns Hopkins University Press, 1996), 6; see also Caruth, introduction to *Trauma: Explorations in Memory*, ed. Cathy Caruth (Baltimore: Johns Hopkins University Press, 1995), 3–12, and compare to Ruth Leys, *Trauma: A Genealogy* (Chicago: University of Chicago Press, 2000), especially chapter 8.

34. LaCapra, *History and Memory after Auschwitz*, 23; see also Dominick LaCapra, *Representing the Holocaust: History, Theory, Trauma* (Ithaca, NY: Cornell University Press, 1994), 18n10; and LaCapra, *Writing History, Writing Trauma* (Baltimore: Johns Hopkins University Press, 2001), 181–86.

35. Liliane Weissberg, introduction to Ben-Amos and Weisberg, *Cultural Memory*, 7–26; see also Yael Zerubavel, *Recovered Roots: Collective Memory and the Making of Israeli National Tradition* (Chicago: University of Chicago Press, 1995), 5, who argues, "Collective memory continuously negotiates between available historical records and current social and political agendas."

36. Wood, *Vectors of Memory*, 2.

37. Richard Terdiman, *Present Past: Modernity and the Memory Crisis* (Ithaca, NY: Cornell University Press, 1993), 34; see also Assmann, *Erinnerungsräume*, 132. Or, as Barbie Zelizer put it, "Collective memories have texture, existing in the world rather than in a person's head"; see Zelizer, *Remembering to Forget: Holocaust Memory through the Camera's Eye* (Chicago: University of Chicago Press, 1998), 4.

38. Angela Keppler, *Tischgespräche: Über Formen kommunikativer Vergemeinschaftung am Beispiel der Konversation in Familien* (Frankfurt, Germany: Suhrkamp, 1994).

39. I am doubtful about the existence of a European collective memory because it is not as yet reproduced in a similar fashion in everyday lives across Europe. With the exception of intellectuals and bureaucrats who convene as colleagues and are paid to discuss and administer European concerns (among others, the question of a European collective memory), a common European collective memory does not yet exist. For discussions of this question, see Luisa Passerini, ed., *The Question of European Identity: A Cultural Historical Approach* (Florence, Italy: European Historical Institute, 1998); Sharon Mcdonald, ed., *Approaches to European Historical Consciousness: Reflections and Provocations* (Hamburg, Germany: Edition Körber,

2000); Rudy Koshar, *From Monuments to Traces: Artifacts of German Memory, 1870–1990* (Berkeley: University of California Press, 2000), 286–96; and especially the empirical data in Richard Herrmann, Thomas Risse, and Marilynn Bewer, eds., *Transnational Identities: Becoming European in the EU* (Lanham, MD: Rowman and Littlefield, 2004). Regardless on what level collective memories are analyzed, it is important to consider the interdependencies between the different levels of collective identity. The larger the collective in question, the more important it is that its memory be reflected and reproduced on a lower level of numeric complexity. For instance, national memories need to be reproduced on the level of families or professions or in other locations where people form emotional attachments in their everyday lives; see Alon Confino, *The Nation as Local Metaphor: Württemberg, Imperial Germany, and National Memory, 1871–1918* (University of North Carolina Press, 1997).

40. Barry Schwartz, *Abraham Lincoln and the Forge of National Memory* (Chicago: University of Chicago Press, 2000), xi.

41. Media events such as *Schindler's List* and Godhagen are just the tip of the iceberg, and they differ from more routine and more prevalent representations of the Holocaust in that they have elicited more intense emotional reactions; for discussions of these media events, see Yosefa Loshitzky, ed., *Spielberg's Holocaust: Critical Perspectives on "Schindler's List"* (Bloomington: Indiana University Press, 1997), and Johannes Heil and Rainer Erb, eds., *Geschichtswissenschaft und Öffentlichkeit: Der Streit um Daniel J. Goldhagen* (Frankfurt, Germany: Fischer, 1998).

42. Matt Matsuda, *The Memory of the Modern* (New York: Oxford University Press, 1996), 8; see also Jeffrey Barash, "The Politics of Memory: Reflections on Practical Wisdom and Political Identity," in Richard Kearney and Mark Dooley, ed., *Questioning Ethics: Contemporary Debates in Philosophy* (London: Routledge, 1999), 33–43.

43. On habit memory and commemorative rituals, see especially Connerton, *How Societies Remember,* 1 and 5.

44. Wickham and Fentress, *Social Memory,* 47.

45. See especially Rudy Koshar, *Germany's Transient Pasts: Preservation and National Memory in the Twentieth Century* (Chapel Hill: University of North Carolina Press, 1998); Koshar, *From Monuments to Traces*; and James Young, *The Texture of Memory* (New Haven, CT: Yale University Press, 1993).

46. Raphael Samuel, *Theatres of Memory,* vol. 1, *Past and Present in Contemporary Culture* (London: Verso, 1994), viii; see also the classic Frances Yates, *The Art of Memory,* new ed. (London: Plimlico, 1999). When discussing images and collective memories, commentators often refer to the work of Aby Warburg, the German art historian, who assembled a laboratory of visual memory studies dedicated to documenting the transmission of ancient motifs to European art during and after the Renaissance; see E. H. Gombrich, *Aby Warburg: An Intellectual Biography* (Oxford: Phaidon, 1970). Warburg's concern with elite memory work illustrates the impressive continuity in style and technology that characterized the media of memory throughout the history of the West, but his work also makes us painfully aware that the technologies of memory experienced a radical transformation in the course of the twentieth century. The transformation was so swift that our scholarly concern for conventional media of memory (that is, art and architecture) assumed a quaint, anachronistic quality. We are only beginning to study the impact on memory caused by the first media revolution of the century represented by film and television, even as we are in the middle the second media revolution, which will force us to come to terms with Internet-based collective memories and new visual and discursive codes.

47. Sherman, *Construction of Memory in Interwar France,* 14. Naturally, images retain that suggestive power even if they are not linked to any authentic experience.

48. Zelitzer, *Remembering to Forget,* 6; Fentress and Wickham, *Social Memory,* 47–49.

49. On the narrative infrastructure of collective memory, see Raymond Vervliet and Annemarie Estor, eds., *Methods for the Study of Literature as Cultural Memory* (Amsterdam:

Rodopi, 2000); Hayden White, *Metahistory* (Baltimore: Johns Hopkins University Press, 1973).

50. Irwin-Zarecka, *Frames of Remembrance*, 4.

51. It is more modest and accurate, although less satisfying, to assume that representations speak primarily to the collective memories of their producers, not their audiences. For an excellent example for this approach that treats journalists as a specific interpretive community, see Barbie Zelizer, *Covering the Body: The Kennedy Assassination, the Media, and the Shaping of Collective Memory* (Chicago: University of Chicago Press, 1992).

52. The problem of reception in memory studies has been emphasized by Alon Confino, "Collective Memory and Cultural History: Problems of Method," *American Historical Review* 102, no. 5 (December 1997): 1386–1403, and Jan-Werner Müller, "Introduction: The Power of Memory, the Memory of Power and the Power over Memory," in Müller, ed., *Memory and Power in Post-war Europe: Studies in the Presence of the Past* (Cambridge: Cambridge University Press, 2002), 1–35; see also Samuel, *Theatres of Memory*; and Irwin-Zarecka, *Frames of Remembrance*, 14.

53. For the collective memory (or nonmemory) of the Korean War in the United States and for notable exceptions on the relative lack of scholarly interest in the history of its memory, see Paul Edwards, *To Acknowledge a War: The Korean War in American Memory* (Westport, CT: Greenwood, 2000), and especially James Kerin, "The Korean War and American Memory" (Ph.D. diss., University of Pennsylvania, 1994).

54. For the news stories about U.S. war crimes in Korea, see Sang Hun Choe, Charles J. Hanley, and Martha Mendoza (all of Associated Press), "G.I.'s Tell of a U.S. Massacre in Korean War," *New York Times*, September 30, 1999, and Michael Cobbs, "Shoot Them All: Half a Century after the Korean War, Members of the 7th Cavalry Regiment Had Hoped for Recognition; Instead They Are Having to Account for What Happened at No Gun Ri," *Washington Post Magazine*, February 6, 2000.

55. The single most widely distributed fictitious images of the war in reruns of the TV series *M.A.S.H.* are frequently not even associated with any referent such as "Korean War" in the minds of its viewers. See Kerin, *Korean War*, 245.

56. Sturken, *Tangled Memories*, 1.

57. Iriwin-Zarecka, *Frames of Remembrance*, 155; Samuel, *Theatres of Memory*, 35, and Winter and Sivan, *War and Remembrance*, 18.

58. Radio listeners, for instance, regularly forget the source of their memories of historical events; they can recall the stories, but they have no conscious recollections of listening to them on the radio. They often attach them to other sources, including television, textbooks, and relatives. See Inge Marssolek and Adelheid von Saldern, eds., *Radiozeiten: Herrschaft, Alltag, Gesellschaft (1924–1960)* (Potsdam, Germany: Verlag für Berlin-Brandenburg, 1999). All these problems and challenges are best illustrated by television, which was the most important medium of historical information in the twentieth century; see Irwin-Zarecka, *Frames of Remembrance*, 155, and Samuel, *Theatres of Memory*, 35.

59. Margaret Archer, *Culture and Agency: The Place of Culture in Social Theory*, 2nd ed. (Cambridge: Cambridge University Press, 1996); see also Francois Dosse, *The History of Structuralism*, 2 vols. (Minneapolis: University of Minnesota Press, 1997).

60. By conducting in-depth interviews, they have tried to reconstruct the evolution of attitudes and feelings about past events as a result of media consumption and personal interaction. See Michael Kohlstruck, "Der Bildungswert von Geschichtsmedien und Deutungskonflikten," in Domansky and Welzer, *Eine offene Geschichte*; Hans-Dieter Kübler, "Medienbiographien," in Manfred Brobrowsky, Wolfgang Duchkowitsch, and Hannes Haas, eds., *Medien—und Kommunikationsgeschichte* (Wien: Braumüller, 1987); and in general, Pruce Chamberlayne and Joanna Bornat, eds., *The Turn to Biographical Methods in Social Science* (London: Routledge, 2000).

61. See Lutz, *Das Geschichtsbewusstsein der Deutschen,* and Rosenzweig and Thelen, *Presence of the Past.*

62. See Werner Bergmann, *Antisemitismus in öffentlichen Konflikten* (Frankfurt, Germany: Campus, 1997).

63. See Elihu Katz, "Viewers Work," in James Hay, Lawrence Grossberg, and Ellen Wartella, eds., *The Audience and Its Landscape,* (Boulder, CO: Westview, 1996), 9–21; see also James Webster, Patricia Phalen, and Lawrence Lichty, eds., *Ratings Analysis: The Theory and Practice of Audience Research,* 2nd ed. (Mahwah, NJ: Lawrence Erlbaum, 2000).

64. In this context, psychological models again play an important role in understanding the everyday interaction between media and their audiences. See Janet Staiger, *Perverse Spectators: The Practices of Film Reception* (New York: New York University Press, 2000); Melvyn Stokes and Richard Maltby, eds., *Identifying Hollywood's Audiences: Cultural Identity and the Movies* (London: BFI, 1999); Bob Mullan, *Consuming Televison: Television and Its Audience* (Oxford: Blackwell, 1997); Tamar Liebes and James Curran, eds., *Media, Ritual, and Identity* (London: Routledge, 1998); and Michael Carlton and Silvia Schneider, eds., *Rezeptionsforschung: Theorien und Untersuchungen zum Umgang mit Massenmedien* (Opladen, Germany: Westdeutscher Verlag, 1997).

65. Steve Anderson, "Loafing in the Garden of Knowledge: History, TV and Popular Memory," *Film and History* 30, no. 1 (2000): 14–23.

66. Assmann, *Erinnerungsräume,* 249–50.

67. Radstone, "Working with Memory," 10.

68. In this respect, collective memory studies also allow us to bring together approaches to culture that consider themselves resolutely scientific and those that prefer to think of themselves as interpretive and closer to the creative arts and thus provide a perfect site for interdisciplinary explorations of culture; see Victoria Bonnell and Lynn Hunt, eds., *Beyond the Cultural Turn: New Directions in the Study of Society and Culture* (Berkeley: University of California Press, 1999), 4–5; see also Mieke Bal, ed., *The Practice of Cultural Analysis: Exposing Interdisciplinary Interpretation* (Stanford, CA: Stanford University Press, 1999).

69. Klein, "On the Emergence of Memory in Historical Discourse," 144.

70. Marius Kwint, "Introduction: The Physical Past," in Marius Kwint and Christopher Breward, ed., *Material Memories* (Oxford: Berg, 1999), 1–16. This position has a number of supporters; see Nick Merriman, introduction to Merriman, ed., *Making Early Histories in Museums* (London: Leicester University Press, 1999), 1–11, who suggests that "meaning is produced through the interaction between the display, the curatorial interpretation and what the visitor brings to the transaction" (6); see also Koshar, *From Monuments to Traces,* 10.

CHAPTER 3

1. Wolfgang Sofsky, "An der Grenze des Sozialen: Perspektiven der KZ-Forschung," in Ulrich Herbert, Karin Orth, and Christoph Dieckmann, eds., *Die nationalsozialistischen Konzentrationslager: Entwicklung und Struktur* (Göttingen, Germany: Wallstein, 1998), 1141–69.

2. Ulrich Herbert, "Der Holocaust in der Geschichtsschreibung der Bundesrepublik Deutschland," in Herbert and Olaf Groehler, *Zweierlei Untergang: Vier Beiträge über den Umgang mit der NS-Vergangenheit in den beiden deutschen Staaten* (Hamburg, Germany: Ergebnisse, 1992), 67–86; Herbert, "Vernichtungspolitik: Neue Antworten und Fragen zur Geschichte des Holocaust," in Herbert, ed., *Nationalsozialistische Vernichtungspolitik, 1939–1945: Neue Forschungen und Kontroversen* (Frankfurt, Germany: Fischer, 1998), 9–66.

3. Peter Novick, *The Holocaust in American Life* (Boston: Houghton Mifflin, 1999); Tim Cole, *Selling the Holocaust: From Auschwitz to "Schindler's List"* (New York: Routledge, 1999).

4. This applies especially to the work of Steven Katz, *The Holocaust in Historical Context,* vol. 1 (New York: Oxford University Press, 1994), who has embarked on a multivolume study

of genocide in world history with the objective of proving the historical uniqueness of the Holocaust; see Berel Lang's review, "The Second Time? The Fifth? The Question of Holocaust-Uniqueness," in Lang, *The Future of the Holocaust* (Ithaca, NY: Cornell University Press, 1999), 77–91.

5. Gavriel Rosenfeld, "The Politics of Uniqueness: Reflections on the Recent Polemical Turn in Holocaust and Genocide Studies," *Holocaust and Genocide Studies* 13, no. 1 (1999): 28–61.

6. Herbert, "Vernichtungspolitik," 21.

7. Jacobson developed this theory of binary opposition in 1956 following Saussure's definition of the syntagmatic and paradigmatic axes in language; see Roman Jacobson, "Two Aspects of Language and Two Types of Aphasic Disturbances," reprinted in Jacobson, *On Language* (Cambridge, MA: Harvard University Press, 1990), 115–33; see also Richard Bradford, *Roman Jacobson: Life, Language, Art* (New York: Routledge, 1994), 9–23; and David Lodge, *The Modes of Modern Writing* (Chicago: University of Chicago Press, 1988), 73–124.

8. Herbert, "Der Holocaust," 81.

9. For the recent debates about German historians during National Socialism, see Winfried Schulze and Otto Gerhard Oexle, eds., *Deutsche Historiker im Nationalsozialismus* (Frankfurt, Germany: Fischer, 1999); see also Wulf Kansteiner, "Mandarins in the Public Sphere: *Vergangenheitsbewältigung* and the Paradigm of Social History in the Federal Republic of Germany," *German Politics and Society* 52, no. 17 (1999): 84–120.

10. Martin Broszat, "Holocaust und die Geschichtswissenschaft," in Broszat, *Nach Hitler: Der schwierige Umgang mit unserer Geschichte* (Munich, Germany: Oldenbourg, 1986), 271–86.

11. See the sources about the history of the "Final Solution" published in the *Vierteljahrshefte für Zeitgeschichte* (VfZ): "Der Gerstein-Bericht," VfZ 1, no. 2 (1953): 177–94; "Denkschrift Himmlers über die Behandlung der Fremdvölkischen," VfZ 5, no. 2 (1957): 194–98; and "Der Generalplan Ost," VfZ 6, no. 3 (1958): 281–325; also Walter Hofer, *Der Nationalsozialismus: Dokumente, 1933–1945* (Frankfurt, Germany: Fischer, 1957), 267–312.

12. Regina Holler, *20. Juli 1944: Vermächtnis oder Alibi?* (Munich, Germany: Saur, 1994), 69–87.

13. Anne Frank, *Das Tagebuch der Anne Frank* (Frankfurt, Germany: Fischer, 1957, originally published in 1949); Eugen Kogon, *Der SS-Staat: Das System der deutschen Konzentrationslager,* 3rd ed. (Frankfurt, Germany: Verlag der Frankfurter Hefte, 1949, 1st ed. 1946).

14. See, for example, Dagmar Barnouw, *Germany 1945: Views of War and Violence* (Bloomington: Indiana University Press, 1996).

15. Norbert Frei, "Auschwitz und Holocaust: Begriff und Historiographie," in Hanno Loewy, ed., *Holocaust: Die Grenzen des Verstehens—Eine Debatte über die Besetzung der Geschichte* (Reinbek, Germany: Rowohlt, 1992), 101–9.

16. Jeffrey Herf, *Divided Memory: The Nazi Past in the Two Germanys* (Cambridge, MA: Harvard University Press, 1997).

17. Kogon, *SS-Staat,* 392.

18. Alexander Mitscherlich and Fred Mielke, eds., *Doctors of Infamy: The Story of the Nazi Medical Crimes* (New York: Schuman, 1949), 151.

19. For this trust in the redemptive power of truthful histories, see Kogon, *SS-Staat,* viii; see also Mitscherlich and Mielke, *Doctors of Infamy,* 153.

20. Herbert, Orth, and Dieckmann, *Die nationalsozialistischen Konzentrationslager,* 2: 19.

21. Kogon, *SS-Staat,* viii. Emphasis in original.

22. Mitscherlich and Mielke, *Doctors of Infamy,* 152.

23. Theodor Adorno and Max Horkheimer, *Dialectic of Enlightenment* (New York: Continuum, 1988).

24. Tobias Freimüller, "Mediziner: Operation Volkskörper," in Norbert Frei, ed., *Karrieren im Zwielicht: Hitlers Eliten nach 1945* (Frankfurt, Germany: Campus, 2001), 13–69.

25. Kogon, *SS-Staat,* vi, and Mitscherlich and Mielke, *Doctors of Infamy,* 151.

344 NOTES TO PAGES 37–42

26. Werner Bergmann, *Antisemitismus in öffentlichen Konflikten: Kollektives Lernen in der politischen Kultur der Bundesrepublik, 1949–1989* (Frankfurt, Germany: Campus, 1997), 187 ff.

27. Norbert Frei, "Der Frankfurter Auschwitz-Prozess und die deutsche Zeitgeschichtsforschung," in Fritz-Bauer-Institut, ed., *Auschwitz: Geschichte, Rezeption, Wirkung* (Frankfurt, Germany: Campus, 1996), 123–36. The expert opinions have been published in Institut für Zeitgeschichte, ed., *Gutachten des Instituts für Zeitgeschichte*, 2 vols. (Munich, Germany: Institut für Zeitgeschichte, 1958 and 1966), and Hans Buchheim, ed., *Anatomie des SS-Staates*, 2 vols. (Olten, Germany: Walter, 1965).

28. Herbert, "Der Holocaust," 75.

29. Wolfgang Scheffler, *Judenverfolgung im Dritten Reich, 1933–1945* (Berlin: Colloquium, 1960), 5.

30. Martin Broszat, ed., *Kommandant in Auschwitz: Autobiographische Aufzeichnungen von Rudolf Höss* (Stuttgart, Germany: Deutsche Verlagsanstalt, 1958), 14.

31. Buchheim, *Anatomie des SS-Staates*, 1: 5,7.

32. Ibid., 8.

33. Uwe Dietrich Adam, *Judenpolitik im Dritten Reich* (Düsseldorf, Germany: Droste, 1972), 360–61; see also H. G. Adler, *Der verwaltete Mensch: Studien zur Deportation der Juden aus Deutschland* (Tübingen, Germany: Mohr, 1974). In his voluminous study, already concluded in 1971, the survivor of Theresienstadt reconstructs every detail of the deportation of Germany's Jews in the name of historical objectivity but reserves his empathy for the demise of the liberal constitutional state under the rule of law xxix–xxx, 1038).

34. Broszat, *Kommandant*, 10, 14, 18, 20, and 21. See also Nicolas Berg, *Der Holocaust und die westdeutschen Historiker: Erforschung und Erinnerung* (Göttingen, Germany: Wallstein, 2003), 580–87.

35. Klaus-Dietmar Henke and Claudio Natoli, eds., *Mit dem Pathos der Nüchternheit: Martin Broszat, das Institut für Zeitgeschichte und die Erforschung des Nationlsozialismus* (Frankfurt, Germany: Campus, 1991).

36. Moishe Postone, "After the Holocaust: History and Identity in West Germany," in Kathy Harms, Lutz Reuter, and Volker Dürr, eds., *Coping with the Past: Germany and Austria after 1945* (Madison: University of Wisconsin Press, 1990), 233–51.

37. Heinrich August Winkler, "Die 'neue Linke' und der Faschismus: Zur Kritik neomarxistischer Theorien über den Nationasozialismus," in Winkler, *Revolution, Staat, Faschismus: Zur Revision des historischen Materialismus* (Göttingen, Germany: Vandenhoeck und Ruprecht, 1987), 65–117.

38. For a summary of the debate, see Ian Kershaw, *Der NS-Staat: Geschichtsinterpretationen und Kontroversen im Überblick*, 3rd ed. (Reinbek, Germany: Rowohlt, 1999), 39–79.

39. Wolfgang Wippermann, "Post-war German Left and Fascism," *Journal of Contemporary History* 4, no. 1 (1976): 192.

40. Georg Iggers, "Introduction," in Iggers, ed., *The Social History of Politics: Critical Perspectives in West German Historical Writing since 1945* (Leamington Spa, UK: Berg, 1985), 1–48.

41. Kershaw, *NS-Staat*, 112–47.

42. Herbert, "Vernichtungspolitik," 21.

43. Helmut Krausnick and Hans-Heinrich Wilhelm, *Die Truppe des Weltanschauungskrieges: Die Einsatzgruppen des Sicherheitsdienstes und des SD 1938–1942* (Stuttgart, Germany: Deutsche Verlagsanstalt, 1981); Eugen Kogon, ed., *Nationalsozialistische Massentötungen durch Giftgas* (Frankfurt, Germany: Fischer, 1983); Militärgeschichtliches Forschungsamt, ed., *Das Deutsche Reich und der Zweite Weltkrieg*, 6 vols. (Stuttgart, Germany: Deutsche Verlagsanstalt, 1979–1988).

44. Otto D. Kulka, "Singularity and Its Relativization: Changing Views in German Historiography on National Socialism and the 'Final Solution,'" *Yad Vashem Studies* 19 (1988): 151–86; Otto D. Kulka, "Major Trends and Tendencies in German Historiography on Na-

tional Socialism and the 'Jewish Question,'" in Yisrael Gutman and Gideon Greif, eds., *The Historiography of the Holocaust Period* (Jerusalem: Yad Vashem, 1988), 1–51.

45. For such exceptions, see Falk Pingel, *Häftlinge unter SS-Herrschaft: Widerstand, Selbstbehauptung und Vernichtung im Konzentrationslager* (Hamburg, Germany: Hoffmann und Campe, 1978), and Christian Streit, *Keine Kameraden* (Stuttgart, Germany: Deutsche Verlagsanstalt, 1978).

46. Hans Mommsen, "Holocaust und die Deutsche Geschichtswissenschaft," in Gutman and Greif, *Historiography*, 79–97; see also, less equivocally, Broszat, "Holocaust," 271.

47. Konrad Kwiet, "Zur historiographischen Behandlung der Judenverfolgung im Dritten Reich," *Militärgeschichtliche Mitteilungen* 27, no. 1 (1980): 149–92.

48. Kershaw, *NS-Staat*, 148–206, and Michael Marrus, *The Holocaust in History* (New York: Meridian, 1987), 31–46.

49. Martin Broszat, "Hitler und die Genesis der 'Endlösung': Aus Anlass der Thesen von David Irving," in Broszat, *Nach Hitler*, 187–229 (originally published in 1977); Hans Mommsen, "Die Realisierung des Utopischen: Die 'Endlösung der Judenfrage' im 'Dritten Reich,'" in Mommsen, *Der Nationalsozialismus und die deutsche Gesellschaft* (Reinbek, Germany: Rowohlt, 1991, originally published in 1983), 184–232; see also Adam, *Judenpolitik*.

50. Eberhard Jäckel and Jürgen Rohwer, *Der Mord an den Juden im Zweiten Weltkrieg* (Frankfurt, Germany: Fischer, 1987), 242.

51. Yehuda Bauer, "Auschwitz," ibid., 164–73.

52. Rosenfeld, "Politics of Uniqueness," 35.

53. Yehuda Bauer, "A Past That Will Not Go Away," in Michael Berenbaum and Abraham Peck, eds., *The Holocaust and History: The Unknown, the Disputed, and the Reexamined* (Bloomington: Indiana University Press, 1998), 12–22; see also Yehuda Bauer, *A History of the Holocaust* (New York: Watts, 1982), 332.

54. Saul Friedlander, "The 'Final Solution': On the Unease in Historical Interpretation," in Friedlander, *Memory, History, and the Extermination of the Jews of Europe* (Bloomington: Indiana University Press, 1993), 102–16; see also Friedlander, "Some Aspects of the Historical Significance of the Holocaust," *Jerusalem Quarterly* 1, no. 1 (1976): 36–59.

55. Steven Aschheim, "On Saul Friedlander," *History and Memory* 9, nos. 1 and 2 (1997): 11–46.

56. Mommsen, "Realisierung des Utopischen," 184; Mommsen, "Der Weg zum Völkermord an den europäischen Juden," in Bernd Faulenbach and Helmut Schütte, eds., *Deutschland, Israel und der Holocaust: Zur Gegenwartsbedeutung der Vergangenheit* (Essen, Germany: Klartext, 1998), 19–30; Eberhard Jäckel, "Die Entschlussbildung als historisches Problem," in Jäckel and Rohwer, *Mord an den Juden*, 9–17; Jäckel, "The Holocaust: Where We Are, Where We Need to Go," in Berenbaum and Peck, *Holocaust and History*, 23–29.

57. Wolfgang Benz, *Der Holocaust* (Munich, Germany: Beck, 1995), 7; see also Benz, *Dimension des Völkermords: Die Zahl der jüdischen Opfer des Nationalsozialismus* (Munich, Germany: Oldenbourg, 1991), 8, and Peter Longerich, *Politik der Vernichtung: Eine Gesamtdarstellung der nationalsozialistischen Judenverfolgung* (Munich, Germany: Piper, 1998), 17.

58. Andreas Hillgruber, "Der geschichtliche Ort der Judenvernichtung," in Jäckel and Rohwer, *Mord an den Juden*, 211–24; see also Hillgruber, *Zweierlei Untergang*. Martin Broszat embraced the idea of the Holocaust's metahistorical quality in Stuttgart; see Jäckel and Rohwer, *Mord an den Juden*, 64; however, he repeatedly voiced doubts before and after; see Broszat, "Genesis," 195; Broszat, "Plädoyer," 159; and Christian Meier, "Der Historiker Martin Broszat," in Henke and Natoli, *Pathos der Nüchternheit*, 11–38.

59. Rudolf Augstein et al., *Historikerstreit: Die Dokumentation der Kontroverse um die Einzigartigkeit der nationalsozialistischen Judenvernichtung* (Munich, Germany: Piper, 1987), 165. For a contextualization of the Historians' Debate, see chapter 4; for an interpretation of the Historians' Debate from a psychoanalytical perspective, see Dominick LaCapra, *Representing the Holocaust:*

History, Theory, Trauma (Ithaca, NY: Cornell University Press, 1994), 43–67, and LaCapra, *History and Memory after Auschwitz* (Ithaca, NY: Cornell University Press, 1998), 43–72.

60. Augstein et al., *Historikerstreit*, 73.

61. Ibid., 71.

62. Nicolas Berg, "'Auschwitz' und die Geschichtswissenschaft: Überlegungen zu Kontroversen der letzten Jahre," in Berg, Jess Jochimsen, and Bernd Stiegler, eds., *Shoah: Formen der Erinnerung* (Munich, Germany: Fink, 1996), 31–52.

63. See, for example, Eberhard Jäckel, "Die elende Praxis der Untersteller: Das Einmalige der nationalisozialistischen Verbrechen lässt sich nicht leugnen," in Rudolf Augstein et al., *Historikerstreit: Die Dokumentation der Kontroverse um die Einzigartigkeit der nationalsozialistischen Judenvernichtung* (Munich, Germany: Piper, 1987), 115–22, and Hans-Ulrich Wehler, *Entsorgung der deutschen Vergangenheit: Ein polemischer Essay zum "Historikerstreit"* (Munich, Germany: Beck, 1988), 100.

64. Norbert Frei, "Farewell to the Era of Contemporaries: National Socialism and Its Historical Examination en Route into History," *History and Memory* 9, nos. 1–2 (1997): 59–79.

65. Not surprisingly, this new social history was vigorously criticized by practitioners of the "old" social history for its methodological naïveté and lack of theoretical foundations; see, Franz Josef Brüggemeier and Jürgen Kocka, eds., *Geschichte von unten—Geschichte von innen: Kontroversen um die Alltagsgeschichte* (Hagen, Germany: Fernuniversität, 1985).

66. Monika Richarz, *Jüdisches Leben in Deutschland: Zeugnisse zur Sozialgeschichte 1918–1945*, vol. 3 (Stuttgart, Germany: Deutsche Verlagsanstalt, 1982), 7, 40.

67. Dan Diner, "Zwischen Aporie und Apologie: Über Grenzen der Historisierbarkeit des Nationalsozialismus," in Diner, ed., *Ist der Nationalsozialismus Geschichte? Zur Historisierung und Historikerstreit* (Frankfurt, Germany: Fischer, 1987), 62–73; see also Diner, "Perspektivenwahl und Geschichtserfahrung: Bedarf es einer besonderen Historik des Nationalsozialismus?" in Walter Pehle, ed., *Der historische Ort des Nationalsozialismus* (Frankfurt, Germany: Fischer, 1990), 94–113, and Diner, "Gedächtnis und Methode: Über den Holocaust in der Geschichtsschreibung," in Fritz-Bauer-Institut, *Auschwitz*, 11–22.

68. Walter Manoschek, *"Serbien ist judenfrei:" Militärische Besatzungspolitik und Judenvernichtung in Serbien 1941/42* (Munich, Germany: Oldenbourg, 1993); Dieter Pohl, *Von der "Judenpolitik" zum Massenmord: Der Distrikt Lublin des Generalgouvernements, 1939–1944* (Frankfurt, Germany: Lang, 1993); Thomas Sandkühler, *"Endlösung in Galizien": Der Judenmord in Ostpolen und die Rettungsinitiativen von Berthold Beitz, 1941–1944* (Bonn, Germany: Dietz, 1996); Christian Gerlach, *Krieg, Ernährung, Völkermord: Forschungen zur deutschen Vernichtungpolitik im Zweiten Weltkrieg* (Hamburg, Germany: Hamburger Edition, 1998); and especially Gerlach, *Kalkulierte Morde: Die deutsche Wirtschafts—und Vernichtungspolitik in Weissrussland 1941 bis 1944* (Hamburg, Germany: Hamburger Edition, 1999).

69. Members of the institute mounted a controversial exhibit about the involvement of the Wehrmacht in ethnic cleansing and genocide, which has been more successful in undermining the persistent myth of the chivalrous German army than twenty years of scholarship; see Hamburger Institut für Sozialforschung, ed., *Vernichtungskrieg: Verbrechen der Wehrmacht 1941–1944* (Hamburg, Germany: Hamburger Edition, 1995).

70. Wolfgang Schneider, *Vernichtungspolitik: Eine Debatte über den Zusammenhang von Sozialpolitik und Genozid im nationalsozialistischen Deutschland* (Hamburg, Germany: Junius, 1991); see also Norbert Frei, "Wie modern war der Nationalsozialismus?" *Geschichte und Gesellschaft* 19, no. 3 (1993): 367–87; Axel Schmidt, "NS-Regime, Modernisierung und Moderne: Anmerkungen zur Hochkonjuktur einer andauernden Diskussion," *Tel Aviver Jahrbuch für deutsche Geschichte* 23 (1994): 3–22; and Michael Burleigh, *Ethics and Extermination: Reflections on Nazi Genocide* (Cambridge: Cambridge University Press, 1997), 169–82.

71. Ulrich Herbert, *Best: Biographische Studien über Radikalismus, Weltanschauung und Vernunft, 1903–1989* (Bonn, Germany: Dietz, 1996).

72. Herbert, "Vernichtungspolitik," 27.

73. Ibid., 65.

74. Ibid.

75. Götz Aly, "Wider das Bewältigungs-Kleinklein," in Loewy, *Holocaust: Grenzen des Verstehens*, 42–51; see also Götz Aly and Susanne Heim, "Editorial," in Aly et al., eds., *Sozialpolitik und Judenvernichtung: Gibt es eine Ökonomie der Endlösung* (Berlin: Rotbuch, 1987), 7–9; and Götz Aly and Susanne Heim, *Vordenker der Vernichtung: Auschwitz und die deutschen Pläne für eine neue europäische Ordnung* (Hamburg, Germany: Hoffmann and Campe, 1991), 11.

76. Götz Aly, *"Final Solution": Nazi Population Policy and the Murder of the European Jews* (New York: Oxford University Press, 1999), 245, 253.

77. Götz Aly, "The Planning Intelligentsia and the 'Final Solution,'" in Michael Burleigh, ed., *Confronting the Nazi Past: New Debates on Modern German History* (New York: St. Martin's Press, 1996), 140–53; see also Aly and Heim, *Vordenker der Vernichtung*, 492.

78. On the Goldhagen debate, see especially Johannes Heil and Rainer Erb, eds., *Geschichtswissenschaft und Öffentlichkeit: Der Streit um Daniel J. Goldhagen* (Frankfurt, Germany: Fischer, 1998), and Geoff Eley, ed., *The "Goldhagen Effect": History, Memory, Nazism—Facing the German Past* (Ann Arbor: Michigan University Press, 2000).

79. See Winfried Schulze and Otto Gerhard Oexle, eds., *Deutsche Historiker im Nationalsozialismus* (Frankfurt, Germany: Fischer Taschenbuch, 1999).

80. See, for example, Ludolf Herbst, *Das nationalsozialistische Deutschland, 1933–1945* (Frankfurt, Germany: Suhrkamp, 1996), esp. 374 and 397.

81. The symbolic, generational change of the guard was theatrically enacted at the Historikertag of 1998, when the new generation did not directly attack their just retired teachers but instead exposed the collaborative behavior of the teachers' teachers during the Third Reich; see Kansteiner, "Mandarins in the Public Sphere," 102–9.

82. Sofsky, "An der Grenze des Sozialen," 1154.

CHAPTER 4

1. On the Jenninger affair, see Armin Laschet and Heinz Malangré, eds., *Philip Jenninger: Rede und Reaktion* (Aachen, Germany: Einhard, 1989), and Peter Reichel, *Politik mit der Erinnerung: Gedächtnisorte im Streit um die nationalsozialistische Vergangenheit* (Munich, Germany: Hanser, 1995), 313–20.

2. Weizsäcker's speech and the favorable reactions have been documented in Ulrich Gill and Winfried Steffani, eds., *Eine Rede und ihre Wirkung: Die Rede des Bundespräsidenten Richard von Weizsäcker vom 8. Mai 1985* (Berlin: Rainer Röll, 1986); see also chapter 11.

3. See Lutz Niethammer, "Jenninger: Vorzeitiges Exposé zur Erforschung eines ungewöhnlich schnellen Rücktritts," *Babylon* 5 (June 1989): 40–46.

4. Ibid., 44.

5. Elisabeth Domansky, "'Kristallnacht,' the Holocaust and German Unity: The Meaning of November 9 as an Anniversary in Germany," *History and Memory* 4 (Spring–Summer 1992): 60–94.

6. On Jenninger's poor performance, see the entertaining critique by Klaus Theweleit, "Kann es denn Zeitungen geben 'nach Auschwitz'?" *Taz hoch 10: Zehn Jahre Pressefreiheit* (special tenth-anniversary edition of the leftist daily *die tageszeitung* in 1989), 16–23, and Katherina Oehler, "Glanz und Elend der öffentlichen Erinnerung: Die Rhetorik des Historischen in Richard von Weizsäckers Rede zum 8. Mai und Philipp Jenningers Rede zum 9. November," *Jahrbuch für Geschichtsdidaktik* 3 (1991–1992): 121–35.

7. On the definition of the Hitler Youth generation, see note 83. For an interpretation of Jenninger's speech as symptomatic for the return of the repressed in West Germany's political

culture, see Hans-Jürgen Wirth, "Der Fall Jenninger und unsere Schwierigkeiten mit der deutschen Vergangenheit," *Psychosozial* 11 (1988–1989): 55–61.

8. Martin Broszat, "A Plea for the Historicization of National Socialism," in Peter Baldwin, ed., *Reworking the Past: Hitler, the Holocaust, and the Historians' Debate* (Boston: Beacon, 1990), 77–87; Saul Friedlander, "Some Reflections on the Historicization of National Socialism," in Baldwin, ed., *Reworking the Past,* 88–101; and Martin Broszat and Saul Friedlander, "A Controversy about the Historicization of National Socialism," in Baldwin, ed., *Reworking the Past,* 102–34; see also chapter 5.

9. The best introductions and analyses of the Historians' Debate in English have been supplied by Charles Maier, *The Unmasterable Past: History, Holocaust, and German National Identity* (Cambridge, MA: Harvard University Press, 1988); Richard Evans, *In Hitler's Shadow: West German Historians and the Attempt to Escape from the Nazi Past* (New York: Pantheon, 1989); and Peter Baldwin, "The Historikerstreit in Context," in Baldwin, ed., *Reworking the Past,* 3–37. For a succinct introduction, see Ulrich Herbert, "Der Historikerstreit: Politische, wissenschaftliche, biographische Aspekte," in Martin Sabrow, Ralph Jessen, and Klaus Grosse Kracht, eds., *Zeitgeschichte als Streitgeschichte: Grosse Kontroversen seit 1945* (Munich, Germany: Beck, 2003), 94–113.

10. The concept of historical culture, *Geschichtskultur,* has been developed by Jörn Rüsen; see Rüsen, "Geschichtskultur als Forschungsproblem," *Jahrbuch für Geschichtsdidaktik,* 3 (1991–1992): 39–50, and Rüsen, "Was ist Geschichtskultur? Überlegungen zu einer neuen Art, über Geschichte nachzudenken," in Klaus Füßmann, Heinrich Theodor Grütter, and Jörn Rüsen, eds., *Historische Faszination: Geschichtskultur heute* (Cologne, Germany: Böhlau, 1994), 3–26.

11. The most complete bibliography of the Historians' Debate has been compiled by Helmut Donat, Diether Koch, and Martin Rohrkrämer, "Bibliographie zum Historikerstreit," in Helmut Donat and Lothar Wieland, eds., *"Auschwitz erst möglich gemacht?" Überlegungen zur jüngsten konservativen Geschichtsbewältigung* (Bremen, Germany: Donat, 1991), 150–214.

12. The core texts by the main protagonists, which represent only a fraction of all the texts published during the Historians' Debate, have been assembled in the documentation Rudolf Augstein et al., *Historikerstreit: Die Dokumentation der Kontroverse um die Einzigartigkeit der nationalsozialistischen Judenvernichtung* (Munich: Piper, 1987); a bad translation of the volume was published under the title Rudolf Augstein et al., *Forever in the Shadow of Hitler: The Dispute about the Germans' Understanding of History* (Atlantic Highlands: Humanities Press, 1993); a different, unauthorized collection of shortened versions of texts dating from the first phases of the debate has been edited, with commentary, by Reinhard Kühnl, *Streit ums Geschichtsbild: Die "Historikerdebatte": Dokumentation, Darstellung und Kritik* (Cologne, Germany: Pahl-Rugenstein, 1987); for a collection of translations of some of the original contributions, see also Baldwin, *Reworking the Past*; the events of the Historians' Debate have been commented on in a number of edited volumes that take the perspective of the liberal historians: Dan Diner, ed., *Ist der Nationalsozialismus Geschichte? Zu Historikerstreit und Historisierung* (Frankfurt, Germany: Fischer, 1987); Donat and Wieland, *"Auschwitz"*; Gernot Erler, ed., *Geschichtswende? Entsorgungsversuche zur deutschen Geschichte* (Freiburg, Germany: Dreisam, 1987); Wieland Eschenhagen, ed., *Die neue deutsche Ideologie* (Darmstadt, Germany: Luchterhand, 1988); Hilmar Hoffmann, ed., *Gegen den Versuch, Vergangenheit zu verbiegen* (Frankfurt, Germany: Athenäum, 1987; Landeszentrale für politische Bildung Nordrhein-Westfalen, ed., *Streitfall deutsche Geschichte: Geschichts—und Gegenwartsbewußtsein in den 80er Jahren* (Essen, Germany: Hobbing, 1988); and Niedersächsische Landeszentrale für politische Bildung, ed., *Von der Verdrängung zur Bagatellisierung: Aspekte des sogenannten Historikerstreits* (Hannover, Germany: Saade, 1988). The perspective of the liberal historians was also further developed in two monographs: Hans Mommsen, *Auf der Suche nach historischer Normalität: Beiträge zum Geschichtsbildstreit in der Bundesrepublik* (Berlin: Argon, 1987), and especially Hans-Ulrich

Wehler, *Entsorgung der deutschen Vergangenheit: Ein polemischer Essay zum Historikerstreit* (Munich, Germany: Beck, 1988). In addition to the collection edited by Kühnl mentioned earlier, four other volumes offer a critique of the Historians' Debate from a position left of the Social-Democratic/liberal perspective: Heide Gerstenberger and Dorothea Schmidt, eds., *Normalität oder Normalisierung: Geschichtswerkstätten und Faschismusanalyse* (Münster, Germany: Westfälisches Dampfboot, 1987); Wolfgang Fritz Haug, *Vom hilflosen Faschismus zur Gnade der späten Geburt*, 2nd ed. (Hamburg, Germany: Argument, 1987); Eike Hennig, *Zum Historikersteit: Was heißt und zu welchem Ende studiert man Faschismus?* (Frankfurt, Germany: Athenäum, 1988; and Heinrich Senfft, *Kein Abschied von Hitler: Ein Blick hinter die Fassaden des "Historikerstreits"* (Cologne, Germany: Volksblatt, 1990). On the conservative side, the only collaborative effort in response to the Historians' Debate consisted of a high-power conference, the proceedings of which have been published by Klaus Hildebrand, ed., *Wem gehört die deutsche Geschichte? Deutschlands Weg vom alten Europa in die Europäische Moderne* (Cologne, Germany: Bachem, 1987). In addition, Ernst Nolte felt the need to further develop and defend his position in two volumes of essays: Nolte, *Das Vergehen der Vergangenheit: Antwort an meine Kritiker im sogenannten Historikerstreit* (Berlin: Ullstein, 1987), and Nolte, *Lehrstück oder Tragödie: Beiträge zur Interpretation der Geschichte des 20. Jahrhunderts* (Cologne, Germany: Böhlau, 1991). Nolte provided these collections in addition to his voluminous study on the issues under debate, which he concluded prior to but which was only published in the midst of the Historians' Debate, Nolte, *Der Europäische Bürgerkrieg 1917–1945: Nationalsozialismus und Bolschewismus* (Berlin: Propyläen, 1987). The only joint endeavor of critics and participants from both sides of the political spectrum has been documented in Hans-Hermann Wiese, ed., *Die Gegenwart der Vergangenheit: Historikerstreit und Erinnerungsarbeit* (Bad Segeberg, Germany: Wäser, 1989). There have been two unsuccessful attempts at reconciliation, advanced by Christian Meier, *Vierzig Jahre nach Auschwitz: Deutsche Geschichtserinnerung heute*, 2nd ed. (Munich, Germany: Beck, 1990), and Imanuel Geiss, *Die Habermas-Kontroverse: Ein deutscher Streit* (Berlin: Siedler, 1988); see also Geiss, *Der Hysterikerstreit: Ein unpolemischer Essay* (Bonn, Germany: Bouvier, 1992). The German radical nationalistic right took note of the debate in two publications: Rolf Kosiek, *Historikerstreit und Geschichtsrevision*, 2nd ed. (Tübingen, Germany: Grabert, 1988), and Dirk Kunert, *Deutschland im Krieg der Kontinente: Anmerkungen zum Historikerstreit* (Kiel, Germany: Arndt, 1987). Among the numerous survey and review articles published in scholarly journals that summarize and comment on the debate, five stand out in retrospect. For the liberal side: Bernd Faulenbach, "Der Streit um die Gegenwartsbedeutung der NS-Vergangenheit: Ein Literaturbericht," *Archiv für Sozialgeschichte* 28 (1988): 607–33; Bernd Faulenbach, "Die Bedeutung der NS-Vergangenheit für das deutsche Selbstverständnis: Weitere Beiträge zum 'Historikerstreit' und zur Frage der deutschen Identität," *Archiv für Sozialgeschichte* 30 (1990): 532–74; Peter Steinbach, "Der 'Historikerstreit': Ein verräterisches Ereignis," *Politische Vierteljahresschrift-Literatur* 28, no. 2 (1987): 159–69; and Detlev Peukert, "Wer gewann den Historikerstreit? Keine Bilanz," in Peter Glotz et al., eds., *Vernunft riskieren: Klaus von Dohnanyi zum 60. Geburtstag* (Hamburg, Germany: Christians, 1988), 38–50; and for the conservative side: Eckhard Jesse, "'Vergangenheitsbewältigung' in der Bundesrepublik Deutschland," *Der Staat* 26, no. 4 (1987): 539–65, and Jesse, "Der sogenannte 'Historikerstreit': Ein deutscher Streit," in Thomas Gauly, ed., *Die Last der Deutschen: Kontroversen zur deutschen Identität* (Cologne, Germany: Wissenschaft und Politik, 1988), 9–54.

13. Walter H. Pehle,"Vorbemerkungen des Herausgebers," in Pehle, ed., *Der historische Ort des Nationalsozialismus: Annäherungen* (Frankfurt, Germany: Fischer, 1990), 7.

14. According to information provided by the historical archives of the ARD and the ZDF, neither of the two public television stations of the Federal Republic dedicated a whole show to the issues of the debate in their national programs. Coverage was limited to short clips in news magazines and to two productions in the regional channels of the ARD network.

15. Hennig, *Zum Historikerstreit*, 35.

16. Nolte's Bürgerkrieg drew heavy fire when it was published at the end of 1987 but did not introduce any new aspects into the debate; see the reviews by Hans Mommsen, "Das Ressentiment als Wissenschaft," *Geschichte und Gesellschaft* 14, no. 4 (1988): 495–512, and Wolfgang Schieder, "Der Nationalsozialismus im Fehlurteil philosophischer Geschichtsschreibung," *Geschichte und Gesellschaft* 15, no. 1 (1989): 88–114.

17. This, of course, is also true for Habermas's work, which was never considered during the debate, although the theme of his critique is developed straight from his philosophical writings.

18. Throughout the chapter and the book, the term *liberal* designates a political position left of center but within the political mainstream. In West German party politics, this position has been occupied by the Social Democratic Party. Thus, applied to intellectuals, the term covers members of the Social Democratic Party as well as persons of similar convictions who are not members. The term is not used in the sense of the German word *liberal*, which is commonly associated with the Free Democratic Party. The Free Democrats formed a coalition with the Social Democrats as junior partners from 1969 through 1982 and are therefore historically linked to the liberal reform era in West German politics. However, since they switched sides in 1982 and entered a coalition with the conservative Christian Union, they have gradually evolved into a special interest group for (West) German economic elites.

19. See, for the most overt declaration of victory, Wehler, *Entsorgung*, 197–98.

20. On the various recent interpretations of National Socialism as a specifically modern event, see chapter 5.

21. That applies in particular to Immanuel Geiss, who was ridiculed by the Left for his self-appointed role as arbiter, most vehemently by Volker Ulrich, "Der Schlichter als Provokateur — Immanuel Geiss und der 'Historikerstreit,'" in Donat and Wieland, *"Auschwitz,"* 140–49; Geiss revisited the site of the Historians' Debate in print in 1993, see Geiss, *Hysterikerstreit*, and Geiss, *Habermas-Kontroverse*.

22. The best critique of Nolte's comparisons and the best exploration of the methodological problems of comparative history raised by the Historians' Debate has been provided by Charles Maier, "A Holocaust Like the Others? Problems of Comparative History," in Maier, *Unmasterable Past*, 66–99; see also Herbert Jäger, "Über die Vergleichbarkeit staatlicher Großverbrechen: Der Historikerstreit aus kriminologischer Sicht," *Merkur* 43, no. 6 (1989): 499–513; Hans-Heinrich Nolte, "Inwieweit sind russisch-sowjetische und deutsche Massenmorde vergleichbar?," in Niedersächsische Landeszentrale, *Verdrängung*, 49–58.

23. For a critique and contextualization of Andreas Hillgruber's *Zweierlei Untergang: Die Zerschlagung des Deutschen Reiches und das Ende des europäischen Judentums* (Berlin: Siedler, 1986), see Wehler, *Entsorgung*, 47–68; Adelheid von Saldern, "Hillgrubers 'Zweierlei Untergang'—der Untergang historischer Erfahrungsanalyse," in Gerstenberger and Schmidt, *Normalität*, 160–69; and Perry Anderson, "On Emplotment: Two Kinds of Ruin," in Saul Friedlander, ed., *Probing the Limits of Representation: Nazism and the "Final Solution"* (Cambridge, MA: Harvard University Press, 1992).

24. On the Bitburg affair, see especially Geoffrey Hartman, ed., *Bitburg in Moral and Political Perspective* (Bloomington: Indiana University Press, 1986), and Hajo Funke, "Bergen-Belsen, Bitburg, Hambach: Bericht über eine negative Katharsis," in Funke, ed., *Von der Gnade der geschenkten Nation* (Berlin: Rotbuch, 1988), 20–34.

25. The interdependence between historical writing and the question of national identity in the Federal Republic has been covered by: Faulenbach, "Bedeutung," 627–33; Meier, *Vierzig Jahre*, 50–76; Hennig, *Historikerstreit*, 108–15; and Wehler, *Entsorgung*, 171–74. Stürmer's position is most clearly developed in two collections of essays: Stürmer, *Dissonanzen des Fortschritts: Essays über Geschichte und Politik in Deutschland* (Munich, Germany: Piper, 1986), and Stürmer, *Deutsche Fragen oder die Suche nach der Staatsräson: Historisch-politische Kolumnen* (Munich, Germany: Piper, 1988).

26. On the renaissance of geopolitical explanatory models, see especially Wehler, *Entsorgung*, 174–89.

27. For a summary and evaluation of this aspect of the debate, see, for instance, Bianka Pietrow, "Deutschland im Juni 1941—Ein Opfer sowjetischer Aggression?" *Geschichte und Gesellschaft* 14, no. 1 (1988): 116–35.

28. A bibliography of the debate about the two museum projects is integrated in the general bibliography of the Historians' Debate, see Donat, Koch, and Rohkrämer, "Bibliographie." The debate is documented in Christoph Stölzl, ed., *Deutsches Historisches Museum: Ideen, Kontroversen, Perspektiven* (Berlin: Propyläen, 1988), and Geschichtswerkstatt Berlin, ed., *Die Nation als Austellungsstück: Planungen, Kritik und Utopien zu den Museumsgründungen in Bonn und Berlin* (Hamburg, Germany: VSA, 1987); see also chapter 11.

29. For an excellent example of this mentality, see Wehler, *Entsorgung*, 189–96.

30. When the Social Democratic/Free Democratic coalition fell apart in 1982, the Free Democrats switched sides and, literally overnight, came to an agreement with the oppositional Christian Democrats. As a result, Helmut Kohl replaced Helmut Schmidt as chancellor.

31. On the transformation of the cultural and political spheres of the Federal Republic, initiated by the student movement of 1968 but institutionalized by the subsequent expansion of the civil service sector, the educational reforms of the 1970s, and extensive state subsidies for free-lance cultural and educational projects, see Hermann Glaser, *Die Kulturgeschichte der Bundesrepublik Deutschland III: Zwischen Protest und Anpassung, 1968–1989* (Frankfurt, Germany: Fischer, 1990), 289–98.

32. The journal *Geschichte und Gesellschaft*, founded in 1975, marks the institutionalization of social history in the Federal Republic, represented especially by a number of historians at the University of Bielefeld.

33. To name just four examples: Eberhard Jäckel, Stuttgart, 1967; Hans Mommsen, Bochum, 1968; Wolfgang Mommsen, Düsseldorf, 1968; and Hans-Ulrich Wehler, Bielefeld, 1971; see also the statistics provided by Wolfgang Weber, *Priester der Klio: Historisch-sozialwissenschaftliche Studien zur Herkunft und Karriere deutscher Historiker und zur Geschichte der Geschichtswissenschaft, 1800–1970* (Frankfurt, Germany: Lang, 1984), 536–77.

34. Allegations of political conspiracy abound in the texts of the Historians' Debate; Hillgruber's statement that Habermas's critique "amounts to nothing but the unleashing of a campaign of character assassination," which was quickly implemented by Habermas's "fellow-travelers and disciples," represents one of the most blunt accusations of this kind; see Andreas Hillgruber, "Jürgen Habermas, Karl-Heinz Janßen, and the Enlightenment in the Year 1986," in Augstein et al., *Forever in the Shadow*, 222–36, 223.

35. For comments from the "independent" Left, see Senfft, *Kein Abschied*; Haug, *Antifaschismus*; and Hennig, *Historikerstreit.*36. Hillgruber, "Habermas."

37. This continuity in the interpretation of Nazism by conservative politicians is very well illustrated in Reichel, *Politik*, see also chapters 9 and 10.

38. See Nolte, "Between Historical Legend and Revisionism," in Augstein et al., *Forever in the Shadow*, 8–9; and Nolte, "The Past That Will Not Pass," in Augstein et al., *Forever in the Shadow*, 21–22.

39. See, for instance, Kosiek, *Historikerstreit*, 49–53; for Nolte's ambivalent relationship to positions espoused by neo-Nazis and revisionists, see Nolte, *Streitpunkte: Heutige und künftige Kontroversen um den Nationalsozialismus* (Berlin: Propyläen, 1993), 304–19.

40. See, in particular, Uwe Backes, Eckhard Jesse, and Rainer Zitelmann, eds., *Die Schatten der Vergangenheit: Impulse zur Historisierung des Nationalsozialismus* (Berlin: Propyläen, 1990).

41. See Jürgen Habermas, "A Kind of Settlement of Damages," in Augstein et al., *Forever in the Shadow*, 34–44.

42. On Stürmer's motives and background, see Volker Berghahn, "Geschichtswissenschaft und Große Politik," *Aus Politik und Zeitgeschichte* 11 (March 1987): 25–37, and Hans-Jürgen

Puhle, "Die neue Ruhelosigkeit: Michael Stürmers nationalpolitischer Revisionismus," *Geschichte und Gesellschaft* 13, no. 3 (1987): 382–99.

43. Georg G. Iggers, *Geschichtswissenschaft im 20. Jahrhundert* (Göttingen, Germany: Vandenhoek und Ruprecht, 1993), 75.

44. Although Alltagsgeschichte has been widely discussed as a historiographical paradigm, its history as a social and historical phenomenon still remains to be written; for the astonishing impact of Alltagsgeschichte, see Volker Ullrich, "Entdeckungsreise in den historischen Alltag: Versuch einer Annäherung an die 'neue Geschichtsbewegung,'" *Geschichte in Wissenschaft und Unterricht* 36, no. 16 (1985): 403–15; Gerhard Paul and Bernhard Schoßig, "Geschichte und Heimat," in Paul and Schoßig, ed., *Die andere Geschichte*, 15–30; and Detlev Peukert, "Das 'Dritte Reich' aus der Alltagsperspektive," *Archiv für Sozialgeschichte* 26 (1986).

45. On the intellectual origins and the development of Alltagsgeschichte, see Geoff Eley, "Labor History, Social History, Alltagsgeschichte: Experience, Culture, and the Politics of the Everyday—A New Direction for German Social History?" *Journal of Modern History* 61, no. 1 (1989): 297–343; Iggers, *Geschichtswissenschaft*, 73–87; Alf Lüdke, "Einleitung: Was ist und wer treibt Alltagsgeschichte?" in Lüdtke, ed., *Alltagsgeschichte: Zur Rekonstruktion historischer Erfahrungen und Lebensweisen* (Frankfurt, Germany: Campus, 1989), 9–47; and Winfried Schulze, ed., *Sozialgeschichte, Alltagsgeschichte, Mikro-Historie* (Göttingen, Germany: Vandenhoek und Ruprecht, 1994).

46. The most theoretically precise historian of Alltagsgeschichte is Alf Lüdtke, whose important contributions have been assembled in Lüdtke, *Eigensinn: Fabrikalltag, Arbeitererfahrungen und Politik vom Kaiserreich bis in den Faschismus* (Hamburg, Germany: Ergebnisse, 1993).

47. On the origins, further developments, and demise of the history workshops in Germany, see Alfred Georg Frei, "Geschichtswerkstätten als Zukunftswerkstätten," in Gerhard Paul and Bernhard Schossig, eds., *Die andere Geschichte: Geschichte von unten, Spurensicherung, ökologische Geschichte, Geschichtswerkstätten* (Cologne, Germany: Bund, 1986), 258–80, and Frei, "Die Geschichtswerkstätten in der Krise," in Berliner Geschichtswerkstatt, ed., *Alltagskultur, Subjektivität und Geschichte* (Münster: Westfälisches Dampfboot, 1994), 315–27.

48. Due to the exceedingly long training period for academic personnel in Germany, the expansion of the university system in the 1960s had provided secure employment for the historians of the Hitler Youth generation and not, as in other professions, for the first postwar generation. For the figures illustrating the expansion in the 1960s, see Udo Wengst, "Geschichtswissenschaft und 'Vergangenheitsbewältigung' in Deutschland," *Geschichte und Gesellschaft* 46 (1995): 189–205.

49. Eley, "Labor History," 298.

50. See chapters 6 and 7. The interpretation of Alltagsgeschichte on West German television is based on research conducted in the archives of the ZDF, the second West German public television station, which provided approximately 50 percent of the national television programming between the early 1970s and the mid-1980s. In the history of the program of the ZDF, four phases of Alltagsgeschichte stand out in retrospect: an early "trial" phase between 1971 and 1972, two ambitious and successful phases between 1978 and 1979 and 1982 and 1984, and another series of successful shows between 1987 and 1988.

51. For an assessment of the contribution of the history workshops to the study of fascism, see Gerstenberger and Schmidt, *Normalität*. Among the numerous discussions about the problems and virtues of Alltagsgeschichte, see, in particular, the following documentations: Franz Brüggemeier and Jürgen Kocka, eds., *"Geschichte von unten—Geschichte von innen": Kontroversen um die Alltagsgeschichte* (Hagen, Germany: Fernuniversität, 1985), and Institut für Zeitgeschichte, ed., *Alltagsgeschichte der NS-Zeit: Neue Perspektiven oder Trivialisierung* (Munich, Germany: Oldenbourg, 1984).

52. For the media events *Holocaust* and *Heimat*, which have been studied closely, see especially Peter Märtesheimer and Ivo Frenzel, eds., *Im Kreuzfeuer: Der Fernsehfilm Holocaust—Eine Nation ist betroffen* (Frankfurt, Germany: Fischer, 1979); Yizhak Ahren, ed., *Das Lehrstück "Holo-*

caust": Wirkungen und Nachwirkungen eines Medienereignisses (Opladen: Westdeutscher Verlag, 1982); the special issue on *Heimat* of the *New German Critique* 36 (1985); and Anton Kaes, *From Hitler to "Heimat": The Return of History as Film* (Cambridge, MA: Harvard University Press, 1989), 161–92.

53. For Lübbe's concepts of historical and moral identity, see chapters 12 and 14–17 in Lübbe, *Geschichtsbegriff und Geschichtsinteresse* (Basel, Switzerland: Schwabe, 1977); Lübbe, "Handlungssinn und Lebenssinn: Über die Reichweite von Rationalitätspostulaten," in Lübbe, ed., *Handlungssinn und Lebenssinn: Zum Problem der Rationalität im Kontext des Handelns* (Freiburg, Germany: Karl Alber, 1987), 11–35; Lübbe, "Die Politik, die Wahrheit und die Moral," *Geschichte und Gegenwart* 3, no. 4 (1984): 288–304; and Lübbe, "Aneignung und Rückaneignung," in Georg Kohler and Heinz Kleger, *Diskurs und Dezision: Politische Vernunft in der wissenschaftlich-technischen Zivilisation* (Vienna: Passagen, 1990), 335–71. For a critique of Lübbe's position, see Emil Angehrn, *Geschichte und Identität* (Berlin: de Gruyter, 1985), 297–303, and especially Jörn Rüsen, "Zur Kritik des Neohistorismus," *Zeitschrift für philosophische Forschung* 33 (1979): 243–63.

54. Hermann Lübbe, "Der Nationalsozialismus im deutschen Nachkriegsbewußtsein," *Historische Zeitschrift* 236, no. 3 (1983): 579–99; Lübbe, "Verdrängung? Über eine Kategorie zur Kritik des deutschen Vergangenheitsverhältnisses," in Wiebe, *Gegenwart*, 94–106; and Lübbe, "Der Nationalsozialismus im politischen Bewußtsein der Gegenwart," in Martin Broszat, ed., *Deutschlands Weg in die Diktatur: Internationale Konferenz zur nationalsozialistischen Machtübernahme* (Berlin: Siedler, 1983), 329–49. The conference volume also documents a long discussion of Lübbe's paper by journalists, politicians, and historians: "Podiumsdiskussion zum Thema des Abschlußvortrages," in Broszat, *Deutschlands Weg*, 350–78.

55. Alexander Mitscherlich and Margarete Mitscherlich, *Die Unfähigkeit zu trauern*, 21st ed. (Munich, Germany: Piper, 1990), and Margarete Mitscherlich, *Erinnerungsarbeit: Zur Psychoanalyse der Unfähigkeit zu trauern* (Frankfurt, Germany: Fischer, 1987).

56. For Habermas's concept of postnational identity, see his contributions to the Historians' Debate: Habermas, "Kind of Settlement," in Augstein et al., *Forever in the Shadow*, 43–44; Habermas, "On the Public Use of History," in Augstein et al., *Forever in the Shadow*, 162–70; and especially Habermas, "Historical Consciousness and Post-traditional Identity: The Federal Republic's Orientation to the West," in Habermas, *The New Conservatism: Cultural Criticism and the Historians' Debate* (Cambridge, MA: MIT Press, 1989), 249–67, as well as Habermas, "Grenzen des Neohistorismus," in Habermas, *Die nachholende Revolution* (Frankfurt, Germany: Suhrkamp, 1990), 149–56. For the philosophical underpinnings of the concept, see Richard Wolin, "Introduction," in Habermas, *Conservatism*, vii–xxxi; and Martin Matustik, *Postnational Identity: Critical Theory and Existential Philosophy in Habermas, Kierkegaard, and Havel* (New York: Guilford, 1993), esp. 3–28.

57. Habermas's philosophical works on discourse ethics comprise three major contributions: Habermas, *Moral Consciousness and Communicative Action* (Cambridge, MA: MIT Press, 1990); Habermas, *Justification and Application: Remarks on Discourse Ethics* (Cambridge, MA: MIT Press, 1993); and especially Habermas, *Between Facts and Norms: Contributions to a Discourse Theory of Law and Democracy* (Cambridge, MA: MIT Press, 1996). For an introduction to Habermas's discourse ethics, see William Rehg, *Insight and Solidarity: A Study in the Discourse Ethics of Jürgen Habermas* (Berkeley: University of California Press, 1994).

58. About the relationship between social analysis and reflections on an ideal society in his writings, see Habermas, *Vergangenheit als Zukunft: Das alte Deutschland im neuen Europa? Ein Gespräch mit Michael Haller* (Munich, Germany: Piper, 1993), 132–35.

59. See especially Habermas, "Historical Consciousness," 250, 255–56; Habermas, "Neohistorismus," 151–52; and Habermas, "On the Public Use," 166.

60. Claussen, "Vergangenheit mit Zukunft: Über die Entstehung einer neuen deutschen Ideologie," in Eschenhagen, *Die neue deutsche Ideologie*, 7–30; see also Lüdtke, "Was ist und wer treibt Alltagsgeschichte," 16, and the excellent critique by Barbara Hahn, and Peter Schöttler,

"Jürgen Habermas und 'das ungetrübte Bewußtsein des Bruchs,'" in Gerstenberger and Schmidt, *Normalität,* 170–77.

61. In this respect, Lutz Niethammer argued: "Both projects in philosophical politics mistakenly assume that the case of the Federal Republic fits current global societal tendencies and they also overestimate the power of philosophical consciousness." See Niethammer, "Konjunkturen und Konkurrenzen kollektiver Identität: Ideologie, Infrastruktur und Gedächtnis in der Zeitgeschichte," *Prokla* 96 (September 1994): 378–99.

62. Wolfram Schütte quoted after Kaes, *From Hitler,* 183.

63. At least indirectly, this phenomenon is corroborated by the almost complete lack of identification of the West German population with East Germans after 1989/1990 on the grounds that the latter had joined the nation or the sphere of influence of the constitution. The continued separation between East and West Germany even after unification is illustrated in Werner Weidenfeld, *Deutschland: Eine Nation—Doppelte Geschichte* (Cologne, Germany: Verlag Wissenschaft und Politik, 1993). The exceptional persistence of regional identities in West Germany is well illustrated by Celia Applegate's recent case study on the Pfalz, see Applegate, *A Nation of Provincials: The German Idea of Heimat* (Berkeley: University of California Press, 1990). The lack of German national identity among West Germans has been constantly lamented by conservative intellectuals; see, for example, Klaus Weigelt, ed., *Heimat und Nation: Zur Geschichte und Identität der Deutschen* (Mainz, Germany: Hase und Kohler, 1984).

64. It is not possible to develop all these references in detail; at this stage, three examples should suffice. Nolte's comparison of Nazi and Soviet crimes, for instance, again raised the question of the scientific viability of the concepts of totalitarianism and fascism, which German scholars had debated in the 1960s when phenomenological and neo-Marxist studies of fascist movements in Europe competed with and partly displaced earlier comparative analyses of the power structure of the Nazi and the Soviet regime. In the same way, Hillgruber's call to identify with the German troops on the eastern front recalled the heated debates between social historians, who advanced a Weberian-type structural analysis of modern industrial societies, and neohistoricists, who favored the more traditional study of elite decision-making processes. These methodological discussions commenced in the 1960s but, with regard to the study of Nazism, climaxed only in the early 1980s when German scholars debated Hitler's position and importance within the Nazi system and subsequently disagreed about the genesis of the "Final Solution." Lastly, the critique of Nolte and Hildebrand for attempting to remove Nazism from its particular German context refers back to the dispute about Germany's special path to modernity that erupted in the early 1980s.

65. On the Fischer Debate, see John A. Moses, *The Politics of Illusion: The Fischer-Controversy in German Historiography* (London: Prior, 1975); Wolfgang Jäger, *Historische Forschung und politische Kultur in Deutschland: Die Debatte 1914–1980 über den Ausbruch des Ersten Weltkrieges* (Göttingen, Germany: Vandenhoek und Ruprecht, 1984), and especially the account by Fischer's student Imanuel Geiss, "Die Fischer-Kontroverse: Ein kritischer Beitrag zum Verhältnis zwischen Historiographie und Politik in der Bundesrepublik," in Geiss, *Studien über Geschichte und Geschichtswissenschaft* (Frankfurt, Germany: Suhrkamp, 1972), 108–98.

66. Most recently, Geiss, *Habermas-Kontroverse,* 14–16. However, Volker Berghahn has shown that by 1980, Fischer's thesis had not found its way into the applicable surveys and handbooks on German and European history of the twentieth century; see Berghahn, "Die Fischerkontroverse—15 Jahre danach," *Geschichte und Gesellschaft* 6, no. 13 (1980): 403–19. Apparently, little has changed since 1980. The most recent survey, Klaus Hildebrand's *Das vergangene Reich: Deutsche Außenpolitik von Bismarck bis Hitler* (Stuttgart, Germany: Deutsche Verlagsanstalt, 1995) also dismisses most of Fischer's arguments.

67. On the postwar historiography, see Georg Iggers, *The German Conception of History: The National Tradition of Historical Thought from Herder to the Present,* rev. ed. (Middletown,

CT: Wesleyan University Press, 1983), 252–64, and Winfried Schulze, *Deutsche Geschichtswissenschaft nach 1945* (Munich, Germany: Oldenbourg, 1989), 46–76.

68. On the concept of totalitarianism, see Kershaw, *Nazi Dictatorship*, 20–23, 30–35; Karl Dietrich Bracher, *Zeitgeschichtliche Kontroversen: Um Faschismus, Totalitarismus, Demokratie* (Munich, Germany: Piper, 1984), 34–62; and especially Uwe Backes and Eckhard Jesse, *Totalitarismus, Extremismus, Terrorismus* (Opladen, Germany: Leske und Budrich, 1984), 47–102.

69. For the development of the paradigm of social history in the Federal Republic, see Nicolas Berg, *Der Holocaust und die westdeutschen Historiker: Erforschung und Erinnerung* (Göttingen, Germany: Wallstein, 2003), and Iggers, *New Directions in European Historiography*, rev. ed. (Middletown, CT, Wesleyan University Press, 1984), 90–122.

70. Otto Dov Kulka, "Singularity and Its Relativization: Changing Views in German Historiography on National Socialism and the 'Final Solution,'" *Yad Vashem Studies* 19 (1988): 151–86. On the study and representation of the Holocaust in West German historiography, see also chapter 3.

71. On the Sonderweg debate, see Jürgen Kocka, "German History before Hitler: The Debate about the German Sonderweg," *Journal of Contemporary History* 23, no. 1 (1988): 3–16; Helga Grebing, *Der deutsche Sonderweg in Europa 1806–1945: Eine Kritik* (Stuttgart, Germany: Kohlhammer, 1986); Bernd Faulenbach, "Eine Variante europäischer Normalität? Zur neusten Diskussion über den 'deutschen Weg' im 19. und 20. Jahrhundert," *Tel Aviver Jahrbuch für deutsche Geschichte* 16 (1987): 285–309; and Institut für Zeitgeschichte, ed., *Deutscher Sonderweg—Mythos oder Realität?* (Munich, Germany: Oldenbourg, 1982).

72. The essay that coined the terms *structuralist* and *intentionalist* is now more easily available in Timothy Mason's collected essays, edited by Jane Kaplan. See Mason, "Intention and Explanation: A Current Controversy about the Interpretation of National Socialism," in Mason, *Nazism, Fascism, and the Working Class* (Cambridge: Cambridge University Press, 1995), 212–30. On the debate between structuralists and intentionalists, see also Saul Friedlander, "From Anti-Semitism to Extermination: A Historiographical Study of Nazi Policies toward the Jews and an Essay in Interpretation," in François Furet, *Unanswered Questions: Nazi Germany and the Genocide of the Jews* (New York: Schocken, 1989), 3–31; Christopher Browning, "Beyond 'Intentionalism' and 'Functionalism': The Decision for the Final Solution Reconsidered," in Browning, *The Path to Genocide: Esays on Launching the Final Solution* (Cambridge: Cambridge University Press, 1992), 86–121; and Kershaw, *Nazi Dictatorship*, 82–106.

73. Some commentators have pointed out that the heated debates between functionalists and intentionalists displayed lines of argumentation similar to the Historians' Debate, albeit in reverse. In the early 1980s, the social historians emphasized the normal aspects of the Holocaust, but several years later, during the Historians' Debate, the same scholars insisted on the Holocaust's exceptionality in a different interpretative and political context. See Baldwin, "Historikerstreit," 21. What remains from the former consensus is Eberhard Jäckel's explicit definition "that the National-Socialist murder of the Jews was unique because never before had a nation with the authority of its leader decided and announced that it would kill off as completely as possible a particular group of humans, including old people, women, children, and infants, and actually put this decision into practice, using all the governmental power at its disposal," Jäckel, "The Impoverished Practice of Insinuation," in Augstein et al., *Forever in the Shadow*, 74–78. During and after the Historians' Debate, the historians on the Left somewhat helplessly reiterated this formula, hoping to be able to restore the former tacit agreement. For that purpose, they mistakenly treated the highly abstract notion of uniqueness as a factual statement; see Wehler, *Entsorgung*, 100.

74. This applies especially to the work of Rainer Zitelmann; see Zitelmann, *Hitler: Selbstverständnis eines Revolutionärs* (Stuttgart, Germany: Klett, 1987). For a critique of Zitelmann's work, see Stefan Berger, "Historians and Nation-Building in Germany after Reunification," *Past and Present* 148 (August 1995): 187–222, esp. 197–98, and chapter 5.

75. Helga Grebing, "Deutsche Vergangenheit und politische Moral," *Niemandsland* 1 (1987): 5–15, and esp. Hennig, *Historikerstreit*, 83–102.

76. Hübner-Funk, "Die 'Hitlerjugend'-Generation: Umstrittenes Objekt und streitbares Subjekt der deutschen Zeitgeschichte," *Prokla* 80 (December 1990): 84–98.

77. Karl Mannheim, "Das Problem der Generationen," in Mannheim, *Wissenssoziologie: Auswahl aus dem Werk* (Berlin: Luchterhand, 1964), 509–65, esp. 541–55.

78. The term "the grace of late birth" (Gnade der späten Geburt) was first coined by the liberal journalist Günter Gaus and later adopted and transformed by Helmut Kohl, also a member of the Hitler Youth generation. Kohl's interpretation of the phrase is more accurately translated as the privilege of late birth, a privilege he claimed in a number a public venues, most notably during his visit to Israel in 1984. The interesting career of the phrase, wandering from the moderate left to the moderate right of the political spectrum, nicely illustrates that the members of this generation shared a similar perception of the Nazi period.

79. There have been various approaches to the study of the Hitler Youth generation in postwar West German sociology and historiography. In his classical 1957 study, Helmut Schelsky focuses on the postwar (West) German youth between 1945 and 1955, which he calls the skeptical generation. Since he defines youth as the age-group between fourteen and twenty-five, he deals with the age-groups born from 1920 through 1945. However, Schelsky avoids any clear dividing lines and allows for a lot of overlap between the skeptical generation and its predessessor, the "political youth" who joined the youth organizations of the parties of the Weimar Republic beginning in the early 1920s. For the definitions, see Schelsky, *Die skeptische Generation: Eine Soziologie der deutschen Jugend* (Düsseldorf, Germany: Eugen Diedrichs, 1957), 5, 57, 66–67, and 87. The historian Rolf Schörken defines the Hitler Youth generation as the male age-groups born between 1921 and 1929, which he further divides into three subcategories: the age-group born between 1921 and 1925/1926, the members of which served as soldiers in World War II; the age-group born between 1926 and 1928, which represents the so-called Flakhelfer-generation, adolescents who staffed the antiaircraft defense in the last years of the war; and the age-group of 1929, which was not drafted into the antiaircraft units but was called up for other supportive duties. Schörken adds that for women, the dividing line was 1926; women who were 19 or older in 1944 had to support the war effort in various positions. See Schörken, *Jugend 1945: Politisches Denken und Lebensgeschichte* (Frankfurt, Germany: Fischer, 1994), 10–15. The Flakhelfergeneration is most closely analyzed in Heinz Bude, *Deutsche Karrieren: Lebenskonstruktionen sozialer Aufsteiger aus der Flakhelfer-Generation* (Frankfurt, Germany: Suhrkamp, 1987). Bude also highlights the different experiences of the various age-groups within the Hitler Youth generation; see Bude, *Bilanz der Nachfolge: Die Bundesrepublik und der Nationalsozialismus* (Frankfurt, Germany: Suhrkamp, 1992), 81. Eike Hennig divides the age-groups in question into two distinct generations: the war generation, comprising the age-groups born between 1920 and 1927, and the generation of Germany's postwar reconstruction, consisting of the age-groups born from 1928 through 1935; see Hennig, *Historikerstreit*, 90–91. For our limited purposes, Sibylle Hübner-Funk's general definition, cited earlier, suffices. On the Hitler Youth generation, see also Gabriele Rosenthal, ed., *Die Hitlerjugend-Generation: Biographische Verarbeitung als Vergangenheitsbewältigung* (Essen, Germany: Blaue Eule, 1986).

80. Schelsky, *Skeptische Generation*, 84–95.

81. Mannheim, "Das Problem der Generationen," 537.

82. The dilemma of the intellectuals of the Hitler Youth generation represents an extreme example of the peculiar way in which modern Western societies deal with their pasts and which Pierre Nora has explained (see chapter 2). During the Historians' Debate, West German historians certainly aspired to provide sites of memory for the population at large but only succeeded in capturing the attention of their traditional audience. The most successful collection of essays of the Historians' Debate sold seventy thousand copies within eight years. This figure indicates that its readership remained limited to the "educated public."

83. For Assmann's definition of cultural and communicative memory, see chapter 2.

84. Lutz Niethammer, "Diesseits des 'Floating Gap': Das kollektive Gedächtnis und die Konstruktion von Identität im wissenschaftlichen Diskurs," in Kristin Platt and Mihran Dabag, eds., *Generation und Gedächtnis: Erinnerungen und kollektive Identitäten* (Opladen, Germany: Leske und Budrich, 1995), 25–50; see also Niethammer, "Konjunkturen."

85. Kaes, *From Hitler*, 196.

86. Notice the absence in the debate of historians such as Lutz Niethammer, Klaus Tenfelde, Alf Lüdtke, and Detlev Peukert.

87. Berger, "Historians," 213; for a postunification endorsement of the category of national history in conjunction with a critical assessment of the social history of the Bielefeld School, see Harold James, *Vom Historikerstreit zum Historikerschweigen* (Berlin: Siedler, 1993).

88. For a recent example, see Yael Zerubavel, *Recovered Roots: Collective Memory and the Making of Israeli National Tradition* (Chicago: University of Chicago Press, 1995).

89. For the press coverage of the recycling of Jenninger's speech, see Arno Widmann, "Ignatz Bubis und die Jenninger-Rede," *Die Zeit*, December 8, 1995; "Gedenkreden: 'Falsches Bild,'" *Der Spiegel* 49 (1995); and "Trauer oder Pflichterfüllung: Bubis wiederholte die umstrittene Jenninger-Rede," *die tageszeitung*, December 1, 1995. Only *die tageszeitung* gave the news a prominent place in its coverage. See also Holger Siever, *Kommunikation und Verstehen: Der Fall Jenninger als Beispiel einer semiotischen Kommunikationsanalyse* (Frankfurt, Germany: Lang, 2001), 428–38.

CHAPTER 5

1. For instance, Perry Anderson, "On Emplotment: Two Kinds of Ruin," in Saul Friedlander, ed., *Probing the Limits of Representation: Nazism and the "Final Solution"* (Cambridge, MA: Harvard University Press, 1992), 54–65.

2. Hayden White, "Interpretation in History," reprinted in White, *Tropics of Discourse: Essays in Cultural Criticism* (Baltimore: Johns Hopkins University Press, 1978), 51–80, and White, *Metahistory: The Historical Imagination in Nineteenth-Century Europe* (Baltimore: Johns Hopkins University Press, 1973).

3. Nancy Struever, "Topics in History," *History and Theory* 19, no. 4 (1980): 66–79, esp. 66–67 and 75–76; Dominick LaCapra, *Rethinking Intellectual History: Texts, Contexts, Language* (Ithaca, NY: Cornell University Press, 1983), 76–77; Lionel Gossman, *Between History and Literature* (Cambridge, MA: Harvard University Press, 1990), 286–87; and Sande Cohen, *Historical Culture: On the Recoding of an Academic Discipline* (Berkeley: University of California Press, 1987), 81–87.

4. Hayden White, *The Content of the Form: Narrative Discourse and Historical Representation* (Baltimore: Johns Hopkins University Press, 1987), 44; for an analysis of the development of White's theory of historical writing and the criticism it received, see Wulf Kansteiner, "Hayden White's Critique of the Writing of History," *History and Theory* 32, no. 3 (1993): 273–95.

5. White, *Content of the Form*, 80.

6. "In the case of the emplotment of the events of the Third Reich in a 'comic' or 'pastoral' mode, we would be eminently justified in appealing to 'the facts' in order to dismiss it from the lists of 'competing narratives' of the Third Reich"; see White, "Historical Emplotment and the Problem of Truth," in Friedlander, *Probing the Limits*, 37–53; reprinted in White, *Figural Realism: Studies in the Mimesis Effect* (Baltimore: Johns Hopkins University Press, 1999), 27–42.

7. White, *Content of the Form*, 76.

8. For an emphatic critique, see Carlo Ginzburg, "Just One Witness," in Friedlander, *Probing the Limits*, 82–96; Gossman, *Between History and Literature*, 303; and Christopher

Norris, *Deconstruction and the Interests of Theory* (Norman: University of Oklahoma Press, 1989), 16.

9. White, *Content of the Form*, 40, 43, and 45.

10. Norbert Frei, "Wie modern war der Nationalsozialismus?" *Geschichte und Gesellschaft* 19, no. 3 (1993): 367–87.

11. White, *Metahistory*, 7–11.

12. Detlev Peukert, *Volksgenossen und Gemeinschaftsfremde: Anpassung, Ausmerze und Aufbegehren unter dem Nationalsozialismus* (Cologne, Germany: Bund, 1982), 16.

13. See, for example, Götz Aly, *Hitlers Volksstaat: Raub, Rassenkrieg und nationaler Sozialismus* (Frankfurt, Germany: Fischer, 2005).

14. Martin Broszat, "Plädoyer für eine Historisierung des Nationalsozialismus," *Merkur* 39 (May 1985): 373–85; Saul Friedlander, "Some Reflections on the Historicization of National Socialism," *Tel-Aviver Jahrbuch für deutsche Geschichte* 16 (1987): 310–24; and Martin Broszat and Saul Friedlander, "Um die 'Historisierung des Nationalsozialismus': Ein Briefwechsel," *Vierteljahrshefte für Zeitgeschichte* 36, no. 2 (1988): 339–72; all of these works are included, where applicable in English translation, in Peter Baldwin, ed., *Reworking the Past: Hitler, the Holocaust, and the Historians' Debate* (Boston: Beacon, 1990); see also Martin Broszat, "Was heißt Historisierung des Nationalsozialismus," *Historische Zeitschrift* 247, no. 1 (1988): 1–14, and Saul Friedlander, "Martin Broszat und die Historisierung des Nationalsozialismus," in Klaus-Dietmar Henke and Claudio Natoli, eds., *Mit dem Pathos der Nüchternheit: Martin Broszat, das Institut für Zeitgeschichte und die Erforschung des Nationalsozialismus* (Frankfurt, Germany: Campus, 1991), 155–71; for discussions of the project of historicization and its problems, see Ian Kershaw, *The Nazi Dictatorship: Problems and Perspectives of Interpretation*, 2nd ed. (London: Arnold, 1989), 150–67; Otto Dov Kulka, "Singularity and Its Relativization: Changing Views in German Historiography on National Socialism and the 'Final Solution,'" *Yad Vashem Studies* 19 (1988): 151–86; Dan Diner, "Zwischen Aporie und Apologie: Über die Grenzen der Historisierbarkeit des Nationalsozialismus," in Diner, ed., *Ist der Nationalsozialsmus Geschichte? Zu Historisierung und Historikerstreit* (Frankfurt, Germany: Fischer, 1987), 62–73; Jörn Rüsen, "The Logic of Historicization: Metahistorical Reflections on the Debate between Friedlander and Broszat," *History & Memory* 9, nos. 1 and 2 (1997): 113–44; and Robert Eaglestone, *The Holocaust and the Postmodern* (Oxford: Oxford University Press, 2004), 173–93.

15. Broszat, "Plädoyer," 373, 375, 382.

16. Broszat and Friedlander, "Controversy about the Historicization of National Socialism," in Baldwin, ed., *Reworking the Past*," 107–9, 117.

17. Broszat, "Plädoyer," 378, 384–85.

18. Friedlander, "Some Reflections," 323; see also Saul Friedlander, "The 'Final Solution': On the Unease in Historical Representation," *History and Memory* 1, no. 2 (1989): 61–73; and Friedlander, "Introduction," in Friedlander, *Probing the Limits*, 1–21.

19. Broszat's choice of perspective may have reflected his own burden of the past. In 2003, fourteen years after Broszat's death, it was revealed that he had been a member of the Nazi party, although he never acknowledged that fact during his lifetime. See Nicolas Berg, *Der Holocaust und die westdeutschen Historiker: Erforschung und Erinnerung* (Göttingen, Germany: Wallstein, 2003), 420.

20. The reevaluation of the Weimar Republic as a period in its own right with the potential for both self-destruction and democratic consolidation illustrates this aspect of historicization. See Hans Mommsen, *Die verspielte Freiheit: Der Weg der Republik von Weimar in den Untergang, 1918–1933* (Berlin: Propyläen, 1989), and Detlev Peukert, *Die Weimarer Republik* (Frankfurt, Germany: Suhrkamp, 1987).

21. Niklas Berg, *Der Holocaust und die westdeutschen Historiker: Erforschung und Erinnerung* (Göttingen, Germany: Wallstein, 2003); Georg Iggers, *The German Conception of History: The*

National Tradition of Historical Thought from Herder to the Present, rev. ed. (Middletown, CT: Wesleyan University Press, 1983), 254–56; Hans Mommsen, "Haupttendenzen nach 1945 und in der Ära des Kalten Krieges," in Bernd Faulenbach and Andreas Dorpalen, eds., *Geschichtswissenschaft in Deutschland: Traditionelle Positionen und gegenwärtige Aufgaben* (Munich, Germany: Beck, 1974), 112–20; Hans-Ulrich Wehler, "Geschichtswissenschaft heute," in Jürgen Habermas, ed., *Stichworte zur "Geistigen Situation der Zeit,"* vol. 2 (Frankfurt, Germany: Suhrkamp, 1979), 709–53; see also Winfried Schulze, *Deutsche Geschichtswissenschaft nach 1945* (Munich, Germany: Oldenbourg, 1989).

22. Immanuel Geiss, cited in Iggers, *German Conception of History,* 260.

23. Mommsen, "Haupttendenzen nach 1945," 119.

24. Helmuth Plessner, *Die verspätete Nation: Über die politische Verführbarkeit bürgerlichen Geistes* (Stuttgart, Germany: Kohlhammer, 1959), and Fritz Rene Allemann, *Bonn ist nicht Weimar* (Cologne, Germany: Kiepenheuer und Witsch, 1956). For a summary and critical evaluation of the debates about the German Sonderweg, see Helga Grebing, *Der "deutsche Sonderweg" in Europa: Eine Kritik,* (Stuttgart, Germany: Kohlhammer, 1986).

25. Jürgen Kocka, "German History before Hitler: The Debate about the German 'Sonderweg,'" *Journal of Contemporary History* 23, no. 1 (1988): 3–16.

26. David Schoenbaum, *Hitler's Social Revolution: Class and Status in Nazi Germany, 1933–1939* (Garden City, NY: Doubleday, 1966), and Ralf Dahrendorf, *Society and Democracy in Germany* (Garden City, NY: Doubleday, 1967). For an analysis of the differences between Schoenbaum and Dahrendorf, see especially J. Alber, "Nationalsozialismus und Modernisierung," *Kölner Zeitschrift für Soziologie und Sozialpsychologie* 41, no. 2 (1989): 346–65; see also Kershaw, *Nazi Dictatorship,* 135–40.

27. See H. Matzerath and H. Volkmann, "Modernisierungstheorie und Nationalsozialismus," in Jürgen Kocka, ed., *Theorien in der Praxis des Historikers: Forschungsbeispiele und ihre Diskussion* (Göttingen, Germany: Vandenhoeck und Ruprecht, 1977), 86–102, Wolfgang Abelshauser and Anselm Faust, *Wirtschafts- und Sozialpolitik: Eine nationalsozialistische Sozialrevolution?* (Tübingen, Germany: DIFF, 1983), 117–18; and Karl-Otto Albrecht, *Wie sozial waren die Nationalsozialisten?* (Frankfurt, Germany: R. G. Fischer, 1997).

28. See, for instance, W. Dirks, "Der restaurative Charakter der Epoche," *Frankfurter Hefte* 5 (1950): 942, and Eugen Kogon, "Die Aussichten der Restauration,"*Frankfurter Hefte* 7 (1952): 165; about the question of restoration, see Jürgen Kocka, "1945: Neubeginn oder Restauration?" in Carola Stern and Heinrich August Winkler, eds., *Wendepunkte deutscher Geschichte* (Frankfurt, Germany: Fischer, 1979), 141–68.

29. For a conclusive critique of the theories of fascism of the New Left, see Heinrich August Winkler, *Revolution, Staat, Faschismus: Zur Revision des historischen Materialismus,* (Göttingen, Germany: Vandenhoeck und Ruprecht, 1978), especially chapter 3, "Die 'neue Linke' und der Faschismus: Zur Kritik neomarxistischer Theorien über den Nationalsozialismus," 65–117.

30. For the debate caused by David Blackbourn and Goeff Eley, *Mythen deutscher Geschichtsschreibung,* (Frankfurt, Germany: Ullstein, 1980), see Grebing, *Der "deutsche Sonderweg,"* 17–22, and Kershaw, *Nazi Dictatorship,* 19–20, and compare to Thomas Nipperdey, "1933 und die Kontinuität der deutschen Geschichte," *Historische Zeitschrift* 227, no. 1 (1978): 86–111.

31. Lutz Niethammer, "Zum Wandel in der Kontinuitätsdiskussion," in Ludolf Herbst, ed., *Westdeutschland 1945 bis 1955* (Munich, Germany: Oldenbourg, 1986), 65–84.

32. Detlev Peukert, *Max Weber's Diagnose der Moderne* (Göttingen, Germany: Vandenhoeck und Ruprecht, 1989), 64.

33. Ibid., 69.

34. Peukert, *Volksgenossen und Gemeinschaftsfremde;* Peukert, "Das 'Dritte Reich' aus der Alltagsperspektive," *Archiv für Sozialgeschichte* 26 (1986): 533–57; Peukert, "Alltag und Barbarei:

Zur Normalität des Dritten Reiches," in Diner, *Ist der Nationalsozialismus Geschichte?*, 51–61; Peukert, "Die Genesis der 'Endlösung' aus dem Geiste der Wissenschaft," in Forum für Philosophie Bad Homburg, ed., *Zerstörung des moralischen Selbstbewußtseins: Chance oder Gefährdung? Praktische Philosophie in Deutschland nach dem Nationalsozialismus* (Frankfurt, Germany: Suhrkamp, 1988), 24–44, reprinted in Peukert, *Max Weber*, 102–21; Peukert, "Rassismus und 'Endlösungs'—Utopie: Thesen zu Entwicklung und Struktur der nationalsozialistischen Vernichtungspolitik," in Christoph Klessmann and Ute Frevert, eds., *Nicht nur Hitlers Krieg: Der Zweite Weltkrieg und die Deutschen* (Düsseldorf, Germany: Droste, 1989), 71–82; Peukert, "Zur Erforschung der Sozialpolitik im Dritten Reich," in Hans-Uwe Otto and Heinz Sünker, eds., *Soziale Arbeit und Faschismus* (Frankfurt, Germany: Suhrkamp, 1989), 36–46. Peukert's approach to the problem of Nazism and modernity is critically assessed in Moshe Zimmermann, "Negativer Fixpunkt und Suche nach positiver Identität: Der Nationalsozialismus im kollektiven Gedächnis der alten Bundesrepublik," in Hanno Loewy, ed., *Holocaust: Die Grenzen des Verstehens—Eine Debatte über die Besetzung der Geschichte* (Reinbek, Germany: Rowohlt, 1992), 128–43; Frank Bajohr, "Detlev Peukert's Beiträge zur Sozialgeschichte der Moderne," in Frank Bajohr, ed., *Zivilisation und Barbarei: Die widersprüchlichen Potentiale der Moderne* (Hamburg, Germany: Christians, 1991), 7–16; and especially Gisela Bock, "Krankenmord, Judenmord und nationalsozialistische Rassenpolitik: Überlegungen zu einigen neuen Forschungshypothesen," in Bajohr, *Zivilisation und Barbarei*, 283–306.

35. Peukert, *Volksgenossen und Gemeinschaftsfremde*, 296; Peukert, "Alltag und Barbarei," 60; Peukert, "Rassismus und 'Endlösungs'—Utopie," 78–80; Peukert, "Genesis der 'Endlösung,'" 37–38 and 40–41.

36. Peukert, "Genesis der 'Endlösung,'" 26.

37. Ibid., 28–29; Peukert, *Max Weber*, 78–82.

38. Peukert, *Max Weber*, 78–82; Peukert, "Genesis der 'Endlösung,'" 36; Peukert, "Alltag und Barbarei," 57.

39. Peukert, "Genesis der 'Endlösung,'" 39; Peukert, "Rassismus und 'Endlösungs'— Utopie," 72.

40. Peukert, "Genesis der 'Endlösung,'" 44.

41. Bajohr, "Detlev Peukerts Beiträge," 13.

42. For Peukert's comments about Zitelmann, see Peukert, *Max Weber*, 134n19, and Peukert, "Zur Erforschung der Sozialpolitik," 45n15; for his critical remarks on Aly and Heim, see Peukert, "Genesis der 'Endlösung,'" 45–46n8.

43. Götz Aly and Susanne Heim, "Die Ökonomie der 'Endlösung': Menschenvernichtung und wirtschaftliche Neuordnung," in Aly, ed., *Sozialpolitik und Judenvernichtung: Gibt es eine Ökonomie der 'Endlösung'?* (Berlin: Rotbuch, 1987), 11–90; Götz Aly and Susanne Heim, *Vordenker der Vernichtung: Auschwitz und die deutschen Pläne für eine neue europäische Ordnung* (Hamburg, Germany: Hoffmann und Campe, 1991); Götz Aly and Susanne Heim, "Sozialplanung und Völkermord: Thesen zur Herrschaftsrationalität der nationalsozialistischen Vernichtungspolitik," in Wolfgang Schneider, ed.,*"Vernichtungspolitik": Eine Debatte über den Zusammenhang von Sozialpolitik und Genozid im nationalsozialistischen Deutschland* (Hamburg, Germany: Junius, 1991), 11–23; Susanne Heim and Götz Aly, "Wider die Unterschätzung der nationalsozialistischen Politik: Antwort an unsere Kritiker," in Schneider, *"Vernichtungspolitik,"* 165–75; Susanne Heim and Götz Aly, "Einleitung," in Aly, ed., *Bevölkerungsstruktur und Massenmord: Neue Dokumente zur deutschen Politik der Jahre 1938–1945* (Berlin: Rotbuch, 1991), 7–12; Götz Aly and Susanne. Heim, "The Economics of the Final Solution: A Case Study on the General Government," *Simon Wiesenthal Center Annual* 5 (1988): 3–48; see also Götz Aly and Karl Heinz Roth, *Die restlose Erfassung: Volkszählen, Identifizieren, Aussondern im Nationalsozialismus* (Berlin: Rotbuch, 1984), and Götz Aly, "Erwiderung auf Dan Diner," *Vierteljahrshefte für Zeitgeschichte* 41, no. 4 (1993): 621–35. Aly and Heim's approach to Nazism, the "Final Solution," and modernity was discussed at length by various scholars in *Konkret*, vols.

10–12 (1989) and 1–6, 9–11 (1990); all contributions have been reprinted in Schneider, *"Vernichtungspolitik.*" For additional critiques, see Hermann Graml, "Irregeleitet und in die Irre führend: Widerspruch gegen eine 'rationale' Erklärung von Auschwitz," in *Jahrbuch für Antisemitismusforschung* 1 (1992): 286–95; Dan Diner, "Rationalisierung und Methode: Zu einem neuen Erklärungsversuch der 'Endlösung,'" *Vierteljahrshefte für Zeitgeschichte* 40, no. 3 (1992): 359–82; and particularly Karl Heinz Roth, "Europäische Neuordnung durch Völkermord: Bemerkungen zu Götz Alys und Susanne Heims Studie über die 'Vordenker der Vernichtung,'" in Schneider, *"Vernichtungspolitik,"* 179–95; and Frei, "Wie modern war der Nationalsozialismus?"

44. Aly and Heim, *Vordenker der Vernichtung,* 485; Aly and Heim, "Wider die Unterschätzung," 169.

45. Aly and Heim, "Bevölkerungsstruktur," 12.

46. Aly and Heim, *Vordenker der Vernichtung,* 10, 13–15, 485, 491; Aly and Heim, "Sozialpolitik und Judenvernichtung," 7, 14.

47. Aly and Heim, "Die Ökonomie der 'Endlösung,'" 20–30; Aly and Heim, *Vordenker der Vernichtung,* 33–47, 276; Aly and Heim, "Sozialplanung und Judenvernichtung," 14.

48. Aly and Heim, "Die Ökonomie der 'Endlösung,'" 30–31; Aly and Heim, *Vordenker der Vernichtung,* esp. 276–81.

49. Aly and Heim, "Sozialplanung und Judenvernichtung," 19; Aly and Heim, *Vordenker der Vernichtung,* 489.

50. Aly and Heim, "Wider die Unterschätzung," 174.

51. Ulrich Herbert, "Rassismus und rationales Kalkül," in Schneider, *"Vernichtungspolitik,"* 25–36; Diner, "Perspektive," 72; Köhler, "Das Morden," 90, 100; Diner, "Rationalisierung und Methode," 379, 381–83; Roth, "Europäische Neuordnung," 194; Peter Longerich, review of Aly and Heim, *Sozialpolitik and Judenvernichtung* in *Historische Zeitschrift* 251, no. 1 (1990): 211–12. For Aly and Heim, the theories of fascism developed by the student movement and the New Left represent a point of reference but more in the sense that they expose and alleviate their shortcomings. They show that the "Final Solution" was not a minor tactical question in regard to which the Nazi leaders managed to ascertain their temporal independence from the otherwise complete control of capitalists, as Reinhard Kühnl argued at one point; see Kühnl, "Probleme einer Theorie über den internationalen Faschismus," *Politische Vierteljahresschrift* 16, no. 1 (1975): 89–121. Nor do they agree that the "economics of the 'Final Solution'" can be reduced to the industries' need for slave labor, as R. Opitz has argued; see Reinhard Opitz, "Über die Entstehung und Verhinderung von Faschismus," *Argument* 16 (November 1974): 543–603, 572. For a good analysis of the NS administration's temporary oscillation between exploitation and extermination in the concentration camps, see Wolfgang Sofsky, *Die Ordnung des Terrors: Das Konzentrationslager* (Frankfurt, Germany: Fischer, 1993).

52. Köhler, "Das Morden," 89.

53. Herbert, "Rassismus," 25–26, 33; Cristopher Browning, "Vernichtung und Arbeit," in Schneider,*"Vernichtungspolitik,"* 37–52; Diner, "Rationalisierung und Methode," 369, 371. The criticism that Aly underestimates the importance of ideological factors has also been raised about his more recent work; see Yehuda Bauer, *Rethinking the Holocaust* (New Haven, CT: Yale University Press, 2001), 89–92, in his comments on Götz Aly, *"Final Solution": Nazi Population Policy and the Murder of the European Jews* (London: Arnold, 1999). See also Michael Burleigh, *Ethics and Extermination: Reflections on Nazi Genocide* (Cambridge: Cambridge University Press, 1997), 169–82, and Steven Aschheim, *Culture and Catastrophe: German and Jewish Confrontations with National Socialism and Other Crises* (New York: New York University Press, 1996), 132–35.

54. See the friendly critique by Roth, "Europäische Neuordnung durch Völkermord," who talks about the "schrille Abwehrpolemik" (shrill, defensive polemic), which characterizes Aly and Heim's work.

55. In their eagerness to identify *the* group of people responsible for the "Final Solution," Aly and Heim—and also some of their critics—fail to recognize that the texts they have uncovered lose none of their relevance even if the texts might "only" represent rationalizations that helped their authors fulfill their assigned role in the realization of the "Final Solution."

56. White, *Metahistory*, 9.

57. On explanation by formal argument, see White, *Metahistory*, 11–22.

58. Rainer Zitelmann, "Nationalsozialismus und Moderne: Eine Zwischenbilanz," in W. Süß, ed., *Übergänge: Zeitgeschichte zwischen Utopie und Machbarkeit* (Berlin: Duncker und Humblot, 1989), 195–223; Rainer Zitelmann, "Die totalitäre Seite der Moderne," in Michael Prinz and Rainer Zitelmann, eds., *Nationalsozialismus und Modernisierung* (Darmstadt, Germany: Wissenschaftliche Buchgesellschaft, 1991), 1–20; Uwe Backes, Eckhard Jesse, and Rainer Zitelmann, "Was heißt: 'Historisierung' des Nationalsozialismus," in Backes, Jesse, and Zitelmann, eds., *Die Schatten der Vergangenheit: Impulse zur Historisierung des Nationalsozialismus* (Frankfurt, Berlin: Ullstein, 1990), 25–57; Rainer Zitelmann, *Hitler: Selbstverständnis eines Revolutionärs*, 3rd rev. ed. (Stuttgart, Germany: Klett-Cotta, 1990), 34–36; Zitelmann, *Adolf Hitler: Eine politische Biographie* (Göttingen, Germany: Muster-Schmidt, 1989); Zitelmann, "Adolf Hitler—'Der Führer,'" in Ronald Smelzer and Rainer Zitelmann, eds., *Die braune Elite: 22 biographische Skizzen* (Darmstadt, Germany: Wissenschaftliche Buchgesellschaft, 1989), 134–58.

59. Zitelmann, "Nationalsozialismus und Moderne," 210–15; Zitelmann, *Selbstverständnis*, 138, 141; and Zitelmann, *Hitler*, 119–20. In these passages, Zitelmann also refers to the secularization of the school system that the Nazis realized against considerable resistance by both churches and that the Social Democrats had demanded for some time, albeit for different reasons.

60. Zitelmann, *Selbstverständnis*, 18, 132–33, 498; Zitelmann, *Hitler*, 120–22; Zitelmann, "Nationalsozialismus und Moderne," 202–4.

61. Zitelmann, *Selbstverständnis*, 44–45, 493; Zitelmann, *Hitler*, 119–20, 123–24, 148–49; Zitelmann, "Nationalsozialismus und Moderne," 209.

62. Zitelmann, *Selbstverständnis*, 230; Zitelmann, *Hitler*, 115–16; and Zitelmann, "Nationalsozialismus und Moderne," 205–6. Zitelmann fails to point out that even the very term *Wirtschaftswunder* (economic miracle) was coined during the NS period and then reintroduced in the 1950s.

63. According to his remarks, Hitler was particularly interested in recruiting future members of the functional elite from the working classes, which he considered an untapped resource. See Zitelmann, *Selbstverändnis*, 122–23, 144–45, 223–24, and Zitelmann, "Nationalsozialismus und Moderne," 213.

64. Zitelmann, *Selbstverständnis*, 306–7, 334, 354–58; Zitelmann, *Hitler*, 160–61; and Zitelmann, "Nationalsozialismus und Moderne," 206–7.

65. Zitelmann, *Selbstverständnis*, 20, see also 498.

66. In his work on the development of the social status of white-collar workers in the Weimar Republic and Nazi Germany, Michael Prinz concludes that Schoenbaum and Dahrendorf's theory about the inadvertent modernizing effect of National Socialism might have to be revised. Although "many aspects of the modernizing impact related to the Third Reich were unintended side effects of its policies or its collapse," the changes it caused with regard to the status and mentality of white-collar workers were clearly intended by the NS leadership; see Prinz, *Vom neuen Mittelstand zum Volksgenossen: Die Entwicklung des sozialen Status der Angestellten von der Weimarer Republik bis zum Ende der NS-Zeit* (Munich, Germany: Oldenbourg, 1986), 335–36. Prinz also warns against reducing the "relative modernity of National-Socialism" to Hitler's intentions and decisions. Thus, he contradicts Zitelmann's stark intentionalism and writes instead in relatively abstract terms about "social energies" and "analogical problems" that help explain the consistency of the NS social policies; see Prinz,

"Die soziale Funktion moderner Elemente in der Gesellschaftspolitik des Nationalsozialismus," in Prinz and Zitelmann, *Nationalsozialismus und Modernisierung*, 295–327; see also Michael Prinz, "Wohlfahrtsstaat, Modernisierung und Nationalsozialismus: Thesen zu ihrem Verhältnis," in Otto and Sünker, *Soziale Arbeit und Faschismus*, 47–62.

67. On this point, also see the review of Zitelmann's *Hitler* by Klaus Hildebrand in *Historische Zeitschrift* 251, no. 1 (1990): 200–201; the critical review of Zitelmann's *Selbstverständnis*, by Marie-Luise Recker in *Neue Politische Literatur* 32, no. 1 (1987): 163–65; and the otherwise favorable review of Zitelmann's *Selbstverständnis* by Jost Dülfer in *Frankfurter Allgemeine Zeitung*, July 7, 1987.

68. These problems are most apparent in Zitelmann, "Nationalsozialismus und Moderne." For a notable exception, see his analysis of the anachronistic use of the term *Chancengleichheit* in Zitelmann, *Selbstverständnis*, 122–23.

69. Frei, "Wie modern war der Nationalsozialismus?"; Hans Mommsen, "Nationalsozialismus als vorgetäuschte Modernisierung," in Mommsen, *Der Nationalsozialismus und die deutsche Gesellschaft* (Reinbek, Germany: Rowohlt, 1991), 405–27; Albers, "Nationalsozialismus und Modernisierung"; Karl Heinz Roth, "Verklärung des Abgrunds: Zur nachträglichen 'Revolutionierung' der NS-Diktatur durch die Gruppe um Rainer Zitelmann," *1999: Zeitschrift für Sozialgeschichte des 20. und 21. Jahrhunderts* 7, no. 1 (1992): 7–11; and G. Elsner, "'. . . in gewisser Hinsicht war Robert Ley der deutsche William Beveridge'—Zur Diskussion über Modernisierungselemente in der nationalsozialistischen Sozialpolitik," *1999: Zeitschrift* 7, no. 4 (1992): 83–100. See also the critical reviews of Zitelmann, *Selbstverständnis*, by Peter Longerich, "Adolf Hitler—Ein Revolutionär?" *Die Zeit*, October 2, 1987, 39–40; by F. Ryszka, in *Vierteljahrshefte für Zeitgeschichte* 4 (1988): 785–90; and the review of Prinz and Zitelmann's *Nationalsozialismus und Moderne* by K. Linne, in *1999: Zeitschrift* 7, no. 1 (1992): 129–32.

70. See the following reviews of Zitelmann's *Selbstverständnis*: Peter Krüger, *Historische Zeitschrift* 247, no. 1 (1988): 736–37; Krüger, *Historische Zeitschrift* 255, no. 1 (1992): 225–26 (review of the 2nd ed.); Andreas Hillgruber, *Die Welt*, May 30, 1987; G. Ueberschär, *Das historisch-politische Buch* 35, no. 9 (1987): 289; Uwe Backes, *Der Tagesspiegel*, July 14, 1988; Klaus Hildebrandt, *Süddeutsche Zeitung*, September 29, 1987; Jost Dülfer, *Frankfurter Allgemeine Zeitung*, July 7, 1987; and Eckhard Jesse, *Rheinischer Merkur*, April 4, 1988.

71. White, *Metahistory*, 9.

72. Alexander Ruoff, *Verbiegen, Verdrängen, Beschweigen: Die Nationalgeschichte der "Jungen Freiheit"* (Münster, Germany: Unrast, 2001).

73. The latter example and its success are particularly telling because before the Historikerstreit, it would have been considered an unacceptable, apologetic representation of Nazism. Only the Historikerstreit canceled the agreement among all historians of Nazism that the Nazi crimes were to be represented as the focal point of histories of the Third Reich.

74. See, for example, the works of the German sociologist Wolfgang Sofsky, *Die Ordnung des Terrors*, and of the British sociologist Zygmunt Bauman. The latter shows, in particular, that an emphasis on the modern traits of Nazism and the "Final Solution" does not entail renouncing its historical singularity. Bauman argues that the "Holocaust is unique in a double sense. It is unique among other cases of genocide because it is modern. And it stands unique against the quotidianity of modern society because it brings together some ordinary factors of modernity which normally are kept apart. In this second sense of its uniqueness, only the combinations of factors is universal and rare, not the factors which are combined"; see Bauman, *Modernity and the Holocaust* (Ithaca, NY: Cornell University Press, 1989), 94. He also shows that considerations about the interdependence between Nazism and modernity profit from probing the theoretical dimensions of the relationship, an undertaking clearly lacking in recent German historiography.

75. White, *Metahistory*, 8.

76. White, "Historical Emplotment and the Problem of Truth," 52.

CHAPTER 6

1. *Holokaust* (documentary miniseries, ZDF, October 17, October 24, October 31, November 7, and November 14, 2000).

2. See, for instance, Thomas Gehringer, "NS-Kitsch: Fernsehen und Zeitgeschichte—Eine Auseinandersetzung," *Tagesspiegel*, June 16, 1998.

3. The ZDF had adopted the title *Holokaust* on the suggestion of Eberhard Jäckel, who was also a consultant during the production of the series. Before making the decision about the title of the series, the station had sought the advice of other academics, among them Walter Jens, who came to the surprising conclusion that "one should use the term 'Holokaust' for the fact that millions were turned to ashes because the term is precise and offers additional insight through aesthetic alienation"; see Edo Reents, "Zur rechten Zeit," *Süddeutsche Zeitung*, June 13, 2000, and especially Henryk Broder's entertaining comments about the choice of terminology, "Kopyright auf Holokaust: Die ZDF-Schreibung für 'Holocaust' steht für den deutschen Sündenstolz," *Tagesspiegel*, October 18, 2000.

4. See the positive reviews by Kirsten Decker, "Ganz verbrennen: Nach *Holocaust*, nach *Shoah*—Wie das ZDF den Mord an den Juden dokumentiert," *Tagesspiegel*, October 14, 2000, and especially Norbert Frei, "Mässige Zuschauerzahlen, enttäuschende Resonanz; Warum die ZDF-Reihe *Holokaust* gut war, aber kein Erfolg," *Süddeutsche Zeitung*, November 21, 2000; compare to "Ästhetisierte Vernichtung," *die tageszeitung*, October 17, 2000.

5. See, for example, Jürgen Tremper, "Vor allem beschrieben und zu wenig hinterfragt: *Holokaust*-Serie des ZDF klebt am Geschichtsbild der 60er Jahre und praktiziert 'Kunst des Weglassens,'" *Nordkurier*, November 18, 2000.

6. "Hitlers Frauen beliebt," *Der Spiegel*, April 30, 2001; Iris Ockenfels, "Stoltes Helfer: ZDF setzt im neuen Jahr auf Knopp, Alsmann und die Klitschkos," *Tagesspiegel*, August 16, 2001.

7. See especially the recent British Broadcasting Corporation (BBC) series *The Nazis*.

8. See, in addition, the data in chapter 7.

9. For general information on Germany's television revolution after 1983, see Dietrich Schwarzkopf, ed., *Rundfunkpolitik in Deutschland*, 2 vols. (Munich, Germany: dtv, 1999); Knut Hickethier, *Geschichte des deutschen Fernsehens* (Stuttgart, Germany: Metzler, 1998), 414–33; more specifically, Stefan Wehmeier, *Fernsehen im Wandel* (Constance, Germany: UVK Medien, 1998); and Udo Michael Krüger, *Programmprofile im dualen Fernsehsystem, 1985–1990* (Baden-Baden, Germany: Nomos, 1992).

10. For instance, the series *Hitlers Helfer* was broadcast in forty-two countries; see Thomas Gehringer, "Der totale Knopp: Geschichte satt bis 2000," *Tagesspiegel*, October 25, 1997.

11. For the changes in West Germany's historical culture during the 1960s, see Peter Reichel, *Vergangenheitsbewältigung in Deutschland: Die Auseinandersetzung mit der NS-Diktatur von 1945 bis heute* (Munich, Germany: Beck, 2001), and Werner Bergmann, *Antisemitismus in öffentlichen Konflikten: Kollektives Lernen in der politischen Kultur der Bundesrepublik, 1949–1989* (Frankfurt, Germany: Campus, 1997).

12. See the ZDF programs *Die Juden von Prag: Bericht über ihre tausendjährige Geschichte* (feature, October 11, 1968); *Jiddisch: Die deutsche Sprache der Juden* (feature, October 26, 1969); and *Juden am Rhein* (feature, April 20, 1973).

13. Erica Burgauer, *Zwischen Erinnerung und Verdrängung: Juden in Deutschland nach 1945* (Reinbek, Germany: Rowohlt, 1993), 104; see also Frank Stern, *Whitewashing of the Yellow Badge: Antisemitism and Philosemitism in Postwar Germany* (Oxford: Pergamon, 1992), 310–26.

14. Walter Fabian, "Pathetische Proklamationen," *epd/Kirche und Rundfunk*, October 15, 1988; see also Susanne Wankell, "Nur abgefragt," *FUNK-Korrespondenz*, October 21, 1988.

15. Anonymous review of the ZDF feature *Die Juden von Prag*, October 11, 1968, in *Gong* 44 (1968).

16. Quote from "Alles nur Schicksal," *Badische Zeitung,* March 8, 1978, a review of *Es verfolgt mich bis auf den heutigen Tag: Ein deutsch-jüdisches Schicksal,* March 6, 1978, which aired after 11 p.m.

17. See the ZDF broadcasts *Der neunte Kreis* (Yugoslav movie, November 20, 1963); *Zwei Halbzeiten in der Hölle* (Hungarian movie, June 21, 1965); *Romeo, Julia und die Finsternis* (Czech movie, November 15, 1965); *Die Passagierin* (Polish movie fragment, October 24, 1966); and *Das Geschäft an der Hauptstrasse* (Czech movie, November 21, 1966).

18. See, for example, the ZDF programs *Zwei Tage von vielen* (TV play, November 11, 1964); *Geheimbund Nächstenliebe* (TV play, March 14, 1964); *Bernhard Lichtenberg* (docuplay, July 20, 1965); *Kirche, Staat und Katholiken* (documentary miniseries, see especially pt. 5 and 6, November 1 and November 5, 1967); *Priester auf dem Schafott* (documentary miniseries, April 21, May 5, May 19, and June 16, 1968); and *Nicht Lob, noch Furcht* (TV play, September 16, 1972).

19. For this type of resistance stories, see the ZDF programs *Es geschah am 20. Juli* (German movie, July 20, 1963); *20. Juli–20 Jahre danach* (documentary, July 20, 1964); *Canaris* (German movie, January 9, 1966); *Der 20. Juli* (German movie, July 22, 1966); *Deutsche gegen Hitler* (documentary, July 20, 1969); *Claus Graf Stauffenberg* (docuplay, July 17, 1970); and *General Oster* (docuplay, August 28, 1970). Christoph Classen has come to similar results in his research of the historical programming of the ARD during the first ten years of its existence; see Classen, *Bilder der Vergangenheit: Die Zeit des Nationalsozialismus im Fernsehen der Bundesrepublik Deutschland, 1955–1965* (Cologne, Germany: Böhlau, 1999).

20. The lack of acknowledgment and financial support for surviving rescuers was appropriately pointed out in a 1972 ZDF documentary, *Wer ein Menschenleben rettet . . . "Judenhelfer": Damals gefährdet—heute vergessen?* (documentary, March 22, 1972).

21. As Hellmut Lange argued succinctly in his review of the docuplay *Feldwebel Schmid,* "Dank an den Lebensretter Feldwebel Schmid," *Schwäbische Zeitung,* March 29, 1968.

22. *Feldwebel Schmid* (docuplay, ZDF, March 22, 1968).

23. The ZDF historian and editorial staff member Franz Neubauer carefully researched the factual accuracy of the script and found numerous mistakes and misrepresentations; see his internal reports about the script addressed to Werner Murawski, the director of the section docuplay, dated August 10, 1966, and January 31, 1967.

24. Hermann Adler showered his ZDF contacts with letters and ultimately distanced himself from the finished product; for one of many examples, see Adler's letter to Werner Murawski dated December 22, 1967.

25. Letter of Hans Günther Imlau to the ZDF director general, Karl Holzamer, dated July 24, 1967.

26. See the reviews by Klaus Hamburger, "Nachgespielte Vernichtung," *FUNK-Korrespondenz,* March 29, 1968, and "Ein Fall von List," *Vorwärts,* April 5, 1968.

27. "Packendes Dokumentarspiel von 'unbewältigter Vergangenheit,'" *Funk-Uhr* 14 (1968).

28. Letter of Hermann Adler to Werner Murawski dated December 22, 1967.

29. The topic of German rescuers was redefined by *Schindler's List.* Coming from abroad, the movie could be enjoyed without qualms because the film was clearly not linked to any self-serving moral agenda. That fact helps explain the movie's extraordinary success in Germany. *Schindler's List* was seen by over six million Germans between March 1994 and May 1995.

30. See, for instance, the ZDF programs *Eli: Mysterienspiel vom Leiden Israels* (theater production, March 8, 1970); *Wer ein Menschenleben rettet: Judenhelfer—Damals gefährdet, heute vergessen* (documentary, March 22, 1972); *Janusz Korczak: Zur Verleihung des Friedenspreises des deutschen Buchhandels* (feature, September 18, 1972); *Der alte Mann und das Kind* (French movie, October 8, 1975); and *Der Märtyrer* (German-Israeli movie, March 8, 1976); in contrast, see the remarkable exceptions *Mendel Schainfeld's zweite Reise nach Deutschland* (documentary, March 17, 1972), and *Dr. W: Ein SS-Arzt in Auschwitz* (documentary, September 16, 1977).

31. See especially Daniel Levy and Natan Sznaider, *Erinnerung im globalen Zeitalter: Der Holocaust* (Frankfurt, Germany: Suhrkamp, 2001), and Moshe Zuckermann, *Zweierlei Holocaust: Der Holocaust in den politischen Kulturen Israels und Deutschlands* (Göttingen, Germany: Wallstein, 1998); for the rise of the survivor paradigm in U.S. television, see Jeffrey Shandler, *While America Watches: Televising the Holocaust* (New York: Cambridge University Press, 1999), 179–210.

32. The ZDF programs *Die Geschwister Oppermann* (TV play, January 30 and January 31, 1983); *Die Bertinis* (TV play, October 31, November 1, November 6, November 7, November 8, 1988); *Die Durchreise* (TV play, March 6, March 7, March 8, March 9, March 10, March 11, and March 14, 1993); *David* (German movie, March 7, 1983); *Regentropfen* (German movie, June 13, 1983); *Feuersturm* [The Winds of War] (U.S. TV play, January 25, January 26, January 27, January 28, January 31, February 1, and February 2, 1986); *Der Schrei nach Leben* [For Those I Love] (TV play, November 17, November 19, and November 23, 1986); *Recht, nicht Rache* [Murderers among Us] (TV play, November 20 and November 21, 1989); *Spiel um Zeit* [Playing for Time] (U.S. TV play, March 9 and March 10, 1981); and *Sophies Entscheidung* [Sophie's Choice] (U.S. movie, March 8, 1992). See also *Cella oder die Überwinder* (TV play, March 13, 1978); *Das letzte Ghetto: 40 Jahre nach der Reichskristallnacht* (documentary, November 8, 1978); *Nacht und Nebel* (documentary, November 9, 1978); *Der Boxer* (TV play, March 3, 1980); *Die Überlebenden des Holocaust in Israel* (documentary, July 21, 1981); *Das Boot ist voll* (Swiss movie, May 17, 1982); *Hiobs Revolte* (TV play, March 11, 1984); *Santa Fe* (TV play, March 2, 1986); *Eine blassblaue Frauenschrift* (TV play, July 13 and July 14, 1986); and *Bittere Ernte* (German movie, March 8, 1987).

33. These connections are emphasized by Judith Keilbach, "Fernseh-Geschichte: Holocaust und Nationalsozialismus im amerikanischen und im bundesdeutschen Fernsehen," in Elisabeth Domansky and Harald Welzer, eds., *Eine offene Geschichte: Zur kommunikativen Tradierung der nationalsozialistischen Vergangenheit* (Tübingen, Germany: diskord, 1999), 118–44; see also Michael Geissler, "The Disposal of Memory: Fascism and Holocaust on West German Television," in Bruce Murray and Chris Wickham, eds., *Framing the Past: The Historiography of German Cinema and Television* (Carbondale: Southern Illinois University Press, 1992), 220–60.

34. This characterization of the representation of Fania Fenelon in *Playing for Time*, by the film scholar Anette Insdorf, applies to the representation of many Holocaust survivors on television; see Anette Insdorf, *Indelible Shadows: Film and the Holocaust*, 2nd ed. (New York: Cambridge University Press, 1989), 20.

35. Thomas Thieringer, "Psychoschocker," *Süddeutsche Zeitung*, November 21, 1986, review of *Der Schrei nach Leben*.

36. For such "standard" stories of victimization and survival, see the ZDF programs *Wiedersehen mit Laupheim* (feature, April 12, 1968); *30 Jahre nach Auschwitz* (January 26, 1975); *Herbst der Welt: Samuel Bak—Ein Maler aus Israel* (feature, February 8, 1976); *Es verfolgt mich bis auf den heutigen Tag: Ein deutsch-jüdisches Schicksal* (interview, March 6, 1978); *Wenn ich wieder ins Leben zurückkehre: Fania Fenelon und die Jahre nach Auschwitz* (interview, March 9, 1981); *. . . damit es nie wieder geschieht: Die Überlebenden des Holocaust in Israel* (documentary, July 21, 1981); *Aber vergessen, das kann ich nicht: Ein jüdischer Kulturkritiker erinnert sich* (feature, October 24, 1983); *Schreiben und Überleben: Das ungewöhnliche Leben der Krystyna Zywulska* (feature, October 20, 1985); *Im Zeichen des Feuers: Zur Verleihung des Friedensnobelpreises an Elie Wiesel* (feature, December 10, 1986).

37. See the ZDF broadcasts *Beschrieben und vergessen: Simon Wiesenthal oder Ich jagte Eichmann* (feature, March 2, 1978); *Zeugen des Jahrhunderts: Simon Wiesenthal im Gespräch mit Guido Knopp* (interview, December 6, 1982); *Sonntagsgespräch: Simon Wiesenthal* (interview, November 8, 1987); *Recht nicht Rache: Die Geschichte des Simon Wiesenthal, 1 and 2* (TV play, November 20, November 21, 1989).

38. "Simon Wiesenthal: Ein Eiferer für die Gerechtigkeit," *Neue Züricher Zeitung*, March 12, 1978; see also "Kritisch gesehen: Simon Wiesenthal," *Stuttgarter Zeitung*, March 8, 1978.

39. Momos [Walter Jens], "Jenseits von Auschwitz," *Die Zeit*, January 31, 1975.

40. See, for example, the ZDF philo-Semitic programs *Juden in Deutschland*, pt. 1, *Spur des Leidens: Vom Ghetto zum Vernichtungslager* (documentary, March 26, 1978); *Wus gewejn . . . es war einmal: Reise durch alte jüdische Zentren*, pts. 1–3 (documentary, June 17, June 19, and July 1, 1985); *Denk ich Ostern an Deutschland: Juden erinnern sich an ihre christlichen Mitbürger* (feature, April 11, 1990); and *Unter der Last der Jahrhunderte gebeugt: Die Gräber der Juden* (feature, November 20, 1990); also see the following rescue narratives: *Gertrud Luckner : Die Not ist immer schneller als die Hilfe* (feature, June 9, 1985); *Lebendig begraben: Das ungeklärte Schicksal des Raoul Wallenberg* (documentary, March 7, 1985); and *Zehn Gerechte : Erinnerungen aus Polen an die deutsche Besatzungszeit* (feature, December 27, 1989).

41. See the documentary *Cäsar, Cäsar: Erinnerungsversuche in Rendsburg*, (March 5, 1990), and the ZDF children's program *Dawids Tagebuch: Ein jüdisch-polnisches Kinderschicksal*, (March 4, 1991); *Cäsar, Cäsar* was very favorably reviewed, see Fritz Wolf, "Verkürzte Nahsicht," *epd/Kirche und Rundfunk*, March 14, 1990. The script of the documentary was published as *Dokumentarfilm-Protokoll: Cäsar,Cäsar! Erinnerungsversuche in Rendsburg* (Mainz, Germany: ZDF, 1990).

42. This small group of programs includes a 1987 BBC remake of the *Diary of Anne Frank*, broadcast by the ZDF in the afternoon in four parts under the title *Das Tagebuch der Anne Frank* (September 3, September 10, September 17, and September 24, 1988); and the ZDF broadcasts of the movie *Regentropfen* (June 13, 1983); and the excellent TV plays *Hiobs Revolte* (March 11, 1984), and *Martha und ich* (November 17, 1991).

43. This strategy was employed very forcefully in Claude Lanzmann's *Shoah*. There are no examples for such aggressive interview strategies in the ZDF sample, although Guido Knopp came closest in his 1992 documentary *Kinder des Feuers: Die Zwillinge von Auschwitz*, (March 15, 1992). Knopp's documentary focuses on Mengele's medical experiments with twins in Auschwitz, and he purposefully represents the victims' physical and psychological trauma as they overcome their own resistances and express their painful memories in front of the camera. The program raises the ethical question if "one may today expose the 50 to 60 year old victims of the sadistic 'twin research' . . . to the flood light and the camera for the purpose of documentation?"; see Klaus Hamburger, "Ehe die Steine schreien," *FUNK-Korrespondenz*, March 19, 1992.

44. Ralph Giordano, *Die Bertinis* (Frankfurt, Germany: Fischer, 1982); the novel sold almost 140,000 copies between 1982 and 1988, 56,000 of which were purchased immediately before and after the broadcast of the TV play on October 31, November 1, and November 6–8, 1988 (internal ZDF memo of Claus Henning Voss dated November 11, 1989); see also Egon Monk's script published as ZDF, ed., *Die Bertinis: Ein ZDF-Fernsehfilm von Egon Monk nach dem Roman von Ralph Giordano* (Frankfurt, Germany: Fischer, 1988), and *Spiel im ZDF* 11 (November 1988): 8–9.

45. Monk, a student of Brecht's, has written and directed a classic didactic play; see Dietrich Leder, "Denkform," *FUNK-Korrespondenz*, November 18, 1988, and "Kraft der Askese," *Frankfurter Rundschau*, November 10, 1988.

46. "Kritisch gesehen: Die Bertinis," *Stuttgarter Zeitung*, November 10, 1988.

47. In addition to the "normal" advertisement, the TV play became the reason for a serious conflict between two of Germany's foremost filmmakers. Eberhard Fechner, who had originally signed on for the project and had already finished a script, could not complete the project because of failing health and agreed to be replaced by Egon Monk. Fechner was under the impression that Monk would use his script, but Monk wrote and directed his own adaptation of the novel; see Dieter Feder, "An den 'Bertinis' zerbrach eine Freundschaft," *Gong*, August 14, 1987, and *Stern TV Magazin*, January 26, 1989; see also the letter by Monk addressed to Fechner dated March 7, 1989, and Fechner's response of March 20, 1989, which did not lead to any resolution. Fechner died in 1992.

48. The household ratings of the five parts were 17, 19, 21, 21, and 22 percent, respectively; see GfK-Fernsehforschung, *Nationaler Wochenbericht*, weeks 44 and 45, 1988.

49. But Monk could be faulted for the fact that he idealized the main protagonists, since the father is depicted much more critically in the book; see Sigrid Schniederken, "Trugschluss," *FUNK-Korrespondenz*, November 18, 1988.

50. Letter of Ralph Giordano to Gyula Trebitsch (one of the producers of the TV play) dated September 19, 1988.

51. *Die Geschwister Oppermann*, pts. 1 and 2 (ZDF, January 30 and January 31, 1983). The script was published as ZDF, ed., *Fernsehfilm Die Geschwister Oppermann* (Frankfurt, Germany: Fischer, 1982); see also *Das Fernsehspiel im ZDF* 39 (November 1982): 31–34.

52. Egon Monk in an interview with Karl Prümm, "Was unsere Zeit noch in Bewegung hält," *epd/Kirche und Rundfunk*, February 5, 1983. Monk had already made statements to the same effect in 1966; see Geisler, "Disposal of Memory," 260n65. The film received rave reviews; for some of many positive reviews, see Karl Prümm, "Weder abstrakt noch gefühlsselig," *epd/Kirche und Rundfunk*, February 9, 1983, and Peter Steinbach, "Das Lehrstück von der grossen Illusion," *Bild-Zeitung*, February 2, 1983; see also the internal ZDF review of Monk's script by Elke Gilliotte-Redlich dated June 25, 1980. Marta Feuchtwanger was also very pleased with the TV play; see her letter to the ZDF dated February 23, 1983. Incidentally, *Die Geschwister Oppermann* was the first German production ever to be broadcast in Israel; see "Israel sah deutschen TV-film," *Badische Neueste Nachrichten*, February 16, 1983.

53. "Was unsere Zeit noch in Bewegung hält: *Geschwister Oppermann?* Ein epd-Interview mit Regisseur Egon Monk," *epd: Kirche und Rundfunk*, February 5, 1983.

54. See Marcel Reich-Ranicki, "So war es nicht," *FAZ*, March 10, 1976, and Elisabeth Bauschmid, "Das Grauen heruntergespielt," *Süddeutsche Zeitung*, March 10, 1976; see also the other program on Korczak aired by the ZDF: *Janusz Korczak: Zur Verleihung des Friedenspreises des Deutschen Buchhandels 1972* (feature, ZDF, September 18, 1972). Other attempts include *Der Schrei nach Leben 2; Recht, nicht Rache 1;* and *Die Passagierin*; compare to *Nacht und Nebel* (documentary, ZDF, November 9, 1978). The tremendous distance that German television productions kept from the center of the Holocaust has also been emphasized by Michael Geisler, "Disposal of Memory."

55. *Mendel Schainfelds zweite Reise nach Deutschland* (ZDF, March 17, 1972).

56. Wolfgang Ruf, "Portrait eines Menschen," *epd/Kirche und Rundfunk*, March 25, 1972; see also Friedrich Weigend, "Mendel Schainfelds zweite Reise nach Deutschland," *Stuttgarter Zeitung*, March 20, 1972.

57. Television has much more aggressively pursued the more general question of why the German people voted for the Nazis and supported the regime, especially during the early phase when its hold on power had not yet been firmly established. These TV plays and docuplays about the Nazi rise to power clearly illustrate that similar fictions could have been produced about the more specific question of the public reactions to the Holocaust. For ZDF programs about the Nazi seizure of power and the popular support of the regime, see *Der Pedell* (TV play, December 1, 1971); *Der 21. Juli* (TV play, December 27, 1972); *Mit dem Strom* (docuplay, August 25, 1972); *Leutersbronner Geschichten* (TV play, January 25, 1982); Die Kinder aus Nr. 67 (TV play, March 9, 1982); *Der letzte Zivilist*, pt. 2 (TV play, November 13, 1984); *Jokehnen oder Wie lange faehrt man von Ostpreussen nach Deutschland?* pt. 1 (TV play, June 21, 1987); *Zum Beispiel Kaltenkirchen: Machtergreifung auf dem Lande* (documentary, January 28, 1983); *Tadelloeser und Wolff*, pts. 1 and 2 (TV play, May 1 and May 3, 1975); *Rotation* (East German movie, October 10, 1976); and *Die Mitläufer* (TV play, January 4, 1988).

58. See especially Jörg Friedrich, *Die kalte Amnestie: NS-Täter in der Bundesrepublik* (Frankfurt, Germany: Fischer, 1984), and Joachim Perels, *Das juristische Erbe des "Dritten Reiches"* (Frankfurt, Germany: Campus, 1999), 203–22.

59. *Romeo, Julia, und die Finsternis* (ZDF, November 15, 1965).

60. Christian Crull. "Dosierte Kritik," *Frankfurter Rundschau*, November 19, 1965.

61. Barbara Sichtermann, "Das Tabu," *Die Zeit,* November 11, 1988. In his recent survey of German television documentaries about the Third Reich, Frank Bösch has also admonished the lack of perpetrator biographies; see Bösch, "Das Dritte Reich ferngesehen: Geschichtsvermittlung in der historischen Dokumentation," *Geschichte in Wissenschaft und Unterricht* 50, no. 4 (1999): 204–20.

62. An informative ZDF documentary that refrained from any commentaries on the state of Vergangenheitsbewältigung in France was aired on the occasion of the opening of the Klaus Barbie trial in May 1987: *Der Fall Barbie: Spuren eines Kriegsverbrechers* (May 11, 1987). The ZDF also broadcast Marcel Ophüls's acclaimed documentary *Hotel Terminus: Leben und Zeit des Klaus Barbie* in a substantially reduced format and late at night on March 26 and March 28, 1990.

63. *Meinungen über Gustav Franz Wagner* (ZDF, June 24, 1979).

64. *Ich habe Eichmann entführt* (ZDF, February 1, 1981). The program on the capture of Eichmann, told from the viewpoint of the Israeli officer in charge of the mission, is the only show on the perpetrators of the Holocaust that was aired during prime time.

65. *Der Holocaust-Befehl: 50 Jahre nach der Wannsee-Konferenz* (January 19, 1992).

66. *Dr. W.—Ein SS-Arzt in Auschwitz* (ZDF, September 12, 1978). The documentary on Eduard Wirths was included in the late-night lineup on short notice, as were two other perpetrator programs: *Die letzte Station* (ZDF, January 11, 1964), and *Der Holocaust-Befehl* (ZDF, January 19, 1992).

67. "Man *muss* das sehen und hören!" *epd/Kirche und Rundfunk,* September 18, 1976; see also Momos, "Schatten eines Mörders," *Die Zeit,* September 17, 1976.

68. See chapter 8 for more details and precise dates of broadcast.

69. This category includes such famous movies as *Das Geschäft an der Hauptstrasse* (Czech movie, November 21, 1966), *Bittere Ernte* (German movie, March 8, 1987), and *Auf Wiedersehen Kinder* (French movie, November 6, 1989); see also *Tagebuch eines Italieners* (Italian movie, March 13, 1984).

70. The ending of the movie, which shows the soldier joining the partisans, was removed prior to the release of the film in West Germany but ultimately added before *Sterne* was aired by the ZDF on September 23, 1983; see internal memo of Dieter Krusche to Herrn Brüne dated August 14, 1964, and letter from Klaus Brüne to Beta Film GmbH of June 10, 1965. *Sterne* was broadcast by the ZDF in an exceptionally unfavorable time slot, after 11:20 p.m.

71. Letter of Klaus Brüne to Beta Film GmbH dated April 10, 1968; see also internal memo of Gerhard Prager to Klaus Brüne dated June 16, 1967.

72. These findings are confirmed by Jürgen Wilke's study of the television coverage commemorating the fiftieth anniversary of the end of World War II; see Wilke, "Fünfzig Jahre nach Kriegsende: Die Rethematisierung im deutschen Fernsehen 1995," in Wilke, ed., *Massenmedien und Zeitgeschichte* (Constance, Germany: UVK Medien, 1999), 260–76, and compare to the data in Wolfgang Becker and Siegfried Quandt, *Das Fernsehen als Vermittler von Geschichtsbewusstsein: 1989 als Jubiläumsjahr* (Bonn, Germany: Bundeszentrale für politische Bildung, 1991).

73. The foreign coverage of German public television is discussed by Peter Zimmermann, "Geschichte von Dokumentarfilm und Reportage von der Adenauer-Ära bis zur Gegenwart," in Peter Ludes, Heidemarie Schumacher and Peter Zimmermann, eds., *Informations- und Dokumentarsendungen: Geschichte des Fernsehens in der Bundesrepublik Deutschlands,* vol. 3 (Munich, Germany: Fink, 1994) 213–324. On a few occasions, German producers even explored episodes in the history of other nations during World War II, for instance, the politics of Vichy (*Der Opportunist oder vom Umgang mit den Besatzern,* ZDF, April 12, 1978) and the anti-Communist aspirations of the Soviet officer corps (*Der Überläufer: Dokumentarspiel zum Fall Wlassow,* docuplay, ZDF, August 19, 1977). As noted earlier, ZDF administrators also frequently purchased Holocaust films produced abroad.

74. For notable exceptions, see the ZDF broadcasts of *Aktion T4* (theater production, January 5, 1964); *Grafeneck: Die Zeit des Lebens* (feature, June 4, 1984); and especially *Eine Liebe in*

Deutschland (German-Polish movie, December 9, 1985), and *Das Heimweh des Waalerjan Wrobel* (TV play, October 24, 1993).

75. "Die Passagierin," *Rheinpfalz,* October 26, 1966.

76. This development was anticipated by Martin Broszat in 1985: "Plädoyer für eine Historisierung des Nationalsozialismus," reprinted in Broszat, *Nach Hitler: Der schwierige Umgang mit unserer Geschichte* (Munich, Germany: Oldenbourg, 1986), 159–73; see also chapter 5.

CHAPTER 7

1. Steve Anderson, "Loafing in the Garden of Knowledge: History, TV, and Popular Memory," *Film and History* 30, no. 1 (2000): 14–23; see also Andrew Hoskins, "New Memory: Mediating history," *Historical Journal of Film, Radio and Television* 21, no. 4 (2001): 333–46.

2. The quantitative aspects of television consumption in West Germany have been documented as part of a series of studies conducted in 1964, 1970, 1974, 1980, 1985, 1990, and 1995. Initiated to research the impact of television on West Germany's print media, especially with regard to advertising revenues, the studies provide a valuable survey of the distribution and use of television, radio, and daily papers since the 1960s. See five volumes by Klaus Berg and Marie-Luise Kiefer: *Massenkommunikation* (Mainz, Germany, 1978); *Massenkommunikation,* vol. 2 (Frankfurt, Germany, 1982); *Massenkommunikation,* vol. 3 (Frankfurt, Germany, 1987); *Massenkommunikation,*vol. 4 (Baden-Baden, Germany, 1992); and *Massenkommunikation,* vol. 5 (Baden-Baden, Germany, 1996); see also the yearly reports on the parameters of German television production and consumption published in *Media Perspektiven.*

3. For the history of television viewing in the Federal Republic, see Knut Hickethier, "Rezeptionsgeschichte des Fernsehens—Ein Überblick," in Walter Klinger and Gunnar Rolers, eds., *Medienrezeption seit 1945,* 2nd ed. (Baden-Baden, Germany: Nomos, 1999), 129–41, and Axel Schildt, *Moderne Zeiten: Freizeit, Massenmedien und "Zeitgeist" in der Bundesrepublik der 50er Jahre* (Hamburg, Germany: Christians, 1995), 283–300.

4. The best synthetic history of German television has been provided by Knut Hickethier, *Geschichte des Deutschen Fernsehens* (Stuttgart, Germany: Metzler, 1998). For the history of German broadcasting policies and institutions, see also Hans Bausch, *Rundfunkpolitik nach 1945,* 2 vols. (Munich, Germany: dtv, 1980), and Dietrich Schwarzkopf, ed., *Rundfunkpolitik in Deutschland,* 2 vols. (Munich, Germany: dtv, 1999). In addition to the two national channels, the member stations of the ARD launched five independent regional channels between 1964 and 1969. The so-called third channels, which originally featured mainly intellectual and educational programs, did not have a significant impact on national programming, with the exception of the broadcast of *Holocaust* in 1979. On the development of the third channels, see Fritz Eberhardt, "Die fünf dritten Programme im Vergleich," *epd-Kirche und Rundfunk* 33, no. 34 (1976): 1–43.

5. See the market-share data published in *ZDF-Jahrbuch 1996* (Mainz, Germany: ZDF, 1997), 217, and *ZDF-Jahrbuch 1997* (Mainz, Germany: ZDF, 1998), 218; compare to *ZDF-Jahrbuch 1993* (Mainz, Germany: ZDF, 1994), 202, which lists data for the years 1985 through 1993.

6. Michael Buss, "Formen der Programmnutzung: Lässt sich das Publikum verplanen?" in Ralph Weiss, ed., *Aufgaben und Perspektiven des öffentlich-rechtlichen Fernsehens* (Baden-Baden, Germany: Nomos, 1991), 144–54.

7. Jürgen Trimborn, *Fernsehen der 90er: Die deutsche Fernsehlandschaft seit der Einführung des Privatfernsehens* (Cologne, Germany: Teiresias, 2000).

8. The ZDF has redefined its prime-time hours several times during its history in attempts to adapt to viewers' needs and capture a larger share of the audience. The most significant change occurred in 1973, when the ZDF pushed the beginning of prime time from 8 p.m. to

7:30 p.m. Since viewers reacted very positively, the decision enhanced the station's profile, increased its audience share, and effectively expanded the most valuable airtime by thirty minutes. As important as this change might have been, it also illustrated the severe limitations that programmers encounter when they try to make their productions available to large audiences.

9. For the different political generations and their contributions to Germany's historical culture, see Harold Marcuse, *Legacies of Dachau: The Uses and Abuses of a Concentration Camp, 1933–2001* (Cambridge: Cambridge University Press, 2001), and Heinz Bude, *Bilanz der Nachfolge* (Frankfurt, Germany: Suhrkamp, 1992).

10. Christoph Classen has found similar strategies in the programs of the ARD between 1955 and 1965. Far more than the later programs of the ZDF, the earlier ARD contributions tended to dehistoricize Nazism by presenting it as the result of existential human fallibility, the totalitarian potential of modernity, or simply the power of evil in history; see Christoph Classen, *Bilder der Vergangenheit: Die Zeit des Nationalsozialismus im Fernsehen der Bundesrepublik Deutschland, 1955–1965* (Cologne, Germany: Böhlau, 1999); see also Knut Hickethier, "Der Zweite Weltkrieg und der Holocaust im Fernsehen der Bundesrepublik der fünfziger und frühen sechziger Jahre," in Michael Greven and Oliver von Wrochem, eds., *Der Krieg in der Nachkriegszeit* (Opladen, Germany: Leske und Budrich, 2000), 93–112, and Michael Geisler, "The Disposal of Memory: Fascism and Holocaust on West German Television," in Bruce Murray and Chris Wickham, eds., *Framing the Past: The Historiography of German Cinema and Television* (Carbondale: Southern Illinois University Press, 1992), 220–60.

11. The suffering of the German population was emphasized in the TV documentaries *Familie ohne Eltern* (ZDF, August 25, 1963); *Russlandheimkehrer* (ZDF, September 9, 1963); *Kriegsopfer* (ZDF, January 19, 1966); *Narben werden nicht vererbt* (ZDF, July 14, 1968); *Jugend in Deutschland: Die betrogene Generation* (ZDF, September 17, 1968); *Sie hinken immer hinterher* (ZDF, March 15, 1970); and the docuplay *Elsa Brandström* (ZDF, March 26, 1971).

12. See, for example, the TV plays *Zwei Tage von vielen* (ZDF, March 11, 1964); *Geheimbund Nächstenliebe* (ZDF, March 14, 1964); *Bernhard Lichtenberg* (ZDF, July 20, 1965); *Nicht Lob, noch Furcht* (ZDF, September 16, 1972); and the two TV documentary miniseries *Kirche, Staat und Katholiken* (ZDF, November 1 and November 5, 1967), and *Priester auf dem Schafott* (ZDF, April 21, May 5, May 19, and June 16, 1972).

13. See the broadcasts of the German movies *Es geschah am 20. Juli* (ZDF, July 20, 1963); *Canaris* (ZDF, January 9, 1966); *Der 20. Juli* (ZDF, July 22, 1966); and the TV documentaries *20. Juli–20 Jahre danach* (ZDF, July 20, 1964), and *Deutsche gegen Hitler* (ZDF, July 20, 1969), as well as the docuplays *Claus Graf Stauffenberg* (ZDF, July 17, 1970), and *General Oster* (ZDF, August 28, 1970). The first and for many years the only acknowledgment of the Communist resistance was the docuplay *Ein Mann, der nichts gewinnt* (ZDF, May 1, 1967).

14. See, for example, the German movies *Hunde, wollt ihr ewig leben* (ZDF, January 29, 1968), and *Nacht fiel über Gotenhafen* (ZDF, May 18, 1968), as well as the docuplay *Flucht über die Ostsee* (ZDF, January 13, 1967).

15. See the TV documentaries *Die Brücke von Remagen* (ZDF, January 13, 1967); *Stalingrad: Hintergründe einer verlorenen Schlacht* (ZDF, January 30, 1968); *Als Feuer vom Himmel fiel: Hintergründe eines verlorenen Luftkrieges* (ZDF, February 17, 1970); and the docuplay *Peenemünde* (ZDF, August 12 and August 14, 1970). Even during the second phase of engagement, the ZDF's coverage still did not acknowledge the crimes of the army.

16. The first programs about Hitler appeared only in the 1970s and focused on his life prior to 1933; see the docuplays *Der Hitler-Ludendorff Prozess* (ZDF, November 5, 1971), and *Ein junger Mann aus dem Innviertel* (ZDF, November 30, 1973).

17. The first critical ZDF TV plays about the burden of the past were written by Oliver Storz: *Prüfung eines Lehrers* (ZDF, December 2, 1968), and *Die Beichte* (ZDF, November 11, 1970).

18. See the docuplays *Geld—Geld—Geld* (ZDF, June 15, 1965), and *Der Fall Sorge* (ZDF, February 20, 1970), among many others.

19. Wolfgang Becker and Norbert Schöll, *In jenen Tagen . . . : Wie der deutsche Nachkriegsfilm die Vergangenheit bewältigte* (Opladen, Germany: Leske und Budrich, 1995), and Heide Fehrenbach, *Cinema in Democratizing Germany: Reconstructing National Identity after Hitler* (Chapel Hill: University of North Carolina Press, 1995); see also Norbert Frei, *Vergangenheitspolitik: Die Anfänge der Bundesrepublik und die NS-Vergangenheit* (Munich, Germany: Beck, 1996).

20. For such rescue stories, see the programs listed in note 14 and the TV documentary *Judenhelfer* (ZDF, March 22, 1972), as well as the docuplay *Feldwebel Schmid* (ZDF, March 2, 1968). The philo-Semitic programs include the TV documentaries *Juden in Deutschland heute: Bilanz eines Verlustes* (ZDF, November 8, 1963); *Die Juden von Prag* (ZDF, October 11, 1968); and *Jiddisch: Die deutsche Sprache der Juden* (ZDF, October 26, 1969).

21. These films from Eastern Europe include *Der neunte Kreis* (ZDF, November 20, 1963); *Romeo, Julia und die Finsternis* (ZDF, November 15, 1965); and *Das Geschäft an der Hauptstrasse* (ZDF, November 21, 1966).

22. Ulrich Herbert, "Vernichtungspolitik: Neue Antworten und Fragen zur Geschichte des Holocaust," in Herbert, ed., *Nationalsozialistische Vernichtungspolitik* (Frankfurt, Germany: Fischer, 1998), 9–66.

23. The most notable Holocaust programs were the documentaries *30 Jahre nach Auschwitz* (ZDF, January 26, 1975); *Mendel Schainfelds zweite Reise nach Deutschland* (ZDF, March 17, 1972); and *Dr. W—Ein NS-Arzt in Auschwitz* (ZDF, September 12, 1976), as well as the docuplay *Reinhard Heydrich—Manager des Terrors* (ZDF, July 22, 1977). The paradigm of Alltagsgeschichte was already brought to screen in the TV plays *Kurze tausend Jahre* (ZDF, April 25, 1975); *Tadellöser und Wolff* (ZDF, May 1 and May 3, 1975); *Ein ganz gewöhnliches Leben* (ZDF, April 7, 1977), and the documentary *Das Leben der Gerda Siepenbrink* (ZDF, November 20, 1975).

24. The biographical data of the scriptwriters of the ZDF fiction and nonfiction programs indicate that the changing of the guard occurred in the mid-1970s. Until 1971, the great majority of scriptwriters were born before 1926 and thus were adults at the end of the war. After a few years of even distribution between members of the older and the younger cohorts, the scales tipped decisively in 1977. From this point on, members of the Hitler Youth generation (born between 1926 and 1937) and members of the first postwar generation (born from 1938 on) make up the overwhelming majority of the ZDF scriptwriters. The data were assembled on the basis of the ZDF's weekly press releases about the upcoming programming and Klaus Brüne, *Autorenlexikon deutschsprachiger Drehbücher für Kino und Fernsehen* (Cologne, Germany, 1994); Egon Netenjakob, *TV-Filmlexikon: Regisseure, Autoren, Dramaturgen, 1952–1992* (Frankfurt, Germany, 1994); and the on-line catalog of the Deutsche Bibliothek Frankfurt at http://z3950gw.dbf.ddb.de/.

25. On *Holocaust* in Germany, see Y. Ahren et al., eds., *Das Lehrstück Holocaust* (Opladen, Germany: Westdeutscher Verlag, 1982).

26. See the documentaries *Simon Wiesenthal oder ich jagte Eichmann* (ZDF, March 2, 1978); *Das letzte Ghetto: 40 Jahre nach der Reichskristallnacht* (ZDF, November 8, 1978); *Nacht und Nebel* (ZDF, November 9, 1978); *Die Überlebenden des Holocaust in Israel* (ZDF, July 21, 1981), and the TV plays *Cella oder die Überwinder* (ZDF, March 13, 1978); *Der Boxer* (ZDF, March 3, 1980); *Spiel um Zeit* (ZDF, March 9 and March 10, 1981); *Die Geschwister Oppermann* (ZDF, January 30 and January 31, 1983); *Hiobs Revolte* (ZDF, March 11, 1984); *Santa Fe* (ZDF, March 2, 1986); *Eine blassblaue Frauenschrift* (ZDF, July 13 and July 14, 1986); *Der Schrei nach Leben* (ZDF, November 17, November 19, and November 23, 1986), as well as the feature films *Das Boot ist voll* (ZDF, May 17, 1982); *Regentropfen* (ZDF, June 13, 1983); and *Bittere Ernte* (ZDF, March 8, 1987).

27. See, for instance, the TV plays *Das tausendunderste Jahr* (ZDF, February 25, 1979); pts. 4, 5, and 6 of *Alpensaga* (ZDF, March 12, October 6, and October 13, 1980); *Ein Kapitel für sich*

(ZDF, December 26 and December 28, 1979); *Gruppenbild mit Dame* (ZDF, May 19, 1980); *Leutersbronner Geschichten* (ZDF, January 25, 1982); *Die Kinder aus Nr. 67* (ZDF, March 9, 1982); *Ringstrassenpalais* (ZDF TV play series beginning February 26, 1983); *Das Dorf* (ZDF, June 17, June 19, and June 20, 1983); *Lebenslinien: Elisabeth* (ZDF, February 26, 1984); *Der letzte Zivilist* (ZDF, November 11 and November 13, 1983); and *Jokehnen* (ZDF, June 21, June 22, and June 23, 1987).

28. On the concept of everyday history in German historiography, see Alf Lüdtke, ed., *The History of Everyday Life* (Princeton, NJ: Princeton University Press, 1995).

29. See, for example, Peter Christian Hall and Joachim Haubrich, eds., *Kritik am Markt: Was kosten Qualität und Quote* (Mainz, Germany: Hase und Koehler, 1993); Gerhard Maletzke, "Empirische Zuschauerforschung: Zusammenfassung und Ausblick," in Karsten Renckstorf and Will Teichert, eds., *Empirische Publikumsforschung: Fragen der Medien-Praxis—Antworten der Medienwissenschaft* (Hamburg, Germany: Hans Bredow Institut, 1983), 96–117; and Hanjörg Bessler, *Hörer—und Zuschauerforschung,* (Munich, Germany: dtv, 1980), 244–46.

30. Susanne Schmidt, *Es muss ja nicht gleich Hollywood sein: Die Produktionsbedingungen des Fernsehspiels und die Wirkungen auf seine Ästhetik* (Berlin: Sigma, 1994), 167.

31. Ien Ang, *Desparately Seeking the Audience* (New York: Routledge, 1991), 1, 7.

32. Advertising agencies have traditionally been much more interested in the precise demographics of television audiences than in their absolute and relative sizes. For a critique of the ratings system from the perspective of German business, see Thomas Koch, "Gutes nach Art des Hauses: Der Umgang mit den Quoten grenzt oft an Scharlatanerie," in Tilmann Gangloff and Stefan Aarbanell, eds., *Liebe, Tod und Lottozahlen: Fernsehen in Deutschland,* (Hamburg, Germany: Steinkopf, 1994), 321–24.

33. During the summer months, television consumption in Germany decreases noticeably, and even during prime time, ratings usually decline after 9:00 p.m. On the seasonal variation of television consumption as reflected in the ratings, see *ZDF-Jahrbuch 1977* (Mainz, Germany: ZDF, 1978), 157; on variations according to day of the week, see *ZDF-Jahrbuch 1974* (Mainz, Germany: ZDF, 1975), 135; the development of ratings throughout the day are represented in *ZDF-Jahrbuch 1978* (Mainz, Germany: ZDF, 1974), 166; see Infratest, *Der Fernsehzuschauer* (Munich, Germany: Infratest, 1965), 11–28, and *Nutzung und Beurteilung des ZDF-Programms, 1963–1967, aufgegliedert nach Programmsparten und -untersparten* (Mainz, Germany: Infratest, 1969), 3–4. For more recent data, see Udo Michael Krüger, *Programmprofile im dualen Fernsehsystem 1985–1990* (Baden-Baden, Germany: Nomos, 1992); and Krüger, *Programmprofile im dualen Fernsehsystem 1991–2000* (Baden-Baden, Germany: Nomos, 2001).

34. In particular, competition can massively influence audience size; see Infratest, *Das Fernsehspiel im Urteil der Zuschauer* (Munich, Germany: Infratest, 1967), 34.

35. Elihu Katz, "Viewers Work," in James Hayes, Lawrence Grossberg, and Ellen Wartella, eds., *The Audience and Its Landscape* (Boulder, CO: Westview, 1996), 9–21.

36. The history of audience measurement in Germany is discussed in detail by Bessler, *Zuschauerforschung;* see also Bernd Büchner, *Der Kampf um den Zuschauer* (Munich, Germany: Fischer, 1989). On the technology of audience measurement, see also Raymond Kent, ed., *Measuring Media Audiences* (London: Routledge, 1994), and especially James Webster et al., *Ratings Analysis,* 2nd ed. (Mahwah, NJ: Lawrence Erlbaum, 2000).

37. Infratam, *Fernsehzuschauer-Forschung in der Bundesrepublik Deutschland: Methodenbeschreibung* (Wetzlar, Germany: Infratam, 1972).

38. Bernward Frank, "Kritische Anmerkungen zu den Tages- und Sendungsanalysen von Infratest," typescript dated Mainz 1971.

39. Critics admonished, for instance, that Infratam provided no data on personal usage, as opposed to household usage, and thus failed to offer any insights into the social structure of television audiences; see Bessler, *Zuschauerforschung,* 206.

40. Hansjörg Bessler, "Teleskopie-Zuschauerforschung: Ein neues System der quantitativen Zuschauerforschung," in Georg Feil, ed. *Fernsehforschung: Feedback oder Anpassung* (Berlin:

Spiess, 1977), 69–73; Bernward Frank, "Die teleskopie-Zuschauerforschung," *Media Perspektiven* 2 (1976): 401–9. The new system had an advantage in that the data from the 1,200 and later 1,500 representative households could be transferred by phone overnight. But the data transmittal by phone created serious problems during the first year of the new service because the Bundespost had not been able to deliver as many modems and lines as promised. As a result, the ratings during the first six months in 1975 were not representative and have never been released by the stations; see Jürgen Pfifferling, "Zuschauerdaten auf dem Prüfstand," *Media Perspektiven* 7 (1982): 309–24. Unfortunately, a couple of important programs on Nazism were aired during this period, most notably Eberhard Fechner's production of Walter Kempowski's novel *Tadellöser und Wolff*.

41. Unfortunately, the data about the social structure of the audience have not been managed and published consistently over the years and cannot be used effectively for historical analysis. Therefore, the ratings analyzed in this chapter are the old standard of household ratings, which have been collected and published in the same fashion for over three decades.

42. The people-meter employed by GfK was also better adapted to West Germany's rapidly diversifying television landscape because it could process more data; see Michael Buss and Michael Darkow, "Der Weg zur GfK-Fernsehforschung," in Dieter Prokop, ed., *Medienforschung,* vol. 1, *Wünsche, Zielgruppen, Wirkungen* (Frankfurt, Germany: Fischer, 1985), 185–99.

43. Klaus Wehmeier, *Die Geschichte des ZDF, 1961–1966* (Mainz, Germany: Hase und Koehler, 1979), 141–42. Due to the limited reach of the ZDF transmitters, the ZDF ratings for the years from 1963 through 1967 are generally reported in two ways; Infratam published both the percentage of all actual television households tuned to the ZDF and a projected figure based on the theoretical assumption that all television households could already choose between ARD and ZDF. Since only the second, projected figure assures comparability to later years, I will ignore the percentage of actual households.

44. Bernward Frank, "Zuschauerreaktionen und das ZDF-Programm von 1963 bis 1972," in *ZDF-Jahrbuch 1972* (Mainz, Germany: ZDF, 1973), 171–79.

45. *ZDF-Jahrbuch 1978* (Mainz, Germany: ZDF, 1979), 163–69; *ZDF-Jahrbuch 1980* (Mainz, Germany: ZDF, 1981), 195; and *ZDF-Jahrbuch 1993* (Mainz, Germany: ZDF, 1994), 202.

46. In 1987, the commercial stations reached a market share of 2.7 percent, up from less than 1 percent the year before. In subsequent years, that share consistently rose from almost 10 percent in 1988 to over 40 percent in 1993, when, for the first time, one of the private stations, RTL Plus, became the market leader. In the same period, from 1987 to 1993, the ZDF's market share dropped from 41 percent to 19 percent; see Heinz Gehrhard, "Zweiertle Erfolg," in *ZDF-Jahrbuch 1993,* 201–3.

47. See especially two classics, Alexander Mitscherlich and Margarete Mitscherlich, *Die Unfähigkeit zu trauern* (Munich, Germany: Piper, 1967), and Theodor Adorno, *Erziehung zur Mündigkeit* (Frankfurt, Germany: Suhrkamp, 1970); also see Jörg Friedrich, *Die kalte Amnestie* (Frankfurt, Germany: Fischer, 1984), and Ralph Giordano, *Die zweite Schuld* (Hamburg, Germany: Rasch und Röhrig, 1987).

48. Infratest, *Das Fernsehspiel im Urteil,* 36–44; Infratest, *Der Fernsehzuschauer,* 29–53; Infratest, *Dokumentation wichtiger Ergebnisse der Fernsehforschung,* IV, *Fernsehspiele und Theaterübertragungen* (Wetzlar, Germany: Infratest, 1975), 26–28, 60–63, 89–93, and 128–32.

49. Infratest, *Das Fernsehspiel im Urteil,* 20–21; Infratest, *Der Fernsehzuschauer,* 50–52. These findings are also supported by a number of in-depth analyses of the reception of documentary and TV play series dedicated to the topic of Nazism; see Infratest, *Gesamtübersicht über die Zuschauerreaktionen auf die vom Deutschen Fernsehen aus Hamburg ausgestrahlte Sendereihe "Eine Epoche vor Gericht"* (Munich, Germany: Infratest, 1961); Infratest, *Die Zuschauerreaktionen zu der Sendereihe "Das Dritte Reich"* (Munich, Germany: Infratest, 1961); and Infratest, *Dokumentation wichtiger Ergebnisse der Fernsehforschung,* vol 4.

50. More accurately, the noticeable decrease in the ratings lasted for three and a half years, since no ratings were published for the first six months of 1975; see note 44.

51. Webster, Phalen, and Lichti, *Ratings Analysis,* 75, 158–84.

52. Hickethier, *Geschichte des Deutschen Fernsehens,* 400.

53. On viewers' selection of programs on the basis of information distributed by television guides and other print media, see Claus Wilkens, *Presse und Fernsehen: Die Funktion der Presse bei der gesellschaftlichen Rezeption des Fernsehens* (Düsseldorf, Germany: Bertelsmann, 1972), 94–96; Herbert Honsowitz, *Fernsehen und Programmzeitschriften: Eine Aussageanalyse der Programmpresse* (Berlin: Spiess, 1975), 132–43; and Volker Reissmann, *Fernsehprogrammzeitschriften: Ein Überblick über die bundesdeutsche Programmpresse mit einer inhaltsanalytischen Untersuchung* (Munich, Germany: Fischer, 1989).

54. Lutz Huth and Michael Krezeminski, *Zuschauerpost—Ein Folgeproblem massenmedialer Kommunikation* (Tübingen, Germany: Niemeyer, 1981). To give just one example, between 1970 and 1993, the ZDF received an average of seven hundred calls per year about its programs on Nazism and World War II.

55. Webster, Phalen, and Lichty, *Ratings Analysis,* 164.

56. On the fundamental changes in West Germany's historical culture starting in the late 1950s, see Werner Bergmann, *Antisemitismus in öffentlichen Konflikten: Kollektives Lernen in der politischen Kultur der Bundesrepublik, 1949–1989* (Frankfurt, Germany: Campus, 1997), 187–311; Helmut Dubiel, *Niemand ist frei von der Geschichte: Die nationalsozialistische Herrschaft in den Debatten des Deutschen Bundestages* (Munich, Germany: Hauser, 1999), 79–127; Michael Kohlstruck, "Das zweite Ende der Nachkriegszeit: Zur Veränderung der politischen Kultur um 1960," in Gary Schaal and Andreas Wöll, eds., *Vergangenheitsbewältigung: Modelle der politischen und sozialen Integration in der bundesdeutschen Nachkriegsgeschichte* (Baden-Baden, Germany: Nomos, 1997), 113–27.

57. On the lack of intergenerational communication about the Nazi past, see Jürgen Müller-Hohagen, *Verleugnet, verdrängt, verschwiegen: Die seelischen Auswirkungen der Nazizeit* (Munich, Germany: Kösel, 1988), and Gesine Schwan, *Politik und Schuld: Die zerstörerische Macht des Schweigens* (Frankfurt, Germany: Fischer, 1997).

CHAPTER 8

1. Karsten Linne, "Hitler als Quotenbringer—Guido Knopps mediale Erfolge," *1999: Zeitschrift für Sozialgeschichte des 20. und 21. Jahrhunderts* 17, no. 2 (September 2002): 90–101.

2. It has to be emphasized from the outset that it is difficult to determine the question of authorship in any traditional sense for many of the programs that will be discussed in this chapter. In contrast to auteur documentaries by filmmakers such as Leiser and Fest, the programs of the ZDF Division for Contemporary History depend more on teamwork, as is the rule in television. Guido Knopp certainly screens all productions quite carefully, and the ZDF's public relations experts present him as the mastermind of the new discourse of history, but it is impossible to determine from the outside who in the team actually developed the radical editing strategies in the 1990s. The cutters, not the scriptwriters, are the real authors of these films.

3. For an excellent critique of the Knopp aesthetics, see Judith Keilbach, "Fernsehbilder der Geschichte: Anmerkungen zur Darstellung des Nationalsozialismus in den Geschichtsdokumentationen des ZDF," *1999: Zeitschrift für Sozialgeschichte des 20. und 21. Jahrhunderts* 17, no. 2 (September 2002): 104–13. See also the insightful review by Barbara Sichtermann, "Auf den Effekt kalkuliert," *Die Welt,* November 23, 1995.

4. The sound tracks of Knopp's TV productions have been effectively criticized by Joachim Westhoff, "TV-Kritik," *Westfälische Rundschau,* November 11, 1995, and Karin Hanig, "Am Mythos nur gekratzt," *Sächsische Zeitung,* December 13, 1995.

5. Adolf Hitler, *Mein Kampf* (Erwin Leiser, Minerva; Sweden, 1959); *Hitler—Eine Karriere* (Christian Herrendoerfer and Joachim Fest, Interart; Germany, 1976–1977). The most recent

addition to this list, produced after Knopp's Hitler programs, is *Der Untergang* (Oliver Hirsch-biegel, Constantin Film; Germany/Italy/Austria, 2004).

6. Prior to Knopp's Hitler programs, the ZDF had only aired three programs specifically about Hitler in the thirty-one years between 1963 and 1993, if Chaplin's *The Great Dictator* (*Der grosse Diktator,* ZDF, June 24, 1979) is excluded. The programs in question are the docu-drama *Wie er es wurde: Ein junger Mann aus dem Innviertel—Adolf Hitler* (ZDF, November 30, 1973); a public reading of *Mein Kampf* by the actor Helmut Qualtinger, *Helmut Qualtinger liest: Adolf Hitler: "Mein Kampf"* (ZDF, August 27, 1974); and the U.S. TV play *Der Führerbunker* (ZDF, November 8, 1981).

7. See Peter Zimmermann's very helpful survey, "Geschichte von Dokumentarfilm und Reportage von der Adenauer-Ära bis zur Gegenwart," in Peter Ludes, Heidemarie Schu-macher, and Peter Zimmermann, eds., *Geschichte des Fernsehens in der Bundesrepublik Deutsch-land* vol. 3, *Informations- und Dokumentarsendungen* (Munich, Germany: Fink, 1994), 213–324, esp. 288–91.

8. *Die deutsche Einheit: Hoffnung, Alptraum, Illusion?* (ZDF, May 27, 1979).

9. For the impact of *Holocaust* in Germany, see Peter Märtesheimer and Ivo Frenzel, eds., *Im Kreuzfeuer: Der Fernsehfilm Holocaust: Eine Nation ist betroffen* (Frankfurt, Germany: Fis-cher, 1979).

10. Uwe Magnus, "*Holocaust* in der Bundesrepublik: Zentrale Ergebnisse der Begleitun-tersuchungen aus der Sicht der Rundfunkanstalten," *Rundfunk und Fernsehen* 28, no. 4 (1980): 534–42.

11. *Narben: Danzig—oder: Wie Menschen Geschichte erleiden,* pt. 1, *Menschen am Kreuzweg* (ZDF, May 3, 1981); *Narben: Danzig—oder: Wie Menschen Geschichte erleiden,* pt. 2, *Treibjagd* (ZDF, May 7, 1981); and *Narben: Danzig—oder: Wie Menschen Geschichte erleiden,* pt. 3, *Stadt im Sturm* (ZDF, May 17, 1981). *Narben* was specifically designed to bring emotionally com-pelling Alltagsgeschichte to the screen in order to implement the lessons of *Holocaust;* see Detlev Sprickmann, "Im Mittelpunkt der Zeitgeschichte steht der Mensch," *ZDF Jahrbuch 1979* (Mainz, Germany: ZDF, 1980), 101–6. Sprickmann anticipated additional international coproductions about the history of the Nazi era in the spirit of reconciliation, but he thought primarily about British, French, and U.S. television stations, not Soviet/Russian TV, which be-came Knopp's partner of choice in the 1990s.

12. Internal memo of director general of the ZDF, Karl-Günther von Hase, to the head of the section for society and politics, Detlev Sprickmann, dated March 28, 1980, and internal memo of Detlev Sprickmann to the deputy editor in chief, Volker von Hagen, dated February 27, 1980.

13. Teleskopie Gesellschaft für Fernsehzuschauerforschung, ed., *Telejour: Einschalt—und Sendeverhalten zu den Sendungen von ARD und ZDF: 18. Woche 1981* (Bonn, Germany: Teleskopie, 1981), 8; Teleskopie, ed., *Telejour: 19. Woche* (Bonn, Germany: Teleskopie, 1981), 4; and Teleskopie, ed., *Telejour: 20. Woche 1981* (Bonn, Germany: Teleskopie, 1981), 8.

14. Armin Biergann, "*Narben:* Holprig und zu betulich," *Kölnische Rundschau,* May 19, 1981, and "Nicht schön, aber notwendig," *Main-Echo,* May 19, 1981.

15. Guido Knopp's internal application ("Vorlage zur Stoffzulassung") to develop the con-cept for a roundtable discussion after the broadcast of *Narben* dated October 10, 1980.

16. *Narben: Was steht noch zwischen Polen und Deutschen?* (ZDF, May 17, 1981). Von Hase had "suggested" including a moderate expellee who would be acceptable to the expellee or-ganizations in the Federal Republic; see von Hase's notes on the permission to develop the concept (Zulassungsbescheid) dated October 29, 1980.

17. Minutes of the ZDF telephone staff (Protokoll des Telefondienstes) of May 17, 1981.

18. "Ein sehr ehrenwerter Versuch," *Westdeutsche Allgemeine Zeitung,* May 19, 1981; Sigrid Schniederken, "Authentizität will gewagt sein," *Funk-Korrespondenz,* May 20, 1981.

19. Officially, Detlev Sprickmann remained in control of the subdivision for contemporary history, which he had led since it was formed in 1978. But in April 1981, Knopp became his

temporary replacement because Sprickmann was transferred to Tokyo for three years. The unit for temporary history was officially disbanded in 1982 but reemerged in 1984, with Knopp officially at the helm. See *ZDF Jahrbuch 1978* (Mainz, Germany: ZDF, 1979), 244; *ZDF Jahrbuch 1980* (Mainz, Germany: ZDF, 1981), 38, 270; *ZDF Jahrbuch 1984* (Mainz, Germany: ZDF, 1986), 48; *ZDF Jahrbuch 1985*, 8, 315.

20. *"Der Deutschen Mai:" Hambach heute—Jubelfeier oder Auftrag?* (ZDF, May 23, 1982), and *Keine Angst vor Kernkraft?* (ZDF, November 29, 1982). Under the series title *Fragen der Zeit*, the ZDF broadcast between thirty-five and fifty interviews with scholars and scientists each year. The series was replaced in 1984 by the more historically oriented series *Damals— Vor vierzig Jahren*. Before Knopp became a media star, these low-profile programs, broadcast on Sunday and Saturday afternoons and performed in front of small audiences, were the bread and butter of his work at the ZDF.

21. *Warum habt Ihr Hitler nicht verhindert?* (ZDF, January 23, 1983), and *Warum habt Ihr Hitler widerstanden?* (ZDF, July 18, 1984); see also the review of Thomas Thieringer, "Bombenerfolg," *Süddeutsche Zeitung*, January 25, 1983.

22. *Der Verführer: Anmerkungen zu Goebbels* (ZDF, November 29, 1987).

23. Sigrid Schniederken, "Übereilige 'Fertigstellung,'" *FUNK-Korrespondenz*, December 11, 1987, and Sybille Simon-Zülch, "Alle gleich honorig," *epd: Kirche und Rundfunk*, December 5, 1987.

24. *Warum habt Ihr Hitler nicht verhindert?*

25. Hans Janke, "Räsonables Resümee," *epd: Kirche und Rundfunk*, February 2, 1983, and Uwe Walter, "Fernsehen kritisch: *Warum habt Ihr Hitler nicht verhindert?*" *Stuttgarter Nachrichten*, January 25, 1983.

26. *Keine Zeit für Tränen: Frauen zwischen Tod und Trümmern* (ZDF, November 30, 1986).

27. For contemporary scholarly debates about Alltagsgeschichte, see Institut für Zeitgeschichte, ed., *Alltagsgeschichte der NS-Zeit: Neue Perspektiven oder Trivialisierung* (Munich, Germany: Oldenbourg, 1984). For an excellent review of *Keine Zeit für Tränen*, see Hans Messias, "Unstatthafter Blick auf deutsche Vergangenheit," *FUNK-Korrespondenz*, December 5, 1986.

28. Between 1981 and 1988, Knopp produced ten documentaries about the Nazi past, which were broadcast after 10 p.m. and reached an average of 12 percent of television households. Although nonfiction programs about other topics (for instance, animal shows) were often more successful, Knopp's ratings compare favorably to the audience sizes of other historical documentaries aired in similar time slots. In addition to Knopp's programs, the ZDF broadcast twenty-seven other documentaries about different aspects of the Nazi past during the same years; they only reached an average of 9 percent of TV households.

29. Representative for this repeated charge, see Lutz Hachmeister, "So und so," *epd: Kirche und Rundfunk*, October 11, 1986, a review of *Das Urteil von Nürnberg* (ZDF, September 28, 1986).

30. For a survey of the politics of memory of the Kohl administration, see Siobhan Kattago, *Ambiguous Memory: The Nazi Past and German National Identity* (Westport, CT: Praeger, 2001), 48–57; Rupert Seulhe, *"Geistig-moralische Wende?" Der politische Umgang mit der NS-Vergangenheit in der Ära Kohl am Beispiel von Gedenktagen, Museums- und Denkmalprojekten* (Frankfurt, Germany: Lang, 2001); and chapter 11.

31. The anniversary of the constitution was remembered in the following Knopp productions: *So entstand die Bundesrepublik: Teil 1: Kalter Krieg um Deutschland* (ZDF, May 7, 1989); *So entstand die Bundesrepublik: Teil 2: Provisorisch, aber gründlich* (ZDF, May 8, 1989); and *Ein Grund zum Feiern? 40 Jahre Bundesrepublik* (ZDF, May 23, 1989). Unification became the subject of a six-part series in 1990: *Die deutsche Einheit*, pt. 1, *Teilung auf Befehl* (ZDF, July 15, 1990); *DdE*, pt. 2, *Ungenutzte Chancen* (ZDF, July 17, 1990); *DdE*, pt. 3, *Getrennte Wege* (ZDF, July 22, 1990); *DdE*, pt. 4, *Kleine Schritte* (ZDF, December 23, 1990); *DdE*, pt. 5, *Zwei Staaten— Eine Nation* (ZDF, December 26, 1990); and *DdE 6*, pt. 6, *Der Weg nach Deutschland* (ZDF, December 30, 1990).

32. *ZDF-Jahrbuch 1990* (Mainz, Germany: ZDF, 1991), 315.

33. An average of less than three million West German viewers were interested in *So entstand die Bundesrepublik* and *Die deutsche Einheit*, *ZDF-Jahrbuch 1990*, 299, and *ZDF-Jahrbuch 1989* (Mainz, Germany: ZDF, 1990), 287.

34. See, for instance, the great review of Momos (Walter Jens) of the fiftieth anniversary coverage of July 20, 1944, in ARD and ZDF, "Schmierentheater," *Die Zeit*, July 26, 1984.

35. A particularly insightful review of Knopp's *"Was soll aus Deutschland werden": Die Konferenz von Potsdam* (ZDF, July 28, 1985) pointed out this deficit but also applauded Knopp for avoiding dry academic discourse and trying to develop a new visual language for television history; see "Kritisch gesehen: *Potsdamer Konferenz*," *Stuttgarter Zeitung*, July 30, 1985. For Knopp's programmatic statements, see note 42.

36. For the impact of *Holocaust* on West German television programming, see Knut Hickethier, *Geschichte des Deutschen Fernsehens* (Stuttgart, Germany: Metzler, 1998), 355–56, and Michael Geisler, "The Disposal of Memory: Fascism and the Holocaust on West German Television," in Bruce Murray and Christopher Wickham, eds., *Framing the Past: The Historiography of German Cinema and Television* (Carbondale: Southern Illinois University Press, 1992), 220–60. Edgar Reitz's eleven-part TV miniseries *Heimat*, which was broadcast by the ARD between September 16 and October 24, 1984, represented a conscious German response to *Holocaust* and helped define the genre of Alltagsgeschichte on television; see Anton Kaes, *From Hitler to "Heimat": The Return of History as Film* (Cambridge, MA: Harvard University Press, 1989), 161–92.

37. That applies in particular to the productions *Warum habt Ihr Hitler nicht verhindert?; Warum habt Ihr Hitler widerstanden?; Was soll aus Deutschland werden?;* and *Ich wurde von Deutschen versteckt* (ZDF, July 20, 1983).

38. See, for instance, the review of *Die Mauer* (ZDF, August 12 and August 13, 1986) by Heinrich von Nussbaum, "Mediengedenktag," *epd: Kirche und Rundfunk*, August 20, 1986. As Knopp's visibility increased on the screen, he was also criticized for his allegedly narcissistic tendency of casting himself in front of the camera; see Dietrich Leder, "Die Zehnminuten-Geschichts-Terrine," *FUNK-Korrespondenz*, July 25, 1991. Leder reviewed the first sequels of Knopp's series *Bilder, die Geschichte machten*, which presented famous photos and their historical context in short, ten-minute features. Begun in 1991, the series was continued in 1992 and 1994, with ten episodes each year.

39. The reactions to Knopp's *Als die Synagogen brannten . . . : Novemberpogrom '38 — Hitlers Reichskristallnacht* (ZDF, November 8, 1988) illustrate this response; see Eberhard Fehre, "Zeitzeugen," *Westdeutsche Zeitung*, November 11, 1988, and Barbara Sichtermann, "Angst und Scherben," *Die Zeit*, November 18, 1988.

40. On the transformation of German television after the introduction of commercial networks, see Dietrich Schwarzkopf, ed., *Rundfunkpolitik in Deutschland: Wettbewerb und Öffentlichkeit*, 2 vols. (Munich, Germany: dtv, 1999).

41. Sound was added in *Warum habt Ihr Hitler widerstanden?*, and scenic reconstructions figured prominently in *Die Mauer* and *Als die Synagogen brannten*.

42. Guido Knopp, "Zwischen Krieg und Frieden: Zeitgeschichte im ZDF 1989," *ZDF-Jahrbuch 1989*, 80–84; see also Knopp, "Geschichte im Fernsehen: Perspektiven der Praxis," in Guido Knopp and Siegfried Quandt, eds., *Geschichte im Fernsehen: Ein Handbuch* (Darmstadt, Germany: Wissenschaftliche Buchgesellschaft, 1988), 1–9; and Knopp, "Zeitgeschichte im ZDF," in Jürgen Wilke, ed., *Massenmedien und Zeitgeschichte* (Constance, Germany: UVK Medien, 1999), 309–16.

43. *Die Saat des Krieges*, pt. 1, *Der erkaufte Frieden* (ZDF, August 20, 1989), and *Die Saat des Krieges*, pt. 2 *Der erzwungene Krieg* (ZDF, August 24, 1989).

44. Some reviewers shared this assessment; see, for instance, Patrick Bahners, "Der kostümierte Diktator," *Frankfurter Allgemeine Zeitung*, August 26, 1989.

45. The first six programs of 1991 were: *Der verdammte Krieg: Das Unternehmen Barbarossa*, pt. 1, *Der Wahn vom Lebensraum* (ZDF, June 16, 1991); *DvK: DUB*, pt. 2, *Der Überfall* (ZDF, June 17, 1991); *DvK: DUB*, pt. 3, *Die Illusion des Sieges* (ZDF, June 18, 1991); *DvK: DUB*, pt. 4, *Der Kampf um Leningrad* (ZDF, June 19, 1991); *DvK: DUB*, pt. 5, *Den Kreml im Visier* (ZDF, June 21, 1991); and *DvK: DUB*, pt. 6, *Der Anfang vom Ende* (ZDF, June 23, 1991); see also the live discussion *Nach fünfzig Jahren: Deutsche und Russen diskutieren* (ZDF, June 23, 1991). The second installment of five programs was broadcast in 1993: *Der verdammte Krieg: Entscheidung Stalingrad*, pt. 1, *Tödliche Weisung* (ZDF, January 1, 1993); *DvK: ES*, pt. 2, *Hass wider Hass* (ZDF, January 20, 1993); *DvK: ES*, pt. 3, *Leningrad will leben* (ZDF, January 21, 1993); *DvK: ES*, pt. 4, *Die Falle schnappt zu* (ZDF, January 22, 1993); and *DvK: ES*, pt. 5, *Das Ende an der Wolga* (ZDF, January 24, 1993). The last installment of six programs aired in 1995: *Der verdammte Krieg: Bis zum bitteren Ende*, pt. 1, *Der Feuersturm* (ZDF, March 5, 1995); *DvK: BzbE*, pt. 2, *Verbrannte Erde* (ZDF, March 12, 1995); *DvK: BzbE*, pt. 3, *"Die Russen kommen!"* (ZDF, March 19, 1995); *DvK: BzbE*, pt. 4, *Der Zusammenbruch* (ZDF, March 26, 1995); *DvK: BzbE*, pt. 5, *Die Schlacht um Berlin* (ZDF, April 2, 1995); and *DvK: BzbE*, pt. 6, *Triumph und Tragödie* (ZDF, April 9, 1995).

46. Heiko Strech, "Blitz und Donner," *Tages-Anzeiger,* June 19, 1991.

47. *ZDF Pressedienst* 26, 1991, Anmerkungen 13; see also the elaborate pamphlet that the ZDF distributed to the press, ZDF, ed., *Der verdammte Krieg: Das Unternehmen Barbarossa* (Mainz, Germany: ZDF, 1991).

48. *ZDF Pressedienst* 26, 1991, Anmerkungen 13. Although the ZDF public relations office emphasized the allegedly single, indivisible historical truth represented in the production, the partners in Mainz and Moscow could not agree on an identical voice-over commentary for the broadcast in Germany and in the Soviet Union; see Peter Carstens, "Auf geistigen Feldhernhügeln." *Frankfurter Allgemeine Zeitung,* June 20, 1991.

49. In fact, the pride of broadcasting over such a large territory recalls the famous Nazi radio Christmas program of 1942, which featured live coverage from many faraway places of the extended front, including Stalingrad.

50. Quoted from the voice-over commentary of the second installment of *Der verdammte Krieg: Entscheidung Stalingrad*; see Jan Ross, "Gemeinsam zu den Gräbern," *Frankfurter Allgemeine Zeitung,* January 19, 1993.

51. Quoted from the voice-over commentary at the end of *Der verdammte Krieg: Entscheidung Stalingrad*, pt. 1, *Tödliche Weisung* (January 19, 1993).

52. Carstens, "Auf geistigen Feldherrnhügeln"; Ulrich von Sanden, "Geschichte als Völkerverständigung," *Stuttgarter Nachrichten,* June 18, 1991.

53. Very perceptive on this point is Bettina Schulte, "Barbarischer Feldzug," *Badische Zeitung,* June 20, 1991, and Tilmann Gangloff, "Gedankenloses Kriegsspiel," *Mannheimer Morgen,* June 25, 1991.

54. Quote from Knopp's closing remarks in *Der verdammte Krieg: Das Unternehmen Barbarossa*, pt. 5, *Den Kreml im Visier.*

55. See, for example, Hans Bachmüller, "Auflösung eines Feindbildes," *epd: Kirche und Rundfunk,* July 3, 1991, and Dieter Mahnecke, "Der verdammte Krieg," *Das Parlament,* July 12, 1991.

56. See, especially, Martina Wengierek, "Sorgfältige Spurensuche," *Kieler Nachrichten,* January 19, 1993; Christian Hörburger, "Der verdammte Krieg," *Tagesspiegel,* January 19, 1993; and Ross, "Gemeinsam zu den Gräbern."

57. *ZDF Jahrbuch 1991* (Mainz, Germany: ZDF, 1992), 323; *ZDF Jahrbuch 1993* (Mainz, Germany: ZDF, 1994), 339; and *ZDF Jahrbuch 1995* (Mainz, Germany: ZDF, 1996), 342.

58. *ZDF Jahrbuch 1993*, 202, and *ZDF Jahrbuch 1995*, 199.

59. For the interpretations of ratings, see James Webster, Patricia Phalen, and Lawrence Lichty, eds., *Ratings Analysis: The Theory and Practice of Audience Research*, 2nd ed. (Mahwah, NJ: Lawrence Erlbaum, 2000).

60. The minutes of the ZDF telephone staff indicate that the fifty documentaries and TV discussions that Knopp produced between 1981 and 1993 received an average of thirty-five calls despite the fact that the programs were often aired after 10 p.m. During the same years, even the ZDF's prime-time programs on the topic of Nazism received only an average of twenty-four calls per broadcast.

61. See, for example, the minutes of the ZDF telephone staff ("Protokoll des Telefondienstes") of June 16, 17, 18, 19, 21, and 23, 1991.

62. The ZDF subdivision for contact with viewers (Referat Zuschauerpost—und Telefonredaktion) compiles a weekly report about the quantity and most important trends in the feedback from the audience; see the reports for the weeks of June 20 through 26, 1991, and June 27 through July 3, 1991, dated June 28 and July 5, 1991.

63. Bettina Schulte, "Friedensgeste," *Badische Zeitung,* June 25, 1991, and "Nach fünfzig Jahren," *Mannheimer Morgen,* June 25, 1991.

64. Knopp, "Zwischen Krieg und Frieden," 80.

65. *Hitler—Eine Bilanz,* pt. 1, *Der Privatmann* (ZDF, November 9, 1995); *HEB,* pt. 2, *Der Verführer* (ZDF, November 12, 1995); *HEB,* pt. 3, *Der Erpresser* (ZDF, November 19, 1995); *HEB,* pt. 4, *Der Diktator* (ZDF, November 26, 1995); *HEB,* pt. 5, *Der Kriegsherr* (ZDF, December 3, 1995); and *HEB,* pt. 6 *Der Verbrecher* (ZDF, December 10, 1995).

66. Guido Knopp, "Keine Angst vor Hitler?—50 Jahre danach," *ZDF Jahrbuch 1995,* 88–90.

67. Ibid., 90.

68. Knopp, "Zwischen Krieg und Frieden," 81; see also *ZDF Pressedienst* 3, 1997, 66.

69. *ZDF Jahrbuch 1995* (Mainz, Germany: ZDF, 1996), 342.

70. Heinz Braun, "Im direkten Kontakt mit dem Zuschauer," *ZDF Jahrbuch 1995,* 204–6.

71. Minutes of the ZDF telephone staff of November 9, 19, and 26 and December 3, 1995.

72. The TV discussion *Hitler heute* (ZDF, December 10, 1995), which was broadcast live after the last sequel of *Hitler—Eine Bilanz* from 10:56 p.m. to 11:57 p.m., prompted 462 phone calls to the station. These calls were received in addition to the calls to the special phone number the ZDF had leased to screen and process questions from viewers; see minutes of the ZDF telephone staff of December 10, 1995.

73. "Hitler und kein Ende," *Stuttgarter Zeitung,* November 11, 1995; Rolf Potthoff, "Ein Hitler-Portrait mit Bildern wie Blendwerk," *Westdeutsche Allgemeine Zeitung,* December 1, 1995; and Karin Hanig, "Am Mythos nur gekratzt," *Sächsische Zeitung,* December 13, 1995. It is also remarkable that *Hitler—Eine Bilanz* received significantly fewer reviews than Knopp's earlier programs. Apparently, as Knopp was celebrating his most successful series up to that point and clearly moving audiences, the critics were losing interest.

74. This strategy of representation is reminiscent of Philip Jenninger's botched speech in the German parliament in November 1988, as his empathetic attempt to explore the popularity of Hitler with the German people cost him his job as the president of that parliament; see chapter 4.

75. With the exception of some of the sequels, the following series did not deal with the Nazi past: *Top-Spione,* six sequels (ZDF, between November 6 and December 11, 1994); *Skandal: Die grossen Affairen,* four sequels (ZDF, between June 16 and July 7, 1996); *Vatikan: Die Macht der Päpste,* five sequels (ZDF, between October 30 and November 26, 1997); and *Kanzler,* six sequels (ZDF, between April 6 and May 11, 1999). *Unser Jahrhundert: Deutsche Schicksalstage,* three sequels (ZDF, between May 19 and June 2, 1998), which continued with a second installment of twelve sequels in 1999, featured a number of programs on NS history.

76. *ZDF Jahrbuch 1996,* 61, and 276–77.

77. The global reach of the ZDF historians has been proudly advertised on many occasions; see, for example, *ZDF Pressedienst* 3, 1997, 66. For the relative size of the subdivision of contemporary history, see *ZDF Jahrbuch 1998,* 269–73.

78. Dieter Stolte, "Vom Markt zur Marke: Marktstrategien für das öffentlich-rechtliche Progamm der Zukunft," *ZDF Jahrbuch 1995,* 45–50, and Dieter Schwarzenau, "Marken

markieren: Anmerkungen zur Pressearbeit in einem verschärften Wettbewerb," *ZDF Jahrbuch 1995*, 195–97. For the rise of the star system in German television, see Hickethier, *Geschichte des deutschen Fernsehens*, 530.

79. Knopp had already published a book for the first documentary he produced with the ZDF, *Warum habt Ihr Hitler nicht verhindert?* (Frankfurt, Germany: Fischer, 1983), but the business really took off with *Der verdammte Krieg* and Knopp's collaboration with Bertelsmann, including: *Der verdammte Krieg: Das Unternehmen Barbarossa* (Gütersloh, Germany: Bertelsmann, 1991); *Entscheidung Stalingrad* (Gütersloh, Germany: Bertelsmann, 1993); and *Das Ende 1945* (Gütersloh, Germany: Bertelsmann, 1995). Ever since, each new series of the ZDF's Division of Contemporary History has been accompanied by a volume based on the research undertaken in preparation for the programs, written by the members of Knopp's staff or a professional writer (for instance, Rudolf Gültner in the case of the three volumes for *Der verdammte Krieg*) and marketed under Knopp's name.

80. *Hitlers Helfer*, pt. 1, *Der Stellvertreter — Rudolf Hess* (ZDF, January 14, 1997); *HH*, pt. 2, *Der Vollstrecker — Heinrich Himmler* (ZDF, January 21, 1997); *HH*, pt. 3, *Der Brandstifter — Josef Goebbels* (ZDF, January 28, 1997); *HH*, pt. 4, *Der Zweite Mann — Hermann Göring* (ZDF, February 4, 1997); *HH*, pt. 5, *Der Architekt — Albert Speer* (ZDF, February 18, 1997); *HH*, pt. 6, *Der Nachfolger — Karl Dönitz* (ZDF, February 25, 1997); and *Hitlers Helfer — Die Diskussion* (ZDF, February 25, 1997). The second installment of six more sequels followed in 1998: *Hitlers Helfer: Täter und Vollstrecker*, pt. 1, *Eichmann — Der Vernichter* (ZDF, April 7, 1998); *HH: TV*, pt. 2, *Ribbentrop — Der Handlanger* (ZDF, April 14, 1998); *HH: TV*, pt. 3, *Freisler — Der Hinrichter* (ZDF, April 21, 1998); *HH: TV*, pt. 4, *Bormann — Der Schattenmann* (ZDF, April 28, 1998); *HH: TV*, pt. 5, *Schirach — Der Hitlerjunge* (ZDF, May 5, 1998); and *HH: TV*, pt. 6, *Mengele — Der Todesarzt* (ZDF, May 12, 1998).

81. *Hitlers Krieger*, pt. 1, *Rommel — Das Idol* (ZDF, October 13, 1998); *HK*, pt. 2, *Manstein — Der Stratege* (ZDF, October 27, 1998); *HK*, pt. 3, *Paulus — Der Gefangene* (ZDF, November 3, 1998); *HK*, pt. 4, *Udet — Der Flieger* (ZDF, November 10, 1998); *HK*, pt. 5, *Canaris — Der Verschwörer* (ZDF, November 17, 1998); *HK*, pt. 6, *Keitel — Der Gehilfe* (ZDF, November 24, 1998); and *Hitlers Krieger — Die Diskussion* (ZDF, November 24, 1998); see also Lutz Kinkel, "Viele Taten, wenig Täter: Die Wehrmacht als Sujet neuerer Dokumentationsserien des öffentlich-rechtlichen Rundfunks," in Michael Greven and Oliver von Wrochem, eds., *Der Krieg in der Nachkriegszeit: Der Zweite Weltkrieg in Politik und Gesellschaft der Bundesrepublik* (Opladen, Germany: Leske und Budrich, 2000), 113–30.

82. "Von Hess bis Goebbels: Sechsteiler über die wichtigsten Nazi-Schergen," *Hamburger Abendblatt*, January 14, 1997.

83. The precise figure of 6.85 million viewers on average corresponds to an excellent market share of 21.1 percent; see *ZDF Jahrbuch 1997* (Mainz, Germany: ZDF, 1998), 349. The single most successful program was the show on Goebbels, which attracted an unprecedented 7.38 million viewers, corresponding to a 22.6 percent market share; see GfK-Fernsehforschung, *ZDF Einschaltquoten für Dienstag, 28. Januar 1997*.

84. *Hitlers Krieger*, pt. 1, *Rommel — Das Idol*.

85. Ibid.

86. One of the Jewish eyewitnesses was Inge Deutschkron, who survived the Third Reich in hiding and has published and lectured about her experience; see Deutschkron, *Ich trug den gelben Stern* (Munich, Germany: Deutscher Taschenbuch-Verlag, 1985).

87. *Hitlers Krieger*, pt. 1, *Rommel — Das Idol*.

88. Ralf Schlüter, "Gespenstisch," *Berliner Zeitung*, January16, 1997, and Fritz Wolf, "Zur Metaphysik ist es nicht weit," *epd medien*, February 5, 1997.

89. Knopp moderated one of the TV discussions with Daniel Goldhagen; see *Hitlers willige Helfer? Die Deutschen und der Holocaust* (ZDF, September 8, 1996).

90. Thomas Gehringer, "Der totale Knopp: Geschichte satt bis 2000," *Tagesspiegel*, October 25, 1997; see also Knopp, "Zeitgeschichte im ZDF," 313.

91. For the changes in television programming in the 1990s, see especially Hickethier, *Geschichte des deutschen Fernsehens*, 517–43.

92. Peter Arens, "Dokus in voller Fahrt: Über die wundersame Rennaissance des IQ-Fernsehens," *ZDF Jahrbuch 1997*, 92–94.

93. Explicitly referring to *Hitlers Helfer*, Oswald Ring attested to "the drastically improved competitiveness of modernized information television"; see Ring, "Beratung und Orientierung sind gefragt," *ZDF Jahrbuch 1996*, 65–68.

94. See Klaus Naumann's excellent summary and analysis of the debate in Naumann, "Der totale Knopp: Der Erfinder des 'ZDF-Docutainments' Guido Knopp gibt der Geschichte dramaturgische Nachhilfe," *Die Woche*, May 15, 1998.

95. Thomas Gehringer, "'NS-Kitsch:' Fernsehen und Zeitgeschichte: Eine Auseinandersetzung," *Tagespiegel*, June 16, 1998; see also Hans-Jürgen Krug. "Geschichte, Fernsehen, Geschichtsfernsehen: Wie das Medium Fernsehen sich der Historie bedient," *Frankfurter Rundschau*, August 22, 1998.

96. Rudolf Grimm, "Aufklärung braucht Reichweite: Historiker und Publizisten zwiespältig im Urteil über die ZDF-Reihe *Hitlers Helfer*," *Tagespiegel*, May 12, 1998, and Guido Knopp, "Aufklärung braucht Reichweite," *ZDF Jahrbuch 1999*, 68–69.

97. Matthias Arning, "Eindimensional," *Frankfurter Rundschau*, October 15, 1998.

98. *Hitlers Frauen*, five sequels (ZDF, April 25 and May 2, May 23, May 30, and June 13, 2001); *Hitlers Kinder*, pt. 1, *Verführung* (ZDF, March 14, 2001); *Hitlers Kinder*, pt. 2, *Hingabe* (ZDF, March 21, 2001); *Hitlers Kinder*, pt. 3, *Zucht* (ZDF, March 28, 2001); *Hitlers Kinder*, pt. 4, *Einsatz* (ZDF, April 4, 2001); and *Hitlers Kinder*, pt. 5, *Opferung* (ZDF, April 14, 2001), five sequels (ZDF, March 14, March 21, and March 28, 2001).

99. The first of twenty-one sequels of *Der Jahrhundertkrieg* was broadcast in January 2002; see Reinhard Lüke, "Schiffe versenken: Guido Knopps Mammutreihe 'Der Jahrhundertkrieg,'?" *Frankfurter Rundschau*, January 10, 2002.

100. *Die grosse Flucht*, pt. 1, *Der grosse Treck, Kampf um Ostpreussen* (ZDF, November 20, 2001); *DgF*, pt. 2, *Der Untergang der Gustloff* (ZDF, November 27, 2001); *DgF*, pt. 3, *Die Festung Breslau* (ZDF, December 4, 2001); *DgF*, pt. 4, *Die Stunde der Frauen: Überleben in Pommern* (ZDF, December 11, 2001); and *DgF*, pt. 5, *Die verlorene Heimat* (ZDF, December 18, 2001).

101. The Walser-Bubis debate is documented in Frank Schirrmacher, ed., *Die Walser-Bubis-Debatte: Eine Dokumentation* (Frankfurt, Germany: Suhrkamp, 1999).

102. Günter Grass, *Im Krebsgang* (Göttingen, Germany: Steidl, 2002); see also "Eine Katastrophe, aber kein Verbrechen," *Stern*, February 14, 2002, and Thomas Schmidt, "Ostdeutscher Totentanz," *Die Zeit*, February 14, 2002.

103. On the decreasing audiences for Knopp's programs, see the graph "Schwindendes Interesse: Dokumentationen im ZDF über die Hitler-Zeit," *Der Spiegel*, April 3, 2000, and the graph "Marktanteile der ZDF-Reihen," *Der Spiegel*, November 20, 2000. One notable exception was the program on Eva Braun, which attained 19 percent market shares in April 2001; see "Hitlers Frauen beliebt," *Der Spiegel*, April 30, 2001.

104. Tom Peukert, "Warten auf Hitlers Hunde," *Tagesspiegel*, February 11, 2000; see also Oliver Maria Schmitt, "Der Fluch der Verknoppung," *die tageszeitung*, March 16, 2000.

105. Tina Angerer, "Hitler—Ein Witz? Der Nazi-Diktator als Comedy-Figur hat Konjunktur im deutschen Fernsehen," *Tagespiegel*, January 29, 2000.

106. For an attempt to develop a didactic program in response to the Hitler wave of the 1970s, see Anneliese Mannzmann, *Hitlerwelle und historische Fakten* (Königstein, Germany: Scriptor, 1979).

107. Norbert Frei, *1945 und wir: Das Dritte Reich im Bewusstsein der Deutschen* (Munich, Germany: Beck, 2005), 7.

108. Lothar Machtan, *Hitlers Geheimnis: Das Doppelleben eines Diktators* (Berlin: Alexander Fest, 2001).

109. Volker Ulrich, "So viel Hitler war nie," *Neue Gesellschaft/Frankfurter Hefte* (May 2005): 44–47.

110. Susan Sontag, *Im Zeichen des Saturns* (Munich, Germany: Hanser, 1981); Saul Friedlander, *Reflections of Nazism* (New York: Harper and Row, 1984).

111. Sontag, *Im Zeichen des Saturns*, 117, and Friedlander, *Reflections of Nazism*, 33.

112. That applies, for instance, to the first Hitler wave of 1977; see Mannzmann, *Hitlerwelle*.

113. "Quoten: Hitlers Frauen beliebt," *Der Spiegel*, April 30, 2001.

114. *Olympia*, Leni Riefenstahl, Olympia-Film, Germany, 1936–1938; Knopp's production was *Der schöne Schein: Olympia '36* (ZDF, July 27, 1986).

115. *Nuit et Brouillard*, Alain Resnais, Como and Argos, France, 1955; *Le Chagrin et la Pitié*, Marcel Ophüls, Rencontre/SSR/NDR, Switzerland and Germany, 1969; *Hitler, ein Film aus Deutschland*, Hans-Jürgen Syberberg, TMS/Solaris/WDR/INA/BBC, Germany, France, and England, 1976–1977; *Shoah*, Claude Lanzmann, Les Films Aleph/Historia Films, France, 1974–1985.

116. Hans Jürgen Syberberg, *Vom Unglück und Glück der Kunst in Deutschland nach dem letzten Kriege* (Munich, Germany: Matthes und Seitz, 1990).

117. Eike Wenzel, *Gedächtnisraum Film: Die Arbeit an der deutschen Geschichte in Filmen seit den sechziger Jahren* (Stuttgart, Germany: Metzler, 2000).

118. See the succinct, insightful remarks by Stefan Bauer, "Geschichte auf Hochglanz," *Gong* 23 (January 1997).

119. For the politics of culture and the political effects of the Nazi film industry, see Eric Rentschler, *The Ministry of Illusion: Nazi Cinema and Its Afterlife* (Cambridge, MA: Harvard University Press, 1996), esp. 215–23.

120. Knopp, "Zeitgeschichte im ZDF," 311.

121. Ibid.

122. See, in this context, the concluding remarks by Frank Bösch, "Das 'Dritte Reich' ferngesehen: Geschichtsvermittlung in der historischen Dokumentation," *Geschichte in Wissenschaft und Unterricht* 50, no. 4 (1999): 204–20.

123. See the exceptionally insightful text of Barbara Sichtermann, "Das Tabu," *Die Zeit*, November 11, 1988.

CHAPTER 9

1. On the problem of the continuity in the ranks of the civil service, see Gregg Kvistad, "Building Democracy and Changing Institutions: The Professional Civil Service and Political Parties in the Federal Republic of Germany," in John Brady, Beverly Crawford, and Elise Willarty, eds., *The Postwar Transformation of Germany: Democracy, Prosperity and Nationhood* (Ann Arbor: University of Michigan Press, 1999), 63–93.

2. Eike Wolgast, *Die Wahrnehmung des Dritten Reiches in der unmittelbaren Nachkriegszeit (1945/46)* (Heidelberg, Germany: C. Winter, 2001), 15.

3. The essence of the international ideological consensus of antitotalitarianism is best represented in Carl Friedrich and Zbigniew Brezezinski, *Totalitarian Dictatorship and Autocracy* (Cambridge, MA: Harvard University Press, 1956).

4. Heinrich Pothoff and Susanne Miller, *Kleine Geschichte der SPD 1848—2002*, 8th updated and enlarged ed. (Bonn, Germany: Dietz, 2002), 190.

5. On East German antifascism, see Antonia Grunenberg, *Antifaschismus: Ein deutscher Mythos* (Hamburg, Germany: Rowohlt, 1993).

6. See the remarks in Manfred Görtemaker, *Geschichte der Bundesrepublik Deutschland: Von der Gründung bis zur Gegenwart* (Munich, Germany: Beck, 1999), 31–32.

7. The postwar German victims discourse has been studied in great detail. For a recent compelling critique, see Habbo Knoch, *Die Tat als Bild: Fotografien des Holocaust in der deutschen Erinnerungskultur* (Hamburg, Germany: Hamburger Edition, 2001), 225–28.

8. Frank Stern, *Im Anfang war Auschwitz: Antisemitismus und Philosemitismus im deutschen Nachkrieg* (Gerlingen, Germany: Bleicher, 1991), 351–58 and passim.

9. Peter Reichel, *Erfundene Erinnerung: Weltkrieg und Judenmord in Film und Theater* (Munich, Germany: Hanser, 2004), 215–41; Anat Feinberg, *Wiedergutmachung im Programm: Jüdisches Schicksal im deutschen Nachkriegsdrama* (Cologne, Germany: Prometh, 1988), 33–46; Ernestine Schlant, *The Language of Silence: West German Literature and the Holocaust* (New York: Routledge, 1999), 51–98.

10. As seen in chapter 4, the concept of generational memory has a long tradition in German memory studies. It has been most consistently applied in Harold Marcuse, *Legacies of Dachau: The Uses and Abuses of a Concentration Camp* (Cambridge: Cambridge University Press, 2001), esp. the table on 292–93.

11. Daniel Rogers, *Politics after Hitler: The Western Allies and the German Party System* (New York: New York University Press, 1995), 20–48; see also Wolfgang Benz, *Deutschland unter Alliierter Besatzung, 1945–1949/1955* (Berlin: Akademie, 1999), 150–57.

12. A detailed analysis of the forced merger is provided in Bernd Faulenbach and Heinrich Potthoff, eds., *Sozialdemokraten und Kommunisten nach Nationalsozialismus und Krieg: Zur historischen Einordnung der Zwangsvereinigung* (Essen, Germany: Klartext, 1998), esp. chapter 5, 83–121.

13. Rebecca Boehling, "US Military Occupation, Grass Roots Democracy, and Local German Government," in Jeffry Diefendorf, Axel Frohn, and Hermann-Josef Rupieper, eds., *American Policy and the Reconstruction of West Germany, 1945–1955* (Cambridge: Cambridge University Press, 1993), 281–306.

14. See the "Aufruf des Zentralkommittees, vol. 11, Juni 1945," reprinted in Ossip Flechtheim, ed., *Dokumente zur parteipolitischen Entwicklung in Deutschland seit 1945*, vol. 3 (Berlin: Wendler, 1963), 313–17.

15. Wolgast, *Wahrnehmung des Dritten Reiches*, 28–31, 43.

16. Ute Schmidt, "Hitler ist tot und Ulbricht lebt: Die CDU, der Nationalsozialismus und der Holocaust," in Werner Bergmann, Rainer Erb, and Albert Lichtblau, eds., *Schwieriges Erbe: Der Umgang mit Nationalsozialismus und Antisemitismus in Österreich, der DDR und der Bundesrepublik Deutschland* (Frankfurt, Germany: Campus, 1995), 65–101.

17. Norbert Frei, "Von deutscher Erfindungskraft oder: Die Kollektivschuldthese in der Nachkriegszeit," in Gary Smith, ed., *Hannah Arendt Revisited: "Eichmann in Jerusalem" und die Folgen* (Frankfurt, Germany: Suhrkamp, 2000), 163–76. See also the analysis of postwar discussions about collective guilt by Barbro Eberan, who argues that assumptions about Germany's collective guilt were especially pronounced among conservative politicians in Western Europe and the United States; see Eberan, *Luther? Friedrich "der Grosse?" Wagner? Nietzsche? Wer war an Hitler schuld? Die Debatte um die Schuldfrage, 1945–1949*, 2nd enlarged ed. (Munich, Germany: Minerva, 1985), 23–24.

18. Helmut Dubiel, *Niemand ist frei von der Geschichte: Die nationalsozialistische Herrschaft in den Debatten des Deutschen Bundestages* (Munich, Germany: Hanser, 1999), 71.

19. "Aufruf des Zentralkommittees," 314; Wolgast, *Wahrnehmung des Dritten Reiches*, 30–32.

20. Wolgast, *Wahrnehmung des Dritten Reiches*, 36–40.

21. Ibid., 68–70. It is interesting to note that Werner Conze, a doyen of West German social history, failed to highlight Kaiser's decisive rejection of anti-Semitism in his study of Kaiser's postwar career; see Werner Conze, *Jakob Kaiser: Politiker zwischen Ost und West 1945–1949* (Stuttgart, Germany: Kohlhammer, 1969). These omissions might reflect Conze's own troublesome use of anti-Semitic invectives in his scholarly publications during the Third Reich; see Thomas Etzemüller, *Sozialgeschichte als politische Geschichte: Werner Conze und die*

Neuorientierung der westdeutschen Geschichtswissenschaft nach 1945 (Munich, Germany: Oldenbourg, 2001), 27–29.

22. Wolgast, *Wahrnehmung des Dritten Reiches*, 120–21.

23. Heinrich Potthoff, "Die Auseinandersetzung der SPD und der Gewerkschaften mit dem NS-System und dem Holocaust," in Bergmann, Erb, and Lichtblau, *Schwieriges Erbe*, 120–37.

24. In the case of Maier, the blunt criticism was based on personal experiences: married to a Jewish woman, he had had many opportunities to observe the indifference of his fellow Germans; see chapter 5, "Bedrängte Familie," in Klaus Jürgen Matz, *Reinhold Maier (1989–1971): Eine politische Biographie* (Düsseldorf, Germany: Droste, 1989), 156–66.

25. Ulrich Baumgärtner, *Reden nach Hitler: Theodor Heuss—Die Auseinandersetzung mit dem Nationalsozialismus* (Stuttgart, Germany: Deutsche Verlagsanstalt, 2001), 80–92, and Jeffrey Herf, *Divided Memory: The Nazi Past in the Two Germanys* (Cambridge, MA: Harvard University Press, 1997), 233–37.

26. Herf, *Divided Memory*, 209–20.

27. Peter Reichel, *Vergangenheitsbewältigung in Deutschland: Die Auseinandersetzung mit der NS-Diktatur von 1945 bis heute* (Munich, Germany: Beck, 2001), 46–47, 59; Jürgen Wilke, Birgit Schenk, Akiba Cohen, and Tamar Zemach, *Holocaust und NS-Prozesse: Die Presseberichterstattung in Israel und Deutschland zwischen Aneignung und Abwehr* (Cologne, Germany: Böhlau, 1995), 128–29.

28. Nobert Frei, *Vergangenheitspolitik: Die Anfänge der Bundesrepublik und die NS-Vergangenheit* (Munich, Germany: Beck, 1996), 133–306; Ulrich Brochhagen, *Nach Nürnberg: Vergangenheitsbewältigung und Westintegration in der Ära Adenauer* (Hamburg, Germany: Junius, 1994), 35–41, 78–81, and 97–113.

29. The classic study on the topic of denazification remains Lutz Niethammer, *Die Mitläuferfabrik: Die Entnazifizierung am Beispiel Bayern*, 2nd ed. (Berlin: Dietz, 1982); see also Frei, *Vergangenheitspolitik*, 54–69, and Reichel, *Vergangenheitsbewältigung*, 30–41.

30. Frei, *Vergangenheitspolitik*, 29–53, 100–131.

31. David Forster, *"Wiedergutmachung" in Österreich und der BRD im Vergleich* (Innsbruck: Studienverlag, 2001), 39.

32. Reichel, *Vergangenheitsbewältigung*, 77.

33. Hermann-Josef Brodesser, Bernd Fehn, Tilo Franosch, and Wilfried Wirth, *Wiedergutmachung und Kriegsfolgenliquidation: Geschichte—Regelungen—Zahlungen* (Munich, Germany: Beck, 2000), 10–16.

34. Jürgen Lillteicher, "Die Rückerstattung in Westdeutschland: Ein Kapitel deutscher Vergangenheitspolitik?" in Hans Günter Hockerts and Christiane Kuller, eds., *Nach der Verfolgung: Wiedergutmachung nationalsozialistischen Unrechts in Deutschland?* (Göttingen, Germany: Wallstein, 2003), 61–78; Reichel, *Vergangenheitsbewältigung*, 79–80.

35. Brodesser, Fehn, Franosch, and Wirth, *Wiedergutmachung*, 18.

36. Hans Dieter Kreikamp, "Zur Entstehung des Entschädigungsgesetzes der amerikanischen Besatzungszone," in Ludolf Herbst and Constantin Goschler, eds., *Wiedergutmachung in der Bundesrepublik Deutschland* (Munich, Germany: Oldenbourg, 1989), 61–75.

37. Forster, *"Wiedergutmachung*," 50–54.

38. The German resistance against restitution and compensation explains the scandalous treatment that many survivors experienced at the hands of the West German compensation bureaucracy; see Christian Pross, *Wiedergutmachung: Der Kleinkrieg gegen die Opfer* (Frankfurt, Germany: Athenäum, 1988); see also Reichel, *Vergangenheitsbewältigung*, 96, and compare to the much more positive assessment in Brodesser, Fehn, Franosch, and Wirth, *Wiedergutmachung*, 225.

39. Ulrich Herbert, "Nicht entschädigungsfähig? Die Wiedergutmachungsansprüche der Ausländer," in Herbst and Goschler, *Wiedergutmachung*, 273–302.

40. Brodesser, Fehn, Franosch, and Wirth, *Wiedergutmachung,* 34.

41. Forster, *"Wiedergutmachung,"* 65–71; Pross, *Kleinkrieg,* 56–72; on the opposition to the agreements within the Adenauer administration, see especially Michael Wolffsohn, "Global-entschädigung für Israel und die Juden? Adenauer und die Opposition in der Bundesregierung," in Herbst and Goschler, *Wiedergutmachung,* 161–90.

42. See, for example, Dubiel, *Niemand ist frei von der Geschichte,* and Reichel, *Vergangen-heitsbewältigung,* and compare to the excellent coverage of expellee affairs in Robert Moeller, *War Stories: The Search for a Usable Past in the Federal Republic of Germany* (Berkeley: University of California Press, 2001).

43. Michael Hughes, *Shouldering the Burden of Defeat: West Germany and the Reconstruction of Social Justice* (Chapel Hill: University of North Carolina Press, 1999), 43–63.

44. Ibid., 73–80; see also Peter Paul Nahm, "Lastenausgleich und Integration der Ver-triebenen und Geflüchteten," in Hans-Peter Schwarz, ed., *Die zweite Republik: 25 Jahre Bun-desrepublik—Eine Bilanz* (Stuttgart, Germany: Seewald, 1974), 817–42.

45. Hughes, *Shouldering the Burden,* 85; Hans Günter Hockerts, "Metamorphosen des Wohlfahrtsstaats," in Martin Broszat, ed., *Zäsuren nach 1945: Essays zur Periodisierung der deutschen Nachkriegsgeschichte* (Munich, Germany: Oldenbourg, 1990), 35–45.

46. That near consensus is succinctly expressed in Görtemaker, *Bundesrepublik Deutsch-land,* 171; compare to the more nuanced and skeptical remarks in Hughes, *Shouldering the Burden,* 197–98.

47. Pertti Ahonen, *After the Expulsion: West Germany and Eastern Europe, 1945–1990* (Ox-ford: Oxford University Press, 2003), 24–38.

48. Reinhold Schillinger, "Der Lastenausgleich," in Wolfgang Benz, *Die Vertreibung der Deutschen aus dem Osten: Ursachen, Ereignisse, Folgen* (Frankfurt, Germany: Fischer, 1985), 183–92.

49. Ahonen, *After the Expulsion,* 65.

50. Hughes, *Shouldering the Burden,* 176–78, and Nahm, "Lastenausgleich."

51. Ahonen, *After the Expulsion,* 66–67, and Josef Foschepoth, "Potsdam und danach: Die Westmächte, Adenauer und die Vertriebenen," in Benz, *Vertreibung,* 70–90.

52. Schillinger, "Lastenausgleich," 190; at the same time, Adenauer and his ministers ex-cluded the expellees from any foreign policy decisions, see Ahonen, *After the Expulsion,* 108–9.

53. The SPD courted the expellees as aggressively as the CDU/CSU and made similar un-realistic promises regarding the former German possessions in Poland and the Soviet Union; see Ahonen, *After the Expulsion,* 70–72.

54. Schillinger, "Lastenausgleich," 188.

55. Forster, *"Wiedergutmachung,"* 68.

56. Incidentally, the balancing act between these two types of claims has led to similar total payments on both sides of the perceived divide. The payments in the context of "Wiedergut-machung" and the "Lastenausgleich" amount to approximately 160 and 140 billion marks, re-spectively. But these payments have been dwarfed by the support that German veterans and their families have received over the decades, which amount to over 400 billion marks; see Reichel, *Vergangenheitsbewältigung,* 74; Karl Doehring, Bernd Josef Fehn, and Hans Günter Hockerts, *Jahrhundertschuld—Jahrhundertsühne: Reparationen, Wiedergutmachung, Entschädi-gung für nationalsozialistisches Kriegs- und Verfolgungsunrecht* (Munich, Germany: Olzog, 2001), 142; and especially Brodesser, Fehn, Franosch, and Wirth, *Wiedergutmachung,* 177–79, 246–51.

57. Reichel, *Vergangenheitsbewältigung,* 111.

58. Frei, *Vergangenheitspolitik,* 69–72.

59. Ibid., 79–81.

60. Forster, *"Wiedergutmachung,"* 62–63.

61. Reichel, *Vergangenheitsbewältigung,* 113.

62. The politicians' motives became quite obvious in the parliamentary debates about the law that took place in September 1950 and April 1951; see Frei, *Vergangenheitspolitik*, 75–82.

63. Manfred Kittel, *Die Legende von der "Zweiten Schuld": Vergangenheitsbewältigung in der Ära Adenauer* (Berlin: Ullstein, 1993), 117. In the 1980s, the critique of the implementation of paragraph 131 intensified again; see, for example, Jörg Friedrich, *Die kalte Amnestie: NS-Täter in der Bundesrepublik* (Frankfurt, Germany: Fischer), 272–81.

64. Armin Pfahl-Traughber, "Der organisierte Rechtsextremismus in Deutschland nach 1945: Zur Entwicklung auf den Handlungsfeldern 'Aktion'—'Gewalt'—'Kultur'—'Politik,'" in Wilfried Schubarth and Richard Stöss, eds., *Rechtsextremismus in der Bundesrepublik Deutschland: Eine Bilanz* (Opladen, Germany: Leske und Budrich, 2001), 71–100, and Lee McGowan, *The Radical Right in Germany: 1870 to the Present* (London: Longman, 2002), 150–52.

65. Many commentators have linked the courts' empathy for incorrigible Nazis to the fact that the West German judiciary of the postwar decades was largely identical with the judiciary of the Third Reich; see the rigorous indictment in Ingo Müller, *Furchtbare Juristen: Die unbewältigte Vergangenheit unserer Justiz* (Munich, Germany: Knaur, 1989), and Joachim Perels, *Das juristische Erbe des "Dritten Reiches": Beschädigung der demokratischen Rechtsordnung* (Frankfurt, Germany: Campus, 1999), 181–202.

66. The Hedler case is one of the best-researched case studies in the history of West German anti-Semitism; see Werner Bergmann, *Antisemitismus in öffentlichen Konflikten: Kollektives Lernen in der politischen Kultur der Bundesrepublik, 1949–1989* (Frankfurt, Germany: Campus, 1997), 117–45; see also Frei, *Vergangenheitspolitik*, 309–25.

67. Frei, *Vergangenheitspolitik*, 326–48, 351–60; Reichel, *Vergangenheitsbewältigung*, 139–140; compare to the antitotalitarian reading of the ban of the SRP in Kittel, *Zweite Schuld*, 159–161, and Uwe Backes and Eckhard Jesse, *Politischer Extremismus in der Bundesrepublik Deutschland* (Berlin: Propyläen, 1993), 62–65.

68. Regina Holler, *20.Juli 1944: Vermächtnis oder Alibi?* (Munich, Germany: Saur, 1994), 121–28; Frei, *Vergangenheitspolitik*, 348–51.

69. Frei, *Vergangenheitspolitik*, 361–74; a more positive assessment of the government is given in Kittel, *"Zweite Schuld,"* 341–49.

70. Frei, *Vergangenheitspolitik*, 380–96.

71. For example, Adenauer and Heuss only settled the question of the national anthem in 1952 when, according to Adenauer's wishes, the third stanza of the traditional German anthem became the official West German anthem; see Udo Wengst, "Die Prägung des präsidialen Selbstverständnisses durch Theodor Heuss, 1949–1959," in Eberhard Jäckel, Horst Möller, and Hermann Rudolph, eds., *Von Heuss bis Herzog: Die Bundespräsidenten im politischen System der Bundesrepublik* (Stuttgart, Germany: Deutsche Verlagsanstalt, 1999), 65–76.

72. Since the constitutional council also passed the constitution on May 8, that event could not serve as a reference point for a national holiday; see Kirsch, *Der 8. Mai als politischer Gedenktag*.

73. Baumgärtner, *Reden*, 173–75.

74. Edgar Wolfrum, *Geschichtspolitik in der Bundesrepublik Deutschland: Der Weg zur bundesrepublikanischen Erinnerung, 1948–1990* (Darmstadt, Germany: Wissenschaftliche Buchgesellschaft, 1999), 84.

75. Baumgärtner, *Reden*, 183.

76. Theodor Heuss, *Die grossen Reden*, vol. 1 (Tübingen, Germany: Wunderlich, 1965), 99–107.

77. Ibid. After absolving his audience of any legal and political responsibility, Heuss also expressed his faith in the future of German-Jewish dialogue and cooperation—as if the two sides had simply been kept apart for a while and could now resume normal relations.

78. Herf is slightly more positive in his interpretation of Heuss's contribution in *Divided Memory*, 329.

79. Baumgärtner. *Reden*, 261–78.

80. Heuss, *Die grossen Reden*.

81. Ahonen, *After the Expulsion*, 28.

82. For the persistence of this type of victims discourse over several political generations, see the analysis of the Hohmann affair in chapter 12.

83. Wolgast, *Wahrnehmung des Dritten Reiches*, 39–40; Aleida Assmann and Ute Frevert, *Geschichtsvergessenheit—Geschichtsversessenheit: Vom Umgang mit deutschen Vergangenheiten nach 1945* (Stuttgart, Germany: Deutsche Verlagsanstalt, 1999), 163.

84. Wolfrum, *Geschichtspolitik*; Potthoff and Miller, *Kleine Geschichte der SPD*, 186–89; and Thomas Berger, *Cultures of Antimilitarism: National Security in Germany and Japan* (Baltimore: Johns Hopkins University Press, 1998), 61–62.

85. Dubiel, *Niemand ist frei von der Geschichte*, 75; compare to the much more positive assessment of antitotalitarian consensus in Kittel, *"Zweite Schuld,"* 62–65.

86. Ahonen, *After the Expulsion*, 56–57.

87. The awkward philosemitic phrase *our Jewish fellow citizens* was already introduced into the vocabulary of German memory in 1945; see Wolgast, *Wahrnehmung des Dritten Reiches*, 68.

88. Dubiel, *Niemand ist frei von der Geschichte*, 14–16, 69–77.

89. Assmann and Frevert, *Geschichtsvergessenheit*, 116–17, 126–28, 140.

90. Hermann Lübbe, "Der Nationalsozialismus im deutschen Nachkriegsbewusstsein," *Historische Zeitschrift* 236, no. 3 (1983): 579–99.

91. Konrad Adenauer, "Regierungserklärung vom 20. September 1949," in Klaus Stüwe, ed., *Die grossen Regierungserklärungen der deutschen Bundeskanzler von Adenauer bis Schröder* (Opladen, Germany: Leske und Budrich, 2002), 35–47.

92. Kurt Schumacher, "Die Opposition ist Bestandteil des Staatslebens," in Horst Ferdinand, ed., *Reden, die die Republik bewegten*, 2nd ed. (Opladen, Germany: Leske und Budrich, 2002), 44–64.

CHAPTER 10

1. Norbert Frei, *Vergangenheitspolitik: Die Anfänge der Bundesrepublik und die NS-Vergangenheit* (Munich, Germany: Beck, 1996), 406; Ulrich Brochhagen, *Nach Nürnberg: Vergangenheitsbewältigung in der Ära Adenauer* (Hamburg, Germany: Junius, 1994), 299–306, 341–45.

2. Marc von Miquel, *Ahnden oder Amestieren? Westdeutsche Justiz und Vergangenheitspolitik in den sechziger Jahren* (Göttingen, Germany: Wallstein, 2004), 376. In the late 1950s and early 1960s, the state governments also ordered a large-scale revision of history textbooks and curricula in response to the lackluster performance of the teaching profession in the field of contemporary history; see Peter Dudek, *"Der Rückblick auf die Vergangenheit wird sich nicht vermeiden lassen": Zur pädagogischen Verarbeitung des Nationalsozialismus in Deutschland (1945–1990)* (Opladen, Germany: Westdeutscher Verlag, 1995), 264.

3. Jan-Werner Müller, *Another Country: German Intellectuals, Unification, and National Identity* (New Haven, CT: Yale University Press, 2000), 37–42; see also Michael Geyer, "Cold War Angst: The Case of West German Opposition to Rearmament and Nuclear Weapons," in Hanna Schissler, ed., *The Miracle Years: A Cultural History of West Germany, 1949–1968* (Princeton, NJ: Princeton University Press, 2001), 376–408. These explicit political interventions were preceded by a string of youth riots that peaked in the summer of 1956 and that rattled the conservative political elite; see Uta Poiger, *Jazz, Rock and Rebels: Cold War Politics and American Culture in a Divided Germany* (Berkeley: University of California Press, 2000), 76–84.

4. Werner Bergmann, *Antisemitismus in öffentlichen Konflikten: Kollektives Lernen in der politischen Kultur der Bundesrepublik* (Frankfurt, Germany: Campus, 1997), 190–91.

5. Habbo Knoch, *Die Tat als Bild: Fotografien des Holocaust in der deutschen Erinnerungskultur* (Hamburg, Germany: Hamburger Edition, 2001).

6. Alice Förster and Birgit Beck, "Post-Traumatic Stress Disorder and World War II: Can a Psychiatric Concept Help Us Understand Postwar Society?" in Richard Bessel and Dirk

Schumann, eds., *Life after Death: Approaches to a Cultural and Social History of Europe during the 1940s and 1950s* (Cambridge: Cambridge University Press, 2003), 15–35.

7. Grete Klingenstein, "Über Herkunft und Verwendung des Wortes Vergangenheitsbe-wältigung," *Geschichte und Gegenwart* 7, no. 4 (1988): 301–12; Peter Dudek, "'Vergangenheits-bewältigung': Zur Problematik eines umstrittenen Begriffs," *Aus Politik und Zeitgeschichte* 42, no. 1–2 (1992): 44–53; and Manfred Kittel, *Die Legende von der "Zweiten Schuld": Vergangen-heitsbewältigung in der Ära Adenauer* (Berlin: Ullstein, 1993), 21–28.

8. Theodor Adorno, *Erziehung zur Mündigkeit* (Frankfurt, Germany: Suhrkamp, 1970); Alexander Mitscherlich and Margarete Mitscherlich, *The Inability to Mourn: Principles of Col-lective Behavior* (New York: Grove, 1975); see also Margarete Mitscherlich, *Erinnerungsarbeit: Zur Psychoanalyse der Unfähigkeit zu trauern* (Frankfurt, Germany: Fischer, 1993); and Ralph Giordano, *Die zweite Schuld oder Von der Last Deutscher zu sein* (Hamburg, Germany: Rasch und Röhrig, 1987). For Lübbe's work, see chapter 4, note 54.

9. Bergmann, *Antisemitismus*, 139–41.

10. Annette Weinke, *Die Verfolgung von NS-Tätern im geteilten Deutschland* (Paderborn, Germany: Schönigh, 2002), 118–30.

11. Compare, for instance, the extensive references to national press coverage in Bergmann, *Antisemitismus*, and Brochhagen, *Nach Nürnberg*, to Axel Schildt's very appropriate characteri-zation of the West German media landscape of the 1950s. In Schildt's opinion, because of the commercialization of the West German print media during the 1950s, critical political cover-age was increasingly limited to a few national dailies and weeklies, which reached only a rela-tively small audience. The truly popular titles such as *Bildzeitung* and *Hör Zu* represented the conservative mainstream and hardly fostered the self-reflexive collective memories; see Schildt, "Massenmedien im Umbruch der fünfziger Jahre," in Jürgen Wilke, ed., *Mediengeschichte der Bundesrepublik Deutschland* (Cologne, Germany: Böhlau, 1999), 633–48. Any attempt to re-construct national memory trends on the basis of the national print media will, by definition, reflect the sociological bias inherent in the sources and fail to detect cultural developments that cut across different media and different audiences. Therefore, the systematic analysis of popular channels of communication is extremely important for the reconstruction of some types of collective memories. For West Germany in the 1950s, see Knoch, *Die Tat als Bild*, and Michael Schornstheimer, *Bombenstimmung und Katzenjammer—Vergangenheitsbewältigung: Quick and Stern in den 50er Jahren* (Cologne, Germany: Pahl-Rugenstein, 1989)

12. See, for example, Richard Bessel, "Charismatisches Führertum? Hitlers Image in der deutschen Bevölkerung," in Martin Loiperdinger et al., eds., *Führerbilder: Hitler, Mussolini, Roo-sevelt, Stalin in Fotografie und Film* (Munich, Germany: Piper, 1995), 14–26. On the media cov-erage of the Nuremberg trials, see especially Jürgen Wilke, Birgit Schenk, Akiba Cohen, and Tamar Zemach, *Holocaust und NS-Prozesse: Die Presseberichterstattung in Israel und Deutsch-land zwischen Aneignung und Abwehr* (Cologne, Germany: Böhlau, 1995).

13. Some of the most interesting legal cases involved former Nazis who wanted to claim their spot in the sun of the economic miracle. In essence, they sought "reclassification" from the side of the visible Nazis to the side of the invisible Nazis in a public forum and thus tested the limits of tolerance of an already exceedingly generous society.

14. Wolfgang Becker and Norbert Schöll, *In jenen Tagen . . . : Wie der deutsche Nachkriegsfilm die Vergangenheit bewältigte* (Opladen, Germany: Leske und Budrich, 1995), 132–40; see also Knoch, *Die Tat als Bild*, 533–88, and chapter 7.

15. Although Adenauer and his associates had no interest in destabilizing the interpretive paradigm, which had served them so well, some of their actions had unforeseeable and un-intended side effects. In 1955, for instance, Adenauer managed to bring home the last Ger-man POWs from Moscow. The trip was a prime public relations opportunity, allowing Ade-nauer to revel in his roles as patriarch of the nation and successful diplomat; see Robert Moeller, *War Stories: The Search for a Usable Past in the Federal Republic of Germany* (Berkeley:

University of California Press, 2001), 88–122. Few commentators remarked at the time that he was also bringing home some of the henchmen of the Nazi regime. Their presence in West Germany and the impudent attempt of a Holocaust perpetrator and former police director to regain his civil service job helped launch a new round of trials against Nazi perpetrators in the 1960s; see Reichel, *Vergangenheitsbewältigung*, 183–84.

16. There are some obvious exceptions, among them the exhibit "Ungesühnte Nazijustiz," which was organized by the West Berlin chapter of the SDS and opened to the public in February 1959; it represents an early manifestation of the critical perspective of the postwar generation; see Annette Wenke, *Die Verfolgung von NS-Tätern im geteilten Deutschland: Vergangenheitsbewältigung 1949–1969 oder Eine deutsch-deutsche Beziehungsgeschichte im Kalten Krieg* (Paderborn, Germany: Schöningh, 2002), 101.

17. The alleged decency of the bystanders of the Third Reich is one of the key subjects of the postwar German film; see Frank Stern, "Film in the 1950s: Passing Images of Guilt and Responsibility," in Hanna Schissler, ed., *The Miracle Years: A Cultural History of West Germany, 1949–1968* (Princeton, NJ: Princeton University Press, 2001), 266–80.

18. Bergmann, *Antisemitismus*, 192–97, 208–14; Manfred Kittel, *Die Legende von der "Zweiten Schuld": Vergangenheitsbewältigung in der Ära Adenauer* (Berlin: Ullstein, 1993), 304–8.

19. Reichel, *Vergangenheitsbewältigung*, 150–51.

20. Bergmann, *Antisemitismus*, 254; Reichel, *Vergangenheitsbewältigung*, 152–54.

21. Von Miquel, *Ahnden oder amnestieren*, 204–7.

22. Reichel, *Vergangenheitsbewältigung*, 151.

23. Siobhan Kattago, *Ambiguous Memory: The Nazi Past and German National Identity* (Westport, CT: Praeger, 2001), 88; Brochhagen, *Nach Nürnberg*, 228–30.

24. Ingo Haar, *Historiker im Nationalsozialismus: Die deutsche Geschichtswissenschaft und der "Volkskampf" im Osten* (Göttingen, Germany: Vandenhoeck und Ruprecht, 2000); see also chapter 5.

25. Philipp-Christian Wachs, *Der Fall Theodor Oberländer (1905–1998): Ein Lehrstück deutscher Geschichte* (Frankfurt, Germany: Campus, 2000).

26. John Teschke, *Hitler's Legacy: West Germany Confronts the Aftermath of the Third Reich* (New York: Lang, 1999), 113–32.

27. Gerd Bucerius, "Was ist mit den Nazis in Bonn?" *Die Zeit,* January 19, 1960.

28. Wachs, *Der Fall Theodor Oberländer;* Teschke, *Hitler's Legacy,* 144–51.

29. Götz Aly and Susanne Heim, *Vordenker der Vernichtung: Auschwitz und die deutschen Pläne für eine neue europäische Ordnung* (Hamburg, Germany: Hoffmann und Campe, 1991); see also chapter 5.

30. Norbert Jacobs, "Der Streit um Dr. Hans Globke in der öffentlichen Meinung der Bundesrepublik Deutschland, 1949–1973" (Ph.D. diss., University of Bonn, 1992), 32–43; Teschke, *Hitler's Legacy,* 174–86.

31. Michael Schwabb-Trapp, *Konflikt, Kultur und Interpretation: Eine Diskursanalyse des öffentlichen Umgangs mit dem Nationalsozialismus* (Opladen, Germany: Westdeutscher Verlag, 1996), 124; Jacobs, *Der Streit um Dr. Hans Globke,* 127–33.

32. See, for example, Executive Council of the National Front of Democratic Germany, ed., *Brown Book: Nazi Criminals in the Federal Republic and in West Berlin* (East Berlin: Zeit im Bild, 1968), 30, 317–19; Teschke, *Hitler's Legacy,* 197–98.

33. Jacobs, *Der Streit um Dr. Hans Globke,* 88–104.

34. Norden organized high-profile show trials against Oberländer and Globke. In the case of Oberländer, the proceedings still influenced the decisions in Bonn. Oberländer was forced to resign before the trial ended on April 29, 1960; see Wachs, *Der Fall Oberländer,* 266–308. See also the early rebuttal of the East Berlin show trial by Hermann Raschhofer, *Der Fall Oberländer: Eine vergleichende Rechtsanalyse der Verfahren in Pankow und Bonn* (Tübingen, Germany: Schlichtenmayer, 1962). The trial against Globke began in July 1963 after he had al-

ready been in retirement for several months; see Teschke, *Hitler's Legacy*, 203–6. Both Oberländer and Globke were sentenced to life imprisonment in absentia. Although the Ludwigsburg agency and several other prosecutors investigated Oberländer, most recently in 1996, he was never charged by courts in the Federal Republic; see Wachs, *Der Fall Oberländer*, 480.

35. Helga Haftendorn, *Deutsche Aussenpolitik zwischen Selbstbeschränkung und Selbstbehauptung* (Stuttgart, Germany: Deutsche Verlagsanstalt, 2001), 173–78; Manfred Görtemaker, *Geschichte der Bundesrepublik Deutschland* (Munich, Germany: Beck, 1999), 399–400.

36. Klaus Stüwe, ed., *Die Grossen Regierungserklärungen der deutschen Bundeskanzler von Adenauer bis Schröder* (Opladen, Germany: Leske und Budrich, 2002), 120–45; Helmut Dubiel, *Niemand ist frei von der Geschichte: Die nationalsozialistische Herrschaft in den Debatten des Deutschen Bundestages* (Munich, Germany: Hanser, 1999), 91–92.

37. Edgar Wolfrum, *Geschichtspolitik in der Bundesrepublik Deutschland: Der Weg zur bundesrepublikanischen Erinnerung 1948–1990* (Darmstadt, Germany: Wissenschaftliche Buchgesellschaft, 1999), 247; Dubiel, *Niemand is frei von der Geschichte,* 92–93.

38. For a concise history of the trials, see Adalbert Rückerl, *NS-Verbrechen: Versuch einer Vergangenheitsbewältigung* (Heidelberg, Germany: Müller, 1984), 105–219. The political impact of the trials is, for instance, discussed in Peter Steinbach, *Nationalsozialistische Gewaltverbrechen: Die Diskussion in der deutschen Öffentlichkeit nach 1945* (Berlin: Colloquium, 1981), 74–89, and Wilke et al., *Holocaust und NS-Prozesse;* regarding the Auschwitz trial, see Fritz-Bauer-Institut, ed., *"Gerichtstag halten über uns selbst . . .": Geschichte und Wirkung des ersten Frankfurter Auschwitz-Prozesses* (Frankfurt, Germany: Campus, 2001).

39. Dudek, *Zur pädagogischen Verarbeitung des Nationalsozialismus,* 284–91; Bergmann, *Antisemitismus,* 261–66.

40. Fritz Raddatz, *Summa iniuria oder Durfte der Papst schweigen? Hochhuths "Stellvertreter" in der öffentlichen Kritik* (Reinbek, Germany: Rowohlt, 1963); Jan Berg, *Hochhuths "Stellvertreter" und die "Stellvertreter"-Debatte: "Vergangeheitsbewältigung" in Theater und Presse der sechziger Jahre* (Kronberg, Germany: Scriptor, 1977).

41. The new history schoolbooks and curricula, adopted by the states in response to the wave of anti-Semitic actions in 1959 and 1960, equated National Socialism with communism, emphasized the resistance of the churches, and highlighted Europe's superior cultural legacy. But many teachers still resented having to teach NS history and therefore failed to respond to the new requirements; see Karin Herbst, *Didaktik des Geschichtsunterrichts zwischen Traditionalismus und Reformismus* (Hannover, Germany: Schroedel, 1977), 131–39.

42. Joachim Perels, "Staatliche Kontinuität nach 1945?" in Martin Bennhold, ed., *Spuren des Unrechts: Recht und Nationalsozialismus* (Cologne, Germany: Pahl-Rugenstein, 1989), 83–99;

43. Von Miquel, *Westdeutsche Justiz und Vergangenheitspolitik,* 194–208; Reichel, *Vergangenheitsbewältigung,* 185–86.

44. The 1965 parliamentary debate about the statute of limitations for murder is generally considered one of the highlights and turning points in the history of West German memory politics. Although many of the fifteen speakers of the day delivered impressive speeches, parliament did not fundamentally change its position about punishment of Nazi perpetrators. In the end, the statute was only extended by four years, which made another debate and extension necessary. See Reichel, *Vergangenheitsbewältigung in Deutschland,* 186–91; Dubiel, *Niemand ist frei von der Geschichte,* 105–10; Hoffmann, *Stunden Null? Vergangenheitsbewältigung in Deutschland, 1945 und 1989* (Bonn, Germany: Bouvier, 1992), 160–65; and, most detailed in its analysis of the national and international aspects of the debate, von Miquel, *Westdeutsche Justiz und Vergangenheitspolitik,* 224–319.

45. Weinke, *Verfolgung,* 272–78.

46. Norbert Madloch, "Rechtsextremismus in Deutschland nach dem Ende des Hitlerfaschismus," in Klaus Kinner and Rolf Richter, eds., *Rechtsextremismus und Antifaschismus* (Berlin: Dietz, 2000), 57–205, 114–24.

47. Jörg Friedrich, *Die kalte Amnstie: NS-Täter in der Bundesrepublik* (Frankfurt: Fischer, 1984), 408–12; Weinke, *Verfolgung*, 301–6.

48. Klarsfeld herself became a victim of the state's overreaction when she was sentenced to a year in prison within a few hours after the assault; see Nick Thomas, *Protest Movements in 1960s West Germany: A Social History of Dissent and Democracy* (Oxford: Berg, 2003), 168–76, 192–93; see also Rita Thalmann, "Beate Klarsfeld," in Claudia Fröhlich and Michael Kohlstruck, eds., *Engagierte Demokraten: Vergangenheitspolitik in kritischer Absicht* (Münster, Germany: Westfälisches Dampfboot, 1999), 289–98, and Wolfgang Kraushaar, *1968: Das Jahr, das alles verändert hat* (Munich, Germany: Piper, 1998), 282–84.

49. In their efforts to instrumentalize the Nazi past of West German politicians for political purposes, the student activists occasionally became the victims of East German manipulation. Albrecht Norden's campaign against West German president Heinrich Lübke, for instance, was based on forged documents but wholeheartedly embraced by the members of the student movement; see Wolfgang Kraushaar, *1968 als Mythos, Chiffre und Zäsur* (Hamburg, Germany: Hamburger Edition, 2000), 39–40.

50. Dubiel, *Niemand ist frei von der Geschichte*, 119–21.

51. Heinrich Potthof and Susanne Miller, *Kleine Geschichte der SPD*, 8th ed. (Bonn, Germany: Dietz, 2002).

52. Peter Merseburger, *Willy Brandt: 1913–1992, Visionär und Realist* (Stuttgart, Germany: Deutsche Verlagsanstalt, 2002), 410–20; Bernd Rother, "Willy Brandt," in Fröhlich and Kohlstruck, *Engagierte Demokraten*, 299–308.

53. Willy Brandt, *Erinnerungen* (Frankfurt, Germany: Propyläen, 1989), 186; Klaus Harpprecht, *Willy Brandt: Portrait und Selbstportrait* (Munich, Germany: Kindler, 1970), 31.

54. With hindsight, an interesting pattern emerges in the evolution of West Germany's memory politics. Although the Social Democrats were called on to administer the phase of crisis and transition, the communicative as well as the cultural memory of the Third Reich, at least as far as the federal government was concerned, were primarily crafted under the auspices of conservative CDU chancellors.

55. Dubiel, *Niemand ist frei von der Geschichte*, 139–45.

56. The first comprehensive history of the "Radikalenerlass," published under the pseudonym Manfred Histor, emphasized Brandt's direct involvement in creating the directive and estimated that over ten thousand people were prevented from pursuing careers in the civil service; see Histor, *Willy Brandts vergessene Opfer: Geschichte und Statistik der politisch motivierten Berufsverbote in Westdeutschland, 1971–1988* (Freiburg, Germany: Ahriman, 1989).

57. Dubiel, *Niemand ist frei von der Geschichte*, 151; see also Jeremy Varon, *Bringing the War Home: The Weather Underground, the Red Army Faction, and Revolutionary Violence in the Sixties and Seventies* (Berkeley: University of California Press, 2004), 258.

58. Peter Bender, *Die "Neue Ostpolitik" und ihre Folgen: Vom Mauerbau bis zur Vereinigung,* 3rd ed. (Munich, Germany: dtv, 1995), 200–205; for a survey of the literature and concise summary of Ostpolitik, see Frank Fischer, *"Im deutschen Interesse": Die Ostpolitik der SPD von 1969 bis 1989* (Husum, Germany: Matthiesen, 2001), 20–21, 29–57; and Haftendorn, *Deutsche Aussenpolitik*, 177–95. For an interesting yet misleading attempt to reinterpret Brandt's foreign policy as an accomplishment of SPD *and* CDU that has been misrepresented by historians, see Werner Link, "Détente: Entspannungs—und Ostpolitik der siebziger Jahre im Widerstreit," in Jürgen Aretz, Günter Buchstab, and Jörg-Dieter Gauger, eds., *Geschichtsbilder: Weichenstellungen deutscher Geschichte nach 1945* (Freiburg, Germany: Herder, 2003), 103–21.

59. Horst Ferdinand, ed., *Reden, die die Republik bewegten*, 2nd ed. (Opladen, Germany: Leske und Budrich, 2002), 347–63. See also four high-profile interviews with Brandt published in *Der Spiegel* between April 1970 and April 1972, reprinted in Erich Böhme and Klaus Wirtgen, eds., *Willy Brandt: Die Spiegel-Gespräche, 1959–1992* (Stuttgart, Germany: Deutsche Verlagsanstalt, 1993), 182–205 and 220–43.

60. Willy Brandt, *Friedenspolitik in Europa* (Frankfurt, Germany: Fischer, 1968).

61. The CSU MPs were particularly blunt in the criticism; see especially the May 1970 parliamentary speech by the CSU foreign policy expert Guttenberg, in Ferdinand, *Reden, die die Republik bewegten*, 365–83.

62. The CDU's ambivalent opposition against the treaties is well documented in Clay Clemens, *Reluctant Realists: The Christian Democrats and West German Ostpolitik* (Durham, NC: Duke University Press, 1989), 91–94, 115–18, and passim. Not surprisingly, the expellee organizations were more explicit in their rejection of the Ostverträge but therefore lost political influence with Social Democrats and Christian Democrats; see Pertti Ahonen, *After the Expulsion: West Germany and Eastern Europe, 1945–1990* (Oxford: Oxford University Press, 2003), 245–53. For a postunification assessment of the Ostverträge by one of leaders of the expellee organization in the 1970s, see Herbert Czaja, *Unterwegs zum kleinsten Deutschland? Mangel an Solidarität mit den Vertriebenen* (Frankfurt, Germany: Knecht, 1996), 330–62.

63. Auswärtiges Amt, ed., *Die Auswärtige Politik der Bundesrepublik Deutschland* (Cologne, Germany: Wissenschaft und Politik, 1972), 743.

64. Brandt, *Erinnerungen*, 215.

65. Adam Kreminski, "Der Kniefall," in Etienne Francoise and Hagen Schulze, eds., *Deutsche Erinnerungsorte*, vol. 1 (Munich, Germany: Beck, 2001), 639–53; Christoph Schneider, "Der Warschauer Kniefall: Zur Geschichte einer Charismatisierung," in Bernhard Giesen and Christoph Schneider, eds., *Tätertrauma: Nationale Erinnerungen im öffentlichen Diskurs* (Constance, Germany: UVK, 2004), 195–235.

66. Brandt, *Erinnerungen*, 186.

67. Jan-Holger Kirsch, *"Wir haben aus der Geschichte gelernt": Der 8. Mai als politischer Gedenktag in Deutschland* (Cologne, Germany: Böhlau, 1999), 52–55; Dubiel, *Niemand ist frei von der Geschichte*, 133–39.

68. Wolfrum, *Geschichtspolitik*, 291.

69. Lothar Gall, *Fragen an die deutsche Geschichte: Ideen, Kräfte, Entscheidungen von 1800 bis zur Gegenwart* (Stuttgart, Germany: Kohlhammer, 1974).

70. Heinemann considered his election "one step in the transfer of power" from the Christian to the Social Democrats; see Görtemaker, *Geschichte der Bundesrepublik*, 496.

71. Eberhard Jäckel, "Gustav Heinemann als Bundespräsident," in Haus der Geschichte der Bundesrepublik Deutschland, ed., *Gustav Heinemann und seine Politik* (Berlin: Nicolai, 1999), 54–60.

72. Wolfrum, *Geschichtspolitik*, 258–63, quote on 260; see also Aleida Assmann and Ute Frevert, *Geschichtsvergessenheit—Geschichtsversessenheit: Vom Umgang mit deutschen Vergangenheiten nach 1945* (Stuttgart, Germany: Deutsche Verlagsanstalt, 1999), 235–37.

73. Wolfrum, *Geschichtspolitik*, 279, 283.

74. Gustav Heinemann, "Die Freiheitsbewegungen in der deutschen Geschichte: Ansprache des Bundespräsidenten aus Anlass der Eröffnung der 'Erinnerungsstätte in Rastatt am 26. Juni 1974'," in Hans Clauser, Martina Jesse, and Wolfgang Michalka, eds., *Einigkeit und Recht und Freiheit: Erinnerungsstätte für die Freiheitsbewegungen in der deutschen Geschichte* (Bönen, Germany: Kettler, 2002), 21–24; see also the comparison of the Rastatt memorial site and the 1971 Reichstag exhibit in Assmann and Frevert, *Geschichtsvergessenheit*, 247–50.

75. Herbert Weichmann, "Der Gustav-Heinemann-Preis," in Heinrich Böll, Helmut Gollwitzer, and Karl Schmid, eds., *Anstoss und Ermutigung: Gustav W. Heinemann* (Frankfurt, Germany: Suhrkamp, 1974), 57–65.

76. Wolfrum, *Geschichtspolitik*, 284–86.

77. For Schmidt's own assessment of the increasing and, in his mind, unavoidable distance between politicians and intellectuals, see Helmut Schmidt, *Weggefährten: Erinnerungen und Reflexionen* (Berlin: Siedler, 1996), 91–114.

78. Schmidt was a junior officer in Hitler's army, and his pragmatic outlook on professional politics and his aversion to political ideologies make him an ideal representative of Schelsky's sociological model of the skeptical generation; see chapter 4.

79. See, for example, Regina Holler, *20. Juli 1944: Vermächtnis oder Alibi?* (Munich, Germany: Saur, 1994), 227–29. The most notable exception to this trend was President Walter Scheel, who was elected in 1974. It is safe to assume, however, that his attempts to foster a genuine West German historical consciousness from the top down had only limited success under the circumstances. For Scheel's identity politics, see Wolfrum, *Geschichtspolitik*, 308–9.

80. Peter Glotz suggested that two completely different cultures developed in West Germany in the late 1970s. See Sabine von Dierke, *"All Power to the Imagination": The West German Counterculture from the Student Movement to the Greens* (Lincoln: Nebraska University Press, 1997), 105.

81. Werner Bergmann argues that the topic of National Socialism almost completely disappeared from the public agenda during the 1970s when the West German media focused on the extraparliamentary opposition and the rise of left-wing terrorism. See Bergmann, *Antisemitismus*, 313. That assessment might underestimate the many implicit and explicit references to the Nazi past that the discussions about terrorism contained. See, for example, Dubiel, *Niemand ist frei von der Geschichte*, 139–60. But it is not clear to what extent the interpretations of fascism and Nazism advanced by the terrorists and their opponents penetrated the mainstream media. Moreover, it is quite possible that contemporaries of the terrorism crisis perceived it as an event with little historical resonance, whereas memory scholars tend to see collective memory at work throughout the confrontation between Baader-Meinhof, the Rote Armee Fraction, and the West German state. For the terrorists themselves, the Nazi past certainly provided an important interpretive and autobiographical reference point. See Varon, *Bringing the War Home*, 245–51 and passim.

82. Janusz Bodek, *Die Fassbinder Kontroversen: Entstehung und Wirkung eines literarischen Textes* (Frankfurt, Germany: Lang, 1991).

83. Anneliese Mannzmann, *Hitlerwelle und historische Fakten* (Königstein, Germany: Scriptor, 1979).

84. See chapter 7.

85. Harald Schmid, "Die 'Stunde der Wahrheit' und ihre Voraussetzungen: Zum geschichtskulturellen Wirkungskontext von 'Holocaust,'" in Zeitgeschichte-online, Thema: Die Fernsehserie "Holocaust"—Rückblicke auf eine "betroffene Nation," March 2004, http://www.zeitgeschichte=online.de/md=FSHolocaust-Schmid.

86. Hochhuth's story, *A German Love Story* (Boston: Little Brown, 1980), was turned into a movie by director Andrzej Wajda in 1983 and broadcast by the ZDF on December 9, 1985.

87. Rolf Hochhuth, "Schwierigkeiten, die wahre Geschichte zu erzählen," *Die Zeit*, February 17, 1978.

88. The key texts of the Filbinger scandal are collected and commented on in Rosemarie von dem Knesebeck, *In Sachen Filbinger gegen Hochhuth: Die Geschichte einer Vergangenheitsbewältigung* (Reinbek, Germany: Rowohlt, 1980); see also Schwab-Trapp, *Konflikt, Kultur und Interpretation*, 130–62; and Teschke, *Hitler's Legacy*, 261–63. For the best defense of Filbinger's wartime and postwar record, see Bruno Heck, ed., *Hans Filbinger: Der "Fall" und die Fakten* (Mainz, Germany: Hase und Koehler, 1980).

89. Rupert Seuthe, *"Geistig-moralische Wende?": Der politische Umgang mit der NS-Vergangenheit in der Ära Kohl am Beispiel von Gedenktagen, Museums- und Denkmalprojekten* (Frankfurt, Germany: Peter Lang, 2001), 77; see also Julia Kölsch, *Politik und Gedächtnis: Zur Soziologie funktionaler Kultivierung von Erinnerung* (Wiesbaden, Germany: Westdeutscher Verlag, 2000), 223–24. Schmidt's participation in the central memorial event in Cologne that had been organized by West Germany's Jewish communities happened in the context of a major, grassroots reinvention of Kristallnacht as a site of memory. Throughout the republic, cities, churches, history workshops, unions, and political parties organized public ceremonies in memory of the victims of November 9, 1938. The national political elite, including President Walter Scheel and the president of parliament Karl Carstens, participated in these memory endeavors, although they tended to repeat the old memorial formulas of previous decades; by contrast, those

involved in the grassroots events, as well as the electronic media, already had experimented with new formats of collective memory. See the detailed analysis of the fortieth anniversary of Kristallnacht in Harald Schmid, *Erinnern an den "Tag der Schuld": Das Novemberpogrom von 1938 in der deutschen Geschichtspolitik* (Hamburg, Germany: Ergebnisse, 2001), 325–93.

90. Von Miquel, *Westdeutsche Justiz*, 364–69; Bergmann, *Antisemitismus*, 369–70.

91. Dubiel, *Niemand ist frei von der Geschichte*, 160–74.

92. Knesebeck, *Filbinger gegen Hochhuth*, 112.

CHAPTER 11

1. Hermann Lübbe, "Der Nationalsozialismus im deutschen Nachkriegsbewusstsein," *Historische Zeitschrift* 236, no. 3 (1983): 579–99. See also Jerry Muller, "German Neo-conservatism, ca. 1968–1985: Hermann Lübbe and Others," in Jan-Werner Müller, ed., *German Ideologies since 1945: Studies in the Political Thought and Culture of the Bonn Republic* (New York: Palgrave, 2003), 161–84, and chapter 3.

2. Habbo Knoch, *Die Tat als Bild: Fotografien des Holocaust in der deutschen Erinnerungskultur* (Hamburg, Germany: Hamburger Edition, 2001), 134–56; Cornelia Brink, *Ikonen der Vernichtung: Öffentlicher Gebrauch von Fotografien aus nationalsozialistischen Konzentrationslagern nach 1945* (Berlin: Akademie, 1998), 46–99.

3. The term *externalization* is used here to describe the objectification and concretization of collective memories in the context of the transition from communicative to cultural memory; see Jan Assmann, "Collective Memory and Cultural Identity," *New German Critique* 65 (Spring–Summer 1995): 125–33. Rainer Lepsius used the word in a different way in his comparison of strategies of coming to terms with past Nazism in Austria, the GDR, and the Federal Republic of Germany. In his intervention, externalization designates Austrian strategies of representation that exclude the problem of the Nazi past from Austrian history and project it onto German history and, more specifically, the history of the Federal Republic; see Lepsius, "Das Erbe des Nationalsozialismus und die politische Kultur der Nachfolgestaaten des 'Grossdeutschen Reiches,'" in Max Haller, ed., *Kultur und Gesellschaft: Verhandlungen des 24. Deutschen Soziologentags* (Frankfurt, Germany: Campus, 1989), 247–64.

4. Clemens Vollnhals, "Zwischen Verdrängung und Aufklärung: Die Auseinandersetzung mit dem Holocaust in der frühen Bundesrepublik," in Ursula Büttner, ed., *Die Deutschen und die Judenverfolgung im Dritten Reich* (Hamburg, Germany: Christians, 1992), 357–92; Michal Bodemann, *In den Wogen der Erinnerung: Jüdische Existenz in Deutschland* (Munich, Germany: dtv, 2002), 22–28.

5. Aleida Assman and Ute Frevert, *Geschichtsvergessenheit—Geschichtsversessenheit: Vom Umgang mit deutschen Vergangenheiten nach 1945* (Stuttgart, Germany: Deutsche Verlagsanstalt, 1999), 258–71; Wolfrum, *Geschichtspolitik in der Bundesrepublik Deutschland: Der Weg zur bundesrepublikanischen Erinnerung* (Darmstadt, Germany: Wissenschaftliche Buchgesellschaft, 1999), 316–19.

6. Germany's architectural memory landscape, that is, the representation of the past in monuments, memorials, historical buildings, and similar media, is one of the best-researched aspects of Germany's historical culture. For a general survey, see Rudy Koshar, *From Monuments to Traces: Artifacts of German Memory, 1870–1990* (Berkeley: University of California Press, 2000), especially from 143 forward. A number of scholars have integrated the local and everyday history of historical preservation into the history of German collective memory; see especially Harold Marcuse, *Legacies of Dachau: The Uses and Abuses of a Concentration Camp, 1933–2001* (Cambridge: Cambridge University Press, 2001), and Gavriel Rosenfeld, *Munich and Memory: Architecture, Monuments, and the Legacy of the Third Reich* (Berkeley: University of California Press, 2000).

7. A complete, two-volume catalog of German memorials for the victims of National Socialism has been published by the Bundeszentrale für Politische Bildung. The first volume presents the memorials in the former West Germany, the second those in the former East Germany; see Ulrike Puvogel and Martin Stankowski, *Gedenkstätten für die Opfer des Nationalsozialismus*, vol. 1, 2nd enlarged ed. (Bonn, Germany: Bundeszentrale für politische Bildung, 1995); and Stefanie Endlich, *Gedenkstätten für die Opfer des Nationalsozialismus*, vol. 2 (Bonn, Germany: Bundeszentrale für politische Bildung, 1999); see also G. E. Schafft and Gerhard Zeidler, *Die KZ-Mahn- und Gedenkstätten in Deutschland* (Berlin: Dietz, 1996), and for a publication on the topic that reflects the memory rhetoric of the 1980s, see Detlef Garbe, ed., *Die vergessenen KZs? Gedenkstätten für die Opfer des NS-Terrors in der Bundesrepublik* (Bornheim-Merten, Germany: Lamuv, 1983). Unfortunately, the comprehensive catalog by Puvogel, Stankowski, and Endlich does not provide any statistical analysis. But the map in volume 2 illustrates that the former East German government aggressively fostered the memory of NS victimization and that the less densely populated and more conservative areas in the north and south of the Federal Republic have made only modest contributions to the memorial wave of the 1980s.

8. For the history of camp memorials in the 1950s and 1960s, see the succinct summary in Assman and Frevert, *Geschichtsvergessenheit*, 206–8.

9. Brigitte Hausmann, *Duell mit der Verdrängung: Denkmäler für die Opfer des Nationalsozialismus in der Bundesrepublik Deutschland, 1980 bis 1990* (Münster, Germany: Lit, 1997), 13. The turning point in preservation politics of the late 1970s and early 1980s is well described in Rudy Koshar, *Preservation and National Memory in the Twentieth Century* (Chapel Hill: University North Carolina Press, 1998), 319–23.

10. See especially the case studies on local memory disputes in East and West Germany after unification in Klaus Neumann, *Shifting Memories: The Nazi Past in the New Germany* (Ann Arbor: University of Michigan Press, 2000).

11. For the most explicit discussions of such intentions, see Michael Stürmer, *Deutsche Fragen oder Die Suche nach der Staatsräson* (Munich, Germany: Piper, 1988), 34, 63, 70–72, 77–78, and passim.

12. Margit Mayer and John Ely, *The German Greens: Paradox between Movement and Party* (Philadelphia: Temple University Press, 1998).

13. Bergmann, *Antisemitismus*, 385–91; Bodemann, *Erinnerung*, 85–87; Michael Wolffsohn, *Ewige Schuld: 40 Jahre deutsch-jüdisch-israelische Beziehungen* (Munich, Germany: Piper, 1988), 43–44; and especially Michael Schwab-Trapp, "Pleiten, Pech und Pannen: Kohls Spaziergang durch die Fettnäpfchen: Typische Argumente in einem Streit um Helmut Kohls Israelreise," in Thomas Herz and Michael Schwab-Trapp, *Umkämpfte Vergangenheit: Diskurse über den Nationalsozialismus seit 1945* (Opladen, Germany: Westdeutscher Verlag, 1997), 139–66.

14. Dubiel, *Niemand ist frei von der Geschichte*, 150–54.

15. The notion of historicization has been best conceptualized by the liberal historian Martin Broszat (see chapter 5). The concept provides a good example for generational affinities that cut across political divides, since Broszat belonged to the moderate Left of West Germany's political spectrum.

16. Many key texts of the Bitburg affair are collected in Geoffrey Hartman, ed., *Bitburg in Moral and Political Perspective* (Bloomington: Indiana University Press, 1986). See also Jan-Holger Kirsch, *"Wir haben aus der Geschichte gelernt": Der 8. Mai als politischer Gedenktag in Deutschland* (Cologne, Germany: Böhlau, 1999), 71–95.

17. Marcuse, *Legacies of Dachau*, 359–60.

18. Hajo Funke, "Bergen-Belsen, Bitburg, Hambach: Bericht über eine negative Katharsis," in Funke, ed., *Von der Gnade der geschenkten Nation: Zur politischen Moral der Bonner Republik* (Berlin: Rotbuch, 1988), 20–34.

19. Shlomo Shafir, *Ambiguous Relations: The American Jewish Community and Germany since 1945* (Detroit, MI: Wayne State University Press, 1999), 299–315; William Bole, "Bitburg: The American Scene," in Hartman, *Bitburg*, 66–79.

20. Rupert Seuthe, *"Geistig-moralische Wende"? Der politische Umgang mit der NS-Vergangenheit in der Ära Kohl am Beispiel von Gedenktagen, Museums- und Denkmalprojekten* (Frankfurt, Germany: Lang, 2001), 60–61.

21. Peter Reichel, *Politik mit der Erinnerung: Gedächtnisorte im Streit um die nationalsozialistische Vergangenheit* (Munich, Germany: Hanser, 1995), 283.

22. For the role of the media in the Bitburg affair, see especially Bergmann, *Antisemitismus*, 391–422.

23. Seuthe, *NS-Vergangenheit in der Ära Kohl*, 73–74.

24. Elizabeth Noelle-Neumann and Renate Köcher, *Allensbacher Jahrbuch der Demoskopie, 1984–1992* (Munich, Germany: Saur, 1993), 976.

25. Bergmann, *Antisemitismus*, 399.

26. Weizsäcker was elected by the highest margin of a first-term president in the history of the Federal Republic; see Horst Ferdinand, ed., *Reden, die die Republik bewegten* (Opladen, Germany: Leske und Budrich, 2002), 470.

27. Weizsäcker's speech and reactions to the speech from Germany and abroad have been collected in Ulrich Gill and Winfried Steffani, eds., *Eine Rede und ihre Wirkung: Die Rede des Bundespräsidenten Richard von Weizsäcker vom 8. Mai 1985* (Berlin: Böll, 1986).

28. Seuthe, *NS-Vergangenheit in der Ära Kohl*, 47. The expellees clearly understood Weizsäcker's message as the critical reaction of one of their officials indicated; see Herbert Czaja, "Recht auf die Heimat—Für Alle? Kritische Fragen zur Rede—Ein Jahr danach," in Gill and Steffani, *Eine Rede*, 91–100.

29. Dubiel, *Niemand ist frei von der Geschichte*, 212.

30. Reichel, *Politik mit der Erinnerung*, 295–96.

31. It was probably particularly important for the popular acceptance of the speech that Weizsäcker, like many of his predecessors, carefully differentiated between the guilty Nazi leadership and German people; see Julia Kölsch, *Politik und Gedächtnis: Zur Soziologie funktionaler Kultivierung von Erinnerung* (Opladen, Germany: Westdeutscher Verlag, 2000), 135–42.

32. Dubiel, *Niemand ist frei von der Geschichte*, 209; Kirsch, *Der 8. Mai*, 106

33. See chapter 3.

34. Sabine Moller, *Die Entkonkretisierung der NS-Herrschaft in der Ära Kohl* (Hannover, Germany: Offizin, 1998), 28–31.

35. On the debates about the concept of constitutional patriotism, see Wolfrum, *Geschichtspolitik*, 291–96.

36. Seuthe, *NS-Vergangenheit in der Ära Kohl*, 164, 186–88.

37. Klaus Stüve, ed., *Die grossen Regierungserklärungen der deutschen Bundeskanzler von Adenauer bis Schröder* (Opladen, Germany: Leske und Budrich, 2002), 271–88 and 289–311.

38. Lothar Gall, ed., *Überlegungen und Vorschläge zur Errichtung eines Hauses der Geschichte der Bundesrepublik Deutschland in Bonn* (Bonn, Germany: Bundesministerium des Innern, 1984).

39. Christoph Stölzl, ed., *Deutsches Historisches Museum: Ideen-Kontroversen-Perspektiven* (Berlin: Propyläen, 1988), 310–33.

40. See, for example, Hans Mommsen, "Stellungnahme zum Gutachten 'Überlegungen und Vorschläge zur Errichtung eines Hauses der Geschichte in Bonn,'" in Freimut Duve, ed., *Materialien der Arbeitsgruppe "Kunst und Kultur" der SPD-Bundestagsfraktion* (Bonn, Germany: SPD, 1984).

41. Seuthe, *NS-Vergangenheit in der Ära Kohl*, 199.

42. Duve, *Materialien*; Moller, *Entkonkretisierung*, 88–94.

43. Die Grünen, ed., *Wider die Entsorgung der deutschen Geschichte: Streitschrift gegen die geplanten historischen Museen in Berlin und Bonn* (Bonn, Germany: Die Grünen im Bundestag,

. pages

1986), and Moller, *Entkonkretisierung*, 102–3; see also the critical essays in Geschichtswerkstatt Berlin, ed., *Die Nation als Ausstellungsstück: Planungen, Kritik und Utopien zu den Museumsgründungen in Bonn und Berlin* (Hamburg, Germany: VSA-Verlag, 1987), especially the entertaining polemic by Lutz Niethammer, "Selbstgespräche eines Sachwalters: Über einige technische Probleme beim Bau eines Nationalmuseums," 29–40.

44. See chapter 4.

45. See the detailed description of the West German memorial events marking the fiftieth anniversary of Kristallnacht in Harald Schmid, *Erinnern an den "Tag der Schuld": Das Novemberpogrom von 1938 in der deutschen Geschichtspolitik* (Hamburg, Germany: Ergebnisse, 2001), 411–49.

46. Bodemann, *Gedächtnistheater*, 85–86. The most comprehensive analysis of the miscommunication between Jenninger and his audience and the general social context of the event has been provided by Holger Siever, *Kommunikation und Verstehen: Der Fall Jenninger als Beispiel einer semiotischen Kommunikationsanalyse* (Frankfurt, Germany: Lang, 2001).

47. Dubiel, *Niemand ist frei von der Geschichte*, 197–98.

48. Dietmar Schiller, *Die inszenierte Erinnerung: Politische Gedenktage im öffentlich-rechtlichen Fernsehen der Bundesrepublik Deutschland zwischen Medienereignis und Skandal* (Frankfurt, Germany: Lang, 1993), 88–89. See also the contributions in Gisela Müller-Brandeck, *Deutsche Europapolitik von Adenauer bis Schröder* (Opladen, Germany: Leske und Budrich, 2002).

49. See, for example, James McAdams, *Judging the Past in Unified Germany* (Cambridge: Cambridge University Press, 2001).

50. Wolfgang Dümcke and Fritz Wilmar, eds., *Kolonialisierung der DDR: Kritische Analysen und Alternativen des Einigungsprozesess* (Münster, Germany: Agenda, 1996).

51. On Habermas's problems of adapting his concept of constitutional patriotism to the political conditions after unification and especially his failure in integrating East German experiences into his blueprint for a postnational republican identity, see Jan-Werner Müller, *Another Country: German Intellectuals, Unification and National Identity* (New Haven, CT: Yale University Press, 2000), 107–12.

52. The political importance of antitotalitarianism during the process of unification is confirmed in exemplary fashion in the voluminous report of the parliamentary commission for the "analysis of the history and consequences of the SED-dictatorship in Germany," which parliament discussed and accepted in June 1994; see Karl Heinz Roth, *Geschichtsrevisionismus: Die Wiedergeburt des Totalitarismus* (Hamburg, Germany: Konkret, 1999), 87–104. For a typical scholarly postunification confirmation of the concept and ideology of antitotalitarianism, see Eckhard Jesse, Christiane Schroeder, and Thomas Grosse-Gehling, *Totalitarismus im 20. Jahrhundert: Eine Bilanz der internationalen Forschung*, 2nd ed. (Baden-Baden, Germany: Nomos, 1999).

53. Jeffrey S. Lantis, *Strategic Dilemmas and the Evolution of German Foreign Policy since Unification* (Westport, CT: Praeger, 2002), 18–27.

54. The most comprehensive analysis of the public debates about the Gulf War has been provided by Michael Schwab-Trapp, *Kriegsdiskurse: Die politische Kultur des Krieges im Wandel, 1919–1999* (Opladen, Germany: Leske und Budrich, 2002), 87–111.

55. Scott Erb, *German Foreign Policy: Navigating a New Era* (Boulder, CO: Lynne Rienner, 2003), 151–52, and Schwab-Trapp, *Kriegsdiskurse*, 92.

56. Lantis, *Strategic Dilemmas*, 24–25.

57. Schwab-Trapp, *Kriegsdiskurse*, 95–96. The peace movement was, in turn, massively criticized not only by conservatives, who argued that it was time for Germany to step up to the plate and assume military responsibilities, but also by liberal commentators, who interpreted the lack of solidarity with Israel as a symptom of troublesome anti-Semitic continuities; see, for example, Henryk Broder, "Israel und die Friedensbewegung," *die tageszeitung*, January 2, 1991, and, in much more detail, Eike Geisel, *Die Banalität der Guten: Deutsche Seelenwanderungen* (Berlin: Tiamat, 1992), 115–65.

58. The first prominent liberal to break rank with the peace movement was the songwriter and former GDR dissident Wolf Biermann; "Damit wir uns missverstehen: Ich bin für den Krieg am Golf," *Die Zeit*, February 1, 1991. He was quickly followed by the poet and novelist Hans Magnus Enzensberger, who equated Saddam Hussein with Hitler in a widely discussed piece in early February; "Hitlers Wiedergänger," *Der Spiegel*, February 4, 1991. For an extensive discussion of this comparison, see Moshe Zuckermann, *Zweierlei Holocaust: Der Holocaust in den politischen Kulturen Israels und Deutschlands*, 2nd ed. (Cologne, Germany: Wallstein, 1999), 78–97. Less than two weeks later, Jürgen Habermas declared his support of the war in the most sophisticated intellectual intervention during the campaign; "Wider die Logik des Krieges," *Die Zeit*, February 14, 1991. The public pronouncements of some of Germany's leading intellectuals were prompted by militarily insignificant but symbolically devastating SCUD missile attacks that Iraq launched against Israel in the second half of January. In response to the attacks and the publicity surrounding them, the Social Democrats toned down their opposition to the war; Michael Prince, "Under Construction: The Berlin Republic," *Washington Quarterly* 22, no. 3 (1999): 109–36. Popular support for the intervention in Iraq increased significantly, see Lantis, *Strategic Dilemmas*, 35.

59. Schwab-Trapp, *Kriegsdiskurse*, 107.

60. Dubiel, *Niemand ist frei von der Geschichte*, 249–56; Werner Süss, "The Germans and Their Capital: A Plea to Continue the Debate," in Howard Williams, Colin Wight, and Norbert Kapferer, eds., *Political Thought and German Reunification* (New York: St. Martin's Press, 2000), 116–38.

61. See the case studies in Hajo Funke, *Paranoia und Politik: Rechtsextremismus in der Berliner Republik* (Berlin: Schiler, 2002), chapter 1.

62. Lee McGowan, *The Radical Right in Germany: 1870 to the Present* (London: Longman, 2002), 197.

63. On the collective memory of the New Right, see Johannes Klotz and Ulrich Schneider, eds., *Die selbstbewusste Nation und ihr Geschichtsbild: Geschichtslegenden der Neuen Rechten* (Cologne, Germany: PapyRossa, 1997), and Alexander Ruoff, *Verbiegen, Verdrängen, Beschweigen: Die Nationalgeschichte der "Neuen Freiheit"* (Münster, Germany: Unrast, 2001).

64. For a careful analysis of the origins and dynamics of postunification right-wing violence, see Funke, *Paranoia und Politik,* and Norbert Madloch, "Rechtsextremismus in Deutschland nach dem Ende des Hitlerfaschismus," in Klaus Kinner and Rolf Richter, eds., *Rechtsextremismus und Antifaschismus* (Berlin: Dietz, 2000), 57–214.

65. Rainer Erb, "Public Responses to Antisemitism and Right-Wing Extremism," in Hermann Kuerthen, Werner Bergmann, and Rainer Erb, eds., *Antisemitism and Xenophobia in Germany after Unification* (New York: Oxford University Press, 1997), 211–23; Dubiel, *Niemand ist frei von der Geschichte*, 248.

66. Donald Phillips, *Post-national Patriotism and the Feasibility of Post-national Community in Unified Germany* (Westport, CT: Praeger, 2000), 121–40; Friedemann Schmidt, *Die Neue Rechte und die Berliner Republik: Parallel laufende Wege im Normalisierungsdiskurs* (Wiesbaden, Germany: Westdeutscher Verlag); J. H. Brinks, *Children of a New Fatherland: Germany's Postwar Right-Wing Politics* (London: Tauris, 2000), 129–42.

67. On the development of xenophobic and anti-Semitic crimes since the mid-1990s, see Helmut Willems, "Rechtsextreme Straftaten in Deutschland: Entwicklung, Strukturen, Hintergründe," in Thomas Grumke and Bernd Wagner, eds., *Handbuch Rechtsextremismus: Personen—Organisationen—Netzwerke vom Neonazismus bis in die Mitte der Gesellschaft* (Opladen, Germany: Leske und Budrich, 2002), 141–57.

68. For a concise history of the Neue Wache, see Klaus Kühnel, "Die Ideologiekathedrale: Berlins Neue Wache in Geschichte und Gegenwart," in Thomas Schmidt, Ernst Mittig, and Vera Böhm, eds., *Nationaler Totenkult—Die Neue Wache: Eine Streitschrift zur zentralen deutschen Gedenkstätte* (Berlin: Karin Kramer Verlag, 1995), 27–40, and, in much greater detail, Jürgen Tietz, "Schinkels Neue Wache Unter den Linden: Baugeschichte 1816–1993," in Christoph

Stölzl, ed., *Die Neue Wache unter den Linden: Ein deutsches Denkmal im Wandel der Geschichte* (Munich, Germany: Koehler und Amelang, 1993), 9–93.

69. On the frustration with the existing memorial in Bonn, see Ulrich Schlie, *Die Nation erinnert sich: Die Denkmäler der Deutschen* (Munich, Germany: Beck, 2002), 144–47. In response to these frustrations, Helmut Schmidt had also suggested building a national memorial site in 1981; see Bernhard Schulz, "Kein Konsens im Land der Menschenketten," in Stölzl, *Neue Wache*, 172–82.

70. The proposal is reprinted in Freimut Duve, ed., *Anhörung der SPD Bundestagsfraktion am 3. Juli 1985: Mahnmal für die Opfer von Krieg und Gewaltherrschaft in Bonn* (Bonn, Germany: SPD Bundestagsfraktion, 1985), 106–15.

71. Susanne Thoma, *"Vergangenheitsbewältigung" am Beispiel der Auseinandersetzungen um die Neue Wache* (Berlin: Scheibel, 1995), 31–32.

72. See especially Duve, *Anhörung der SPD Bundestagsfraktion*.

73. Moller, *Entkonkretisierung*, 31–39.

74. Thoma, *"Vergangenheitsbewältigung,"* 72.

75. Seuthe, *NS-Vergangenheit in der Ära Kohl*, 249–50.

76. In fact, the East German government contemplated installing a Kollwitz sculpture in the Neue Wache when it turned the building into a memorial for the "victims of fascism and the world wars" in 1960 but ultimately settled on a more abstract design; see Reichel, *Politik mit der Erinnerung*, 238–39.

77. This was the criticism of Walter Jens, the president of the national academy of the arts; see his "Offener Brief an den Bundeskanzler Dr. Helmut Kohl," in Stölzl, *Die Neue Wache*, 189–90; see also Eberhard Roters, "Die Skulptur—Der Raum—Das Problem," in Akademie der Künste, ed., *Streit um die Neue Wache: Zur Gestaltung einer zentralen Gedenkstätte* (Berlin: Akademie der Künste, 1993), 7–18.

78. Most persistent and compelling on this point was the historian Reinhart Koselleck, "Bilderverbot—Welches Totengedenken?" *FAZ*, April 8, 1993; see also Reinhart Koselleck, Andrea Seibel, and Siegfried Weichlein, "'Mies, medioker und provinziell,'" in Schmidt et al., *Nationaler Totenkult*, 107–10; and Moller, *Entkonkretisierung*, 61–64.

79. Seuthe, *NS-Vergangenheit in der Ära Kohl*, 253.

80. Thoma, *"Vergangenheitsbewältigung,"* 46; Seuthe, *NS-Vergangenheit in der Ära Kohl*, 255.

81. Moller, *Entkonkretisierung*, 56–57.

82. See, for example, Assmann and Frevert, *Geschichtsvergessenheit*, 273–74; Kattago, *Ambiguous Memory*, 133–134; Reichel, *Politik mit der Erinnerung*, 233; and Moller, *Entkonkretisierung*, 68–70.

83. Seuthe, *NS-Vergangenheit in der Ära Kohl*, 257–62.

84. Benedikt Erenz, "Geschenk an die Jugend, Jahrmarkt mit Peinlichkeiten: In Bonn wurde das Haus der Geschichte der Bundesrepublik Deutschland eröffnet," *Die Zeit*, June 24, 1994; see also Seuthe, *NS-Vergangenheit in der Ära Kohl*, 180–81.

85. Christian Semler, "Wie Kohl Geschichte schreiben lässt," *die tageszeitung*, June 15, 1994.

86. Reichel, *Politik mit der Erinnerung*, 252.

87. Christel Dormagen, "Die Ware BRD," *Die Woche*, June 16, 1994.

88. Stiftung Haus der Geschichte der Bundesrepublik Deutschland, ed., *Tätigkeitsbericht*, *1995–1996* (Bonn, Germany: Haus der Geschichte der Bundesrepublik Deutschland, 1997), 40–43, 105–6.

89. When the museum opened, this historicization effect apparently worked very well. Most reviewers, including reviewers from abroad, praised the exhibit for acknowledging the Nazi crimes without noticing that it also systematically undercut the relevance of that past for the Federal Republic; see Moller, *Entkonkretisierung*, 117–18.

90. See the museum's Web site at http://www.dhm.de/ausstellungen/index.html.

91. Seuthe, *NS-Vergangenheit in der Ära Kohl*, 221–22.

CHAPTER 12

1. Theodor Heuss had already developed this memory theme in 1946; see Ulrich Baumgärt-ner, *Reden nach Hitler: Theodor Heuss—Die Auseinandersetzung mit dem Nationalsozialismus* (Stuttgart, Germany: Deutsche Verlagsanstalt, 2001), 107.

2. Jan-Holger Kirsch, *"Wir haben aus der Geschichte gelernt": Der 8. Mai als politischer Gedenk-tag in Deutschland* (Cologne, Germany: Böhlau, 1999), 153–64.

3. Rupert Seuthe, *"Geistig-moralische Wende?": Der politische Umgang mit der NS-Vergangenheit in der Ära Kohl am Beispiel von Gedenktagen, Museums- und Denkmalprojekten* (Frankfurt, Germany: Lang, 2001), 106.

4. Some of the media offerings during the anniversary months are documented in Stiftung Lesen, ed., *1945: Literatur gegen das Vergessen—Programme zur Erinnerung* (Mainz, Germany: Stiftung Lesen, 1995).

5. Maybe Mitterand's generosity was a result of his own memory problems. In 1994, his civil service career during the Vichy regime and his failure to reveal the details of that service became the subject of intense public scrutiny in France; see Stanley Hoffman et al., "Sympo-sium on Mitterand's Past," *French Politics and Society* 13, no. 1 (1995): 4–28.

6. Seuthe, *NS-Vergangenheit in der Ära Kohl,* 108.

7. Ibid., 110–16; Kirsch, *Der 8. Mai als politischer Gedenktag,* 180–84.

8. "Mai 1945—Gegen das Vergessen," *FAZ,* April 7, 1995, reprinted in slightly changed form on April 28 and May 5, 1995. On the political objectives behind the initiative, see Alexan-der Ruoff, *Verbiegen, Verdrängen, Beschweigen: Die Nationalgeschichte der "Jungen Freiheit"* (Münster, Germany: Unrast, 2001).

9. Bill Niven, *Facing the Nazi Past: United Germany and the Legacy of the Third Reich* (London: Routledge, 2002), 114–16.

10. Presse und Informationsamt der Bundesregierung, ed., *Zum 50. Jahrestag des Endes des Zweiten Weltkrieges: Staatsakt am 8. Mai* (Bonn: Presse und Informationsamt der Bun-deskgierung, 1995), 48–56.

11. Roman Herzog, "Zum 50. Jahrestag des Endes des Zweiten Weltkrieges: Ansprache am 8. Mai 1995 beim Staatsakt im Konzerthaus am Gendarmenmarkt in Berlin," in Fried-helm Ost, ed., *Die Deutschen und das Kriegsende: Die Reden der Bundespräsidenten von Weiz-säcker und Herzog zum 40. und 50. Jahrestag des Kriegsendes* (Paderborn, Germany: Bonifatius, 1997), 27–38, 29.

12. Ibid., 33–35.

13. Michael Schwab-Trapp, *Kiegsdiskurse: Die politische Kultur des Krieges im Wandel 1991–1999* (Opladen, Germany: Leske und Budrich, 2002), 115–20. The position of the conservative camp had been bolstered by a July 1994 decision of the constitutional court stipulating that, in contrast to long-held assumptions, the constitution did not prohibit the deployment of Ger-man troops as part of an internationally sanctioned military intervention; see Jeffrey Lantis, *Strategic Dilemmas and the Evolution of German Foreign Policy since Unification* (Westport, CT: Praeger, 2002), 108.

14. Schwab-Trapp, *Kriegsdiskurse,* 125–32.

15. Ibid., 124–25.

16. Andrei Markovits and Simon Reich, *The German Predicament: Memory & Power in the New Europe* (Ithaca, NY: Cornell University Press, 1998), 145.

17. David Rohde, *Endgame: The Betrayal and Fall of Srebrenica—Europe's Worst Massacre since World War II* (New York: Farrar, Straus and Giroux, 1997).

18. "Bosnische Konsequenz: Auszüge des Briefes, den Joschka Fischer gestern an die Bundestagsfraktion und die Partei Bündnis 90/Die Grünen schickte," *die tageszeitung,* Au-gust 2, 1995; see also Scott Erb, *German Foreign Policy: Navigating a New Era* (Boulder, CO: Lynne Riener, 2003), 164.

19. That was Krista Sager's self-reflexive contribution to the discussions within the Green Party; see Krista Sager, "'Möchte gern, kann nicht:' Bündnisfähig für PDS wie CDU, ein Flügel für Kampfeinsätze, der andere dagegen: Wo stehen die Grünen? Ein Plädoyer für eine Grundsatzdebatte," *die tageszeitung*, September 14, 1995.

20. The Green Party debated the new foreign policy options most vigorously and only gradually abandoned the traditional pacifist positions that had helped bring the party to the national stage in the early 1980s; see Markovits and Reich, *German Predicament*, 145–48, and Schwab-Trapp, *Kriegsdiskurse*, 160–77. The liberal daily *die tageszeitung* made the same transition from pacifism to interventionism during the summer of 1995; see Ruoff, *Verbiegen, Verdrängen, Beschweigen*, 125–31.

21. Schwab-Trapp, *Kriegsdiskurse*, 183.

22. Habermas expressed his support in an interview published in *Der Spiegel*, August 7, 1995; see also Ralph Giordano, "'Uns steht kein Fluchtweg offen': Ein Militäreinsatz in Bosnien ist unvermeidlich geworden," *die tageszeitung*, August 11, 1995.

23. See the catalog of the exhibit: Hannes Heer and Klaus Naumann, *Vernichtungskrieg: Verbrechen der Wehrmacht, 1941–1944* (Hamburg, Germany: Hamburger Edition, 1995).

24. Gauweiler's intervention was extreme but not unprecedented. In most cities where it was shown, the exhibit tended to divide the local political establishment into supporters and critics, with Greens, SPD, and a somewhat reluctant FDP defending the Hamburg Institute against critics from the ranks of the CDU/CSU; Niven, *Facing the Nazi Past*, 144. These local battles provided free advertisement, and they illustrate the importance of local politics for the construction of collective memories. Specifically for the responses in Munich, see Kulturreferat München, ed., *Bilanz einer Ausstellung: Dokumentation der Kontroverse um die Ausstellung "Vernichtungskrieg—Verbrechen der Wehrmacht 1941 bis 1944" in München* (Munich, Germany: Knaur, 1998).

25. The exhibit lost some credibility when scholars from Eastern Europe proved that some of the photos depicted crimes committed by the Soviet Secret Service. As a result of the criticism, the show was closed in November 1999 and reopened in a corrected version in November 2001; see the new catalog, Jan Philipp Reemtsma, Ulrike Jureit, and Hans Mommsen, *Verbrechen der Wehrmacht: Dimensionen des Vernichtungskrieges, 1941–1944* (Hamburg, Germany: Hamburger Edition, 2002).

26. The parliamentary debate is reprinted in Hans-Günther Thiele, ed., *Wehrmachtsausstellung: Dokumentation einer Kontroverse* (Bremen, Germany: Edition Temmen, 1997), 170–208; see also Helmut Dubiel, *Niemand ist frei von der Geschichte: Die nationalsozialistische Herrschaft in den Debatten des Deutschen Bundestages* (Munich, Germany: Hanser, 1999), 22–33.

27. Helga Haftendorn, *Deutsche Aussenpolitik zwischen Selbstbeschränkung und Selbstbehauptung, 1945–2000* (Stuttgart, Germany: Deutsche Verlagsanstalt, 2001), 413–17.

28. For a typical justification of the intervention that contains a few references to Germany's past and inadvertently reveals the excitement that Germany's political leaders felt during the NATO campaign against Serbia, see the war memoirs of Germany's defense minister Rudolf Scharping, *Wir dürfen nicht wegsehen: Der Kosovo-Krieg und Europa* (Berlin: Ullstein, 1999); see also Wolfgang-Uwe Friedrich, Wolfgang Ischinger, and Rudolf Scharping, *The Legacy of Kosovo: German Politics and Policies in the Balkans* (Washington, DC: American Institute for Contemporary German Studies, 2000); Schwab-Trapp, *Kriegsdiskurse*, 250, 257–60; and Michael Jeismann, *Auf Wiedersehen Gestern: Die deutsche Vergangenheit und die Politik von morgen* (Stuttgart, Germany: Deutsche Verlagsanstalt, 2001), 33–34.

29. Jürgen Habermas, "Bestialität und Humanität: Ein Krieg an der Grenze zwischen Recht und Moral," *Die Zeit*, April 29, 1999, and Dan Diner, "Ein Schlüsselereignis," *Die Zeit*, June 10, 1999. With hindsight, it is clear that this political utopia has not yet been realized and certainly not in Kosovo; see Jürgen Elsässer, *Kriegsverbrechen: Die tödlichen Lügen der Bundesrepublik und ihre Opfer im Kosovo-Konflikt* (Hamburg, Germany: Konkret, 2000).

30. For an indictment of the militarization of German memory from the perspective of the peace movement, see Wolf Wetzel, *Krieg ist Frieden: Über Bagdad, Srebrenica, Genua, Kabul nach . . .* (Münster, Germany: Unrast, 2002), 98–105 and passim.

31. Schwab-Trapp, *Kriegsdiskurse*, 308–15, and Erb, *German Foreign Policy*, 172–73.

32. Richard Meng, *Der Medienkanzler: Was bleibt vom System Schröder?* (Frankfurt, Germany: Suhrkamp, 2002), 111–24, and Erb, *German Foreign Policy*, 198–203.

33. Elazar Barkan, *The Guilt of Nations: Restitution and Negotiating Historical Injustices* (New York: Norton, 2000).

34. Jeismann, *Auf Wiedersehen Gestern*, 139–48. For a similar argument, see Antonia Grunenberg, *Die Lust an der Schuld: Von der Macht der Vergangenheit über die Gegenwart* (Berlin: Rowohlt, 2001), esp. 202–3.

35. Atina Grossmann, "The 'Goldhagen Effect': Memory, Repetition, and Responsibility in the New Germany," in Geoff Eley, ed., *The "Goldhagen Effect": History, Memory, Nazism—Facing the German Past* (Ann Arbor: University of Michigan Press, 2000), 89–129.

36. See the comparison between the age profile of the first Schröder cabinet and that of the previous administration in Frank Pfetsch, "Die rot-grüne Aussenpolitik," in Christoph Egle, Tobias Ostheim, and Reimut Zohlnhöfer, *Das rot-grüne Projekt: Eine Bilanz der Regierung Schröder, 1998–2002* (Opladen, Germany: Westdeutscher Verlag, 2003), 381–98.

37. Sylvia Meichsner suggests that Schröder and Fischer also share a keen ability to build and deploy symbolic capital, especially through the media. In Fischer's case, that includes deriving political legitimacy within his own party from evoking the memory of his political resistance efforts during the 1970s; see Meichsner, *Zwei unerwartete Laufbahnen: Die Karriereverläufe von Gerhard Schröder und Joschka Fischer im Vergleich* (Marburg, Germany: Tectum, 2002), 149–53. On at least one occasion, however, Fischer's past in the West German subculture caused a temporary public relations problem. In January 2001, photos surfaced that depicted Fischer attacking a police officer during clashes with the police in Frankfurt in April 1973, and it took several months before his popularity rebounded; see Ottmar Berbalk, "Linke Gewalt: Bilder vom blutigen Samstag," *Focus*, January 8, 2001.

38. The history of the memorial is one of the best-researched subjects in the rapidly expanding literature on Germany's efforts to come to terms with the Nazi past. The strong academic interest in the origins of the memorial reflects the important role that academics and intellectuals have played in the long and controversial discussions about the memorial plans. In this case, as in many studies in collective memory, academics are particularly interested in reconstructing the memories of collectives to which they belong. The most comprehensive among several collections of documents and critiques is Ute Heimrod, Günter Schlusche, and Horst Severens, *Der Denkmalstreit—Das Denkmal? Die Debatte um das "Denkmal für die ermordeten Juden Europas"* (Berlin: Philo, 1999). In addition, three monographs have already been published about the topic: Jan-Holger Kirsch, *Nationaler Mythos oder historische Trauer? Der Streit um ein zentrales "Holocaust-Mahnmal" für die Berliner Republik* (Cologne, Germany: Böhlau, 2003); Hans Georg Stavginski, *Das Holocaust-Denkmal: Der Streit um das "Denkmal für die ermordeten Juden Europas" in Berlin (1988–1999)* (Paderborn, Germany: Schöningh, 2002); and Sibylle Quack, *Auf dem Weg zur Realisierung: Das Denkmal für die ermordeten Juden Europas und der Ort der Information—Architektur und historisches Konzept* (Stuttgart, Germany: Deutsche Verlagsanstalt, 2002).

39. Seuthe, *NS-Vergangenheit in der Ära Kohl*, 265–69; Kirsch, *Nationaler Mythos*, 85–91. Shortly after the memorial plans had been made public, representatives of the Sinti and Roma voiced objections to a memorial because it would establish a hierarchy of victimhood; see Stavginski, *Holocaust-Denkmal*, 36–42 and 58–61.

40. Stavginski, *Holocaust-Denkmal*, 97–101; about the design of the Berlin artist Christine Jacob-Marks, see especially Kirsch, *Nationaler Mythos*, 241–54.

41. Seuthe, *NS-Vergangenheit in der Ära Kohl*, 272–79.

42. Stavginski, *Holocaust-Denkmal*, 154–59.

43. Ibid., 195–97. Together with seventeen other public figures, Grass and Jens signed an appeal to abandon the project; it was published in several dailies, including the *Frankfurter Rundschau*, on February 5, 1998.

44. For a discussion of the Eisenman/Serra design, see Kirsch, *Nationaler Mythos*, 288–312, and Quack, *Realisierung*.

45. Kirsch, *Nationaler Mythos*, 122, and Niven, *Facing the Nazi Past*, 194; the Walser-Bubis debate is documented in Frank Schirrmacher, *Die Walser-Bubis-Debatte: Eine Dokumentation* (Frankfurt, Germany: Suhrkamp, 1999). Schröder's primary interest in pleasing the different constituencies involved in the debate is nicely illustrated by his Freudian slip when saying he would prefer a memorial that "the people like to visit"; see Lars Rensmann, "Baustein der Erinnerung: Die politische Textur der Bundestagsdebatte über ein zentrales 'Holocaust-Mahnmal,'" in Micha Brumlik, Hajo Funke, and Lars Rensmann, *Umkämpftes Vergessen: Walser-Debatte, Holocaust-Mahnmal und neue deutsche Geschichtspolitik* (Berlin: Das Arabische Buch, 2000), 135–67.

46. Christof Siemens, "Noch Fragen? Das Holocaust-Denkmal wird gebaut: Rückblicke, Prognosen und Seitenhiebe," *Die Zeit*, July 1, 1999; see also Gerhard Matzig, "Labyrinthische Suche nach der richtigen Erinnerung," *Süddeutsche Zeitung*, June 26, 1999; and Michael Jeismann, "Die Entscheidung ist gefallen," *Frankfurter Allgemeine Zeitung*, June 26, 1999.

47. Josef Joffe, "Metaphysik eines Mahnmals," *Süddeutsche Zeitung*, June 26, 1999.

48. Konrad Schuller, "Der Tag, an dem im Bundestag in Bonn ein Nationaldenkmal in Berlin beschlossen wurde," *Frankfurter AllgemeineZeitung*, June 26, 1999; Hans-Jörg Heims, "Debatte ohne Leidenschaft," *Süddeutsche Zeitung*, June 26, 1999; Roderich Reifenrath, "Das Mahnmal," *Frankfurter Rundschau*, June 26, 1999; and Rensmann, "Baustein der Erinnerungspolitik."

49. Richard Breitstein, "Holocaust Legacy: Germans and Jews Debate Redemption," *New York Times*, October 29, 2003.

50. "Holocaust-Denkmal: Fragezeichen statt eines Schlusspunkts," *Süddeutsche Zeitung*, May 10, 2005.

51. Philipp Grassmann, "Versteckspiele im Stelenwald," *Süddeutsche Zeitung*, May 16, 2005; and "Hakenkreuze am Holocaust-Mahnmal," *Spiegel Online*, June 1, 2005, http://www.spiegel.de/politik/deutschland/0,1518,358617,00.html.

52. Bettina Schneuer, "'Mama, das ist doch kein Grab,'" *Stern*, May 19, 2005; Miguel Sanches, "Ein Mahnmal als Spielplatz," *Westfälische Rundschau*, May 21, 2005; and Jörg Lau, "Stelenhüpfen: Der Alltag und das Holocaust-Mahnmal," *Die Zeit*, May 25, 2005.

53. Stefan Berg and Henryk Broder, "Jedem das Seine," *Der Spiegel*, January 5, 2004.

54. Nigel Biggar, ed., *Burying the Past: Making Peace and Doing Justice after Civil Conflict* (Washington, DC: Georgetown University Press, 2001); Andrew Rigly, *Justice & Reconciliation: After the Violence* (Boulder, CO: Lynne Rienner, 2001).

55. Janna Thompson, *Taking Responsibility for the Past: Reparations and Historical Injustice* (Cambridge: Blackwell, 2002); John Torpey, ed., *Politics and the Past* (Lanham, MD: Rowman and Littlefield, 2003); and Cherif Bassiouni, ed., *Post-conflict Justice* (Ardsley, NJ: Transnational, 2002).

56. See, in general, Avi Beker, *The Plunder of Jewish Property during the Holocaust* (Houndmills, UK: Palgrave, 2001), and specifically about Switzerland, the most infamous Holocaust culprit in the 1990s, Philippe Braillard, *Switzerland and the Crisis of Dormant Assets and Nazi Gold* (London: Kegan Paul, 2001).

57. Jonathan Wiesen has shown how effectively West Germany's economic leaders reinvented themselves as benevolent, antitotalitarian entrepreneurs in the postwar decade; see Wiesen, *West German Industry & the Challenge of the Nazi Past, 1945–1955* (Chapel Hill: University of North Carolina Press, 2001).

58. Despite the reluctance to enter into any comprehensive agreements, the Adenauer and Erhard administrations concluded limited compensation treaties with all West European part-

ners between 1959 and 1964, and very limited agreements, specifically concerning the victims of medical experiments, were also negotiated with Poland, Yugoslavia, and Czechoslovakia; see Hans Günter Hockerts, "Wiedergutmachung: Ein umstrittener Begriff und ein weites Feld," in Hockerts and Christiane Kuller, eds., *Nach der Verfolgung: Wiedergutmachung national-sozialistischen Unrechts in Deutschland?* (Göttingen, Germany: Wallstein, 2003), 7–33, 16–18.

59. To avoid further reparations claims, the Kohl administration carefully crafted the two-plus-four negotiations and treaties in such a fashion that they would not appear like peace negotiations and treaties, but this interpretation was successfully challenged in the 1990s; see Karl Doehring, Bernd Josef Fehn, and Hans Günter Hockerts, *Jahrhundertschuld Jahrhundert-sühne: Reparationen, Wiedergutmachung, Entschädigung für nationalsozialistisches Kriegs—und Verfolgungsunrecht* (Munich, Germany: Olzog, 2001), 138–40.

60. In support of the Bonn position, see Hermann-Josef Brodesser, Bernd Josef Fehn, Tilo Franosch, and Wilfried Wirth, *Wiedergutmachung und Kriegsfolgenliquidationen: Geschichte-Regelungen-Zahlungen* (Munich, Germany: Beck, 2000), 186–87, and compare to Matthias Arning, *Späte Abrechnung: Über Zwangsarbeiter, Schlussstriche und Berliner Verständigungen* (Frankfurt, Germany: Fischer, 2001), 32–33. Due to the substantial difference in the standard of living between East and West, even a fairly modest financial effort from Bonn sufficed to ward off more aggressive demands—at least for the time being.

61. Hockerts, "Wiedergutmachung," 18–21.

62. On the legal tool of class-action suits, see Clemens Kregelius-Schmidt, "Besonderheiten einer Sammelklage nach US-amerikanischem Prozessrecht aus rechtsvergleichender Perspektive," in Peer Zumbansen, ed., *Zwangsarbeit im Dritten Reich: Erinnerung und Verantwortung* (Baden-Baden, Germany: Nomos, 2002), 213–31; on the alien tort statute, see Ralph Steinhardt and Anthony D'Amato, eds., *The Alien Tort Claims Act: An Analytical Anthology* (Ardsley, NJ: Transnational, 1999).

63. Susanne-Sophia Spiliotis, *Verantwortung und Rechtsfrieden: Die Stiftungsinitiative der deutschen Wirtschaft* (Frankfurt, Germany: Fischer, 2003), 53–55.

64. Hilene Flanzbaum, ed., *The Americanization of the Holocaust* (Baltimore: Johns Hopkins University Press, 1999), and Peter Novick, *The Holocaust in American Life* (Boston: Houghton Mifflin, 1999).

65. Spiliotis, *Verantwortung und Rechtsfrieden*, 30–33, and Libby Adler and Peer Zumbansen, "The Forgetfulness of Noblesse: A Critique of the German Foundation Law Compensating Slave and Forced Laborers of the Third Reich," in Zumbansen, *Zwangsarbeit im Dritten Reich*, 333–92.

66. For the perspective of the German business community, see especially Spiliotis, *Verantwortung und Rechtsfrieden*.

67. On the Volkswagen case, see Michaela Lorenz, "Der Fall Volkswagen," in Zumbansen, *Zwangsarbeit im Dritten Reich*, 103–18.

68. Matthias Arning, *Späte Abrechnung: Über Zwangsarbeiter, Schlußstriche und Berliner Verständigungen* (Frankfurt, Germany: Fischer, 2001), 69, 75.

69. Bündnis 90 and Die Grünen, eds., *Anerkennung, Rehabilitierung, Entschädigung: Politische Initiativen für die Opfer des Nationalsozialismus 50 Jahre nach Kriegsende* (Cologne, Germany: Bündnis 90 and Die Grünen im Bundestag, 1995), and David Forster, *Wiedergutmachung in Österreich und der BRD im Vergleich* (Innsbruck, Austria: Studienverlag, 2001), 104.

70. For a concise summary of the complex treaties, see Günter Saathoff, "Entschädigung für Zwangsarbeiter? Entstehung und Leistungen der Bundesstiftung 'Erinnerung, Verantwortung und Zukunft' im Kontext der Debatte um die 'vergessenen Opfer,'" in Hockerts and Kuller, eds., *Nach der Verfolgung*, 241–73. The most important guarantee came from the U.S. government, which, in an international treaty with the Federal Republic, promised to advise all U.S. courts to desist from future litigation in this matter. In fact, in fulfillment of a German precondition for payment, almost all the pending suits had been dismissed by summer 2001. Moreover, the U.S. government explicitly stated that no unresolved reparation issues

stemming from World War II existed between the two countries, and that statement also undercut any future claims by other parties involved in the negotiations.

71. Ironically, this elegant evasion of one key element of responsibility was shrouded in language full of reverence for the suffering of the former slaves; see Adler and Zumbansen, "Forgetfulness of Noblesse."

72. Some CEOs argued that their predecessors at the helm of the companies never had a choice about the use of slave labor or, an even more offensive statement, that the former slaves should be thankful because they survived significantly longer than other camp inmates. Others maintained that compensation problems could only be settled through diplomatic channels, which, by definition, excluded private enterprise; see Arning, *Späte Abrechnung.*

73. Gruppe Offene Rechnungen, ed., *The Final Insult: Das Diktat gegen die Überlebenden—Deutsche Erinnerungsabwehr und Nichtentschädigung der NS-Sklavenarbeit* (Münster, Germany: Unrast, 2003).

74. See the protocol of the plenary session posted at http://www.nsberatung.de/doku/regierung/protokoll-bundestag-6-7-2000.html; and Lars Rensmann, "Entschädigungspolitik, Erinnerungsabwehr und Motive des sekundären Antisemitismus," in Rolf Suhrmann, ed., *Das Finkelstein-Alibi: "Holocaust-Industrie" und Tätergesellschaft* (Cologne, Germany: PapyRossa, 2001), 126–53.

75. Malte Lehming, "Der Westen findet sich," *Der Tagesspiegel,* June 7, 2004. The chancellor's unprecedented visit in Normandy was widely covered by the German media, and as it often did with war topics, the ZDF went over the top with a three-hour, live broadcast featuring Guido Knopp, plenty of military music, and generous praise for the courageous German soldiers; see Jan Freitag, "Tote auf Friedhöfen—Wie eine Königshochzeit: Das ZDF sendete live von den D-Day Feiern, Ursachenketten haben da keinen Platz," *die tageszeitung,* June 8, 2004.

76. All quotes from "Schröders Rede im Wortlaut," *Die Welt,* June 7, 2004. If Schröder's speech had any critical edge at all, it was directed against the visitor from the United States. Schröder assured Bush that "Europe's citizens and politicians now have to make sure that war mongers, war criminals, and terrorists do not stand a chance anywhere else" and that Germans are no pacifists, but he added unequivocally that "we also do not use military means lightly."

77. "Der Auftritt von Bundeskanzler Gerhard Schröder bei den D-Day-Feiern in der Normandie findet international Anerkennung," *Kölner Stadtanzeiger,* June 8, 2004; consider also the unusual praise in the liberal *tageszeitung,* Stefan Reinicke, "Ein Lob der zweiten Reihe—Gerhard Schröders Auftritt bei den D-Day-Feiern in der Normandie war angemessen," *die tageszeitung,* June 8, 2004.

78. "Lob für Schröders Teilnahme an D-Day Gedenkfeier—'Simpler Akt mit immensem Symbolwert,'" *Süddeutsche Zeitung,* June 8, 2004; Jochen Hehn, "Unter Brüdern," *Die Welt,* June 7, 2004.

79. The routine seems to develop in three textual stages. First, a particular cultural or political event is declared pathbreaking or scandalous. Second, if the declaration is successful, the event's implications are discussed in detail in the national press. Third, the debates are documented in edited volumes, which make them accessible to German and foreign scholars for further analysis.

80. Martin Walser, "Erfahrungen beim Abfassen einer Sonntagsrede," in Schirrmacher, *Walser-Bubis-Debatte,* 7–17.

81. Günter Grass, *Im Krebsgang* (Göttingen, Germany: Steidl, 2002). Incidentally, Grass consciously returns to the memory paradigm of the 1950s when he appreciatively cites Frank Wisbar's 1959 film *Nacht fiel über Gotenhafen;* see Grass, *Krebsgang,* 135.

82. The renewed focus on German suffering in World War II has been noticeable in a number of media, including literature, television, and popular historiography; see, for example,

W. G. Sebald's controversial essay *Luftkrieg and Literatur* (Munich, Germany: Hanser, 1999); Guido Knopp's television documentary *Die grosse Flucht*, mentioned in chapter 8, note 100; and Jörg Friedrich, *Der Brand: Deutschland im Bombenkrieg, 1940–1945* (Berlin: Propyläen, 2002); see also Lothar Kettenacker, ed., *Ein Volk von Opfern? Die neue Debatte um den Bombenkrieg, 1940–1945* (Berlin: Rowohlt, 2003).

83. See, for example, "Stoiber auf Sudetendeutschen Tag: 'Tschechiens Vertreibungs-dekrete belasten EU,'" *Süddeutsche Zeitung*, May 30, 2004. The enhanced national profile of the expellee organization was also the result of improved leadership. The new chairperson, Erika Steinbach, a CDU MP from Frankfurt, has reestablished the organization in the political mainstream by attaching the organization's special agenda to general discussions about human rights; see Thomas Kröter, "Vom rechten Rand der Union," *Frankfurter Rundschau*, November 10, 2003.

84. "Rede von Bundeskanzler Schröder zum 60. Jahrestag des Warschauer Aufstandes," published by the German government at http://www.bundeskanzler.de/www.bundeskanzler .de-.7698.691262/Rede-von-Bundeskanzler-Schroeder-zum-60.-Jahrest . . . htm; see also Nico Fried, "Schröder gedenkt in Warschau des Aufstandes vor 60 Jahren: 'Versöhnung mit Polen wirkt wie ein Wunder,'" *Süddeutsche Zeitung*, August 2, 2004. Even in this context, however, Schröder acknowledged guilt in an indirect, strangely convoluted way, running somewhere along the following semantic lines: "We are sorry that you became the victims of people about whom we know that they started the war."

85. "Rede von Bundeskanzler Schröder zum 60. Jahrestag des Warschauer Aufstandes."

86. "Rede von Bundeskanzler Gerhard Schröder in der Feierstunde zum Gedenken an den Widerstand gegen die nationalsozialistische Gewaltherrschaft am 20. Juli 2004 in Berlin," published by the German government at http://www.bundesregierung.de/Reden-Interviews/ Bulletin-,11639.688841/bulletin/Rede-von-Bundeskanzler-Gerhard.htm.

87. Gerhard Schröder, "'Wir stehen erst am Ende einer langen Nachkriegszeit,'" *Süddeutsche Zeitung*, May 7, 2005. Note the contradictory title of Schröder's article. Like many of his predecessors, Schröder wanted to make clear that Germans had reached the end of the postwar period. At the same time, however, he did not want to be perceived as a particularly eager Schlussstrich-advocate and therefore conceded that it has been an especially long postwar period and that Germans were only just reaching its end.

88. Well known for his anti-Israel and pro-Arabic stance, Möllemann also encouraged a former Green Party state representative, a man who had accused Israel of using Nazi methods in the occupied territories, to join the FDP; see Eberhard Seidel, "Karsli-Krise wird zum Fall Möllemann," *Die Tageszeitung*, May 21, 2002; on the Möllemann affair, see also Lars Rensmann, "'Alte' und 'neue' Formen des Antisemitismus: Judenfeindliche Vorurteile und Bestrebungen vor und nach den Terroranschlägen von New York und Washington," in Gruppe Offene Rechnungen, *Final Insult*, 159–90.

89. Having lost his leadership position within the party, Möllemann left the FDP in March 2003 and was accused of violating campaign finance laws; he committed suicide in June 2003. In an interesting twist worthy of any TV drama, Friedman was convicted of cocaine possession a few weeks after Möllemann's death and had to resign from his job and his position with the Central Council; see Robin Detje, "Im freien Fall: Antisemitische Anhaftungen," *Die Zeit*, June 18, 2003; see also Frank Drieschner, "'Die Abwehrkräfte sind intakt:' Judenfeind-schaft unter dem Deckmantel der Israelkritik—Ein *Zeit*-Gespräch mit Wolfgang Benz," *Die Zeit*, May 23, 2002.

90. See especially Wolfgang Benz, "Lupenreines Exempel: Martin Hohmanns juden-feindlicher Diskurs," *Süddeutsche.de*, November 10, 2003.

91. Hohmann's speech has been posted at http://www.heise.de/bin/tp/issue/dl-print .cgi?artikelnr=15981&rub_ordner=inhalt&mode=print. Hohmann was a typical backbencher who never played an important role in the CDU/CSU faction. Ironically, however, he was the

faction point person for NS retribution matters, a job he promptly lost after his speech became public knowledge.

92. Christian Semler, "Antisemitismus im Konjunktiv," *die tageszeitung*, November 1, 2003.

93. See http://www.heise.de/bin/tp/issue/dl-print.cgi?artikelnr=15981&rub_ordner=inhalt&mode=print.

94. "Erst einen Monat nach der Rede des CDU-Hinterbänklers wird deren Brisanz zum Thema: Wie die Rede bekannt wurde," *Kölner Stadtanzeiger*, November 1, 2003.

95. "Juden als Tätervolk verunglimpft," *Kölner Stadtanzeiger*, October 31, 2003.

96. Romanus Otto, "In der Affäre um Hohmann wächst Kritik an Merkel," *Financial Times Deutschland*, November 10, 2003.

97. Detlef Esslinger, "Wenn ein Ort in Deckung geht," *Südddeutsche Zeitung*, November 8, 2003, and "Keine Mehrheit für Rauswurf von Hohmann in Sicht," *Financial Times Deutschland*, November 7, 2003.

98. Susanne Höll, "Trotz wachsenden Unmuts in der Union: Hessen-CDU will Hohmann nicht ausschliessen," *Südddeutsche Zeitung*, November 10, 2003.

99. Peter Dausend, "Merkel geht auf Distanz zu Hohmann," *Die Welt*, November 1, 2003.

100. Susanne Höll, "Das versammelte Schweigen der Fraktion," *Süddeutsche Zeitung*, November 6, 2003.

101. German law clearly advises soldiers and officers to act with restraint in all political matters. Sending an unsolicited letter of support to a controversial politician on Bundeswehr letterhead certainly violated that provision; see "'Diktion der Neuen Rechten': Polit iloge Gessenharter über General Günzel und innere Probleme der Bundeswehr," *Frankfurter Rundschau*, November 6, 2003.

102. Höll, "Das versammelte Schweigen."

103. "Hohmann vor Aussschluss aus Partei und Fraktion," *Süddeutsche.de*, November 10, 2003.

104. "Rausschmiss durch die Nebentür," *Süddeutsche.de*, November 14, 2003.

105. "Antisemitismus-Affäre: CDU schliesst Hohmann aus," *Süddeutsche.de*, July 20, 2004; see also "Geplanter Hohmann-Ausschluss: Die CDU-Basis rebelliert," *Süddeutsche.de*, November 13, 2003.

106. "Freundschaftlich verbunden," *Süddeutsche Zeitung*, November 6, 2003.

107. Excellent on the transition from the critical and moralistic to the self-serving and irrational stages in the memory discourse of the student movement is Bernd-A. Rusinek, "Von der Entdeckung der NS-Vergangenheit zum generallen Faschismusverdacht—Akademische Diskurse in der Bundesrepublik der 60er Jahre," in Axel Schildt, Detlev Siegfried, and Karl Christian Lammers, eds., *Dynamische Zeiten: Die 60er Jahre in den beiden deutschen Gesellschaften* (Hamburg, Germany: Christians, 2000), 114–47.

CONCLUSION

1. That is one of the few problems with Habbo Knoch's magisterial *Die Tat als Bild: Fotografien des Holocaust in der deutschen Erinnerungskultur* (Hamburg, Germany: Hamburger Edition, 2001); for another example, see Aleida Assmann and Ute Frevert, *Geschichtsvergessenheit–Geschichtsversessenheit: Vom Umgang mit deutschen Vergangenheiten nach 1945* (Stuttgart, Germany: Deutsche Verlagsanstalt, 1999).

2. Niklas Luhmann, *Social Systems* (Stanford, CA: Stanford University Press, 1995), and Pierre Bourdieu, *Distinction: A Social Critique of the Judgement of Taste* (Cambridge, MA: Harvard University Press, 1984). For successful applications, see Werner Bergmann, *Antisemitismus in öffentlichen Konflikten: Kollektives Lernen in der politischen Kultur der Bundesrepublik,*

1949–1989 (Frankfurt, Germany: Campus, 1997), and Michael Schwab-Trapp, *Kriegsdiskurse: Die politische Kultur des Krieges im Wandel, 1991–1999* (Opladen, Germany: Leske und Budrich, 2002).

3. See, for example, Julia Kölsch, *Politik und Gedächtnis: Zur Soziologie funktionaler Kultivierung von Erinnerung* (Wiesbaden, Germany: Westdeutscher Verlag, 2000).

4. See the data in Rüdiger Schulz, "Nutzung von Zeitungen und Zeitschriften," in Jürgen Wilke, ed., *Mediengeschichte der Bundesrepublik Deutschland* (Cologne, Germany: Böhlau, 1999), 401–25.

5. See, in this context, the interesting qualitative and quantitative data about the historical consciousness of Germans assembled by Felix Philipp Lutz. Lutz describes five types of historical consciousness and suggested that two types of people—skeptics and those with a pronounced sense of historical responsibility—are particularly likely to visit historical exhibit, lectures, and so forth. Lutz comes to the perhaps overly optimistic conclusion that these active consumers of Germany's historical culture represent almost 40 percent of the population. See Lutz, *Das Geschichtsbewusstsein der Deutschen: Grundlagen der politischen Kultur in Ost und West* (Cologne, Germany: Böhlau, 2000), 193–95, 257.

6. Lutz Niethammer, ed., *"Die Jahre weiss man nicht, wo man die heute hinsetzen soll": Faschismuserfahrungen im Ruhrgebiet : Lebensgeschichte und Sozialkultur im Ruhrgebiet 1930 bis 1960* (Berlin: Dietz, 1983); Niethammer, ed., *"Hinterher merkt man, dass es richtig war, dass es schiefgegangen ist": Nachkriegserfahrungen im Ruhrgebiet* (Berlin: Dietz, 1983).

7. Harld Welzer, Sabine Moller, and Karoline Tschuggnall, *"Opa war kein Nazi": Nationalsozialismus und Holocaust im Familiengedächtnis* (Frankfurt, Germany: Fischer, 2001).

8. This point of criticism is very appropriately developed in Rupert Seuthe, *"Geistigmoralischen Wende?": Der politische Umgang mit der NS-Vergangenheit in der Ära Kohl am Beispiel von Gedenktagen, Museums- und Denkmalprojekten* (Frankfurt, Germany: Lang, 2001), 299–300.

9. The value of historians as reality effects has created an interesting consulting relationship between select historians and public TV networks. For relatively generous fees, historians check the accuracy of film scripts or pose as interview partners without having any control over the final product. Some notable exceptions to this one-sided relationship have resulted in true intellectual cooperation between historians and TV makers; see Norbert Frei, ed., *Karrieren im Zwielicht: Hitlers Eliten nach 1945* (Frankfurt, Germany: Campus, 2001).

10. Some television makers have abandoned the cloak of impartiality, including Guido Knopp, who has come to support a center for expulsion history in Berlin, and Lea Rosh, who has been one of the driving forces behind the Holocaust memorial. But each of these individuals occupies an exceptional position in the German media environment.

11. See Daniel Levy and Natan Szaider's concept of cosmopolitan memory, *Erinnerung im globalen Zeitalter: Der Holocaust* (Frankfurt, Germany: Suhrkamp, 2001).

12. The split between elite and nonelite identities is confirmed by empirical research on the evolution of transnational European identities; compare part 2 and part 3 in Richard Hermann, Thomas Risse, and Marilynn Brewer, eds., *Transnational Identities: Becoming European in the EU* (Lanham, MD: Rowman and Littlefield, 2004).

13. Daniel Levy and Natan Sznaider, *Erinnerung im globalen Zeitalter: Der Holocaust* (Frankfurt, Germany: Suhrkamp, 2001), 219–24, 228, 232; see also Alison Landsberg, *Prosthetic Memory: The Transformation of American Remembrance in the Age of Mass Culture* (New York: Columbia University Press, 2004), 148–52.

14. These moments are acknowledged in some of the publications on German memory studies; see Alexander von der Borch-Nitzling, *Das Dritte Reich im stern: Vergangenheitsverarbeitung, 1949–1995* (Göttingen, Germany: Schmerse, 2000), 1–13.

SELECTED BIBLIOGRAPHY

Ahonen, Pertti. *After the Expulsion: West Germany and Eastern Europe, 1945–1990*. Oxford: Oxford University Press, 2003.

Ahren, Yizhak, Christoph Melchers, Werner Seifert, and Werner Wagner, eds. *Das Lehrstück "Holocaust": Wirkungen und Nachwirkungen eines Medienereignisses*. Opladen: Westdeutscher Verlag, 1982.

Aly, Götz. *Final Solution: Nazi Population Policy and the Murder of the European Jews*. New York: Oxford University Press, 1999.

Aly, Götz, and Susanne Heim. *Vordenker der Vernichtung: Auschwitz und die deutschen Pläne für eine neue europäische Ordnung*. Hamburg, Germany: Hoffmann und Campe, 1991.

Ang, Ien. *Desperately Seeking the Audience*. London: Routledge, 1991.

Antze, Paul, and Michael Lambek, eds. *Tense Past: Cultural Essays in Trauma and Memory*. New York: Routledge, 1996.

Archer, Margaret. *Culture and Agency: The Place of Culture in Social Theory*. 2nd ed. Cambridge: Cambridge University Press, 1996.

Aretz, Jürgen, Günter Buchstab, and Jörg-Dieter Gauger, eds. *Geschichtsbilder: Weichenstellungen deutscher Geschichte nach 1945*. Freiburg, Germany: Herder, 2003.

Arning, Matthias. *Späte Abrechnung: Über Zwangsarbeiter, Schlussstriche und Berliner Verständigungen*. Frankfurt, Germany: Fischer, 2001.

Assmann, Aleida. *Erinnerungsräume: Formen und Wandlungen des kulturellen Gedächtnisses*. Munich, Germany: Beck, 1999.

Assmann, Aleida, and Ute Frevert. *Geschichtsvergessenheit—Geschichtsversessenheit: Vom Umgang mit deutschen Vergangenheiten nach 1945*. Stuttgart, Germany: Deutsche Verlagsanstalt, 1999.

Assmann, Jan. "Collective Memory and Cultural Identity." *New German Critique* 65 (Spring–Summer 1995): 125–33.

———. *Das kulturelle Gedächtnis: Schrift, Erinnerung und politische Identität in den frühen Hochkulturen*. Munich, Germany: Beck, 1992.

Augstein, Rudolf, et al. *Historikerstreit: Die Dokumentation der Kontroverse um die Einzigartigkeit der nationalsozialistischen Judenvernichtung*. Munich, Germany: Piper, 1987.

Backes, Uwe, Eckhard Jesse, and Rainer Zitelmann, eds. *Die Schatten der Vergangenheit: Impulse zur Historisierung des Nationalsozialismus*. Berlin: Propyläen, 1990.

Bal, Mieke, Jonathan Crewe, and Leo Spitzer, eds. *Acts of Memory: Cultural Recall in the Present*. Hanover, NH: University Press of New England, 1999.

Baldwin, Peter, ed. *Reworking the Past: Hitler, the Holocaust and the Historians' Debate*. Boston: Beacon, 1990.

Barkan, Elazar. *The Guilt of Nations: Restitution and Negotiating Historical Injustices*. New York: Norton, 2000.

Barnouw, Dagmar. *Germany, 1945: Views of War and Violence*. Bloomington: Indiana University Press, 1996.

Bassiouni, Cherif, ed. *Post-conflict Justice*. Ardsley, NJ: Transnational, 2002.

Bauman, Zygmunt. *Modernity and the Holocaust*. Ithaca, NY: Cornell University Press, 1989.

Baumgärtner, Ulrich. *Reden nach Hitler: Theodor Heuss—Die Auseinandersetzung mit dem Nationalsozialismus*. Stuttgart, Germany: Deutsche Verlagsanstalt, 2001.

Bausch, Hans. *Rundfunkpolitik nach 1945*. 2 vols. Munich, Germany: dtv, 1980.

Becker, Wolfgang, and Siegfried Quandt. *Das Fernsehen als Vermittler von Geschichtsbewusstsein: 1989 als Jubiläumsjahr*. Bonn, Germany: Bundeszentrale für politische Bildung, 1991.

Becker, Wolfgang, and Norbert Schöll. *In jenen Tagen . . . : Wie der deutsche Nachkriegsfilm die Vergangenheit bewältigte*. Opladen, Germany: Leske und Budrich, 1995.

Beker, Avi. *The Plunder of Jewish Property during the Holocaust*. New York: New York University Press, 2001.

Benz, Wolfgang. *Die Vertreibung der Deutschen aus dem Osten: Ursachen, Ereignisse, Folgen*. Frankfurt, Germany: Fischer, 1985.

Berg, Jan. *Hochhuths "Stellvertreter" und die Stellvertreter-Debatte: Vergangenheitsbewältigung in Theater und Presse der sechziger Jahre*. Kronberg: Scriptor, 1977.

Berg, Klaus, and Marie Luise Kiefer. *Massenkommunikation*. Vol. 1. Mainz, Germany: Hase und Koehler, 1978.

———. *Massenkommunikation*. Vols. 2 and 3. Frankfurt, Germany: Metzner, 1982 and 1987.

———. *Massenkommunikation*. Vols. 4 and 5. Baden-Baden, Germany: Nomos, 1992 and 1996.

Berg, Nicolas. *Der Holocaust und die westdeutschen Historiker: Erforschung und Erinnerung*. Göttingen, Germany: Wallstein, 2003.

Berger, Stefan. *The Search for Normality: National Identity and Historical Consciousness in Germany since 1800*. Providence, RI: Berghahn, 1997.

Berger, Thomas. *Cultures of Antimilitarism: National Security in Germany and Japan*. Baltimore: Johns Hopkins University Press, 1998.

Bergmann, Werner. *Antisemitismus in öffentlichen Konflikten*. Frankfurt, Germany: Campus, 1997.

Bergmann, Werner, Rainer Erb, and Albert Lichtblau, eds. *Schwieriges Erbe: Der Umgang mit Nationalsozialismus und Antisemitismus in Österreich, der DDR und der Bundesrepublik Deutschland*. Frankfurt, Germany: Campus, 1995.

Bessel, Richard, and Dirk Schumann, eds. *Life after Death: Approaches to a Cultural and Social History of Europe during the 1940s and 1950s*. Cambridge: Cambridge University Press, 2003.

Bessler, Hanjörg. *Hörer- und Zuschauerforschung*. Munich, Germany: dtv, 1980.

Biggar, Nigel. *Burying the Past: Making Peace and Doing Justice after Civil Conflict*. Washington, DC: Georgetown University Press, 2001.

Bodemann, Michal. *Gedächtnistheater: Die jüdische Gemeinschaft und ihre deutsche Erfindung*. Hamburg, Germany: Rotbuch, 1996.

———. *In den Wogen der Erinnerung: Jüdische Existenz in Deutschland*. Munich, Germany: dtv, 2002.

Bodnar, John. *Remaking America: Public Memory, Commemoration, and Patriotism in the Twentieth Century*. Princeton, NJ: Princeton University Press, 1992.

Böhme, Erich, and Klaus Wirtgen, eds. *Willy Brandt: Die Spiegel-Gespräche, 1959–1992*. Stuttgart, Germany: Deutsche Verlagsanstalt, 1993.

Bonnell, Victoria, and Lynn Hunt, eds. *Beyond the Cultural Turn: New Directions in the Study of Society and Culture*. Berkeley: University of California Press, 1999.

Borch-Nitzling, Alexander von der. *Das Dritte Reich im* stern: *Vergangenheitsverarbeitung, 1949–1995*. Göttingen, Germany: Schmerse, 2000.

Bösch, Frank. "Das Dritte Reich ferngesehen: Geschichtsvermittlung in der historischen Dokumentation." *Geschichte in Wissenschaft und Unterricht* 50, no. 4 (1999): 204–20.

Brady, John, Beverly Crawford, and Elise Willarty, eds. *The Postwar Transformation of Germany: Democracy, Prosperity and Nationhood*. Ann Arbor: University of Michigan Press, 1999.

Braese, Stephan. *Deutsche Nachkriegsliteratur und der Holocaust*. Frankfurt, Germany: Campus, 1998.

Braillard, Philippe. *Switzerland and the Crisis of Dormant Assets and Nazi Gold*. London: Kegan Paul, 2001.

Brink, Cornelia. *Ikonen der Vernichtung: Öffentlicher Gebrauch von Fotografien aus nationalsozialistischen Konzentrationslagern nach 1945*. Berlin: Akademie, 1998.

Brinks, Jan Hermann. *Children of a New Fatherland: Germany's Post-war Right-Wing Politics*. London: Tauris, 2000.

Brochhagen, Ulrich. *Nach Nürnberg: Vergangenheitsbewältigung und Westintegration in der Ära Adenauer*. Hamburg, Germany: Junius, 1994.

Brodesser, Hermann-Josef, Bernd Fehn, Tilo Franosch, and Wilfried Wirth. *Wiedergutmachung und Kriegsfolgenliquidation: Geschichte—Regelungen—Zahlungen*. Munich, Germany: Beck, 2000.

Broszat, Martin. *Nach Hitler: Der schwierige Umgang mit unserer Geschichte*. Munich, Germany: Oldenbourg, 1986.

———, ed. *Zäsuren nach 1945: Essays zur Periodisierung der deutschen Nachkriegsgeschichte*. Munich, Germany: Oldenbourg, 1990.

Brüggemeier, Franz Josef, and Jürgen Kocka, eds. *Geschichte von unten—Geschichte von innen: Kontroversen um die Alltagsgeschichte*. Hagen, Germany: Fernuniversität, 1985.

Brumlik, Micha, Hajo Funke, and Lars Rensmann. *Umkämpftes Vergessen: Walser-Debatte, Holocaust-Mahnmal und neue deutsche Geschichtspolitik*. Berlin: Das Arabische Buch, 2000.

Brüne, Klaus. *Autorenlexikon deutschsprachiger Drehbücher für Kino und Fernsehen*. Cologne, Germany: KIM, 1994.

Bude, Heinz. *Das Altern einer Generation: Die Jahrgänge 1938–1948*. Frankfurt, Germany: Suhrkamp, 1995.

———. *Bilanz der Nachfolge: Die Bundesrepublik und der Nationalsozialismus*. Frankfurt, Germany: Suhrkamp, 1992.

———. *Deutsche Karrieren: Lebenskonstruktionen sozialer Aufsteiger aus der Flakhelfer-Generation*. Frankfurt, Germany: Suhrkamp, 1987.

Burgauer, Erica. *Zwischen Erinnerung und Verdrängung: Juden in Deutschland nach 1945*. Reinbek, Germany: Rowohlt, 1993.

Carlton, Michael, and Silvia Schneider, eds. *Rezeptionsforschung: Theorien und Unter-suchungen zum Umgang mit Massenmedien.* Opladen, Germany: Westdeutscher Verlag, 1997.

Caruth, Cathy. *Unclaimed Experience: Trauma, Narrative, and History.* Baltimore: Johns Hopkins University Press, 1996.

Classen, Christoph. *Bilder der Vergangenheit: Die Zeit des Nationalsozialismus im Fernsehen der Bundesrepublik Deutschland, 1955–1965.* Cologne, Germany: Böhlau, 1999.

Clemens, Clay. *Reluctant Realists: The Christian Democrats and West German Ostpolitik.* Durham, NC: Duke University Press, 1989.

Cohen, Sande. *Historical Culture: On the Recoding of an Academic Discipline.* Berkeley: University of California Press, 1987.

Cole, Tim. *Selling the Holocaust: From Auschwitz to Schindler's List.* New York: Routledge, 1999.

Confino, Alon. "Collective Memory and Cultural History: Problems of Method." *American Historical Review* 102, no. 5 (December 1997): 1386–1403.

———. *The Nation as Local Metaphor: Württemberg, Imperial Germany, and National Memory, 1871–1918.* Chapel Hill: University of North Carolina Press, 1997.

Connerton, Paul. *How Societies Remember.* Cambridge: Cambridge University Press, 1989.

Diefendorf, Jeffry, Axel Frohn, and Hermann-Josef Rupieper, eds. *American Policy and the Reconstruction of West Germany, 1945–1955.* Cambridge: Cambridge University Press, 1993.

Dierke, von Sabine. *"All Power to the Imagination": The West German Counterculture from the Student Movement to the Greens.* Lincoln: University of Nebraska Press, 1997.

Diner, Dan. *Beyond the Conceivable: Studies on Germany, Nazism, and the Holocaust.* Berkeley: University of California Press, 2000.

———, ed. *Ist der Nationalsozialismus Geschichte: Zur Historisierung und Historikerstreit.* Frankfurt, Germany: Fischer, 1987.

Doehring, Karl, Bernd Josef Fehn, and Hans Günter Hockerts. *Jahrhundertschuld—Jahrhundertsühne: Reparationen, Wiedergutmachung, Entschädigung für nationalsozialistisches Kriegs- und Verfolgungsunrecht.* Munich, Germany: Olzog, 2001.

Domansky, Elisabeth. "'Kristallnacht,' the Holocaust and German Unity: The Meaning of November 9 as an Anniversary in Germany." *History and Memory* 4 (Spring–Summer 1992): 60–94.

Domansky, Elisabeth, and Harald Welzer, eds. *Eine offene Geschichte: Zur kommunikativen Tradierung der nationalsozialistischen Vergangenheit.* Tübingen, Germany: diskord, 1999.

Donat, Helmut, and Lothar Wieland, eds. *"Auschwitz erst möglich gemacht?": Überlegungen zur jüngsten konservativen Geschichtsbewältigung.* Bremen, Germany: Donat, 1991.

Dower, John. *Embracing Defeat: Japan in the Wake of World War II.* New York: Norton, 1999.

Dubiel, Helmut. *Niemand ist frei von der Geschichte: Die nationalsozialistische Herrschaft in den Debatten des Deutschen Bundestages.* Munich, Germany: Hanser, 1999.

Dudek, Peter. *"Der Rückblick auf die Vergangenheit wird sich nicht vermeiden lassen"*: *Zur pädagogischen Verarbeitung des Nationalsozialismus in Deutschland (1945–1990)*. Opladen, Germany: Westdeutscher Verlag, 1995.

Dümcke, Wolfgang, and Fritz Wilmar, eds. *Kolonialisierung der DDR: Kritische Analysen und Alternativen des Einigungsprozesess*. Münster, Germany: Agenda, 1996.

Eberan, Barbro. *Luther? Friedrich "der Grosse"? Wagner? Nietzsche? Wer war an Hitler schuld? Die Debatte um die Schuldfrage, 1945–1949*, 2nd enlarged ed. Munich, Germany: Minerva, 1985.

Egle, Christoph, Tobias Ostheim, and Reimut Zohnlhöfer. *Das rot-grüne Projekt: Eine Bilanz der Regierung Schröder, 1998–2002*. Opladen, Germany: Westdeutscher Verlag, 2003.

Eley, Geoff, ed. *The "Goldhagen Effect": History, Memory, Nazism—Facing the German Past*. Ann Arbor: University of Michigan Press, 2000.

———. "Labor History, Social History, Alltagsgeschichte: Experience, Culture, and the Politics of the Everyday—A New Direction for German Social History." *Journal of Modern History* 61, no. 1 (1989): 297–343.

Elsässer, Jürgen. *Kriegsverbrechen: Die tödlichen Lügen der Bundesrepublik und ihre Opfer im Kosovo-Konflikt*. Hamburg, Germany: Konkret, 2000.

Endlich, Stefanie, ed. *Gedenkstätten für die Opfer des Nationalsozialismus*. Vol. 2. Bonn, Germany: Bundeszentrale für politische Bildung, 1999.

Erb, Scott. *German Foreign Policy: Navigating a New Era*. Boulder, CO: Lynne Rienner, 2003.

Etzemüller, Thomas. *Sozialgeschichte als politische Geschichte: Werner Conze und die Neuorientierung der westdeutschen Geschichtswissenschaft nach 1945*. Munich, Germany: Oldenbourg, 2001.

Faulenbach, Bernd, and Helmut Schütte, eds. *Deutschland, Israel und der Holocaust: Zur Gegenwartsbedeutung der Vergangenheit*. Essen, Germany: Klartext, 1998.

Faulstich, Werner, ed. *Vom "Autor" zum Nutzer: Handlungsrollen im Fernsehen (Geschichte des Fernsehens in der Bundesrepublik Deutschland, vol. 5)*. Munich, Germany: Fink, 1994.

Fehrenbach, Heide. *Cinema in Democratizing Germany: Reconstructing National Identity after Hitler*. Chapel Hill: University of North Carolina Press, 1995.

Feinberg, Anat. *Wiedergutmachung im Programm: Jüdisches Schicksal im deutschen Nachkriegsdrama*. Cologne, Germany: Prometh, 1988.

Fentress, James, and Chris Wickham. *Social Memory*. London: Blackwell, 1992.

Ferdinand, Horst, ed. *Reden, die die Republik bewegten*. 2nd ed. Opladen, Germany: Leske und Budrich, 2002.

Fischer, Frank. *"Im deutschen Interesse": Die Ostpolitik der SPD von 1969 bis 1989*. Husum, Germany: Matthiesen, 2001.

Flanzbaum, Hilene, ed. *The Americanization of the Holocaust*. Baltimore: Johns Hopkins University Press, 1999.

Forster, David. *"Wiedergutmachung" in Österreich und der BRD im Vergleich*. Innsbruck, Austria: Studienverlag, 2001.

Francoise, Etienne, and Hagen Schulze, eds. *Deutsche Erinnerungsorte*. 3 vols. Munich, Germany: Beck, 2001.

Frei, Norbert. *1945 und Wir: Das Dritte Reich im Bewußtsein der Deutschen*. Munich, Germany: Beck, 2005.

————, ed. *Karrieren im Zwielicht: Hitlers Eliten nach 1945*. Frankfurt, Germany: Campus, 2001.

————. *Vergangenheitspolitik: Die Anfänge der Bundesrepublik und die NS-Vergangenheit.* Munich, Germany: Beck, 1996.

Friedlander, Saul. *Memory, History, and the Extermination of the Jews of Europe.* Bloomington: Indiana University Press, 1993.

————, ed. *Probing the Limits of Representation: Nazism and the "Final Solution."* Cambridge, MA: Harvard University Press, 1992.

————. *Reflections of Nazism: An Essay on Kitsch and Death.* New York: Avon, 1986.

Friedrich, Jörg. *Der Brand: Deutschland im Bombenkrieg, 1940–1945.* Berlin: Propyläen, 2002.

————. *Die kalte Amnestie: NS-Täter in der Bundesrepublik.* Frankfurt, Germany: Fischer, 1984.

Fritsche, Christiane. *Vergangenheitsbewältigung im Fernsehen: Westdeutsche Filme über den Nationalsozialismus in den 1950er und 60er Jahren.* Munich, Germany: Meidenbauer, 2003.

Fritz-Bauer-Institut, ed. *"Gerichtstag halten über uns selbst . . . ": Geschichte und Wirkung des ersten Frankfurter Auschwitz-Prozesses.* Frankfurt, Germany: Campus, 2001.

Fröhlich, Claudia, and Michael Kohlstruck, eds. *Engagierte Demokraten: Vergangenheitspolitik in kritischer Absicht.* Münster, Germany: Westfälisches Dampfboot, 1999.

Füßmann, Klaus, Heinrich Grütter, and Jörn Rüsen, eds. *Historische Faszination: Geschichtskultur heute.* Cologne, Germany: Böhlau, 1994.

Funke, Hajo. *Paranoia und Politik: Rechtsextremismus in der Berliner Republik.* Berlin: Schiler, 2002.

————, ed. *Von der Gnade der geschenkten Nation.* Berlin: Rotbuch, 1988.

Gangloff, Tilmann, and Stefan Aarbanell, eds. *Liebe, Tod und Lottozahlen: Fernsehen in Deutschland.* Hamburg, Germany: GEP, 1994.

Gerlach, Christian. *Kalkulierte Morde: Die deutsche Wirtschaft- und Vernichtungspolitik in Weissrussland 1941 bis 1944.* Hamburg, Germany: Hamburger Edition, 1999.

Gerstenberger, Heide, and Dorothea Schmidt, eds. *Normalität oder Normalisierung: Geschichtswerkstätten und Faschismusanalyse.* Münster, Germany: Westfälisches Dampfboot, 1987.

Geschichtswerkstatt Berlin, ed. *Die Nation als Austellungsstück: Planungen, Kritik und Utopien zu den Museumsgründungen in Bonn und Berlin.* Hamburg, Germany: VSA, 1987.

Giesen, Bernhard. *Intellectuals and the German Nation: Collektive Identity in an Axial Age.* Cambridge: Cambridge University Press, 1998.

Giesen, Bernhard, and Christoph Schneider, eds. *Tätertrauma: Nationale Erinnerungen im öffentlichen Diskurs.* Constance, Germany: UVK. 2004.

Gill, Ulrich, and Winfried Steffani, eds. *Eine Rede und ihre Wirkung: Die Rede des Bundespräsidenten Richard von Weizsäcker vom 8. Mai 1985.* Berlin: Rainer Röll, 1986.

Giordano, Ralph. *Die zweite Schuld oder Von der Last Deutscher zu sein.* Hamburg, Germany: Rasch und Röhring, 1987.

Görtemaker, Manfred. *Geschichte der Bundesrepublik Deutschland: Von der Gründung bis zur Gegenwart*. Munich, Germany: Beck, 1999.

Greven, Michael, and Oliver von Wrochem, eds. *Der Krieg in der Nachkriegszeit: Der Zweite Weltkrieg in Politik und Gesellschaft der Bundesrepublik*. Opladen, Germany: Leske und Budrich, 2000.

Grunenberg, Antonia. *Antifaschismus: Ein deutscher Mythos*. Hamburg, Germany: Rowohlt, 1993.

———. *Die Lust an der Schuld: Von der Macht der Vergangenheit über die Gegenwart*. Berlin: Rowohlt, 2001.

Gruppe Offene Rechnungen, ed. *The Final Insult: Das Diktat gegen die Überlebenden— Deutsche Erinnerungsabwehr und Nichtentschädigung der NS-Sklavenarbeit*. Münster, Germany: Unrast, 2003.

Haar, Ingo. *Historiker im Nationalsozialismus: Die deutsche Geschichtswissenschaft und der "Volkskampf" im Osten*. Göttingen, Germany: Vandenhoeck und Ruprecht, 2000.

Habermas, Jürgen. *Die nachholende Revolution*. Frankfurt, Germany: Suhrkamp, 1990.

———. *The New Conservatism: Cultural Criticism and the Historians' Debate*. Cambridge, MA: MIT Press, 1989.

———. *Die Normalität einer Berliner Republik*. Frankfurt, Germany: Suhrkamp, 1995.

Haftendorn, Helga. *Deutsche Aussenpolitik zwischen Selbstbeschränkung und Selbstbehauptung*. Stuttgart, Germany: Deutsche Verlagsanstalt, 2001.

Halbwachs, Maurice. *La Mémoire collective*. Published posthumously by Jeanne Alexandre. Paris: Presses Universitaire, 1950.

Hartman, Geoffrey, ed. *Bitburg in Moral and Political Perspective*. Bloomington: Indiana University Press, 1986.

Haug, Wolfgang Fritz. *Vom hilflosen Faschismus zur Gnade der späten Geburt*, 2nd ed. Hamburg, Germany: Argument, 1987.

Hausmann, Brigitte. *Duell mit der Verdrängung: Denkmäler für die Opfer des Nationalsozialismus in der Bundesrepublik Deutschland 1980 bis 1990*. Münster, Germany: Lit, 1997.

Hay, James, Lawrence Grossberg, and Ellen Wartella, eds. *The Audience and Its Landscape*. Boulder, CO: Westview Press, 1996.

Heer, Hannes, and Klaus Naumann. *Vernichtungskrieg: Verbrechen der Wehrmacht, 1941–1944*. Hamburg, Germany: Hamburger Edition, 1995.

Heil, Johannes, and Rainer Erb, eds. *Geschichtswissenschaft und Öffentlichkeit: Der Streit um Daniel J. Goldhagen*. Frankfurt, Germany: Fischer, 1998.

Heimrod, Ute, Günter Schlusche, and Horst Seveerens. *Der Denkmalstreit—Das Denkmal? Die Debatte um das "Denkmal für die ermordeten Juden Europas."* Berlin: Philo, 1999.

Henke, Klaus-Dietmar, and Claudio Natoli, eds. *Mit dem Pathos der Nüchternheit: Martin Broszat, das Institut für Zeitgeschichte und die Erforschung des Nationalsozialismus*. Frankfurt, Germany: Campus, 1991.

Herbert, Ulrich. *Best: Biographische Studien über Radikalismus, Weltanschauung und Vernunft, 1903–1989*. Bonn, Germany: Dietz, 1996.

———, ed. *Nationalsozialistische Vernichtungpolitik, 1939–1945: Neue Forschungen und Kontroversen*. Frankfurt, Germany: Fischer, 1998.

———, ed. *Wandlungsprozesse in Westdeutschland: Belastung, Integration, Liberalisierung, 1945–1980*. Göttingen, Germany: Wallstein, 2002.

Herbst, Ludolf, and Constantin Goschler, eds. *Wiedergutmachung in der Bundesrepublik Deutschland.* Munich, Germany: Oldenbourg, 1989.

Herf, Jeffrey. *Divided Memory: The Nazi Past in the Two Germanys.* Cambridge, MA: Harvard University Press, 1997.

Herrmann, Richard, Thomas Risse, and Marilynn Brewer, eds. *Transnational Identities: Becoming European in the EU.* Lanham, MD: Roman and Littlefield, 2004.

Herz, Thomas, and Michael Schwab-Trapp. *Umkämpfte Vergangenheit: Diskurse über den Nationalsozialismus seit 1945.* Opladen, Germany: Westdeutscher Verlag, 1997.

Hickethier, Knut. *Geschichte des deutschen Fernsehens.* Stuttgart, Germany: Metzler, 1998.

———. *Institution, Technik und Programm: Rahmenaspekte der Programmgeschichte des Fernsehens (Geschichte des Fernsehens in der Bundesrepublik Deutschland, vol. 1).* Munich, Germany: Fink, 1993.

Hirsch, Marianne. *Family Frames: Photography, Narrative, and Postmemory.* Cambridge, MA: Harvard University Press, 1997.

Hockerts, Hans Günter, and Christiane Kuller, eds. *Nach der Verfolgung: Wiedergutmachung nationalsozialistischen Unrechts in Deutschland?* Göttingen, Germany: Wallstein, 2003.

Hoffmann, Christa. *Stunden Null? Vergangenheitsbewältigung in Deutschland, 1945 und 1989.* Bonn, Germany: Bouvier, 1992.

Holler, Regina. *20. Juli 1944: Vermächtnis oder Alibi?* Munich, Germany: Saur, 1994.

Hughes, Michael. *Shouldering the Burden of Defeat: West Germany and the Reconstruction of Social Justice.* Chapel Hill: University of North Carolina Press, 1999.

Hutton, Patrick. *History as an Art of Memory.* Hanover, NH: University Press of New England, 1993.

Huyssen, Andreas. *Twilight Memories: Marking Time in a Culture of Amnesia.* New York: Routledge, 1995.

Iggers, Georg. *The German Conception of History: The National Tradition of Historical Thought from Herder to the Present.* Rev. ed. Middletown, CT: Wesleyan University Press, 1983.

———. *Geschichtswissenschaft im 20. Jahrhundert.* Göttingen, Germany: Vandenhoek und Ruprecht, 1993.

Insdorf, Anette. *Indelible Shadows: Film and the Holocaust.* 2nd ed. New York: Cambridge University Press, 1989.

Institut für Zeitgeschichte, ed. *Alltagsgeschichte der NS-Zeit: Neue Perspektiven oder Trivialisierung.* Munich, Germany: Oldenbourg, 1984.

Irwin-Zarecka, Iwona. *Frames of Remembrance: The Dynamics of Collective Memory.* New Brunswick, NJ: Transaction, 1994.

Jäckel, Eberhard, and Jürgen Rohwer, eds. *Der Mord an den Juden im Zweiten Weltkrieg.* Frankfurt, Germany: Fischer, 1987.

Jäckel, Eberhard, Horst Möller, and Hermann Rudolph, eds. *Von Heuss bis Herzog: Die Bundespräsidenten im politischen System der Bundesrepublik.* Stuttgart, Germany: Deutsche Verlagsanstalt, 1999.

Jacobs, Norbert. "Der Streit um Dr. Hans Globke in der öffentlichen Meinung der Bundesrepublik Deutschland, 1949–1973." Ph.D. diss., University of Bonn, 1992.

Jarausch, Konrad, and Michael Geyer. *Shattered Past: Reconstructing German Histories*. Princeton, NJ: Princeton University Press, 2003.

Jeismann, Michael. *Auf Wiedersehen Gestern: Die deutsche Vergangenheit und die Politik von morgen*. Stuttgart, Germany: Deutsche Verlagsanstalt, 2001.

Jesse, Eckhard , Christiane Schroeder, and Thomas Grosse-Gehling. *Totalitarismus im 20. Jahrhundert: Eine Bilanz der internationalen Forschung*. 2nd ed. Baden-Baden, Germany: Nomos, 1999.

Kaes, Anton. *From Hitler to Heimat: The Return of History as Film*. Cambridge, MA: Harvard University Press, 1989.

Kansteiner, Wulf. "Genealogy of a Category Mistake: A Critical Intellectual History of the Cultural Trauma Metaphor." *Rethinking History* 8 (2004): 193–221.

———. "Hayden White's Critique of the Writing of History." *History and Theory* 32, no. 3 (1993): 273–95.

Kattago, Siobhan. *Ambiguous Memory: The Nazi Past and German National Identity*. Westport, CT: Praeger, 2001.

Keilbach, Judith. "Fernsehbilder der Geschichte: Anmerkungen zur Darstellung des Nationalsozialismus in den Geschichtsdokumentationen des ZDF." *1999: Zeitschrift für Sozialgeschichte des 20. und 21. Jahrhunderts* 17, no. 2 (2002): 104–13.

Kent, Raymond, ed. *Measuring Media Audiences*. London: Routledge, 1994.

Keppler, Angela. *Tischgespräche: Über Formen kommunikativer Vergemeinschaftung am Beispiel der Konversation in Familien*. Frankfurt, Germany: Suhrkamp, 1994.

Kettenacker, Lothar, ed. *Ein Volk von Opfern? Die neue Debatte um den Bombenkrieg, 1940–45*. Berlin: Rowohlt, 2003.

Kinner, Klaus, and Rolf Richter, eds. *Rechtsextremismus und Antifaschismus*. Berlin: Dietz, 2000.

Kirsch, Jan-Holger. *Nationaler Mythos oder historische Trauer? Der Streit um ein zentrales "Holocaust-Mahnmal" für die Berliner Republik*. Cologne, Germany: Böhlau, 2003.

———. *"Wir haben aus der Geschichte gelernt": Der 8. Mai als politischer Gedenktag in Deutschland*. Cologne, Germany: Böhlau, 1999.

Kittel, Manfred. *Die Legende von der "Zweiten Schuld": Vergangenheitsbewältigung in der Ära Adenauer*. Berlin: Ullstein, 1993.

Klein, Kerwin Lee, "On the Emergence of Memory in Historical Discourse." *Representations* 69 (Winter 2000): 127–50.

Klinger, Walter, Gunnar Roters, and Maria Gerhards, eds. *Medienrezeption seit 1945*. 2nd ed. Baden-Baden, Germany: Nomos, 1999.

Klotz, Johannes, and Ulrich Schneider, eds. *Die selbstbewusste Nation und ihr Geschichtsbild: Geschichtslegenden der Neuen Rechten*. Cologne, Germany: PapyRossa, 1997.

Knesebeck, Rosemarie von dem. *In Sachen Filbinger gegen Hochhuth: Die Geschichte einer Vergangenheitsbewältigung*. Reinbek, Germany: Rowohlt, 1980.

Knigge, Volkhard, and Norbert Frei, eds. *Verbrechen erinnern: Die Auseinandersetzung mit Holocaust und Völkermord*. Munich, Germany: Beck, 2002.

Knoch, Habbo. *Die Tat als Bild: Fotografien des Holocaust in der deutschen Erinnerungskultur*. Hamburg, Germany: Hamburger Edition, 2001.

Knopp, Guido, and Siegfried Quandt. *Geschichte im Fernsehen: Ein Handbuch.* Darmstadt, Germany: Wissenschaftliche Buchgesellschaft, 1988.

Kohlstruck, Michael. *Zwischen Erinnerung und Geschichte: Der Nationalsozialismus und die jungen Deutschen.* Berlin: Metropol, 1997.

Kölsch, Julia. *Politik und Gedächtnis: Zur Soziologie funktionaler Kultivierung von Erinnerung.* Wiesbaden, Germany: Westdeutscher Verlag, 2000.

König, Helmut. *Die Zukunft der Vergangenheit: Der Nationalsozialismus im politischen Bewusstsein der Bundesrepublik.* Frankfurt, Germany: Fischer, 2003.

König, Helmut, Michael Kohlstruck, and Andreas Wöll, eds. *Vergangenheitsbewältigung am Ende des zwanzigsten Jahrhunderts.* Opladen, Germany: Westdeutscher Verlag, 1998.

Koshar, Rudy. *From Monuments to Traces: Artifacts of German Memory, 1870–1990.* Berkeley: University of California Press, 2000.

———. *Germany's Transient Pasts: Preservation and National Memory in the Twentieth Century.* Chapel Hill: University of North Carolina Press, 1998.

Kraushaar, Wolfgang. *1968 als Mythos, Chiffre und Zäsur.* Hamburg: Hamburger Edition, 2000.

Krüger, Udo Michael. *Programmprofile im dualen Fernsehsystem, 1985–1990.* Baden-Baden, Germany: Nomos, 1992.

LaCapra, Dominick. *History and Memory after Auschwitz.* Ithaca, NY: Cornell University Press, 1998.

———. *Representing the Holocaust: History, Theory, Trauma.* Ithaca, NY: Cornell University Press, 1994.

Landsberg, Alison. *Prosthetic Memory: The Transformation of American Remembrance in the Age of Mass Culture.* New York: Columbia University Press, 2004.

Langer, Lawrence. *Holocaust Testimonies: The Ruins of Memory.* New Haven, CT: Yale University Press, 1991.

Lantis, Jeffrey S. *Strategic Dilemmas and the Evolution of German Foreign Policy since Unification.* Westport, CT: Praeger, 2002.

Laschet, Armin, and Heinz Malangre, eds. *Philip Jenninger: Rede und Reaktion.* Aachen, Germany: Einhard, 1989.

Leonhard, Nina. *Geschichts- und Politikbewusstsein im Wandel: Die politische Bedeutung der nationalsozialistischen Vergangenheit im Verlauf von drei Generationen in Ost- und Westdeutschland.* Münster, Germany: Lit, 2002.

Lepsius, Rainer. "Das Erbe des Nationalsozialismus und die politische Kultur der Nachfolgestaaten des 'Grossdeutschen Reiches.'" In Max Haller, Hans-Joachim Hoffmann-Nowotny, and Wolfgang Zapf, eds., *Kultur und Gesellschaft: Verhandlungen des 24. Deutschen Soziologentags,* 247–64. Frankfurt, Germany: Campus, 1989.

Levy, Daniel, and Natan Sznaider. *Erinnerung im globalen Zeitalter: Der Holocaust.* Frankfurt, Germany: Suhrkamp, 2001.

Loewy, Hanno, ed. *Holocaust: Die Grenzen des Verstehens—Eine Debatte über die Besetzung der Geschichte.* Reinbek, Germany: Rowohlt, 1992.

Loshitzky, Yosefa, ed. *Spielberg's Holocaust: Critical Perspectives on "Schindler's List."* Bloomington: Indiana University Press, 1997.

Lowenthal, David. *The Past Is a Foreign Country.* Cambridge: Cambridge University Press, 1985.

Lübbe, Hermann. "Der Nationalsozialismus im deutschen Nachkriegsbewußtsein." *Historische Zeitschrift* 236, no. 3 (1983): 579–99.

Ludes, Peter, Heidemarie Schumacher, and Peter Zimmermann, eds. *Informations-und Dokumentarsendungen (Geschichte des Fernsehens in der Bundesrepublik Deutschlands, vol. 3)*. Munich, Germany: Fink, 1994.

Lüdtke, Alf. *The History of Everyday Life*. Princeton, NJ: Princeton University Press, 1995.

Lutz, Felix Philipp. *Das Geschichtsbewusstsein der Deutschen: Grundlagen der politischen Kultur in Ost und West*. Cologne, Germany: Böhlau, 2000.

Maier, Charles. *The Unmasterable Past: History, Holocaust, and German National Identity*. Cambridge, MA: Harvard University Press, 1988.

Manig, Bert-Oliver. *Die Politik der Ehre: Die Rehabilitierung der Berufssoldaten in der frühen Bundesrepublik*. Göttingen, Germany: Wallstein, 2004.

Mannheim, Karl. "Das Problem der Generationen." In Mannheim, *Wissenssoziologie: Auswahl aus dem Werk*, 509–65. Berlin: Luchterhand, 1964.

Marcuse, Harold. *Legacies of Dachau: The Uses and Abuses of a Concentration Camp, 1933–2001*. Cambridge: Cambridge University Press, 2001.

Markovits, Andrei, and Simon Reich. *The German Predicament: Memory & Power in the New Europe*. Ithaca, NY: Cornell University Press, 1998.

Marssolek, Inge, and Adelheid von Saldern, eds. *Radiozeiten: Herrschaft, Alltag, Gesellschaft (1924–1960)*. Potsdam, Germany: Verlag für Berlin-Brandenburg, 1999.

Märtesheimer, Peter, and Ivo Frenzel, eds. *Im Kreuzfeuer: Der Fernsehfilm Holocaust—Eine Nation ist betroffen*. Frankfurt, Germany: Fischer, 1979.

Matsuda, Matt. *The Memory of the Modern*. New York: Oxford University Press, 1996.

Meng, Richard. *Der Medienkanzler: Was bleibt vom System Schröder?* Frankfurt, Germany: Suhrkamp, 2002.

Merseburger, Peter. *Willy Brandt: 1913–1992—Visionär und Realist*. Stuttgart, Germany: Deutsche Verlagsanstalt, 2002.

Michman, Dan, ed. *Remembering the Holocaust in Germany, 1945–2000*. New York: Peter Lang, 2002.

Miquel, Marc von. *Ahnden oder Amnestieren? Westdeutsche Justiz und Vergangenheitspolitik in den sechziger Jahren*. Göttingen, Germany: Wallstein, 2004.

Mitscherlich, Margarete. *Erinnerungsarbeit: Zur Psychoanalyse der Unfähigkeit zu trauern*. Frankfurt, Germany: Fischer, 1987.

Mitscherlich, Margarete, and Alexander Mitscherlich. *The Inability to Mourn*. New York: Grove, 1975.

Möller, Robert. *War Stories: The Search for a Usable Past in the Federal Republic of Germany*. Berkeley: University of California Press, 2001.

Moller, Sabine. *Die Entkonkretisierung der NS-Herrschaft in der Ära Kohl*. Hannover, Germany: Offizin, 1998.

Mommsen, Hans. *Der Nationalsozialismus und die deutsche Gesellschaft*. Reinbek, Germany: Rowohlt, 1991.

Mullan, Bob. *Consuming Televison: Television and Its Audience*. Oxford: Blackwell, 1997.

Müller, Ingo. *Furchtbare Juristen: Die unbewältigte Vergangenheit unserer Justiz*. Munich, Germany: Knaur, 1989.

Müller, Jan-Werner. *Another Country: German Intellectuals, Unification, and National Identity*. New Haven, CT: Yale University Press, 2000.

———, ed. *German Ideologies since 1945: Studies in the Political Thought and Culture of the Bonn Republic*. New York: Palgrave, 2003.

———, ed. *Memory and Power in Post-war Europe: Studies in the Presence of the Past*. Cambridge: Cambridge University Press, 2003.

Müller-Brandeck, Gisela, ed. *Deutsche Europapolitik von Adenauer bis Schröder*. Opladen, Germany: Leske und Budrich, 2002.

Murray, Bruce, and Chris Wickham, eds. *Framing the Past: The Historiography of German Cinema and Television*. Carbondale: Southern Illinois University Press, 1992.

Netenjakob, Egon. *TV-Filmlexikon: Regisseure, Autoren, Dramaturgen, 1952–1992*. Frankfurt, Germany: Fischer, 1994.

Neumann, Klaus. *Shifting Memories: The Nazi Past in the New Germany*. Ann Arbor: University of Michigan Press, 2000.

Niethammer, Lutz. *Deutschland danach: Postfaschistische Gesellschaft und nationales Gedächtnis*. Bonn, Germany: Dietz, 1999.

———. *Kollektive Identitäten: Heimliche Quellen einer unheimlichen Konjunktur*. Reinbek, Germany: Rowohlt, 2000.

———. *Lebenserfahrung und kollektives Gedächtnis: Die Praxis der "Oral History."* Frankfurt, Germany: Syndikat Autoren- und Verlagsgesellschaft, 1980.

———. *Die Mitläuferfabrik: Die Entnazifizierung am Beispiel Bayern*. 2nd ed. Berlin: Dietz, 1982.

Niven, Bill. *Facing the Nazi Past: United Germany and the Legacy of the Third Reich*. London: Routledge, 2002.

Nolte, Ernst. *Streitpunkte: Heutige und künftige Kontroversen um den Nationalsozialismus*. Berlin: Propyläen, 1993.

Nora, Pierre, ed. *Realms of Memory: Rethinking the French Past*. 3 vols. New York: Columbia University Press, 1996–1998.

Novick. *The Holocaust in American Life*. Boston: Houghton Mifflin, 1999.

Olick, Jeffrey. "Collective Memory: The Two Cultures." *Sociological Theory* 17 (1999): 333–48.

Olick, Jeffrey, and Joyce Robbins. "Social Memory Studies: From 'Collective Memory' to the Historical Sociology of Mnemonic Practices." *American Review of Sociology* 24 (1998): 105–40.

Passerini, Luisa, ed. *The Question of European Identity: A Cultural Historical Approach*. Florence, Italy: European Historical Institute, 1998.

Paul, Gerhard, and Bernhard Schossig, eds. *Die andere Geschichte: Geschichte von unten, Spurensicherung, ökologische Geschichte, Geschichtswerkstätten*. Cologne, Germany: Bund, 1986.

Peukert, Detlev. "Die Genesis der 'Endlösung' aus dem Geiste der Wissenschaft." In Forum für Philosophie Bad Homburg, ed., *Zerstörung des moralischen Selbstbewußtseins: Chance oder Gefährdung?* 24–48. Praktische Philosophie in Deutschland nach dem Nationalsozialismus. Frankfurt, Germany: Suhrkamp, 1988.

———. *Volksgenossen und Gemeinschaftsfremde: Anpassung, Ausmerze und Aufbegehren unter dem Nationalsozialismus*. Cologne, Germany: 1982.

Phillips, Donald. *Post-national Patriotism and the Feasibility of Post-national Community in Unified Germany.* Westport, CT: Praeger, 2000.

Platt, Kristin, and Mihran Dabag, eds. *Generation und Gedächtnis: Erinnerungen und kollektive Identitäten.* Opladen, Germany: Leske und Budrich, 1995.

Poiger, Uta. *Jazz, Rock and Rebels: Cold War Politics and American Culture in a Divided Germany.* Berkeley: University of California Press, 2000.

Pross, Christian. *Wiedergutmachung: Der Kleinkrieg gegen die Opfer.* Frankfurt, Germany: Athenäum, 1988.

Puvogel, Ulrike, and Martin Stankowski. *Gedenkstätten für die Opfer des Nationalsozialismus.* Vol. 1, 2nd. enlarged ed. Bonn, Germany: Bundeszentrale für politische Bildung, 1995.

Quack, Sibylle. *Auf dem Weg zur Realisierung: Das Denkmal für die ermordeten Juden Europas und der Ort der Information—Architektur und historisches Konzept.* Stuttgart, Germany: Deutsche Verlagsanstalt, 2002.

Raddatz, Fritz. *Summa iniuria oder Durfte der Papst schweigen? Hochuths "Stellvertreter" in der öffentlichen Kritik.* Reinbek, Germany: Rowohlt, 1963.

Radstone, Susannah, ed. *Memory and Methodology.* Oxford: Berg, 2000.

Reichel, Peter. *Erfundene Erinnerung: Weltkrieg und Judenmord in Film und Theater.* Munich, Germany: Hanser, 2004.

———. *Politik mit der Erinnerung: Gedächtnisorte im Streit um die nationalsozialistische Vergangenheit.* Munich, Germany: Hanser, 1995.

———. *Vergangenheitsbewältigung in Deutschland: Die Auseinandersetzung mit der NS-Diktatur von 1945 bis heute.* Munich, Germany: Beck, 2001.

Reissmann, Volker. *Fernsehprogrammzeitschriften: Ein Überblick über die bundesdeutsche Programmpresse mit einer inhaltsanalytischen Untersuchung.* Munich, Germany: Fischer, 1989.

Rensmann, Lars. *Demokratie und Judenbild: Antisemitismus in der politischen Kultur der Bundesrepublik Deutschland.* Wiesbaden, Germany: VS, 2004.

Rentschler, Eric. *The Ministry of Illusion: Nazi Cinema and Its Afterlife.* Cambridge, MA: Harvard University Press, 1996.

Rigly, Andrew. *Justice & Reconciliation: After the Violence.* Boulder, CO: Lynne Rienner, 2001.

Rogers, Daniel. *Politics after Hitler: The Western Allies and the German Party System.* New York: New York University Press, 1995.

Rohde, David. *Endgame: The Betrayal and Fall of Srebrenica—Europe's Worst Massacre since World War II.* New York: Farrar, Straus and Giroux, 1997.

Rosenfeld, Gavriel. *Munich and Memory: Architecture, Monuments, and the Legacy of the Third Reich.* Berkeley: University of California Press, 2000.

Rosenthal, Gabriele, ed. *Die Hitlerjugend-Generation: Biographische Verarbeitung als Vergangenheitsbewältigung.* Essen, Germany: Blaue Eule, 1986.

Rosenzweig, Roy, and David Thelen. *The Presence of the Past: Popular Uses of History in American Life.* New York: Columbia University Press, 1998.

Roth, Karl Heinz. *Geschichtsrevisionismus: Die Wiedergeburt des Totalitarismus.* Hamburg, Germany: Konkret, 1999.

Rückerl, Adalbert. *NS-Verbrechen: Versuch einer Vergangenheitsbewältigung.* Heidelberg, Germany: Müller, 1984.

Ruoff, Alexander. *Verbiegen, Verdrängen, Beschweigen: Die Nationalgeschichte der "Neuen Freiheit."* Münster, Germany: Unrast, 2001.

Rüsen, Jörn. *Geschichte im Kulturprozess.* Cologne, Germany: Böhlau, 2002.

———. *History: Narration, Interpretation, Orientation.* New York: Berghahn, 2004.

Rüsen, Jörn, and Jürgen Straub, eds. *Die dunkle Spur der Vergangenheit: Psychoanalytische Zugänge zum Geschichtsbewusstsein.* Frankfurt, Germany: Suhrkamp, 1998.

Sabrow, Martin, Ralph Jesse, and Klaus Grosse Kracht, eds. *Zeitgeschichte als Streitgeschichte: Grosse Kontroversen seit 1945.* Munich, Germany: Beck, 2003.

Samuel, Raphael. *Theatres of Memory.* Vol. 2, *Past and Present in Contemporary Culture.* London: Verso, 1994.

Schaal, Gary, and Andreas Wöll, eds. *Vergangenheitsbewältigung: Modelle der politischen und sozialen Integration in der bundesdeutschen Nachkriegsgeschichte.* Baden-Baden, Germany: Nomos, 1997.

Schafft, G. E., and Gerhard Zeidler. *Die KZ-Mahn- und Gedenkstätten in Deutschland.* Berlin: Dietz, 1996.

Schanze, Helmut, and Bernhard Zimmermann, eds. *Das Fernsehen und die Künste (Geschichte des Fernsehens in der Bundesrepublik Deutschland, vol. 2).* Munich, Germany: Fink, 1994.

Scharping, Rudolf. *Wir dürfen nicht wegsehen: Der Kosovo-Krieg und Europa.* Berlin: Ullstein, 1999.

Schildt, Axel. *Moderne Zeiten: Freizeit, Massenmedien und "Zeitgeist" in der Bundesrepublik der 50er Jahre.* Hamburg, Germany: Christians, 1995.

Schildt, Axel, Detlev Siegfried, and Karl Christian Lammers, eds. *Dynamische Zeiten: Die 60er Jahre in den beiden deutschen Gesellschaften.* Hamburg, Germany: Christians, 2000.

Schiller, Dietmar. *Die inszenierte Erinnerung: Politische Gedenktage im öffentlich-rechtlichen Fernsehen der Bundesrepublik Deutschland zwischen Medienereignis und Skandal.* Frankfurt, Germany: Lang, 1993.

Schirrmacher, Frank, ed. *Die Walser-Bubis-Debatte: Eine Dokumentation.* Frankfurt, Germany: Suhrkamp, 1999.

Schissler, Hanna, ed. *The Miracle Years: A Cultural History of West Germany, 1949–1968.* Princeton, NJ: Princeton University Press, 2001.

Schlant, Ernestine. *The Language of Silence: West German Literature and the Holocaust.* New York: Routledge, 1999.

Schlie, Ulrich. *Die Nation erinnert sich: Die Denkmäler der Deutschen.* Munich, Germany: Beck, 2002.

Schmid, Harald. *Erinnern an den "Tag der Schuld": Das Novemberpogrom von 1938 in der deutschen Geschichtspolitik.* Hamburg, Germany: Ergebnisse: 2001.

Schmidt, Friedemann. *Die Neue Rechte und die Berliner Republik: Parallel laufende Wege im Normalisierungsdiskurs.* Wiesbaden, Germany: Westdeutscher Verlag.

Schmidt, Susanne. *Es muss ja nicht gleich Hollywood sein: Die Produktionsbedingungen des Fernsehspiels und die Wirkungen auf seine Ästhetik.* Berlin: Sigma, 1994.

Schmidt, Thomas, Ernst Mittig, and Vera Böhm, eds. *Nationaler Totenkult—Die Neue Wache: Eine Streitschrift zur zentralen deutschen Gedenkstätte.* Berlin: Karin Kramer Verlag, 1995.

Schneider, Wolfgang, ed. *Vernichtungspolitik: Eine Debatte über den Zusammenhang von Sozialpolitik und Genozid im nationalsozialistischen Deutschland.* Hamburg, Germany: Junius, 1991.

Schornstheimer, Michael. *Bombenstimmung und Katzenjammer—Vergangenheitsbewältigung: Quick and Stern in den 50er Jahren.* Cologne, Germany: Pahl-Rugenstein, 1989.

Schubarth, Wilfried, and Richard Stöss, eds. *Rechtsextremismus in der Bundesrepublik Deutschland: Eine Bilanz.* Opladen, Germany: Leske und Budrich, 2001.

Schulze, Winfried. *Deutsche Geschichtswissenschaft nach 1945.* Munich, Germany: Oldenbourg, 1989.

———, ed. *Sozialgeschichte, Alltagsgeschichte, Mikro-Historie.* Göttingen, Germany: Vandenhoek und Ruprecht, 1994.

Schulze, Winfried, and Otto Gerhard Oexle, eds. *Deutsche Historiker im Nationalsozialismus.* Frankfurt, Germany: Fischer, 1999.

Schwab-Trapp, Michael. *Konflikt, Kultur und Interpretation: Eine Diskursanalyse des öffentlichen Umgangs mit dem Nationalsozialismus.* Opladen, Germany: Westdeutscher Verlag, 1996.

———. *Kriegsdiskurse: Die politische Kultur des Krieges im Wandel 1919–1999.* Opladen, Germany: Leske und Budrich, 2002.

Schwarzkopf, Dietrich, ed. *Rundfunkpolitik in Deutschland.* 2 vols. Munich, Germany: dtv, 1999.

Sebald, W. G. *Luftkrieg and Literatur.* Munich, Germany: Hanser, 1999.

Seixas, Peter, ed. *Theorizing Historical Consciousness.* Toronto, Canada: University of Toronto Press, 2004.

Seuthe, Rupert. *"Geistig-moralische Wende?": Der politische Umgang mit der NS-Vergangenheit in der Ära Kohl am Beispiel von Gedenktagen, Museums- und Denkmalprojekten.* Frankfurt, Germany: Peter Lang, 2001.

Shafir, Shlomo. *Ambiguous Relations: The American Jewish Community and Germany since 1945.* Detroit, MI: Wayne State University Press, 1999.

Shandler, Jeffrey. *While America Watches: Televising the Holocaust.* New York: Cambridge University Press, 1999.

Siever, Holger. *Kommunikation und Verstehen: Der Fall Jenninger als Beispiel einer semiotischen Kommunikationsanalyse.* Frankfurt, Germany: Lang, 2001.

Smith, Gary, ed. *Hannah Arendt Revisited: "Eichmann in Jerusalem" und die Folgen.* Frankfurt, Germany: Suhrkamp, 2000.

Sofsky, Wolfgang. *Die Ordnung des Terrors: Das Konzentrationslager.* Frankfurt, Germany: Fischer, 1993.

Sontag, Susan. *Under the Sign of Saturn.* New York: Farrar, Straus and Giroux, 1980.

Spiliotis, Susanne-Sophia. *Verantwortung und Rechtsfrieden: Die Stiftungsinitiative der deutschen Wirtschaft.* Frankfurt, Germany: Fischer, 2003.

Staiger, Janet. *Perverse Spectators: The Practices of Film Reception.* New York: New York University Press, 2000.

Stavginski, Hans Georg. *Das Holocaust-Denkmal: Der Streit um das "Denkmal für die ermordeten Juden Europas" in Berlin (1988–1999).* Paderborn, Germany: Schöningh, 2002.

Steinbach, Peter. *Nationalsozialistische Gewaltverbrechen: Die Diskussion in der deutschen Öffentlichkeit nach 1945.* Berlin: Colloquium, 1981.

Stern, Frank. *Whitewashing of the Yellow Badge: Antisemitism and Philosemitism in Postwar Germany.* Oxford: Pergamon, 1992.

Stokes, Melvyn, and Richard Maltby, eds. *Identifying Hollywood's Audiences: Cultural Identity and the Movies.* London: BFI, 1999.

Stölzl, Christoph, ed. *Deutsches Historisches Museum: Ideen, Kontroversen, Perspektiven.* Berlin: Propyläen, 1988.

———, ed. *Die Neue Wache unter den Linden: Ein deutsches Denkmal im Wandel der Geschichte.* Munich: Koehler und Amelang, 1993.

Straub, Jürgen, ed. *Erzählung, Identität und historisches Bewusstsein: Die psychologische Konstruktion von Zeit und Geschichte.* Frankfurt, Germany: Suhrkamp, 1996.

Sturken, Marita. *Tangled Memories: The Vietnam War, the AIDS Epidemic, and the Politics of Remembering.* Berkeley: University of California Press, 1997.

Stüwe, Klaus ed. *Die grossen Regierungserklärungen der deutschen Bundeskanzler von Adenauer bis Schröder.* Opladen, Germany: Leske und Budrich, 2002.

Terdiman, Richard. *Present Past: Modernity and the Memory Crisis.* Ithaca, NY: Cornell University Press, 1993.

Teschke, Klaus. *Hitler's Legacy: West Germany Confronts the Aftermath of the Third Reich.* New York: Lang, 1999.

Thiele, Hans-Günther, ed. *Wehrmachtsausstellung: Dokumentation einer Kontroverse.* Bremen, Germany: Edition Temmen, 1997.

Thoma, Susanne. *"Vergangenheitsbewältigung" am Beispiel der Auseinandersetzungen um die Neue Wache.* Berlin: Scheibel, 1995.

Thomas, Nick. *Protest Movements in 1960s West Germany: A Social History of Dissent and Democracy.* Oxford: Berg, 2003.

Thompson, Janna. *Taking Responsibility for the Past: Reparations and Historical Injustice.* Cambridge: Blackwell, 2002.

Torpey, John, ed. *Politics and the Past.* Lanham, MD: Rowman and Littlefield, 2003.

Trimborn, Jürgen. *Fernsehen der 90er: Die deutsche Fernsehlandschaft seit der Einführung des Privatfernsehens.* Cologne, Germany: Teiresias, 1999.

Varon, Jeremy. *Bringing the War Home: The Weather Underground, the Red Army Faction, and Revolutionary Violence in the Sixties and Seventies.* Berkeley: University of California Press, 2004.

Vervliet, Raymond, and Annemarie Estor, eds. *Methods for the Study of Literature as Cultural Memory.* Amsterdam: Rodopi, 2000.

Wachs, Philipp-Christian. *Der Fall Theodor Oberländer (1905–1998): Ein Lehrstück deutscher Geschichte.* Frankfurt, Germany: Campus, 2000.

Webster, James, Patricia Phalen, and Lawrence Lichty. *Ratings Analysis: The Theory and Practice of Audience Research.* 2nd ed. Mahwah, NJ: Lawrence Erlbaum, 2000.

Wehmeier, Stefan. *Fernsehen im Wandel.* Constance, Germany: UVK Medien, 1998.

Weinke, Annette. *Die Verfolgung von NS-Tätern im geteilten Deutschland.* Paderborn, Germany: Schöningh, 2002.

Welzer, Harald. *Das kommunikative Gedächtnis: Eine Thoerie der Erinnerung.* Munich, Germany: Beck, 2002.

Welzer, Harald, Sabine Moller, and Karoline Tschuggnall. *"Opa war kein Nazi": Nationalsozialismus und Holocaust im Familiengedächtnis.* Frankfurt, Germany: Fischer, 2002.

Wende, Waltraud, ed. *Geschichte im Film: Mediale Inszenierungen des Holocaust und kulturelles Gedächtnis*. Stuttgart, Germany: Metzler, 2002.

Wenzel, Eike. *Gedächtnisraum Film: Die Arbeit an der deutschen Geschichte in Filmen seit den sechziger Jahren*. Stuttgart, Germany: Metzler, 2000.

Wetzel, Wolf. *Krieg ist Frieden: Über Bagdad, Srebrenica, Genua, Kabul nach . . .* Münster, Germany: Unrast, 2002.

White, Hayden. *The Content of the Form: Narrative Discourse and Historical Representation*. Baltimore: Johns Hopkins University Press, 1987.

———. *Metahistory*. Baltimore: Johns Hopkins University Press, 1973.

Wiesen, Jonathan. *West German Industry & the Challenge of the Nazi Past, 1945–1955*. Chapel Hill: University of North Carolina Press, 2001.

Wilke, Jürgen, ed. *Massenmedien und Zeitgeschichte*. Constance, Germany: UVK Medien, 1999.

———, ed. *Mediengeschichte der Bundesrepublik Deutschland*. Cologne, Germany: Böhlau, 1999.

Wilke, Jürgen, Birgit Schenk, Akiba Cohen, and Tamar Zemach. *Holocaust und NS-Prozesse: Die Presseberichterstattung in Israel und Deutschland zwischen Aneignung und Abwehr*. Cologne, Germany: Böhlau, 1995.

Williams, Howard, Colin Wight, and Norbert Kapferer, eds. *Political Thought and German Reunification*. New York: St. Martin's Press, 2000.   .

Winter, Jay, and Emmanuel Sivan, eds. *War and Remembrance in the Twentieth Century*. Cambridge: Cambridge University Press, 1999.

Wolfrum, Edgar. *Geschichtspolitik in der Bundesrepublik Deutschland: Der Weg zur bundesrepublikanischen Erinnerung, 1948–1990*. Darmstadt, Germany: Wissenschaftliche Buchgesellschaft, 1999.

Wolgast, Eike. *Die Wahrnehmung des Dritten Reiches in der unmittelbaren Nachkriegszeit (1945/46)*. Heidelberg, Germany: Winter, 2001.

Wolffsohn, Michael. *Ewige Schuld: 40 Jahre deutsch-jüdisch-israelische Beziehungen*. Munich, Germany: Piper, 1988.

Wood, Nancy. *Vectors of Memory: Legacies of Trauma in Postwar Europe*. Oxford: Berg, 1999.

Young, James. *At Memory's Edge: After-Images of the Holocaust in Contemporary Art and Architecture*. New Haven, CT: Yale University Press, 2000.

———. *The Texture of Memory*. New Haven, CT: Yale University Press, 1993.

Zelizer, Barbie. *Covering the Body: The Kennedy Assassination, the Media, and the Shaping of Collective Memory*. Chicago: University of Chicago Press, 1992.

———. *Remembering to Forget: Holocaust Memory through the Camera's Eye*. Chicago: University of Chicago Press, 1998.

Zerubavel, Yael. *Recovered Roots: Collective Memory and the Making of Israeli National Tradition*. Chicago: University of Chicago Press, 1995.

Zuckermann, Moshe. *Zweierlei Holocaust: Der Holocaust in den politischen Kulturen Israels und Deutschlands*. Göttingen, Germany: Wallstein, 1998.

Zumbansen, Peer, ed. *Zwangsarbeit im Dritten Reich: Erinnerung und Verantwortung*. Baden-Baden, Germany: Nomos, 2002.

INDEX